Physical Education for Elementary School Children

Physical Education for Elementary School Children

Ninth Edition

Glenn Kirchner

Simon Fraser University

Graham J. Fishburne

University of Alberta

WCB Brown & Benchmark
PUBLISHERS

Madison, Wisconsin · Dubuque, Iowa

Book Team

Editor *Scott Spoolman*
Production Editor *Jayne Klein*
Designer *Lu Ann Schrandt*
Art Editor *Brenda Ernzen*
Photo Editor *Shirley Lanners*
Permissions Coordinator *LouAnn Wilson*
Production Manager *Beth Kundert*
Visuals/Design Freelance Specialist *Mary L. Christianson*
Marketing Manager *Pamela S. Cooper*

**WCB Brown &
Benchmark**

A Division of Wm. C. Brown Communications, Inc.

Executive Vice President/General Manager *Thomas E. Doran*
Vice President/Editor in Chief *Edgar J. Laube*
Vice President/Marketing and Sales Systems *Eric Ziegler*
Vice President/Production *Vickie Putman*
National Sales Manager *Bob McLaughlin*

 Wm. C. Brown Communications, Inc.

President and Chief Executive Officer *G. Franklin Lewis*
Senior Vice President, Operations *James H. Higby*
Corporate Senior Vice President and President of Manufacturing *Roger Meyer*
Corporate Senior Vice President and Chief Financial Officer *Robert Chesterman*

Consulting Editor Aileen Lockhart

Cover photo supplied by Glenn Kirchner

Copyedited by Marilyn Frey

A Times Mirror Company

Library of Congress Catalog Card Number: 94–70334

ISBN 0–697–15248–0

Printed in the United States of America by Wm. C. Brown Communications, Inc.,
2460 Kerper Boulevard, Dubuque, IA 52001

10 9 8 7 6 5 4 3 2

To Diane, my wife and
best friend. Glenn Kirchner

This book is dedicated to my mother. Her love and
support continue to be my source of
inspiration. Graham J. Fishburne

Brief Contents

Part 5
Game and Movement Activities

Part 6
Gymnastic and Movement Activities

Part 7
Dance and Movement Activities

Contents

Part 3
Physical Education Curriculum

Part 4
Provision for Special Programs

Part 5
Game and Movement Activities

Part 6
Gymnastic and Movement Activities

Part 7
Dance and Movement Activities

Preface

T he ninth edition of *Physical Education for Elementary School Children* includes several major changes. One is the addition of coauthor Dr. Graham J. Fishburne, professor of education at the University of Alberta. His major areas of expertise are in motor learning, motor development, and teaching strategies. Dr. Fishburne has taught at all levels in the public schools and has given numerous seminars and workshops in his areas of expertise. For his contributions in this area he has received several awards of excellence, including the 1990 3M Canadian Universities National Teaching Award. Dr. Fishburne's background in the areas of effective teaching and motor development, coupled with his general knowledge in the field of elementary school physical education, bring additional strength to the text and accompanying lesson plans.

The changes and new material in this ninth edition of *Physical Education for Elementary School Children* reflect our continuing emphasis on a developmentally based curriculum. Each chapter continues to accommodate the three developmental levels established in previous editions. Level I represents the beginning phase of acquiring game, dance, gymnastic, and movement concepts and skills that children pass through in the early primary years. As children move into level II, they begin to show an increased proficiency in all fundamental and manipulative skills, coupled with an improved ability to perform more coordinated movement patterns with greater speed and accuracy. Developmental level III is a period of refinement in all game, dance, and gymnastic activities. Since children at each chronological age can vary as much as four or five years in physical maturity and have markedly different physical education experiences, the three developmental levels are considered to be "signposts" along a continuum of concept and motor skill development. To accommodate these basic differences, each activity area in this book allows the teacher to choose activities from the most appropriate level for each child or group of children.

The key changes in this edition were made to accommodate the contemporary needs of the elementary school physical education program. One of the main modifications has been in the area of integrating physical education with other subject areas. In previous editions, one chapter was devoted to this topic. Because of the growing importance of using the medium of physical activity to teach academic concepts and skills, we have expanded on this topic within several chapters. In parts 5, 6, and 7 the reader will find lists of game, gymnastic, and dance activities that can be used to teach a variety of academic concepts and skills in language arts, mathematics, science, and other subject areas. Special sections titled "Using . . . to teach academic concepts and skills" are also provided at the end of several chapters.

Another emphasis in this edition is the health-related concerns for children. Development of an "active lifestyle" is essential for all children if they are to benefit from a program of physical education. Bridging school, community, and home lives is crucial. Ideas to achieve this, and to monitor and encourage involvement in physical activity, are presented in chapter 9. This chapter also includes new ideas to evaluate and assess children's progress. Portfolios and journal writing are presented as additional forms of assessment to help the teacher build a profile of each child's growth and development in physical education.

Classroom activities and cooperative games have been expanded to present the general classroom teacher with many ideas for using the classroom for physical activities and to integrate physical education with other subject areas. The cooperative games chapter has been expanded to include many new games created by children from all parts of the world.

Every chapter has also been updated with new material and complemented by more than 150 new photographs and illustrations. This edition contains more photographs and illustrations than any other book in its field. It also contains some of the most extensive lists of game, dance, and gymnastic skills and activities to be found in any competing book. One of this book's features is the way in which a discussion of Laban's movement concepts and skills has been integrated into every game, dance, and gymnastic activity. This integration allows the teacher to select and emphasize structured skills, movement concepts, or both, according to the developmental level, interest, and background of the children in each class.

The basic organization of this book consists of seven parts. Part 1 describes the meaning and purpose of physical education and outlines the developmental characteristics of elementary school children. Part 2 discusses Laban's four elements of movement; locomotor, nonlocomotor, and manipulative skills; and motor learning.

Part 3 is concerned with the process of curriculum design, implementation, and evaluation. Chapter 6 begins this discussion by explaining and illustrating how to plan a yearly program, units of instruction, and daily lesson plans. Chapter 7 follows with ideas about class management, facilities, and equipment. Chapter 8 deals with teaching strategies, motivational techniques, and discipline maintenance. Chapter 9 covers the observational and evaluative techniques of assessing student progress. Chapter 10 covers the legal responsibilities of a teacher.

Part 4 describes the various ways of handling special problems within instructional and extraclass programs. Chapter 11 provides important background information on the structure and functions of the body. Chapter 12 covers the methods of assessing and improving physical fitness. This is an extremely important chapter in light of recent national concerns about decreasing levels of physical fitness among the elementary school population. Chapter 13 discusses the methods of integrating children with special needs into instructional and extraclass programs. Chapter 14 describes how the classroom can be used to teach physical education activities. The concluding chapter in part 4 explains how to design and supervise intramural and interschool sports programs.

The last three parts of this book contain separate resource sections for game, dance, and gymnastic activities. Part 5 offers a variety of individual and team games for the three developmental levels. Each chapter within this resource section suggests a sequence for presenting motor skills, practice activities, lead-up games, and evaluative techniques. Part 6 contains a comprehensive coverage of gymnastic and movement activities that are performed on the floor and with small and large equipment. Part 7 covers rhythmic activities, traditional and contemporary dances, and creative movement. Throughout these sections are suggestions for teaching such activities through both direct and indirect methods.

Throughout this book, the pronouns *she* and *her* are generally used when referring to the teacher, for the sake of simplicity and consistency. Likewise, the pronouns *he* and *his* are used to describe the student, although feminine pronouns are used to refer to female students in the illustrations. The use of the word *gender* has also been widely used throughout this text.

An expanded glossary and appendixes include new information about audiovisual resources, equipment, and supplies. The revised *Instructor's Manual* accompanying this text provides a summary outline for each chapter, along with teaching suggestions and evaluative techniques. The manual offers an overview of each chapter and acquaints the teacher with the updated written and audiovisual resources that are available.

This edition blends theory, research findings, and sound pedagogical knowledge related to child development into practical ideas for the generalist classroom teacher. The book continues to serve as a university/college textbook and as an excellent resource for administrators, school boards, curriculum developers, and educational consultants, in addition to elementary school teachers.

A strong ancillary package accompanies this new edition. The lesson plans, now called *Yearly Programs, Units, and Daily Lesson Plans,* have been substantially revised and expanded by Glenn Kirchner and Graham Fishburne. Also revised, with new and improved test items, the *Instructor's Manual/Test Item File* is available to adopters, along with the powerful new *MICROTEST* testing program for personal computers. A new set of *overhead transparencies* is also provided for adopters of this edition. Additionally, the authors have produced three *videotapes* to illustrate the content and the strategies used to teach game, gymnastic, and dance activities to elementary school children. Each videotape is accompanied by a user manual, which includes brief descriptions of each scene and its approximate location on the videotape. Finally, Brown & Benchmark offers *Fitness Tracker* fitness assessment software, available for IBM-compatible and Apple computers, for use in elementary school physical education classes.

Acknowledgments

Once again, the many content changes and photographs are the result of the generous assistance of teachers and children from several schools in the United States, Canada, and several other countries. Special thanks to Lynne Tomlinson, Caufeild Elementary School; Mrs. D. Fishburne, Idylwylde Elementary School; Deborah Rowley, and Donna Goodwin, school consultants; Ms. Jennifer Bennett, Glenlyon Norfolk School; and to all their talented children. We also wish to express our appreciation to Claire Palo, Dana and Keith Wagschal, Katie Halloran, Mathew Clark, Loren and Ema Megan, Rebecca and Stephanie Fishburne, and Christie Jenvey for being such excellent models for all the new photographs in this edition. And to Dru Marshall and the staff at the University of Alberta's fitness unit for their generous assistance. Many of the numerous content changes in this edition were made on the basis of the suggestions provided by elementary school teachers, colleagues and the following reviewers:

Barbara A. Thompson
Florida A&M University

Todd M. Cotton
Adams State College

Stuart G. Robbins
York University

Rick Bell
University of Victoria

Virginia Foster Chadwick
California State University, Fresno

Cindy J. Bross
Meredith College

Tina E. Gabriele
University of Calgary

Gillian D. Ratray
Pennsylvania State University

To each, our sincere appreciation. The extensive changes found in chapter 13 are due to the excellent suggestions made by Dr. M. Miller, Saint Bonaventure University. Our thanks to Bob Birch for drawing the new illustrations for this ninth edition. Finally, a very special thanks to our wives, Diane and Dianne, for their support, ideas, and suggestions.

Physical Education and the Growing Child

 art 1 is designed to provide teachers with a basic understanding of the meaning and purpose of physical education and the characteristics and needs of young children ■

Chapter 1
Elementary School Physical Education

Chapter 2
Children and Activity

Elementary School Physical Education

The process of developing an elementary school physical education curriculum must begin with a clear statement of its general aim, goals, and objectives before discussing appropriate content and teaching strategies. This chapter will deal with this first important step. It will provide a statement of beliefs that is used as a foundation from which the general aim and objectives of physical education are derived. The stated objectives are used in this book as a basis for the way in which it is organized, for the inclusion and emphasis of certain teaching strategies, and for the diversity of activities provided in the resource sections ■

Statement of Beliefs

The following statement of beliefs is based on several sources of information. First, general statements about the nature and role of education are derived from a set of philosophical tenets concerning life and education. They are not the result of science or surveys; rather, they are the end products of critical thinking about the way we see ourselves in society. Second, other statements relating to why and how children learn are based on a body of knowledge that includes many disciplines. Third, some statements about teaching, children, and physical education are based, in part, on intuition and experience. Taken collectively, the following beliefs provide a basis for the general aims and objectives of elementary physical education. In turn, these will act as guidelines for the programs and strategies provided in the following chapters of this book.

About Education and Teaching

1. Education should be a process through which all students are able to reach their greatest potential.
2. Teaching is an art and a science of helping children reach their greatest potential.

The first statement means that all children must be treated as equal, participating members of society. From this perspective, the second belief implies that teachers should use all of the scientific knowledge available about how and why children learn, as well as their own ingenuity and common sense, to guide children to realize their greatest potential. In addition, all teaching must be done within a democratic environment that recognizes the worth and integrity of every child.

About the Child

1. All children are unique individuals who learn according to their own level of ability and style of learning.
2. All children are capable of making their own decisions; however, a child must learn to do so in a gradual and systematic way.

Since children of similar age vary greatly in maturity and ability, we must provide variety in the learning tasks and the time needed to complete them. Different styles of learning indicate the need to offer not only a variety of activities within each lesson and throughout the curriculum, but also a variety of teaching methods and approaches will be necessary to accommodate the unique individual needs of each child. Since children are rational individuals, we must provide many experiences, in a graduated way, to allow each child opportunities to learn how to make correct and effective decisions. Our task, then, is to help each child become a self-directed and independent learner who will constantly seek new challenges (figure 1.1).

Figure 1.1 Every child is a unique individual.

About Physical Education

1. Physical education has a unique, but not exclusive, role to play in the education of children. This role is twofold—to enhance children's physical fitness and well-being and to teach them a wide variety of motor skills.
2. Physical education, through its activities and experiences, can and *must* contribute to the shared goals of education, such as enhancing self-direction, self-esteem, and cooperative behavior.
3. Physical education should be an enjoyable and satisfying experience for every child.

The first belief sets a priority for physical education. Whatever else we profess to do, we must provide experiences that will enhance children's levels of health and fitness, and we must teach them concepts and motor skills inherent in a wide selection of physical activities. As we perform these tasks, we can also contribute to other goals of the elementary school curriculum through the way we structure the environment and the teaching styles and techniques we choose to use. Finally, in order to make physical education an enjoyable and satisfying experience, we must provide opportunities for all children to reap success every time they are involved in a movement experience. Physical education must be an enjoyable and satisfying experience for all children.

Historical Development of Physical Education

A study of the history of education reveals that physical education has always been present but regarded with varying degrees of importance. In the age of the classical Greeks the idea of harmony of body and mind was emphasized in the education of their citizens. This concept of unity and balance involved the harmonious development of the mental, physical, and spiritual aspects of the human personality. Consequently, physical education was considered an integral component of the educational program with similar purposes but unique contributions. Plato expressed this idea in his writings and by personal exemplifications of his participation in physical exercise. Although strength and physical prowess were important, the Greeks' ideals embraced more than mere strength alone; for example, they included the grace and beauty of movement and other moral expectations. Indeed, the Greek sport festivals celebrating the magnificence of movement is the Greek legacy that is the basis of the modern Olympic Games. During this period of history, where mind and body were considered in a balanced view and where physical activity was valued, there was intellectual and cultural development rarely equalled in the generations that followed. The balanced view, however, gave way to the military concerns of physical strength and fitness, with the warlike Spartans emphasizing the physical training of the body for military purposes. Repetition of the latter emphasis has been recorded in virtually every civilization since. One major exception was the aesthetics, which, throughout the Middle Ages, stressed the spiritual to the complete neglect of the physical and social aspects of human development.

From the period of Enlightenment to the twentieth century, education primarily emphasized intellectual development. Physical education expressed in terms of natural play or organized activities, such as gymnastics and games, was emphasized by such writers as Locke, Rousseau, and Spencer. The purposes of such programs, however, were conceived in terms of "training" the body to enhance optimum intellectual development. Although connections were made, the "mind–body" distinction was still firmly in place. It has only been during the twentieth century that a move has been seen in the philosophy of education toward the return of the Greek ideal of balance and harmony between mind and body.

Since the beginning of the twentieth century there have been profound changes in the philosophy, content, and methods of teaching at all levels in the public school. These changes toward "education for democratic living" did not happen by chance. New theories of learning, such as those presented by Thorndike and Gestalt psychology, produced significant changes in the way children were taught. Dewey and his disciples made their interpretations of the nature of learning chiefly in terms of social and philosophical rationale. The combined influences of philosophers, economists, and educators provided the impetus and rationale for the transition toward a liberal or general education for all citizens.

Physical education underwent profound changes in the nature of activities and methods of teaching. At the turn of the century rigid gymnastic programs were still strongly emphasized, although games were beginning to be accepted as a valid part of elementary and secondary school physical education programs. The influence of Dewey, particularly during the period between 1930 and 1940, created major changes in the philosophy of education and thereby influenced both the teaching and content of physical education. Gymnastics were almost eliminated from the program, while games were given a predominant role. Because the educational emphasis was on "learning by doing," with children allowed to determine their own needs and interests, play through games was considered to be a strong contributor to social adjustment. Only minor emphasis was placed on skill and physical development.

During the early 1940s and until the latter part of the 1960s, physical education programs were changed substantially. Increased attention was given to the professional preparation of specialists in physical education as well as classroom teachers. Various state laws and educational requirements of certification upgraded both the caliber of physical education teaching and its perceived degree of importance in the educational milieu. Extensive research in such areas as growth and development, motor learning, and physical performance brought back the rationale for a balanced program of physical activities for all levels of public and private education. For reasons of national survival, a special emphasis was still placed on physical fitness.

The past 30 years have seen further changes in the content and teaching of physical education. Again, these changes reflect philosophy, economic needs, and new knowledge regarding children's growth and development. Trends in automation and urbanization throughout the western world have presented physical educators with new challenges. Programs in harmony with contemporary philosophies of education have been designed to develop within each child sufficient knowledge, skill, health, and fitness, and a positive attitude toward participation in wholesome recreational activities that can be continued throughout life. To accommodate this, there has been a shift in elementary school physical education programs from group-paced instruction toward more individualized programs. Teaching techniques that emphasize self-direction through exploratory and problem-solving methods have been implemented.

Contemporary Physical Education

The move toward a concern for the individual has been reflected by two major thrusts in recent years. The first is the move toward a developmentally appropriate physical education program. Here the activities, teaching methods, practices, and so on, are designed to meet the developmental needs of the individual child. The child's current level of development determines the starting point for the physical education teacher. The second major thrust has been a decrease in the emphasis on physical fitness for military purposes and an increase in individual's personal health. Burgeoning health care costs have seen governments struggle to meet society's health care needs. Improving the health of people through the development of active and healthy lifestyles is one of the major aims of today's education systems. This view is reflected in the role physical education is now playing in public health. The development of active lifestyles is one of the major driving forces behind current physical education programs. Although developmentally appropriate activities that will develop active lifestyles is the desired outcome of contemporary physical education programs, achieving this will not be easy.

There are approximately 80,000 elementary schools in the United States teaching 31 million children. Schools vary in size from rural, one-room schools to large, urban schools exceeding 1,000 children. Physical education facilities also vary from large gymnasia and outdoor playgrounds to multistory inner-city schools without gymnasia or adequate playground facilities. According to the National Children and Youth Fitness I and II (1983, 1985), the current status of physical education throughout the United States is relatively low. This study indicates that a surprising 97 percent of all children in grades one through four participate in a physical education program 3.1 times per week. However, only 36.4 percent of the children in the first four grades, 18.4 percent in the fifth grade, and 27.4 percent in the sixth grade participate in daily physical education. It was also found that 37.2 percent of grades one through four, 48.4 percent of fifth grades, and 42 percent of sixth grades are scheduled for only one or two classes per week. With respect to time allotments, the average class period is 33.4 minutes for grades one through four and 90 minutes per week for fifth- and sixth-grade children. These are the basic facts about the current status of elementary school physical education. The next section, dealing with aims, goals, and objectives, draws from the initial statement of beliefs as well as other educational and social factors in order to state what should be the general aim and basic goals and objectives of physical education.

General Aim, Goals, and Objectives of Physical Education

An educational aim is a statement that identifies the expectation that should result from the overall educational experience. For example, "the aim of the elementary school science curriculum is to. . . ." Once the general aim has been identified, specific goal statements need to be established in order to understand what goals will need to be achieved in order to meet the aim. Finally, goal statements can be broken down into even more specific statements outlining the objectives that need to be met in order to ensure that goals are realized. Since objectives describe in greater detail the specific content that make up goals, these statements play an important role in the teaching/learning process. For example, both unit plan objectives and lesson plan objectives are

essential components in a teacher's planning since these statements describe the specific content to be covered and desired learning outcomes. The book of lesson plans that accompanies this text describes in detail the process of translating goal statements into clearly stated unit and lesson plan objectives. The organizational make-up of aims, goals, and objectives is a commonly accepted framework for identifying educational outcomes.

It can be said the aim of physical education is to produce physically educated individuals. However, this statement alone is insufficient, since it does not identify what a physically educated individual must possess in order to be viewed in this manner. To clarify this position, educational goals need to be considered. In 1986, the United States Secretary of Education stated that the general goals of elementary education are "to build for every child a strong foundation for further education, for democratic citizenship, and for eventual entry into responsible adulthood" (Bennett, 1986). Translated into goal statements for physical education, the major goals would be to assist each child to develop an optimum level of health and well-being and to acquire the attitudes, knowledge, and movement skills that will lead to lifelong participation in enjoyable and wholesome physical activities. Achieving these goals is the aim of physical education.

It is possible to describe a set of specific physical education objectives based on the above goals, the previous statement of beliefs about education and teaching, the child, and physical education as a unique subject area in the elementary school curriculum. Some physical educators (Dauer and Pangrazi 1992; Morris and Stiehl 1985; and Gallahue, 1993), as well as local and national organizations, have expressed similar objectives to those that follow. They are used in this book as basic criteria for the selection and emphasis of activities, for the inclusion of numerous teaching methods and techniques, and for the blending of Laban's Movement Education concepts with contemporary game, dance, and gymnastic activities.

Physical Fitness and Well-Being

Objective: To help each child develop and maintain an optimum level of health and well-being and to acquire the knowledge, attitude, and ability to maintain this state of well-being throughout life

Prior to 1980, physical fitness was broadly defined as having sufficient strength and energy to meet daily life activities. However, virtually every physical fitness test that was used measured motor fitness performance, which is an individual's ability to perform motor tasks involving such factors as agility and power. In most instances, physical fitness was also looked upon as an end in itself, rather than a process of understanding and achieving a positive state of health. The publication of AAHPERD's *Health Related Fitness Test* (1980) and its revised edition, *Physical Best Test* (1989), redefined physical fitness in terms of health

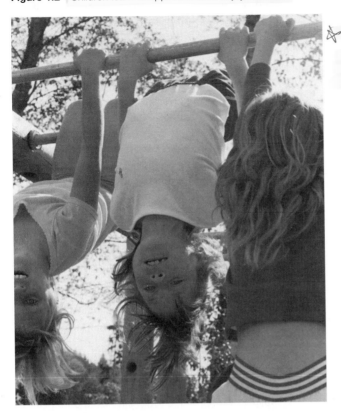

Figure 1.2 Children learn to appreciate and enjoy wellness.

rather than motor performance. Physical fitness is more broadly defined as "a physical state of well-being that allows people to (1) perform daily activities with vigor, (2) reduce their risk of health problems related to lack of exercise, and (3) establish a fitness base for participation in a variety of physical activities."

This change toward understanding and maintaining a positive state of well-being is also reflected in the report *Healthy People 2000: National Health Promotion and Disease Prevention Objectives.* This document was released in 1991 by the office of the U.S. Surgeon General and outlines realistic health objectives to be achieved by the year 2000. These objectives were established by representatives from more than 300 national organizations. The major focus of this report is on health as represented by a high quality of life and a sense of well-being. Such a focus has major implications for physical education programs. Since the interpretation of health-related fitness now includes strength, cardiorespiratory endurance, flexibility, and body composition, these components must be stressed in the program and, of course, on an individual basis. Programs must be designed to help children understand how their bodies function, the effects of exercise, and how to create one's own physical fitness program. If children are to leave elementary school with a positive and sustained interest in maintaining a healthy lifestyle, the physical education program must be taught in a way that children learn to appreciate and enjoy wellness (figure 1.2). The

developmental approach that is emphasized in this book provides content and strategies that can accomplish this objective.

Growth and Development

Objective: To provide opportunities for children to participate in activities that will enhance their own level of physical growth and development

All children are born with certain inherited characteristics that determine their approximate height, weight, and general physique. Such environmental factors as proper nutrition, amount of sleep, exposure to disease, and general parental care also affect the child's growth and development. In addition, substantial evidence has shown that normal growth and development of bone as well as connective and muscle tissue occur only when a child receives adequate and continuous exercise throughout the growing period. Regular exercise, for example, increases bone width and mineralization (Rarick 1973). Similarly, lack of exercise can severely limit the potential growth of other bodily systems and organs.

There is growing evidence of the important role physical education can play in the prevention of coronary heart disease. Although heart disease is usually manifest in adulthood, it has been suggested that it is frequently of pediatric origin. Indeed, autopsy studies have revealed fatty streaks in the aortas of children younger than three years in age (Armstrong and Bray, 1986). The build–up of fatty streaks in the inner lining of the arterial wall is the first step toward coronary heart problems. Childhood would therefore appear to be the appropriate time to commence the fight against cardiovascular heart disease. For many adults, the coronary heart risk factors of physical inactivity and poor diet may have their roots in the habits, attitudes, and interest levels established in early school experiences. It is well documented that regular vigorous physical activity is associated with low incidence of coronary heart disease in adult life. Participation in developmentally appropriate physical activity as a child will increase the likelihood of participation as an adult. Clearly, the elementary school physical education program offers the potential to influence development over the total life span.

Body Management and Useful Physical Skills

Objective: To provide opportunities to help children develop effective body management and useful physical skills

All the movements used in everyday activities, such as the locomotor and nonlocomotor skills of walking, dodging, and stopping, and the movement skills and concepts of transfer of weight and moving with a change of speed and direction, are useful physical skills. Some of these skills are used to help children control their bodies while moving on or over apparatus or through space. Other skills are used in combination with one or more locomotor and movement skills to form the complex skills and movement patterns involved in sports, gymnastics, and dance activities. Regardless of the nature and type of skill, they are usually learned through a systematic program of instruction.

Poorly developed motor abilities such as hand-eye coordination, balance, and finger dexterity will severely restrict the success associated with performing most physical skills. Children need to develop their motor abilities to their fullest potential. Since environmental experiences influence development of basic motor abilities, the physical education program has an important role to play in fostering both motor skill and motor ability development. With well-developed motor abilities, a person has the prerequisite foundation for the acquisition of motor skills.

The values of efficient and skillful movements, particularly in sports and dance, are many. Children who demonstrate ease and grace of movement are usually physically fit and well adjusted among their peers. Furthermore, a child who displays a skill in an activity, such as basketball or swimming, not only experiences a great deal of enjoyment through participation but usually pursues the activity for many years. Adults should understand this lesson well, for we generally participate in activities in which we show a reasonable degree of skill; rarely do we actively pursue or enjoy a sport that we cannot master at least in part.

Understanding and Appreciating Human Movement

Objective: To help children understand and appreciate the knowledge and concepts relating to effective and efficient movement

The intent of this objective is to help children understand the components of each skill they learn and how the laws and principles of gravity and motion affect their performance. Knowledge of Laban's movement concepts and skills also expands children's movement vocabulary and helps them design, perform, and appreciate a unique movement sequence. In addition, a knowledge of game skills and rules, of dance steps and patterns, and of gymnastic movements and safety skills helps all learners execute each movement with ease, efficiency, and an appreciation of the efforts and intricacies involved in human movement.

Active Lifestyle

Objective: To help each child develop and acquire the knowledge, skills, attitude, ability, and desire to maintain an active lifestyle

One of the major goals of elementary school physical education is to educate children toward the development of an active lifestyle. Children must achieve what Armstrong (1989) terms "activity independence." That is, they must be active as part of their normal lifestyles rather than only when a teacher offers instruction. In a way, the physical education teacher should have an easy task. When they enter school, most children possess a reasonably high level of physical fitness, an interest in the joy of moving, a desire to move, and abundant energy and enthusiasm. In fact, many children have difficulty sitting still! Children have a natural penchant for movement—they will run to the gymnasium. A teacher's task, then, is to maintain this natural interest and motivation as the child progresses through school.

Sadly, statistics too frequently reveal that students' fitness and activity levels deteriorate as they progress through school; this is more true for girls than for boys. Clearly, the social influences of watching television, diet, inactivity, and the lack of good role models outside of school play an influencing part. Schools cannot make all the changes in isolation of these other factors. However, the physical education program can play an important role in providing a child with an appropriate environment where the child develops the necessary prerequisites for an active lifestyle. In order to participate in physical endeavors, children will need to acquire skills. Without skill, there will be little success. Without success, there will be little motivation. Without motivation, there will be little interest, and without interest an attitude commensurate with inactivity will develop. Skills alone will likely not be sufficient to maintain an active lifestyle. Knowledge, a prerequisite degree of fitness (necessary to achieve success), and a desire to achieve will all be necessary. A child will need to be physically educated (the aim of the program) in order to support an active lifestyle. Further, the influences outside of school must foster and support the education within the school. This latter point has implications for parental and community involvement, assessment and reporting procedures, developmentally appropriate activities, and instructional methods that promote "transfer." Each of these areas is covered within the text.

Enjoyment Through Play

Objective: To provide opportunities for children to experience enjoyable play experiences

The meaning of enjoyment goes far beyond "having fun" or "being amused" in playing a game or performing a dance movement. Enjoyment, as used in this objective, relates to the intrinsic value of the activity to the child. If the child truly enjoys what she is doing, it often becomes the main reason for continuous participation in the activity, as well as the motivation for the child to seek higher levels of performance. Joy of movement may be the key to excellence—a goal we want all learners to achieve (figure 1.3). Therefore, this objective should be given a high priority in the physical education program.

Fostering Intellectual Growth

Objective: To provide opportunities to help children develop their intellect competency

The intellectual growth of a young child involves the cognitive skills of acquiring, ordering, and communicating

Figure 1.3 Joy of movement may be the key to excellence.

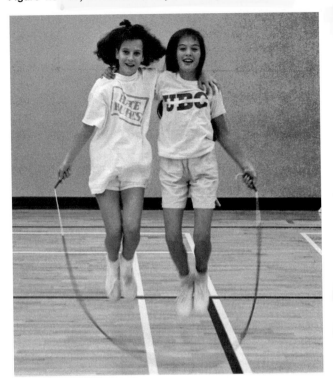

knowledge and ideas. It also involves the ability to communicate one's ideas and feelings in a creative way and through a variety of modes of expression. Although the physical education program should be predominantly physical, it should encourage the acquisition of vocabulary and concepts as well as exercise the thinking process of every child. For example, in gymnastics and dance activities, when children plan a movement sequence, they are required to understand movement terms and concepts and to join together mentally a series of movements that answer a movement challenge efficiently, safely, and creatively. In a similar manner, creative and cooperative game activities provide an effective medium in which young children exercise their thinking processes in active and inventive ways.

Physical activities can also be used as an effective mode to teach a variety of academic skills and concepts. Simple games, such as Steal the Bacon and Squirrel in the Trees, can be used to teach adding, subtracting, sets, and many other mathematical concepts. Gymnastic movements can be an effective way of explaining balance, force, or geometrical shapes. Physical education can provide a rich source of activities through which academic skills and concepts can be taught or reinforced in an exciting, effective, and enjoyable way.

Personal and Social Development

Objective: To provide opportunities for children to develop positive personal and social development

Five-year-old children enter school with certain feelings and attitudes about themselves, their parents, and the people who have affected their lives in various ways. In terms of enhancing personal and social development, physical education provides an effective environment in which each child can learn to behave in a variety of social settings. Through small- and large-group activities, such as in games, dance, and aquatic activities, primary children begin to learn to test their tolerance and perseverance and to explore alternatives in a nonthreatening environment. As children progress through this type of program, they begin to learn the meaning of patience, honesty, fair play, and team loyalty—valuable lessons for the future citizens of a democratic society.

Self-image

Objective: To provide opportunities for every child to develop a positive self-image

Self-image is essentially a child's feelings about himself. Children develop feelings about their intellectual abilities, popularity among peers, and ability to perform physical activities. If there is reasonable success in each of these dimensions, children normally have positive feelings about their personal worth. A child who has positive feelings is generally eager to attempt new challenges. However, children who constantly experience failure in any of these areas normally have a very low opinion of themselves. Too often this leads to withdrawal or other forms of undesirable behavior. Classroom teachers clearly understand the implications of such children's problems in learning tasks and in getting along with classmates.

The physical education environment can either foster or impede the development of a child's positive self-image. If the activities are presented so that each child, regardless of physical ability, can achieve a measure of success, the child's feelings about himself are enhanced. One needs only to see a young child perform a successful roll or swim his first few strokes to observe the joy of success and the eagerness to try again. On the other hand, a child who is repeatedly required to attempt movement skills beyond his capabilities generally develops a negative attitude.

Since self-image is one of the most important factors in learning motor skills, physical education activities must be presented in such a way that every child achieves some success. New methods and techniques described in later chapters can assist teachers in providing this type of program for all children.

Creative Talents

Objective: To provide opportunities for all children to develop their own creative talents

Contemporary public education stresses the development of creativity at all levels. Creativity, however, is a difficult concept to define. A work of art, such as a painting, sculpture, or musical score, is creative in that it is unique in composition, color, or form. In physical education, creativity is defined in terms of the way in which a movement or series of movements is performed or by the degree of inventiveness of a movement.

According to Gladys Andrews and her colleagues, creativity is what one thinks, feels, sees, and expresses in terms of oneself and in one's own way (Andrews, Saurborn, and Schneider 1960). Since every child has a potential ability to be creative, the physical education program should provide numerous opportunities for each child to explore and express creativity through movement (figure 1.4).

Outcomes of Quality Physical Education Programs

Outlining objectives, goals, and aims provides an understanding of the learning outcomes associated with a quality physical education program. The outcomes identified here are similar to those identified by other professional groups concerned with quality physical education programs. For example, in 1992 the National Association for Physical Education and Sport (NASPE) published a nationally endorsed guide on the desired outcomes of quality physical education programs. The guide identifies similar outcomes to those stated above and provides direction toward the development of standards for student achievement. Further reference to the NASPE outcome statements is made in chapter 9, where the evaluation of student progress is considered.

Factors Influencing the Nature and Direction of Physical Education

During the past three decades, the elementary physical education curriculum has been profoundly influenced by the changing philosophy of elementary education, by new federal and state laws and regulations, and by new developments in the content and teaching strategies of physical education. A few of the major trends, which are discussed in the following paragraphs, illustrate how these factors are shaping the future elementary physical education curriculum.

Individualized and Personalized Instructional Programs

Perhaps one of the most significant trends affecting every subject area in the elementary school curriculum is the shift toward individualized and personalized instruction. This form of teaching creates an environment for successful

Figure 1.4 Every child has a potential ability to be creative.

personal encounter, fostering the free and open expression of ideas, facts, and feelings. It is an environment in which learning activities integrate the personal interests of the students with the goals of the school. In physical education, this means we no longer teach according to our own predetermined goals, exclusively choose the types of physical activities for the program, or use only a formal method of instruction. Rather, we shift from group-paced instruction toward a process of teaching that is a shared enterprise between the learner and the teacher.

Movement Education

Just prior to the Second World War, Rudolph Laban, an Austrian dance teacher, moved to England and brought a new way of analyzing all forms of human movement. During the war, English primary teachers, most of whom had little or no training in physical education, began to use Laban's movement analysis and more problem-solving methods in their physical education programs. Gradually this new analysis of movement, coupled with more exploratory methods, became known as the Movement Education approach. During the past thirty years, Movement Education as a curriculum model has received mixed reviews. Some proponents have used Movement Education as the structure on which all movement concepts and skills are taught (Graham, Holt-Hale, and Parker 1980; Logsdon 1984; Wall and Murray 1990). There has been some success with the model in the primary grades; however, very few intermediate programs have been successful in adopting Movement Education as an all-inclusive approach to teaching physical education.

One of the most significant trends has been the integration of Laban's movement concepts and skills with all content areas of the elementary school physical education program. At times, particularly during early primary years, the Movement Education approach is used exclusively as the curriculum model. As children grow older, the physical education program still emphasizes the basic movement concepts in a complementary way to acquiring individual and team game skills, gymnastic movements, and many folk dance movement patterns. Creative dance programs throughout every grade in the elementary school use Laban's four elements of movement as a basic structure to teach creative movement activities. The contemporary developmental model, which is emphasized throughout this book, is an example of how the Movement Education approach has been integrated into new and exciting elementary school physical education curriculum models.

Integration of Subjects

A growing trend in elementary education is toward more conceptual development through an integrated or interdisciplinary approach to learning (Werner and Burton 1979). Such common concepts as *geometrical forms, stability,* and *rhythm* are no longer viewed as the sole property of one subject or another. Rather, teachers are using a variety of subject areas when teaching a single concept. Physical education is seen as an effective medium for teaching basic concepts from such subjects as mathematics, science, language arts, and music. The fundamental implication is that both the classroom teacher and the physical education specialist must view the process of integration as a two-way street. Opportunities exist for physical education teachers to emphasize a particular concept arising from another subject area and for classroom teachers to reinforce concepts arising from the medium of physical education.

One of the fundamental themes throughout this book is that physical education makes unique contributions to the general goals of elementary education. Through a broadbased program of activities and effective teaching strategies, young children progressively increase their physical attributes and learn the knowledge and skills of a variety of physical activities. Through the medium of play, a child also learns about self-control and cooperative behavior.

Elementary school teachers fully realize that learning in one area, such as arithmetic, can be strengthened by another area, as when adding the number of points in a game played in a physical education lesson. Research evidence provided by Humphrey (1990) and Cratty (1967) supports this general point of view. Their studies strongly indicate that children tend to learn certain academic concepts better through the motor activity medium than through the traditional medium. Also, teaching academic skills and concepts through a kinesthetic medium seems to be more favorable for children with average or below average intelligence. These findings are not surprising. Plato wrote in *The Republic* more than 2,000 years ago, "do not my friend keep children to their studies by compulsion but by play" (cited in Kline, 1977, p. 199). No doubt Plato realized the importance of sensory experiences when a child is learning. Unfortunately, teachers generally rely almost entirely on vision and hearing as the major forms of sensory learning experience. To limit learning opportunities to these forms of experience is to miss out on other areas of sensory stimulation. In terms of information processing, Steinhaus (1966) wrote more than a quarter of a century ago that in the human brain,

A larger portion of the nervous system is devoted to receiving and integrating sensory input originating in the muscles and joint structures than is devoted to the eye and ear combined (p. 38).

It is not surprising to find positive results reported by researchers who have integrated movement experiences into all areas of learning. Indeed, Johnson (1987) demonstrates in his work on "The Body in the Mind" how all knowledge originates from bodily experiences.

Contemporary education uses the term *integration* to describe this mutual relationship between subject areas. As explained above, integration implies a two-way street in which each subject area has a unique place and role in the child's total education. Whenever a concept or skill in one subject area can be fortified or acquired through another subject, the relationship should be consciously planned. This may occur in two ways in the elementary school. The first approach is to use the assigned time for an academic subject, such as math, and use physical activities within this time period to teach or reinforce a particular skill or concept. A simple example of this approach would be a first-grade teacher using a grid to teach number recognition or simple addition. The grid could be drawn on the floor of the classroom or outside on the blacktop (see p. 231). The essential point is that the time spent on this grid activity is not considered part of the allocated time for physical education.

The second approach is, first, to plan a well-balanced physical education program for a particular grade. Once the program is established, the classroom teacher can modify activities within each unit to reinforce academic skills and concepts concurrently taught in the classroom. To illustrate, a third-grade teacher is teaching the concept of sets in math and a games unit in physical education to emphasize controlling the ball with the hands. Without changing the main emphasis of the games unit, she substitutes Squirrel in the Forest (p. 256), Doubles Hopscotch (p. 295), and Loose Caboose (p. 268) for three previously selected games. The three new games now emphasize the games skills as well as sets. In addition, she designs a series of creative game challenges that includes sets as part of each challenge. These changes show how the teacher meets the objectives of her games unit and reinforces learning in another subject area.

Multicultural Society

Most of the early American immigrants were white Anglo-Saxon Protestants. The remaining early settlers were either black, Hispanic, or of Asian origin. As the public educational system became established, it attempted to assimilate all students into a single new culture. The resulting mix became known as the "melting pot" and has unfairly forced students to accept a white-dominated, Anglo-Saxon culture, regardless of their own heritage. During the past thirty years, there has been a positive shift toward a multicultural or pluralistic society. Today the population of the United States is rapidly changing from a white majority to a society composed of Middle East and South Asians, Hispanics, black Americans, and Native Americans. By the third or fourth decade of the next century, people with black or yellow skin color will outnumber the white population.

Multicultural education emphasizes the need to accept and respect the rights and cultural heritage of all people. It also recognizes that ethnic diversity enriches everyone's life. For example, physical education has played an important role in teaching games and dances from other countries. This trend will continue to stress a very broad-based multicultural program of physical activities at all levels of the public school system. These programs will be found not just in special schools where there is a major shift in the cultural background of their school population but in all schools regardless of the initial make-up of their population (figure 1.5).

National Physical Fitness Programs

In 1953 Dr. Hans Kraus released the results of his physical fitness survey, which showed the level of physical fitness of American children to be far lower than that of European children. The resulting impact of this study created a wave of interest in physical fitness throughout North America and from primary- to university-level programs. Within a few years, the federal government created the President's Council on Physical Fitness, which in turn had a major effect on the elementary and secondary physical education programs in North America. The Council's Physical Fitness Test and recommended programs were adopted by numerous school districts from New York to California. Other organizations, such as AAHPERD and several state departments of education, also produced their own physical fitness tests and special programs to raise the level of physical fitness of elementary and secondary school children. Although other trends and programs, such as lifetime sports and Movement Education, have changed the nature and direction of elementary school physical education, the emphasis on physical fitness that was started in 1953 is still felt today. The contemporary trend toward human wellness and active living is, in many respects, a continuation of this trend but with a major change in the meaning of physical fitness toward more health-related aspects.

Human Wellness and Positive Lifestyle

During the past few years, many elementary physical fitness programs have incorporated more health-related aspects of human wellness. The excessive number of either overweight or undernourished children has created a need for programs that help children assess their eating habits and plan effective weight-control programs. Problems relating to stress

Figure 1.5 A positive shift toward a multicultural society.

management and alcohol and drug addiction have also prompted the physical education profession to redefine and emphasize new aspects of physical fitness. For example, AAHPERD's *Physical Best Fitness Test Manual* emphasizes cardiorespiratory function; body composition (leanness/fatness); and abdominal, arm and shoulder girdle, and lowback-hamstring muscular skeletal function (AAHPERD 1989). This direction toward an emphasis on a positive state of well-being, which is further supported by the *Healthy People 2000* document, has created a need for programs that help children understand how their bodies work, how they can monitor body changes, and how they can design personal fitness programs for improving and maintaining optimum levels of health.

Active Living

Health-related concerns have prompted a move toward an "active living" concept. This thrust has been seen throughout North America. U.S. documents such as *Healthy People 2000* and findings stemming from the monumental research work of Sallis and McKenzie (1991) highlight the need to develop programs that promote active living. Similar support is seen in Canada through the Canadian Association for Health, Physical Education and Recreation's foundation document *Physical Education 2000* (CAHPER, 1992) and through their coordination of a program entitled "The Canadian Active Living Challenge." The idea is that if children are engaged in developmentally appropriate activities throughout their school years, then their natural interest in movement will be nurtured and developed from

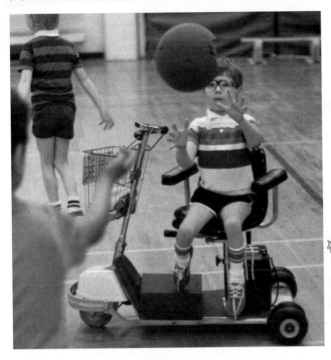

Figure 1.6 A child with a disability can participate in a regular physical education program according to the limits of his capabilities.

childhood through to adulthood. The active living concept is important since there is overwhelming evidence that exercise of the appropriate type, intensity, frequency, and duration will improve all health related aspects of children's physical fitness. Further, apart from the obvious benefits of physical and motor development, there is also evidence that regular physical activity has beneficial effects on mental health, including decreased anxiety and depression, a more positive mood, and elevated levels of self-esteem. Clearly, fostering and maintaining a physically active lifestyle throughout the entire life span is deemed desirable from a health point of view.

Equal Opportunity for All Children

Two laws that have dramatically affected all aspects of physical education are the Educational Amendment Act of 1972 (Title IX), and Section 504 of the Rehabilitation Act of 1973. A definition of each law follows, along with a brief explanation of the implications of these laws to teachers of elementary school children.

The Educational Amendment Act of 1972 (Title IX)

Title IX of this act states that "no person in the United States shall, on the basis of sex, be excluded from participation in, be denied the benefits of, or be subjected to discrimination under any education program or activity receiving federal financial assistance" (AAHPERD 1976). This law now requires all schools to provide equal opportunities to girls

and boys within the instructional and extracurricular program. This includes such aspects as facilities, time allotment, and equal employment of the teaching staff. This law, however, allows students to be grouped by ability and is applied without regard to gender. It also allows students to be separated by gender within the instructional program when this is deemed appropriate.

The most significant result of this act is that virtually all elementary physical education classes are now coeducational. As a result, this law has provided an opportunity for much greater social interaction among boys and girls. In addition, it has placed sports participation into a more natural lifetime environment. As a consequence of this law, AAHPERD has published an extensive guide describing a variety of methods and techniques for implementing the basic requirements of Title IX.

Section 504 of the Rehabilitation Act of 1973 (Public Law 93–112)

This law states that "no otherwise qualified handicapped individual shall, solely by reason of his handicap, be excluded from participation in, be denied the benefits of, or be subject to discrimination under any program or activity receiving federal financial assistance." This law requires schools to provide equal opportunities for any child with a disability to participate in all programs offered by the school. The interpretation of this law includes the regular instructional program, intramurals, and interschool athletics. The act has required schools to provide (1) special access to buildings for special needs children, (2) appropriate transportation, (3) appropriate curricular adjustments, and (4) appropriate adaptations in activities. The latter would include changes in rules and regulations, special ramps, and adjustments to playing equipment (figure 1.6).

The general implications of laws dealing with negligence have helped teachers improve the general care and safety of the children within their care. In very direct ways, such laws help teachers focus on the key points of teaching, on the quality of facilities and equipment, and on the general supervision of children. In a similar way, the laws dealing with children with disabilities have forced teachers and administrators to adjust facilities and modify teaching strategies to allow these children greater access to and participation in the physical education program.

Research Findings and Platform Statements

Other factors directly affecting the nature and direction of elementary physical education programs have resulted from research findings and statements by influential individuals or groups interested in the education and welfare of children. Numerous studies, for example, have been conducted to determine the effect of exercise on such factors as bone and muscle growth, perceptual-motor efficiency, and academic achievement. Two outstanding publications provide a comprehensive summary of research findings relating to children and physical activity. *Physical Activity and Well-Being* (1986) is written by leading researchers in the fields of health and physical education and is published by AAHPERD. *Children and Exercise XI* (1985), published by Human Kinetics Publishers, provides similar information. The investigations cited in these two publications clearly indicate that young children must receive appropriate daily exercise to ensure that their bodies grow and develop in a normal, functional manner.

Long-term studies, such as the Vanves program (Albinson and Andrews 1976), in which one third of the school day was devoted to physical education, have shown dramatically that children with strong, healthy bodies tend to do very well academically. These studies do not imply, however, that increases in strength, endurance, or motor coordination increase a child's intelligence. They simply demonstrate that physically fit children who possess good motor control do well academically. These investigations also show that strong, robust children can meet everyday personal and social pressures and challenges with relative ease.

The American Medical Association (AMA) and numerous other influential organizations have issued statements supporting the importance of daily physical education for children and youths. Such support has encouraged state and local officials to construct playing fields and facilities for physical education and athletic programs.

Public and private organizations have also influenced the direction and emphasis of instructional and extraclass programs. For example, the efforts of the President's Council on Physical Fitness and Sports, the AMA, and numerous other organizations have encouraged and supported physical education programs emphasizing physical fitness, intramural activities, or specific types of interschool competitive athletics. With respect to the latter, the publication *Guidelines for Children's Sports,* prepared by the American Alliance for Health, Physical Education, Recreation and Dance (AAHPERD 1979) and approved by the American Academy of Pediatrics, has had a major impact on all forms of children's athletics.

The collective influence of these factors and trends has required teachers to add new objectives to the elementary physical education program. This influence has also required teachers to set new priorities and to place renewed emphasis on key objectives of the program. This is *not* an undesirable situation because schools, being a mirror of society, must constantly adapt to legitimate trends and influences.

Toward a Developmentally Based Physical Education Curriculum

The term *developmentally appropriate* has been used for many years in the field of early childhood education. In 1987 the National Association for the Education of Young Children (NAEYC) provided an official definition of developmentally appropriate practice (Bredekamp, 1987). NAEYC defines "developmentally appropriate" programs as

those which are based on knowledge of what is age-appropriate for the group of children served as well as information about what is individually appropriate (i.e., the needs and interests of individual children within the program) (Bredekamp, 1992, p. 31).

If children are to grow and develop to their full potentials, then they must be provided with the most conducive learning environments. Unfortunately this is not always the case, as many children experience failure and frustration in a physical education setting. Designing a curriculum around developmentally appropriate practices provides the necessary focus to ensure that all children experience success and develop to their full potentials.

A developmentally based curriculum is based on several important factors. First, every child passes through a series of developmental stages. For example, in the process of learning to throw a ball, every child progresses through an initial and somewhat jerky stage, to a more focused second stage, to a final automatic step in which the movement is performed smoothly and effortlessly. A second important factor is that, although the majority of children follow similar sequences of motor development and arrive at developmental points at approximately the same age level, the rate of motor development varies; hence the rate of development is not age-dependent. Children pass through each developmental stage according to their own level of maturity and ability, rather than according to chronological age or grade level. Although it is impossible for a classroom teacher to individualize a program for each child, it is possible to use new organizational techniques, new content areas, and new teaching strategies to allow children within any given learning experience in physical education to develop and learn according to their own levels of interest, ability, and previous experience.

Since an understanding of social, emotional, and cognitive development, in addition to psychomotor development, will be needed if developmentally appropriate programs are to be achieved, all these areas of development are highlighted within the text.

Each part of this book is designed to help teachers create their own developmentally based curriculum. Parts 1 through 4 are sequential, beginning with background information, progressing through the nature and analysis of movement and designing a curriculum, and finishing with several chapters dealing with programs to accommodate special needs and interests. The latter three parts contain resource materials relating to game, dance, and gymnastic activities. The appendices contain information relating to facilities, equipment, and supplies.

Selected References

AAHPERD. (1980). *Personalized Learning in Physical Education.* Reston, VA: AAHPERD.

———. (1989). *Physical Best Program.* Reston, VA: AAHPERD.

Albinson, J. G., and Andrews, G. (1976). *Child in Sport and Physical Activity.* Baltimore: University Park Press.

Andrews, G., Saurborn, J., and Schneider, E. (1960). *Physical Education for Today's Boys and Girls.* Boston: Allyn and Bacon.

Armstrong, N. (1989). Children Are Fit But Not Active! *Education and Health, 7*(2), 28–32.

Armstrong, N., and Bray, S. (1986). The Role of the Physical Education Teacher in Coronary Prevention. In B. Wright and G. Donald (Eds.), *Trends and Developments in Physical Education.* London: E. & F. N. Spon Ltd. pp. 346–352.

Bennett, W. J. (1986). *First Lessons: A Report on Elementary Education in America.* Washington, DC: U.S. Government Printing Office.

Bredekamp, S. (1987). *Developmentally Appropriate Practice in Early Childhood Programs Servicing Children From Birth Through Age 8.* Washington, DC: National Association for the Education of Young Children.

Bredekamp, S. (August, 1992). What Is "Developmentally Appropriate" and Why Is It Important? *Journal of Physical Education, Recreation and Dance,* 31–32.

CAHPER. (1992). *Physical Education 2000.* Gloucester, Ontario: CAHPER Pub.

COPEC. (1992). *Developmentally Appropriate Physical Education Practices for Children.* A statement of the Council on Physical Education for Children.

Cratty, R. J. (1967). *Movement Behavior and Motor Learning,* Second Edition. Philadelphia: Lea & Febiger.

Dauer, V. P., and Pangrazi, R. P. (1992). *Dynamic Physical Education for Elementary School Children,* Eighth Edition. New York: Macmillan Publishing Co.

Fishburne, G. J., and Haslam, I. R. (1992). Critical Issues in Elementary School Education: Integration and the Curriculum. In T. Williams, L. Almond, and A. Sparkes (Eds.), *Sport and Physical Activity.* London: E. & F. N. Spon Ltd. pp. 132–137.

Gallahue, D. L. (1993). *Developmental Physical Education for Today's Children.* Dubuque, IA: Brown & Benchmark.

Graham, G., Holt-Hale, S. A., and Parker, M. (1993). *Children Moving,* Third Edition. Mountain View, CA: Mayfield Publishing Co.

Haywood, K. M. (1991). The Role of Physical Education in the Development of Active Lifestyles. *Research Quarterly for Exercise and Sport, 62*(2), 151–156.

Healthy People 2000: National Health Promotion and Disease Prevention Objectives. (1991). Report Issued by the U.S. Surgeon General.

Hellison, D. R. (1985). *Goals and Strategies for Teaching Physical Education.* Champaign, IL: Human Kinetics Publishers, Inc.

Humphrey, J. H. (1990). *Integration of Physical Education in the Elementary School Curriculum.* Springfield, IL: Charles C. Thomas Publishers.

Jewett, A. E., and Bain, L. L. (1985). *The Curriculum Process in Physical Education.* Dubuque, IA: Wm. C. Brown Publishers.

Johansen, J. H., Collins, H. W., and Johnson, J. A. (1990). *American Education: An Introduction to Teaching,* Sixth Edition. Dubuque, IA: Wm. C. Brown Publishers.

Johnson, M. (1987). *The Body in the Mind: The Bodily Basis of Meaning.* Chicago: University of Chicago Press.

Kline, M. (1977). *Why the Professor Can't Teach: Mathematics and the Dilemma of University Education.* New York: Academic Press.

Logsdon, R. J. (1984). *Physical Education for Children: A Focus on the Teaching Process.* Second Edition. Philadelphia: Lea & Febiger.

Morris, D. G. S., and Stiehl, J. (1985). *Physical Education: From Intent to Action.* Columbus: Merrill Publishing Co.

NASPE (1992). *Outcomes of Quality Physical Education Programs.* Reston, VA: NASPE/AAHPERD Publication.

Rarick, G. L. (1973). *Physical Activity and Human Growth and Development.* New York: Academic Press.

Sallis, J. F., and McKenzie, T. L. (1991). Physical Education's Role in Public Health. *Research Quarterly for Exercise and Sport, 62*(2), 124–134.

Steinhaus, A. H. (1966, September). Your Muscles See More than Your Eyes. *Journal of Health, Physical Education, and Recreation,* 38–40.

Thomas, J. R., Lee, A. M., and Thomas, K. T. (1988). *Physical Education for Children: Concepts into Practice.* Champaign, IL: Human Kinetics Publishers, Inc.

U.S. Department of Health and Human Services. (1985). "Summary of Findings from National Children and Youth Fitness Study." *Journal of Physical Education, Recreation and Dance,* 56(1), NCYFS 1–48.

———. (1987). "Summary of Findings from National Children and Youth Fitness Study II." *Journal of Physical Education, Recreation and Dance,* 58(1), NCYFS 1–48.

Wall, J., and Murray, N. (1994). *Children and Movement: Physical Education in the Elementary School,* Second Edition. Dubuque, IA: Wm. C. Brown Publishers.

Werner, P. H., and Burton, E. G. (1979). *Learning Through Movement: Teaching Cognitive Content Through Physical Activities.* St. Louis: C. V. Mosby Co.

2

Children and Activity

Contemporary education focuses on helping children develop to their full potential. As teachers of physical education, we must understand children's growth and development stages in order to choose appropriate activities and movement experiences. For example, a cursory knowledge of bone growth during childhood clearly indicates that vigorous daily exercise is necessary for normal development of bone tissue. Such knowledge also shows that excessive weight bearing or severe blows caused by a sport like contact football are harmful to virtually every elementary school child. Teachers and parents of elementary school children should be aware of the potential harm of this type of activity and oppose the adoption of such activities for this age level.

Physiological changes, however, are not the sole criterion for selecting activities or teaching methods. Psychological changes involving self-image and attention span as well as motivation and sociological changes relating to peer group importance also have significant implications for the physical education program.

This chapter summarizes the important physical, psychological, and social changes children experience as they move through three levels of development. A few important implications of these changes for primary and intermediate physical education programs are also provided ■

Human Development

The purpose of any educational environment is to create the most conducive situation for optimum learning and development. This will allow students to develop to their true potential. Since children develop and grow in unique ways, it is imperative that those individuals who structure children's learning environments are knowledgeable about the developmental level of students for whom the learning experience is intended. In order to provide developmentally appropriate activities, teachers of physical education must be cognizant of human development.

Studying human development is an extremely complex undertaking. As Bower (1979), a developmental psychologist, aptly stated:

We enter this world small and helpless, with few capacities and few behaviors. Within two decades, however, we have the full range of human skills at our disposal, for whatever purposes we desire. Within another two decades the inexorable decline in powers and skills through aging begins, and will continue until death. The human adult is the lord of creation, the most successful organism ever evolved. Yet no other primate—indeed no other mammal—is as dependent as we are at birth. How does anything as helpless as a human baby become something as competent as an adult? (p. 3)

Development is a difficult area to study due to the interaction of nature and nurture. Whatever area of development is considered, be it intellectual, social, or physical, the same problem is always encountered: What part does nature play and what is the influence of nurture? Teasing out the precise benefits of environmental influence (nurture) is difficult due to the complex interaction that constantly occurs with heredity (nature). As difficult as the problem may seem, some headway has been made through systematic observation, experimentation, and careful analysis of human behavior. Some of the major developmental findings in the physical and motor domain follow. However, before undertaking a review of children's physical and motor development, it will be helpful if several terms are clarified.

Definition of Terms

Developmentalists have gained some insights through first defining the terms under study. Defining terms such as skill and ability, for example, can be an extremely valuable start to gaining an understanding of child development. The following terms have been identified and agreed on by most developmental psychologists.

Growth: refers to a quantitative increase in size. In terms of physical growth, this refers to quantitative changes in body mass. For example, an increase in the size of the calf muscle would represent growth.

Maturation: refers to the physical and behavioral changes that are primarily a product resulting from an innate process of growth rather than being influenced by direct experiences with the environment. For example, as a baby grows (matures) there is a natural progress toward walking. Maturation is a qualitative advancement and refers to progress toward maturity.

Development: implies a continuous process of change. Development may occur in the form of quantitative and/or qualitative change. For example, a young child develops language and speech through the interaction of growth, maturation, and learning opportunities.

Motor development: implies a continuous process of change in the motor area. That is, as children grow, mature, and learn, both quantitative and qualitative changes occur in their motor proficiency. For example, a young child will develop proficiency in catching a small ball through the interaction of growth, maturation, and learning opportunities. Motor development refers to such a process of change.

Motor task: refers to the specific movement activity. For example, the motor task may be to throw a ball at a target.

Motor performance: refers to the actual movement performance that occurs when an attempt is made to complete a motor task. For example, hitting the center of a target with a ball.

Motor learning: The term motor refers to movement. Hence, motor learning deals with aspects of learning involving body movement. Improving motor performance through practice would constitute motor learning. Hence, improving catching performance through practice would be classified as motor learning.

Motor learning and motor performance: Performance can be thought of as observable behavior. Learning, on the other hand, is an internal phenomenon that cannot be observed directly. Learning is inferred from performance. If permanent changes in motor performance occur over trials (practices), it is suggested that learning has occurred. However, all that is observable is performance. This is reflected in definitions of motor learning. For example, Magill (1993) defines motor learning as: "A change in the capability of a person to perform a skill that must be inferred from a relatively permanent improvement in performance as a result of practice or experience" (p. 44). As can be seen, Magill's definition of motor learning has to rely on observable motor performance since learning can only be inferred from performance.

Motor behavior: is a general term that is often used when both learning and performance of movement are to be addressed. For example, it is possible to observe a child's motor behavior.

Motor skill and motor ability: The terms skill and ability are often used in the educational setting. Sometimes these terms are used interchangeably, with little regard for any real differences between them. However, careful examination of these two terms is extremely helpful to a teacher of young children.

Motor skill: refers to the degree of proficiency in performing a motor task. Skill, therefore, is task oriented and is judged on a continuum from poor (unskillful) to excellent (highly skilled). For example, a child who performs the motor task of catching a small ball would perform observable behavior. When a judgment of proficiency is assigned to this motor performance, this refers to the level of skill exhibited.

Motor ability: Fleishman (1964) has suggested that motor skills depend on motor abilities. Individuals bring with them to each situation a set of underlying traits (abilities), which are utilized when making a motor performance. For example, the level of proficiency (skill) exhibited when catching a small ball will depend on motor abilities such as hand-eye coordination, finger dexterity, wrist-finger speed, and arm-hand steadiness.

Now that these terms have been defined, it is appropriate to move to the significance of these defined areas in terms of children's motor and physical development. Understanding developmental changes of elementary-school-age children will provide a foundation from which developmentally appropriate activities and strategies of teaching can be determined.

Physical Growth and Development

Young children experience significant changes as they grow and develop. For example, they experience changes in height and weight and in other areas of body composition. Knowledge of children's physical growth and development is essential if a developmentally appropriate program of physical education is to be realized.

Height and Weight

Two of the most common measures of a child's growth pattern are height and weight. In figures 2.1 and 2.2, the average heights of boys and girls are plotted according to age and expressed in percentiles to show relative position for children within any particular age level. To illustrate, a nine-year-old boy whose height is 51.2 inches is at the 25th percentile on the chart. This means that 75 percent of all nine-year-olds are taller than he is and 25 percent are shorter.

The first period of rapid growth for both sexes occurs during infancy. During the early primary period (approximately ages five to seven), there is a time of steady growth of about 2 to 3 inches per year. At around nine years for girls and eleven years for boys, the adolescent growth spurt begins. Girls reach their peak of this growing period by age twelve

Figure 2.1 Girls' height by age and expressed in percentiles. The central line represents the mean, or 50th centile. The two lines above and below it represent the 75th and 25th centiles (i.e., 25 percent of the cross-sectional sample fell below the lower line and 25 percent above the upper line). Other centile lines are also provided. (From David L. Gallahue, *Understanding Motor Development,* 2d edition, Copyright © 1989 by Benchmark Press, Inc. Reprinted by permission of Wm. C. Brown Communications, Inc., Dubuque, IA. All Rights Reserved.)

children and activity

Figure 2.2 Boys' height by age and expressed in percentiles. (From David L. Gallahue, *Understanding Motor Development*, 2d edition, Copyright © 1989 by Benchmark Press, Inc. Reprinted by permission of Wm. C. Brown Communications, Inc., Dubuque, IA. All Rights Reserved.)

or thirteen, whereas boys reach their maximum gains by their fourteenth or fifteenth year. Boys' height gain is much greater than girls' by the time both have reached early adolescence.

The average gains in weight, which appear in figures 2.3 and 2.4, show a relatively steady increase until they reach a peak for girls at age twelve and for boys at age fourteen. It should also be noted that the peak in weight is about six to eight months behind the peaking of height for both sexes. There is a major problem in the interpretation of age-height charts, since weight values give no indication of how fat or thin children are at any given age. For example, an eight-year-old boy who weighs 55 pounds and is 45 inches tall may look thin because his proportionate weight is due to relatively heavy bones. To obtain more information about children's growth as it relates to weight, we are now beginning to use a measure of body leanness/fatness measured by a simple estimate of body composition, which will be described in the next section.

The period of steady and fairly even growth of boys and girls during the latter part of early childhood (five to seven years) and partially through middle childhood (eight to nine years) provides a stable period to acquire and improve many basic locomotor and manipulative skills. Since there are negligible differences between the sexes in weight and height until the beginning of the adolescent growth spurt, it is appropriate to combine boys and girls for instruction in physical education. Further, during this period of time, there is no reason to expect boys to show a superior performance in using motor skills. If they do, such performance levels may be attributed to the relative time each sex devotes to practice and playing physical activities than to any inherent physiological differences between boys and girls.

Body Composition

Body composition is the proportionate amount of total body mass that is lean (bone, muscle, organs, and tissues) or fat (adipose tissue). The total amount of body fat in any individual cannot be directly measured. Fairly reliable and valid estimates of an individual's proportionate body fat can be obtained, however, by placing a caliper over a fold of skin and underlying fat tissue. Since approximately 50 percent of the fat stored in the body is in a layer just below the skin, skinfold measurements, such as those now used in the AAHPERD Fitness Test (see chapter 12), are accurate indicators of a child's proportionate amount of fat.

However, a few important points should be noted when evaluating the body composition of elementary school children. For example, some children may look overweight, yet, when measured with the skinfold calipers, they do not register a high level of body fat. Conversely, a child may look thin but register a high percentage of body fat. Many young children, particularly those who have not reached puberty, have not developed a high percentage of muscle mass and, hence, record a higher-than-expected percentage of body fat.

The contemporary estimates of elementary-school-age children with excessive proportions of fatty tissue to lean body mass, or what is commonly called overweight or obesity, is somewhere between 20 and 35 percent. Recent surveys suggest the incidence of obesity among children is rising. Such surveys have prompted some medical practitioners to claim it is a form of child abuse to allow young children to become obese. The health-related implications associated with obesity are significant. For example, the chances of developing diabetes, hypercholesterolemia, hypertension, and respiratory and orthopedic problems are all increased for the obese person over a "normal" weight person. In fact, everything from flat feet to cancer is more likely in obese people. Obese children are more likely to become obese adults and therefore at greater risk of heart disease, stroke,

Figure 2.3 Girls' weight by age. (Reprinted with permission of Ross Laboratories, Columbus, OH 43216, from NCHS Growth Charts, © 1986 Ross Laboratories. Adapted from: Hamill PVV, Drizd TA, Johnson CL, Reed RB, Roche AF, Moore WM, *Physical Growth: National Center for Health Statistics Percentiles.* AM J CLIN NUTR 32:607–629, 1979. Data from the National Center for Health Statistics [NCHS], Hyattsville, Maryland.)

the most effective approach to combating obesity. As Haywood (1986) states:

> The increased number of calories expended by increased activity permits weight reduction while maintaining caloric intake at safe levels. Exercise, then, plays an important role in weight reduction at any age, but particularly in children. (p. 236)

It is unlikely that physical education programs alone will be able to address the issue of obesity among children. Integration of other subject areas, which is a feature of this text, is one avenue of opportunity to help combine the need of diet with regular physical activity. Integrating health curriculum topics of nutrition and diet with physical education offers a valuable educational opportunity. However, without parental support, even this combined approach may not be sufficient. Intervention techniques to help alleviate obesity are usually tied to continued participation by the child and family support. Hence the need for an active lifestyle

and the many other ailments and diseases cited. It is imperative that elementary school physical education programs address this problem. It has been suggested that overeating in young children is quite rare (Mayer, 1968); rather, inactivity is the common characteristic of obese children. Reducing caloric intake without exercising may result in the loss of lean body tissue as well as fat weight. Further, a reduction of caloric intake to the 1,000 calorie-per-day level can temporarily slow down or even arrest growth. Obviously, a combination of diet and activity is needed for

both within and outside of school. Unfortunately, children who are overweight or obese have difficulty in performing virtually all motor skills. As children gain proportionately more fat than lean body tissue, they normally display early fatigue and a decrease in participation in all forms of physical activity. A sound nutritional diet helps decrease the percentage of body fat, but, without daily vigorous physical activity, overweight children continue to be overweight or become obese as they enter adolescence and adulthood. A major challenge for teachers of physical education programs is to develop activities that help each overweight and obese child, on an individual basis, to begin to become more physically active and to maintain this lifestyle throughout the life span.

Physique

Physique refers to body build and is made up of a composite of body proportion and body characteristics. We normally use three body somatotypes (Sheldon, Dupertuis, and McDermott, 1954) to describe general physiques. A tall and relatively thin, or Ichabod Crane-like, person is classified as an ectomorph. The second, more proportionate and muscular looking person is known as a mesomorph. Finally, a person who is round in contour with a tendency toward fatness and obesity has an endomorphic physique.

There appears to be little relationship between body type and strength among the three somatotypes during early, middle, and late childhood. Also, performance in locomotor or manipulative skills is largely unaffected by body physique except for unusually tall or excessively obese children (figure 2.5).

Body Proportion

Changes occur in both body form and proportion as a child moves from newborn through to adulthood. A child is not a miniature adult who merely gains in height each year. Body proportions change as the child grows. As the infant's body begins to grow and develop, dramatic proportional changes take place in the size of various parts of the body. For example, the head changes from one quarter of the body length at birth to approximately one

sixth at age six and one eighth at maturity. Legs increase five times and the trunk three times from birth to maturity. During early childhood, the center of gravity for boys and girls is near the umbilicus, causing some difficulties in maintaining balance when catching balls or while performing balance movements on small and large apparatus. As children mature, the center of gravity lowers to the pelvic area, creating a greater degree of stability for all motor activities.

As boys and girls reach the beginning of puberty, they start to show proportionate differences in the width of their shoulders and hips. Girls begin to increase hip width relatively more than shoulder width. Boys do not

Figure 2.5 A child's physique.

Figure 2.6 Growth of long bones.

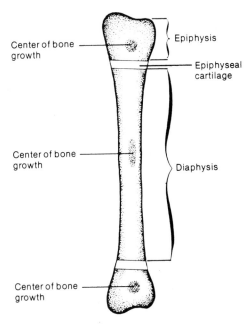

show any increase in shoulder width over hip width until around ten years. As both sexes reach adolescence, boys develop greater shoulder width than girls and proportionately longer legs, giving them an advantage in activities involving forceful arm actions and running speed.

Skeletal Growth and Development

The bones of an elementary school child undergo continuous change in length, width, and general composition. The long bones, such as the humerus (upper arm) and femur (upper leg), have one center of growth in the middle of the bone called diaphysis and one or more centers at each end of the bone called epiphysis (figure 2.6). Growth occurs from the center of the bone toward the ends and from the ends toward the center. When these centers merge into a solid bone, bone maturation is complete.

It should be noted that research has shown that bones attain their greatest mass and strength through appropriate weight-bearing activities. This probably accounts for the natural propensity of children to climb and swing during their normal play activities.

Since the bones of an elementary school child are relatively soft and flexible, they normally can absorb many jars or blows without fracturing. However, severe blows, such as those experienced in contact football, and excessive weight bearing on any joint should be avoided. Since the ends of the bones and other connecting tissues around the joints are extremely supple, however, children can bend and stretch all parts of their body farther than even the most fit adult.

Boys and girls from age five to approximately eleven show a steady increase in bone growth. During this period the bone structure is still relatively weak and flexible. As a child reaches puberty, bone growth appears to be more rapid; this is quite evident with eleven- and twelve-year-old girls in the fifth and sixth grades.

Bones have many functions, some of which are not obvious. In addition to providing shape and form of the body, support and protection for internal organs, and limbs for locomotion and movement, they perform many other vital bodily functions. For example, bones provide a site for blood formations, are a basic component of the body's immune system, and provide a dynamic reservoir for calcium and phosphate (Bailey, Martin, Houston, and Howie, 1986). The body uses the calcium and phosphate reservoir to supply the nerves, the heart and the muscles, and the metabolic pathways. Bones go through a process of deposit and withdrawal. The development and maintenance of strong healthy bones is necessary to provide the mineralization (calcium and phosphate) reservoir. It is essential to develop strong bones in order to keep the mineralization reservoir in balance with the withdrawal demands made by the body. The most efficient way of developing strong and healthy bones is through physical activity.

When the calcium and phosphate withdrawal is greater than the mineralization deposit, osteoporosis can occur. This is the most common skeletal disorder in North America and is the result of progressive bone loss. A suggested remedy and prevention for osteoporosis is the intake of calcium supplements. However, epidemiologic evidence does not support the hypothesis that larger intakes of calcium are associated with increased

children and activity

bone density or the decreased incidence of fractures (Martin and Houston, 1987). The research evidence suggests that regular physical activity is probably the most effective way of maintaining the mineralization reservoir. Martin and Houston (1987) state,

Regular physical activity, started early in childhood, can increase the peak bone mass of early adulthood, delay the onset of bone loss and reduce the rate of loss. (p. 591)

In other words, regular physical activity is probably more beneficial to the integrity of bone development than the intake of milk or other calcium supplement. Just as parents and teachers encourage the intake of milk for bone growth, of equal or greater importance to the integrity of bone development is regular physical activity.

Children should be denied neither milk nor regular physical activity. It should also be remembered that the movement experiences children undertake must include careful, but necessary, weight-bearing activities. The teacher cannot rely on "recess" to provide these opportunities but must structure an environment that will provide developmentally appropriate activities for optimum bone development.

Maturation

Certain changes, relatively independent of environmental influence, take place as growth proceeds. For example, there are changes in a child's motor performance as growth proceeds. At approximately four months of age a baby can sit with support. At seven months the infant can sit alone. Creeping, climbing, and eventually standing occur as the child matures and is able to increase control over voluntary movements. Such development is, as Hottinger (1980) states, predictable.

Since all human life is subject to this same basic process it is logical to believe that characteristics subject to the maturational process will be broadly predictable in all normal children. (p. 15)

Motor milestones have therefore been identified and are used as developmental checks to establish if a child is proceeding along the normal path of development. For example, if an infant was not walking at twenty months of age then there would be some concern regarding the child's motor development. For the interested reader, a comprehensive list of motor milestones can be found in Espenschade and Eckert (1980), and Haywood (1986). In addition to motor milestones, there are two other areas of development that need to be considered if a developmentally appropriate program of physical education is to be realized.

Cephalocaudal and Proximodistal Development

Growth tends to proceed from the head toward the feet, or in a "cephalocaudal" direction. Both growth and motor function follow this pattern. The nervous system develops from the brain downward. Hence, the child gains control of the head before the trunk. Control of the legs follows the trunk. Hence, based on this knowledge of development, the sequencing of the motor milestones mentioned earlier can be understood.

Growth also tends to proceed from the center of the body to the periphery, or in a "proximodistal" direction. Again, both growth and function follow this pattern. Motor control proceeds from the trunk to arms and then to hands and fingers. Also, control proceeds from the hips to legs, then to feet and toes. Further, there will be control of gross muscle movements before fine muscle movement.

Evidence of proximodistal development is seen with those kindergarten children who cannot perform the fine motor task of tying a shoelace. Apart from the cognitive aspects involved in this task, many children have difficulty due to a lack of finger dexterity. This motor ability has not yet fully developed. To solve the problem, some teachers demand that children wear slip-on or easy-to-fasten shoes when they attend school. This may solve the teacher's problem, but it may not be in the best interest of child development to mainly provide gross motor tasks and ignore practice of fine manipulative abilities. Since there is evidence of sensitive periods or times in development when a child needs to experience certain activities, then a full range of experiences should be provided.

Muscular Growth and Development

Prior to birth, the muscles of the developing embryo increase in the number of muscle cells (hyperplasia) and in the size of each cell (hypertrophy). After birth, hyperplasia continues for a brief period; however, thereafter muscle growth is only activated by an increase in the size of the muscle fibers. With respect to school-age children, an initial rapid growth in muscle tissue occurs between ages five and six. However, from ages seven to eleven or twelve, growth of muscle mass is relatively gradual and continuous. By age twelve, the average child has nearly double the amount of muscle tissue he had at age six. Experts in the growth and development field indicate that increases in the size and strength of muscles, particularly in children in the middle elementary grades (grades three to five), make this a period of restlessness for most children. As with all other systems of the human body, muscle tissue must be exercised if its full potential is to be reached.

The majority of physical fitness norms show that boys are slightly stronger than girls between five and twelve years of age. This difference, particularly prior to puberty, is not the result of an inherent difference in muscular systems but is normally due to social factors—boys tend to participate in vigorous activities, whereas girls lean toward less active and less physically demanding activities. However, this tendency clearly is being reduced by social and cultural changes, along with the current policy of giving equal time to both sexes in all publicly supported sport and physical activity programs. Once they reach puberty, however, boys begin to show significant increases in muscle mass and strength, and physiological changes in girls create proportionately less muscular mass and more fatty tissue. These changes, coupled with other structural changes in both sexes, produce a major difference in the strength of boys and girls as they enter adolescence.

Cardiorespiratory Growth and Development

The heart is a special kind of muscle; however, it grows and develops in the same way as skeletal muscle tissue. The growth of the heart muscle and lungs is almost proportional to the growth of bones and muscles throughout the elementary school years. At six, the average heart rate for boys and girls is around ninety beats per minute. Girls' heart rates are two to three beats higher at this age than boys'. Respiration rate for both sexes is approximately twenty a minute. Thus, easy fatigue and rapid recovery are characteristic of this age.

At age twelve, boys' heart rates drop to about seventy and girls' to around seventy-two. Respiration rate is between fifteen and twenty breaths a minute. Children between nine and twelve have more cardiorespiratory endurance, although girls with early signs of puberty may tire sooner. Maximum heart rate, which is the fastest the heart beats during heavy exercise, is around 212 beats per minute for six-year-old children. This maximum rate declines slightly to around 205 beats for both sexes by the time they reach early adolescence.

Factors Affecting Growth and Development

The growth and developmental process of every child is determined by two interdependent factors: heredity and the environment. Heredity sets the limits on growth, physique, and ultimate performance. Environmental factors, such as nutrition and exercise, also play an important role in this developmental process. The following four environmental factors are particularly important in determining whether children will reach their potential.

Nutrition

One of the most important environmental factors affecting growth is nutrition. During periods of rapid growth, the body must have sufficient quantities of proteins, carbohydrates, fats, water, minerals, and vitamins. Without sufficient quantities of these basic elements, the growing child will not reach maximum height. Chronic malnutrition can also cause delay in puberty and serious disease such as rickets and scurvy. Furthermore, children who suffer from chronic malnutrition during infancy and early childhood may not resume a normal growth and developmental pattern once an adequate diet is provided.

Exercise

As stated earlier, scientific evidence indicates that exercise is necessary during the formative years for normal bone growth. Therefore, an active lifestyle will be necessary for the development of strong bones and muscles. It has also been shown that long periods of inactivity cause some decalcification of bones (Albinson and Andrews 1976). The result of this demineralization is weaker and brittler bone, which is more susceptible to fractures and other injuries. On the other hand, regular physical activity increases bone mineralization and density, which makes the bone more resistant to stress and trauma. It has also been established that an appropriate dose of daily physical activity increases muscle mass. Exercise causes the muscle fiber to increase in size but it does not increase the number of muscle cells. Regular exercise also decreases the amount of body fat. However, in some cases, particularly with long-term exercise programs, a child will lose body fat but will not lose weight, due to a proportionate increase in muscle tissue.

Geography and Climate

Several physical environmental factors, such as climate, geographical location, and altitude, seem to affect normal growth patterns. To illustrate, short, stocky physiques are more common in cold climates and tall, thin physiques are prevalent in hot climates. Other related factors, such as diet, types of exercise, and genetic inheritance, may have overriding influences. Nevertheless, the trend is common throughout the world. Children who are raised in high altitudes, such as in the Himalayas, have proportionately smaller bodies and slower growth rates than children who live at lower altitudes. This may be due to an insufficient supply of oxygen, which is needed for normal growth and development. At high altitudes, two other factors—a colder climate and poor nutrition—may combine with altitude to simultaneously affect normal growth patterns.

Motor Ability Development

Children improve their motor skills through practice. However, frequently they are faced with new motor tasks never before performed, yet they can often turn to the new task and produce a fairly satisfactory motor performance. How can children perform motor skills that have never been specifically practiced? One view to explain such "transfer" effects is the idea of a general motor ability.

Figure 2.7 A child uses fine manipulative abilities to catch a small ball.

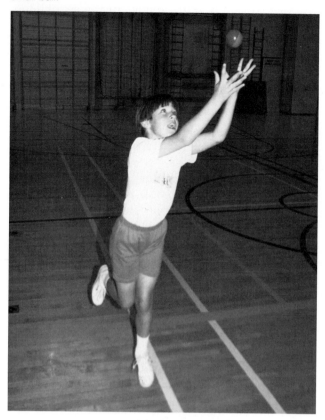

Figure 2.8 A child uses fine manipulative abilities to type.

Just as psychologists have searched to measure and define a general intellectual ability (IQ), so too has there been a drive to isolate a similar correlate in the motor domain. Two of the main proponents who have attempted to isolate and define motor ability are Fleishman (1954) and Guilford (1958). Guilford postulated a matrix of psychomotor abilities. Fleishman's work indicated that a general motor ability could not be found; instead, several categories of motor abilities were identified. His position is that individuals bring with them to each situation a set of underlying motor abilities that determine to a large degree the level of proficiency to which a skill will be performed.

To explain transfer effects, it is only necessary to present one of the four categories here, namely "fine manipulative abilities." The fine manipulative abilities category consists of four basic motor abilities: arm-hand steadiness, wrist-finger speed, finger dexterity, and manual dexterity. Consider now the two dissimilar motor tasks of catching a small ball and typing, as shown in figures 2.7 and 2.8. If the four motor abilities in the fine manipulative category were not developed to a high degree in the performer, then a poorly skilled performance would result when each of the motor tasks were attempted. The same underlying motor abilities necessary for performing a sport skill are needed to perform many other skills well outside the realm of sport.

In essence then, a performer who has well-developed motor abilities has many of the prerequisites for performing all motor skills. Transfer effects can now be explained, since a performer who has well-developed motor abilities can turn to a novel motor task and use the developed abilities to make an adequate motor performance. Obviously, the cognitive aspects and precise nuances associated with each unique motor skill will affect the performance too, but the basic motor abilities will be of primary importance.

One other finding of importance reported by Fleishman (1964) was the changes noted in the development of motor abilities. He stated that motor abilities are themselves the "product of learning and develop at different rates, mainly during childhood and adolescence" (p. 9). Since there are sensitive times early in life for developing motor abilities, it is imperative that a rich environment occur in the elementary school years to ensure that children develop to their maximum potential. Elementary school teachers must provide opportunities for children to develop their underlying motor abilities. Having children involved in a whole variety of movement activities, with lots of opportunity for practice, will ensure that each child has the chance of developing to full potential. Providing experiences mainly in gross motor activities and limiting opportunities to develop motor abilities through fine motor tasks (e.g., tying shoelaces) may not be in the best interests of the child. Obviously, attempting motor tasks that provide little or no success may result in frustration. Thus, a variety of different motor tasks of varying levels of difficulty (developmentally appropriate) must be provided to ensure

Table 2.1　Stages of Motor Skill Development

Babyhood	Early childhood	Middle childhood	Late childhood
(age one month through second year)	(ages three to seven)	(ages eight to nine)	(ages ten to twelve)
Stage one: rudimentary skills	*Stage two: fundamental movement skills*	*Stage three: refined movement skills*	*Stage four: specific sport, dance, or specialized skills*
Rudimentary skills—sit, crawl, creep, stand, walk	Basic locomotor skills—walk, run, leap, jump, hop	Combination and refinement of one or more fundamental skills—run and jump, slide and stop, land and roll, catch and throw, dribble and kick	Advanced and refined versions of sports, dance, or other specialized skills—running long jump, football pass, Scottish sword dance, hand spring
	Combined locomotor skills—skip, slide, stop, and dodge		
	Basic nonlocomotor skills—bend, stretch, twist, turn, push, pull, swing		
	Basic manipulation skills—throw, catch, strike		

success. Threading ropes of various thicknesses through a variety of different sized holes is one way of controlling level of difficulty for the development of fine manipulative abilities. When children practice these motor skills, they are contributing to the development of their motor abilities. Early childhood through to adolescence should be a time of continuing to refine basic motor skills, while at the same time developing underlying motor abilities to their full potential. Once a solid foundation of basic motor abilities has been established, there exists the opportunity to transfer such abilities to new situations in order to perform and learn new motor skills with some ease.

Returning once more to the four motor abilities that make up the category of fine manipulative abilities, the teacher must realize that when movement experiences are used to develop these fine manipulative abilities, it is not for the sole purpose of learning sport skills. As mentioned earlier, the same motor abilities used to catch a small ball are needed to perform many other motor skills well outside the realm of sport. For example, typing, handwriting, drawing and drafting, playing a musical instrument, and sewing all require fine manipulative motor abilities. This is why the curriculum area is termed physical education and not merely sports education. The aim of a developmentally appropriate program of physical education is to develop physically educated children.

Motor Skill Development

The development of motor skills, from birth to late childhood, follows an orderly sequence through four overlapping age ranges (table 2.1). The first stage, known as babyhood or infancy, begins about one month after birth and lasts to the end of the second year. During this period, a child displays reflex responses and then proceeds to the

Figure 2.9　A child begins to develop basic manipulative skills.

rudimentary skills of sitting, crawling, creeping, climbing, standing, and walking (figure 2.9).

The next stage, known as early childhood, continues from age three to approximately the seventh year. During this period, a child develops the fundamental locomotor and nonlocomotor skills of running, jumping, leaping, hopping, skipping, sliding, dodging, stopping, swinging, twisting, bending, turning, and stretching. A child also begins to develop the basic manipulative skills of throwing, catching, and striking.

As children move into middle childhood, they begin to show greater ease and efficiency in performing fundamental motor skills and develop more complex

Figure 2.10 A child begins to develop complex combinations.

Figure 2.11 A child becomes more fluid and creative.

combinations of locomotor, nonlocomotor, and manipulative skill patterns (figure 2.10). During third and fourth grades, increases in physical size and strength, coupled with improved perceptual and cognitive development, contribute to a child's ability to perform more coordinated movement patterns with greater speed and accuracy.

During late childhood, the more specific movement skills required of games, dance, and gymnastics begin to show some refinement. In game activities, such as soccer, fifth- and sixth-graders learn to dribble with changing speeds as well as to add feints and other tactics necessary for moving a ball through a variety of complex game situations. Similarly, dance and gymnastic skills become more fluid and creative as the performers acquire greater skill and understanding of the finer aspects of a movement or sequence of movements (figure 2.11). As children move into adolescence, they continue to refine these more specialized game, dance, and gymnastic skills to acquire new skills that are more related to their social and future leisure activities.

These four developmental stages, coupled with the tremendous individual differences existing at each grade level, have a direct bearing on a teacher's choice of activities, the way in which these activities are taught, and the learning expectations of every child. The primary program should be a time for acquiring minimal form in the fundamental and manipulative skills. This program should emphasize exposure to these movement concepts and skills and include numerous opportunities for experimenting with different ways of moving and manipulating balls, bats, and a variety of other small equipment. It is clearly not a time for refinement or specialization.

As children enter middle childhood, they become interested in improving specific motor skills; therefore, they devote more time and energy to acquiring these

skills. They also are keenly interested in playing more organized and challenging games. Teachers of these children should not only show them how to improve their performances and provide interesting and challenging game and dance activities, but they should also provide opportunities for exploration and creative expression regardless of the nature of the activity. Children in this age range enjoy competition, but they also like cooperative activities that provide avenues for positive interpersonal relationships.

Late childhood is essentially a continuation of the previous stage, characterized by a keener interest in improving performance. Differences in physiological maturity, particularly for girls who have entered puberty, present some problems with respect to activity interests and gender preferences in playing or performing some activities. These problems, however, can be dealt with by using more individualized teaching strategies, as suggested in later chapters.

Personal and Social Development

The personal and social characteristics of children, as well as their physical growth and motor development, must be considered when planning a physical education program. This section describes some of the more common personal and social characteristics of children in early childhood (three to seven years), middle childhood (eight to nine years), and late childhood (ten to twelve years).

Early Childhood (Five to Seven Years)

Five- and six-year-old children are quite egocentric; hence, they enjoy playing by themselves or with one or two other children. They have boundless curiosity and enthusiasm, but they tire easily (figure 2.12). These children need to explore many types of physical activities and challenges—but without pressure and with generous

chapter 2

Figure 2.12 These children need to explore many types of activities.

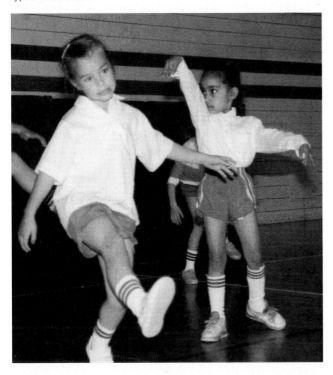

Figure 2.13 Children's interests shift toward more group activities.

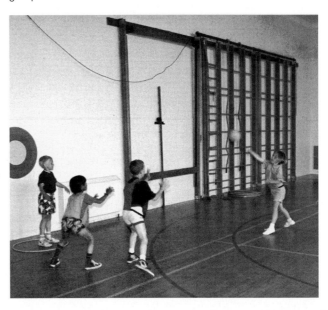

praise for their accomplishments. As they enter grade two, they become much more cooperative and they display an interest in all types of physical activity, although for relatively short periods of time. Teachers find that seven-year-olds seek adult approval much more than they did just a year earlier.

Middle Childhood (Eight to Nine Years)

As children enter middle childhood, their interests shift toward more group activities and group success (figure 2.13). They show a keen interest in more complex game and dance activities and a willingness to practice to improve their individual skills. Although these children seem to display a great deal of group or team loyalty, they tend toward adult-supervised activities. It is very important that teachers provide challenging activities *with many opportunities for each child to be successful.* Middle childhood is a period during which children begin to test their abilities within a group setting. If all challenges end in failure, the child's self-image reaches a very low ebb, and continued interest in physical activities becomes doubtful. Therefore, it is important that instructors provide children with a strong base for coping with the failures that everyone experiences during a lifetime.

Late Childhood (Ten to Twelve Years)

Physical maturation influences the social and psychological development of children in this age group, creating

a period of transition and differentiation in the interests and behavior of both boys and girls (Arnold 1968) (figure 2.14). Both sexes enjoy highly complex team games and, like the previous age range, are willing to practice for long periods to improve their playing ability. They have an intense need to become responsible for their own actions; hence, they enjoy planning, organizing, and supervising their own activities, which has major implications for daily instructional, intramural, and interschool programs.

Boys tend to be less concerned with dress and appearance, are keenly interested in vigorous competitive sports, and show a strong concern about their peers and a great deal of confidence in adults. Hero worship, particularly of well-known athletes, is a rule rather than the exception.

Girls' attitudes toward active participation in all types of vigorous physical activities are changing. More girls are now participating in organized intramural and interschool team sports. Community clubs for gymnastics, swimming, and soccer are also experiencing a major increase in the number of girls wishing to participate in their sports programs. Although this is a significant trend, girls of this age level still become increasingly concerned with their personal femininity; therefore, they tend toward less vigorous activities. They are, however, keenly interested in current fad dances and will participate in this type of activity with great vigor.

No magic line separates one age from another; teachers of grades five and six are aware of the tremendous diversity in the psychological characteristics of these children. However, as with the younger age range, some basic considerations should be made when planning a

children and activity

Figure 2.14 A period of transition and differentiation in interests and abilities.

physical education program for children in the intermediate grades (see p. 97).

Cognitive Development

For many years, physical education has been justified on the basis of enhancing the physical fitness of children and teaching them a variety of physical activities. These objectives are still the cornerstone of most physical education programs; however, the shift toward a more developmental approach now requires a greater emphasis on cognitive development. The basic philosophy of the developmental approach is to teach children the underlying concepts and principles of health and movement. When they understand their bodies' functions, the principles of exercise, and body mechanics, they learn to appreciate the importance of maintaining optimum levels of well-being and to acquire and enjoy a variety of physical activities. A conscious effort has been made throughout this text to provide the basic knowledge and important concepts for each content area of the program.

For many years, classroom teachers have recognized the value of using the medium of movement to teach a variety of academic skills and concepts. For example, the use of the game Squirrel in the Tree to reinforce the concept of sets or the modification of Steal the Bacon to teach adding and subtracting is not new to classroom teachers. The premise of using physical activities to enhance academic concepts and skills is based on three important factors. First, children have a greater chance of learning an academic skill when they are actively involved in the learning. Games and other exciting movement activities that also emphasize an academic skill can accomplish this task. Second, children learn through a variety of experiences. Some learn best through auditory modes; others through visual modes; and others through an active and enjoyable game, dance, or gymnastic activity. Third, to learn and retain an academic concept, a child must practice it many times through different media. Numerous suggestions are provided throughout this text for integrating physical education with other academic subject areas.

Implications for the Physical Education Program

The choice of an activity, as well as the manner in which children are motivated to learn, must be based on the characteristics and needs of children within each level of development. The previous discussion on growth and development has provided a general understanding of elementary school children. They are children, who, through a period of seven years, undergo major physiological, psychomotor, cognitive, personal, and social changes. The major changes and their implications for the physical education program are summarized in tables 2.2, 2.3, and 2.4. The three developmental levels are provided as guidelines to help teachers plan developmentally appropriate activities and teaching strategies to meet the needs and interests of each age group.

Table 2.2 Developmental Level I (Early Childhood, Five to Seven Years)

Characteristics	Implications for physical education program
Physical growth and development	
Height and weight gains moderate and steady.	Provide daily vigorous activity, particularly running, climbing, and swimming, with frequent rest intervals. Discourage long periods of inactivity. Encourage recess and period breaks throughout the school day that incorporate vigorous and total body movement.
Heart and breathing rates relatively high.	Attend to postural development; early detection of structural anomalies is important. Children of this age have relatively small bodies; hence, consider the relative size of supplies and equipment.
Steady growth in strength and muscular endurance. Both sexes maintain high level of flexibility.	Expect the same level of performance from both sexes.
Motor skill development	
Hand-eye coordination shows steady improvement.	Provide for manipulation (catching, throwing, kicking, etc.) of balls of various size. Initial instruction should include relatively low speeds of throwing with short distances. Gradually increase speed, use of small objects, and distance as skill develops.
Reaction time is slow but shows persistent increase throughout this stage.	Encourage participation in numerous activities involving a change of speed, direction, and level.
Locomotor and manipulative skills show continuous improvement.	
Static and dynamic balance skill shows steady improvement.	Provide opportunities to practice balance and agility movements on small and large apparatus.
Rhythmic and dance skills show increase in quality and complexity of movement.	Provide a variety of rhythmic, folk, and creative dance activities.
Cognitive development	
Gradual increase in attention span.	Provide a large variety of activities within the instructional period. Initiate games for the individual and for small groups. Keep them simple in purpose, rules, and directions.
Extremely creative.	Provide material and content that foster creative interests and movements (creative dance and movement education).
Enjoy rhythm and music.	Provide various forms of dance experiences, including singing games and creative dance.
Keen desire to repeat activities they know and perform well.	Allow children to choose activities, such as playing the same game each recess period. In dance and gymnastic activities, chronic interest in one activity is characteristic. With patience, children soon run the course and move on to other challenges. Your challenge is to provide more interesting and challenging activities.
Curious—want to know how things work.	
Can work with simple movement concepts.	Take time to answer questions and explain reasons for activities whenever the opportunities arise.
Personal and social development	
Individualistic but show a need for adult approval.	In one respect, five-to-seven-year-olds are basically individualistic. Therefore, provide numerous individual activities for all children regardless of ability. Children of this age level also need adult approval.
Enjoy working in small groups.	
General lack of fear and an extremely high spirit of adventure.	Encourage the spirit of adventure (climbing, testing one's own ability with other children). At the same time, develop within each child concern for personal safety and a general awareness and concern for the safety of others. Extensively use the Movement Education approach with gymnastic activities.
Little concern for the opposite sex during early grades.	
Very sensitive to feeling and criticism of adults.	Provide frequent and generous praise and encouragement to all children.
Egocentric.	Provide situations in which children learn to take turns, to share equipment, and to win and lose gracefully.

Table 2.3 Developmental Level II (Middle Childhood, Eight to Nine Years)

Characteristics	Implications for physical education program
Physical growth and development	
Height and weight gains continue to be moderate and steady. Girls begin to show early signs of puberty.	Continue to provide daily vigorous physical activities.
Heart and lungs continue to develop at a slow and steady rate.	Continue to give close attention to postural development, particularly to girls who begin early growth spurt.
Early signs of poor posture.	Use simple postural screening tests.
Steady growth in strength.	
Slight decrease in flexibility, particularly in boys.	Provide activities that enhance flexibility.
Motor skill development	
Eye-hand coordination continues to improve, along with major improvements in manipulative skills.	Introduce basic sports skills and lead-up games.
General improvement in reaction time.	Stress form rather than speed, distance, or accuracy.
General improvement in balance skills.	Provide more complex balance and agility skills with small and large apparatus.
General improvement in rhythmic and dance skills.	Provide more complex rhythmic and folk dance activities.
Cognitive development	
Continued increase in attention span.	Continue to provide a variety of more complex activities, which require closer attention and cooperative behavior.
Continue to be very curious, particularly about their own abilities.	Teach the mechanical principles relating to performing movement skills. Encourage children to invent their own games and movement sequences.
General movement toward more group activities.	Continue to provide challenging tasks on apparatus and on the playing field. Stress personal and group safety throughout this age range.
Beginning to show interest in ways and means of improving personal fitness.	
Personal and social development	
Continued high spirit of adventure.	Plan game, dance, and gymnastic activities that boys and girls can participate in together. When "fierce" antagonism and/or major differences in skill levels exist, particularly in combative activities and ball games, separate the sexes.
Gradual trend of mutual antagonism toward the opposite sex.	
Lack of discrimination on the basis of race, color, or religion.	Take care in the methods and techniques used to choose teams, leaders, and various social groupings. The essential teaching characteristic should be fairness to all children.
Accept just punishment for self and for group.	Do not punish a whole group for the wrongdoings of one child. Children recognize inconsistencies in degrees of punishment; therefore, be consistent and fair with the type and amount of discipline and punishment. Because of the "social awareness" and inherent fairness of children, stress group control through self-discipline.
Display honesty, team loyalty, and strong group identity.	

Table 2.4 Developmental Level III (Late Childhood, Ten to Twelve Years)

Characteristics	**Implications for physical education program**

Physical growth and development

Rapid height and weight gains after beginning of puberty. Girls normally reach puberty between ten and eleven years, whereas boys begin approximately two years later. Marked differences in height and weight gains occur in grades five and six.	Continue to provide vigorous activities, emphasizing strength and endurance for longer periods of time. Although girls, particularly those who have reached the early stages of puberty, may show a general disinterest in vigorous activities, remember that normal growth and development depend on vigorous and continuous activity.
Heart and lungs increase in size and capacity proportionate to height and weight gains.	Postural development for this age group is a particular problem. The problem has been intensified by excessive viewing of television and video games, and general sedentary living. Therefore, observe sitting and walking postures of students, and plan activities for general posture development. Give special attention to girls who have reached puberty and tend toward sloping shoulders to compensate for height and chest development.
Muscle strength increases with boys and girls; differences in strength between boys and girls during this age level may be due to the type of activities in which they participate rather than to inherent structural or physiological changes within each sex.	
Flexibility decreases with boys showing greater losses than girls.	Continue to provide activities that enhance flexibility.

Motor skill development

Muscle coordination continues to improve with both sexes.	Provide more highly organized and competitive individual and team sports. If there is a marked difference in level of skill between boys and girls, separate them when playing team games to allow both sexes to develop according to their own level of skill and interest.
Boys and girls begin to show major differences in level of skill in team sport activities.	Both sexes, however, require extensive practice in the refinement of throwing, catching, and kicking skills. Separate and solid unit construction is appropriate, particularly in the upper grades. Provide more complex challenges in small and large apparatus activities. Provide more socially based folk and square dance activities.

Cognitive development

Marked increase in attention span.	Provide more complex and challenging activities. This applies to individual and team games where allowance is made for extensive practice in learning skills, rules, and complex team strategy. Similarly, with dance and gymnastic activities, allow time for developing complex and creative movements.
General increase in intellectual curiosity.	Teach concepts and principles of movement related to the physical and motor skills the children are learning. Through the application of the problem-solving method, test and challenge a child's intellectual ability through movement tasks.
Genuine interest in knowing about the human body and how to improve health and performance.	
Curiosity leading to tendency to constantly ask questions and challenge reasons for studying or performing activities.	Provide good reason and rationale for your decisions. Encourage open discussion and debate whenever possible.

Personal and social development

Increased control of emotions in individual and group situations.	Select activities commensurate with the emotional development of each age group. Outbreaks of emotions in tense game situations are normal and, in some situations, desirable. Make provision for each child to experience leadership roles.
Girls tend to be more self-conscious in the presence of boys as well as when performing within their own sex grouping.	The essence of good teaching should be the development of self-direction on the part of each child. Independence is a natural tendency for this age group and must be provided for both in methods and appropriate activities. Teacher-directed approaches should not be completely abandoned but should be blended with other approaches that call for greater freedom and responsibility on the part of the learner. Pay special attention to the kinds of groupings that provide for identification as well as foster team cooperation and loyalty.
General increase toward independence and peer group identity.	
Major differences in attitude toward opposite sex as well as toward different types of activities. Boys and girls alike, particularly during upper grades, show a lack of sympathy and understanding toward each other. Boys tend toward more rough team sports, increased concern for physique and skill, and a dominant interest in competition. Girls begin to show concern for personal appearance and activities involving graceful and creative movements.	Make provisions within the instructional and extraclass program for children to participate in both individual sex and mixed group activities. Allow extensive opportunities for boys and girls to plan and direct activities. The latter not only contributes to the development of cooperation, leadership, and team loyalty, but also allows children to develop other important social traits and personal friendships.
Social acceptance is more peer-centered than adult-centered.	Use discretion when asking girls (particularly fifth- and sixth-graders) to demonstrate skills or movements in a mixed setting. Although girls are normally more graceful than boys in gymnastic-type movements, they tend to be embarrassed when asked to demonstrate. The reverse, however, is generally true with ball skills, where girls are usually less proficient than boys. Develop an understanding and appreciation for the differences that exist between boys and girls of this age level.

Selected References

Albinson, J., and Andrews, G. (1976). *Child in Sport and Physical Activity.* Baltimore: University Park Press.

Arnold, P. J. (1968). *Education, Physical Education and Personality Development.* London: Heinemann Educational Books.

Bailey, D. A., Martin, A. D., Houston, C. S., and Howie, J. L. (1986). Physical Activity, Nutrition, Bone Density, and Osteoporosis. *Australian Journal of Science and Medicine in Sport, 18*(3), 3–8.

Bower, T. G. R. (1979). *Human Development.* San Francisco: W. H. Freeman and Company.

Corbin, C. (1980). *A Textbook of Motor Development,* Second Edition. Dubuque, IA: Wm. C. Brown Publishers.

Espenschade, A. S., and Eckert, H. D. (1980). *Motor Development.* Columbus, OH: Charles E. Merrill.

Fishburne, G. J. (1983). Explaining the Mystery of Movement. *Elements: A Journal for Elementary Education, 15*(1), 18–21.

Fishburne, G. J. (1988). Sensitive Periods During Brain Development: Implications for the Development of Motor Abilities. In D. McNair (Ed.), *Proceedings for the 1986 ICHPER World Conference* (pp. 170–188). London: Foresee Enterprise Ltd.

Fleishman, E. A. (1954). A Dimensional Analysis of Motor Abilities. *Journal of Experimental Psychology, 48,* 437–454.

Fleishman, E. A. (1964). *The Structure and Measurement of Physical Fitness.* Englewood Cliffs, NJ: Prentice Hall.

Fleishman, E. A. (1967). Individual Differences and Motor Learning. In R. M. Gagne (Ed.), *Learning and Individual Differences.* Columbus, OH: Charles E. Merrill.

Gabbard, C. (1992). *Lifelong Motor Development.* Dubuque, IA: Wm. C. Brown Publishers.

Guilford, J. P. (1958). A System of Psychomotor Abilities. *American Journal of Psychology, 71,* 164–174.

Haywood, K. (1986). *Life Span Motor Development.* Champaign, IL: Human Kinetics Publishing, Inc.

Hottinger, W. (1980). Importance of Studying Motor Development. In C. B. Corbin (Ed.), *A Textbook of Motor Development.* Dubuque, IA: Wm. C. Brown Publishers.

Krus, P. H., Bruininks, R. H., & Robertson, G. (1981). Structure of Motor Abilities in Children. *Perceptual and Motor Skills, 52,* 119–129.

Magill, R. A. (1993). *Motor Learning Concepts and Applications.* Dubuque, IA: Brown & Benchmark.

Martin, A. D., & Houston, C. S. (1987). Osteoporosis, Calcium and Physical Activity. *Canadian Medical Association Journal, 136,* 587–593.

Mayer, J. (1968). *Overweight: Causes, Cost, and Control.* Englewood Cliffs, NJ.: Prentice Hall.

Rarick, G. (1973). *Physical Activity: Human Growth and Development.* New York: Academic Press Inc.

Roberton, M., and Halverson, L. (1984). *Developing Children—Their Changing Movement.* Philadelphia: Lea & Febiger.

Sheldon, W. H., Dupertuis, C. W., and McDermott, F. (1954). *Atlas of Man: A Guide for Somatotyping the Adult Male at All Ages.* New York: Harper & Row.

PART 2

Nature and Analysis of Movement

C hapter 3 describes and illustrates the basic movement concepts and skills appropriate for children in the primary and intermediate grades. Chapter 4 covers locomotor and manipulative skills and movement patterns. Chapter 5 deals with the phases of motor development; the process of learning motor skills; and the important principles relating to stability, force, motion, and leverage ■

Chapter 3
Movement Concepts and Skills

Chapter 4
Locomotor, Nonlocomotor, and Manipulative Skills

Chapter 5
Learning Motor Skills

3

Movement Concepts and Skills

Contemporary education is characterized more than ever by an inquiring approach to learning. Through a process that may include guided experience, experimentation, observation, and selection, children make many important discoveries for themselves. The teacher uses concrete materials and visual aids, where suitable and available, to link abstract thought to the real world. In the interest of understanding rather than isolated memorization, the teacher classifies ideas to help children learn to link information to meaningful concepts. At the same time, children learn the skills of classification and analysis. In selecting subject matter, the teacher pays greater attention than ever before to children's intellectual development and to the enormous range of skill and maturity among individuals in any primary or intermediate class.

The developmental model, which is stressed throughout this book, is based on these principles. This approach incorporates the movement concepts and skills of Movement Education into every aspect of game, dance, and gymnastic activities. Each of the movement concepts and skills is described in this chapter, followed by suggestions for primary and intermediate teachers when introducing these concepts.

Movement concepts and skills, as shown in table 3.1, are grouped under the elements of body awareness, space awareness, qualities, and relationships. Body awareness refers to what the body can do—the shapes it can make, the way it balances, and the transfer of weight from one part of the body to another. Space awareness describes the spatial aspects of movement, as well as the skills relating to moving in different directions and to different levels. Qualities describe how the body can move and include skills relating to speed, force, and flow of movement. Relationships refer to the connection between the body and other performers or to the body and small and large apparatus. These four elements of Movement Education are briefly described in the following pages. References are also provided under each subelement to chapters where expanded definitions, illustrations, sample challenges, and lesson plans are provided. Two videotapes described in appendix A were also produced by the authors to explain and illustrate the four elements of Movement Education. *Videotape No. 1: Teaching Gymnastic Activities,* describes each subelement and shows how to integrate these elements with traditional gymnastic activities. *Videotape No. 4: Teaching Creative Dance,* uses the four elements of Movement Education as the basic framework for developing a creative dance lesson (figure 3.1) ■

Table 3.1   Classification of Movement Concepts and Skills

Body awareness (what the body can do)	Space awareness (where the body moves)	Qualities (how the body moves)	Relationships (to whom and what the body relates)
Shapes the body can make	Personal and general space	Speed of moving	To people
Balance on parts of the body	Direction and pathways of moving	Force of moving	To objects
Transfer of weight from one part of the body to another	Levels of moving	Bound and flow movements	

Figure 3.1   The movement concepts and skills of Movement Education.

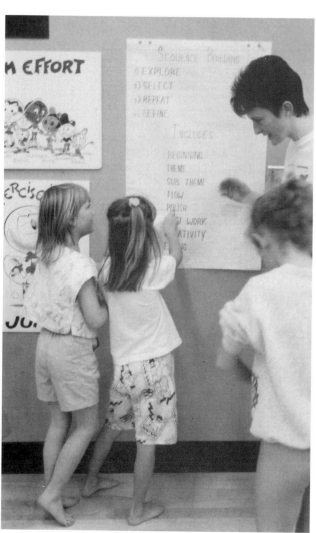

Body Awareness

Body awareness, or what the body can do, is the way in which the body or parts of it can be controlled, moved, or balanced on. This involves three subelements: the *shape* the body can make, the *balance* positions the body can take, and the way the body can *transfer* weight from one part to another. The shapes the body can make will be described and illustrated, followed by a progressive addition of balance, or weight bearing, and transfer of weight.

Shapes the Body Can Make

The human body is capable of forming an infinite variety of shapes. Three basic types form the framework on which children learn how to bend, stretch, and twist their bodies.

Stretched and Curled Shapes

A stretched shape (figure 3.2) is an extension of the whole body or a part of it in various directions. For example, children can stretch upward, to the side, or through their legs. A curled shape (figure 3.3) results from an action that flexes or bends the body or a part of it. Assisting children to find or discover what stretched and curled shapes their bodies are capable of making should start from the familiar and simple, then gradually shift to the more complex. Once a child has developed a "movement vocabulary," which is simply knowing what shapes the body can make, greater freedom should be permitted. Attempting a variety of shapes without concern for form, however, hinders both physical and intellectual development. Progression in shape or combinations of shapes involves thought, repetition, and constant attention on the part of the teacher and child.

Figure 3.2 Stretched shape.

Figure 3.4 Wide shape.

Figure 3.3 Curled shape.

Figure 3.5 Narrow shape.

Wide and Narrow Shapes

Wide and narrow shapes, like curled and stretched ones, are contrasting shapes. A wide shape requires the legs and/or arms to be away from the trunk (figure 3.4). In contrast, the arms or legs must be extended close together or in a thin line with the trunk to form a narrow shape (figure 3.5).

Twisted Shapes

A twisted shape can be performed in two ways. One can hold a part of the body in a fixed or stabilized position, such as on the floor or apparatus, then turn the body or any part of it away from the fixed base. In figure 3.6 the body is stabilized by two feet restricting the degree of twisting

away from this stationary base. A twisted shape can also be made when the body is in flight. In this case, as illustrated in figure 3.7, one part of the body is held in a fixed position while the other part turns away from the fixed part, producing a twisted shape. Although it could be argued that the latter is a "turn" (usually defined as a rotation of the body coupled with a loss of a fixed contact), with young children the synonymous use of "twist" and "turn" is quite acceptable at this stage of development. Later, the meaning can be refined. Once a child has developed an understanding of what shapes the body can make, new challenges should lead to more interesting and complex forms.

Figure 3.6 Twisted shape.

Figure 3.7 Twisted shape in the air.

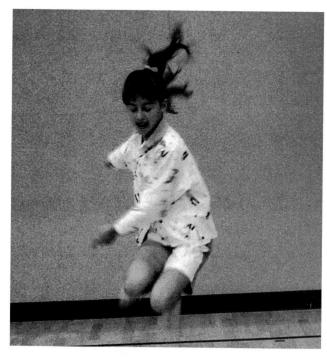

References to Activities Stressing Shapes

1. Suggested progression, photographic illustrations, and combinations with structured skills, chapter 25, p. 463
2. Making shapes of letters and spelling words with parts of the body, chapter 25, p. 467
3. Combined with beanbag activities, chapter 26, p. 480
4. Combined with wand activities, chapter 26, p. 496
5. Combined with balance beam activities, chapter 27, p. 510
6. Combined with rope climbing activities, chapter 27, p. 516
7. Combined with vaulting box activities, chapter 27, p. 522
8. Matching and contrasting shapes, chapter 25, p. 567

Balance, or Weight Bearing

A second important aspect of body awareness is balancing, or "maintaining the weight" on different parts of the body. A child, for example, can balance on one foot or any number of body parts, including the head positioned as in a headstand. (See figure 3.8.)

References to Activities Stressing Balance or Weight Bearing

1. Suggested progression, photographic illustrations, and combinations with structured skills, chapter 25, p. 466
2. Sample lesson plan with balance as the main theme, chapter 25, p. 472
3. Challenge involving weight bearing and individual ropes, chapter 26, p. 491

Figure 3.8 Balance, or weight bearing.

4. Challenge involving balance and vaulting box, chapter 27, p. 522
5. Challenge involving balance and horizontal bar, chapter 27, p. 527

Transfer of Body Weight

The third aspect of body awareness is the transfer of weight from one part of the body to another, while in contact with a surface such as the floor or parts of apparatus (figure 3.9). Sliding on the feet or seat is an exception. Transference of

Figure 3.9 Transfer while in contact with a surface.

Figure 3.11 Transfer through flight.

Figure 3.10 Transfer from one body surface to another.

weight can take place from one foot to another, as in walking. It can take place with a variety of steplike actions, using various permutations of the feet or the hands and feet. It can also take place when one body surface receives the body weight from an adjacent part, as in a forward rolling action (figure 3.10). Flight is also a form of transfer of weight that requires the body to be propelled off the floor or apparatus and to maintain a period of time off the ground. For example, the body can leap off the floor from one or both feet, and it can land on one or both feet (figure 3.11). The body can be thrust into the air from the feet, with the weight received by the hands as in the Cat Spring or jumping onto a rope or vaulting box.

Even when it is in the air, the body has shape. It can be stretched long and thin or spread in a number of directions. The positions and actions of the limbs in flight also alter the shape of the body. Furthermore, the body can perform complete or various degrees of revolution in midair.

Finally, attention must be given to landing. The body weight can be brought back to the floor by one or both feet or hands. The depth of landing or the degree of body resilience can also vary. All landings, however, require "give," or flexion, of the leg joints, especially the knees. When jumping, children should be encouraged to make a deep landing, which brings them into a full knee bend position. This allows them to continue to absorb the momentum of the fall and the shock of impact by rolling.

References to Activities Stressing Transfer of Weight

1. Suggested progression, photographic illustrations and combinations with structured skills, chapter 25, p. 463
2. Sample lesson plan with transfer of weight (flight) as main theme, chapter 30, p. 589
3. Sample dance lesson with transfer of weight as the main theme, chapter 29, p. 554
4. Challenge involving transfer of weight and beanbag activities, chapter 26, p. 480
5. Challenge involving transfer of weight and balance bench activities, chapter 27, p. 510
6. Challenge involving transfer of weight and climbing frame activities, chapter 27, p. 529

Space Awareness: Where the Body Moves

Space awareness is one element of movement that includes concepts relating to general and personal space, direction, pathways, and levels.

General and Personal Space

All space that a child or group of children can use is divided into two types. General space is the total space that can be used by one child or a group of children. In figure 3.12, the gymnasium floor constitutes the general space the child can use when performing a series of movement skills. Personal, or limited, space is the immediate space a child can use around her. The top of the vaulting box constitutes the personal space available to the child when performing a series of balance skills. As the child moves off the top of the box, she enters the general space.

References to Activities Stressing General and Personal Space

1. Definition and photographic illustrations, chapter 25, p. 469
2. Sample lesson plan with general space as the subtheme, chapter 30, p. 587
3. See tables 16.1 and 16.2 for a list of games stressing general and personal space, chapter 16, p. 257

Direction

Direction includes moving forward, backward, sideways, diagonally, and up and down.

References to Activities Stressing Direction

1. Definition and photographic illustrations, chapter 25, p. 469
2. Challenge involving change of direction and bean-bags, chapter 26, p. 480
3. Challenge involving change of direction and individual ropes, chapter 26, p. 491
4. Challenge involving change of direction and musical accompaniment, chapter 28, p. 539
5. Challenge involving change of direction, musical accompaniment, and individual ropes, chapter 28, p. 539
6. Direction as an element in creative folk dance activities, chapter 29, p. 553
7. Sample lesson plan with change of direction as the main theme, chapter 29, p. 555
8. See tables 16.1 and 16.2, for a list of games stressing change of direction, chapter 16, p. 257

Figure 3.12 Space awareness: where the body moves.

Pathways

Pathways are the patterns a child or an object makes when moving on or off the floor. The child in figure 3.12 may leap off the box, travel in a curve followed by a straight pathway, and end in a zigzag pathway.

References to Activities Stressing Pathways

1. Sample lesson plan with pathway as a subtheme, chapter 30, p. 587
2. Pathway as an element in creative folk dance activities, chapter 29, p. 555

Levels

Level refers to the location of the body or body parts to the floor or apparatus. In figure 3.12, the child is high in relation to the top of the box. In figure 3.13, movement is low to the floor; in figure 3.14, movement is at a medium level on all fours; and, in figure 3.15, movement is at a high level in the performance of a cartwheel or leap from the floor. Levels also refers to the relation of one part of the body to another. High movements are those performed above the shoulders; medium movements, between the shoulders and knees; and low movements, from the knees to the toes.

References to Activities Stressing Levels

1. Challenge involving levels, shapes and wands, chapter 26, p. 496

Figure 3.13 Low level.

Figure 3.14 Medium level.

Figure 3.15 High level.

2. Challenge involving levels and the climbing frame, chapter 27, p. 529

Qualities: How the Body Moves

Qualities, or effort (the third element of Movement Education), includes concepts that describe how the body moves from one position to another. Speed, force, and flow of movement are concepts described within this element.

Speed

Speed is the rate of a movement. In figure 3.16, the child runs toward a traffic cone, leaps over it, lands, and slowly rolls across the mat to dissipate the forward momentum.

Figure 3.16 Qualities: how the body moves.

SPEED
quick, slow

run. . . .

FORCE
strong, light

leap. . . .

FLOW
bound, free

movement concepts and skills

Figure 3.17 Light or gentle force.

Figure 3.18 Bound flow.

a

b

c

References to Activities Stressing Speed

1. Definition and photographic illustrations of quick and slow, chapter 25, p. 468
2. Speed as a subtheme of a lesson, chapter 25, p. 472
3. Speed combined with structured skills, chapter 25, p. 472
4. Challenge with speed, pathways, and traffic cones, chapter 26, p. 499
5. Challenge with speed and benches, chapter 27, p. 510
6. Sample lesson plan with speed as the subtheme, chapter 30, p. 587

Force

Force is the effort or tension involved in a movement. A child leaping over a traffic cone, as in figure 3.16, performs a strong thrusting action to gain enough height and distance to clear the obstacle. In dance, however, a child may shift arms lightly from one side to the other to describe something light or gentle (figure 3.17).

References to Activities Stressing Force

1. Definition and photographic illustrations, chapter 25, p. 468
2. Challenge involving force and an individual rope, chapter 26, p. 491
3. Sample lesson plan with strong and light as main theme, chapter 30, p. 589

Flow

Flow is how a movement or series of movements is linked in a purposeful action. Bound flow occurs when a series of movements is stopped, with the balance maintained, then continued to another static movement. For example, two children performing a tumbling routine shift from a roll to a shoulder stand and hold this balance position momentarily before lowering their legs and trunks in preparation for another roll (figure 3.18). Movements that proceed smoothly from one to another are described as free flow.

References to Activities Stressing Flow

1. Definition and photographic illustrations, chapter 25, p. 468
2. Challenge involving flow, hoops, and musical accompaniment, chapter 28, p. 493
3. Challenge involving flow, transfer of weight, and wands, chapter 26, p. 496

Figure 3.19 Relationship with objects and other performers.

Relationships: To Whom and What the Body Relates

The fourth element of movement involves the relationship of an individual or a group to other performers or objects. A relationship to an object is described as the position of a performer relative to an apparatus. For example, in figure 3.19, the child on the left side begins outside the turret, moves around and then over, stopping on the top surface. He is positioned near the apparatus. As he moves toward the other turret, he travels under the beam.

Concepts describing the manner in which performers relate to each other represent another dimension of relationships. The two performers in figure 3.19 are performing matching shapes, with the child on the right turret leading her partner. As they continue their sequence, they will "meet" and "part."

References to Activities Stressing Relationships to People

1. Description and photographic illustrations of relationship to individuals and to groups, chapter 25, p. 470

2. Challenge involving relationship to partner, individual ropes, and force, chapter 26, p. 489

3. Challenge involving partners and shape, chapter 26, p. 481

4. Challenge involving matching and contrasting shapes and wands, chapter 26, p. 496

5. Challenge involving matching and contrasting shapes and balance benches, chapter 27, p. 510

6. Challenge involving relationship of two people and a musical accompaniment, chapter 28, p. 537

References to Activities Stressing Relationship to Equipment and Apparatus

1. Description and photographic illustrations of relationship to equipment, chapter 26, p. 578

2. Challenge involving partners and balancing on a vaulting box, chapter 27, p. 522

3. Challenge involving matching sequences and traffic cones, chapter 26, p. 499

Suggested Teaching Procedure

The success of teaching movement concepts and skills depends on creating an atmosphere in which children can work safely and independently and on the teacher's ability to introduce skills and movement ideas in a systematic, progressive way. One must remember that the contemporary approach to teaching game, dance, and gymnastic activities stresses the importance of the direct method, which requires the teacher to plan what and how each skill is to be performed. In this method of teaching, emphasis is given to following orders rather than encouraging children to think for themselves or produce creative movements. Hence, the shift from a predominantly formal, teacher-directed situation to an informal atmosphere in which the learner assumes responsibility for learning is a tremendous challenge for both teacher and class. However, the rewards inherent in this transition are worth the patience and effort required of the teacher and, of course, the children under her charge.

It is vital, therefore, that the initial lessons, particularly for children beyond level I, be more concerned with establishing the "atmosphere for learning" than with the teaching of introductory movement skills and ideas. The latter will come much more rapidly and effectively when children learn to work independently at their own rate and according to their own ability.

The four elements (body awareness, space awareness, qualities, and relationships) are introduced sequentially in chapter 25 ("Stunts, Tumbling, and Movement Skills"). A sample lesson and unit plan are also provided as a format for developing individual lessons and extended themes. Once a teacher acquires the basic movement vocabulary, she will in turn develop variations in the suggested procedure. Additional sample lesson plans, using one or more movement concepts and skills, are provided in the dance and game resource sections.

Selected References

Graham, G., Holt-Hale, S. A., and Parker, M. (1993). *Children Moving,* Third Edition. Mountain View, CA: Mayfield Publishing Co.

Kirchner, G., Cunningham, J., and Warrell, E. (1978). *Introduction to Movement Education,* Second Edition. Dubuque, IA: Wm. C. Brown Publishers.

Logsdon, et al. (1984). *Physical Education for Children: A Focus on the Learning Process,* Second Edition. Philadelphia: Lea & Febiger.

Morrison, R. (1969). *A Movement Approach to Educational Gymnastics.* London: J. M. Dent and Sons.

Wall, J., and Murray, N. (1994). *Children and Movement: Physical Education in the Elementary School,* Second Edition. Dubuque, IA: Wm. C. Brown Publishers.

Locomotor, Nonlocomotor, and Manipulative Skills

The fundamental motor skills described in this chapter are the important building blocks for more specialized sports, dance, and gymnastic activities. By the time children reach school age, they have acquired some proficiency in such motor skills as running and dodging, as well as a few basic throwing, catching, and hitting skills. However, such factors as lack of physical and mental maturity and lack of opportunities to learn and practice these basic movements leave many primary-age children with low levels of proficiency in these prerequisite motor skills. Since these basic locomotor and manipulative skills are prerequisites for advanced sports and dance movement patterns, they should be learned in a systematic and progressive manner in developmental levels I and II. Once children can perform these motor skills with ease and efficiency, they have the confidence and ability to learn more advanced skills and movement patterns.

In this chapter, under each basic skill are descriptions and illustrations, as well as important mechanical principles and lists of suggested activities. Locomotor skills, such as walking, running, and hopping, are individual skills that are used to move the body through space by shifting the leg movements of the body from one base of support to another. The skills of skipping, stopping, and dodging are traditionally placed in this category; however, they are essentially a combination of locomotor and nonlocomotor movements. Nonlocomotor skills consist of movements of the body where one or more parts of the body maintain contact with the floor or apparatus while other parts of the body move in different directions, pathways, and levels. Manipulative skills, such as throwing, catching, and hitting, are combined movement patterns involving one or more locomotor and nonlocomotor skills with other movement skills and concepts. The organization patterns and teaching strategies that are used to teach these skills are contained in later chapters ■

Figure 4.1 Walking.

a   b   c

Locomotor Skills

The fundamental locomotor and nonlocomotor skills are the foundation for developing everyday utilitarian and safety skills. They are the building blocks for all specialized skills involved in game, dance, and gymnastic activities.

Nine locomotor skills are described and illustrated in this section. The discussion of each skill includes the mechanical principles involved in its proper execution, things to stress, applications of movement concepts and skills, and suggested activities. The nonlocomotor skills will be treated similarly later in this chapter.

The first five locomotor skills described—walking, running, leaping, jumping, and hopping—represent the skeleton on which the child begins to develop complex movement skills. Although skipping, sliding (or galloping), stopping, and dodging combine several of the first five skills, they will be described as separate locomotor skills.

Walking

Walking is the transfer of weight from one foot to the other while moving forward or backward. In a natural and rhythmical walking action, the body is erect and the eyes focus forward. The heel of the stepping foot strikes the ground (figure 4.1a), and the weight of the body is transferred through the ball, then off the toes of the foot. At that moment, the heel of the free-swinging leg touches the ground, and the knee of that leg bends, allowing it to absorb the shock of the weight transferred to this leg (figure 4.1b). In a walking movement, one foot is always in contact with the ground, and the arms swing freely in opposite directions to the feet (figure 4.1c).

Applying Mechanical Principles

1. *Balance:* Walking has been described as a continuous process of losing and gaining balance. Hence, the inner edges of the feet should move along a straight line to allow the center of gravity to shift directly over the base of support. This also prevents unnecessary swaying movements.

Direction of walk →

Too wide

Too narrow

Just right

2. *Production of force:* Since the total effectiveness of a movement is the sum of all the forces, properly synchronized leg and arm movements are essential.

3. *Direction of force:* The force initiated from the back leg should be directed forward and upward through the center of the body weight. If the direction of force is too vertical, the walk will be bouncy and inefficient. If the force is primarily horizontal, the walk will be a shuffle.

4. *Absorption of force:* The force should be gradually dissipated by transferring weight from the heels through the ball of the foot toward the toes.

5. *Momentum:* The forward motion initiated by the backward thrust of the leg is directed forward through the trunk. An unchecked forward movement would carry the trunk beyond the forward base of support too quickly, resulting in a forward fall or a shift to running. To counteract this, the front leg momentarily restrains the forward motion of the trunk, allowing a smooth transfer of weight as the back leg begins to move forward.

Things to Stress

1. Keep body straight, head up, look straight ahead, and move in a relaxed manner.

2. Swing arms freely and naturally, but not too far.

3. Point toes straight ahead and take easy strides to avoid excessive up-and-down and jerky movements.

Applying Movement Concepts and Skills

1. *Body awareness:* Walking in different ways by changing use of body parts, varying size of step, and transferring weight to different parts of the foot

2. *Space awareness:* Walking in different directions, pathways with a change in level

3. *Qualities:* Walking with changes in speed and force and showing bound and flow forms of walking

4. *Relationships:* Walking with a partner, showing relationships such as side-by-side, near and far, and slow and fast

Walking Activities

1. Walk informally about the room in an easy, relaxed, natural way.

2. Same as activity 1, but walk in a circle.

3. Same as activity 2, but change direction.

4. Walk in different ways—short or long steps, fast or slow, hard or soft, high or low.

5. Change speed. Start slowly, walk at a moderate pace, then walk briskly, walk moderately again, walk slowly, then stop.

6. Walk on the heels of the feet, using exaggerated arm movements.

7. Walk on tiptoes.

8. Walk slowly for balance (use two, three, or four beats per measure).

9. Walk sideways by crossing one foot in front of the other.

10. Do pantomimes of a "happy" or "sad" walk, of carrying a heavy or light load, of a young person or old person, of walking through mud or wet concrete.

11. Combine walking with other locomotor skills. Begin with a walk, shift to a run, then shift back to a walk. Repeat with another locomotor skill, such as a skip or slide.

12. Gradually lower and raise the body while walking.

13. Change arm positions and movements while walking (e.g., hands swinging forward and backward above the shoulders).

14. Walk on painted lines, balance benches, planks, and other available apparatus.

15. Walk in step with a partner. Begin walking together slowly, then increase speed, change direction, or use other locomotor movements.

16. Walking skills can be enhanced through the application of the elements of rhythm described in chapter 28. Most of the activities in this list can be performed in time to a musical accompaniment. Rhythmic activities teach children to walk in time to an underlying beat, to change direction on an accented beat, and to develop walking sequences according to measures and phrases of music.

17. Many of the singing games and folk dance activities listed in chapter 29 (see table 29.1, p. 556) stress walking as a main locomotor skill. Through these simple dances children learn to walk in time to a musical accompaniment and to walk with grace and ease of movement.

Running

Running is the transfer of weight from one foot to the other with a momentary loss of contact with the ground by both feet (figure 4.2). In a slow run, such as jogging, the body leans slightly forward; arms, bent at the elbows, swing forward and backward from the shoulders and move in opposition to the leg movements. The knees are bent and the heel of the foot contacts the ground, followed by a shift of the body weight through the ball, then off the toes, of the foot. As the speed of the run increases, so does the forward lean and arm action. In a fast run, the ball of the foot touches the ground first.

Figure 4.2 Running.

a   b   c

Applying Mechanical Principles

1. *Inertia:* Overcoming inertia is most difficult at the takeoff and decreases as the child gains speed. Therefore, take off from a crouched position to gain maximum speed in the shortest period of time; this allows maximum force to be exerted in a horizontal direction.

2. *Momentum:* Any increase in momentum is directly proportional to the force producing it. In running, the greater the power of the backward leg drive, the greater the forward acceleration.

3. *Direction of force:* In running, the body should lean forward about twenty degrees from vertical. This slight forward lean keeps the center of gravity ahead of the forward foot as it contacts the ground and allows the backward extension of the leg to propel the body in a nearly horizontal direction, producing the greatest forward speed and minimizing the inefficient upward movements of the body. To avoid lateral movements of the body, which restrict forward momentum, move the knees directly forward and upward and swing the arms forward and backward.

4. *Absorption of force:* In long-distance running, the heel of the foot touches the ground first, and the force is gradually dissipated through the outer edge of the foot toward the toe. In sprinting, the ball of the foot contacts the ground first. This permits the force to be absorbed by slightly flexed hips, knees, and ankles.

5. *Levers:* By shortening the lever arm, the speed of a movement is increased. Bending the knees and elbows shortens the lever arms to increase running speed.

Things to Stress

1. In jogging, run in a relaxed and rhythmical manner, with a slight forward body lean; gently swing arms with elbows bent and land lightly on the heels.

2. In fast running, increase knee and elbow flexion, swing arms forward and backward, and land on the balls of the feet.

3. In all types of running, breathe naturally; never hold your breath.

Applying Movement Concepts and Skills

1. *Body awareness:* Running in different ways by changing the use of body parts, varying length of stride, and transferring weight to different parts of the foot

2. *Space awareness:* Running in different directions, pathways with a change in level

3. *Qualities:* Running with a change of speed and force

4. *Relationships:* Running with a partner, showing matching form, speed, and changes in direction and level; running with, on, or around small equipment and large apparatus

Running Activities

1. Run informally around the gymnasium.
2. Run with short or long steps.
3. Run with a high knee lift.
4. Run backward and sideward.

Figure 4.3 Leaping.

a   b   c

1. *Momentum:* Since momentum is directly proportional to the force applied, the performer should take several running steps before leaping. The increased momentum gained by the run produces a higher and farther leap.

2. *Direction of force:* The height of the leap is directly proportional to the angle of takeoff, as well as to the backward force of the takeoff leg. To gain maximum height, increase the angle of takeoff and exaggerate the forward and upward movement of the arms.

Things to Stress

1. To gain maximum height, stretch upward with the hands and forward with the lead foot.

2. Execute a short and fast run before leaping.

3. To absorb the shock, flex the knee as soon as the ball of the foot touches the ground.

Applying Movement Concepts and Skills

1. *Body awareness:* Showing different ways to move arms in the leaping action, and changing length of stride

2. *Space awareness:* Changing direction and level of leap

3. *Qualities:* Changing speed and force of leap

4. *Relationships:* Leaping alone or with a partner, through space, over small equipment, or carrying small equipment

Leaping Activities

1. Run a few steps, then leap. Alternate the takeoff foot.

2. Leap for height and distance.

3. Hop in place a few times, then leap forward or sideward.

4. Leap in different directions.

5. Combine leaping with other locomotor skills—run, leap, walk, and so on.

6. Leap over obstacles—rope, beanbag, hoop.

7. Perform a series of consecutive leaps without breaking stride.

8. Leap without using arms.

9. Leap while holding on to small equipment such as hoops or individual ropes.

5. Change speed—begin slowly, run at a moderate speed, then run fast.

6. Run on the heels or tiptoes.

7. Run and change directions.

8. Run and keep in time with a partner.

9. Combine running with other locomotor skills—run, walk, run, slide, and so on.

10. Run around obstacles, such as other children, chairs, or beanbags.

11. Do pantomime running—run like a tall person, a dog, an elephant.

12. Run and jump rope on each step or alternate steps.

13. Many of the games listed in table 16.1 (p. 257) and table 16.2 (p. 269) stress running as the major locomotor skill. These games also help children learn to run at different speeds, change direction, and combine running with one or more locomotor or manipulative skills.

Leaping

Leaping, like running, is the transfer of weight from one foot to the other. The toe of the takeoff foot leaves the floor last, whereas the ball of the landing foot contacts the floor first (figure 4.3). In leaping, however, contact with the ground is lost for a longer period than in running, and greater height and distance are achieved. Also, a leap is usually preceded by a few running steps to achieve a maximum lift through the air.

Applying Mechanical Principles

Since leaping is essentially the same as running, the same mechanical principles apply. In addition, the following principles are important in producing a maximum leap.

Jumping

Jumping is the transfer of weight from one foot or both feet to both feet (figure 4.4). For example, a running long jump

locomotor, nonlocomotor, and manipulative skills

Figure 4.4 Jumping.

a. Long jump

b. High jump

c. Jump-reach

begins with a one-foot takeoff and ends with a two-foot landing action. Other jumping movements, such as the standing broad jump or the jump-reach, start and land with two feet.

Applying Mechanical Principles

There are two types of jumping movements: one for height, such as the vertical or high jump, and the other for distance, such as the standing or running broad jump. The basic mechanical principles for leaping also apply to jumping movements; specific principles follow.

1. *Jumping for distance:* To gain the greatest distance, the jumper should take off with the greatest forward speed and upward thrust. The running broad jump requires maximum speed prior to takeoff; the standing broad jump requires a maximum forward and upward swing of the arms. The angle of takeoff should be about forty-five degrees. As the jumper begins to descend, the arms and body are brought forward, with the knees bent and the feet parallel. The resulting forward momentum prevents the body from falling back on landing and allows the forward momentum to gradually dissipate through the flexed knees and forward arm movements.

2. *Jumping for height:* Maximum height depends on several important factors. The angle of takeoff must be as close to vertical as possible. The hips, knees, and ankles should be flexed in the starting position to permit maximum force to be directed upward by the forceful extension of the strong leg muscles.

Additional height is also attained by forward and upward movement of the arms.

3. *Production of force:* To gain maximum height or distance, the movement must be smooth and synchronized—the sum of all forces.

Things to Stress

1. To gain maximum height or distance, make a few preliminary swings of the arms, then a ballistic but synchronized movement of the various segments of the body through the proper angle of movement.

2. To gain maximum force, flex the ankles and knees prior to initiating the movement.

3. To absorb shock, land on the toes and flex the knees.

Applying Movement Concepts and Skills

1. *Body awareness:* Changing position of arm during vertical and horizontal jumping movements; changing length and height of jump

2. *Space awareness:* Changing direction, pathways, and levels of jumping

3. *Qualities:* Changing speed and force of jumping movements and moving in time to rhythmic accompaniment

Figure 4.5 Hopping.

a b c

Throughout this movement, the arms help maintain balance and assist in the upward movement.

Applying Mechanical Principles

1. *Balance:* Since the hop is performed on one leg, the body should lean slightly in the direction of the jumping leg, allowing the center of gravity to shift slightly away from the midline of the body.

2. *Force:* For maximum height, the angle of takeoff should be as close to vertical as possible. Additional height is gained by moving both arms upward simultaneously.

Things to Stress

1. To gain maximum height, swing arms backward, then vigorously forward and upward.

2. To apply force in the right direction, lean slightly toward the support leg to allow the force to be directed through the body's center of gravity.

3. To absorb shock, land first on the toes, then on the ball of the foot while gradually bending the knee.

Applying Movement Concepts and Skills

1. *Body awareness:* Changing use of different parts of body and hopping in different ways (short, medium, and long hop)

2. *Space awareness:* Changing directions, levels, and pathways

3. *Qualities:* Changing speed and force of hopping movement in time to a rhythmic accompaniment

4. *Relationships:* Hopping with a partner while matching movements, directions, and pathways

Hopping Activities

1. Hop in place. Clear the floor on the first hop, then gradually increase the height of each successive hop.

2. Hop forward, sideward, and backward.

3. Hop in place and make a quarter turn on each hop.

4. Hop in place to a 4/4 rhythm. Perform different positions in the air on ascent, such as right leg forward, arms sideward or overhead.

5. Hop several times on one foot, then switch to the other foot without losing rhythm.

6. Combine hopping with other locomotor skills—run, hop, skip.

7. Hop over floor lines or small equipment such as beanbags or ropes.

4. *Relationships:* Jumping alone or with a partner through space and onto or over small equipment

Jumping Activities

1. Jump with feet together and gradually spread legs with each jump.

2. Jump forward, sideward, and backward.

3. Begin jumping from a crouched position and gradually increase the height of each jump.

4. Jump over small equipment, such as ropes, beanbags, and hoops.

5. Jump up and mark the wall with chalked fingertips.

6. Combine jumping with other locomotion or locomotor skills—run, twist, turn, stretch, and so on.

7. Jump rope activities. See chapter 26 for individual and long rope jumping skills.

8. Jump from various heights—from a box, bench, or other apparatus. Combine this jumping activity with a roll to allow for a gradual dissipation of force.

9. Jump with a partner—with or without a skipping rope.

10. Jump in time to a musical accompaniment (see chapter 28).

11. Pantomime jumping skills in sports (jump shot), dance (seven jumps), and gymnastics (two-foot takeoff).

Hopping

Hopping is the transfer of weight from one foot to the same foot. In the upward phase, the toe leaves the floor last; on the way down, the toe contacts the floor first, then the weight gradually shifts to the ball and heel of the foot (figure 4.5).

8. Hop in time with a partner.
9. Hop and change position of body from high to medium to low.
10. Hop in place or on the move and keep changing arm position.

Skipping

A skip is a combination of a long step and a short hop, alternating the lead foot after each hop. In figure 4.6, the child hops on the left foot and swings the right leg forward, stepping on the ball of the right foot. The next sequence would involve a hop on the right foot, followed by a step on the left foot.

Applying Mechanical Principles

Since skipping combines a step and a hop, the mechanical principles that apply to these skills also apply to the skip. The following additional principles are important.

1. *Balance:* Since the base of support is narrow and alternately shifts from one foot to the other, the arms should extend sideward to help maintain balance.
2. *Force:* Since the extension of the leg on the hop produces the upward movement, the angle of takeoff should be nearly vertical. An exaggerated forward lean on the hop causes too much forward movement and makes it difficult for the child to freely swing the opposite leg forward.

Things to Stress

1. Step and hop on the same foot.
2. Since dance style and rhythm are normally emphasized more than distance or height, keep the length of the step and the height of the hop relatively short and small, and maintain smoothness.

Applying Movement Concepts and Skills

1. *Body awareness:* Changing use of different parts of the body while skipping in different ways; making shapes and varying length and height of skipping action
2. *Space awareness:* Changing direction, level, and pathways, moving in small and large spaces
3. *Qualities:* Changing to quick and slow, strong or light, and bound and flowing movements
4. *Relationships:* Moving with a partner or small group, matching, contrasting or performing movements with or around other objects

Figure 4.6 Skipping.

a   b   c

Skipping Activities

1. Skip forward, backward, in a circle, or in different directions.
2. Cross hands with a partner and skip together, or skip in other dance positions.
3. Skip four long steps forward, then four short steps backward.
4. Skip four steps beginning with the right foot, then four steps beginning with the left foot.
5. Skip diagonally right for three steps (right—left—right) and bring feet together on the fourth count. Repeat to left.
6. Combine a skip with other locomotor skills—run, skip, walk.
7. Skip and change directions on the step phase of the movement.
8. Combine a skip with other body movements, such as change arm movements, snap fingers, or clap in time to musical accompaniment (see chapter 28 for additional ideas).
9. Skip and change body position from high to medium to low.
10. Use the list of singing games and folk dances listed in chapter 29 (table 29.1, p. 556) to teach children to skip in time to a musical accompaniment and to combine skipping skills with other locomotor and nonlocomotor movements.

Figure 4.7 Sliding (galloping).

a. Step   b. Short hop   c. Step
            and slide

Sliding (Galloping)

A slide combines a step and a short leap and can be performed in a forward, sideward, or backward direction. When the direction is forward or backward, the slide is called a *gallop*; when sideways, it is known as a *slide*. The movement is performed by stepping with one foot, then sliding with the other foot. The weight is transferred from the lead foot to the back foot. Once the sliding or galloping action begins, the lead foot is always the same foot (figure 4.7).

Applying Mechanical Principles

Sliding employs many of the mechanical principles listed under walking, running, and leaping. Of these, the following are important for the proper execution of the slide.

1. *Balance:* The center of gravity should be kept within the base of support. When moving to the side, the body should not lean too far, or the center of gravity will fall outside of the body. Similarly, when moving forward, the angle of takeoff for the leap should be close to vertical.
2. *Force:* Forward or sideward momentum is generated by the forceful action of the leap. In dance and sport activities, control rather than height is normally desired. Therefore, the force is controlled or adjusted by the extension of the back leg movement.

Things to Stress

1. Encourage movement in a variety of directions.
2. Emphasize light, smooth actions rather than long, forceful leaps followed by a heavy sliding movement of the following foot.

Applying Movement Concepts and Skills

1. *Body awareness:* Changing use of different parts of the body while sliding or galloping; making shapes and varying the length and height of the stepping action
2. *Space awareness:* Changing direction, level, and pathways, and moving in small and large spaces
3. *Qualities:* Changing to quick and slow, strong and light movements
4. *Relationships:* Moving in groups of two or more persons, matching, contrasting or performing movements with or around small objects

Sliding Activities

1. In a circle or line formation, slide forward, backward, and sideward.
2. Slide four steps to the right, make a half turn, then slide four steps to the left.
3. With partners, slide four steps right, then four steps left.
4. Slide and vary the height of the leap.
5. Slide with the left foot forward, stop, then slide with the right foot forward.
6. Slide in different directions.
7. Combine the slide with other locomotor movements—run, slide, skip.
8. Slide and gallop, changing levels and other body movements.
9. Pantomime sports skills that require a sliding action.
10. Develop sliding routines for partners or small groups.
11. Use the list of singing games and folk dances listed in chapter 29 (table 29.1, p. 556) to teach children to slide in time to a musical accompaniment and to combine sliding skills with other locomotor and nonlocomotor movements.

Stopping

Two basic types of stopping action are used in many sports and daily activities. In the forward stride stop (figure 4.8), the runner simultaneously bends the knees and leans backward while moving the arms sideward. In the skip stop, the performer takes a step and a hop, which allows him to shift upward and lean backward to slow down his forward movement; he then lands in a stride position with the weight over the balls of the feet.

Figure 4.8 Stopping.

Figure 4.9 Dodging.

Applying Mechanical Principles

1. *Absorption of force:* Initiating a preliminary skip and landing in a stride position with knees bent spreads the force over a maximum distance.
2. *Balance:* Landing in a stride position with knees bent and trunk leaning backward provides a low, stable base of support.

Thing to Stress

1. Land with feet apart (stride or parallel) and bend the knees as contact is made.
2. Lean backward from the waist and away from the direction of the movement.
3. Keep your head up.

Applying Movement Concepts and Skills

1. *Body awareness:* Changing different parts of the body and landing in different ways; making shapes in the air before landing; making a sequence of run, jump, land, and roll
2. *Space awareness:* Changing direction in flight, land, and roll
3. *Qualities:* Showing landing movements that vary from light and gentle to forceful and heavy
4. *Relationships:* Moving with a partner, showing matching run, jump, land, and roll, in varying heights, speeds, and over small equipment

Stopping Activities

1. Run forward and stop when the whistle blows.
2. Select a line or spot on the floor. Run and stop with front foot on the line.
3. Run forward, sideward, and diagonally and stop when the whistle blows.

4. With a partner, follow the leader with back player stopping when leader stops. Run side-by-side with one player calling "stop."
5. Run, jump over small equipment, and stop.
6. Repeat activities 1 to 5 using a skip stop.
7. Repeat activities 1 to 5 backward.

Dodging

Dodging is a quick shifting of one part or all parts of the body away from a stationary or moving object. A dodge is normally executed after a momentary stop by bending the knees and then thrusting the body vigorously toward the side. One or both feet may leave the ground as a performer executes a dodging movement (figure 4.9).

Applying Mechanical Principles

1. *Balance:* Since dodging requires a quick shift in position, the center of gravity should be low and close to the center of the base of support just before the shift is made.
2. *Production of force:* To gain maximum force, the knees should be flexed to allow a maximum extension of the powerful muscles of the legs.
3. *Direction of force:* By keeping the body relatively low, the force can be directed through the body in a sideward direction. If the player is standing erect, the direction of force is upward and only slightly toward the side.

Things to Stress

1. Keep the body low with the weight over both feet and the arms to the side.
2. Always lean in the direction of the dodge.

3. Once a dodging movement is made, keep low and shift the center toward the middle of the body in order to prepare for another movement.

Applying Movement Concepts and Skills

1. *Body awareness:* Changing the position of different parts of the body while dodging; developing sequences involving other locomotor movements with dodging (e.g., run, dodge, slide)
2. *Space awareness:* Changing direction and pathways before and after a dodging movement
3. *Qualities:* Changing to quick and slow movements before, during, and after a dodging action
4. *Relationships:* Traveling and dodging around other players or objects; in partners, repeat movements around small and large objects

Dodging Activities

1. Run, stop, move right, then move left.
2. Run to a partner, stop, and change direction.
3. Run around obstacles—beanbags, balls, chairs.
4. Bounce or dribble a ball, stop, and change direction on command.
5. Bounce or dribble a ball around obstacles.
6. See table 16.1 (p. 257) and table 16.2 (p. 269) for lists of games that stress dodging.
7. Combine dodging with other locomotor skills—slide, stop, dodge, run.

Nonlocomotor Skills

Nonlocomotor, or axial, movements (swing, bend and stretch, twist and turn, push and pull), are performed from a relatively stable base of support. These movements are usually performed while standing, kneeling, sitting, or lying; however, they can be combined with locomotor skills.

Swinging

A swing is a pendular or circular movement of the body or its parts around a stationary center (figure 4.10).

Applying Mechanical Principles

The following principles apply to the swinging movements of parts of the body while the body as a whole maintains a stationary standing or sitting position.

1. *Lever:* In movements of the arm, the hand has greater speed when the elbow is kept straight. Similarly, the foot has greater speed when the knee is kept straight.
2. *Momentum:* The momentum of any part of a supported body can be transferred to the rest of the

Figure 4.10 Swinging.

body. For example, swinging an arm sideward and upward moves the whole body in those directions. This transfer takes place only when the body is in contact with a supporting surface.

3. *Gravity:* The movement of a pendulum is caused by the force of gravity. As the pendulum swings downward, its speed increases; as it swings upward, its speed decreases until it stops at the top of the swing. The speed of pendular movement is not increased by body weight; it is increased only by the application of additional muscular force.

Things to Stress

1. Keep swinging movements relaxed, smooth, and rhythmical.
2. Keep swinging movements equal on both sides; hence, do not apply additional muscular force to one side.
3. Dismount swinging bars, rings, or swings at the top of the swing.

Applying Movement Concepts and Skills

1. *Body awareness:* Using different parts of the body to initiate and perform swinging actions; combining body shapes with different swinging movements
2. *Space awareness:* Performing swinging movements while moving and changing directions and pathways
3. *Qualities:* Changing swinging movements from quick to slow, strong to light, and combinations of both
4. *Relationships:* Swinging with light scarves, hoops, or wands; developing sequences with partner, with equipment and while traveling and stopping

Swinging Activities

1. Swing arms forward and backward and from side to side.

2. Swing arms overhead, forward and backward, and sideward.

3. Lie on back and swing arms and legs.

4. Repeat activity 1 with legs.

5. Swing head forward and backward and from side to side.

6. Ask the children how many parts of the body can swing or sway from standing or sitting positions. Allow them to experiment.

7. Swing or sway parts of the body in pantomime. Tell the children to sway like a tree, swing like a windshield wiper, and so on. Change tempo with each pantomime movement.

8. Swing arms or legs with moderate speed, then shift to slower or faster speeds.

9. Stand on a box, step, or other apparatus and swing the leg.

10. Grasp chinning bar and swing body forward and backward. Flex arm and repeat.

11. Swing on a rope and release it at different points on the forward and backward swing. Note that the top of the backswing is the best point to release a rope.

12. Combine swinging with other locomotor skills such as a jump or slide.

13. Hang from a bar or rings, then swing.

Bending and Stretching

A bend is a flexing movement around one or more joints (figure 4.11). A stretch is an extension of one or more joints of the body (figure 4.12). A light or gentle stretch moves the joint partially through its range of movement. A strong forceful stretch, such as a stretch upward and backward, requires maximum extension through many joints.

Things to Stress

1. To increase flexibility, bend in a slow and sustained manner.

2. Encourage children to find, test, and extend different parts of the body that bend. Also, use such terms as *tuck, curl,* and *coil* in place of *bend* or *flex.*

3. Initial stretching movements should be light and gentle; discourage ballistic movements.

4. Encourage children to stretch through the full range of movement.

5. Where possible, combine stretching and bending movements.

6. Encourage stretching movements from a variety of positions and in a variety of ways.

Figure 4.11 Bending.   **Figure 4.12** Stretching.

Applying Movement Concepts and Skills

1. *Body awareness:* Balancing on different parts of the body and seeing how many different parts and ways to bend and stretch; making matching curved and stretched shapes with a partner; using individual ropes, wands, or hoops, designing sequences that involve stretch and curved shapes

2. *Space awareness:* Bending and stretching in different directions, levels, and pathways

3. *Qualities:* Changing from bending and stretching movements with quick and slow and strong and light movements

4. *Relationships:* Developing sequences with partners showing matching and contrasting bending and stretching movements; adding speed, force, and small equipment to the sequence

Bending and Stretching Activities

1. Imitate things that bend—tree, snake, dog, ostrich, giraffe, and so on.

2. Bend one part of the body while keeping another part straight.

3. Combine bending with other locomotor or nonlocomotor movements—bend while stretching, swinging, or jumping.

4. Run and jump, and bend one or more parts while in the air.

5. Stand and stretch trunk, then arms, wrists, and fingers in a slow upward movement. Repeat and move in other directions.

6. Repeat activity 5 from a front or back lying position.

7. Slowly stretch in one direction and slowly curl back to the starting position. Repeat and move quickly back to the curled position.

8. Run, jump, and stretch, then land and bend.

9. Stretch one arm slowly and bend it back rapidly; reverse movement. Do the same with other parts of the body.

10. Bend one part of the body (arms) while stretching another (legs).

11. Stand on a box or step with toes touching near the edge. Keep legs straight and bend forward and down; try to extend the fingers beyond the toes.

12. Pantomime sports movements that require strong sustained stretching movements.

13. Stretch while holding individual ropes, wands, or hoops.

Twisting and Turning

Figure 4.13 Twisting.

A twist is a rotation of parts of the body around its own axis (figure 4.13). Twisting movements usually occur at the neck, shoulders, spine, hips, ankles, and wrists. A turn is a partial or total rotation of the body, accompanied by a shift in the base of support (figure 4.14). A pivot to one side illustrates a turning movement involving a partial rotation and a shift in the base of support. A jump followed by a full rotation in the air illustrates a total rotation and complete change in the base of support.

Things to Stress

1. A twisting movement can take place on or off the ground.

2. The range of the twisting action is determined by the type of joint (hinge joint, ball-and-socket joint, etc.).

3. Keep the part of the body around which the twisting action occurs stable.

4. To increase the speed of a turn, pull the legs and arms close to the body.

5. In activities requiring a quick change of direction, keep the body weight low and the feet about shoulder-width apart.

Figure 4.14 Turning.

Applying Movement Concepts and Skills

1. *Body awareness:* Finding how many different parts of the body on which one can twist and turn; using individual ropes, wands, and hoops, designing sequences involving twisting and turning

2. *Space awareness:* Designing sequences involving twisting and turning in different directions, levels, and pathways

3. *Qualities:* Performing twisting and turning movements quickly and slowly and strongly and lightly

4. *Relationships:* Developing sequences with a partner showing twisting and turning movements that involve changes in direction, level, and speed

Twisting and Turning Activities

1. Twist to pantomime movements—trees and wind.

2. Combine twisting with other locomotor skills—walk, stop, leap, and jump.

3. Twist part of the upper body one way while twisting part of the lower body the opposite way.

4. With a partner, make up twisting routines—together and against each other's body parts.

5. Pantomime athletic and mechanical movements that involve twisting.

6. Turn the body a quarter, half, or full turn to the right, then to the left.

7. Turn the body to music.

8. Turn to pantomime movements—tops, doors, sports skills.

9. Combine twisting and turning movements.

10. Face a partner and pivot toward and away from each other.

11. Begin a turn with arms outstretched, then quickly draw in the arms as the turn is made. Repeat with the legs or legs and arms.

12. Combine turning movements with a walk, run, jump, skip, or slide.

13. Combine a turn with small equipment such as individual ropes, hoops, wands, and traffic cones.

14. Have partners make up sequences involving twisting and turning movements. These can be performed standing, walking, and from different positions.

Pushing and Pulling

Pushing is directing a force or object away from the base of support, such as pushing a door open or pushing against an imaginary object with hands or feet (figure 4.15). Pulling is directing a force or object toward the body (figure 4.16). A pulling action is normally initiated by the hands and arms; however, other parts of the body, such as the foot, knee, or trunk, can also initiate a pulling movement.

Things to Stress

1. For movements requiring excessive force, lower the body to direct the force through the center of the weight.

2. Start strong pushing movements with a wide base of support.

3. Keep the back straight during strenuous pushing movements.

4. When lifting or pulling heavy objects, start with a wide base of support, bent knees, and straight back and pull the object upward toward the body.

5. Keep the pulling action smooth; use a controlled sequence of muscular contractions rather than rigid, ballistic-type movements.

Applying Movement Concepts and Skills

1. *Body awareness:* Finding out how many different parts of the body with which one can push and pull; finding out how many different positions the body can be in, such as lying on the back or side and pushing and pulling with different parts of the body

2. *Space awareness:* Designing sequences involving pushing and pulling in different directions, pathways, and levels

3. *Qualities:* Performing pushing and pulling sequences involving quick and slow and strong and light movements

4. *Relationships:* Developing individual or partner sequences showing pushing and pulling and involving one or more elements of body awareness, qualities, and space awareness

Figure 4.15 Pushing.   **Figure 4.16** Pulling.

Pushing and Pulling Activities

1. Pull in pantomime—pull a wagon or row a boat.

2. Pull objects of varying weights and sizes toward the body. Start with light objects and progress to heavier ones, gradually adjusting the base of support and angle of pull as the weight increases.

3. Use different parts of the body to pull an object, such as a leg, the trunk, or head.

4. Repeat activity 3 but from different positions, such as lying on your back and pulling an object toward your body with the lower leg.

5. Pull an object with different rates of speed—begin pulling slowly, then gradually increase speed.

6. Play tug-o-war with two players. Play as usual, beginning in a standing position; then vary the starting position, and begin by kneeling, lying on one side and the back, and so on.

7. Repeat with four or more players.

8. Push in pantomime—push a box or a wheelbarrow.

9. Push objects of various weights and sizes. Begin with small objects and gradually increase weight and size.

10. Push objects with the hands, feet, and back.

11. Do partner activities—from a standing position, one partner assumes a good base of support and the other attempts to push the other backward. Experiment in various positions with different parts of the body. For example, have both partners face each other on the floor and push their legs or arms against each other. From back-to-back position, one partner pulls the other over his head.

12. Balance on one foot and push a box against a wall or partner. Try same movements, but balance on two

Figure 4.17 Two-hand underhand throw.

a   b   c

feet. Repeat movements, lowering the body and widening the base of support.

13. Pantomime sports skills that require a pushing action.

14. Perform five or six calisthenic exercises or stunts that require a pushing action.

Manipulative Skills

The fundamental manipulative skills of throwing, catching, and striking represent the foundation of all major individual and team sport activities. These skills should be taught to primary children in a systematic manner using a direct and limitation method of teaching and through a variety of running, tag, simple team, and creative game activities. As children progress to the intermediate grades, specialized skills are organized sequentially within each major sport (see part 5). Thus, the following skills should be acquired by boys and girls before they reach level III.

Throwing

Children in levels I and II normally begin with a two-hand underhand throw. They progress to a one-hand underhand throw, and finally tackle the one-hand overhand throw.

Two-Hand Underhand Throw

The child begins with her back straight, feet about shoulder-width apart, and knees slightly bent. Arms are straight and the ball is held with the fingers of both hands (figure 4.17a). Keep the back straight, then swing arms forward and upward, and straighten the knees (figure 4.17b). Release the ball off the fingers and follow through in the direction of the ball (figure 4.17c).

Applying Mechanical Principles

The following mechanical principles apply to all three basic throwing skills.

1. *Momentum:* The momentum of any part of the body can be transferred to the ball. To apply this principle, rotate the body toward the side while shifting the weight to the back foot. Bring back the throwing arm as far as possible. If the forward swinging action is smooth, maximum force will be transferred to the ball as it leaves the hands.

2. *Speed:* Greater speed can be gained by increasing the distance over which the force is applied. This is particularly important in the one-hand underhand and overhand throws. The straighter the arm in the forward throwing movement, the greater the force that is generated and the greater the speed of the ball.

Things to Stress

1. Use a large ball (beach ball or 8½-to-12-inch utility ball) with young children, particularly five-and six-year-olds.

2. Begin a throw with legs far enough apart to provide a good base of support.

3. Rotate the body in the same direction as the ball during the preparatory movement.

4. Keep arms straight on the forward swing, and follow through after the ball has been released.

Applying Movement Concepts and Skills

1. *Body awareness:* Finding different positions and ways of throwing a ball with two hands

2. *Space awareness:* Finding different directions, levels, and distances the ball can be thrown
3. *Qualities:* Experimenting with throwing a ball with different speeds and force
4. *Relationships:* Throwing a ball to a partner, changing ways of throwing and from different levels and distances

Throwing Activities

1. Use large balls (beach balls, playballs) and large targets (walls, lines on floor, colorful targets painted on plywood). Have children begin by throwing a few feet from the target, then gradually increase the distance.
2. Throw and catch with a partner.
3. Have children experiment with different ways of throwing a two-hand side throw (from either side, while kneeling, or while lying on back).
4. Play simple throwing games. Refer to "Classroom Games" (chapter 14), "Incorporating the Inventive Games Approach" (p. 252), and chapter 16 (table 16.1, p. 257 and table 16.2, p. 269).

One-Hand Underhand Throw

The child stands facing the target with legs slightly apart and weight evenly distributed on both feet. She holds the ball in front of her body with both hands slightly under the ball (figure 4.18a). Her right hand swings down and back as her body twists to the right and her weight shifts to her right foot. As her right arm swings forward she steps forward onto her left foot and releases the ball off the fingertips (figure 4.18b).

Things to Stress

1. Use a large ball (beach or utility ball).
2. Begin with a wide base of support and extend arms far enough in the initial backswing.
3. Emphasize a smooth forward swing and follow through after the ball is released.

Applying Movement Concepts and Skills

1. *Body awareness:* Finding different positions and ways of throwing a one-hand underhand throw
2. *Space awareness:* Finding different directions, levels, and distances the ball can be thrown
3. *Qualities:* Experimenting with throwing a ball with different force and speed
4. *Relationships:* Throw a ball to a target or partner, changing way of throwing from different levels and distances

Figure 4.18 One-hand underhand throw.

a   b

Throwing Activities

1. Adapt two-hand side throw activities to the one-hand underhand throw.
2. Adapt two-hand side throw activities using a beanbag or fleece ball.
3. Roll a ball toward a target or partner.
4. Throw various-sized balls into the air and catch them on the volley or after one bounce.
5. Repeat activities 2 to 4 using your other hand.
6. Run, change direction, and throw at a target.
7. Run, stop, turn, and throw at a target.
8. Make up games for individuals or partners that require a one-hand underhand throw.

One-Hand Overhand Throw

The player begins with her left foot forward and her body weight evenly distributed over both feet. She holds the ball with both hands in front of her body. In the first part of the backswing she raises her upper arm, and flexes her wrist so the hand points backward. At this point, her left side faces the direction of the throw; her left arm extends forward; and her weight is on the rear foot (figure 4.19a). In a simultaneous movement, her upper arm lifts up and forward and her left arm moves down and back as her weight shifts to the front foot (figure 4.19b). The ball is released off the fingertips. The follow-through should be in a downward direction, ending with the palm of the throwing hand toward the ground (figure 4.19c).

Figure 4.19 One-hand overhand throw.

a   b   c

Things to Stress

1. Hold the ball with tips of fingers and thumb.
2. Raise upper arm and forearm well above the shoulder on the backward swing.
3. Keep elbow away from the body on the forward throwing action.
4. Snap the wrist and release the ball off the fingertips.
5. Follow through after the ball is released and take a step on the right foot.

Applying Movement Concepts and Skills

1. *Body awareness:* Finding different positions and ways of throwing a one-hand overhand throw
2. *Space awareness:* Finding different directions and levels the ball can be thrown
3. *Qualities:* Experimenting with throwing the ball with different force and speed
4. *Relationships:* Throwing the ball at different targets or to a partner, changing ways of throwing from different levels and distances

Throwing Activities

1. Adapt the two-hand and one-hand underhand activities to the one-hand overhand throw.
2. Refer to practice activities and lead-up games in chapter 22, "Basketball Activities."

3. Refer to practice activities and lead-up games in chapter 23, "Softball Activities."
4. Play simple throwing games listed in chapter 16 (table 16.1, p. 257 and table 16.2, p. 269).

Catching

Catching is one of the more difficult skills for early primary school children. The child must learn to focus on an oncoming object, to move into a correct catching position, and to decide whether to use an underhand or overhand catch. All of these movements take a lot of practice; hence, young children show a great deal of inconsistency with this skill. Using large balls, such as balloon and fleece balls, and throwing from short distances help build confidence and skill during the initial stages of learning to catch. As skill improves, introduce smaller balls and increase other aspects such as catching a ball from different levels and at different rates of speed. These points should be kept in mind when teaching the following catching skills.

Two-Hand Underhand Catch

Use the two-hand underhand catch when the ball approaches below the waist. The player stands with feet about shoulder-width apart, elbows bent, and fingers pointing down. As the ball approaches, the player steps forward, extends her arms, and brings her hands close together (figure 4.20a). The ball is caught with the tips of the fingers and thumbs. The pinkies (baby fingers) should be close together when the ball is caught (figure 4.20b). As the ball is caught, the hands recoil toward the body to soften the force.

Two-Hand Overhand Catch

When the ball approaches above the waist, the two-hand overhand catch should be used. The elbows are bent and held high, and the fingers and thumbs are spread (figure 4.21a). As the ball approaches, the arms extend forward and up. The ball should be caught with the tips of the fingers and thumbs; the thumbs are close together (figure 4.21b). As the ball is caught, the hands recoil toward the body to deaden the force of the oncoming ball.

Figure 4.20 Two-hand underhand catch.

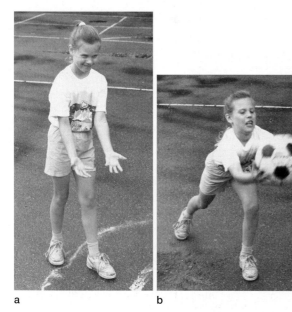

a   b

Figure 4.21 Two-hand overhand catch.

a   b

Applying Mechanical Principles

1. *Center of gravity:* The body should be kept in line with the ball. The legs should be comfortably spread or in a stride position to provide a firm base of support. With the underhand catch, a slightly crouched position lowers the center of gravity, providing an even firmer base of support.

2. *Absorption of force:* To absorb the impact of the oncoming ball, the force should be spread over as large an area as possible or as long a distance as possible, or both. Catch the ball with the arms extended and the fingers spread and cupped, then recoil the arms toward the body to provide the greatest surface and distance for absorbing the force.

Things to Stress

1. Move into a "ready" position, where the body is in line with the oncoming ball.

2. Meet the ball with cupped hands and slightly bent elbows, then recoil back toward the body.

3. Keep feet in a comfortable stride position; for low catches, bend the knees and lean forward in the direction of the oncoming ball.

Applying Movement Concepts and Skills

1. *Body awareness:* Finding different positions and ways to catch a ball

2. *Space awareness:* Exploring different ways of receiving a ball or other small and large objects— along the ground, rebound from floor or wall

3. *Qualities:* Exploring ways of receiving balls, beanbags, and other light objects that are thrown with different speeds and force

4. *Relationships:* Explore throwing and catching with a partner, changing height, distance, and speed of throw

Catching Activities

1. See activities list under one- and two-hand throws.

2. Throw and catch objects of different size (large utility balls, Nerf and tennis balls, beanbags, etc.) from a short distance then gradually increase the distance between players.

3. Throw and catch a large ball over a net or string tied across two chairs.

4. Throw and catch a ball thrown under the string or through a hoop held off the ground by a third player.

5. Play simple throwing and catching games listed in chapter 16 (table 16.1, p. 257, and table 16.2, p. 269).

Striking

Two basic types of striking skills are used in individual, partner, and group games. These striking skills include hitting a ball with the hand or foot and hitting an object with a bat, racquet, or other implement. The basic skills within each of these general areas are described in this section. The more specific sport skills are detailed in chapters 18 to 24.

Figure 4.22 Hitting the ball with an underhand striking action.

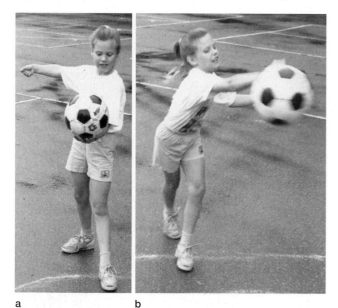

a   b

Figure 4.23 Hitting the ball with a two-hand overhand striking action.

Figure 4.24 Dribbling with the hand.

Striking with the Hand

When striking a ball with the hand or fist, the player stands in line with the oncoming ball. The feet are in a stride position, with the weight on the back foot. If the ball is hit with an underhand striking action (figure 4.22a), the striking arm extends straight back, then forcefully moves forward to contact the ball when it is opposite the front foot (figure 4.22b). The hand of the striking arm is held firm as the ball is contacted. Follow-through is forceful in the direction of the hit. When a ball is hit with a two-hand overhand striking action, the elbows are bent slightly, the fingers are spread apart, and the thumbs face each other (figure 4.23). As the ball drops, the body and arms extend upward and slightly forward, and the ball is hit with "stiff" fingers. Follow-through is an upward and forward motion in the direction of the ball.

When dribbling with the hands, the striking action is downward. The body leans forward slightly and the knees are bent. The wrist of the dribbling hand is flexed, with the fingers cupped and spread (figure 4.24). The forearm extends downward and the ball is "pushed" toward the ground. As the ball rebounds, the fingers, wrist, and arm "ride" back with it.

Applying Mechanical Principles

1. *Stability:* In all striking skills, the legs should be comfortably spread to provide a wide, stable base of support from which to hit the ball. Standing with the knees slightly bent also lowers the center of gravity, further increasing stability.

2. *Action-reaction:* Every action causes an equal and opposite reaction. When a player begins to swing his arm toward the oncoming ball, he is building up force. If he maintains a steady forward momentum at the moment of contact, the ball will recoil with an equal force.

3. *Production of force:* Hitting a ball is basically the transfer of rotary force to linear force. More force can be gained by increasing the distance of the backswing and by cocking the wrist at the top of the backswing. Additional force is also gained by extending the arms as the bat is moved toward the ball.

4. *Direction of force:* The direction in which an object moves is determined by the direction in which the force is applied. If the force is applied in line with the ball's center of gravity, the ball travels in a straight line, but if the bat hits the ball above or below the center of gravity, the ball travels in a rotary motion, losing distance and speed.

5. *Inertia:* An object has its greatest inertia when it is not moving. Once dribbling begins, it should be continued by easy, sequential pushing actions. Each time the ball comes to rest, more force must be applied to overcome the initial inertia.

Things to Stress

1. Keep your eye on the ball.
2. Get in line with the ball.
3. Strike and follow through.
4. When dribbling, push the ball and ride back with the rebound.

locomotor, nonlocomotor, and manipulative skills

Applying Movement Concepts and Skills

1. *Body awareness:* Exploring different ways of hitting a light object, such as a balloon or Nerf ball; using different parts of the body to hit an object and hitting the object from different positions and while moving
2. *Space awareness:* Exploring ways of hitting objects in space—high and far, short and down, etc.
3. *Qualities:* Varying the force and speed of hitting small and large balls
4. *Relationships:* Exploring different ways of hitting a balloon or fleece ball back and forth to a partner

Striking Activities

1. Strike a balloon with the hand or the elbow, then with different parts of the body.
2. Repeat activity 1 with either hand and with both hands.
3. Strike different-sized balls toward a target or to a partner.
4. Attempt to strike a balloon or light Nerf ball into the air three or more times.
5. Make up a sequence of striking, throwing, and catching a balloon or ball.
6. Run, change direction, then strike a Nerf ball toward a target.
7. Strike a ball into the air, perform a stunt, then catch the returning ball.
8. Make up a game for one person or partners that requires a strike.
9. Adapt games from the following chapters that stress striking skills with one or two hands.

   Chapter 14: "Adapting Physical Education Activities to the Classroom"
   Chapter 16: "Locomotor and Manipulative Games"
   Chapter 17: "Cooperative Games"
   Chapter 21: "Volleyball Activities"

10. Play simple striking games listed in chapter 16 (table 16.1, p. 257 and table 16.2, p. 269).

Striking with the Feet

The majority of kicking games played in elementary school involve kicking a stationary or moving ball with the top or side of the instep. Just before the ball is kicked, the nonkicking foot is even with the ball, the head and trunk lean forward slightly, and the kicking leg is well back with the knee slightly bent. The eyes are focused on the ball, and the arms extend sideways. The kicking leg is then brought downward and forward, and the top of the instep contacts the ball (figure 4.25). The kicking leg continues forward and slightly upward.

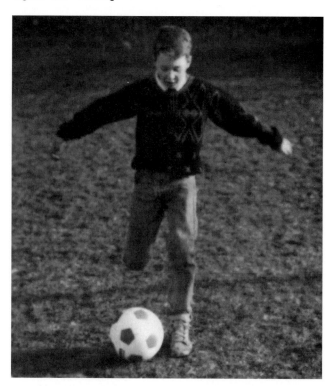

Figure 4.25 Kicking.

Many kicking games also involve a controlled striking or dribbling action of both feet (figure 4.26). In this type of striking action, the body is bent slightly forward with the head over the ball. The ball is moved with short, controlled pushes.

Applying Mechanical Principles

The mechanical principles listed under "Striking with the Hand" also apply to "Striking with the Feet." The following principles apply to kicking a ball.

1. *Acceleration:* A ball that is kicked moves in the direction of the force, and the resulting change of speed is directly proportional to the force acting on it. It is important that the force applied by the kicking foot be directly behind the ball and moving in the direction in which the ball is intended to move.
2. *Increasing linear velocity:* Kicking a ball involves the conversion of angular velocity to linear velocity. Linear velocity can be increased by taking more steps prior to the kick or by extending the lower leg more to create a longer lever and, thus, more force when the ball is contacted.

Things to Stress

1. Never kick with the toes.
2. Bend the knee prior to kicking, and follow through in the direction of the kick.

Figure 4.26 Dribbling with the feet.

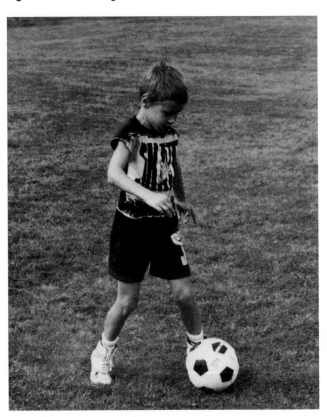

Figure 4.27 Striking a lightweight object with an implement.

Figure 4.28 Batting.

3. When dribbling, push the ball and maintain a steady, rhythmical dribbling action.

Applying Movement Concepts and Skills

Adapt movement ideas listed under "Striking with the Hand."

Kicking Activities

1. Adapt the striking activities listed under "Striking with the Hand" to kicking or dribbling.
2. Adapt practice activities and lead-up games provided in the following chapters to kicking or dribbling a ball.
   Chapter 18: "Soccer Activities"
   Chapter 20: "Flag or Touch Football Activities"
3. Play simple kicking games listed in chapter 16 (table 16.1, p. 257, and table 16.2, p. 269)

Striking with an Implement

When striking with a racquet or paddle, the player stands with feet comfortably apart, knees slightly bent, and elbow flexed and away from the body. Young children begin with lightweight objects such as balloons or sponge balls (figure 4.27). The striking action for these objects involves light elbow and wrist movements.

When striking a ball with a bat, the player stands with feet parallel, about shoulder-width apart. His left side faces the pitcher. He grips the bat comfortably, shifting it to the back of his head about shoulder high. His arms, bent at the elbows, are held away from his body (figure 4.28). As the ball leaves the pitcher's hand, the batter shifts his weight to his rear foot, then swings the bat forward as he shifts his weight to his front foot. He keeps a firm grip on the bat as the ball is hit. After the ball is hit, the bat continues to swing around the left shoulder.

Applying Mechanical Principles

The mechanical principles listed under "Striking with the Hand" apply to "Striking with an Implement."

Applying Movement Concepts and Skills

Adapt movement ideas listed under "Striking with the Hand."

Things to Stress

1. Keep your eye on the ball.
2. Start with feet spread apart and the knees slightly flexed.
3. Maintain a firm grip through the forward swing and follow-through.

locomotor, nonlocomotor, and manipulative skills

Striking Activities

1. Adapt striking activities listed under "Striking with the Hand" to striking with an implement.
2. Play simple striking games listed in chapter 16 (table 16.1, p. 257, and table 16.2, p. 269)
3. Adapt practice activities and lead-up games provided in the following chapters to batting an object.

   Chapter 19: "Hockey Activities"
   Chapter 23: "Softball Activities"

In the primary grades, the fundamental skills of throwing, catching, and striking should be facilitated through an informal exploratory approach. Emphasis should be on exploring different ways of performing each manipulative skill. Gradually, teachers should stress throwing, kicking, or hitting a ball for distance or speed. Accuracy should be of minimal concern during these formative years. The game activities provided in chapters 16 and 17 stress an informal and enjoyable environment for acquiring these fundamental manipulative skills. Equally stressed in each of these chapters is the generous application of exploratory teaching methods and techniques.

Specialized Skills and Movement Patterns

Specialized skills and movement patterns are the more complex skills and movements unique to individual and team sports, folk dance, and gymnastic activities. These specialized skills and movement patterns require a high level of speed and accuracy. In addition, each sport requires a knowledge of rules and an understanding of complex offensive and defensive playing strategies. Hence, proficiency in each sport requires extensive practice according to acceptable form and accuracy. Whenever possible, these skills and movement patterns should be learned through realistic practice activities and lead-up games, as well as in playing the game according to its rules and regulations. Chapters 18 through 24 include a description of skills, a suggested sequence in acquiring them, and a variety of appropriate activities. Although the emphasis within each of these chapters is on acquiring and refining skills and improving playing ability, there is also a discussion of exploratory methods and modified games to cope with individual differences in the levels of ability, needs, and interests of upper elementary school children.

The specialized skills and movement patterns required in folk and square dance activities are quite different than those of individual or team sports. In folk dances, an increased complexity of skill is required in such steps as the waltz or polka. Perhaps more important, however, is the complexity of the dance, style, and finesse of each dancer or group of performers. Because of this, the scope and sequence of the dances provided in chapter 29 are simple guidelines. Teachers should view the suggested level for each dance activity as a very rough guideline and select dance activities according to the class's background in dance and its level of interest in folk and square dance activities.

Creative dance activities do not involve specialized skills, nor does this form of activity adhere to a scope and sequence of skill development. The suggested ideas in chapter 30 will provide a basis for teaching this type of activity to children in primary and intermediate grades.

The basic skills of traditional gymnastic activities are classified as balance, vaulting, climbing, and agility skills. These skills are organized within each category according to their difficulty. Chapter 25, "Stunts, Tumbling, and Movement Skills," includes the basic stunts and tumbling skills appropriate for developmental levels I to III and describes how the movement concepts and skills of body awareness, space awareness, qualities, and relationships can be integrated with these structured skills. Chapters 26 and 27 follow a similar pattern, combining the structured and movement skills used with small equipment and large apparatus.

Selected References

Corbin, C. R. (1980). *A Textbook of Motor Development,* Second Edition. Dubuque, IA: Wm. C. Brown Publishers.

Gallahue, D. L. (1989). *Understanding Motor Development: Infants, Children, Adolescents,* Second Edition. Indianapolis: Benchmark Press.

Graham, G. S., Holt-Hale, S. A., and Parker, M. (1993). *Children Moving,* Third Edition. Mountain View, CA: Mayfield Publishing.

Hammett, C. T. (1992). *Movement Activities for Early Childhood.* Champaign, IL: Human Kinetics Publishers, Inc.

Haywood, K. M. (1986). *Life Span Motor Development.* Champaign, IL: Human Kinetics Publishers, Inc.

Keogh, J., and Sugden, D. (1985). *Motor Skill Development.* New York: Macmillan Publishing Co.

Pica, R. (1991). *Early Elementary Children Moving and Learning.* Champaign, IL: Human Kinetics Publishers, Inc.

Wickstrom, R. L. (1983). *Fundamental Movement Patterns.* Philadelphia: Lea & Febiger.

5

Learning Motor Skills

One of the fundamental objectives in physical education is to teach a variety of games, dance, and gymnastic skills to children from all age levels in the elementary school. Our challenge is to teach these motor skills and concepts to children of varying physical maturity, interests, and abilities. To do this effectively and safely, we must understand *when* it is appropriate to introduce a motor skill and *how* it should be taught. Within the past few decades, researchers in this area have produced a body of knowledge that can help us understand the nature of motor learning and the process of acquiring motor skills and movement concepts.

This chapter will briefly cover several important areas relating to learning a motor skill. It will summarize the current theories of motor learning that provide a framework on which to build a series of working concepts and principles relating to teaching motor skills. The remaining sections include information about the stages of motor skill development, the phases of learning a motor skill, and the concepts relating to the mechanics of movement, as well as some general guidelines for teaching motor skills and concepts. The concepts and principles contained in this chapter are fundamental to all future chapters dealing with teaching game, dance, and gymnastic activities ■

Understanding the Terminology

Since physical education programs are designed to promote motor learning, it is important to consider what is currently known about this area. Motor learning and motor skill were initially defined in chapter 2. In this chapter these terms will be expanded upon and dealt with in more detail. Motor skill was defined as the degree of proficiency with which a person performs a motor task, where "performance" is viewed as the single execution of a movement or sequence of movements and "proficiency" refers to the level of performance at any given time. Motor skill, then, as used throughout this book, includes any muscular activity, under voluntary control of the brain, that is directed toward a specific objective. This term includes all voluntary muscle movements from the large gross motor movements, such as running and jumping, to fine motor movements, such as the creative finger flicking movements in an interpretive dance sequence. This definition also includes static balance positions, since they involve voluntary contractions of skeletal muscles.

The term *motor skill development* was also introduced in chapter 2 and refers to a change in the proficiency and form of a motor skill as a result of growth, maturation, and learning (Stallings, 1973). This term is further clarified by Kathleen Haywood, who states that it is

. . . the sequential, continuous age-related process whereby an individual progresses from simple, unorganized, and unskilled movements to the achievement of highly organized, complex motor skills and finally to the adjustment of skills that accompanies aging. (Haywood 1986)

The latter part of this statement implies that motor skill development continues throughout the life span.

Although growth and maturation influence the acquisition of motor skills, learning plays a significant role. Since learning is an internal phenomenon that cannot be observed directly, it can only be inferred from the observation of a person's performance. Motor learning then, as defined in chapter 2, is viewed as a change in the capability of a person to perform a skill, and this must be inferred from observing a relatively permanent improvement in motor performance that is a result of practice or experience.

Process of Learning a Motor Skill

If you can remember when you first learned a particular skill, such as riding a bicycle, it will provide a basis for understanding the process of learning any motor skill. When you first got on your two-wheel bicycle, (three-wheelers don't count) without training wheels, your parent or friend held the bicycle upright while you sat on the seat. Your initial attempts were chaotic and clumsy—thinking, "How do I do this?" "What happens when this occurs?" and so on. Gradually, you learned to stay upright,

Figure 5.1 With practice, riding a bicycle becomes automatic.

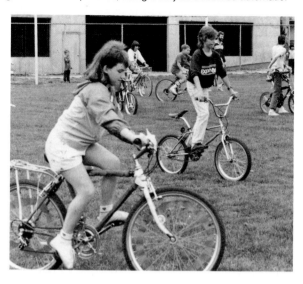

but you still were concerned about how to stop or judge your position in relation to your "proficient" friends, who were "circling, dodging, and deaking" around your bicycle. With practice, you gradually became one of the gang because you reached a phase of riding in which you did not worry about the actual process of riding; it had become automatic (figure 5.1). Your concerns were now on other things, such as playing bicycle hockey or another complex activity involving a high level of proficiency in all aspects of maneuvering a bicycle in and around objects and alluding very tricky opponents.

This scenario illustrates a three-stage model of motor learning. These three stages were first identified by Paul Fitts and Michael Posner (1967) and labeled the *initial, intermediate, and autonomous* phases of learning. This three-stage model will be discussed, along with suggestions and implications for teaching motor skills to children in the primary and intermediate grades.

Initial Phase

The initial phase of learning involves *thinking* about a skill as much as it does trying to perform it. For example, when first introduced to dribbling a soccer ball, a child virtually thinks about each part of the skill, then tries to perform it. Consequently, his movements are somewhat jerky, inaccurate, and inconsistent. Although the child knows the ball should be "pushed," it is usually kicked and chased in the early stages. Unless he is allowed to experiment with various ways of moving the ball with his feet, and then receives gradual and specific assistance from the teacher, he may stay at this phase for a long time.

The implications for the teacher during this phase of motor skill acquisition are provided in the following list.

1. Introduce each skill with clear, simple, and short explanations.

2. Allow the learner to practice the skill by himself. During this initial phase, encourage the child to experiment with a variety of ways of dribbling the ball.

3. Help the child concentrate on one or two main parts of the skill—contacting the ball with both feet, then the sides of both feet, and so on.

4. Provide continuous and positive feedback throughout the beginning phase of this skill.

5. As the child begins to understand how to perform the skill, gradually stress more form. This phase does not include accuracy, distance, or speed.

6. Use practice activities and low organization games that are simple, cooperative, and fun and that require few participants and very few rules.

Intermediate Phase

The second phase in acquiring a motor skill represents a gradual shift from the concentrated thinking and hit-or-miss activities of the initial phase to a more focused effort to refine the skill. As the learner shifts into this phase, he should possess a clear mental picture of the skill so he is not consciously thinking about isolated elements of the movement. Also, many of the basic fundamentals of the skill should have been acquired. For example, while dribbling the ball, the child can detect some of his own errors, such as leaning too far forward, using one foot too often, or not looking up while dribbling. This is the time for keen observations by the teacher in order to give helpful suggestions to improve and refine the skill performance.

This is a very important phase of acquiring any motor skill. Consequently, the following guidelines should be adhered to throughout this phase of motor skill development.

1. Provide numerous practice activities that require increased levels of skill performance.

2. Provide appropriate coaching hints and suggestions throughout practice activities and lead-up games.

3. Gradually increase the rate until the skill is performed to the speed required in the mature form of the activity. This applies to learning games, dance, or gymnastic motor skills.

4. Stress short practice sessions with frequent breaks, rather than long practice sessions with fewer breaks.

5. Stress practice sessions and lead-up activities that are performed with small groups and require maximum participation.

6. Stress practicing the correct form until it is learned or even overlearned. Once a smooth and efficient form has been achieved, begin to emphasize other factors—speed and accuracy.

7. Consider individual differences in the rate and level of ability within and among children of the same chronological age.

Automatic Phase

After the learner has completed numerous practice sessions and performed the skill in a variety of settings, the automatic phase is entered. Once this phase is reached, the motor skill is performed in a way that feels and looks like it is an automatic or habitual movement. In the case of the soccer player, he now can move the ball with short pushes of his feet, giving the impression of a smooth, almost effortless movement of the ball. When this phase is reached, the child no longer has to concentrate mentally on the various components of the skill or on how he is executing each one at any given moment in the game. He now concentrates on his offensive or defensive playing skills, separately or in concert with dribbling the ball. As with all game, dance, and gymnastic skills, this phase is not considered the final, advanced, or terminal phase. If it were, there would be no room for improvement. The automatic phase, thus, always allows time and room for more practice and experience to enhance and fine-tune the motor skill. Most elementary school children reach this phase with the majority of fundamental skills. However, in terms of the specialized skills of game, dance, and gymnastic activities, few children extend beyond the minimum level of the automatic phase of motor skill development.

The implications of this phase of motor skill development for the teacher and learner are provided here.

1. Provide practice sessions that enhance form, style, and accuracy.

2. Provide more qualified coaching techniques, including better skill analysis and effective motivational devices.

3. When plateaus are reached, encourage the learner to experiment with new ideas or a change of pace. Doggedly continuing without improvement or satisfaction may lead to regressive skill performance.

4. Provide greater variety and more intensity in practice sessions, lead-up activities, and in official sport, dance, or gymnastic contests.

In summary, it is obvious that the three phases of motor skill development are not sharply defined. Rather, they are stages along a continuum of acquiring and retaining a motor skill. Hence, the suggestions made within each phase of motor skill learning should be used as guidelines for teaching. Other factors, such as the characteristics and maturity levels of children, also have significant effects on how or when a child can and will learn a motor skill. In addition to these factors, teachers need to understand the following changes that occur during the process of motor learning if they are to provide developmentally appropriate activities and teaching situations.

Changes During the Process of Learning a Motor Skill

Several changes occur at different points in time as the child begins to learn a motor skill. As children move from the initial and intermediate phases of learning toward the automatic phase, they begin to understand what to do and how the motor skill should be performed. They get better in detecting errors in performance and correcting their motor actions. They learn where to direct their attention. They also become more efficient in performing the motor skill, producing smooth coordinated movements that do not waste energy. What follows is a brief description of these changes. Since the teacher's job is to provide children with opportunities to gain the necessary practice and experience to get to the automatic phase of motor learning, understanding the changes that occur during the process of learning a motor skill will help achieve this goal.

Changes in Knowledge

The performer's level of understanding of knowing what to do and how the skill can be performed changes during motor learning. In the initial stage of learning a child will need to know what to do, in addition to knowing how to perform the motor skill. For example, when learning to throw a ball for distance, a child will need to know the effect of gravity and that throwing at an angle of approximately 45 degrees will be the most effective strategy. This will be a new piece of knowledge the child adds as he acquires the motor skill. The terms procedural knowledge and declarative knowledge are used to separate these two types of knowledge. Procedural knowledge refers to "knowing how to perform the motor skill" and declarative knowledge refers to "knowing what to do." These areas of knowledge interact as the child begins to acquire a motor skill.

To illustrate, as the child reaches the automatic stage of learning to throw for distance, he will throw at the 45 degree angle without consciously thinking about gravity or this particular strategy. He has learned to incorporate this declarative knowledge into the motor skill performance of throwing for distance. Practice and experience can now be viewed as the interaction of procedural knowledge (knowing how to perform the skill) with declarative knowledge (knowing what to do). Teachers will not only need to provide children with opportunities to practice motor skills, but at the same time they will need to help them understand what knowledge is important to perform the skill effectively. Background information, such as the 45-degree throwing angle (declarative knowledge), together with information about how to perform the motor skill (procedural knowledge), needs to be provided.

Changes in Error Detection and Correction

As a learner moves toward the highly skilled automatic phase of learning, the capability to detect errors and make appropriate corrections will improve. Throughout all stages of motor skill development children should be taught to detect errors in motor performance, correctly identify appropriate corrections, and be able to carry out the error corrections to improve performance. To achieve this, a teacher must provide children with guidance and accurate feedback on performance. This can be achieved through a variety of teaching methods, ranging from direct instruction to discovery learning (see chapter 8). In the example of learning to throw a ball for distance, guided discovery can be used to pose questions to the child such as "What happens if you throw the ball straight and parallel with the ground?" and "What happens when you throw the ball very high into the sky?" Once these questions have been answered, the following challenge can be given: "Now try to find the best throwing angle between sky and ground that will result in the farthest distance you can throw." Once this knowledge (declarative) is acquired, the child will be in a position to detect errors and offer solutions to improve performance.

A similar form of error detection and correction will need to be applied to the actual throwing movement (procedural knowledge). For example, feedback from a checklist on throwing movement pattern (see chapter 9) can be provided through direct instruction to enable the child to gain an understanding of errors in this area of performance. When completing the checklist, the teacher may notice the child is not extending the arm fully behind himself at the start of the throw. Pointing this out will help the child realize the error and provide a solution to correct it. This procedural knowledge will help the child detect and correct errors in the throwing movement; that is, he learns to know how to perform the motor skill correctly.

Changes in Coordination

Performing a motor skill requires muscles and limbs to work together in a coordinated manner. Throwing a ball, for example, requires different muscles and limbs to work together in one smoothly coordinated movement. In the initial stages of learning, limb movements tend to be locked, with each limb operating somewhat independently. This may account for some of the jerkiness associated with first attempts at a new motor skill. Limb segments need to be flexible to adapt as needed toward a smooth coordinated movement. Getting children to "feel" the sensation of the movement is an important characteristic in motor learning. Children who experience motor learning disabilities (see chapter 13) frequently exhibit very stiff movements. These children tend to have difficulty relaxing their muscles and limbs. Getting these children to concentrate on feeling the sensation of the actual movement is a worthwhile endeavor. Manually moving their limbs through the movement pattern to ensure correct limb movement and coordination is a helpful strategy. Also, as the skill improves, the energy expended to perform the movement decreases. Since young children tire easily, as their skills improve they will experience energy savings that will allow for more continuous movement.

Changes in Visual Attention

In the initial and intermediate phases of learning a motor skill, a child will not know what cues are the most important for performing the skill. Highly skilled performers who have reached the automatic phase of learning are able to select the most appropriate cues in the environment to help produce the desired performance. During motor learning, the teacher may need to point out areas that require the child's attention. For example, if the teacher is trying to develop a child's mature throwing pattern and a right-handed child who is learning to throw for distance puts the right foot forward during the throwing action, the teacher could point out that the opposite (left) foot needs to be placed forward during the throwing action. Getting the child to visually attend to the correct foot action will provide the appropriate cue to ensure the child is performing the correct foot movement. By helping a child to identify the correct things to attend to, the teacher will be assisting in the motor learning process.

Theories of Motor Learning

A theory of learning is a theoretical assumption about how an individual learns. In physical education, the theory must provide a reasonable basis for understanding motor learning and also provide a list of learning principles that can be applied to the teaching and learning of physical activities. Although there is a history of motor learning (Schmidt, 1991), only the most recent theories will be reviewed here. Contemporary theories involve the concepts of motor program and schema to explain motor learning, and it is these two areas that will be addressed.

Motor Program Theory

The concept of motor program was forwarded to explain the accuracy and consistency of movement that occurs when a skill has been learned to the automatic level. For example, once the skill of walking has been learned, it can be consistently performed with accuracy and with minimum conscious thought. It is as if a computer program inside the brain were automatically "running off" the motor responses each time the skill is performed. The concept of the motor program is seen as analogous to a computer program. A motor program is just like a computer program in the brain. When initiated, the motor program automatically sets off all the movements necessary to run off the motor skill with minimum conscious intervention. In the initial phase of learning, the motor program does not exist and thus needs to be developed. With practice and experience the motor program is constantly refined. When the learner reaches the automatic phase of learning, the motor program will have been developed to a point where it can now automatically produce the desired motor skill. Motor program theory views motor learning as the creation and reorganization of motor programs as motor skills improve toward the automatic phase of learning. The key implication for the physical education teacher will be the need to provide children with opportunities for many practices to encourage development of well-organized motor programs. Developing effective motor programs that can run almost unconsciously will free processing space in the brain for other use. Since the children will run the motor programs without much conscious thought, they will be free to concentrate on other important aspects, such as strategies and tactics.

Generalizable Motor Program Theory

Unfortunately, the motor program concept cannot account for all aspects of motor learning. For example, a performer is often capable of performing well-learned skills in a variety of situations, even though these skills were not learned in previous situations. To explain this, motor programs would need to exist that had never been learned or practiced. An attempt to explain some of the transfer effects of motor skills to new situations has been made through the theory of a generalizable motor program.

To illustrate, a person's written signature can be made with a pen between teeth or toes, or the fingers of the nondominant hand. In all cases the signatures will be remarkably similar; that is, consistency and accuracy will be maintained. Regardless of where the pen is held, it is believed that a common motor program for the motor skill of written signature is responsible for the similarity in responses among tasks.

However, it is also possible to write one's signature much larger than normal. For this to occur, significant changes to the motor program would be needed, since it would involve more than merely running off the same (computerized) motor program. Since a person is able to write a large signature resembling the smaller, "normal" one, the concept of a generalizable motor program was developed; a motor program that can be adjusted somewhat to meet the needs of a changing environment. (It should be noted that timing is rather inflexible in a motor program. That is why a person speeds up hand movement when a much larger signature is required. The generalizable motor program attempts to run off the movement from beginning to end in a constant amount of time, regardless of size of movement.)

Even with this degree of flexibility built into the motor program concept, it is still not possible to explain the large variety of transfer effects noted in skilled performances. Also, the number of motor programs that would need to be stored to accommodate the infinite variety of motor skill responses would pose serious limitations on human memory. The concept of schema was therefore invoked to address both storage problems and the infinite variety of motor skills human beings are capable of performing.

Schema Theory

Schema theory addresses the issue of a person being able to perform successfully a novel motor skill response. That is, a person can make a skillful response that has not been made before in exactly the same way. In chapter 2, it was suggested that calling on well-developed motor abilities will account for some of the transfer effects. In addition to these effects, generalizable motor programs and schemas will also play a part in transfer of learning.

According to Schmidt (1991), a schema is a rule or set of rules that is used to provide an individual with a basis for making a decision. A schema is developed by abstracting key pieces of information from experiences, then combining them into a rule. To illustrate, a child's initial contact with an animal, such as the family's pet cat, provides an initial schema. With experience, the child enlarges the concept of the cat to include size, speed, and habits the animal exhibits. Gradually, through extended experience, the child learns there are smaller, larger, fatter, noisier cats, which in turn form an ever-expanding schema for this class of animal. The same idea is believed to hold true in motor learning. Take, for example, the given "class" of movements that would fall under "overhand throw pattern." Whenever overhand throws are made, the performer begins to abstract different pieces of information about each throwing response (figure 5.2). Through continuous and varied experiences a schema is constructed and developed that will allow the performer to successfully carry out a variety of movements where the overhand throw pattern is involved. The response requirements to perform a novel overhand throw are synthesized and generated from the motor response schema. A well-developed schema will allow correct motor responses to be generated, whereas a poorly developed schema will probably result in the production of an incorrect response.

In soccer, for example, the ball does not always remain on the ground—it may arrive in the air and from a variety of angles. A young child who does not have a well-developed motor response schema for dealing with this class of movement responses (controlling the ball with upper-body area) will not be in a position to generate an appropriate motor response. Instead, the child may try to create a response from other motor schemas he already possesses. In all likelihood a child will use his hands to control the ball, even when there is no immediate danger of injury. When a soccer ball is bouncing over the heads of a group of players, hands frequently go out to control the ball (figure 5.3). Adults often chastise children for breaking the soccer rule of "no hand ball," when in fact the children may be aware of the rule (declarative knowledge), yet not be in a position to offer a more appropriate motor response (procedural knowledge) since they have not yet developed the appropriate response schema. This is one reason why playing the full game of soccer or basketball is inappropriate for elementary aged children. Instead, developmentally appropriate activities such as practice activities, lead-up games, and small-sided games (e.g. three versus three) are needed, where schema development can be nurtured. Further, it will be necessary to provide a variety of practices within each class of movements. For example, if teaching the skill of passing in basketball, rather than have the children stand the same

Figure 5.2 A child learns to throw a ball.

Figure 5.3 Hand reaction to a ball in the air.

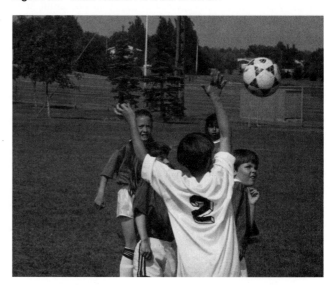

distance apart for the practice activity, vary the distance between the children. Or, if teaching a child to throw a ball at a target, vary the distances and the angles from the target. That is, the children should not only practice throwing from a variety of distances directly in front and in line with the target, they should also practice throwing from a variety of distances from either side of the target.

Based on the aforementioned theories of motor learning, teachers will need to design developmentally appropriate practices to ensure the development of well-organized motor programs and richly developed motor response schemas. If this is accomplished, children will be able to react to a wide range of novel movement situations with a high level of success.

General Guidelines

Theories of learning are just theories; that is, they are assumptions about how individuals learn. Nevertheless, the theories discussed in this text provide a basis for organizing content, developing styles of teaching, and using various types of evaluative techniques. Further knowledge of the benefits associated with different practice schedules will also aid the instructional process. In addition, an understanding of the stages of motor skill development, coupled with the knowledge of how children pass through a three-phased sequence to acquire a motor skill, helps us teach children a variety of physical activities. In a similar way, the following principles of learning motor skills provide a general understanding of the important factors that affect the way we teach and how children should learn motor skills.

Principle of Interest

Any skill, whether it is climbing a rope or throwing a softball, is acquired more efficiently if the child has a motive for learning it. A child's attitude toward learning a skill determines, for the most part, the amount and kind of learning.

It is inherent in this principle that the teacher foster in children a desire to learn motor skills. Learning generally takes place if children experience immediate satisfaction, if they see the necessity of building strong, healthy bodies, or if they value the skill as something they can use during leisure activities. Learning can also occur out of fear or because of an extrinsic reward, such as a star or check put beside one's name.

Implications for Physical Education

1. Select activities appropriate to the child's interests, needs, and capacities.
2. Stress the intrinsic value of the activity.
3. Present activities so that each child achieves a degree of success.

Principle of Practice

Research in motor learning strongly suggests that practice is necessary for the acquisition of a motor skill. The child must practice the skill correctly until it becomes automatic. Once a child has learned to swim, several months may elapse without practice, yet he is still able to swim. In general, the more the skill is practiced, the longer the time before it is lost. When a skill is practiced incorrectly, however, it will not lead to improvement and might even lead to regression.

Implications for Physical Education

1. Select skills appropriate to the group's interests and maturation level.

2. Stress proper form while the skill is being learned. After the skill has been learned, stress other factors, such as speed and distance.
3. Repeat drill activities after several months to ensure retention.

Principle of Distributed Practice

A motor skill is usually performed more effectively with distributed practice periods than with massed practice periods. However, in terms of learning, as measured by degree of retention of the skill, research indicates little difference between distributed and massed practice schedules. Since a greater number of massed practices can occur in a fixed time-frame (single lesson), teachers can plan sessions that have little rest between practice trials. However, a teacher's judgment is crucial here. Since young children tend to tire easily and recover quite quickly, breaks between practice trials will be necessary; hence, some form of distributed practice will be needed. Further, since performance may be higher during distributed practice, this could have corresponding effects on motivation. Hence, it is not only important to consider the time between practice; it is important to consider the overall length of the practice period. As a general rule, a short period of intense effort and attention is better than a half-hearted longer period.

This principle generally applies to all age levels and virtually all skills, but there are times, depending on the interest of the children and the amount of effort required, when the practice period might be longer or shorter than normally considered wise. For example, if children are permitted to practice a forward roll until they become dizzy and fatigued, the practice period is too long and too strenuous regardless of student interest. Self-testing activities for any age group should have a variation so that one part of the body is not overworked.

A teacher working with fifth- and sixth-grade children in an activity like volleyball lead-up games may find that the students remain interested and enthusiastic for ten or fifteen minutes or even longer. As long as interest is high and skill development is fostered, it is not only permissible but desirable to extend the practice period. On the other hand, when the children are indifferent and are not attaining the skill, a change in the lead-up activity or a shorter practice period is suggested.

Implications for Physical Education

1. Adjust the length of the practice period and the spacing of rest periods to the material being taught and to the children's developmental needs.
2. Change an activity whenever the children show fatigue, boredom, and poor skill development.

Principle of Variable Practice

Practice sessions can be organized in blocked or variable schedules. In a blocked schedule, the same motor task is practiced repeatedly. For example, if teaching two gymnastic stunts, a blocked practice would have children complete their practice trials for the first stunt before engaging in practices of the second stunt. In a variable practice schedule, the learner would mix practices between the two stunts. Intuitively, the blocked practice schedule might be considered most effective since this form of practice allows the learner to concentrate on only one task at a time. Numerous studies, however, have shown that although blocked practices do produce superior motor performances at the time of practice (in the lesson), it is variable practice that creates superior learning when measured in terms of retention of the skills between lessons. It might be thought that when two tasks are to be learned together, as in variable practice, they would "interfere" with each other's learning. However, rather than "interfere," it has been suggested that when the "context" for the practice (type of schedule) causes the learner to really concentrate on differences between motor tasks, then superior learning occurs. Hence the term context interference is sometimes used to explain the superior learning associated with variable practice schedules. Although a variable practice schedule has been shown to benefit motor skill learning, a teacher's own judgment as to the best form of practice schedule is also very important. Since motor performance is frequently lower during variable practices, as the learner concentrates to sort out motor response differences between tasks, there may be a drop in motivation. This could easily happen in the initial phase of learning. Changing to a blocked practice will likely heighten performance and may produce a corresponding rise in motivation.

Implications for Physical Education

1. Start children off with blocked practices and quickly move to a variable practice schedule.
2. Variable practices usually result in better retention, and play a major role in developing schemas.
3. If children begin to lose motivation due to slow progress while practicing in a variable practice situation, move to a blocked practice schedule.

Principle of Skill Specificity

A child's ability to acquire a particular skill depends on the child's unique characteristics. A child may excel in one skill but be awkward in others that require about the same maturity and physical effort. A nine-year-old girl may be able to throw, catch, and hit a softball with ease and accuracy but still show a subpar performance in kicking a ball. As discussed in chapter 2, there does not appear to be a general motor ability; instead, many abilities need to be developed.

If different motor abilities are needed to perform two motor skills, then vast differences in performance may occur.

This principle of skill specificity also applies to children who have reached the same psychological and physiological maturity level. After a single demonstration of a skill, one child may be able to perform it in its entirety, whereas another child may need more demonstration and practice to perform even a part of the skill. Differences in schema development will obviously play a part here, in addition to other differences in information processing capacities between children. Hence, developmentally appropriate activities will need to be provided in order to accommodate children's preferred learning styles and differences in their existing knowledge bases.

Implications for Physical Education

1. Provide varied activities at all grade levels.
2. Allow for individual differences in the standards of performance.
3. Allow for variations in the speed at which children acquire the same skill.
4. Develop standards based on the individual's level and rate of development rather that the class average.

Principle of Whole-Part Learning

According to Knapp (1967), material is learned in the *whole method*, by going through it completely again and again. In the *part method*, the material is divided into portions, which are practiced; eventually, the parts are joined as a whole. In physical education, it is difficult to define what is whole and what is a part of the skill or game. Recognizing this difficulty, the available evidence indicates that the whole method is usually superior to the part method in teaching motor skills.

A teacher must decide whether to teach a movement in its entirety or to break it into parts. The choice depends, first, on the complexity of the skill and, second, on the learner's amount and speed of skill development. For example, a teacher demonstrates to her third-grade class a one-foot hop-skipping skill using a single rope. The children then attempt to do the skill in its entirety; this is practice through the whole method. If only a few children learn the skill after repeated attempts, however, it would be better to break down the skill into simpler movements. The children could do a one-foot hop over a long rope turned by two people, then attempt the one-foot hop with a single rope, using a half swing. Finally, with a full turn of the rope, the hopping movement could be integrated into the rhythmic turning of the rope.

Implications for Physical Education

1. Use the whole method whenever the skill represents a single functional movement.

2. It may be desirable to break complex skills into smaller parts. Complexity depends on the skill as well as the learner's ability.

3. Generally, the rate and amount of learning indicate the effectiveness of the method used.

Principle of Transfer

Transfer in physical education can be defined as the effect of the practice of one motor task on the learning or performance of a second, closely related task. Underlying this principle is the assumption that a learner will take advantage of what a new situation has in common with a previous experience. Clearly, many factors account for transfer effects. Drawing upon similar motor abilities, well-developed motor schemas, generalizable motor programs, and existing procedural and declarative knowledge bases will all influence the degree of transfer achieved. This is reflected in current research indicating that transfer depends on the degree of resemblance between skills.

Implications for Physical Education

Proponents of the Movement Education approach have said that Movement Education has a strong carry-over to other skill learning, but no firm evidence indicates a common motor skill transfer factor among all skills. There are, however, many other reasons for incorporating the Movement Education approach. One important reason is that a carry-over does occur with Movement Education in the form of a positive attitude toward other activities. Also, individualized instruction, which is a major feature of the Movement Education approach, will contribute to the development of all the major factors highlighted above that influence transfer effects.

Principle of Skill Improvement

A child does not always learn every physical skill in the same way. Too many factors affect the learning curve, including the complexity of the skill, the child's motivation and physical ability, and the adequacy of instruction.

Generally speaking, however, the initial phase of learning is usually quite rapid. This may be due to the child's enthusiasm for a new activity and the fact that the child learns the easy parts first, using previously acquired skills. Progress slows down gradually, however, even as practice continues, to a period of almost no overt improvement. Numerous explanations have been given for these learning "plateaus," such as lack of motivation, failure to learn a prerequisite skill, and improper instruction. However, even when no obvious improvement in skill performance is visible, there may be consolidation changes occurring in terms of memory reorganization and neuronal connections being made within the brain. Keeping children motivated through this consolidation period is obviously important. After consolidation, with proper analysis and correction, an increase in skill attainment should result.

Implications for Physical Education

1. Recognize children's individual differences in the learning curve for the same activity.

2. After a new skill is introduced, allow sufficient practice time for mastery.

3. Provide positive reinforcement and encouraging feedback to motivate children through learning plateaus.

4. Be aware of physiological limitations that hinder or prevent additional improvement.

Principle of Feedback

Feedback is defined as the information a learner receives from internal or external sources (Drowatzky 1975). Such information, whether it comes from an internal "feeling" about a movement or from an observation made by the teacher, is used to direct or redirect the learner toward a goal. Feedback acts as a positive motivator as well as a strong reinforcer of behavior. However, it should be emphasized that it is not necessary for a teacher to provide feedback on every practice trial. Indeed, providing feedback after every practice has been found to be not as beneficial to learning as providing feedback on an intermittent basis. This is probably due to the learner becoming dependent on the teacher for identifying the errors and possible corrections. When children are provided with appropriate instruction for error detection and correction, spacing feedback will cause children to solve problems themselves. Learning to problem solve is a desirable educational goal since it encourages children to take responsibility for their own learning. Giving guidance and accurate feedback on an intermittent basis provides the necessary reinforcement for continued success. Since it is not possible to provide feedback to each child after every practice trial, the teacher can share feedback time and observations of performance among children, knowing that this form of intermittent feedback is both effective and reinforcing.

Implications for Physical Education

Feedback is an indispensible aspect of learning any cognitive, affective, or psychomotor skill or concept. Virtually all learning involves a form of internal feedback through the visual, auditory, or kinesthetic senses. The following guidelines apply more generally to external feedback methods and techniques.

1. Structure the teaching situation to allow time for the learner to practice alone as well as while being observed by the teacher or a classmate.

2. When observing and guiding a performer, make sure the performer has a clear understanding of the goal. Closely related to this point is not to set the goal too high for the performer.

3. Provide guidance or teaching cues while the student is performing a motor skill. Assistance, such as

auditory clues or touching (spot belts, etc.), as the performer is executing a movement is a very effective form of feedback.

4. Terminal feedback techniques using videotape or individual photographic sequences should be commonplace in elementary school physical education programs.

5. Provide feedback on an intermittent basis, not after every single practice trial.

Feedback is a very important component of teaching and learning. Further aspects of feedback are considered in chapter 8, where teaching styles, motivational strategies, and other effective teaching techniques are discussed.

Older teaching methods were based on the premise that the teacher is the sole authority on what is correct and desirable for children. Children were expected to learn, regardless of their limitations and interests or the inadequacies of the learning situation. Contemporary education has replaced these concepts with principles of learning that are based on tested thinking and experimentation.

All principles of learning are applicable to physical education. Those stated in this chapter, however, are extremely important for selecting physical activities, choosing appropriate methods, and understanding how motor skills are learned. When these principles are considered in relation to the goals of the physical education program and the characteristics of the learner, the scope and direction of the program and the way it should be taught should become abundantly clear.

Applying Mechanical Principles

Basic laws, concepts, and principles affect all movements of the body. The laws of gravity, for example, affect balance and the adjustment of position while moving. The human body is a living machine; it converts food into energy and expends the energy in movement. If the human body is kept in optimum condition and is moved in accordance with the principles of force and motion, expenditure of energy will be proportionate to the task, but if movement is contrary to the laws of motion and force, too much energy will be expended and maximum results will not be achieved.

It is difficult for teachers who have not studied kinesiology (the science of human movement) to understand all the important mechanical principles of human movement. They should, however, understand the following important concepts and principles concerning balance, force, motion, and leverage and be able to apply them when teaching skills and movement patterns.

Figure 5.4 A child resists the force of gravity.

Balance

Balance, or stability, is the ability of the body to maintain a stationary position or to perform purposeful movements while resisting the force of gravity (figure 5.4). Our first consideration, then, is the "law of gravity," which is the natural force that pulls everything toward the center of the earth. Most important to balance is that gravitational pull always occurs through the center of the weight or mass of an object. On the human body, the center of gravity is the point around which the weight is distributed equally in all directions. The human body is in balance when all forces acting on it equal zero. The child in figure 5.5 is lying on his back with all his muscles in a state of relaxation. His body is not resisting gravity; therefore, the center of gravity is the point in the middle of his body weight, indicated by the circle.

Figure 5.5 The center of gravity (circle) is in the middle of the body weight.

Figure 5.6 The center of gravity is in the middle of the hips.

Figure 5.7 The center of gravity rises when the arms are elevated.

Figure 5.8 A wide base of support increases stability.

center of gravity also rises. If the boy relaxes those muscles, he will fall to the ground, obeying the law of gravity.

Principles and Concepts Relating to Balance

The basic principles and concepts relating to balance are important in understanding all stationary and movement skills. When attempting to hold a *static* balance position, a child is concerned with keeping the center of gravity in a stable position. When he is moving, the center of gravity is an important factor in retaining *dynamic balance*, or equilibrium. The ability of the child to maintain stability or balance while in a static position or in motion is governed by the following principles of balance.

Principles of Balance

1. *The wider or broader the base of support, the more stable the body.* This principle is extremely important in many game, dance, and gymnastic skills. For example, in figure 5.8, the hands and head of the child performing a headstand form a wide triangle, or broad base of support. The center of gravity is located through the hips and head and midpoint between the hands. By comparison, the child's hands in figure 5.9 are almost in line with the shoulders, thus greatly reducing the base of support.

   Teachers will observe that a child performing a headstand this latter way will not hold the position very long, since even a slight movement will cause him to fall sideways, backward, or forward, which can result in a severe strain on the neck muscles, as well as a hard thud.

2. *The lower the center of gravity, the greater the stability.* The child in figure 5.10 has assumed the same position as in figure 5.8 but has kept his knees bent, thus dropping the center of gravity closer to his base of support. This example shows that a wide base of support, coupled with a low center of gravity, helps in the performance of numerous balance stunts.

In figure 5.6, the center of gravity is in the middle of the hips. The child is maintaining a state of equilibrium, or balance, through the tension he is applying to his antigravitational muscles (the large muscles of the trunk and legs). When the boy raises his arms, as illustrated in figure 5.7, his

learning motor skills

Figure 5.9 A narrow base of support reduces stability.

Figure 5.10 A wide base of support and a low center of gravity increase stability.

Figure 5.11 A narrow base of support and a high center of gravity do not provide stability when meeting an oncoming force.

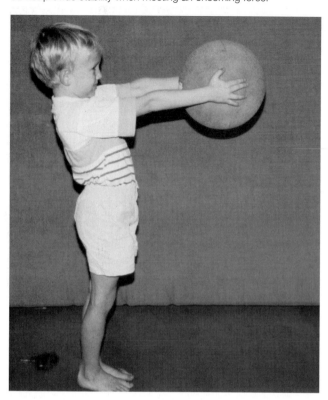

In sports, a stable position is often required when meeting an oncoming force, such as a large ball. A large utility ball thrown with force could knock a young child off balance if he is standing upright with his feet close together, as in figure 5.11. He has a narrow base of support and a high center of gravity. However, in figure 5.12, his legs are spread and his knees are bent, giving him a wider base of support and a lower center of gravity.

3. *The nearer the center of gravity to the middle of the base of support, the greater the stability.* Gravity was defined as the natural force that pulls everything toward the center of the earth. The *line of gravity* is an imaginary line that extends through the center of gravity directly down toward the center of the earth. In skills requiring a very stable base, the child spreads his arms and legs, lowers his body, and makes sure the line of gravity is near the center of the base of support. The child balancing on his hands, knees, and feet in figure 5.13 illustrates this important principle. Notice how the wide base is low to the ground and the line of gravity passes downward through the middle of his body.

There are, however, numerous skills in games, sports, and dance activities where an unstable base of support is necessary to perform the skill correctly.

Figure 5.12 A wide base of support and a low center of gravity increase stability when meeting an oncoming force.

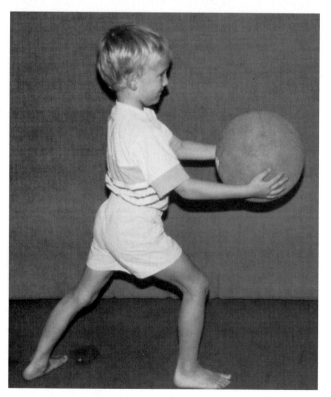

chapter 5

Figure 5.13 When the line of gravity is near the center of the base of support, greater stability is achieved.

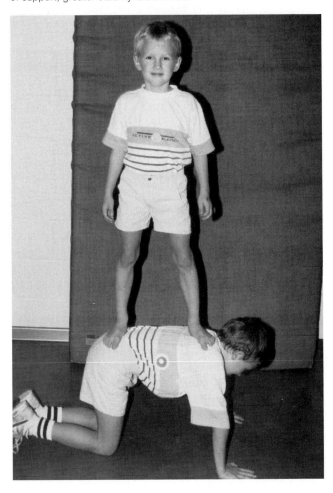

Table 5.1 Skills Requiring an Unstable Base of Support

Activity	Skill	Page
Soccer	Dribbling (fig. 18.11)	312
Track and field	Sprint start (fig. 24.2)	404
Track and field	Hop, step, and jump (fig. 24.14)	410
Gymnastics	Backward roll (fig. 25.20)	429
Gymnastics	Cartwheel (fig. 25.31)	433
Rope jumping	Two foot basic (fig. 26.11)	483
Juggling	Three bags (fig. 26.64)	502
Gymnastics	Straddle vault (fig. 27.38)	520
Dance	Tinikling (fig. 29.11)	579

The principles of balance still apply. Sometimes one must deliberately shift the center of gravity to an unstable position in order to move quickly. When the line of gravity reaches a point outside the base of support, the individual falls in that direction. This happens when we walk or run; we shift our weight forward in order to move. The sprinter in a crouched starting position leans forward considerably, shifting his center of gravity forward (figure 5.14). He then raises his hips higher than his shoulders to further increase the "unstable" position toward the direction in which he intends to move and to place the strong hip muscles in a position to contract effectively.

Other examples of skills requiring an unstable base of support are listed in table 5.1. The three principles of balance described previously are normally taught to elementary school children in the science curriculum. It is hoped the illustrations provided will encourage teachers to use the medium of physical education to further clarify these principles through the child's own movement patterns. In addition, if the following concepts are also explained to children in a meaningful way through the use of their own bodies, they will understand the mechanical advantages of the principles and apply them in sports, games, and other daily activities.

Concepts Relating to Balance

1. To achieve the greatest stability, assume a wide base of support, be low to the ground, and have the line of gravity running through the middle of the base of support.
2. To receive a heavy force or a fast-moving object, widen the base of support in line with the direction of the oncoming force.
3. To apply a forceful movement, widen the base of support in line with the direction of the force.

Figure 5.14 A sprinter shifts his center of gravity (circle) to an unstable position for a quick start.

Table 5.2 Skills Requiring a Stable Base of Support

Activity	Skill	Page	Principle		
			Wide base of support	Lower center of gravity	Center of gravity to middle of base of support
Soccer	Volley kick (fig. 18.4)	309	Partial	X	X
Soccer	Heading (fig. 18.12)	312	Partial	X	X
Field hockey	Scoop shot (fig. 19.7)	333	X	X	X
Touch football	Forward pass (fig. 20.1)	341	X		X
Volleyball	Bumping (fig. 21.2)	356	Partial	X	X
Basketball	Pivoting (fig. 22.12)	374	Partial	X	X
Softball	Batting (fig. 23.11)	392	Partial		X
Track and field	Standing broad jump (fig. 24.7)	406	X	X	X
Gymnastics	Bear dance (fig. 25.66)	444	No	X	X
Gymnastics	Squat on one leg (fig. 27.10)	510	No	X	X

4. To lift or carry a heavy object, keep the object close to the body.

5. To stop quickly, bend the knees and lean away from the direction you are moving.

There are numerous examples in games, dance, and gymnastic activities where the skill illustrates the application of one or more of these principles. Table 5.2 provides a few examples for each activity. Note that the principles of balance may apply mainly to the initial position of each skill.

Motion

Motion is any form of movement that is produced by a force exerted by a push or pull. In the human body, motion is produced by muscular contraction. All movements of the human body, whether they change position, slow down, or start another object in motion, are directly influenced by three laws discovered by Sir Isaac Newton in the seventeenth century. These three laws explain how, where, and why the body moves, as well as how to project or receive an object.

Law of Inertia

The law of inertia states that an object will remain in a state of rest and an object in motion will remain in motion at the same speed and direction unless acted upon by a force.

Inertia is directly proportional to the size or mass of the object and its velocity. This means that the greater an object's mass and velocity, the more difficult it is to change its direction or motion. The force that changes an object's motion or direction could be gravity, wind, another object, or the contraction of muscles.

Understanding this law is extremely important when performing physical movements. For example, a ball thrown toward a target moves in a straight line and at uniform speed until the force of gravity or wind causes it to change direction (figure 5.15). Thus, a child must learn to adjust to or compensate for these forces in all throwing and striking activities.

Another example for understanding and overcoming the effects of the law of inertia is dribbling a soccer ball. The ball will not move until it receives an external force—the foot. A force starts the ball moving (overcoming mass); however, as long as the ball is kept in motion, the effect of inertia is minimal. Performing continuous sit-ups and maintaining a steady running or swimming pace are also good examples of overcoming the effects of inertia.

Law of Acceleration

The law of acceleration states that when an object is acted upon by a force, it will move in the direction of that force. The resulting change of speed (acceleration) of the object will be directly proportional to the force acting on it and inversely proportional to the mass.

To illustrate this second law, consider a volleyball player executing a high "floating" serve (figure 5.16a). The force exerted behind the ball is relatively gentle, producing a slow acceleration. The second serve (figure 5.16b) is a more forceful hit behind the ball, causing a rapid acceleration. In this case, the acceleration is directly proportional to the force. If a player makes the same forceful hit with a tennis ball, the ball's acceleration will be greater because its mass is much less than that of a volleyball. Acceleration in this example is inversely proportional to the mass of the ball.

Figure 5.15 Throwing a ball with a high arc allows for the effects of gravity and wind.

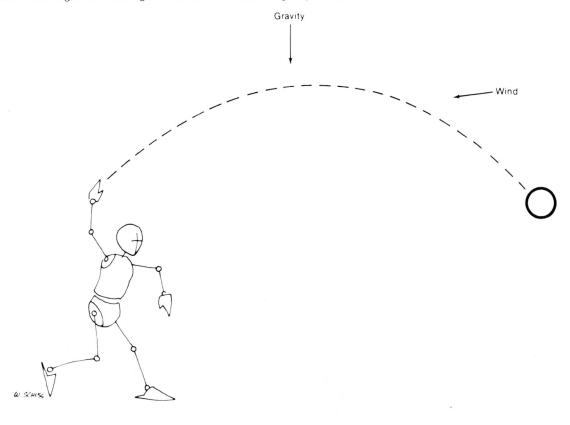

Figure 5.16 The acceleration of a volleyball across the net is directly proportional to the force exerted behind the ball.

a. A gentle force exerted by a volleyball player produces slow acceleration.

b. A strong, forceful hit causes rapid acceleration.

Law of Action-Reaction

The law of action-reaction states that for every action there is an equal and opposite reaction.

Tug-of-war (figure 5.17) can be used to illustrate this law to elementary school children. The distance that team A moves backward is equal to the distance that team B is forced to move forward. When swimming, a child moves forward by pushing backward against the resistance of the water. The water is pushing the child forward with a force equal to the force that he is exerting in his backward body movements.

Although this principle is relatively hard to explain to children, and at times to adults, it applies to all movements directed away from a hard surface. For example, when a child jumps up to tip a basketball, the floor pushes back with a force equal to the force the child exerts downward through his feet. There is an equal and opposite reaction. Also, to receive the maximum reaction force, the surface that the force is exerted against must be stable. For instance, a hard surface (figure 5.18a) allows a runner to push off with maximum thrust because of the equal and opposite reaction between the foot and the hard surface, but on grass (figure 5.18b), soft mud, or sand (figure 5.18c), the surface gives and thus decreases the force that propels the runner forward.

Types of Motion

Linear motion is the movement of a body or an object as a whole in a straight line with uniform speed. An example is the human body being carried by another object such as a car or skis. In this type of motion, the body takes on the same motion as the object carrying it. The human body can also move in a linear pathway, as in a walking or running movement; this, however, is a pathway of movement resulting from the rotary action of the legs at the hip joints.

Rotary motion is a movement that traces an arc or circle around an axis or a fixed point. As the radius of the circle becomes smaller, the rotary speed increases. For example, in the first phase of a forward roll, the radius is large because the legs and trunk are partially extended (figure 5.19a). As the performer tucks and rolls, he decreases the radius

Figure 5.17 Tug-of-war illustrates that every action creates an equal, opposite reaction.

Figure 5.18 Law of action-reaction. The force that propels a runner forward is a result of the action-reaction between his feet and the surface on which he is running.

a. Hard road provides a stable surface.

b. Grass field gives, thus reducing force.

c. Soft sand or mud gives even more, with a much greater decrease in force.

chapter 5

Figure 5.19 Rotary motion during a forward roll.

a. Large radius, slow rotary speed.

b. Short radius, fast speed.

c. Large radius, slow speed.

(figure 5.19b). When the roll is completed, the leg and trunk are extended, thus lengthening the radius and slowing the forward motion (figure 5.19c).

Virtually all physical skills involve a combination of linear and rotary motions. Movements normally begin with a rotary action of the body, then transfer to linear speed. In running, for instance, the rotary action of the legs at the hip joints is converted into linear speed to move the body forward. Similarly, as the ball leaves the thrower's hand, it is converted from the rotary motion of the arm and shoulder into a linear motion. As the ball travels through the air, the motion begins to change into a curvilinear motion because of gravity and air resistance. Curvilinear motion follows a curved pathway, rather than the true arc or circle of rotary motion.

Concepts Relating to Motion

1. Once a human being or an object is in motion, it will continue in motion unless stopped by a force.
2. Once a human being or an object is in motion, less force is required to maintain its speed and direction.
3. The heavier the object, the more force required to move it.
4. The heavier the object and the faster it is moving, the more force is required to stop its motion.
5. When an object moves, another object moves in the opposite direction.
6. When performing rotary movements, shortening the radius of the rotation increases speed, and lengthening the radius decreases speed.
7. When performing linear movements, lengthening the radius increases linear speed and, conversely, shortening the radius decreases linear speed.

Force

According to K. F. Wells (1955), force can be felt and its effect can be seen and measured, but force itself, like the wind, is invisible. Force is the effect one body has on another. This can be the movement of one body by another, such as a child throwing a ball, hitting a softball, or volleying a ball. Force can also be the stopping of one body by another, such as the tackler stopping the ball carrier. Finally, force can be resistance against movements, such as that used in isometric exercises or when a wrestler in a defensive position attempts to prevent his opponent from moving him. Force, then, is the push or pull exerted against something.

Teachers should understand several principles relating to the production, direction, and absorption of force to help children execute movement skills with ease, efficiency, and safety.

Production of Force

The total effective force of a movement is the sum of all forces produced by the muscle groups when applied in the same direction and in proper sequence. The jump-reach stunt illustrates this principle, as well as related factors that must be considered when executing any forceful movement.

Any muscular action that is intended to move the body weight must have a firm base of action (stability). In figure 5.20a, the child's legs are spread reasonably apart and his knees are bent to lower his center of gravity. Strong muscles exert more than weak ones, and the flexed-knee position allows the boy to begin his jump by contracting his thigh muscles, the strongest muscles of the body. As stated earlier, the total effective force of a movement is the sum of all forces produced by the muscle groups in the same direction. This means that the jump should be executed in a continuous movement, beginning with the extension of the legs, then stretching upward (figure 5.20b), and finally fully extending the body (figure 5.20c).

Achieving maximum results in any forceful movement requires continuity of flow from one part through another and the timing of each muscle group contraction. One only needs to swing a softball bat forward to understand the importance of continuity and the cumulative effect of a properly executed forceful action. Refer to table 5.3 for other examples.

Figure 5.20 Production of force in a jump-reach stunt.

a   b   c

Table 5.3   Production, Direction, and Absorption of Force

Sport	Skill	Page	Production of force	Direction of force	Absorption of force
Soccer	Kicking	308	Fig. 18.1(a)	Fig. 18.1 (b)	—
Soccer	Throw-in	313	Fig. 18.13(b)	Fig. 18.13(c)	—
Field hockey	Scoop shot	333	Fig. 19.7(a)	Fig. 19.7(b)	—
Volleyball	Bumping	356	Fig. 21.2(a)	Fig. 21.2(b)	—
Basketball	Lay-up shot	373	Fig. 22.10(a)	Fig. 22.10(b)	—
Track and field	Long jump	406	Fig. 24.8(a)	Fig. 24.8(b)	Fig. 24.8(c)
Gymnastics	Kip	450	Fig. 25.87(a)	Fig. 25.87(b,c)	Fig. 25.87(c)
Gymnastics	Headspring	449	Fig. 25.86(a)	Fig. 25.86(b)	Fig. 25.86(c)
Gymnastics	Squat vault	519	Fig. 27.35(a)	Fig. 27.35(b,c)	Fig. 27.35(d)

Direction of Force

When initiating a forceful movement, the force should be directed through the center of the body weight in the direction intended. In the jumping procedure illustrated in figure 5.20, the weight of the body is directly over and midway between the feet. When making a forward movement, the force should be applied through the center of the weight and in the direction in which it is intended to go. In figure 5.21, the center of gravity is too high and too far back to gain maximum force. By bending and leaning forward (figure 5.22), the child shifts the weight forward in the direction of the intended forceful action.

Perhaps one of the most important areas of concern is the application of force when lifting heavy objects. "Lift with the legs and not the back" is the overriding principle. The child in figure 5.23 is attempting to lift the trunk, but his center of gravity is too high and too far forward. When he applies force, it will be upward and backward, decreasing the maximum forces that could have been applied in an upward direction. He is also in a vulnerable position because too much strain may be placed on his back muscles. The potential force of the leg muscles in assisting the upward movement is almost negligible here. However, in figure 5.24, the child has moved his center of gravity closer to the trunk and lower by flexing his legs. A forceful movement can now be made by extending the weight upward. Refer to table 5.3 for other examples.

Absorption of Force

When it is necessary to absorb the impact of a forceful movement or object, the shock should be spread over as large an area or as long a distance as possible, or both. This principle applies when receiving a blow, landing from a fall, or catching or trapping a ball. The essential point is to gradually decrease the force of the movement or object. In figures 5.25b and 5.25c, the gymnast has landed, flexing his

Figure 5.21 The center of gravity (circle) is too high and too far back to gain maximum force.

Figure 5.23 The center of gravity (circle) is too high and too far forward to gain maximum force.

Figure 5.22 Shifting the center of gravity lower and in the direction of the intended action increases force potential.

Figure 5.24 Shifting the center of gravity (circle) lower and closer to the object increases force potential.

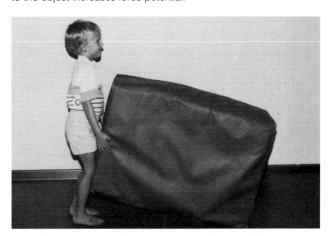

Figure 5.25 Absorption of force. This gymnast executes a forward roll to absorb the force of landing from a stunt.

a   b   c

knees to absorb part of the downward and forward momentum and using the remaining forward momentum to execute the forward roll. He has gradually and systematically dissipated the forward momentum.

Other examples of gradually spreading the shock of a forceful movement are catching an oncoming ball with arms extended forward, then recoiling the arms; or rolling after falling on a ball when playing football. Refer to table 5.3 for other examples.

Concepts Relating to Force

1. The more fully each working muscle group is stretched, the more force can be supplied.

2. Pushing or pulling an object should be done through the center of the weight of the object and in the direction the object is to move.

3. Maximum force is achieved when each body part is involved in sequential order. Sequence for a throwing action would be trunk rotation, shoulder, upper arm, lower arm, hand, and fingers. Sequence for kicking action would be hip, upper leg, lower leg, and foot.

4. When using individual body parts, such as arms or legs, or implements, such as bats or paddles, they should be completely extended at the moment they make contact with the object to be propelled. The longest extension of the arm creates the greatest force.

5. When receiving or absorbing the force of an object, the largest possible area and distance (recoiling) should be used to absorb force.

6. When landing from a jump, each joint should give (bend) to gradually absorb the force.

7. Once maximum force has been applied in throwing, striking, and kicking movements, the movement should continue in a follow-through action to ensure that maximum force has been applied and to allow for a gradual reduction in force.

8. Force is increased by using more muscles and by increasing the speed of the movement.

Leverage

All movement of the body, whether it is a simple bending of the arm or the rapid running action of the legs, is made possible through a system of levers. A lever, as shown in figure 5.26, is a rigid bar that turns around a fixed point (axis or fulcrum) when a force is applied to overcome resistance. The

Figure 5.26 Example A: first-class lever.

functions of a lever are (1) to gain mechanical advantage to increase speed and distance and (2) to reduce the effort necessary to overcome resistance. The three types of levers are classified according to the location of the fulcrum and the point at which force and resistance are applied.

First-Class Lever

A first-class lever has the *fulcrum* between the force and the resistance. The distance between the force and fulcrum is the *force arm* (FA) and the distance between the resistance and the fulcrum is the *resistance arm* (RA). In the seesaw in figure 5.26, the length of the force arm and the resistance arm are equal and the two boys weigh the same. In this example, there is no mechanical advantage to either the force arm or the resistance arm, since both are an equal distance from the fulcrum. In figure 5.27, the force arm (FA) is longer than the resistance arm (RA); therefore, this first-class lever favors force and the doghouse is easily moved. In figure 5.28, the resistance arm (RA) is longer, which means this lever favors speed and range of movement.

Second-Class Lever

A second-class lever has the resistance located between the fulcrum and the force (figure 5.29). Since this type of lever has a longer force arm, it produces force at the expense of

Figure 5.27 Example B: first-class lever.

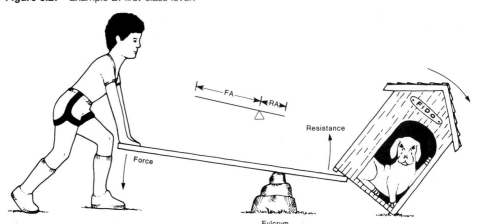

Figure 5.28 Example C: first-class lever.

From oarlock to hand is the force arm

Oarlock is fulcrum

Oar is resistance arm

◄──RA──►◄FA►

Figure 5.29 Second-class lever.

Force

Resistance

Fulcrum

speed and range of movement. Children should remember that, when lifting a wheelbarrow or prying up a heavy object with a plank, the longer the force arm, the less force required to move the object.

Third-Class Lever

A third-class lever has the force between the fulcrum and the resistance. Since this type of lever has a longer resistance arm, it produces speed and range of movement at the expense of force. Most levers of the human body are third-class levers; the bones act as lever arms, the joints as fulcrums, and the muscles as force. In figure 5.30, the elbow joint, where the movement occurs, is the fulcrum. The radius bone in the lower arm acts as the lever, and the bicep muscle (in this case, the point of insertion at the top of the forearm) acts as the force. The resistance is the lower arm that is moved, as well as any additional weight such as a ball or heavy object.

Figure 5.30 Third-class lever.

Resistance

Force

Force

Resistance

Fulcrum

Fulcrum

Most game, dance, and gymnastic movements involve the sequential action of many levers. For example, as an individual begins to swing a softball bat, the speed and force of the movement starts in the body, then transfers the built-up force and speed through the bat to the coming ball.

Concepts Relating to Levers

1. The longer the force arm, the greater the force produced.

2. The longer the resistance arm at the moment of release, the faster the action. When throwing a ball, a straight arm at the moment of release produces the fastest thrown ball. Similarly, when implements (bats or racquets) are used, they must be an extension of the lower arm at the moment of contact to propel the object (ball or bird) back in the fastest possible action.

3. The mechanical advantage of any lever is the ratio between the length of the force arm (from fulcrum to force) to the length of the resistance arm (from fulcrum to resistance).

4. Levers are used in the production and absorption of force.

The concepts and principles relating to balance, motion, force, and leverage are important considerations when teaching virtually every skill and movement pattern. Children should learn these concepts and principles through their own performances and by the teacher explaining the basic concepts in a meaningful way.

Selected References

Drowatzky, J. (1975). *Motor Learning: Principles and Practices.* Minneapolis: Burgess Publishing Co.

Fitts, P. M., and Posner, M. I. (1967). *Human Performance.* Belmont, CA: Brooks/Cole.

French, K. E., and Thomas, J. R. (1987). "The Relation of Knowledge Development to Children's Basketball Performance." *Journal of Sport Psychology, 9,* 15–32.

Haywood, K. M. (1986). *Life Span Motor Development.* Champaign, IL: Human Kinetics Publishers, Inc.

Keogh, J., and Sugden, D. (1985). *Motor Skill Development.* New York: Macmillan Publishing Co.

Knapp, B. (1967). *Skill in Sports.* London: Routledge and Kegan Paul.

Magill, R. A. (1993). *Motor Learning Concepts and Applications,* Fourth Edition. Dubuque, IA: Wm. C. Brown Publishers.

Schmidt, R. A. (1976). "The Schema as a Solution to Some Persistent Problems in Motor Learning Theory." In G. E. Stelmach (Ed.), *Motor Control: Issues and Trends,* (pp. 41–65). New York: Academic Press.

———. (1977). "Schema Theory: Implication for Movement Education." *Motor Skills: Theory into Practice,* 2, 36–48.

———. (1991). *Motor Learning and Performance.* Champaign, IL: Human Kinetics Publishers, Inc.

Stallings, L. M. (1973). *Motor Skill Development and Learning.* Dubuque, IA: Wm. C. Brown Publishers.

Wells, K. F. (1955). *Kinesiology.* Philadelphia: W. B. Saunders Co.

Physical Education Curriculum

The contemporary definition of an elementary school curriculum includes all the experiences of children for which the school accepts responsibility. In physical education, this encompasses all the learning experiences relating to the physical activities provided within the regular instructional period and out of class. The school or teacher can organize the physical education curriculum in several ways. The fundamental purpose of organization is to provide an effective means of choosing activities, developing teaching strategies, and providing experiences that best meet the goals of the program.

Contemporary educational practices, such as individualized teaching strategies, team teaching, and concept development, directly affect the nature and structure of the physical education program. Teachers must also consider the unique characteristics and needs of children within each grade of the elementary school when selecting the length, type, and nature of each instructional unit. In addition, such federal laws as PL 93–112 (1973) and PL 94–142 (1975) require that equal opportunities be provided for all children with physical, psychological, or social disabilities. Each of these factors is considered, weighed, then translated into the broad goals of an elementary physical education curriculum.

The process of developing an elementary physical education curriculum is outlined in the chart on page 92. To accomplish the broad goals, the physical education curriculum is divided into two types of programs: the instructional program and the cocurricular program. The instructional program is the central core within which children acquire knowledge, skills, and understandings relating to human movement; thus, it will be the focus of part 3. The cocurricular program will be covered in part 4 of this text.

Chapter 6 describes how to develop a yearly, unit, and daily instructional program. Chapter 7 is concerned with class management, ways of organizing children, and standards relating to equipment and supplies. Styles of teaching, motivational techniques, and ways of handling discipline problems are the subjects of chapter 8. Observational techniques and evaluative procedures are discussed in chapter 9. Chapter 10 deals with legal responsibilities and the implications of recent laws for elementary physical education programs ■

Chapter 6
Planning a Physical Education Curriculum

Chapter 7
Organizing for Physical Education

Chapter 8
Using Teaching Strategies and Techniques

Chapter 9
Selecting Evaluative Methods and Techniques

Chapter 10
Understanding Legal Responsibilities

Process of Curriculum Development

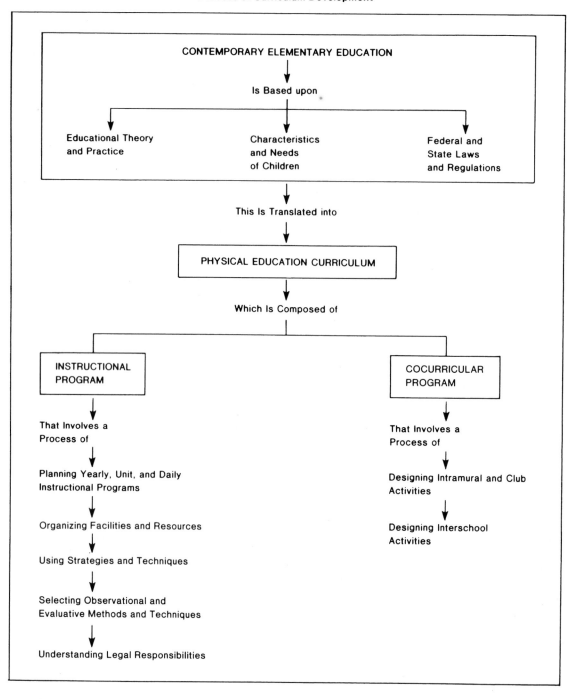

CONTEMPORARY ELEMENTARY EDUCATION

Is Based upon

Educational Theory
and Practice

Characteristics
and Needs
of Children

Federal and
State Laws
and Regulations

This Is Translated into

PHYSICAL EDUCATION CURRICULUM

Which Is Composed of

INSTRUCTIONAL
PROGRAM

COCURRICULAR
PROGRAM

That Involves a
Process of

That Involves a
Process of

Planning Yearly, Unit, and Daily
Instructional Programs

Designing Intramural and Club
Activities

Organizing Facilities and Resources

Designing Interschool
Activities

Using Strategies and Techniques

Selecting Observational and
Evaluative Methods and Techniques

Understanding Legal Responsibilities

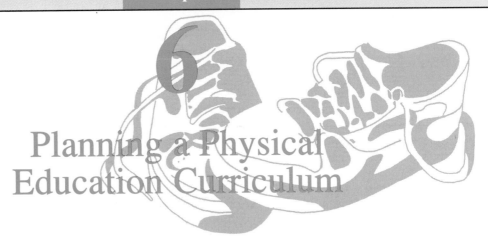

Chapter 6

Planning a Physical Education Curriculum

The instructional program is more than the physical activities that are taught to the class. Rather, it is the total experience of activities, methods, and teaching strategies.

The activities themselves serve two basic functions. First, through the activities, the children learn fundamental locomotor and nonlocomotor skills and the basic movement skills and concepts involved in games, dance, and other organized activities. Mastering these skills, in turn, helps children maintain an optimum level of physical fitness, move their bodies easily and efficiently, and express themselves creatively. Second, physical activities provide a medium within which children learn many intangible, yet important, lessons of life. They learn, for example, to share experiences, to give and take, and to control emotions under a variety of cooperative and competitive situations.

This chapter describes some types of activities and outlines the process of developing yearly, unit, and daily lessons. Sample programs are provided as guidelines for helping teachers develop their own programs, which must always be based on the teachers' stated goals and teaching competence; the characteristics and needs of children; and the available time, facilities, and equipment ■

Types of Curriculum Models

An elementary school curriculum includes all the experiences of children for which the school accepts responsibility. In physical education, this encompasses all the learning experiences related to the physical activities in both the regular instructional period and the intramural and interschool programs. This discussion is limited to the learning experiences that are part of the regular instructional program. The physical education curriculum can take several forms. The fundamental purpose of a curriculum model is to provide an effective means of choosing activities, developing teaching strategies, and providing experiences that meet the objectives of the instructional program.

A review of current elementary school physical education programs and contemporary guides and textbooks indicates that there are about four types of curriculum models. There are variations within and between each model as well as a strong tendency toward one particular type of curriculum. Three of the most common types are described in this section. Although each type of curriculum model can be found throughout Canada and the United States, the developmental model is one of the more prevalent and is stressed throughout this book.

Traditional Model

The traditional model, as outlined in table 6.1, is the oldest type of elementary school physical education curriculum. It is an activity-based program that includes separate content areas of game, dance, gymnastic, and physical fitness activities. A percentage of instructional time is allocated to each activity area according to grade level. The primary level curriculum stresses an informal participation in low organization activities such as running and tag games, singing games, and a variety of stunts and tumbling activities. The general teacher-centered approach to this type of curriculum model is continued in the intermediate grades. However, as outlined in table 6.1, emphasis in each content area shifts to developing more specialized skills. Both primary and intermediate programs stress formal teaching strategies and norm-based progress, particularly in game, gymnastic, and physical fitness activities.

Movement Education Model

The Movement Education model, originally proposed by R. Laban (1960), is based on a different analysis of movement from that of the traditional movement. This model uses Laban's classification system as the structure on which thematic programs are developed throughout the elementary school physical education program. The four elements of body awareness, space awareness, qualities, and relationships represent four content areas of the curriculum. The central idea of this program is that children learn how their bodies move through a variety of mediums such as games, gymnastics, and dance. It is an individualized approach and a child-centered program that teaches children to learn new movement concepts and skills according to their own rate and level of development. The teacher's role is that of a guider rather than a director of the learning experience. As such, teaching strategies stress exploratory methods and techniques. Although physical fitness is listed under both levels in table 6.1, fitness development is not a separate unit or theme; it is integrated into each theme and, thus, is seen as a means to moving effectively and efficiently rather than as an end in itself.

Developmental Model

The developmental model is essentially an eclectic approach that uses a developmental sequence of acquiring movement concepts and motor skills according to each child's level of ability, interest, and maturity. The program is based on a philosophy of education that emphasizes the development of each child's human potential through a personalized and humanistic learning environment. It draws on the knowledge of how children grow and develop, of theories of learning motor skills, and of important social and cultural factors relating to the types of activities children enjoy. In addition, the model considers the long-term concepts and skills children will need to meet the challenges of an exciting future.

The content that is outlined under the developmental model shown in table 6.1 indicates that this approach includes the game, dance, and gymnastic activities of the traditional model, as well as the basic concepts and skills of Movement Education. The developmental model also emphasizes creative and exploratory methods and the acquisition of knowledge and skills that will help children learn how the body works and how to maintain a high level of health and fitness throughout life. It is truly a child-centered program.

Program Emphasis

The developmental approach to curriculum development is based on the premise that each child learns concepts and motor skills according to his own rate and level of development. It is a process-based rather than a product-based curriculum that views each child as progressing through stages of development according to his own time clock. Each stage of development is not a rigid or fixed set of standard academic, motor, and social skills a child must acquire before advancing to the next stage. Rather, developmental stages are approximate time periods from early through late childhood in which children acquire psychomotor, cognitive, and affective concepts, skills, and understandings. In this text, three general levels of development are used as a rough guide for designing appropriate physical education programs.

Table 6.1 Types of Curriculum Models

Traditional model	Movement Education model	Developmental model
Primary level		
Games	*Games*	*Games*
Basic game skills	Body awareness	Basic game skills
Running, tag, and simple team games	Space awareness	Locomotor and nonlocomotor skills
	Qualities	Simple team and creative games
	Relationships	Movement Education concepts and skills
Dance	*Dance*	*Dance*
Locomotor and nonlocomotor skills	Body awareness	Locomotor and nonlocomotor skills
Singing games, folk dance	Space awareness	Rhythmics, singing games, and folk dance
Creative dance	Qualities	
	Relationships	Creative dance stressing Movement Education concepts and skills
Gymnastics	*Gymnastics*	*Gymnastics*
Stunts and tumbling	Body awareness	Stunts and tumbling
Small equipment	Space awareness	Small equipment
Some large apparatus	Qualities	Large apparatus
	Relationships	Movement Education concepts and skills
Fitness	*Fitness*	*Fitness*
Increase and maintain level of physical fitness	Integrated into Movement Education program	Understanding and development of individualized approaches to health-related fitness
Intermediate level		
Games	*Games*	*Games*
Low organization games	Body awareness	Low organization and creative games
Sport skills and games	Space awareness	Sports skills and team sports
Knowledge of rules and playing strategies	Qualities	Knowledge of rules and playing strategies
	Relationships	Movement Education concepts and skills
Dance	*Dance*	*Dance*
Rhythmics	Body awareness	Rhythmics
Folk and square dance	Space awareness	Folk and square dance
Creative dance	Qualities	Creative dance—emphasis on Movement Education
	Relationships	
Gymnastics	*Gymnastics*	*Gymnastics*
Stunts and tumbling	Body awareness	Stunts and tumbling
Small equipment	Space awareness	Small equipment
Large apparatus	Qualities	Large apparatus
	Relationships	Movement Education concepts and skills
Fitness	*Fitness*	*Fitness*
Increase and maintain level of physical fitness	Integrated into Movement Education program	Understanding and development of individualized approaches to health-related fitness

In tables 6.2, 6.3, and 6.4, the term "learning descriptor" is used rather than "outcomes." If the teacher were to state what she wants every child to accomplish within each of these developmental periods, she would violate the premise of this curriculum design. Learning descriptors must be considered as signposts along a child's path of development. Such words as *performs, shows,* and *demonstrates* are used to stress that there are no rigid boundary lines between stages of development. Also, because of a variety of contemporary educational factors, such as previous physical education experiences, number of physical education periods per week, and available equipment and facilities, a standard grade-level approach would be inappropriate. Each level of development, however, provides a general framework on which each teacher can plan a physical education program.

Table 6.2 Learning Descriptors for Developmental Level I

Psychomotor domain	Cognitive domain	Affective domain
Performs locomotor skills of walking, running, jumping, hopping, sliding, and skipping individually or in a simple sequence	Knows the names and locations of the main parts of the body	Shows joy and excitement for movement experiences
Performs nonlocomotor skills of swinging, bending, stretching, twisting, turning, pushing, pulling individually or in simple sequences	Can identify and name simple movements such as run, twist, and catch	Accepts different abilities of others
Moves through general space in a safe and controlled manner	Shows ability to describe simple movements	Accepts responsibility for own efforts
Performs a run, jump, land, and roll	Understands meaning and importance of strength and endurance	Demonstrates willingness to play and share ideas, space, and equipment with others
Performs simple movement sequence	Understands difference between personal and general space	Shows willingness to listen to directions and simple explanations
Moves through personal and general space changing speed and direction	Knows names and meanings of directions, levels, and pathways of moving	Shows willingness to assume responsibility for one's own safety
Executes simple sequences using small equipment and large apparatus	Knows names and meanings of quick and slow, strong and light, and flow	Demonstrates a willingness to create games or other movement sequences with others
Performs a variety of simple balance and agility stunts	Knows names and meanings of weight bearing, shapes, and balance	Shows willingness to stay on-task until the activity is completed
Shows ability to roll a ball with both hands	Understands meaning of simple relationships of self to others and to objects	Demonstrates understanding and tolerance toward classmates who have physical or mental disabilities
Performs two-hand underhand throws with control and accuracy	Shows ability to create and explain simple movement sequences	Demonstrates understanding and tolerance toward classmates who may have different skin color
Performs one-hand underhand and overhand throw with minimum skill and accuracy	Understands meaning of safety of self and others	
Executes a one-hand dribble with either hand	Shows ability to understand simple rules of games and contests	
Shows ability to catch a ball using a two-hand underhand catch	Knows the meaning of sharing, cheating, and other social behaviors	
Shows limited ability to catch a ball using a two-hand overhand catch	Understands meaning of rhythm	
Executes a stationary kick with dominant foot	Knows how to plan simple dance sequences	
Performs a simple dribble using both feet		
Shows basic ability to stop a moving ball with one foot		
Shows ability to play simple running, tag, and team games		
Performs simple striking actions with arm or small implement		
Shows ability to perform locomotor and nonlocomotor movements in time to simple rhythmic accompaniment		
Performs singing games and simple folk dances		
Performs simple pantomime movements		
Shows ability to respond to a variety of stimuli such as stories and poems		

Level I: Early Childhood

The characteristics and needs of children in the early primary grades have a very strong influence on the selection of appropriate physical activities. For example, children's physical immaturity, short attention span, and lack of experience in the content areas indicate that a broad exposure to all types of game, dance, and gymnastic activities is required. Since this is a time for children to explore and discover how their bodies work, emphasis should be placed on movement concepts and skills. These considerations are reflected in the percentage of time allocated for activities in table 6.5. During the first and second year of a child's school life, attention is given to creative and exploratory ways of learning the skills involved in game and gymnastic activities and locomotor and nonlocomotor skills and movement patterns. Dance activities for early primary children should also take a strong creative approach, as they learn rhythmic skills, singing games, and creative movements. The range in the suggested percentage of time for each activity allows each teacher to develop a curriculum that meets the level of maturity and ability of the children in her care.

Table 6.3 Learning Descriptors for Developmental Level II

Psychomotor domain	Cognitive domain	Affective domain
Demonstrates a mature form in all locomotor and nonlocomotor movements	Shows a basic understanding of principles of gravity and force	Continues to show joy and excitement for movement experiences
Adjusts locomotor and nonlocomotor movements to varying rhythm and tempo	Demonstrates increased ability to invent and describe movement sequences for gymnastics and dance	Displays open willingness to work with others who possess different abilities and interests
Performs simple movement sequences involving two or more elements of body awareness, qualities, space awareness, and relationships	Possesses an understanding of major components of physical fitness and how to improve and maintain optimum levels of health-related fitness	Shows increased willingness to work in small and large groups
Shows ability to repeat and improve quality of movement sequences	Shows ability to understand simple team strategies in low-organization games and modified team sports	Shows willingness to assume responsibility for one's own safety as well as for the general safety of the class
Performs a variety of stunts and tumbling skills	Demonstrates a reasonable understanding of sharing, cheating, and other social behavior	Demonstrates willingness to stay on-task for long periods of time
Shows ability to develop movement sequences involving small and large apparatus		Shows a continuous support to work with others of lesser ability
Executes simple movement sequences with a partner and using small and large apparatus		Reveals tolerance toward others of different race and cultural backgrounds
Performs a variety of individual and long rope jumping skills		Demonstrates a willingness to participate in group discussions and abide by the group's decisions on rules and regulations
Shows improved form, speed, and accuracy with underhand and overhand throw		
Demonstrates increased skill in two-hand underhand and overhand catch		
Performs one-hand dribble with either hand with a change in level, speed, and direction		
Shows ability to kick a stationary and moving ball with increased power and accuracy		
Dribbles ball with both feet with a change of direction and speed		
Shows ability to stop a moving ball with feet, legs, and body		
Performs striking actions with large instruments, such as bats and hockey sticks, with increased control and proficiency		
Plays more complex running tag and lead-up games to major team sports		
Performs movement sequences involving locomotor and nonlocomotor movements and in combination with different rhythm patterns		
Performs folk dances with increased skill and style		
Performs creative dance movements with increased skill and expression		

Level II: Middle Childhood

Level II is the important transitional period in a physical education program. According to table 6.5, there is a slight reduction in the time devoted to movement concepts and skills and fundamental skills. As children progress through this age range, they develop an understanding of how their bodies work, they learn more complex skills and strategies, and they become more group oriented than the previous age range. This period of time should reflect participation in group activities, and children should be given many opportunities to increase their level of skill and understanding in a wide variety of physical activities. It is also a time to use creative and exploratory teaching strategies to enhance children's creative expressions in games, gymnastics, and dance.

Level III: Late Childhood

As children move from the latter part of level II to level III, they begin to refine many fundamental motor skills and to develop a fairly proficient level of performance in the more complex skills of sports, dance, and gymnastics. This is

Table 6.4 Learning Descriptors for Developmental Level III

Psychomotor domain	Cognitive domain	Affective domain
Performs complex movement sequences involving four elements of movement	Shows mature understanding of principles of gravity, force, and motion	Continues to show the same joy and excitement for movement experiences as previous levels
Shows increased ability to repeat and improve quality of movement sequences	Demonstrates increased ability to invent and describe movement sequences for gymanstics and dance	Displays a mature and open willingness to work with others who possess different abilities and interests
Executes a wide variety of stunts and tumbling skills and movement patterns in combination with one or more elements of movement	Plans more complex game strategies for individual and team sports	Shows willingness to develop into a self-directed human being
Performs a wide variety of gymanstic skills and movements using small equipment and large apparatus in combination with one or more elements of movement	Understands the factors affecting performance such as body type, conditioning, and training methods	Shows mature ways and means of working with children with special needs
Performs motor skills and movement patterns with good mechanics and efficacy of performance	Shows understanding and ability to discriminate between a poor and good performance in game, dance, and gymnastic activities	Shows a mature tolerance toward others of different races and cultural backgrounds
Performs basic sport skills and movement patterns with increased proficiency	Demonstrates an increased knowledge of health-related fitness and how to design individual programs to improve and maintain one's own physical fitness	Demonstrates a mature understanding and manner in dealing with safety of self and others
Applies concepts and skills of Movement Education while playing individual and team sports	Understands the basic principles of exercise and how to apply them in an exercise program	Shows an appreciation for the ideas and physical abilities of others
Demonstrates increased defensive and offensive playing strategies in individual and team sports	Demonstrates a mature understanding of acceptable social behavior	Displays a mature attitude toward criticisms by the teacher and fellow students
Executes track and field skills with increased style and performance		Shows a positive attitude toward cooperative and competitive attitudes of others
Applies effective spotting techniques in stunts, tumbling, and other gymanstic activities		Displays an active and positive attitude toward learning new types of physical activity
Demonstrates increased style and form in folk, square, and social dance activities		Shows an attitude and direction toward activities that are intrinsically motivating
Performs expressive dance sequences using numerous types of stimuli with increased creativity and form		Demonstrates a positive attitude toward game, dance, and other movement activities from other countries
		Demonstrates an increased willingness to participate in group discussions and to abide by majority rule

Table 6.5 Percentage of Time for Activities

Type of activity	Suggested yearly percentage of time		
	Level I	Level II	Level III
Movement Education skills and concepts	15–25	10–20	10–15
Locomotor and nonlocomotor skills	15–20	5–10	2–5
Game activities	20–25	20–35	30–40
Dance activities	20–25	20–25	15–20
Gymnastic activities	20–30	20–25	15–20
Physical fitness activities	5–15	10–15	15–20
Special interest activities	5–20	5–20	12–20

reflected in table 6.6, where there is a significant increase in time devoted to sport activities. However, these children still enjoy running, tag, and individual and cooperative games. Although less time is allotted for dance activities within each intermediate grade, the proportionate percentage of time for this area supports its value.

There is a slight reduction in time allotments for gymnastic activities from grade four through grade six. The major change with this program, however, is the shift toward more artistic types of gymnastic movements and a decrease in the emphasis on Laban's movement concepts and skills. There is, though, a good argument to blend these two approaches in order to cope with varying levels of interest and ability and to provide a program that fosters creative expression.

Table 6.5 provided between 12 and 20 percent for special interest activities in level III. This time allotment can be used for such programs as swimming or for other special outdoor pursuits that are popular and important to unique

Table 6.6 Physical Education Activities

	Chapter	Level I	Level II	Level III	Page
Physical fitness activities					
Posture activities	11	———	———	——▶	176
Conditioning exercises	12	———	———	——▶	190
Circuit training	12		———	——▶	199
Obstacle course	12		———	——▶	200
Rope jumping	26		——	——▶	481
Jogging	12		———	——▶	201
Aerobic dancing	12		———	——▶	202
Movement Education					
Body awareness	25	———	———	——▶	466
Space awareness	25	———	———	——▶	469
Qualities	25	———	———	——▶	468
Relationships	25	———	———	——▶	470
Locomotor activities	4	———	———	——▶	48
Nonlocomotor activities	4	———	———	——▶	57
Game activities					
Basic game skills	4	———	——▶		61
Running, tag, and simple team games	16	———	———	——▶	257
Individual and partner games	16	———	———	——▶	257
Cooperative games	17		———	——▶	295
Classroom games	14	———	———	——▶	227
Soccer activities	18		———	——▶	314
Hockey activities	19		———	——▶	331
Football activities	20		——	——▶	346
Volleyball activities	21		———	——▶	358
Basketball activities	22		———	——▶	375
Softball activities	23		———	——▶	393
Track and field activities	24		———	——▶	404
Gymnastic activities					
Stunts and tumbling skills	25	———	———	——▶	424
Movement skills	25	———	———	——▶	463
Pyramid building	25		——	——▶	450
Beanbag activities	26	———	———	——▶	478
Individual and long rope activities	26	———	———	——▶	482
Hoop activities	26	———	———	——▶	492
Wand activities	26	———	———	——▶	493
Parachute activities	26	———	———	——▶	497
Indian clubs, traffic cones	26	———	———	——▶	499
Juggling activities	26		———	——▶	500
Balance beam and benches	27	———	———	——▶	507
Climbing ropes	27	———	———	——▶	512
Springboard, vaulting box	27		———	——▶	517
Horizontal bar, ladder, stall bars	27	———	———	——▶	522
Agility apparatus	27	———	———	——▶	529
Outdoor apparatus	27	———	———	——▶	530
Dance activities					
Elements of rhythm	28	———	———	——▶	536
Rhythm activities	28	———	———	——▶	539
Singing games	29	———	——▶		551
Folk dance	29		———	——▶	556
Creative dance	30	———	———	——▶	583

planning a physical education curriculum

geographical areas of North America. These may include cross-country skiing, canoeing, and orienteering programs. Many educators have stressed the importance of including a basic drown-proofing swimming unit as part of all elementary physical education programs. If local budgets can afford such programs, contracts can be made with local recreational agencies, such as the YMCA or Red Cross, to provide this program on a contractual basis. Finally, this unscheduled time allotment can be used to cope with special interests in any one of the main categories or to introduce new activities, such as rhythmic gymnastics or European handball, into the curriculum.

The relative percentage of time suggested for each activity area in table 6.5 provides a very rough guideline as to what types of activities should be taught at various developmental levels. Table 6.6 goes one step further by providing an overview of the specific activities recommended for each level. This table will be used extensively in the next section, dealing with planning a yearly program.

Developing a Yearly Program

In the majority of elementary schools in the United States and Canada, the classroom teacher is mainly responsible for planning the yearly physical education program. Her task is to translate her goals, and those expressed by school officials and parents, into a broad-based activity program that meets the needs and interests of the children.

If every class were assigned thirty to forty-five minutes a day for physical education; if the interests and abilities of each class were equal, or at least similar; and if all facilities, equipment, and supplies were available for any activity selected, then a basic program with specific percentages of time allocated for specific activities would be suggested for each class. This ideal situation simply does not exist in elementary schools in the United States and Canada. There are, for example, local cultural factors to consider, such as a large local population of German- or Spanish-speaking families who may wish certain dances or game activities taught to their children. The climate also has a direct bearing on the selection of activities and when they are taught. Also, as mentioned earlier, the teacher's background and competence in physical education directly affect the nature and direction of every aspect of the program. School conditions, such as time allotments, class size, and available equipment and facilities must also be given consideration before beginning the first step in planning a yearly program. Once these are considered, the following five-step plan provides a framework on which the classroom teacher can develop her own program.*

*The five-step process in developing a yearly physical education curriculum is explained in detail in Kirchner and Fishburne's book titled *Yearly Programs, Units, and Daily Lesson Plans.* See Selected References.

Step 1: Establish the Basic Objectives of the Program

The basic objectives of an elementary physical education program discussed in chapter 1 can be used as a starting point for the classroom teacher. Of course, these objectives may be modified or others may be added to reflect the philosophy of the local school district or the wishes of parents and school officials. The developmental curriculum, described earlier, used Bloom's (Bloom, 1976) three domains to outline the learning descriptors for the proposed three levels in the elementary school physical education program. These three domains are also used below as a framework to state the basic objectives of the proposed curriculum.

Psychomotor Domain

1. To enhance physical growth and development through the provision of a quality daily physical education program
2. To help each child develop and maintain an optimum level of health-related fitness
3. To help children develop a wide variety of physical skills that can and will be used to achieve long-term enjoyment through wholesome and recreational activities

Cognitive Domain

1. To help each child understand how the body works, the ways of learning skills and movement concepts, and the basic principles and mechanics of movement
2. To develop children's knowledge and understanding of a wide variety of game, dance, gymnastic, and body management principles, concepts, and strategies
3. To provide opportunities for all children to enhance their innate creative talents
4. To provide opportunities to enhance academic concepts and skills through the medium of physical activity

Affective Domain

1. To develop within each child a feeling of joy and excitement through movement
2. To enhance a child's positive self-image
3. To develop within each child a willingness to listen to and accept the ideas and opinions of others
4. To develop a child's conscious feeling for the safety and protection of self and other classmates
5. To develop a child's understanding and appreciation for differences in ethnic and cultural backgrounds, abilities, and disabilities

Table 6.7   Yearly Program Planning Sheet: Ms. Green's Third-Grade Class

Activities	Chapter	Value		Student interest		Safety risk		Teacher competence		Facilities	Equipment	No. of lessons
Teacher-learner and administrative considerations		High	Low	High	Low	High	Low	High	Low			
Game activities												
Unit 1: Ball Skills (hand-eye)	16	X		X			X	X		Adequate	Class sets of balls	15
Unit 2: Ball skills (foot-eye)	16	X		X			X	X		Adequate	Class sets of balls	15
Unit 3: Cooperative games	17	X		X			X	X		Adequate	Class sets of balls	10
Unit 4: Ball skills	18	X		X			X	X		Adequate	Class sets of balls	15
Gymnastic activities												55 lessons
Unit 1: Gymnastics	25–27	X		X		X			X	Adequate	Small equipment sufficient	15
Unit 2: Gymnastics	25–27	X		X		X			X	Adequate	Large equipment limited	15
Unit 3: Gymnastics	25–27	X		X		X			X	Adequate	Large equipment limited	15
Unit 4: Gymnastics	25–27	X		X		X			X	Adequate	Large equipment limited	10
Dance activities												55 lessons
Unit 1: Rhythmics	28	X			X	X		X		Adequate	Tapes	5
Unit 2: Creative folk dance	29	X			X	X		X		Adequate	Tapes	10
Unit 3: Folk dance	29	X			X	X		X		Adequate	Tapes	15
Unit 4: Creative dance	30	X			X	X		X		Adequate	Tapes and instruction	15
Other activities	Reserved 25 lessons for extras											25 lessons

Game activities: 55 lessons · Dance activities: 45 lessons

↑ In terms of your stated goals. · ↑ In terms of class's needs and interests. · ↑ Consider class's age in relation to nature and activity. · ↑ Consider teaching skills and experiences in each activity. · ↑ Consider quality and quantity of facilities and equipment: Describe situation for each unit. · ↑ Attempt to provide a balanced program of activities.

Note: Physical fitness and movement concepts and skills have been incorporated into each respective unit of instruction.

Step 2: Select General Activity Areas

Selecting and allocating a percentage of time to game, dance, and gymnastic activities is a difficult task for the classroom teacher. In the first place, classes are usually organized according to age rather than ability. Ability in physical education, as with other subject areas, varies immensely within any age level. For example, a class of second graders, ranging in age from late six to early eight, may vary as much as five years in physiological maturity. In addition, differences occur in prior experience of children, teacher competence in each activity area, and available facilities and equipment. The following teaching situation illustrates how this important step in selecting appropriate activities can be accomplished.

This example illustrates how Ms. Green, a third-grade teacher, used the "Yearly Program Planning Sheet" shown in table 6.7 to develop a balanced program of activities. Her teaching situation included 180 teaching days,

		Suggested percentage	Total percentage	Number of days
180 days of instruction	Games	20	30	54
30-minute lessons	Dance	25	25	45
5 lessons/week or 36 weeks of instruction (180 ÷ 5)	Gymnastics	30	30	54
	Movement concepts	10		
	Fitness (stress in each area)	5	5	9
	Nonscheduled	10	10	18
			100%	180 days

each having a thirty-minute physical education class with access to indoor and outdoor facilities.

Ms. Green's first decision was to allocate a percentage of time to one or more of the activity areas outlined in table 6.5. She decided to take 10 percent allocated for Movement Education skills and concepts and use it for game activities (see Worksheet A). The movement skills and concepts were going to be emphasized in her gymnastic program, so she felt the 30 percent allocation of time would be adequate to handle her gymnastic program. The 5 percent for physical fitness activities would be represented in the warm-up activities for all lessons within each content area. The remaining 10 percent was reserved for other activities.

According to Ms. Green's checks and written comments in table 6.7, she has made a preliminary selection of activities and indicated where problems might arise. For example, she was concerned about the high risk of gymnastic activities and her general low level of competence to teach these activities using the Movement Education approach. Consequently, she would need to participate in in-service programs and perhaps eliminate the more high-risk large apparatus activities she felt unsure of teaching. She also saw the importance of creative dance activities but noted the low interest of her class. This lack of interest will require a review of more creative and appropriate teaching strategies for this activity. After reviewing the teaching and administrative considerations, she decided to teach four units within each activity area.

The "Yearly Program Planning Sheet" provides a means of allocating the available instructional time to appropriate activities. It does *not,* however, indicate what should be emphasized within each activity area or the month of the year when these activities should be taught. Table 6.8 is used to accomplish this task. Ms. Green has decided to block the activities according to the way she had planned her original units, that is, in blocks of one, two, or three weeks. She started the program with the first games unit, then followed a general pattern of alternating activities until the end of April. With the five remaining weeks, sufficient school funds were available for a two-week swimming program that would be handled by a local YMCA. After taking a course in orienteering in March, she decided to try out a few ideas during the first week in May. The activities of the last two weeks were chosen by the children.

The format illustrated in this general outline is perhaps the easiest method to organize the full year's program of activities. However, other factors—such as climate, age of children, and available facilities—may indicate other patterns of organizing the program. The various types of units are discussed under the next step in the process of developing a physical education curriculum.

Step 3: Develop an Instructional Unit

An instructional unit is one segment of the yearly program, which normally emphasizes one type of activity and lasts for a set period of time. Although there is no standard format for a unit plan, it usually contains the following seven items:

A. Objectives
B. Sequential list of concepts and skills to be learned
C. Selection of activities
D. Organization and teaching strategies
E. Equipment and facilities
F. Evaluation
G. Resources

A clarification of each item is provided, along with suggestions to help each teacher construct her own unit plans.

A. Objectives

The objectives of a unit are normally expressed in terms of general objectives, then broken down into learning descriptors. For example, a fifteen-lesson soccer unit for a fifth-grade class might have the following general objectives:

1. To teach children to play soccer
2. To teach children to appreciate the rules and strategies of soccer
3. To provide for positive interpersonal relations
4. To enhance leadership qualities, fair play, and sportsmanship

Table 6.8   General Outline of a Yearly Program (Level II)

September

Week

1	Unit 1: game skills (hand-eye)
2	Unit 1: game skills (hand-eye)
3	Unit 1: game skills (hand-eye)
4	Unit 2: gymnastics—level 1 (Movement Education)

October

Week

5	Unit 2: gymnastics—level 1 (Movement Education)
6	Unit 2: gymnastics—level 1 (Movement Education)
7	Unit 3: rhythmics
8	Unit 4: cooperative games
9	Unit 4: cooperative games

November

Week

10	Unit 5: folk dance
11	Unit 5: folk dance
12	Unit 5: folk dance
13	Unit 6: gymnastics—level 2 (Movement Education)

December

Week

14	Unit 6: gymnastics—level 2 (Movement Education)
15	Unit 6: gymnastics—level 2 (Movement Education)

January

Week

16	Unit 7: games (foot-eye)
17	Unit 7: games (foot-eye)
18	Unit 7: games (foot-eye)
19	Unit 8: dance—creative folk

February

Week

20	Unit 8: dance—creative folk
21	Unit 9: gymnastics—level 3 (Movement Education)
22	Unit 9: gymnastics—level 3 (Movement Education)
23	Unit 9: gymnastics—level 3 (Movement Education)

March

Week

24	Unit 10: dance—creative
25	Unit 10: dance—creative
26	Unit 10: dance—creative
27	Unit 11: games—ball skills

April

Week

28	Unit 11: games—ball skills
29	Unit 11: games—ball skills
30	Unit 12: gymnastics—level 4 (Movement Education)
31	Unit 12: gymnastics—level 4 (Movement Education)

May

Week

32	Unit 13: orienteering
33	Unit 14: swimming
34	Unit 14: swimming
35	Unit 15: track and field

June

Week

36	Unit 16: softball

Although these objectives are global and, at times, difficult to evaluate, they are extremely important guidelines for selecting activities, for developing teaching strategies, and for dealing with other related parts of an instructional unit.

Once the general objectives for a unit are established, a list of learning descriptors must be stated. These are outlined in table 6.4 on page 98. For example, in the soccer unit cited, the learning descriptors would be as follows:

1. Shows how to kick a stationary and moving ball with the instep and side of foot
2. Possesses the ability to trap a ball with the chest, leg, shin, and foot
3. Performs dribble and pass with reasonable accuracy
4. Shows how to head a ball with reasonable accuracy
5. Demonstrates positional play and team strategy
6. Understands one's own level of ability prior to and after a unit of soccer.
7. Shows mature tolerance toward others with different levels of ability
8. Demonstrates willingness to participate in team discussions and to abide by majority rule

These learning descriptors provide guideposts for the teacher to follow. They can tell the direction a child in each level should be moving, but they cannot demand that he reach the signpost at a certain time or restrict him if his level of maturity and ability demand higher levels of performance and achievement.

B. Sequential List of Concepts and Skills

Learning outcomes help identify the skills and concepts for each unit of instruction. The previous soccer unit can be used to illustrate the sequential listing of introductory skills, rules, and strategies. After referring to the "Suggested Sequence of Presenting Soccer Skills and Rules" (see chapter 18) the teacher would make the following tentative list:

1. Instep kick
2. Heading
3. Corner and penalty kicks
4. Pass and trap
5. Throw in
6. Positional play

After administering a skill test and observing the children play a few lead-up games, the teacher would be able to properly sequence the selected activities to meet the general level of interest and ability of her class.

C. Selection of Activities

The activities for a unit are the medium through which the general objectives are accomplished. In the soccer unit, appropriate activities would include:

1. A list of practice activities, page 315
2. A list of lead-up games, page 316
3. Rules and regulations of soccer, page 323

D. Organization and Teaching Strategies

This part of the instructional unit outlines the various organizational techniques and teaching strategies used throughout the unit. The fifth-grade teacher of the soccer unit might outline the methods and techniques she will use throughout the unit as follows:

Organization	Teaching Strategies
Modified unit	Stress progression from
Station work	individual to partner to
Rotational team or group	group activities
leaders	Stress balance between
Reduce size of outdoor	structured drills and lead-
instructional area	up games with inventive
Improvise: size and type of	activities
balls, location and	Stress individual progress
number of goals	and self-evaluation

E. Equipment and Facilities

The success of any instructional unit depends on adequate facilities and sufficient equipment for all participants. In the games program, balls and related small equipment should be procured for each games unit. Different-sized balls and improvised equipment should be acceptable in schools with budget limitations. Gymnastic units involving a large number of small and larger equipment may require the use of "pooled" apparatus or a revamping of the gymnastic units of instruction to cope with limitations in the type and number of apparatus. Finally, dance units normally require tedious hours of selecting and taping musical accompaniments. If all teachers in a school agree on a standardized procedure of copying and storing tapes, many hours can be saved by each teacher. The construction of improvised instruments shown in appendix B can also be used in most creative dance programs.

F. Evaluation

Formative and summative evaluative procedures should be established for every instructional unit. A list of appropriate subjective and objective evaluative instruments is provided in chapter 9.

G. Resources

Two basic types of resources should be listed in each unit plan: (1) written materials, such as textbooks, individual activity units, and other printed materials, and (2) audio-visual materials, such as films, videotapes, or demonstration charts. It is wise to include order forms for films and tapes to confirm their availability before the instructional unit begins.

This type of instructional plan is appropriate for most structured activities within game, dance, and gymnastic programs. Instructional units involving creative dance or the Movement Education approach in gymnastics must be adapted to meet the unique conditions relating to a theme approach to sequencing as well as to methods of evaluation.

Selecting the appropriate type of instructional unit is one of the most important tasks within this area. Following are three basic types of units that can be used in the primary and intermediate grades. Each teacher should select the unit that most readily meets the needs of her class and is in harmony with her basic teaching approach.

Multiple Teaching Unit

The multiple teaching unit is actually two or three units taught concurrently throughout the year. In other words, game, dance, and gymnastic activities are taught on alternate days for an indefinite period (see table 6.9). Kindergarten activities might include games on Monday, gymnastics on Tuesday, dance on Wednesday, and singing games (representing dance) on Thursday to start the second rotation. In this case, the rotation system has been modified by having similar activities two days in a row.

Advantages of this approach are its variety of activities and its flexibility; therefore, it can be used in kindergarten and first-grade classes to cope with the short attention spans of five- and six-year-olds. The facilities and equipment available may determine whether this method can be adopted. Whatever the reasons for selecting the multiple unit, the teacher should make sure that game, dance, and gymnastic activities are given the appropriate amount of emphasis.

Modified Teaching Unit

The modified teaching unit is a block of time allocated primarily for the instruction of one type of activity. For example, dance might be emphasized 90 percent of the time during a three- or four-week period, while the remaining 10 percent is devoted to game and gymnastic activities. Table 6.10 exemplifies a third-grade class with a thirty-minute physical education period scheduled every day in the gymnasium. During the first week of the unit, dance activities are taught on Monday, Tuesday, Thursday, and Friday. Wednesday is set aside for gymnastics or outdoor games.

This method provides both continuity and variety. For example, "Paw Paw Patch" is introduced on Monday and repeated

Table 6.9   Sample Weekly Plan for Level I (Multiple Unit)

Monday *Game skills*	Tuesday *Floor stunts*	Wednesday *Rhythmic activities*	Thursday *Singing games*	Friday *Classroom games*
Bouncing practice activities 1. Bounce and catch 2. Bounce several times 3. Bounce to partner	Camel walk, elevator, tightrope walk	Pantomime animal walks, such as bears, lions, dogs, and horses	"London Bridge"	"Ringmaster"

Table 6.10   Dance Unit for Level II (Modified Unit)

	Monday	Tuesday	Wednesday	Thursday	Friday
1st week	*Introduce:* "Paw Paw Patch"	*Review:* "Paw Paw Patch" *Introduce:* "Bleking"	*Games:* Stunts Relay Pinch-oh	*Review:* "Bleking" "Skip to My Lou"	*Review:* "Paw Paw Patch" "Bleking" "Skip to My Lou"
2nd week	*Review:* "Skip to My Lou" *Introduce:* "Pease Porridge Hot"	*Review:* "Pease Porridge Hot" "Skip to My Lou"	*Gymnastics:* Stunts Balance beam Rope skipping	*Review:* "Bleking" "Pease Porridge Hot"	*Review:* "Skip to My Lou" *Introduce:* Jiffy Mixer
3rd week	*Review:* Jiffy Mixer *Introduce:* "Shoo Fly"	*Review:* Jiffy Mixer "Shoo Fly"	*Review:* Games or stunts	*Review:* "Paw Paw Patch" "Bleking" "Skip to My Lou"	*Review:* "Pease Porridge Hot" "Skip to My Lou" Jiffy Mixer

Table 6.11   Softball Unit for Level III (Solid Block Approach)

	Monday *(40 min.)*	Tuesday *(15 min.)*	Wednesday *(40 min.)*	Thursday *(15 min.)*	Friday *(40 min.)*
1st week	*Explain:* Underhand throw (pitching) *Practice:* Zigzag passing *Lead-up:* Center ball	*Practice:* Throwing *Lead-up:* Shuttle throw	*Explain:* Bunting *Practice:* Swing at four *Lead-up:* Twenty-one softball	*Review:* Shuttle throw Twenty-one	*Explain:* Grounders *Practice:* Zigzag passing *Lead-up:* Bat ball

Note: Continue the above pattern during the second, third, and fourth weeks.

on Tuesday so that the basic skills and dance patterns are learned. Later in the Tuesday lesson, "Bleking" is introduced. To provide variety, Wednesday is set aside for vigorous running and tag games, which could be played in the gymnasium or outdoors. The remaining two days are devoted to dance activities. This pattern continues throughout the second and third weeks.

The modified block, unlike the multiple unit, provides continuity in learning skills and has certain desirable instructional features. It permits the teacher to plan one type of activity for an extended period, rather than three different types each week. Furthermore, planning a one-year program is much easier using the modified unit than the multiple approach.

Solid Teaching Unit

A solid teaching unit is an extended period of instruction—from one to several weeks—devoted exclusively to one type of activity. Its value lies in its continuity, as there is no disruption in the type of skill development. Perhaps the solid unit has its greatest application in team teaching, where the most qualified teacher is used to maximum effectiveness. However, fifth- and sixth-grade teachers who are responsible for their own physical education programs may find this type of unit applicable in teaching activities that are of great interest to their students.

Refer to table 6.11, in which a solid four-week unit of softball has been organized for a sixth-grade class. Note that the physical education period is scheduled for forty minutes on

planning a physical education curriculum

Table 6.12 Structure of a Lesson

Entry activity	Part 1 Introductory activity	Part 2 Skill development	Part 3 Closure
	Stress vigorous warm-up activities	**Games:** Stress acquisition of skills and concepts through individual and partner activities and group games	Stress key points
	Standard for all types of physical education lessons	**Gymnastics:** Stress acquisition of stunts and movement skills and concepts through individual, partner, and small equipment activities and large apparatus	
		Dance: Stress acquisition of skills and movement ideas and concepts through individual, partner, and group activities	

Monday, Wednesday, and Friday but for only fifteen minutes on Tuesday and Thursday. New skills are explained and demonstrated, drills are practiced, and lead-up games are played during the longer periods. The shorter periods are just long enough for a short drill and possibly a lead-up game.

It is suggested that the first week be planned in detail. After four or five days of instruction, the teacher may note that certain skills require additional concentration, or that students are ready for more advanced skills and lead-up games. The remaining three weeks should be planned around the skill level and interests of the class.

It is possible to use both the modified and solid units during the year. Early fall and spring activities are particularly adaptable to the solid unit, while the modified unit may be the only feasible approach for activities requiring the use of indoor facilities.

Step 4: Develop Flexible Lesson Plans

The next important phase in curriculum design is to plan and execute a series of lesson plans for each unit. This is one of the most important aspects of teaching. Good lesson plans set the direction and tone, establish the main focus, minimize confusion and loss of time, and help keep the teacher and class on track throughout each part of the lesson.

A physical education lesson plan should be considered a flexible guideline that includes brief notes and suggestions relating to objectives, equipment, content, organizational procedures, and teaching cues. The lesson plan for teaching game, dance, or gymnastic activities normally contains three parts, as shown in table 6.12. The general progression within each content area is from a warm-up session to skill development, then to larger apparatus or to larger group activities in dance or game activities. All lessons should end with a cooling down time that involves a discussion of the key points of the lesson. The sample lesson plan in table 6.13 will help each teacher develop her own lesson format.

Entry Activities

In table 6.13, the three minutes allocated for entry activities is the time children normally take to come into the gymnasium, change, and wait for the lesson to begin. Although the changing procedures vary from school to school and from grade to grade, a definite procedure should be established to use this time effectively. If children change and enter the gymnasium in a somewhat staggered fashion, establish a routine that will reward the quick changer. In this sample lesson, the teacher placed four containers of balls and small equipment in the four corners of the gymnasium. As soon as a child entered the gymnasium, he was allowed to get a ball and practice kicking it from a stationary position toward the wall. When all the children arrived, the teacher instructed them to put the balls back in the containers and then either sit in their station places or line up in their teams. The lesson is now ready to begin.

Part 1: Introductory Activities

Introductory activities, or what has been known as the warm-up period, serve two general purposes. The first is to provide an activity that involves vigorous movement of all children for the first three to five minutes of the lesson. The second purpose is to include in these activities movements or skills that will be stressed in the remaining parts of the lesson. In a sense, it is "killing two birds with one stone." In the sample lesson, requiring children to roll the ball, then to run and jump over as many balls as possible contributes to general vigorous movement. Rolling the ball and learning to judge its speed and position is part of the lesson emphasis. In most cases, teachers can plan activities that contribute to both purposes. However, there are times when the teacher wants to introduce a change of pace, such as a vigorous lead-up game, a physical fitness circuit, or rope skipping, which may only contribute to the physical fitness purpose and not directly to the main theme of the lesson. This situation should be encouraged.

Part 2: Skill Development

The second part of the lesson sets its focus and direction. Once the first lesson has been taught, the second and all remaining lessons normally begin with a quick review of the key point or skills introduced in the preceding lesson. Following this, new skills are introduced and practiced individually, with a partner, or in small groups. The exact way a

Table 6.13   Unit No. 2: Ball Skills—Foot-Eye

Grade 1

Lesson no. 3: Kicking a moving ball

Objectives: To learn how to kick a moving ball

To learn how to roll and gain possession of the ball

To learn to follow a few simple rules of the game

To learn to stay on-task until the practice activity or game is completed

Equipment: Class set of 8½-inch utility balls or old volleyballs

Content	Organization/cues	Lesson Evaluation
Entry activity (3 minutes)	Place balls and small equipment in four containers Get ball and no equipment	Children used equipment and balls—next time balls only
Part 1: Introductory activities (3 to 5 minutes) Roll and jump over a ball	Roll and jump over as many as possible Repeat with change of direction	Stress safety practices in future lessons
Part 2: Skill development (10 to 15 minutes) *Review:* Kicking Stationary ball *Introduce:* Kick moving ball Gaining possession Kick toward target Partner and kicking game	 Toward wall and kick rebound Roll, chase, kick Roll, chase, kick to wall Repeat above with partner Make up game—partners and two goals Add to game—must kick while ball is rolling	 Check key teaching points Too difficult—make challenge for individual and small equipment
Part 3: Closure (2 minutes) Discuss ball contact on foot and staying on task		

particular skill, game, or movement idea is taught to children will depend on their age and ability and the style of teaching. If children are being taught a specific sport skill, they are normally introduced to the skill by an explanation and demonstration of the key components of the movement. This is followed by individual practice and group drills or movement patterns involving two or more players. The latter phase of part 2 normally includes one or more lead-up or modified games. Gymnastic lessons follow a similar pattern, beginning with the introduction of individual movement concepts or skills on the floor or mats followed by practice on small or large equipment. Dance lessons also begin with individual movements, then progress to partner and group dance activities.

The sample lesson plan in table 6.13 illustrates the use of the direct teaching style. Each skill is explained and demonstrated, followed with individual and partner practice. The teacher could have used more exploratory methods,

particularly with this first-grade class. Her choices, in this case, could have been based on the general maturity or background of the class. However, she changed her style toward the end of part 2.

Part 3: Closure

This short session at the end of the lesson has a twofold purpose. First, it is a time to review the key point of the lesson or to stress a valuable concept that arose during the lesson. The second purpose is to provide a quiet time to allow children to "settle down" before returning to the classroom.

Variations in Lesson Plans

The previous lesson plan was based on a thirty-minute physical education period; however, in many schools, particularly for the primary grades, the period may last only fifteen to twenty minutes. Since it may not be possible to cover three

Figure 6.1 A three-part instructional unit for two class periods.

	← 30 minutes →		
Monday	**PART ONE** *Introductory Activities* (5 minutes)	**PART TWO** *Skill Development* (20 minutes to complete Kick Toward Target)	**PART THREE** *Closure*
Tuesday	(5 minutes) Repeat Monday's Introductory Activities	Begin Partner and Kicking Game plus: add two additional variations	Closure

main parts of a lesson in such a short period, the lesson can begin on one day and continue on the next without any major loss in the continuity of learning. The previous lesson will be used to illustrate such a modification. As shown in figure 6.1, part one and halfway through part two was covered in the twenty-five-minute instructional period on Monday. The second part of the lesson took longer than the teacher had expected. Thus, on Tuesday, the lesson started with a five-minute warm-up, then moved directly to partners making up a game. As this second lesson had five minutes remaining, the teacher added two more variations to the challenge before moving to part three: closure.

Regardless of the time available during the first five or six lessons, a considerable amount must be devoted to skill development. As the children acquire skill and movement understanding, more time can be devoted to group activities. The best guideline for determining the emphasis of the lesson plan is the children's progress. If the skill level appears to be quite low, continue to emphasize practice activities. If there is marked improvement, increase the difficulty of individual and partner activities and give more time and emphasis to group activities.

The amount of detail that a teacher records on her lesson plan depends, of course, on her professional background and experience. Beginning teachers tend to write down more detail. Abbreviated notes under each of the main parts of the lesson usually suffice for the more experienced teacher.

Step 5: Conduct Student and Program Evaluations

The final step in curriculum development is assessing the progress of students and the success of each part of the physical education program. Evaluation, as discussed in chapter 9, is an ongoing process of determining whether program, unit, or lesson plan objectives are being met. Teachers should use formative techniques throughout the yearly program and make appropriate adjustments in content and teaching strategies according to these objective and subjective assessments.

The evaluation of the instructional program that occurs at the end of the year can take many forms. For example, the "Physical Education Program Evaluation Form" (see chapter 9) can be modified to accommodate individual school or district programs. Other methods, such as using external evaluative teams, can be very effective in assessing the total program. The important consideration of the latter type of evaluation is to use the findings to meet revealed deficiencies and, where indicated, to enrich program offerings.

Selected References

Bloom, B. S. (1976). *Human Characteristics and School Learning.* New York: McGraw Hill.

Gabbard, C., Leblanc, E., and Lowy, S. (1987). *Physical Education for Children: Building the Foundation.* Englewood Cliffs, NJ: Prentice-Hall, Inc.

Gallahue, D. L. (1993). *Developmental Physical Education for Today's Children,* Second Edition. Dubuque, IA: Brown and Benchmark Publishers.

Graham, G., Holt-Hale, S. A., and Parker, M. (1987). *Children Moving,* Second Edition. Palo Alto, CA: Mayfield Publishing Co.

Harrison, J. M. (1986). *Instructional Strategies for Physical Education,* Second Edition. Dubuque, IA: Wm. C. Brown Publishers.

Jewett, A. E., and Bain, L. L. (1985). *The Curriculum Process in Physical Education.* Dubuque, IA: Wm. C. Brown Publishers.

Kirchner, G., and Fishburne, G. J. (1994). *Developing Yearly Programs, Units, and Daily Lesson Plans for Physical Education for Elementary School Children,* Ninth Edition. Dubuque, IA: Brown & Benchmark Publishers.

Laban, R., and Ullmann, L. (1960). *The Mastery of Movement.* London: Macdonald and Evans.

Logsdon, B. J., et al. (1977). *Physical Education for Children: A Focus on the Teaching Process.* Philadelphia: Lea & Febiger.

Mosston, M., and Arnsworth, S. (1994). *Teaching Physical Education,* Fourth Edition. New York: Macmillan Publishing Co.

Pangrazí, R. P., and Dauer, V. P. (1992). *Dynamic Physical Education for Elementary School Children,* New York: Macmillan Publishing Co.

Siedentop, D., Mand, C., and Taggart, A. (1986). *Physical Education and Curriculum Strategies for Grades 5–12.* Palo Alto, CA: Mayfield Publishing Co.

Wall, J., and Murray, N. (1994). *Children and Movement,* Second Edition. Dubuque, IA: Wm. C. Brown Publishers.

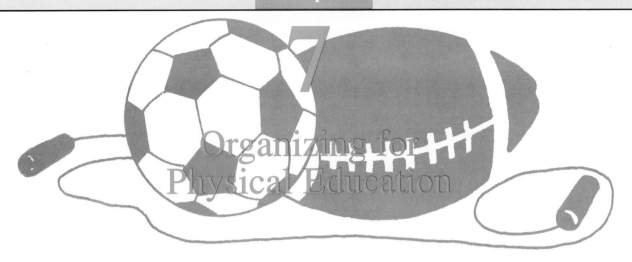

Chapter 7

Organizing for Physical Education

The quality of any physical education program depends primarily on the philosophy and competence of the teacher. Both philosophy and competence are reflected in the way the teacher manages her class and in the way she uses available space and equipment. This chapter provides some ideas and suggestions relating to general class management. It also provides information relating to maintaining and effectively using available facilities, equipment, and supplies ■

Organizational Details

Once the physical education program has been designed and teaching responsibilities have been assigned to the teaching staff, a number of other important organizational details must be completed. Policies and procedures should be established for the following areas before any instructional program begins.

Class Size

Class size in physical education should never exceed the regular number of children within each respective classroom. Assigning two classes to one physical education class is educationally unsound and may create an extremely unsafe teaching environment. Also, if two or more severely handicapped children are enrolled in a physical education class, extra assistance is warranted.

Time Allotment

The recommended amount of time for physical education varies from a minimum of 20 minutes to one hour per day. The most common figure is 150 minutes per week, which translates into daily 30-minute classes. Within the intermediate grades, the 150 minutes may be arranged into three 50-minute classes per week to provide for showering and longer periods of instruction. However, the 150 minutes per week does not include recess, supervised free play, or other intramural or interschool activities.

Scheduling

The problems of scheduling physical education vary from school to school. If the principal and staff are cooperative, it is wise to schedule all physical education classes first. This is not favoritism; it simply permits the most appropriate scheduling of a limited number of physical education facilities. Whenever limited facilities exist for the number of classes, equal access should be given to primary and intermediate classes. In previous years, intermediate classes were normally scheduled indoor or outdoor first, leaving the remaining time to primary classes. This also included specialist help if it was available. Today all classes, regardless of grade level, must be given equal access to facilities and specialist assistance.

With respect to whether a class should be scheduled for the first or last period of the instructional day, there is no evidence to support one or the other time period. If personal preferences can be accommodated within the schedule, the principal should receive this information before classes are scheduled. When several teachers request the same time slot, provisions should be made to rotate their time schedules throughout the school year.

Paraprofessional Assistance

The term *paraprofessional* includes a wide variety of voluntary or paid assistants who have special qualifications but do not normally possess a teaching certificate. A few of the more common types of paraprofessionals used in the elementary physical education program are described in the following paragraphs.

Teaching Assistants

State and local school districts vary with respect to the certification requirements and types of duties that can legally be assigned to a teaching assistant. Normally, a teaching assistant completes a special program in a community college and may be assigned to assist regular teachers or to supervise recess, noon-hour, and intramural activities. This type of teaching assistance and supervisory help has been very popular in virtually all school districts that have hired these paraprofessionals.

Contracted Recreational Specialists

During the past ten years, the trend toward contracting local recreational specialists in such activities as swimming, skiing, and skating has grown in a number of geographical areas. Perhaps the most popular program has been with local YMCA or recreational centers to teach a basic or survival swimming program to a particular grade. In most cases, these specialists have a similar philosophy and instructional approach to teaching young children. These factors should, however, be checked before entering into a contractual agreement with any nonschool agency.

Volunteer Assistance Programs

Under the umbrella term of *volunteer assistance* is a large number of interested and talented parents and neighbors who donate their time and talent to the elementary physical education program. For example, in the city of Nanaimo on Vancouver Island, more than 700 parents have volunteered their time to help teach, supervise, and administer physical fitness tests. Special in-service sessions are given to these volunteers to prepare them for specific tasks within each school program. This program has been in operation for several years and has not only enhanced the quality of the physical education offerings but has created a positive relationship between parents and school officials.

Student Assistance

Two types of student assistance programs appear to be emerging in a large number of school districts. The first uses high school students to assist classroom teachers in the regular instructional program or as supervisors and assistant coaches in the extraclass program. Many teenagers who have worked in this program have received excellent recommendations from principals, teachers, and parents. This early practical experience has also proven a positive method of recruiting mature, talented, and enthusiastic young men and women into the teaching profession.

The second type of student assistance program uses upper-grade students to help classroom teachers and to act as

Figure 7.1 The period of time before a lesson should be used constructively.

coaches, managers, and referees in the intramural program. Studies of these programs seem to indicate that older children work exceptionally well with kindergarten and first-grade children. Fifth- and sixth-graders, who are not always highly skilled but enjoy working with primary children, can develop a strong rapport with young children. In numerous cases, through this program, the younger children develop motor skills as well as demonstrate a very positive self-image and a respect and an appreciation toward their older "idols." It is a program that should be encouraged in virtually every elementary school.

Effective Class Organization

Once a teacher has decided on the basic approach and methods she will stress in her program, several important teaching patterns and formations will assist her in creating an informal and efficient learning environment.

Use of Time Before a Lesson Starts

Normally, children change into physical education uniforms, or at least into tennis shoes, and begin the lesson when everyone is present. The following procedure has been adopted in numerous schools and has proved to be extremely effective in using the time before the lesson officially begins. Although the type of activity and the time available vary from class to class, this procedure can be applied to every physical education lesson, whether in the gymnasium or on the playing field.

Each child should constructively use the free time before the lesson begins (figure 7.1). Thus, simply provide children who enter the gymnasium or go out on the playing field early an opportunity to practice a skill or movement pattern while they wait for the lesson to begin.

The procedure varies slightly, depending on the type of instructional unit. In a game-type lesson, a variety of balls is made available when the children enter the instructional area. A few instructions are given, such as "practice bouncing and catching by yourself or with a partner as soon as you come into the gymnasium." In a gymnastic unit, a variety of small equipment—hoops, beanbags, skipping ropes—is placed on the floor. As the children enter the gymnasium, they are instructed to choose equipment and practice any skill they learned in the previous lesson or to explore any movement they want. Practice with large apparatus, such as climbing ropes, vaulting box, or springboard, should be avoided during the free practice time. Free practice activities prior to a dance lesson could involve ball or other small equipment activities, rather than practice of a specific dance step or movement pattern.

The following suggestions show how this procedure can be used effectively even in the first few lessons. After the children have been instructed how and where to change their clothing, use one or more of these ideas while they are changing:

1. *Balls:* Tell the children that as soon as they have changed they may choose a ball and practice bouncing it (or throwing and catching it, jumping over it, or playing catch with a partner).
2. *Beanbags:* Same as above.
3. *Hoop:* Place on the floor and practice jumping over it, jumping in and out of it, or hopping around it.
4. *Skills:* As skills are taught, indicate one or two that can be practiced during this free practice time.

Since children in the intermediate grades have acquired many gymnastic skills, you need only to require that the children practice one or more of them as they enter the gymnasium:

1. *Balance stunts:* Practice a handstand, cartwheel, one-foot balance, and so on.
2. *Balls:* Require bouncing and change of direction (bounce, throw into air, and make a full turn of body before bouncing again).
3. *Partners:* Do not suggest free practice with partners until the class has demonstrated its ability to work independently in this type of atmosphere.

Individualized Teaching Patterns

The following two individualized teaching patterns allow the teacher to set challenges to meet the level of ability and interest of each member of the class. Task or challenge cards are extremely helpful to beginning teachers, since they can be prepared prior to each lesson. Further, once the class is working on its tasks, the teacher can move about the instructional area, providing assistance and encouragement where needed. The second teaching pattern, known as station work, not only allows for a variety of individualized teaching patterns but, in addition, is an effective method of using all available equipment.

organizing for physical education

Task, or Challenge, Cards

Task, or challenge, cards are an enjoyable way of individualizing game, dance, and gymnastic activities. The value of this technique is that the teacher can prepare a series of tasks, varying from simple to complex movement challenges, to adapt to the differences in ability that exist within a class of thirty or more. The examples provided illustrate how this technique can be applied to game, dance, and gymnastic activities.

Several examples of the application of tasks or challenges are found in later chapters. Refer specifically to chapters 26 and 27 for additional ideas.

Station Work

Station work is the establishment of a number of practice areas within the available instructional space. Students work at one assigned area for a set period of time, then rotate to the next station. Five or six children are assigned to a station for a few minutes to practice the preassigned skill, as shown in the diagram. When the whistle blows, each group rotates clockwise to the next station. This basic form of station work can be used to teach all game, rhythmic, and gymnastic activities. It is also particularly useful in developing physical fitness stations in the gymnasium or out-of-doors. Station work can also be combined with task cards. Combining these two teaching patterns is an excellent way to individualize the tasks for each child and provides valuable time for the teacher to move freely to stations where special help or praise may be needed.

Teaching Formations

Basic formations for organizing physical education activities are the *line, circle,* and *shuttle.* These patterns, shown in table 7.1, are used to divide classes into smaller groups

Challenge Cards

Inventive Games
(Partner Activities)
Make up a game with your partner that includes one ball, a bounce, and a catch.

Gymnastics
(Individual Sequences)
Make up a sequence that includes a stretch, a curl, and a change of direction.

Dance
(Rhythmic Activities: Group Work)
In your group of four, develop a routine that includes clapping, walking, hopping, and two changes in direction. (Music: ''Pluma Blanca'')

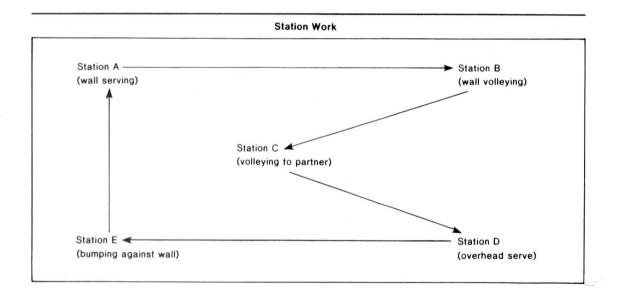

Station Work

Station A (wall serving)
Station B (wall volleying)
Station C (volleying to partner)
Station E (bumping against wall)
Station D (overhead serve)

Table 7.1 Basic Formations

Formation	Explanation	Uses
Circle (diagram of X's arranged in circle with Teacher or Leader marked)	Children may form a circle by following the teacher as she walks around in a circle. Other methods include all joining hands and forming a circle, or having the class take positions on a circle printed on the floor or play area.	Simple games Warm-up exercises Circle relays Teaching simple stunts Teaching basic dance steps Teaching throwing and kicking skills Marching Mimetics
Line (diagram of X's in a vertical line with Teacher or Leader marked)	Place one child for each line desired equidistant apart, then signal the class to line up behind these children. The first child in each line may move out in front of his line or shift to the side as illustrated.	Relays Simple games Marching Teaching stunts on floor or mats Roll taking Teaching basic skills
Fan (diagram of X's in half-circle with Teacher or Leader marked)	The fan formation is used for small group activities. Arrange children in a line facing their leader, then have them join hands and form a half-circle.	Throwing and kicking drills Relays Mimetics Simple floor stunts Teaching dance skills
Shuttle (diagram of X's numbered 6,4,2 and 1,3,5 with Teacher or Leader marked)	Arrange children in two, three, or more equal lines, then separate lines the distance required for the activity. Player 1 performs the skill, then shifts to the rear of the opposite line; player 2 performs and shifts to the rear of the opposite line, etc.	Throwing and kicking drills Relays Tumbling activities from opposite ends of mat Activities requiring close observation by teacher
Zigzag (diagram of X's numbered 1-6 in two lines with arrows, Teacher or Leader marked)	Arrange class or squads into two equal lines, with partners facing each other. Player 1 passes to 2, 2 passes to 3, 3 passes to 4, until the last player is reached.	Throwing, catching, and kicking skills
Scattered (diagram of scattered X's with Teacher or Leader marked)	Allow children to find a spot in the play area. Have each child reach out with his arms to see if he can touch another person. Require the children who can touch others to shift until they are free of obstructions.	Warm-up exercises Mimetics Tag games Simple floor stunts Creative activities

Table 7.2 Order of Team Selection by Captains

Round no.	Captain A	Captain B	Captain C	Captain D
1	1st choice	2nd choice	3rd choice	4th choice
2	8th choice	7th choice	6th choice	5th choice
3	9th choice	10th choice	11th choice	12th choice
4	16th choice	15th choice	14th choice	13th choice
5	17th choice	etc.		

for relays, team games, and drill exercises. Once learned, the patterns can be formed quickly and in an orderly manner at a simple command by the teacher. They save valuable practice and play time, eliminate confusion, and minimize the potential for accidents.

In many cases, the selection of a formation is determined by the activity itself. Running and tag games require a specific formation, and many folk dances begin with the children in a circle or line. Such activities as warm-up exercises, apparatus activities, and low-organization games can be performed from a variety of formations. However, two basic principles should be applied when selecting a formation. First, each squad should be aligned so that all members can see the performer. Second, the activities of one squad should not interfere with those of another.

Grouping Procedures

Grouping children in physical education classes is done by arranging them in squads according to their age, height, ability, or another criterion. The type of grouping technique a teacher selects depends on the activity and the performance levels of her class. For example, a third-grade teacher who wishes to organize the children into four teams for a relay could (1) arrange them into groups of two boys and two girls, (2) number the children from one to four, (3) have four captains choose their own teams, or (4) give every child a random number between 1 and 100, and select teams by pulling out random numbers from a hat. Since the third way is a common method for organizing equal teams, as well as fostering leadership and team loyalty, it is explained here in detail.

The teacher of the class selects four captains. To preclude favoritism, gender preferences, and emotional-social problems stemming from the order in which children are selected, the captains should meet with the teacher before class or, if in the gymnasium, away from the rest of the class. The teacher would explain the rules, then have the four teams selected in the following manner. As illustrated in table 7.2, captain A is awarded first choice; B, second; C, third; and D, fourth. At this point, tell each captain that, if his first choice is a boy, the next choice must be a girl; alternate boy and girl until the last member is chosen. Let us assume captain D selected a boy in round one and that captain D also has the next selection, which must be a girl.

Other methods of organizing children into squads should be used throughout the year to provide opportunities for children to work with different groups, as both leaders and followers. The method chosen will depend on the activity, the space, and the age of the children. Following are some methods:

1. Skill tests or observation of skill ability

2. Numbering off in twos, fives, or whatever other number of teams is desired

3. Arranging the class in a circle, then dividing it into the desired number of squads

4. Selecting teams on the basis of birth dates, for example:

   Team 1: children born between January and March

   Team 2: children born between April and June

   Team 3: children born between July and September

   Team 4: children born between October and December

Once children can effectively move into squads (or teams, groups, section places, or units), such groupings can be highly profitable to both the students and the teacher. From the teacher's point of view, the children can be organized quickly according to a particular criterion selected either by the teacher or jointly with the class.

The duties of the elected or assigned leader should include the following:

1. Maintaining order and general control of the squad

2. Checking routine procedures such as attendance, uniforms, and tardiness

3. Assisting the teacher in daily planning and lesson organizing

4. Setting an example of leadership

The inherent value of squads from a purely organizational standpoint cannot be overemphasized. However, every child should be given the opportunity to experience a leadership role. Whereas some students develop leadership ability in the early primary grades, others need encouragement and subtly planned experiences as leaders. Consequently, captains should be selected on a temporary basis so that each child can test his ability as a captain. There are always moments of frustration when young children are given leadership roles; therefore, both teachers and children must develop tolerance, understanding, and patience.

Routine Procedures

The success of any physical education program depends, to a large extent, on the simple routine procedures a class follows in going to, participating in, and returning from a physical education activity. Primary teachers usually are not confronted with the problems of showering; however, they are concerned with problems relating to changing clothes, class excuses, and class control. At the intermediate level, the teacher must solve problems of changing clothes, showering, and individual excuses.

Physical Education Apparel

Elementary school children usually are not required to wear special uniforms for physical education. The time required to change in relation to the time available, particularly for five-, six-, and seven-year-olds, does not justify a complete change. However, tennis shoes should be worn for games and some dance activities. For gymnastic activities, the teacher should seriously consider letting the children participate in bare feet if the floor is clean and free of hazards. Bare feet assist in balancing activities and encourage freedom of movement. However, this should be a gradual process to allow the children to get used to running, balancing, jumping, and landing on their bare feet. If the children enjoy participating in gymnastic activities with bare feet and there are no adverse effects (plantar warts or excessive bruising), continue the practice. Students should not be allowed to participate in physical activities wearing socks without shoes. Socks are very slippery on the floor or approaches and may lead to accidents or injuries.

Roll Call

Since physical education periods are usually too short anyway, don't lose time in the routine procedure of checking attendance. In most cases, roll call is not necessary in the primary grades, and, regardless of grade, the classroom teacher who is responsible for her own physical education program will know if any child is absent. However, when the use of specialist teachers or team teaching requires a roll-call procedure, the following methods can be used:

1. A line formation based on alphabetical list in the roll book
2. Squads, with one member assigned to take roll

Class Excuses

Excuses for physical education range from permanent waivers because of chronic health conditions to temporary waivers because of colds or other illnesses. It is imperative that the principal, the school nurse, and the teacher establish

Figure 7.2 A third area set aside for large playground apparatus.

policies covering problems encountered in this area. The following situations should be included in the policies:

1. A temporary excuse should be authorized by the school nurse.
2. The school nurse should authorize children to return to physical activity after any illness.
3. Children with disabilities should be encouraged to participate in physical education classes. The amount and type of participation should be indicated by the parents and/or family physician.
4. On the recommendation of the teacher, a child may be excused from participation in a physical education class because of a detectable illness or injury.

Facilities, Equipment, and Supplies

One of the most important considerations in the development of a comprehensive physical education program is the adequacy of facilities, equipment, and supplies. National standards regarding the size of the school property, outdoor play areas, gymnasia, and swimming pools provide guidelines for local districts and individual schools (Athletic Institute 1979). Beyond this point, however, it is the local community's responsibility, along with each school within its jurisdiction, to provide the facilities, equipment, and supplies required to meet the goals of the program. The following provides a basic coverage of these important considerations.

Outdoor Facilities

Elementary schools normally have three types of play areas. The first, open area, is designated for team games and track and field activities. A second facility, a hard surface area, is used for team games, such as volleyball and basketball, as well as for many activities such as four-square and hopscotch. Many schools also have a third area which is set aside for large playground apparatus (figure 7.2).

organizing for physical education

Figure 7.3 A variety of activities.

Open Area

Since the open area is used for running and tag games and team sports, such as soccer, softball, and track and field, it should be a flat turfed area. Lack of sufficient water supply may necessitate the surface to be dirt or another composition. Regardless of the type of surface, there should be good drainage and no hazardous objects such as automobiles, overhead wires, or other obstructions located on or near the playing area. Chalk lines, rather than sticks or permanent and protruding marks, should be used to mark playground lines. A safety zone should also be provided around the marked-off playing areas.

Hard Surface Area

The hard surface area is normally located near the school and is used for a variety of activities (figure 7.3). Part of this area usually has permanently marked-off courts for basketball and volleyball. The remaining surface area is normally covered with hopscotch, four-square, and other game patterns.

Playgrounds

Teachers who are serious about helping children become self-directing individuals capable of expressing themselves creatively must not only practice creative teaching strategies but must also see that the physical environment stimulates the creative process. In many schools, boxlike gymnasia and flat, unobstructive playing fields constitute the physical education facilities. Playground equipment normally includes swings, slides, and unattractive steel climbing apparatus encased in concrete and surrounded by asphalt, concrete, or sand. Although these apparatus may be easy to keep tidy, they are unimaginative and lack educational value.

Basic Criteria for Creative Playgrounds

The following nine criteria (Ledermann and Trachsel 1968) for creative playgrounds provide a guideline for evaluating existing playground facilities and constructing new ones (figure 7.4).

1. Playgrounds must be designed and equipped with their function for play foremost in mind. The playground should not be designed purely from the landscape gardener's aesthetic conception or the educator's concern for children's play habits and needs. It must serve the play characteristics of children and, at the same time, be aesthetic in the selection and arrangement of apparatus, pathways, and greenery.

2. Architects, landscape designers, and educators must work together to produce good solutions to playground problems. Architects, landscape designers, and educators tend to visualize the creative playground from their own points of view. Architects inject their bias toward artistic creations; landscape gardeners are more concerned with tree and flower arrangements than children's play activities; and educators often see the creative playground as an extension of the classroom. Each specialist must recognize the contributions of the others, so that each plan is seen as a cooperative effort.

3. The playground is not meant for passive entertainment. It must encourage active, spontaneous, and creative play. The creative playground should not be a simple collection of commercial equipment, old cars, or concrete tunnels arranged in parallel rows. The apparatus, whether natural or commercial, should

Figure 7.4 Imaginative playground equipment is planned on the basis of its safety and the practical value it has for the children.

Figure 7.5 Playground materials are available locally.

be selected and arranged to stimulate the child's imagination and enhance continuous exploration.

4. Half-finished components and materials for play are more valuable than mechanical equipment. Most playgrounds are dominated by inflexible apparatus such as slides, swings, and a variety of rotary-type equipment. It is not suggested that slides and swings be removed, but that consideration be given to including more creative and, if possible, natural equipment such as large roots of trees or other materials that are available in the local area (figure 7.5).

5. Playground design and equipment must conform to the typical games of the age group for which the playground is intended. In most cases, creative playgrounds are first seen as an addition to the primary school playground area. Children from age five to eight thoroughly enjoy playing on or around a creative playground. Intermediate children appear to be more sophisticated; however, experience shows that children of this age level are equally interested in using creative equipment. Thus, plans should consider the full age range in the elementary school.

6. The playground design must reflect the functions and movements of different games. This involves the total play area of the school. For example, an elementary school playground serves both primary and intermediate children. Consequently, the creative

playground area should be away from the main ball game areas. If the school is near an area with trees, a ravine, or any type of natural area, the creative playground should be put near this site. Of course, safety must be considered; natural areas that are potentially hazardous should not be considered desirable locations.

7. Games of fantasy should not be overlooked. Some children enjoy playing by themselves. Therefore, the creative playground, particularly for primary children, should provide small individual areas on or near apparatus where children can absorb themselves in fantasy or other forms of individual self-expression.

8. Architects and landscape designers should "play" a little while designing the creative playground. The specialists should observe children at play and attempt to visualize the potential area through "the eyes of a child." The designer who does this would not build a square sandbox, place a slide in the middle of an area with slopes and contours, or place equipment in straight lines. Relevance, too, is important. A creative playground near a coast should be representative of the area, with "ships" and "trees"—natural or synthetic—in the general play area. Similar themes for the South and Midwest should be present in the creative playground.

9. Interested groups of people should cooperate in designing, equipping, and maintaining a playground. The majority of creative playgrounds that have been constructed in Canada and the United States are the results of cooperative parent-teacher groups that wished to do something for local school children. Initially, such projects were undertaken because of the lack of tax money to construct this type of outdoor facility. This cooperative action has given the parents an understanding of the value and purpose of such

Figure 7.6 A well-designed gymnasium.

planning new facilities, use of this publication is advisable as a basic reference for nationally acceptable standards of gymnasium construction.

There are, however, recommendations relating to floor dimensions, placement of equipment, and general safety that apply to any gymnasia or multipurpose room that is used for physical education. The following suggestions will assist teachers in organizing an indoor facility for maximum use and optimum safety:

1. Maintain gymnasium temperature between sixty and sixty-five degrees.
2. Paint permanent boundary lines on the floor for activities held most often. Use different colored lines for each—black for basketball, red for volleyball, and green for a large center circle.
3. Provide adequate safety margins for all games. The standard basketball dimensions for elementary school children are seventy-four by forty-two feet. If the facility is only seventy by forty feet, the actual court dimensions should be sixty-seven by thirty-seven feet to provide a minimum three-foot safety zone around the court.
4. Remove all equipment that is not being used during the physical education class.
5. Request that any hazardous fixtures, such as floor-level heating ducts and lighting fixtures, be covered with protective screens.
6. Establish a standard procedure for obtaining and returning equipment to the storage room.

playgrounds and has also significantly reduced the amount of vandalism, as parents and children consider these jointly built facilities community property, and not just for use during school hours.

Indoor Facilities

Physical education can be taught in several locations within a typical elementary school. In geographical areas where there is a need for an indoor facility, gymnasia are normally designed as multipurpose facilities for assemblies, cafeteria lunches, and physical education. In most instances, a single multipurpose room is not sufficient for all classes on a daily basis or even two or three times per week. Other events, such as assemblies, plays, and concerts, too often take precedence over physical education. As a consequence, other areas of the school, such as the classroom, library and hallway, can be used for limited game, dance, gymnastic, and fitness activities. The creative use of each type of indoor facility provides the teacher with several important options for her instructional program.

Gymnasium

The location, size, and special features of the multipurpose room and/or gymnasium should be determined by the philosophy and activities of the physical education program (figure 7.6). Often, incorrect planning results in inadequate court dimensions, low ceilings, and avoidable hazards or obstructions. To help eliminate mistakes in the planning and construction of future elementary school gymnasia, national leaders in the field of health and physical education have developed a guide, *Planning Facilities for Athletics, Physical Education and Recreation* (Athletic Institute 1979). Included in this guide are standard recommendations for floor construction, playing space, storage facilities, and numerous other aspects of a well-planned gymnasium. When

Classroom

In many elementary schools throughout the country, the only available space indoors for physical education is the classroom. Although this is inadequate, some minor furniture adjustments can make the classroom suitable for many different physical activities (see chapter 14). By shifting movable desks and tables, one area of the classroom can be made free of obstructions (figure 7.7). Since most lighting and window fixtures in the classroom are not screened, do not permit activities that in any way create a potentially hazardous situation. Adjustable and movable bars may be placed in doorways, mats can be used for tumbling activities, and four-by-four-inch beams and chairs can be used for balance activities.

Library, Hallway, and Other Locations

The importance of daily physical education has been recognized by parents, teachers, physicians, and other related professional organizations. As a consequence, efforts are being made in many schools throughout the nation to use other large areas of the school in addition to the gymnasium for a variety of physical activities. The primary purpose of the library is obviously to store and use written and audiovisual resources. However, carpeted library floors are a very desirable surface

Figure 7.7 Some minor furniture adjustments can make the classroom suitable for many physical activities.

for gymnastic and creative dance activities. Creative scheduling, coupled with the use of chairs and tables, can provide an adequate teaching area, particularly for primary-level children. Discussions with the principal and the librarian can often lead to opening this room to physical education when it is not being used for library purposes.

In a similar way, the hallway can be used for some game activities such as shufflecurl, hopscotch, and four-square. This area can also be used for a variety of fitness activities and, to a lesser extent, some gymnastic activities. The main problem in using the hallway relates to disturbing adjacent classrooms. Once again, working with teachers in nearby classrooms or creative scheduling can lead to a more open use of the hallway. For example, if teachers in adjacent rooms can schedule the gymnasium and library for the same time, the hallway will become a place another teacher can use with a little more freedom and with a slightly higher acceptable noise level of her class.

Basic Equipment and Supplies

Physical education equipment refers to permanent apparatus such as balance beams and outdoor play apparatus. Generally speaking, these materials last from five to twenty years, even with repeated use. Supplies, on the other hand, are expendable items such as balls, whistles, and tapes. These items last one to two years. Each teacher should list the proper equipment for her grade level and, where budgets are limited, suggest how to make various types of equipment. (See appendix B for diagrams of inexpensive equipment. See appendix C for a list of commercial manufacturers and distributors of equipment and supplies.)

The type of physical education program, the geographic area, and economic conditions, among other things, determine the type of equipment a school will buy. The following suggestions will assist in ordering the proper type and size of equipment and supplies.

Recommended Playground Equipment

Climbing apparatus: climbing cubes, Big Toy apparatus, etc.

Horizontal bar: "chinning" or "turning bar" at three levels—48, 54, and 64 inches—all 5 feet wide

Horizontal ladder: 6½ feet high, length optional

Balance beam: 8 to 12 feet long, three levels—18, 24, or 48 inches with alternate surface of 4 inches and 2 inches

Tetherball standards: minimum of three

Basketball standards: minimum of two; 8 feet high (heavy duty construction)

Volleyball standards: minimum of two with adjustable height

Softball backboards: minimum of two

Soccer goalposts: minimum of two

Creative playground apparatus: see p. 119

Sandbox: 6 × 10 feet, with cover

Track and field equipment: long jump pit, high jump pit and standards, hurdles

Tug-of-war rope

Optional and Homemade Equipment

Automobile tires: suspended on rope or chain, with bottom of line 12 to 14 inches off ground

Movable barrows and kegs

Movable planks: 8 to 12 feet long, with planed edges

Sawhorses: different heights

Concrete sewer pipes: arranged in units of three or four

Obstacle courses: permanent or portable; type and construction should complement the climate and geographic area; see chapter 12

Recommended Indoor Equipment

Tumbling mats: minimum of four; light synthetic material; sizes are optional, although 4 × 7 foot mats are easy to handle and store

Individual mats: 18 × 36 × ¾ inches; minimum of forty, or one per child

Record player (three speeds)

Tape recorder

Dance drum

Balance beam: 1 to 4 feet high, depending on general use, and approximately 12 feet long

Balance benches: reversible for optional use (2 inch and 4 inch sides), plus hook attachment on one end

Horizontal bar: see appendix B

Scooters: 12 × 12 inches with four casters

Volleyball net and standards: adjustable heights

Basketball standards: adjustable heights

Climbing ropes: 15 to 20 feet high; 1½ to 2 inches in diameter

Vaulting box: see appendix B

organizing for physical education

Set of jumping boxes: see appendix B
Springboard or mini-tramp
Sawhorses: minimum of six
Portable agility apparatus: see chapter 27
Hockey nets: two
Cargo nets
Supply cart
Climbing frame

Recommended Supplies

The number of items listed here is a suggested minimum based on a maximum of thirty children using the supplies during one physical education period. If two or more classes meet at the same time, double or triple the number.

Supplies	Minimum number
General supplies: (all areas of program)	
Ball inflater with gauge	1
Balloons	60–100
Braids (cloth)	30
Clipboards	4
Hoops (36-inch and 42-inch)	30–40
Indian clubs or bowling pins	24–30
Measuring tape (50 feet)	1
Parachutes	2
Plastic tape (1-inch, 1½-inch, and 2-inch)	2 rolls of each
Stopwatches	6
Tote bags	10–15
Traffic cones	10–15
Whistles	6–8
Yardsticks	6–8
Dance supplies	
Audiotapes (see part 7)	
Dance drums	6–8
Lummi sticks	60–80
Percussion instruments (castanets, tambourines, bells, etc.)	4 of each
Records (see part 7)	
Tinikling poles	12–16
Game supplies	
Beach balls (12-inch and 16-inch)	6 of each
Beanbags (6 inches × 6 inches, assorted colors)	40–60
Basketballs (junior size)	30
Basketballs (standard size)	30
Basketball nets	6–8
Cageballs (24-inch)	5–10
Colored arm bands	2 sets of 15
Compasses	4–6
Deck tennis rings	10–15

Earth balls	2
Eye-glass protectors	6–8
Field hockey sticks	30–40
Field hockey balls	30
Floor hockey sticks	30–40
Floor hockey pucks	6–8
Fleece balls	40
Footballs (junior size)	10–15
Frisbees	15–20
Gymnasium scooters	30
Horseshoe sets	4–6
Jacks	60
Juggling scarves	90
Juggling bags	90
Nerf balls	15–30
Paddles (tennis, etc.)	30
Repair kit for balls	1
Scoops	30–40
Softballs	10–15
Softball bases	8–10
Softball gloves	10–15
Softball hats	10–15
Softball catcher masks and body protectors	2 of each
Softball batting tees	10–15
Sponge or tennis balls	40–50
Soccer balls (rubber)	30
Utility balls (6½-inch, 8½-inch, and 10½-inch)	10 of each
Volleyballs (rubber)	30
Volleyball nets	4–6
Tetherball sets	6–8
Track and field equipment (batons, crossbars, starter, etc.)	
Gymnastic supplies	
Blocks (4 inches × 4 inches × 1 foot)	15–20
Individual ropes (⅜-inch sash, nylon, or plastic; 10 each of 6, 7, 7½, and 8 feet)	1 set of 40
Long ropes (⅝-inch sash, nylon, or plastic; 13, 14, and 15 feet)	3 of each
Wands (10 each at 3, 3½, 4, and 4½ feet)	1 set of 40
Testing supplies	
Skinfold calipers (plastic)	3–5
Sit and reach boxes	3
Optional and homemade supplies	
Automobile tires	6–8
Assorted small barrels (for dance drums)	

Broom handles	10–15
Rubber bands (cut from inner tubes)	40–60
Shuffleboard supplies	3 sets
Stilts	10–20 pairs
Targets (various sizes)	
Tool chest (saw, hammer, etc.)	
Walking board	1
Walking cans	60

Care and Maintenance of Equipment and Supplies

Because equipment and supplies represent a large expenditure of money, they should be stored, used, and maintained in an effective and prudent manner. The following suggestions should be incorporated into each school's policies and procedures for handling equipment and supplies.

1. All apparatus, equipment, and supplies should be permanently marked with a number and school identification.

2. Each school should establish a set of rules and procedures for handing out and returning equipment and supplies.

3. All apparatus, equipment, and supplies should be checked before they are issued. Any broken equipment should not be issued; it should be repaired as soon as possible and returned to the storage room. Worn-out equipment should be discarded, as it leads to poor skill development and potential accidents.

4. Inflate all balls according to the recommended pressure. Place a chart near the ball inflator and adhere strictly to the recommended pressure for each inflated ball. Store balls during the off-season in a partially inflated shape.

5. Store all materials according to recommended standards.

6. Design your equipment room to permit easy and efficient access to all materials.

7. Each school should make a complete inventory of all physical education materials at the beginning and end of each season. Records of how well such items as rubber volleyballs, mats, and skipping ropes perform will aid in future replacement or purchase policies.

8. When ordering materials, always write out the specifications, such as brand name, size, and required options. If materials are ordered through a central purchasing department, it is extremely important to state the specifications and add "or its equivalent." The latter will guarantee the purchase of a quality item rather than a cheaper, but inferior, second- or third-choice item.

Construction of Inexpensive Equipment and Supplies

Equipment and supplies should be purchased from commercial firms whenever possible. Normally, school districts have clear-cut purchasing policies each school must adhere to. If not, the principal and teaching staff should develop a purchasing plan to secure new equipment and supplies and to provide funds to replace and maintain existing inventory.

If local funds are not available, some equipment can be constructed by interested parents. Appendix B contains examples of locally constructed equipment and supplies. It is strongly recommended that all such homemade equipment be constructed with the best available materials. Furthermore, such equipment should be checked by school maintenance personnel for quality construction and safety before it is used in the program.

Selected References

Athletic Institute. (1979). *Planning Facilities for Athletics, Physical Education and Recreation,* Revised Edition. Reston, VA: AAHPERD.

Bruya, L. D. (Ed.). (1988). *Play Spaces for Children: A New Beginning.* Reston, VA: AAHPERD.

Ellis, M., and Neilson, A. B. (1980). *Play Things.* Willowdale, Ontario: John Degill Co.

Hall, T. (1984). *Inexpensive Movement Material.* Bryon, CA: Front Row Experience.

Ledermann, A., and Trachsel, A. (1968). *Creative Playgrounds and Recreation Centers,* Second Edition. New York: Praeger Publishers.

Moore, R. E., Goltsman, S. M., and Iacofano, D. S. (Eds.). (1987). *Play for All Guidelines: Planning, Design and Management of Outdoor Play Settings for All Children.* Berkeley, CA: MIG Communications.

Stillwell, J. L. (1987). *Making and Using Creative Play Equipment.* Champaign, IL: Human Kinetics Publishers, Inc.

U.S. Consumer Product Safety Commission. (1986). *A Handbook for Public Playground Safety, Vols. I and II.* Washington, DC: U.S. Consumer Product Safety Commission.

Werner, P. H., and Simmons, R. A. (1990). *Homemade Play Equipment for Children,* Reston, VA: AAHPERD.

Using Teaching Strategies and Techniques

Contemporary teaching in the elementary school emphasizes concept development rather than the simple acquisition of knowledge. Accompanying this emphasis is an effort to individualize and personalize the learning process in response to individual differences and to provide a learning atmosphere that enhances positive relationships. Helping children achieve their full intellectual, physical, and creative potential can be done only through an informal learning atmosphere, in which the responsibility for learning is shared by the teacher and child.

Children learn new skills and concepts when they are capable of exploring alternatives. This means they must have a goal, some uncertainty as to how to reach it, and the ability and motivation to attempt to reach it. The essential duties of the teacher of physical education, as with all subjects, are to provide learning tasks that are within each child's reach and to give continuous encouragement and assistance through the learning process.

The many skills and movement concepts of physical education cannot be learned through one approach, however. Each new learning situation must be tailored to the varying degrees of interest and skill found in a class of twenty-five or more young learners. There is no ideal style of teaching, no single set of concepts or learning principles, and no best motivational technique that will guarantee success. The teacher should draw from the areas discussed in this chapter to develop effective styles of teaching, sound motivational techniques, and effective ways of creating good classroom control and positive student behavior ■

Teaching Strategies

The broad goals of physical education, the characteristics of children, and the knowledge of how and why children learn through the medium of physical activities have significantly changed our approach to teaching. Teaching is no longer considered a simplistic form of cohort instruction (AAHPERD 1976), with the teacher teaching the same material to all children in the same way. Differences in each child's maturation, potential ability, and interests have shifted teaching strategies toward more individualized and personalized forms of learning.

Individualized Learning

Individualized learning is based on the premise that teaching should be adapted to the unique abilities and special needs of the learner. This places the learner, not the subject, at the center of the curriculum and teaching (figure 8.1). It must be understood that a teacher who provides individual assistance to one or more children in a class of thirty or more is applying a technique and is in no way teaching an individualized instructional program.

Individualized learning occurs only when there is a sequential plan for every child, including a diagnosis of the child's potential ability and a teaching prescription to develop that potential. True individualization is possible when there is a ratio of one teacher to one child. However, for groups of two or more children with varying degrees of ability, rarely is a true individualized instructional program ever achieved.

The term *individualized instruction* in physical education refers to a process that adjusts the learning to the student. Such a program usually takes two approaches. The first is to vary the time it takes the children to achieve a specific movement task. For example, we can ask three children with varying levels of ability to walk across a narrow balance beam, allowing each child to complete the task in his own time. However, when the task is structured, and the child does not possess the ability to accomplish it regardless of the time given him, this is an exercise in futility. The second approach is to vary the task and, if necessary, the time. Allowing each child to cross the length of the balance beam in any way possible would be varying the task. If a teacher can vary the task, she can provide an individualized program.

Personalized Learning

Personalized learning is a version of individualized learning in which the student's involvement with others in the learning environment is used or emphasized. This may involve the learner in a guider-learner relationship with the teacher, or it may involve learner with learner in a shared experience characterized by mutual trust and respect. Personalizing the learning process enhances the dignity and self-image of each child and creates a learning atmosphere that increases the efficiency of learning by each child.

Figure 8.1 The learner, not the subject, is the center of the curriculum in an individualized instructional program.

Primary and intermediate teachers can individualize and personalize their teaching in several ways. The following section on styles of teaching provides methods that allow the task to be varied and that provide a learning environment that encourages children to share their ideas and creative talents. These approaches also allow all children to progress at their own rate and level of ability, to feel at ease, and to experience success with the task at hand.

Styles of Teaching

A review of contemporary books in elementary school physical education indicates there is no general agreement as to what constitutes an approach, a style, or a method of teaching. In this text, an approach and a style of teaching are considered to be synonymous. They are, in essence, general ways of guiding and controlling the learning experiences of children. In figure 8.2, there are three general styles of teaching derived from Mosston's original spectrum of teaching styles (Mosston 1981). These three general approaches are based on the amount of freedom or choice given to the students in a particular learning task. Each style, described in the following paragraphs, emphasizes one or more methods when teaching movement concepts or skills or when fostering the development of positive behavioral traits. At times, teachers stress the command or task method, whereas, in other situations, the nature of learning requires the more exploratory methods within the combined or indirect teaching styles.

Direct Teaching Style

Direct styles of teaching are classified as teacher-centered because of the way the teacher handles various aspects of the learning process. Within the command and task

Figure 8.2 Three general teaching styles.

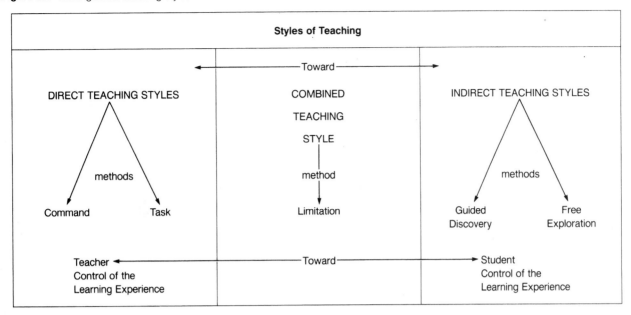

Styles of Teaching

Toward

DIRECT TEACHING STYLES

COMBINED TEACHING STYLE

INDIRECT TEACHING STYLES

methods

method

methods

Command   Task

Limitation

Guided Discovery   Free Exploration

Teacher Control of the Learning Experience   Toward   Student Control of the Learning Experience

---

Table 8.1 Command Method

Aspects of learning	Teacher	Learner
Sets objectives	X	
Chooses content	X	
Chooses methods	X	
Chooses evaluation	X	

Figure 8.3 Teaching the forward roll is a direct method because the choice of the activity and how it is performed are controlled by the teacher.

methods, teachers decide what objectives are to be accomplished, what the content will be, how children should perform, and how they should be evaluated. The characteristics and general applications of each method are described here.

Command Method

The command method of teaching, as described by Mosston (Mosston 1981), is characterized by the teacher making all the decisions in the learning episode (see table 8.1). For example, the teacher arranges the class in lines or in a circle, chooses the activity (such as practicing a basketball chest pass), and prescribes how and where each child will practice the movement. Use of the command method is illustrated in teaching the forward roll (figure 8.3).

1. *Class organization:* The class is scattered or arranged in parallel lines facing a mat, with each child working within her own area. The essential aspect is that all children watch a demonstration and then practice the skill.

2. *Choice of activity:* In this example, the children are restricted to practicing the forward roll. The choice is the teacher's.

Student participation in choosing the activity and how it should be practiced is limited in this method. However, it is the most effective and efficient way, for example, to teach a specific movement skill, a safety procedure, or the rules of a game. Also, when the general level of skill is low, such as for heading in soccer or performing a headstand in gymnastics, the command method is appropriate for illustrating,

Table 8.2	Task Method		
Aspects of learning	**Teacher**	**Learner**
Sets objectives	X	
Chooses content	X	
Chooses methods		X
Chooses evaluation	X	

Table 8.3	Combined Teaching Style		
Aspects of learning	**Teacher**	**Learner**
Sets objectives	X	
Chooses content	X	X
Chooses methods	X	X
Chooses evaluation	X	X

Figure 8.4 Completing a basketball task within a station.

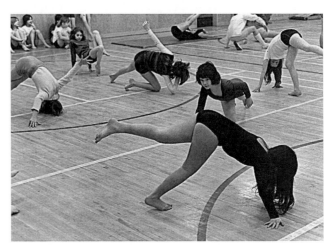

Figure 8.5 Combined teaching style. "Can you balance on three parts of your body?"

clarifying, and practicing various aspects of a skill or movement. In addition, this method can be used to regain control and direction when class discipline is low.

Task Method

The task method is very similar to the command method of teaching in several important aspects. In this way of teaching, the teacher sets the objectives, chooses what should be learned, and evaluates the amount and quality of learning by an individual or a group of learners. An important change for the learner is that the learning task can be graduated from beginner to advanced levels of performance for each skill. It also provides for variations in the time different learners need to acquire the same skill (see table 8.2). An example would be to establish a basketball skill circuit involving dribbling, passing, and shooting skills. All skills would first be explained and demonstrated, and then each student would attempt each task according to his own level of ability (figure 8.4). Task cards would be used by each student to record scores at each station. This method of teaching recognizes individual differences in levels of ability and in different rates of learning motor skills. In addition, it

provides for maximum participation. Finally, this way of teaching allows partners to work together in observing and evaluating each other's skill performance.

Combined Teaching Style

The combined teaching style has come to be known in elementary physical education as the limitation method of teaching. The choice of the activity or how it is performed is limited by the teacher. With this approach, children are given freedom to perform the movement or task in their own way, and at their own pace (see table 8.3). For example, when teaching a forward roll, the teacher might limit the performance by indicating that the forward roll be practiced on the floor or on mats, but, by posing a challenge, such as "practice the forward roll and see how many variations in leg positions you can make," some freedom of interpretation is provided. This freedom is a basic characteristic of the combined style of teaching. Figure 8.5 illustrates this freedom of interpretation.

The combined teaching style has the greatest application and value in virtually all areas of the physical education program. For example, when teaching dance, a

Figure 8.6 "Can you balance on one foot?"

Table 8.4 Indirect Teaching Style

Aspects of learning	Teacher	Learner
Sets objectives	X	
Chooses content	X	X
Chooses method		X
Chooses evaluation	X	X

primary teacher might use the command method initially to teach a skip or gallop step. Once the step has been learned, the limitation method may be applied by providing musical accompaniment and allowing the children to move in any direction to create individual or dual patterns. The single limitation might be that the children use a skip movement.

A few of the more obvious advantages of this style of teaching follow:

1. It allows the teacher to give some direction without restricting the children's free or creative expressions.
2. It allows for physical differences and varying interests of the children.
3. Through a careful choice of activities, it allows the teacher to develop all aspects of movement rather than what might become a "one-sided" development if left solely to each child.
4. Analysis and correction of movement by the teacher is simplified because one type of movement is to be practiced.

One problem that virtually all teachers must overcome when using this style of teaching is being able to shift from *directing* children to perform a movement to *guiding* them through suggestions and challenging questions (figure 8.6). Although each teacher develops her own technique of asking questions, the following phrases and words have proved quite successful:

Can you make a . . . ?

Can you discover a new . . . ?

Can you add to this by . . . ?

Can you find another way of . . . ?

Can you add a different way to . . . ?

Can you vary your . . . ?

Can you improve on the . . . ?

Could you move from . . . ?

Could you shift . . . ?

Could you change . . . ?

Try to add on to . . .

Try to vary . . .

How many different ways . . . ?

Are you able to . . . ?

See if you can . . .

Attempt to do . . .

Is it possible to . . . ?

Discover a new way to . . .

Avoid the words "I want you to do . . ." The key words should stimulate a creative interpretation of a task or challenge. Once you have posed the question, it is usually necessary to give a command to start. Probably the most common, and informal, beginning is "off" or "away you go." Children react extremely well to this type of comment. Other expressions are "and begin" or "start."

Indirect Teaching Style

An indirect teaching style is an approach that allows children degrees of freedom in the choice of an activity, how it should be performed or practiced, and at times how it should be evaluated. This style includes methods of teaching that require the teacher to shift from being a director of the learning experience to being a guide (table 8.4). The following methods also dramatically change the role of the learners; they become increasingly more responsible, creative, and self-directed through the application of these methods.

Guided Discovery Method

This is a sequential series of challenges and observations that leads toward an understanding of predetermined objectives. For example, a third-grade teacher is teaching a three-week gymnastic unit. The main objective of lesson 3 is to teach children that a stable balance position depends on a wide and low base of support. Her first challenge, as shown

Figure 8.7 Guided discovery method.

in figure 8.7, is "Can you balance on one foot?" From this point on, the teacher would observe the class, then present another challenge that would clarify the meaning of these fundamental principles of balance.

In this method of teaching, children are encouraged to use their creative powers to answer each movement challenge. It is a method that allows all children to move at their own rates and levels of ability and understanding. Also, it is a method that allows the teacher to use her knowledge and observational skills in a continuous process of guiding each learner toward a predetermined objective (table 8.5).

Free Exploration Method

This is what Mosston called the "Divergent Style." This method shifts the major responsibility of the learning task and how it should be performed to the learner. Here the teacher simply sets the stage by presenting a general direction or challenge, such as "use small equipment" or "work on flow." The use and ultimate success of this method depend on a gradual shift from direct to indirect methods of teaching. Through this process, children gradually learn to be self-directed learners who show care and concern for their own safety as well as for the other children in the class (figure 8.8).

Techniques of Good Teaching

A review of effective teaching practices in physical education has indicated several key teaching behaviors, which provide a valuable framework for teaching physical education activities to elementary school children.

Structure the Lesson

Structuring refers to helping children organize where the lesson content fits into their learning experiences. Too often in physical education we see children leave the gymnasium or class without understanding why they had to do a particular activity. Structuring is clearly explaining to children why the content of the lesson is being covered and where this fits into

Table 8.5 Guided Discovery Method

Aspects of learning	Teacher	Learner
Sets objectives		X
Chooses content		X
Chooses methods		X
Chooses evaluation	X	X

their learning experiences. Explaining why practices are necessary and why that particular practice has been scheduled and how it connects with the next activity helps make the connecting "links" for the child. A child's community play outside of school usually consists of playing the game, not sequentially practicing skills. Further, many children only see their sports heroes on television or at the ball park, for example. They only see their role models playing the game; rarely do they see the hours of practice that precede the actual event. Hence, children do not make the natural connection between practice and performing; too frequently the teacher hears, "When are we going to play the game?" Apart from pointing out the connection, a school field trip to a professional sport team's practice can be a worthwhile event. Planning and organizing children's learning experiences through structured connections is an essential component of effective teaching. As the old adage says, "Transfer should be sought and taught."

In addition to making connections for students, there is a need for classroom structure and routine, which establishes an environment in which students learn how the teacher will manage the class. It is a process that involves organizing equipment and facilities, establishing routine procedures, and setting codes of behavior. It includes teaching students when to ask questions, telling them how much talking and independent behavior is permissible, and acquainting them with many other day-to-day operational procedures. Once children understand and appreciate the teacher's format of teaching and her fair and consistent ways of handling routine procedures, an on-going positive

chapter 8

Figure 8.8 Children gradually learn to become self-directed learners.

student-teacher rapport is assured, along with effective and efficient use of the instructional time. If a teacher can establish the following structure and basic routine procedures within the first month of the school year, she will have begun the process of effective class management.

1. Procedure for changing and entering the gymnasium or playing area
2. Procedure for getting out and returning equipment (class and extra class time)
3. Procedures for establishing a safe environment
4. Procedure for handling accidents
5. Method of stopping children in order to give instructions (use of whistle, hand signal, etc.)
6. General form of teaching, including the lesson format, the procedure for children to ask questions, and the use of teaching formations
7. Method of selecting leaders and monitors
8. Ways in which praise and punishment are used
9. Method of integrating children with disabilities into the program

Teachers should check for student understanding. It cannot be assumed when instructions are verbally given that all children will clearly understand the information. Developing effective questioning strategies, covered later in this chapter, is an important consideration when checking for student understanding. Task cards involving both written instructions and diagrams will help supplement verbal instructions, as will demonstrations and modeling.

Provide Variety within Each Lesson

Instructional variety refers to the variability or flexibility of delivery during a lesson. Variety has been linked to student attention; if students don't attend to practices and instructions, little learning is likely to occur. Studies have also shown that there is less disruptive behavior when more varied activities and materials are used. It should be remembered that variety does not mean constantly changing, without regard for learning. Teachers need to plan for variety with learning in mind. The following suggestions will help plan for variety with units and lessons.

1. Use stations to set up a variety of activities. For example, if teaching basketball skills, passing activities can take place in one station, dribbling in another, shooting in a third, a two versus two game in a fourth, a creative basketball game in a fifth, and a variation involving a passing and shooting practice in the sixth.
2. Bring out a selection of equipment. For example, provide children with different sized and colored balls when teaching throwing and catching skills. In general, children learn faster when they choose the size and color of the ball.
3. During creative dance activities, use props such as scarves, ribbons, and wands. Provide a variety of music to match the themes being taught.

Monitor Time On-Task

Time on-task is the amount of learning time devoted to the task. As soon as a teacher has established her format and procedures for effective class management, she can begin to develop a teaching strategy that will keep her students on-task. This includes planning well-organized and appropriate units and lessons, using good observational practices, and applying effective motivational techniques. Time on-task (engagement) is a very important learning variable. It should be noted that the teacher may be task oriented but the child may be disengaged. A teacher must monitor for engagement and plan to achieve maximum time on-task. The following general guidelines are important in maintaining a task-oriented atmosphere.

1. Develop lessons that are adaptable to individual levels of ability and interest, that is, developmentally appropriate.
2. Provide opportunities for every child to experience and learn how to develop self-directed techniques.
3. Develop an effective observational plan that includes observation of specific types of behavior or skills and a procedure to carry this out and record the information.
4. Develop an ability to allow for changes in pace and content within a lesson while still moving toward the main objectives.
5. Develop the knowledge and skills necessary to apply the appropriate type and amount of feedback to individuals and groups of students.
6. Try to eliminate line-ups to use equipment. Careful planning and organization will help alleviate waiting.

For example, provide each child with his own equipment (e.g., a ball each), and organize gymnastic stations so that equipment is not in a straight line. Using star shapes and other creative designs where children can have multiple entries onto, through, and around the gymnastic apparatus will allow all the children to work at the same time. Teachers should also reflect on their organizational time to determine the most efficient practices for getting children started as quickly as possible. These practices will assist in getting children engaged in the learning process.

Provide for Success in Each Learning Task

Success rate is the rate at which a child understands and correctly completes activities. In physical education it is quite common to see a teacher move on to the next practice before a child has correctly completed the first activity. The teacher must organize and plan instruction that will yield moderate to high success rates for all children. Observing and monitoring children's progress is very important since achieving success is not only essential for motivation and learning, but has been linked to higher-level problem solving and critical thinking. The following guidelines will help teachers organize successful experiences for all children.

1. Set up a variety of different stations where children can work on activities designed for their level of development. Children can be organized on the basis of ability level (developmental standing) to maximize success rate. Planning developmentally appropriate activities to match children's ability levels with the activities they are engaged in will assist in providing success.
2. Once children experience success they should be challenged to be creative, to problem solve, and to go beyond their current levels of performance. For example, in gymnastics, after a child completes a gymnastic stunt such as the backward roll, a challenge might be given to see how many different variations in leg movement he can achieve. Or when a child has practiced several individual gymnastic stunts, he can be challenged to create a sequence that includes all of the individual stunts.

Use Student Ideas and Contributions

Apart from involving children in their own learning experiences, using students' ideas and contributions establishes the lesson content within the context of their world, within their own "lived experience." They become part of the learning enterprise, have a degree of ownership, and are motivated since they contributed to the learning endeavor. Whenever possible, a teacher should strive to incorporate student ideas and contributions into the lesson. A teacher will find the creative dance activities in chapter 30 and the creative and cooperative games described in chapter 17 helpful since these activities involve using student ideas and contributions in an effective way. The following suggestions will also be of help.

1. Try to understand and incorporate the student's point of view. As human beings, we normally see each situation from our own perspective. For example, when we teach a dance skill, such as the waltz step, we tend to see it as a motor skill that is performed in three-quarter rhythm and as a dance skill that children enjoy when they pair off to dance. A child who is shy, who is from a culture where girls and boys don't dance together, or who particularly dislikes dance, has a different perspective of the dance activity. The essential point is to try to find out the different attitudes that exist in the class, then adjust to cope with some of the more important ones.
2. Learn to understand and improve listening skills. The preceding guidelines are primarily designed to improve a teacher's ability to communicate knowledge, skills, and attitudes to the learner. Of equal, if not more, importance in the learning process, is the ability to receive messages from students. Few people, however, are good listeners, particularly in listening seriously to what children want to say or in reading many of their important nonverbal messages. The following are some ways of improving receiving skills: (a) paraphrase or restate what a child has said and include hidden messages or feelings you may have detected; (b) use effective nonverbal listening gestures such as looking directly at the student, leaning slightly forward, and showing you are attentive by not doing something else as you listen; (c) try to understand and adjust to your own feelings that may affect how you interpret the student's message; and (d) try to be open, honest, and consistent with all students regardless of their skill level or color, or any other social or interpersonal characteristic.

Communicate Effectively

Effective communication is one of the most important skills a teacher must understand and use. In every learning situation, effective communication between the teacher and a student or group of students is a continuous, two-way process of exchanging knowledge, skills, ideas, and feelings (figure 8.9). The teacher's task is to be able to communicate what is to be learned, how it should be learned, and what quality of performance is expected from each student. For example, when teaching the class how to dribble a soccer ball, the teacher has to communicate to every child how the skill is to be performed. This may involve verbally pointing out the main parts of the skill as each student dribbles the ball. At this stage in the process, the learners must be able to ask questions,

Figure 8.9 A two-way process of exchanging knowledge, skills, ideas, and feelings.

Figure 8.10 Use facial expressions or movements to express ideas and feelings.

to seek clarification, and to express their feelings verbally or nonverbally about what is to be learned. As this process continues, the teacher must be able to draw on effective communication skills and strategies and to keep all children on-task and striving toward their highest level of achievement. To accomplish this goal, the teacher needs to develop a set of guidelines she can use to help her communicate with every child in the class. If the following guidelines are adhered to, effective communication between the teacher and her class can be reasonably assured.

1. Use such pronouns as *I, my,* and *mine* to establish personal ownership of what you are going to say. When the teacher says, "I think you need to . . ." rather than "Wouldn't it be better if . . . ," the suggestions are coming from her and she is being open and honest about what she wants to say.

2. Use positive rather than negative reinforcement. If a child performs a structured skill, such as a forward roll, one-hand overthrow, or schottische step, stress the positive aspects of the skill. For example, if a child throws a softball with the one-hand overhand throw and steps forward on the same foot as the throwing arm, begin by emphasizing the correct aspects, such as, "You had good trunk rotation and the ball started from a good throwing position. Keep in mind the opposite foot should come forward with your throwing arm to give you the correct and best throwing action. Try it again and try to get the opposite leg moving with your throwing arm."

3. Be aware of and use nonverbal cues effectively. Nonverbal communication is the use of facial expressions, body alignment, and movement to express a variety of ideas and feelings (figure 8.10).

People use many different types of nonverbal communicative expressions but may or may not be aware they are using them. For example, on returning home from work, a wife may be greeted with, "Don't change, we're going out to dinner with the Wilkinsons." The wife responds, "OK, I'll get ready." Her accompanying unenthusiastic facial expression, coupled with a forward droop of the shoulders, conveys her real feelings about going out for dinner. Teachers need to understand the importance of their own positive and negative nonverbal communication. For example, if a teacher praises a student for performing a headstand and at the same moment does not look at the child or displays a body action of insincerity, the child will read the "action message" with more meaning than the empty words. Each teacher should try to discover what negative nonverbal signals she uses and consciously curtail them. When verbal instruction or praise is accompanied by a smile, nod, or positive body gesture such as clasping two hands together and shaking them in a victory salute, a more positive and effective signal is conveyed.

Develop an Effective Questioning Strategy

A vital component in teaching is asking questions. An average of 100 to 150 questions per class hour are asked in the typical elementary school classroom. In fact, it has been suggested that 80 percent of all school time is devoted to questions and answers. Of these questions, 70 to 80 percent would be considered low-level questions requiring a simple recall of facts, while only 20 to 30 percent require the higher-level thought processes of clarifying, expanding, generalizing, and making inferences. For example, a low-level question would be to ask an upper-elementary-age child a simple basketball game rule, whereas a higher-level question would be to ask for an appropriate strategy to score a basket against a certain defensive set-up. Teachers need to consider carefully the questions they ask since they can elicit different kinds of responses. Further, effective questioning strategies will assist in checking for understanding, mentioned previously under structuring the lesson. Also, as noted earlier in this chapter, different teaching styles demand different kinds of questions. In addition to the kind of question posed, consideration should be given to eliciting student responses. The following guidelines will help the teacher organize effective question-and-answer interactions with children.

1. Probing is related to encouraging students to elaborate upon an answer. Probing may be accomplished through asking more questions, waiting longer than usual for responses, and/or using nonverbal signals. Probing questions may be used to clarify, reframe and redirect new responses. Helping a child to clarify a response will encourage the child to respond to questions in the future.

2. Teachers generally overestimate the time they think they wait for a response. Teachers frequently wait for only one second or less before providing the answer or moving on to a different student for a response. Research indicates that a wait time of at least three seconds is more effective. When this occurs, a teacher can expect longer responses, higher-level responses (not just a repeat of content), an increase in the number of unsolicited responses, more questions from students, and an increase in student confidence when answering questions. During indirect instruction, where questions may require thinking through and evaluating alternatives, up to fifteen seconds in wait time may be appropriate.

3. There is also value in waiting after an initial response to the question is received. Staying with the same child and waiting at least three seconds tends to produce further responses. Nonverbal movements from the teacher, such as head nodding and smiling, will also encourage a child to continue responding.

Demonstrate Positive Personal Characteristics

Enthusiasm, a sense of humor, and nonverbal signals such as movement, facial expression, gestures, and eye contact all are part of a teacher's personal characteristics. Open expressions of warmth, sensitivity, empathy are also part of a teacher's style of teaching. Personal characteristics cannot be overemphasized in effective teaching. These characteristics, in conjunction with other key teaching behaviors, interact to produce the child's learning environment. The teacher plays a vital role in this learning environment, and being a good role model to children is very important. A

Figure 8.11 An effective role model.

teacher who is an effective role model for students displays several important characteristics. One of the most crucial of these is the teacher's genuine interest in the subject. An elementary school teacher has to be "a master of all trades." Because she is required to teach seven or eight subjects, she is not expected to be a specialist in any one of them. It follows, then, that in physical education the teacher does not have to be proficient in a wide variety of motor skills; however, she must show the children that she considers physical education important by planning for and teaching well-organized and exciting lessons. In addition, wherever possible, she should participate in the activities with genuine enthusiasm (figure 8.11). The following guidelines will help develop the essential characteristics and competencies of an effective role model for young children.

1. Attempt to be fair and consistent with all children.
2. Display a sense of confidence and competence in your ability as a teacher.
3. Never use your authority to belittle students or display other forms of aggressive behavior to your students.
4. Communicate your expectations clearly and concisely.
5. Communicate to children that you personally and professionally enjoy teaching them.
6. Dress appropriately for physical education and physical activity. Set the dress code through role modeling, not just through rules.

Motivational Techniques

One of the premises of good teaching is that the amount a child learns depends on the frequency, intensity, and variation of the learning task. We know the importance of practice activities in learning a motor skill. We also understand how important it is for a child to be actively involved in the learning task and the importance of learning the skill or concept in and through different situations. However, even when all three of these learning factors are present, a child may still not learn or retain the concept or motor skill. This may be due to inherent physical or intellectual limitations, immaturity, or inconsistent motor skill development. It also may be due to a lack of motivation; that is, the child does not have a personal desire to achieve the goal. Our task is to find effective ways of helping each child set higher goals and stay on the task until the goal has been reached. Four types of motivational techniques can be used to accomplish this task. As described in the accompanying paragraphs, each has strengths and weaknesses.

Goal Setting

Studies have shown that when children set attainable goals, achievement is usually greater than in a situation where the teacher instructs the child to "try the best you can." This is especially so if a child is personally involved in the goal setting. Involving children in goal-setting decisions motivates them since they now have a responsibility to try to achieve the goals they set for themselves.

Cooperative Learning

Placing children in group situations where competition between children is replaced with the goal of learning together in a cooperative environment can have positive effects on both learning and motivation. To be effective, cooperative learning must include two elements: a group goal and individual accountability. For example, the group goal might be to produce a gymnastic sequence of balances. Individual accountability could involve each child choosing one piece of gymnastic equipment to include in the apparatus set-up. Or, each child must contribute one particular gymnastic stunt to include in the sequence. Individual accountability is required to ensure that all children play a part in the cooperative learning activity.

Studies have shown positive effects when both group goals and individual accountability are present in cooperative learning activities. Small groups of approximately four children of mixed ability level work particularly well. A developmental mix of one high performer (level 1), two average performers (level 2), and one child who is progressing at the lower developmental level 3, has been suggested as the ideal combination for cooperative learning activities. Positive findings resulting from cooperative learning relate to improved self-esteem, intergroup relations, acceptance of special needs children, attitudes toward school, and ability to work cooperatively. Another interesting finding is that even when problems are not correctly solved, motivation remains high among the cooperative group members. The cooperative game ideas presented in chapter 17 will help the teacher establish cooperation among children. Planning cooperative learning activities will also contribute to instructional variety and the use of student ideas, both areas that help keep children motivated.

Figure 8.12 Intrinsic motivation—pleasure derived from the activity.

Intrinsic Motivation

Intrinsic motivation is motivation internally perceived by the learner that keeps him moving toward the goal. This may be the sheer pleasure the child derives from the game or dance activity (figure 8.12). It may also be an increased feeling of pride and self-confidence with each successful trial or movement activity. The child participates in the activity because he wants to and without external pressure. The following suggestions may help teachers create situations within which each child can be intrinsically motivated to participate, enjoy, and retain the required skill or concept.

1. Select activities that are challenging, yet allow each child to reap some immediate success. Good curriculum design will guarantee the proper selection of activities. Create a daily teaching situation within which children find the activities challenging, enjoyable, and successful. All three factors are critical.

2. Show enthusiasm toward the activity. This can be done in many ways, such as participating in the game activity, talking positively about the activity, and indicating where you feel improvement in the class performance and playing skill has occurred.

3. Provide for maximum participation within every learning task. You can keep students' interest as long as they are active and enjoying what they are doing. Playing basketball is fun, but not if one is watching from the sidelines. As a general guideline, increase the number of game situations (two games playing cross court) or decrease the number of players (reduce to three or four per team to provide for more movement and ball contact) in each game situation.

4. Make practice activities and lead-up games as close to a game situation as possible. Boring drills or slow, dull lead-up games do not motivate young children. Numerous suggestions are provided in later chapters for applying the inventive or creative games approach to game activities.

5. Provide praise and positive corrections rather than scorn or negative criticism. Praise is the strongest form of reinforcement. Be honest; that is, give praise for positive achievement. Do not praise or tell a student that his performance has improved when it has not—particularly in front of other children. Also, when praising a child, recognize the personality of the child. Some children love to be praised in front of peers, whereas others prefer that your comments be made quietly and away from earshot of their peers.

Intrinsic motivation is what we seek to instill in all children. Good curriculum design, effective organization, and generous adherence to the suggestions given will help develop learners who are intrinsically motivated toward physical activities.

Extrinsic Motivation

Extrinsic motivation is motivation outside of the learner that encourages him to act in a particular way. This form of motivation is not as desirable as the child's intrinsic motivation for performing an act or movement. However, when the child or class is not personally motivated, extrinsic techniques can start the process.

Achievement charts and points for performance have been used in education for generations. Achievement charts for such activities as gymnastics and physical fitness have several inherent problems that must be addressed. If such charts are solely based on "how much and how high," the lower achiever is guaranteed to be a failure. Design such charts on the basis of individual improvement. On this basis, physically ungifted children who try as hard as they can are capable of receiving the same recognition as any other average or highly skilled performer in the class, even though their performance level is much lower. Closely related to the design and application of achievement charts are various applications of point and award systems. For example, in intramural activities, awarding points only to the winners of events or games is a mistake. Certainly, do reward winners for their efforts. However, rewarding other qualities, such as participation, sportsmanship, and special effort, will open doors heretofore not available to the less-gifted athlete.

There are many philosophical differences with respect to grading in elementary physical education programs. Some schools prefer pass or fail, whereas others insist on letter grades or no grades at all. If the school district's policy is to have a grading system, the solution is to attempt to design a process that is fair to all children and based on

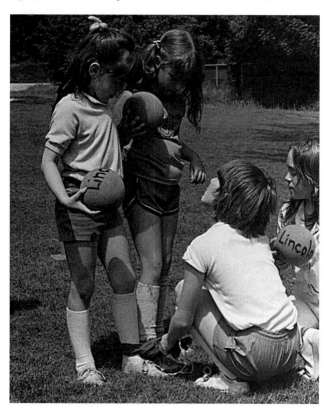

Figure 8.13 Peer recognition—a form of extrinsic motivation.

individual improvement. Wherever possible, such a system should include cumulative records and valid descriptions of the child's performance in the various activities of the physical education program (see chapter 9 for suggestions). Too often, grades are based on fitness scores or simple skill tests.

Regarding the use of peer recognition, help children understand the inherent worth of all children (figure 8.13). This is particularly important for children with disabilities, who are equal participants in the instructional and extra-class programs. If we can guide children to recognize each other's strengths and limitations and to praise and encourage all class members, extrinsic motivation of this nature is highly valued.

Maintaining Discipline

One of the most common concerns of both experienced and new teachers is how to maintain *discipline*. When asked to define this term, however, some describe discipline as a general method of control over the class, whereas others interpret discipline as a way of handling problem cases. In its broadest meaning, discipline is a process of helping children adjust to the school environment and develop acceptable self-control (Harrison 1983). This section will describe some of the more common types of discipline problems, their potential causes, and ways of alleviating the problems or preventing them from arising.

Causes of Misbehavior

Most discipline problems can be traced to the teacher, the learner, or the learning task. A behavior problem arising from something the teacher has created usually is the result of being unfair or inconsistent or of displaying a general lack of enthusiasm or genuine concern for children. A second, closely related source centers on the nature of the learning task. In this case, the motor task, dance, or game may be too easy or too hard or simply played too long. The result is usually one or more undesirable behavior problems. The third cause, which seems to give teachers the most concern, is the misbehavior of children. The underlying reason for a child's misbehavior may be traced to problems at home, to poor interpersonal relations with peers, or to an ignorance of rules or codes of conduct. Regardless of the cause, a child will normally misbehave through the ways described in the next section.

Types of Discipline Problems

The following types of discipline problems occur in virtually every grade in the elementary school. Teachers are concerned with all these behavioral problems. Due to the potential risk in such areas as gymnastics and competitive game activities, teachers must be aware of the following behavior:

1. *Talking:* The most common example of this type of behavior is the child who talks to peers while you are explaining or demonstrating something. Another example is one or more children talking too loud or too much—or both—while engaged in a physical activity.
2. *Not paying attention:* This type of behavior takes many forms, such as looking at something else, daydreaming, or bothering another child while you are explaining something.
3. *Attention seeking:* The most common form of attention seeking is showing off or bothering other classmates.
4. *Dishonesty:* The major problems here relate to violating rules in games, cheating on tests, stealing other students' or school property, and lying to you or classmates.
5. *Overaggressive behavior:* Many physical activities require the learner to be aggressive but in a positive sense, such as to "steal a base" or to "leap higher to tap the ball." The type of aggressive behavior to be concerned about is fighting, bullying, or doing something that may injure another student.

6. *Defiance:* In this type of behavior, the child openly refuses to obey rules or directions. It is poor behavior and may lead to injury or harm to other members of the class.

Techniques to Improve Classroom Control

According to Joyce Harrison, the key to good classroom control comes from an understanding of the worth of each child. In addition, all students need the guidance and security that is only provided by well-defined rules of expected behavior, coupled with the knowledge that the teacher cares enough about them to enforce these rules consistently (Harrison 1983). The best preventive measure is an appropriate curriculum taught through effective styles and techniques. Beyond this, the following suggestions will help in the day-to-day challenge of teaching and dealing with classroom control.

1. Be a role model—set a good example of self-control and concern for others.
2. Be consistent—establish reasonable rules of conduct and stay with them.
3. Be fair to all children—don't pick on one or two, and don't have classroom pets.
4. Be a good teacher and not a pal.
5. Treat every child as an individual. All children should be valued for their true worth and dignity.
6. Change your instructional program when there are significant increases in behavioral problems.
7. Attempt to display a friendly and firm attitude in daily experiences with children.
8. Be prepared with planned strategies to deal with behavior problems. A teacher who is not well prepared usually "reacts" to situations, and this may not produce the desired outcome.
9. Take a deep breath and try to remain calm when dealing with classroom control problems. Emotional responses should be avoided, since they often are not linked to planned strategies and may result in both teacher and students being upset after the interaction.
10. Carefully plan teaching situations. Excellent teaching does not usually occur fortuitously. Well-planned lessons that are interesting and enjoyable engage children. Effective classroom management involves planning.

Techniques to Handle Misbehavior

Experienced teachers are aware of the fact that, no matter how hard they try to be good teachers—to plan and teach appropriate activities—inevitably there will be a discipline problem to solve. There is no single answer to any problem arising from the various types of behavior problems described earlier. The following acceptable practices and suggestions can be used to deal with individuals or groups who have displayed unacceptable behavior.

1. Always try to consider the whole child, including behavior in other classes, as well as available information about the home environment. If the child has a consistent pattern and type of misbehavior, such as attention getting, the solution is to try to find the cause. Also, when there are similar problems with other teachers, check with them to make sure you are all reasonably consistent in your approach to this child's misbehavior.

2. If an individual or a group of children is displaying unacceptable behavior, display an "aggressive waiting stance." This stance should appear to be "quietly aggressive"—for example, frowning, shaking your head, and generally giving the appearance that you disapprove of their behavior. By all means, do not yell at them or try to compete by blowing your whistle louder or harder. Sometimes a serious move toward the trouble spot is sufficient to eliminate the problem. If it is solved, quickly move on to another part of the lesson, rather than giving the troublemakers more time than they deserve.

3. If a child is displaying misbehavior and will not heed your advice, remove him from the activity. This means you should have a location all the children know as the place one goes when one is being disciplined. This can be a bench in the gymnasium or a spot on the sideline of the playing field that is in sight yet away from the area where children are performing: if the child is a potential hazard, he is away from other children, and, by being located in a known spot, he is always under observation.

4. Arrange to meet with the child who has displayed a discipline problem after class. At noon or after school, both of you have had a chance to calm down. Individual conferences provide more time to find out what the cause may be and to solve it in a calm atmosphere. It also provides time to develop a better understanding of the child and the problem and, equally important, to build a greater friendship and trust. In addition to holding a student responsible for his work, he should also be held responsible for his behavior. A student returning from misbehavior time out should make some form of a contract with the teacher to prevent a repeat of the misbehavior; he should not be allowed to just return. However, once the contract is made and the child returns to class, let him know that you start from zero again. Constantly reminding a child of past mistakes will not help, and it certainly will not improve your rapport with him.

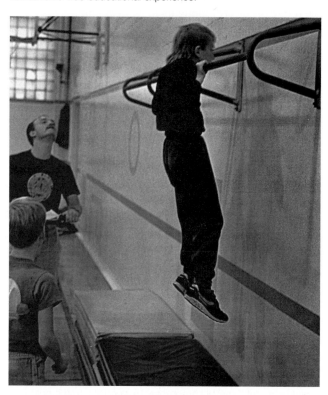

Figure 8.14 The teacher's genuine enthusiasm for the value of physical education is the most critical factor in making physical education a true educational experience.

5. One type of acceptable punishment for misbehavior is a loss of privilege. For example, if a child cheats or misbehaves in an intramural game, he can be denied the privilege of playing for a reasonable number of games. Corporal punishment is banned in virtually all school districts.

A few unacceptable practices have been used in the past but are rarely used in contemporary school programs. These are (1) ridiculing children, (2) punishing the group for the misbehavior of one child, (3) having the children perform calisthenics or other exercise as a form of punishment, (4) forcing an apology, and (5) lowering a grade because of misbehavior. Care should be taken not to revert to these techniques regardless of the pressures of the day.

Qualities of a Good Teacher

The general qualities of "good" teaching have been presented by numerous authorities and apply to physical education as well as any other subject. The teacher's genuine enthusiasm for the value of physical education is one of the most critical factors in making this subject a true educational experience (figure 8.14).

There are many other desirable and sometimes necessary characteristics for teaching physical education. Although the following list is incomplete, if a teacher possesses these qualities, there is more than a reasonable chance that the physical education period will be enjoyable and educational.

1. A teacher should want to acquire more competence in teaching physical education. Classroom teachers are normally required to take one or two professional courses in physical education. This, of course, is inadequate preparation for teaching all the areas of this subject, so it is necessary for teachers to gain new skills and insights through additional courses, texts, films, and other in-service media. Probably of equal importance is that the teacher "have the courage to be imperfect and enjoy it." No teacher can be an expert in every subject. What is more important is the courage to try new ideas and teaching methods, however insecure one might feel. A child's attitude toward a teacher is not based entirely on the teacher's overall competence; it is based on the very simple premise that the child and the teacher are jointly engaged in the search for knowledge and understanding. It is, in essence, a mutual respect for each other's abilities and efforts. When children know the teacher is trying something new for their benefit, they, in turn, will respond in a mature and understanding way.

2. A teacher should possess a sense of humor. Teaching is very hard work, but it is also a very rewarding profession. The ability to laugh at one's own inadequacies and "gentle" errors is vital for the maintenance of sanity and perspective in the day-to-day task of teaching. This is particularly important to classroom teachers who work long hours in confined quarters with children who are extremely demanding of one's patience and understanding.

3. A teacher should possess an optimum level of health. Teachers obviously need to maintain good physical and mental health. Otherwise, the pressure of teaching becomes too demanding, with serious consequences to both teacher and student. Because physical education is physically demanding, a teacher who lacks strength and stamina will tend to neglect this area of the curriculum, with a loss to both the teacher and the class. New teaching methods do not require a high level of motor skill on the part of the teacher. They do, however, require physical effort and enthusiasm.

Selected References

AAHPERD. (1976). *Personalized Learning in Physical Education.* Reston, VA: AAHPERD.

Bellon, J. J., Bellon, E. C., and Blank, M. A. (1992). *Teaching from a Research Knowledge Base.* New York: Macmillan Publishing Co.

Borich, G. D. (1992). *Effective Teaching Methods.* New York: Macmillan Publishing Co.

Gallahue, D. L. (1993). *Developmental Physical Education for Today's Children.* New York: Macmillan Publishing Co.

Harrison, J. M. (1983). *Instructional Strategies for Physical Education.* Dubuque, IA: Wm. C. Brown Publishers.

Heitmann, H. M., and Kneer, M. E. (1976). *Physical Education Instructional Techniques: An Individualized Humanistic Approach.* Englewood Cliffs, NJ: Prentice-Hall Inc.

Johansen, J. H., Collins, H. W., and Johnson, J. A. (1990). *American Education: An Introduction to Teaching.* Dubuque, IA: Wm. C. Brown Publishers.

Mosston, M., and Arnsworth. (1994). *Teaching Physical Education,* Fourth Edition. N.Y. Macmillan College Book Publishing Co.

Siedentop, D. (1983). *Developing Teaching Skills in Physical Education,* Second Edition. Palo Alto, CA: Mayfield Publishing Co.

Selecting Evaluative Methods and Techniques

Evaluation is essential to all phases of the physical education program. A teacher uses the techniques of observation to assess the strengths and weaknesses of her daily lessons in order to make appropriate changes in her teaching strategies. She also uses a variety of objective and subjective evaluational tools to assess performance, to motivate children, and to communicate information to parents and interested citizens.

The value and practical application of a variety of new observational techniques, such as event and duration recording and evaluative tools and procedures relating to student and program development, are discussed in this chapter. In addition, ideas to monitor and promote active living are provided ■

Meaning of Evaluation

Contemporary education favors a "reflective practice" approach to teaching (e.g., see Hellison and Templin, 1991). Just as there is an emphasis today on providing individual children developmentally appropriate experiences, there is an equally important need to reflect on the effectiveness of our teaching practices. Evaluation is an important aspect of the physical education program. In addition to monitoring and reporting student progress, evaluation of both teaching practices and the effectiveness of the overall physical education program will be required. Self-reflection is one of the hallmarks of an effective teacher.

Evaluation in physical education is a process of determining whether the goals of an individual, a group, or a program are being reached. It is an ongoing process of measuring the effectiveness of a teaching strategy, the level of skill development of an individual child or class, and the efficacy of a unit of instruction or a total program. Its purpose can be to evaluate progress, to motivate a child, or to provide effective ways of reporting a child's progress to parents.

Formative and Summative Evaluation

Two types of evaluation are used in the physical education program. Formative evaluation is used within each lesson to assess the progress each child is making toward the goals of the lesson. It is a process of dividing the lesson into smaller units of learning, then evaluating each student's progress in these subparts as the lesson proceeds. With this type of assessment, the teacher can determine how much has been learned and where problem areas have arisen. The teacher can then make consequent changes to the learning task or teaching strategy, or she can redirect the learner to another activity. The second type of evaluation, summative evaluation, occurs at the end of an instructional activity—for example, at the completion of a lesson, unit, or yearly program. The results of this form of evaluation normally produce a cumulative score for determining the achievement of each child or the whole class. This form of evaluation assesses individual levels of achievement, compares individuals or groups, establishes standards of performance, or provides a basis for establishing a grading system.

Norm-Referenced and Criterion-Referenced Tests

The contemporary goals of elementary physical education stress improving physical fitness and well-being, enhancing skill development, fostering good interpersonal relations, and developing positive attitudes toward physical activity. The implication of these goals is that formative and summative evaluations of student progress must include techniques that measure both quantitative and qualitative aspects of the child's development. Quantitative aspects, such as physical fitness and skill development, are usually measured by "norm-referenced" tests. These may be standardized test batteries, such as AAHPERD's Physical Best Test, or a teacher-made test to measure basketball skills. Qualitative aspects, such as the quality and form of a child's movement in dance or gymnastics, are measured by "criterion-referenced" techniques. Both types of evaluative measures will be discussed in the following paragraphs.

Norm-Referenced Tests

Norm-referenced assessment of a child's fitness and skill development has been used in elementary physical education programs for decades. The posture and health-related physical fitness tests described in chapter 12 provide objective measures of a child's posture, cardiorespiratory endurance, body composition, and flexibility. These objective test batteries are used to assess individual levels of fitness and to prescribe remedial programs where warranted.

In a similar way, standardized and teacher-made skill tests have been used to measure levels of skill development. The American Alliance for Health, Physical Education, Recreation and Dance has produced a number of standardized test batteries with accompanying norms for boys and girls, ages ten to eighteen. A series of manuals covering such sports as basketball, football, softball, and volleyball may be purchased through AAHPERD Publications, Dept. V, P.O. Box 704, 44 Industrial Park Circle, Waldorf, MD, 20601. The skill tests described in part 5 are examples of teacher-made tests. Generally, they are product-type tests that measure the number of successive trials, speed of performance, or distance covered.

Each test, whether standard or homemade, should have the following characteristics:

1. Each item in the test battery should accurately measure one important skill (for example, an underhand catch).

2. The test battery should be inexpensive and easy to administer and should yield scores that can be totaled.

3. Each test item should accurately measure the skills and movements of the activity. A dribbling test item in basketball or soccer should include such factors as speed, change of direction, and ball control.

4. Each item in the battery should distinguish between low and high levels of ability. If all children score eight or ten points out of a possible ten on an accuracy test—throwing at a large target from ten feet away—the test would be of little value. The results would indicate that either the distance was too short or the target too large.

Criterion-Referenced Tests

A criterion-referenced assessment evaluates an individual's quality of performance (Morris and Stiehl 1985). It is usually a description of the skill or movement pattern. Table 9.1 is an example of this type of assessment.

Table 9.1 Subjective Rating of Performance in Fundamental Skills

Name: Jim Adams
Date: September 1995

Name of skill	Developmental sequence			Correction indicated
	Initial stage	*Intermediate stage*	*Automatic stage*	
Walking			X	Toes inward
Running			X	Toes inward
Skipping	X			
Leaping	X			
Jumping		X		
Sliding	X			Changes lead foot
Hopping	X			
Swinging and swaying		X		
Rising and falling		X		
Pushing and pulling		X		
Bending and stretching		X		
Striking and dodging		X		

Table 9.2 Activity Chart

Date_____

	Minutes					
	1 2 3 4 5 6	*7 8 9 10 11 12*	*13 14 15 16 17 18*	*19 20 21 22 23 24*	*25 26 27*	*28 29 30*
Stop	X X X X X X		X X X X X X		X X X	X X X
Moving		X X X X X X		X X X X X X		
Parts of lesson	Changing and waiting for class to begin	Introductory activity	Skill development	Skill development	Skill development	Closure

The table provides a description of a child's performance of fundamental skills at the beginning of the school year. Each skill is rated as initial, intermediate, or automatic. Under correction indicated, comments are included for helping the teacher plan activities to correct the child's weaknesses. This type of evaluation sheet can also be developed for specific sport skills and gymnastic activities and is especially useful in explaining a child's level of performance to parents and in pointing out corrective measures that can be undertaken at home.

Evaluating the Teaching Process

Evaluation of the teaching process is an ongoing observational assessment of how well the instructional program is meeting its stated goals. Once the lesson has begun, the teacher must be continuously aware of a series of interrelated instructional and learning factors. For example, she needs to know if the content is appropriate, if the children are keeping on-task and for how long, and if she is providing sufficient guidance and encouragement to all students in the class. Four contemporary systematic observational methods have proven to be effective, reliable, and valid. Several of the following methods—event recording, duration recording, interval recording, and group time sampling—can be used by classroom teachers with slight modifications to cope with the realities of specific teaching situations and the maturity and observational skills of student helpers.

Event Recording

Event recording is defined as the number of times an event occurs within a given time period. One of the first and most important tasks is to define accurately what is to be observed. To illustrate, a second-grade teacher wants to know if the children are physically active during her gymnastic unit. She is using a Movement Education approach and wants to know how much movement occurs during her thirty-minute lesson. A student in the sixth grade is available to observe and record according to the activity chart in table 9.2. The student is taught how to use a stopwatch and when to place an "X" on "Stop" (meaning the whole class is sitting or standing and listening to the teacher) or on "Moving" (meaning the children are engaged in any form of movement). The student then records her observation at intervals of one minute throughout the lesson. Daily observations following this procedure could be made by the sixth-grade student, or the teacher could videotape each session and do her own observation.

This example is only a simple quantitative observation of one aspect of the lesson. Nevertheless, it shows that the teacher is talking too much and the children are not getting sufficient exercise. For example, after the children changed, the introductory activity kept all children moving. During the second part of the lesson, the teacher talked too long (minutes number 13 to 18, and again from 25 to 30). After reviewing this chart, she made a decision to make her comments and instructions shorter to give the children more time to practice their sequences.

Event recording is one of the easiest and most useful methods of observing skills, events, or behavior characteristics. It is essentially a quantitative measurement that can be used as a basis of assessing one or more parts of a lesson or program.

Duration Recording

Duration recording means to record the length of time a student or group of children participates in a given activity. In event recording, the information only revealed two types of activity the whole class was engaged in. With duration recording, the teacher can measure the length of time a child stays on a given task. Using the same class and activity, the teacher wanted to determine whether her tasks involving individual sequences were too easy or too hard for the children. Once again the teacher used four sixth-grade children to observe four children chosen at random. The results indicated that the first and fourth movement tasks were sufficiently challenging and interesting to keep the children engaged for a relatively long period of time. Tasks two and three were too easy and not as demanding, so each child gave each task proportionately less time. Changes were made to tasks number two and three to make them more challenging and, thus, more enjoyable and interesting to this particular group of children. Duration recording has many useful applications in observing and measuring practice sessions,

behavior, and equipment utilization. It is suggested that each teacher design her own form(s) to assess one or more aspects of her own teaching or in assessing the specific motor skills or behavior pattern of her students.

Interval Recording

Interval recording is a sequential method of observing behavior for a short period of time (e.g., ten seconds) followed by a short recording period (e.g., fifteen seconds). During the fifteen-second recording interval, the recorder describes the behavior that occurred during the preceding ten seconds. This type of method is good for observing individual movement patterns or specific behavior characteristics. Since this method requires quick and precise judgments, it cannot be administered by student helpers. Because of this, without adult assistance, interval recording has limited application to the typical elementary physical education program.

Group Time Sampling

Group time sampling is a variation of interval recording. In this method, the observer scans the whole group (usually from left to right) for a short time period (e.g., ten seconds). During this scanning period, the observer quickly counts the number of children engaged in a particular behavior category, such as talking, participating, or fighting. Once again, this is a difficult task for fifth- or sixth-grade helpers; thus, it is of limited use to a classroom teacher. Teachers, however, can use modified scanning techniques to assess general class behavior and whether certain activities or challenges are appropriate for the children. For example, in virtually every lesson, the teacher constantly checks the safety of the equipment, the tone of the class, the noise level, and the effort the children are making, throughout the lesson and from different vantage points. To illustrate this process, let us assume figure 9.1 represents a soccer lesson. The lesson emphasis is dribbling and passing the ball. The first observation is made from a corner of the field a few minutes after the children begin dribbling the ball within the instructional area. As the teacher quickly scans from left to right, she makes a mental note of spacing, colliding, and individual effort. If the pace

Figure 9.1 Group time sampling—soccer.

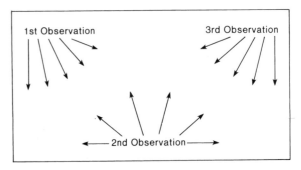

Student	Task Number			
	1	2	3	4
Mary Jones	1.35	.30	.32	2.46
Bill Brown	2.40	.16	.23	2.40
Jill Smith	2.00	.10	.26	1.55
Brian Ward	2.15	.18	.24	2.30

and tone of the class appear satisfactory, she begins observing the main focus points of the lesson. As the lesson progresses, she periodically scans the class from a variety of vantage points and makes appropriate adjustments to alleviate any problem areas.

Lesson Focus Observations

Within each lesson, one or more skills or movement patterns are considered the main focus of the lesson. In the previous example, dribbling and passing the ball was the main emphasis of the lesson. The almost universal question that arises is "What and whom do I observe within my class of thirty children?" The answer to this question is based on the teacher's knowledge of the activity and the potential level of ability of each child in the class. For example, teaching dribbling and passing requires a basic understanding of mechanical principles, progression of skill development, and alternate teaching strategies for enhancing the development of these skills. The teacher must also have a reasonable idea of each child's level of maturity, interest, and motivation. With this general background information, the teacher assesses the child's or group's performance and, where indicated, changes the task or teaching technique to improve performance. Most classroom teachers, however, do not possess this background information and feel frustrated with respect to applying observational skills in a productive manner. The following guidelines will assist each teacher in using observational skills according to her own general background in physical education.

1. Before the lesson begins, select one or two *key focus points,* and, where appropriate, assist individual children or change the direction of the whole class. For example, the two key focus points in dribbling and passing are keeping the ball close to the feet while dribbling and passing the ball with either foot. As the lesson progresses, the teacher is satisfied with the children's ability to keep the ball close; however, she notes most children pass the ball with their right foot only. She stops the class (while they are practicing with partners) and stipulates that every second pass has to be with the left foot. As a teacher's observational skills and competence in an activity improve, she gradually increases the number of key focus points.

2. Make the observation very brief.

3. If the observation is for the benefit of the whole class, make sure each child has a clear view of the performance.

4. Limit the number of observations for the class's benefit to a few demonstrations.

5. When choosing an individual or a group to perform, do not always select the best performers. Every child,

Figure 9.2 Observational skills can be developed and improved.

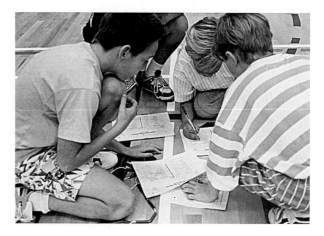

Figure 9.3 Children observing and sharing.

regardless of ability, has something to offer and something to gain when demonstrating a skill or movement idea to peers.

6. When observing a demonstration, provide constructive comments and praise. A child gains from positive, not negative, criticism.

7. When children are asked to observe a performance, specify one or two aspects for them to comment on. Children, like teachers, learn to observe (figure 9.2). Ask them to observe one or two aspects, such as which foot was used to trap the ball or the number of times a player used his right or left foot to pass the ball.

Observational skills are not restricted to teachers; they are equally important to every child in the class. When a child can observe another child's performance he may gain insight into his own performance, acquire another idea, or learn to appreciate the individual differences that exist in each child, whether performing the same skill or answering a movement challenge in a creative way (figure 9.3).

Evaluating Student Progress

The stated objectives of elementary physical education determine the various types of evaluative tools that are used in the program. These objectives indicate a need to evaluate progress in a wide variety of motor skills. Appropriate testing instruments should also be available to measure changes in levels of physical fitness. Knowledge tests relating to movement concepts and skills in game, dance, and gymnastic activities are required for upper elementary school children. Some form of evaluation is required to assess the changes in interpersonal skills and social behavior at all levels of the elementary physical education program.

In chapter 6, a set of learning descriptors for the psychomotor, cognitive, and affective domains was listed for each developmental level. These learning descriptors are to be considered as signposts along a child's path of development. They also provide a rough guideline of what children within each developmental level should be expected to perform, show, or demonstrate. As stated in chapter 1, in 1992 the National Association for Physical Education and Sport (NASPE), an association of the AAHPERD organization, produced a similar set of learning descriptors, which they identified as "benchmarks." These benchmarks, however, are listed by grade level and are produced for kindergarten and grades two, four, six, eight, ten, and twelve. According to NASPE, these time periods were chosen to suggest when assessment might occur. The benchmarks themselves were chosen to indicate what might be assessed in these time periods. Specifically, they consider if the child:

HAS learned skills necessary to perform a variety of physical activities
IS physically fit
DOES participate regularly in physical activity
KNOWS the implications of and the benefits from involvement in physical activities
VALUES physical activity and its contributions to a healthful life-style.

The NASPE benchmarks for kindergarten and grades two, four, and six are provided here for additional reference points that teachers can use as guidelines for developing appropriate evaluative instruments for children within each developmental level.

Examples of Benchmarks—Kindergarten

As a result of participating in a quality physical education program it is reasonable to expect that the student will be able to:

HAS	K	1.	Travel, in different ways, in a large group without bumping into others or falling.
HAS	K	2.	Travel, in forward and sideways directions, and change direction quickly in response to a signal.
HAS	K	3.	Demonstrate clear contrasts between slow and fast speeds while traveling.
HAS	K	4.	Distinguish between straight, curved, and zigzag pathways while traveling in various ways.
HAS	K	5.	Make both large and small body shapes while traveling.
HAS	K	6.	Travel, demonstrating a variety of relationships with objects, (e.g. over, under, behind, alongside, through).
HAS	K	7.	Place a variety of body parts into high, middle, and low levels.
HAS	K	8.	Without falling, walk forward and sideways the length of a bench.
HAS	K	9.	Roll sideways (right or left) without hesitating or stopping.
HAS	K	10.	Toss a ball and catch it before it bounces twice.
HAS	K	11.	Demonstrate the difference between an overhand and underhand throw.
HAS	K	12.	Kick a stationary ball, using a smooth, continuous running approach prior to the kick.
HAS	K	13.	Continuously jump a swinging rope held by others.
HAS	K	14.	Form round, narrow, wide, and twisted body shapes alone and with a partner.
HAS	K	15.	Walk and run using a mature motor pattern.
IS	K	16.	Sustain moderate physical activity.
DOES	K	17.	Participate daily in vigorous physical activity.
KNOWS	K	18.	Identify selected body parts, skills, and movement concepts.
KNOWS	K	19.	Recognize that skill development requires practice.
KNOWS	K	20.	Recognize that physical activity is good for personal well-being.
KNOWS	K	21.	State guidelines and behaviors for the safe use of equipment and apparatus.
VALUES	K	22.	Identify feelings that result from participation in physical activities.
VALUES	K	23.	Enjoy participation alone and with others.
VALUES	K	24.	Look forward to physical education lessons.

As a result of participating in a quality physical education program it is reasonable to expect that the student will be able to:

HAS	2	1.	Travel in a backward direction and change direction quickly, and safely, without falling.
HAS	2	2.	Travel, changing speeds and directions, in response to a variety of rhythms.
HAS	2	3.	Combine various traveling patterns in time to the music.
HAS	2	4.	Jump and land using a combination of one and two foot take-offs and landings.
HAS	2	5.	Demonstrate skills of chasing, fleeing, and dodging to avoid or catch others.
HAS	2	6.	Roll smoothly in a forward direction without stopping or hesitating.
HAS	2	7.	Balance, demonstrating momentary stillness, in symmetrical and asymmetrical shapes on a variety of body parts.
HAS	2	8.	Move feet into a high level by placing the weight on the hands and landing with control.
HAS	2	9.	Use the inside or instep of the foot to kick a slowly rolling ball into the air or along the ground.
HAS	2	10.	Throw a ball hard demonstrating an overhand technique, a side orientation, and opposition.
HAS	2	11.	Catch, using properly positioned hands, a gently thrown ball.
HAS	2	12.	Continuously dribble a ball, using the hands or feet, without losing control.
HAS	2	13.	Use at least three different body parts to strike a ball toward a target.
HAS	2	14.	Strike a ball repeatedly with a paddle.
HAS	2	15.	Consistently strike a ball with a bat from a tee or cone, using a correct grip and side orientation.
HAS	2	16.	Repeatedly jump a self-turned rope.
HAS	2	17.	Combine shapes, levels, and pathways into simple sequences.
HAS	2	18.	Skip, hop, gallop, and slide using mature motor patterns.
IS	2	19.	Move each joint through a full range of motion.
IS	2	20.	Manage own body weight while hanging and climbing.
DOES	2	21.	Demonstrate safety while participating in physical activity.
DOES	2	22.	Participate in a wide variety of activities that involve locomotion, nonlocomotion, and the manipulation of various objects.
KNOWS	2	23.	Recognize similar movement concepts in a variety of skills.
KNOWS	2	24.	Identify appropriate behaviors for participating with others in physical activity.
KNOWS	2	25.	Identify changes in the body during physical activity.
KNOWS	2	26.	State reasons for safe and controlled movements.
KNOWS	2	27.	Appreciate the benefits that accompany cooperation and sharing.
VALUES	2	28.	Accept the feelings resulting from challenges, successes, and failures in physical activity.
VALUES	2	29.	Be considerate of others in physical activity settings.

As a result of participating in a quality physical education program it is reasonable to expect that the student will be able to:

HAS	4	1.	While traveling, avoid or catch an individual or object.
HAS	4	2.	Leap, leading with either foot.
HAS	4	3.	Roll, in a backward direction, without hesitating or stopping.
HAS	4	4.	Transfer weight, from feet to hands, at fast and slow speeds using large extensions (e.g., mulekick, handstand, cartwheel).
HAS	4	5.	Hand dribble and foot dribble a ball and maintain control while traveling within a group.
HAS	4	6.	Strike a softly thrown, lightweight ball back to a partner using a variety of body parts, and combinations of body parts (e.g., the bump volley as in volleyball, the thigh as in soccer).
HAS	4	7.	Consistently strike a softly thrown ball with a bat or paddle demonstrating an appropriate grip, side to the target and swing plane.
HAS	4	8.	Develop patterns and combinations of movements into repeatable sequences.
HAS	4	9.	Without hesitating, travel into and out of a rope turned by others.
HAS	4	10.	Balance, with control, on a variety of moving objects (e.g., balance boards, skates, scooters).
HAS	4	11.	Jump and land for height, and jump and land for distance using a mature motor pattern.
HAS	4	12.	Throw, catch, and kick using mature motor patterns.
HAS	4	13.	Demonstrate competence in basic swimming strokes and survival skills in, on, and around the water.
IS	4	14.	Maintain continuous aerobic activity for a specified time.
IS	4	15.	Maintain appropriate body alignment during activity (e.g., lift, carry, push, pull).
IS	4	16.	Support, lift, and control body weight in a variety of activities.

DOES	4	17.	Regularly participate in physical activity for the purpose of improving skillful performance and physical fitness.
KNOWS	4	18.	Distinguish between compliance and noncompliance with game rules and fair play.
KNOWS	4	19.	Select and categorize specialized equipment used for participation in a variety of activities.
KNOWS	4	20.	Recognize fundamental components and strategies used in simple games and activities.
KNOWS	4	21.	Identify ways movement concepts can be used to refine movement skills.
KNOWS	4	22.	Identify activities that contribute to personal feelings of joy.
KNOWS	4	23.	Describe essential elements of mature movement patterns.
KNOWS	4	24.	Describe healthful benefits that result from regular and appropriate participation in physical activity.
KNOWS	4	25.	Analyze potential risks associated with physical activities.
KNOWS	4	26.	Design games, gymnastics, and dance sequences that are personally interesting.
VALUES	4	27.	Appreciate differences and similarities in others' physical activity.
VALUES	4	28.	Respect persons from different backgrounds and the cultural significance they attribute to various games, dances, and physical activities.
VALUES	4	29.	Enjoy feelings resulting from involvement in physical activity.
VALUES	4	30.	Celebrate personal successes and achievements and those of others.

Examples of Benchmarks—Sixth Grade

As a result of participating in a quality physical education program it is reasonable to expect that the student will be able to:

HAS	6	1.	Throw a variety of objects demonstrating both accuracy and distance (e.g., Frisbees, deck tennis rings, footballs).
HAS	6	2.	Continuously strike a ball to a wall, or a partner, with a paddle using forehand and backhand strokes.
HAS	6	3.	Consistently strike a ball, using a golf club or a hockey stick, so that it travels in an intended direction and height.
HAS	6	4.	Design and perform gymnastics and dance sequences that combine traveling, rolling, balancing, and weight transfer into smooth, flowing sequences with intentional changes in direction, speed, and flow.
HAS	6	5.	Hand dribble and foot dribble while preventing an opponent from stealing the ball.
HAS	6	6.	In a small group keep an object continuously in the air without catching it (e.g., ball, foot bag).
HAS	6	7.	Consistently throw and catch a ball while guarded by opponents.
HAS	6	8.	Design and play small group games that involve cooperating with others to keep an object away from opponents (basic offensive and defensive strategy) (e.g., by throwing, kicking, and/or dribbling a ball).
HAS	6	9.	Design and refine a routine, combining various jump rope movements to music, so that it can be repeated without error.
HAS	6	10.	Leap, roll, balance, transfer weight, bat, volley, hand and foot dribble, and strike a ball with a paddle, using mature motor patterns.
HAS	6	11.	Demonstrate proficiency in front, back, and side swimming strokes.
HAS	6	12.	Participate in vigorous activity for a sustained period of time while maintaining a target heart rate.
IS	6	13.	Recover from vigorous physical activity in an appropriate length of time.
IS	6	14.	Monitor heart rate before, during, and after activity.
IS	6	15.	Correctly demonstrate activities designed to improve and maintain muscular strength and endurance, flexibility, and cardiorespiratory functioning.
DOES	6	16.	Participate in games, sports, dance, and outdoor pursuits, both in and outside of school, based on individual interests and capabilities.
KNOWS	6	17.	Recognize that idealized images of the human body and performance, as presented by the media, may not be appropriate to imitate.
KNOWS	6	18.	Recognize that time and effort are prerequisites for skill improvement and fitness benefits.
KNOWS	6	19.	Recognize the role of games, sports, and dance in getting to know and understand others of like and different cultures.
KNOWS	6	20.	Identify opportunities in the school and community for regular participation in physical activity.
KNOWS	6	21.	Identify principles of training and conditioning for physical activity.
KNOWS	6	22.	Identify proper warm-up, conditioning, and cool-down techniques and the reasons for using them.
KNOWS	6	23.	Identify benefits resulting from participation in different forms of physical activities.
KNOWS	6	24.	Detect, analyze, and correct errors in personal movement patterns.
KNOWS	6	25.	Describe ways to use the body and movement activities to communicate ideas and feelings.
VALUES	6	26.	Accept and respect the decisions made by game officials, whether they are students, teachers, or officials outside of school.
VALUES	6	27.	Seek out, participate with, and show respect for persons of like and different skill levels.
VALUES	6	28.	Choose to exercise at home for personal enjoyment and benefit.

NASPE Benchmarks for kindergarten, grade two, grade four, and grade six. Reprinted from *Outcomes of Quality Physical Education Programs* with the permission of the National Association for Sport and Physical Education, 1900 Association Drive, Reston, VA 22091.

Table 9.3 Locomotor Skill Checklist

1st check ___(date)___ 2nd check ___(date)___ 3rd check ___(date)___ Correct form Incorrect	Walk			Run			Leap			Jump			Hop			Skip			Slide			Stop			Dodge		
Student	1st check	2nd check	3rd check	1st check	2nd check	3rd check	1st check	2nd check	3rd check	1st check	2nd check	3rd check	1st check	2nd check	3rd check	1st check	2nd check	3rd check	1st check	2nd check	3rd check	1st check	2nd check	3rd check	1st check	2nd check	3rd check
1. _____																											
2. _____																											
3. _____																											
4. _____																											
5. _____																											
6. _____																											
7. _____																											

Motor Skills

In most elementary school physical education programs, the majority of instructional time is devoted to learning motor skills. As children mature both physically and in motor skill performance, the emphasis, particularly in the upper elementary grades, shifts to acquiring advanced motor skills and movement patterns in game, dance, and gymnastic activities. The following sample testing instruments are used in the primary and intermediate grades.

Checklists

Children in the primary grades do not perform reliably on most standardized or teacher-made motor skill tests. A more appropriate form of testing is your own checklist and rating scales. The checklist in table 9.3 illustrates how a teacher can use a formative evaluation to determine whether a child can perform each of the important fundamental locomotor skills. If this form is used in the first part of the school year, it generally indicates the locomotor skills that need to be stressed in the physical education program. The fact that it does not distinguish among good, average, and poor levels of performance is the main limitation of the checklist. However, rating scales can provide this type of information.

Rating Scales

A rating scale is an instrument that measures the degree or level of performance of a skill or movement pattern. Table 9.4 uses the three phases of skill development described on page 70. Since this scale is intended for early and late primary, some children are not able to perform at the minimum "initial level." Hence, a zero rating has been added.

The value of rating scales is that they can give each teacher an overview of the skills that need greater attention. They also provide general guidelines to help each child acquire the important manipulative skills according to his own level of skill and ability. Rating scales are also used in the intermediate grades to assess game skills, as well as dance and gymnastic movement skills and patterns.

Checklists and rating scales are valuable tools for teachers in both the primary and intermediate grades. The following suggestions will help in the design and use of these instruments.

1. In designing checklists and scales, limit each observation to one skill or concept.
2. Try to understand the key aspect of each skill being assessed. This means reading about the skill, checking videotapes that describe the execution of the skill, or seeking help from physical education specialists.
3. Keep the skill as simple as possible until you gain greater knowledge of the skills and movement patterns involved in the specific activity.
4. Observe each child performing the specific movement several times before making an assessment.
5. Record observations for every child under the same conditions and in the same sequence. In the previous example, all children should be rated on the first skill before the first child on the list is assessed on the second skill.

Skill Tests

As children move through the upper primary and into the intermediate grades, there is an increased need to measure

Table 9.4 Manipulative Skills

Date_____

Rating scale (see stages of skill development) 0 Cannot perform 1 Initial stage 2 Intermediate stage 3 Automatic stage	One-hand underhand throw			One-hand overhand throw			One-hand underhand catch			Two-hand overhand catch			Striking with hand			Striking with an implement			Kicking a ball			Dribbling a ball		
	1st check	2nd check	3rd check	1st check	2nd check	3rd check	1st check	2nd check	3rd check	1st check	2nd check	3rd check	1st check	2nd check	3rd check	1st check	2nd check	3rd check	1st check	2nd check	3rd check	1st check	2nd check	3rd check
Name																								
1. _____																								
2. _____																								
3. _____																								
4. _____																								
5. _____																								
6. _____																								
7. _____																								

performance levels in a wide variety of game skills. There are a few standardized skill tests produced by AAHPERD (1989); however, the majority of skill tests used to assess game, gymnastic, and dance skills are developed by local school districts and individual teachers.

Table 9.5 is an example of a teacher-made battery test for measuring throwing and catching skills; it is simple, inexpensive, and easy to administer. Each test item can be modified to meet the skill levels of several grades. The first four tests measure form and accuracy; the fifth measures distance.

Test 1: underhand catch. The teacher stands twenty feet from the child and throws consecutively ten balls, which the child must catch with an underhand catch. One point is awarded for each successful catch.

Test 2: overhand catch. Repeat test 1, but require an overhand catch.

Test 3: one-hand underhand throw. The child stands fifteen feet from a wastepaper basket and attempts to throw ten softballs into it. The underhand throw must be used. One point is awarded for each successful throw.

Test 4: two-hand chest throw. Repeat test 3, but with a two-hand chest throw and a larger utility ball.

Test 5: throw for distance. The child throws a softball three times. The total distance is divided by three and recorded against a linear scale of 1 to 10. For example, distances of 0 to 10 feet may receive a score of "1," 11 to 20 feet a "2," and so on, up to 91 to 100 feet, which would receive a "10." This scale can be adjusted to meet the developmental level of the children being tested. The important criterion is that test number 5, for distance, be measured under the same weighting as all other tests. In this example, each test is scored "out of 10." This helps eliminate bias between test items. If the distance throw was not scaled down to fit a weighting of "10," then a child who throws the ball a long distance will be awarded a high grade regardless of performance on the other four test items.

A teacher-made skill test should be devised so that the individual scores can be totaled to provide a means of ranking children, as well as indicating where additional emphasis should be placed in the selection of practice activities and lead-up games. Several sample teacher-made tests are provided in part 5 of this text.

Movement Education Skills Concepts

When teaching Movement Education concepts and skills, there is no common standard by which to judge progress. The essential purpose of these skills is to help children use their bodies in a variety of ways on and off apparatus; each movement task should produce different shapes and movement patterns for each child. Thus, performance is an individualized matter and must be evaluated on that basis. The sequence of development chart illustrates how a simple checklist can be used to evaluate a child's understanding of a movement challenge and the quality of his performance. The movement challenge was to make up a sequence that included stretched, curled, and twisted shapes. According to

Table 9.5 Objective Skill Test

Name of student	Throwing and catching skills					Total	Grade
	Test 1: underhand catch	Test 2: overhand catch	Test 3: one-hand underhand throw	Test 4: two-hand chest throw	Test 5: throw for distance		
1. John Smith	7	5	6	5	8	31	B
2. Mary Able	6	4	5	5	5	25	C
3.							
4.							

the chart, Jill Wells included a stretch and a curl but no twisted shape. Also, the teacher judged her sequence to be somewhat jerky. Bill Smith's sequence included a stretch and a twist but lacked a curled shape. Nevertheless, he moved smoothly from one shape to the other.

Student	Sequence of Development				
	stretch	curl	twisted	flow	
				smooth	jerky
Jill Wells	✔	✔			✔
Bill Smith	✔		✔	✔	

The sample criterion-type evaluations of these two students placed emphasis on the developmental aspect of movement. As teachers become more experienced with this form of evaluation, it can be expanded to include other concepts and skills, as well as additional items that describe the quality of the movement. Finally, developmental assessment can and should be made jointly by the teacher and the child. Since each child learns to progress at his own rate and according to his potential ability, the teacher's assessment is based on whether the child is sufficiently challenged and is continually improving his ability to produce more difficult shapes and movements. Progress, then, is as much concerned with the quality of movement as with the individuality and variety of movements the child performs.

Physical Fitness

The physical fitness test developed by AAHPERD (1989) is an excellent example of a standardized norm-referenced test battery. The items in this test battery include measures of cardiorespiratory endurance, body composition, flexibility, abdominal strength and endurance, and arm and shoulder girdle strength and endurance. This test is described in chapter 12.

Personal Activity Log—PAL

The contemporary move toward promoting active living will require changes to many of the traditional approaches physical education has taken in the past. The move to a developmentally appropriate approach is one positive change that will provide children with the necessary background to enjoy an active lifestyle. However, even with quality daily physical education, there will be a need to foster transfer to the child's world outside of school. The physical education curricula will need to be integrated into the child's life outside of school if the goal of "activity independence" outlined in chapter 1 is to be achieved. In line with a reflective practice approach to teaching has been a move toward understanding children's individual needs by encouraging children to keep personal journals. Through journals, children can express their own personal needs, desires, aspirations, feelings, experiences, and so on. The journals will reflect the "lived experiences" of the children. Reviewing journal entries will form part of a teacher's reflective practices, where she can reflect on the congruency between children's needs and her own teaching practices. As a result, the teacher should be in a better position to plan developmentally appropriate activities.

In a similar way, a personal activity log (PAL) can be arranged for each child; as the acronym suggests, this journal is the child's "pal." Not only can children express their own lived experiences, they can use the journals for goal setting, planning activities that are commensurate with their own environments outside of school. As noted in chapter 8, goal setting usually produces superior performance over merely asking a child to "try the best you can." This is especially true if children are personally involved in the goal setting. For example, if a child enjoys riding a bicycle, the child may set the personal goal of cycling twice around a local park on Saturday. The parent of the child can then become involved in monitoring this activity and signing the log book to state that permission to pursue the activity was granted and that indeed the goal was achieved. The child's PAL serves many purposes; not only does it cater to the child's home and local community activities, it provides an avenue for getting parents involved in monitoring and taking an interest in the child's active lifestyle.

Traditionally, Homework is not usually assigned in physical education. Through the child's PAL, homework becomes a natural part of the interlink between school activities and community and home life. Further, the homework activity is designed by the child; hence, children learn to take responsibility for their own learning. In addition, the children's PAL activities can in turn be linked back to school and integrated with physical education and other areas of curricula. In the example cited above, cycling can be discussed and integrated with fitness and health curricula in terms of aerobic fitness, balance, strength, and endurance, for example. Cycling might also be linked to social studies through events such as races that are common to most countries, for example the "Tour de France." Orienteering skills of map reading and planning routes that are considered safe for cycling might be linked to community cycle paths. Language arts activities could include writing stories about cycling trips or cycling holidays, and research projects could involve studying the history surrounding the invention and development of the bicycle. Research projects linked to the science curriculum might include studying the mechanical principles that allow the bicycle to convert human movement into movement speed that far exceeds the capability of a human or studying the engineering designs that have resulted in differences between the mountain bike and the racing bicycle. Linking the mechanical principles of balance, motion, force, and leverage, outlined in chapter 5, with bicycling will help increase the child's (declarative) knowledge base in this area.

Clearly, teacher direction and planning will be required to assist children with their PALS. As noted in chapter 8, setting realistic goals that are achievable to ensure success is essential for motivation. Also, parental permission is essential before any of the planned activities occur out of the school setting. Further, younger children, children with disabilities, and others who experience difficulty in writing will have problems responding through journal writing. Modifications may be necessary since these children will require help in filling out their PALS.

Many teachers do not plan for daily physical education since the gymnasium or other specified physical education area is not always available. Rather than lose the opportunity of daily physical education, classroom activities can be arranged (see chapter 14). In addition, classroom time can be set aside on a regular basis for children to work on their PALS. Planning and monitoring for an active lifestyle can be undertaken at this time. Also, planning for group, cooperative, and individual projects that integrate PAL content with school work can be done. The time could also be used for assessment and acquisition of other areas of declarative knowledge associated with physical education.

Knowledge

One objective of physical education is to acquire a knowledge and understanding of physical activities and their contribution to physical and mental health. When children know the team positions, rules, and strategy of a game, there is less chance of misunderstandings and misbehavior. Furthermore, as indicated in chapter 5, declarative knowledge of the rules of a team sport, the verses in a singing game, or the parts of a complex gymnastic skill enhances motor learning.

In the primary grades, verbal questions are used to teach simple rules and verses in singing games and to stimulate creative thought through interpretive movements. Written tests can be used in the upper grades in all phases of the physical education program. Written tests are rarely used in physical education. The major emphasis is usually assessment of procedural knowledge and not declarative. Written tests offer the opportunity to address this imbalance. Also, a child may not possess well-developed procedural knowledge skills but may still be knowledgeable in terms of declarative knowledge. This child will likely benefit from written tests. Further, research has shown that when people are told that the material they are learning in class will form part of the content for later written testing, greater retention and achievement scores usually occur. Planning for written testing of declarative knowledge would appear to be an effective teaching strategy. The choice of true-false, multiple-choice, or short-answer tests depends on the teacher and the capabilities of her students. Regardless of the type of test chosen, care should be taken to pose questions that are clear and appropriate to the physical activity.

Social Development

The traits represented in the term *social development* do not lend themselves readily to either subjective or objective measurement. For example, the ability to get along with others, team loyalty, and sportsmanship cannot be measured accurately by a rating scale, an anecdotal record, or even an expert's judgment. Nevertheless, these are extremely important qualities that we profess to develop within the physical education program. Consequently, an attempt, however meager, should be made to evaluate the development of these qualities. Some of the more practical techniques follow.

Teacher Observations

Probably the most commonly used technique for assessing individual social growth is the daily observation a teacher makes while the children are playing in a structured situation or during free-play activities. Behavioral problems, such as cheating and poor sportsmanship, may be noted by the teacher. The manner of coping with adjustment problems varies from a change in the method of instruction to a complete change in activities.

Interview

A personal interview between the teacher and the child and/or parent is another technique used to gain a better understanding of a child's general behavior. Usually, specific adjustment problems are discussed with the child or, when appropriate, the parent to determine the reasons behind certain behavioral problems. The teacher should take care, however, not to lecture, but to win the child's confidence and show genuine concern for the child. When a child respects and trusts the teacher, chances are he will gain an understanding of his problem and make appropriate changes.

Sociogram

The sociogram is a technique used to study the relationships within a group. By posing such key questions as "With whom would you like to practice catching skills during recess?" or "Who would you like to have on your team?" it is possible to identify children who appear to be well adjusted within the group and those who are isolated and rejected. To obtain the best results from this technique, it is wise to keep the following procedures in mind when asking students such questions (Kozman, Cassidy, and Jackson 1967):

1. Make sure the situation for which students are asked to make choices is a real one.
2. Use the choices to group students according to their preferences.
3. Make sure the atmosphere is informal and friendly.
4. Let the students understand that their answers will be confidential.
5. Give no clues to the student about how to choose.

The results of the sociogram can help identify children who need assistance. By drawing circles on a sheet to represent each child and lines to each child as the answers dictate, it becomes quite clear who are the popular children and the rejected children in a particular social group. By a simple regrouping, the shy and retiring child can be brought into a more favorable group without making the reasons for such a change obvious. Furthermore, undesirable group situations can also indicate possible variations in methods of class organization, selection of team captains, and type of group activities.

Grading and Reporting

The purpose of grading in physical education is identical to that in all other subjects—to report the child's progress. Although the majority of elementary school report cards require only an *S* or *U*, or *P* or *F*, additional information relating to skill performance, physical fitness, and social adjustment should be available in the form of a cumulative record. When the parent asks, "How is my child doing in physical education?" and the answer is, "He is well adjusted in his group" or "He is doing fairly well in physical skills," very little insight has been gained and the parent may come away with an unfavorable impression of the program.

To overcome the weakness of the *P* or *F* grading and reporting system, many schools require a cumulative record in physical education. This is particularly true in districts where children are given physical fitness tests in the fall and spring. After the spring test has been given, the physical fitness scores are reported to parents or passed on to the next grade to assist the new teacher in setting reasonable limits for the child. Additional information about skill performance in rhythmic, game, and gymnastic activities should be recorded within the cumulative record. The child's evaluation should then be based on his improvement rather than on how he ranks with others in the class. However, improvement alone is not the only consideration. Due to known sensitive times in development (see chapter 2), certain minimum levels of achievement should be in place as the child progresses through the elementary years. The "mature" form of fundamental motor patterns (automatic phase) associated with basic motor skills of running, jumping, throwing, catching, and kicking (see chapter 4) can be expected to be in place by age eight. If a child is reaching the upper grades of elementary school, yet is still exhibiting "immature" movement patterns in these basic movement tasks (early or associative phases), then individualized practices should be scheduled to help the child move along the skill/learning continuum. As the child reaches adolescence and beyond, it will become increasingly more difficult to change these fundamental motor patterns. The checklists cited earlier, together with the NASPE benchmarks, will be helpful to teachers in both monitoring and reporting motor development to parents, administrators, and policy makers.

Portfolio Assessment

Traditionally portfolios have been used in subject areas other than physical education, yet they can be a useful assessment tool. Portfolios have the potential to portray growth and development about a variety of student outcomes that are difficult to assess using traditional methods. Portfolios are more than a collection of folders containing examples of children's work. They are a purposeful collection of student work that shows both progress and achievement in given areas. What to include in a portfolio is a matter of teacher (and often student) choice. Children's involvement in the process provides an opportunity for ownership in their own educational process. Portfolios in physical education can include a variety of material, including videotaped recordings of student accomplishments. A videotape of dance or gymnastic performances, for example, may capture the essence of the child's accomplishment better than many other forms of assessment and evaluation. It would also be possible in small classes to videotape before and after shots of a given locomotor or manipulative skill. A visual record of motor development would add substantially to other forms of assessment. A computer disk for each child, which might contain journal entries and other forms of declarative knowledge gained through the physical education program, could also be included in the portfolio. Adding the child's personal activity log (PAL) to the portfolio would offer further evidence of student progress. In addition, if the developmentally appropriate activities covered in physical education have been integrated into other areas of the school curriculum, then a variety of student work to represent these connections and topics could be gathered to include in the portfolio. Sharing these accomplishments with both the child and parent can offer a unique insight into the child's achievement and progress. A portfolio is not meant to replace other forms of assessment and evaluation; it merely offers the opportunity to purposefully gather various forms of evidence to display both progress and achievement. The portfolio adds another dimension to the evaluation process.

Evaluating the Program

The physical education program in its broadest form includes all the organized experiences, the facilities, and the teachers involved in teaching and supervisory roles. Evaluative techniques for measuring all these factors are simply not available. Even if they were, the time element alone would prohibit extensive assessments. There are, however, periodic evaluations teachers should make about program content, daily lessons, facilities, equipment, and their own effectiveness. Most of the following suggestions apply to each teacher; however, joint evaluative programs, involving the principal, supervisors, or other teachers should be encouraged for providing greater expertise and support to areas of the program where improvement or redirection is indicated.

Program Content

The content of a physical education curriculum can be effectively and formally evaluated by external organizations, such as state department of instruction or an official accrediting agency. Such evaluations normally use highly refined evaluative instruments and include many items of a physical education program. Another way of evaluating the program content is for each classroom teacher to develop her own self-appraisal scale that covers key elements in her instructional program. The sample scale shown in table 9.6 will help the teacher judge how well she is meeting a particular goal or providing a particular service to her students.

Daily Lesson

Perhaps the most important evaluation procedure that teachers make is the ongoing assessment of each physical education lesson. If the following areas are checked routinely, teachers can gauge whether the objectives of the lesson are being reached and where specific changes in content and teaching strategies are needed.

Since the time available for physical education is usually quite short, each lesson must be planned carefully to encourage maximum participation. The teacher should, therefore, assess the following:

1. The time children take to change and enter the gymnasium
2. The amount of time devoted to explaining and demonstrating skills: most teachers spend so much time explaining that they allow too little time for practice
3. The time available for each child to practice each skill or movement

Effective Routine Procedures

Many unnecessary problems and wasted time can be avoided when children know what is expected of them in the gymnasium. Simple routine procedures, therefore, should be established and followed from the first lesson. These should include the following:

1. Arrangement of apparatus—who should be responsible
2. Rotation procedure—moving from one piece of equipment or apparatus to another
3. Carrying and putting away equipment and apparatus

Sufficient Challenge to Children

When teachers are continually confronted with disciplinary problems, the reason could be lack of challenge in the tasks they give children. The teacher should constantly observe the amount of concentration and effort the children are giving to the task. Specific things to look for are:

1. After introducing a new skill, game, or challenge, is there a demonstration of general boredom or a general rise in noise?
2. Are various children moving away from their assigned working area to be with friends or to irritate other children?
3. Is there a marked increase in irrelevant questions and comments by the children?

Individual Observation and Guidance

In any learning situation, each child needs some guidance and encouragement, regardless of ability. Too often, the outstanding performer is selected for demonstrations and praise, while the low achiever, who really needs attention and encouragement, is neglected. Hence, consideration should be given to:

1. Observing, correcting, and encouraging as many children as possible
2. Selecting many different children for demonstrations
3. Recording important and successful techniques that will assist in future lessons

Table 9.6 Physical Education Program Evaluation Form

Program area	Excellent compliance	Adequate compliance	Needs improvement
1. Objectives of the program are clearly stated.			
2. Objectives of the program are used as a guideline for selecting and emphasizing program content.			
3. The written curriculum is an up-to-date program that provides adequate scope and sequence for each grade level.			
4. The curriculum contains a variety of activities appropriate for children in the primary or intermediate grades.			
5. Provision is made for periodic revisions of the physical education curriculum.			
6. Program content reflects a consideration of the needs and interests of both sexes.			
7. Program content reflects a consideration of children with special needs.			
8. Provisions are made to integrate program content of physical education with other subject areas in the elementary school curriculum.			
9. Time allotments for physical education meet school district, state, or national standards.			
10. Provisions are made for student involvement in the selection of activities.			
11. Provisions are made for the involvement of parents and interested citizens in the selection of activities.			
12. Children are required to have a physical examination by a qualified physician on a scheduled basis. The actual schedule is a written policy of the school.			
13. An up-to-date professional physical education library is available within the district.			
14. Flexible plans are followed with respect to the nature and length of instructional units.			
15. An evaluation of the program content is made on a yearly schedule by the classroom teacher and/or other school personnel.			

Facilities and Equipment

The majority of school districts have established policies for the allocation of funds for physical education. Normally, each school receives an annual equipment and supplies grant based on the number of children in the school. Teachers should refer to the list of suggested equipment and supplies in chapter 7 as a basic guideline. It is extremely valuable for each school district to establish its own recommended list so teachers have a reasonable idea of the quantity and quality of equipment they can expect to receive.

Facilities and equipment should also be inspected prior to and during each lesson for the following:

1. Safety of playing space and equipment
2. Appropriateness of space and equipment. For example, if the instructional space is too large for good control, reduce its size by markers or another device. If balls, bats, or the size and height of equipment or apparatus is too small or too large for the learners, make immediate and appropriate adjustments. Finally, is there equipment in the gymnasium or outdoor playing area that is not recommended for use in the elementary school program? Serious consideration should be given to such apparatus as merry-go-rounds, swings with steel or wooden seats, and such gymnastic equipment as the trampoline and mini-tramp. The latter two pieces of equipment are desirable for upper elementary, provided competent teachers are present to teach skills on them.
3. Adequate supply of equipment. If the number of balls or other pieces of small equipment are insufficient for the number of children, introduce such techniques as "station work" to provide for maximum participation.

Teacher Effectiveness

Every teacher should appraise her teaching to determine how she can improve her effectiveness in the classroom and gymnasium. Since the field of physical education is undergoing extensive changes, both in content and methods of instruction, teachers should assess whether they are as up-to-date in this area as they are in other subjects. Consideration should be given to the following areas:

1. New developments in health-related physical fitness tests, movement education, and cooperative and creative games
2. New textbooks in the general field of physical education and specialized texts in game, dance, and gymnastic activities
3. New developments in audiovisual materials for physical education (films, filmstrips, and videotapes)
4. New developments in equipment and apparatus, particularly the new agility apparatus
5. Related research in motor learning, teaching academic concepts through movement, perceptual motor development, and physical education
6. New program developments, particularly programs supported by federal and state funds

Information and general assistance in these areas can be secured from state and local district supervisors of physical education. Numerous national organizations, such as the American Alliance of Health, Physical Education, Recreation and Dance (AAHPERD), the Office of Education, and the Athletic Institute, provide information on request.

Evaluation should be an ongoing process of assessing whether goals are being achieved. Adequate program evaluation primarily involves the day-to-day assessment of each lesson in order to make modifications in activities and methods of instruction. Contemporary programs also include student evaluation of the program. Although the children cannot always see the value of and reason for all activities, they can provide valuable assistance with respect to their needs and interests. Provision should be made for children to participate actively in program evaluation. When children are respected for their contributions, they, in turn, will generally provide the effort and enthusiasm to make the program a success.

Selected References

AAHPERD. (1989). *Physical Best Instructor's Guide*, Reston, VA: AAHPERD.

Baumgartner, T. A., and Jackson, A. S. (1987). *Measurement for Evaluation in Physical Education and Exercise Science,* Third Edition. Dubuque, IA: Wm. C. Brown Publishers.

Darst, P. W., Mancini, V. H., and Zakrajsek, D. B. (1988). *Systematic Observation Instrumentation for Physical Education,* Second Edition. Champaign, IL: Human Kinetics Publishers, Inc.

Hellison, D. R., and Templin, T. J. (1991). *A Reflective Approach to Teaching Physical Education.* Champaign, IL: Human Kinetics Publishers, Inc.

Kirkendall, D. R., Gruber, J. J., and Johnson, R. E. (1987). *Measurement and Evaluation for Physical Educators,* Second Edition. Dubuque, IA: Wm. C. Brown Publishers.

Kozman, H. C., Cassidy, R., and Jackson, C. O. (1967). *Methods in Physical Education,* Fourth Edition. Dubuque, IA: Wm. C. Brown Publishers.

Morris, D. G. S., and Stiehl, J. (1985). *Physical Education: From Intent to Action.* Columbus: Charles E. Merrill Publishing Co.

NASPE. (1992). *Outcomes of Quality Physical Education Programs.* Reston, VA: NASPE/AAHPERD Publication.

Safrit, M. J. (1990). *Introduction to Measurement in Physical Education and Exercise Science,* Second Edition. St. Louis: Times Mirror/Mosby College Publishing.

Siedentop, D. (1983). *Developing Teaching Skills in Physical Education,* Second Edition. Palo Alto, CA: Mayfield Publishing Co.

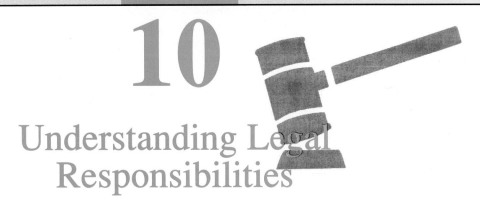

10

Understanding Legal Responsibilities

During the past few years, several legal developments have produced significant effects on public education in general, and on physical education specifically. This chapter will provide a basic coverage of legal liability and maintenance of a safe environment in the gymnasium and on the playground ■

Our Legal System

In our criminal legal system, a person is punished for breaking the law by imprisonment, by the restriction of personal freedom, or by the imposition of fines. The court takes such action on behalf of the state against a person(s) who has committed a crime. When an individual (called the "plaintiff") is wronged by another person(s) (called the "defendant(s)"), tort law allows the plaintiff to be compensated for any losses or injury he or she may have suffered because of the action(s) of the defendant.

A tort is a "civil wrong for which the court will provide some remedy in the form of an action for damages" (Brown 1977). One type of tort is an intentional tort such as "assault and battery." This is a situation in which the wrongdoer is aware of and specifically desires the outcome of his or her actions. A second type of tort is an unintentional tort, which is the result of an act of negligence. The definition of negligence is "the omission to do something which a reasonable man, guided by these considerations which ordinarily regulate the conduct of human affairs, would do, or the doing of something which a prudent and reasonable person would not do" (Brunt 1969).

Legal Liability

In virtually every school situation, the teacher acts "in loco parentis"—that is, in the place of the parent. The definition of a reasonable and careful parent comes from a famous English case in 1893 (Williams v. Eady 1893), which states:

as to the law on the subject there should be no doubt; and it was correctly laid down by the learned judge, that the schoolmaster was bound to take such care of his boys as a careful father would take of his boys, and there could not be a better definition of the duty of a schoolmaster. (CAHPER 1978)

This definition of a reasonably careful parent has become the standard definition of the school teacher's duty of care. A teacher, whether in the classroom or gymnasium, on the playground or on a class trip, should act in a reasonable and responsible manner with respect to the welfare and safety of the children in her care. Reasonable behavior of an elementary school teacher is interpreted by the courts on the basis of what one would expect of a person with ordinary intelligence, ordinary perception, ordinary memory (Koehler 1987), and specified academic and professional credentials.

The important professional implication of the previous paragraph is to select and teach those physical activities the teacher feels competent to teach in order to prevent any serious injury to the children in her care. This statement does not mean that teachers should eliminate virtually every game, gymnastic, or dance activity that has the slightest element of risk. Children need to learn how to climb, fall, and roll correctly in order to learn to move with ease

and competence in a variety of life's activities. This is a part of a child's education that is expected to be learned in physical education. With this in mind, the following hypothetical situation will help you understand the meaning of legal liability.

The hypothetical situation involves fifth-graders participating in a physical education class (figure 10.1). After several practice activities, the teacher arranges the class into two teams to play a full game of softball. A fly ball is hit into the field and a fielder runs to catch it but trips and falls, breaking his arm. This child, William Brown, and his parents become the plaintiffs. The plaintiffs can initiate, through a civic court, a legal action charging the teacher and/or school board with an act of negligence. The teacher, Ms. Buchan, and her school board become the defendants.

If the plaintiff takes this action to court, the case is based on the assumption that a tort, in this case an action resulting in injury, has been committed. If the defendant is found to be legally responsible for the injury, she and/or her school board can be held liable and can be forced to pay compensation to the plaintiff. The following description of the various types of negligence will be followed by suggestions for preventing such acts from occurring within the various parts of the physical education program.

Elements of Negligence

As stated earlier, negligence is the failure to act as a reasonably careful and prudent person would act under the circumstances involved in the specific situation. A teacher, principal, or school board may be held liable if the following four elements of negligence are proven.

Established Duty

This duty involves an obligation that has grown out of a special relationship between the teacher and the student. It requires the teacher (1) to anticipate foreseeable risk in an activity, (2) to take reasonable steps to prevent injuries, (3) to provide a warning relating to any risk that is inherent in the task or activity, (4) to provide aid to the injured student, and (5) to prevent an increase in the severity of the injury.

Breach of Duty

In breach of duty, a teacher fails to conform to her required duties. There are two general areas in which this may occur. The first is a situation in which the teacher fails to do something that should have been done (an act of omission). Normally, in this case, a teacher fails to teach an activity according to an acceptable progression or fails to provide equipment or apparatus that is safe to use. The second area of breach of duty is a situation in which the teacher does something that is not supposed to be done (an act of commission). Examples of this type of breach of duty would be allowing a player to continue playing a game after severely

Figure 10.1 Understanding legal liability.

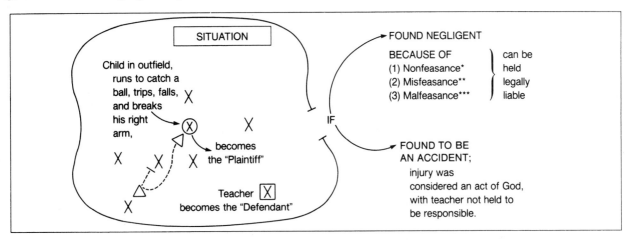

*Nonfeasance is failing to do what is required, such as failing to teach proper landing skills in gymnastics.

**Misfeasance is doing something incorrectly, such as moving an injured student improperly.

***Malfeasance is doing something illegal, such as administering medical advice.

injuring his leg, striking a student for not performing a movement correctly, or failing to allow players to drink water during practice.

Injury

With respect to every potential negligent act, the injury must have occurred while the student was under the care and safety of the teacher. To illustrate, if a student runs after a soccer ball, trips and falls on a broken bottle, and cuts himself, an obvious injury has occurred. In a second example, the teacher permits a student to use a broken vaulting box; in the process of leaping over it, the student sustains no injury. In the latter case, even though the elements under "established duty" or "breach of duty" were not adhered to, there are no grounds for civil tort action, because no injury has occurred.

Proximate Cause

Proximate cause is a situation in which the teacher's behavior is the main factor in an injury to the student. The following case illustrates how the court interprets the relationship of the teacher's presence and behavior and the cause of the injury.

Gard v. Board of School Trustees of Duncan (1946)

An eleven year old boy was injured in the eye by another player's stick while playing in a pick-up grass hockey game after school on the school grounds. At the time of the injury, there was general supervision of the playground by teachers, however, there was no special supervision of the game. The teacher in charge of grass hockey had given the children permission to play, but she was not able to supervise the game immediately as she first had to attend a staff meeting. It was also noted that both boys had played about five scheduled games under the teacher's supervision and the rules had been clearly explained to them. (CAPHER 1978)

The court applied the classic "reasonably careful parent" test to the facts of this case and ruled there was no breach of duty of care owed to the student. In this case, the absence of the teacher was not judged to be the main cause of the injury.

Types of Negligence

As stated previously, negligence is an individual's failure to act as a reasonably careful and prudent person would act under the circumstances of any particular situation. To be held liable for a negligent act, the elements of established duty, breach of duty, injury, and proximate cause must be proven. Proven negligence is due to one of the following types of negligent behavior on the part of the defendant.

Malfeasance

Malfeasance is an unlawful act. With respect to teaching, it occurs when a teacher does something that is illegal and usually results in an injury or adverse effect on the student. Examples of malfeasance would be using unauthorized corporal punishment; failing to spot children while they perform a difficult vault; or discriminating against a child on the basis of nationality, race, or religious beliefs.

Misfeasance

Misfeasance is improperly performing a lawful act. In this instance, the teacher adheres to the law and/or established procedures but does not perform her duties according to an established standard of conduct. The resulting effect of the teacher's performance usually results in injury or psychological harm to the student. One of the most common forms of misfeasance relates to the teacher administering improper first aid treatment to an injury that results in further damage or permanent disability. Other types of misfeasance involve improper spotting techniques and violations of safety codes and regulations.

Nonfeasance

Nonfeasance is failing to perform a required act. In this instance, the teacher knows the proper procedures to follow but fails to perform them. It is essentially an act of omission. In the previous example of misfeasance in which the teacher administered improper first aid treatment, injury resulted from subpar performance. In nonfeasance, the teacher knows what first aid procedure should be applied to an injured student but fails to do so.

Contributory and Comparative Negligence

Contributory negligence is the failure of an injured party to exercise due care for his or her own good and welfare (Koehler 1987). In several states, the courts normally hold that a person who is contributorily negligent cannot recover damages (Delon 1977). During the past few years, this aspect of the law has gradually changed in many states. A more reasonable legal doctrine, called comparative negligence, has begun to replace contributory negligence (Ware 1958). Under comparatory negligence, plaintiffs may collect compensation based on a percentage of their negligence. Comparative negligence, therefore, is more reasonable, logical, and fair to the plaintiff and the defendant.

Act of God (Nature)

An act of God is considered to be a situation that is completely unexpected and due to the forces beyond the control of the defendant (teacher or supervisor). An example of an act of God would be a child playing on the school grounds and a strong and sudden wind blows a branch off a tree, striking and injuring the child. In a legal case, if the injury is ruled to be caused by an act of God, negligence cannot be charged against the defendant (teacher, supervisor, or principal).

Areas in Which Negligence May Occur

Five general areas in the physical education program may give rise to a legal action. Each of these areas will be discussed, along with a set of guidelines that will help maintain an educationally sound and safe learning environment.

Instructional Program

The instructional program is probably the most vulnerable area for teachers, particularly for activities in which an element of risk is involved. According to many legal experts, proper instruction should include teaching students (1) how to perform the activity through an acceptable teaching procedure, (2) how to use equipment and apparatus, (3) how to apply proper safety precautions, and (4) to communicate to students the amount of risk that is inherent in the activity (Appendzeller 1970). The teacher should also be able to foresee and prevent malicious conduct by any child under her care. The class must adhere to a standard of conduct that includes respect and consideration for the safety of every class member. This is usually stated by the teacher (and better yet, agreed on by the pupils) in the form of "rules of conduct" that the children must follow. When one child's malicious behavior causes injury to another, the "case" against the teacher would depend on an evaluation of the teacher's ability, the situation, and a thorough investigation of the incident.

Since the instructional program is one of the most common areas in which potential cases of negligence occur, the following guidelines should be adhered to.

1. Use an approved written curriculum, arrange activities into sequential units of instruction, and follow written lesson plans.
2. Use acceptable teaching methods and techniques for the age, ability, and maturity levels of the class.
3. Provide effective safety precautions. For example, lifeguards, mats, jumping pits, and protective headgear should be provided according to the specifications outlined by the school board. Where spotting techniques are used, teachers should provide this service according to the policy of the school district. When students are used as spotters, they must be taught the proper methods before being permitted to spot a fellow student.
4. Explain to students that the decision to perform any activity that has an inherent risk rests with the student. No student should be required to perform a movement that he is afraid of or thinks may cause physical harm.
5. Activities taught off campus should be thoroughly planned, documented, and agreed on by the principal and/or school board.
6. Develop within students an attitude of self-discipline and a consideration for the safety of other members of the class.
7. Require students to wear appropriate clothing and footwear and to remove watches and jewelry.

Supervision

The general policy followed in all public school situations is that all activities under the jurisdiction of the school must be supervised. The degree of supervision within a school varies according to the type of activity. During a regular instructional class, the teacher needs to be present at all times and to perform her duties carefully. This ensures that the class is following established rules and regulations and high-risk activities are being taught properly and closely supervised or spotted by the teacher. During recess, noon hour, or after-school or school-sponsored events, general supervision policy requires the teacher or a school district–appointed person to be present in the general area in which the activity is taking place. The person in charge of general supervision is primarily concerned with maintaining a safe environment and ensuring that children follow established rules and regulations.

There have been more successful liability cases brought against physical education teachers concerning supervision than in any other area of a teacher's responsibilities (CAHPER 1978). The following guidelines will help maintain a safe and properly supervised physical education environment.

1. List rules and regulations and insist that all students adhere to them while under your supervision.

2. Be present at all delegated supervisory activities. When forced to leave the area because of a student injury or another legitimate reason, make sure another qualified person assumes your supervisory activities. If a teacher cannot get a qualified substitute, it may be wise and prudent to cancel the activity.

3. Use safe, tested, school-approved apparatus and equipment.

4. Establish a standard procedure for checking out and returning equipment and supplies.

Facilities and Equipment

Quality and safety standards for all facilities and equipment are normally established by the school district. Each teacher, however, should routinely inspect instructional equipment and areas for problems such as broken glass, nails, holes, or defective equipment. Also, activities that require running and other general vigorous movements should be played in areas that are clear of obstructions such as gymnastic apparatus, chairs, or other movable equipment. Adequate safety zones should also be provided around the perimeter of playing areas, particularly where they border walls or potentially hazardous obstructions.

The following guidelines will help keep your facilities and equipment in good working order and prevent unnecessary accidents.

Figure 10.2 Sample equipment and supply checklist form.

Equipment and Supply Checklist					
Equipment / Supplies	Quantity	Good	Poor	Comments	Date
Equipment					
Example No. 1					
Vaulting Box					
(1) Surface Condition		x		small tear	
(2) Section Locks		x		stable	
(3) Wood Surface		x		clear	
List other equipment, such as climbing ropes and wall apparatus in a similar format.					
Supplies					
Example No. 2					
Hoops – 36"	22	19	3	3 destroyed	
Hoops – 42"	24	24	0	complete set	
List other supplies such as individual ropes, balls, and bats in a similar format.					

Date inventory completed_____

Teacher's signature_____

Original submitted to the principal on_____

Copy of original filed_____

1. Routinely check all facilities and equipment before using them. When you find something that is too hazardous to use or needs to be repaired, refrain from using it and write a memo to the principal.

2. Purchase equipment according to quality and safety standards established by the school board or other agencies.

3. List the rules and regulations for locker and shower rooms. These should include codes of behavior, traffic patterns, and time limits that should be strictly enforced.

4. Limit the use of outdoor apparatus according to weather conditions.

The responsibility for checking, maintaining, and ordering equipment and supplies may be delegated to the physical education specialist or to a classroom teacher. Some school districts have their own form and a standard procedure for checking inventory and submitting the completed form to the principal. This checklist should itemize all equipment and supplies, describe their condition, and indicate what should be repaired or replaced. If a school district does not have a standard checklist form, the sample form in figure 10.2 can be modified to meet local school conditions. Teachers should refer to the standard list of equipment and supplies in chapter 7 when designing their own checklist. A well-designed form can help maintain a safe teaching environment and assist teachers in ordering needed equipment and supplies.

Emergency Care

A basic guideline all teachers should adhere to when administering first aid is to provide immediate and temporary care needed to preserve life and to prevent further injury until medical care becomes available. All teachers, and particularly those who teach physical education, should possess a first aid certificate. This certificate stresses the meaning of emergency first aid and certifies that the holder has the required knowledge and skill to administer proper first aid. Negligence usually results from the teacher attempting to do too much, causing further injury, or doing too little, causing permanent damage.

The following suggestions will assist in treating a person and adhering to proper follow-up procedure after an injury occurs.

1. Establish a standard procedure for administering emergency care.
2. Establish a standard procedure for removing an injured person from the instructional area and for notifying administrators and parents.
3. Establish a standard procedure for completing an accident form similar to the one in figure 10.3. This form should be completed immediately, in triplicate, after the injured person has been taken care of.
4. After a student is injured, contact the parent or guardian as soon as possible.
5. Obtain a standard first aid and CPR certificate at the earliest possible date.

Transportation

The transportation of students from school to off-campus locations involves school vehicles, commercial vehicles, or private cars. The most sensible and prudent choice is to use school buses or commercial vehicles. Commercial vehicles must adhere to strict safety standards, as well as possess adequate liability coverage. If teachers use their own vehicles or parents' vehicles, the school board should provide insurance riders to cover the car owner and the children in the owner's care.

The following guidelines will help ensure safe transportation for students to and from school-sponsored activities.

1. Prepare detailed travel plans and have them approved by the principal or appropriate school administrator.
2. Hire licensed drivers and school-approved commercial vehicles.

Figure 10.3 Student accident report form.

Student Accident Report Form

Name of injured student: _____ Phone: _____

Age: _____   Address: _____

P.E. class: _____   _____

Homeroom: _____   _____

School: _____

Date of accident: _____ A.M. / P.M.
                  (time) (day) (month)

Place of accident: _____

Date reported: _____

Location and description of accident: _____
_____
_____
_____

Nature of injury: _____
_____

Condition of environment: _____
_____

Supervising person: _____

Type of activity: _____

First-aid treatment: _____
_____

Where taken: _____

Parents contacted: yes ☐ no ☐   Time: _____

School nurse contacted: yes ☐ no ☐ Time: _____

Witnesses: (1) _____
(2) _____
(3) _____

Signature _____

Date _____

White copy: Superintendent's office
Pink copy: Principal's office
Green copy: Teacher's copy

3. If teachers and/or parents, and their vehicles, transport students, obtain adequate liability coverage to cover potential lawsuits.
4. Require all travelers to be properly seated and to use seat belts. Do not use vehicles such as vans without seats, open bed trucks, or vehicles that do not meet adequate maintenance and safety standards.

5. Prior to embarking on any official school trip, check vehicle for such items as tires, lights, extra keys, and emergency equipment, such as, fire extinguisher, blankets, and first aid kit.

6. Establish a standard procedure for seating travelers, loading and unloading equipment, and administering emergency care.

Liability Insurance

Who should purchase liability insurance varies from district to district. Policies are normally held by local school districts, teacher associations, or individual teachers. Since the costs incurred in this area of responsibility are excessive, each teacher should consult with local school officials regarding the extent of liability coverage. If no policy exists to cover teaching responsibilities, particularly in the area of physical education, a personal policy is warranted.

Selected References

AAHPERD. (1976). *Complying with Title IX of Education Amendments of 1972 in Physical Education and High School Sports Programs.* Washington, DC: AAHPERD.

Alberta, Alberta Education, Curriculum Branch. (1992). *Better Safe Than Sorry: Safety Guidelines for Elementary and Secondary School Physical Education.* Learning Resources Distributing Center, 12360: 142 Street, Edmonton, Alberta, Canada, T5L 4X9.

Appendzeller, H. (1970). *From the Gym to the Injury.* Charlottesville, VA: Michie Company Law Publishing.

Arnold, D. E. (1983). *Legal Considerations in the Administration of Public School Physical Education and Athletics Programs.* Springfield, IL: Charles C. Thomas.

Bailey, J. A., and Matthews, D. L. (1984). *Law and Liability in Athletics, Physical Education and Recreation.* Boston: Allyn and Bacon.

Brown, R. (1977). "Tort Liability As a Form of Social Control over Violence in Sports." Unpublished paper, Faculty of Law, University of Windsor, Ontario.

Brunt, R. T. (1969). "Tortious Liability of Canadian Physical Education and Recreation Practitioners." Unpublished Master's thesis, University of Alberta.

CAHPER. (1978). *Legal Liability in Physical Education.* Vanier, Ontario: CAHPER.

Clement, A. (1985). *Law in Sport and Physical Education.* Dubuque, IA: Brown & Benchmark.

Della-Giustina, D. E., and Yost, C. P. (1991). *Teaching Safety in the Elementary School.* Reston, VA: AAHPERD Publications.

Delon, F. G. (1977). "Tort Liability," *Yearbook of School Law.* Shannon v. Addison Trial, 339 N.E., 2d 372.

Federal Register. (1977). Vol. 42, August 23, 1977 (part II), page 42480.

Kaiser, R. A. (1986). *Liability and the Law in Recreation, Parks and Sports.* Englewood Cliffs, NJ: Prentice-Hall.

Koehler, R. W. (1987). *Law, Sport Activity and Right Management.* Champaign, IL: Stripes Publishing Co.

Selby, R. (1977). "What's Wrong (and Right!) with Coed Physical Education Classes: Secondary School Physical Educators' Views on Title IX Implementation." *The Physical Educator,* 29, 60.

Ware, M. (1958). "Is the Teacher Liable?" *National Education Association Journal,* 47: 603.

Provision for Special Programs

S pecial needs and interests must be met within the instructional and extraclass programs. Chapter 11 provides background information relating to the structure and function of the skeletal, muscular, and cardiovascular systems. Chapter 12 explains how to assess and improve health-related physical fitness. Chapter 13 discusses how special needs children can be integrated effectively into the regular program. Chapter 14 describes a variety of ways to use the classroom to teach game, dance, gymnastic, and fitness activities. The last chapter in part 4 covers the ways and means of organizing intramural and interschool programs ■

11

Learning About the Human Body and Wellness

In 1980, the Public Health Service of the U.S. Department of Health and Human Resources established a set of health objectives for the nation. The objectives included health protection (seat belt legislation, fluoridation, etc.), preventive health (immunization, disease control, etc.), and health promotion (physical fitness, nutrition, etc.). In the past ten years, many of the goals set under health protection and prevention have been met. For example, numerous states now have effective laws relating to wearing seat belts and pollution control. In addition, there are numerous national programs relating to the early detection of heart disease, cancer, and diabetes. The one area in which the goals have not been reached is health promotion.

To meet the objectives of health promotion, our profession has developed the concept of human wellness to include fitness, nutrition, stress management, and the avoidance of all forms of substance abuse. Human wellness, however, is not simply the absence of disease; it is viewed as a positive health life-style. This new concept requires every individual to be responsible for setting one's own life-style goals in a self-directed manner. This means embarking on a life-long program of reaching and maintaining optimum levels of health and fitness, good nutrition, effective stress management, and an avoidance of substance abuse.

The physical education program can play an effective role in laying the foundation for each child to develop his own health life-style. If we preach to children, we will accomplish little in terms of developing long-term health-related goals. However, if we can provide programs that allow children to discover how their bodies work and how to develop their own fitness programs, there is a reasonable chance they will want to continue the programs indefinitely. Toward this goal, the material in this chapter should be used to help children understand how the body works. Knowledge and concepts about bones, muscles, posture, nutrition, stress management, and substance abuse can be taught in a variety of ways. At times, there are "teachable moments" when facts about how a muscle works or about ways to control stress can be covered individually. At other times, it is appropriate to meet with the children for a few minutes at the end of a gymnastic lesson to discuss the principles of balance and strength they have been attempting to execute. The next chapter, "Assessing and Improving Physical Fitness," will continue to provide knowledge about levels of fitness and individualized ways to use this information to maintain an optimum level of fitness throughout life ■

Skeletal System

The human skeleton consists of 208 bones that work together with the muscles and connective tissues to move the body, to support it, and to protect the internal organs (figure 11.1). Bones are divided into two broad groups, known as axial and appendicular bones. *Axial bones* consist of the skull, spine, and ribs and provide the basic structure to which the *appendicular bones,* consisting of the arms and legs, are attached.

A joint is a meeting point between bones. For example, the knee joint (figure 11.2) is a hinge joint that allows the leg to flex and extend. The shoulder and hip joints are ball-and-socket joints, which allow rotary movements in several directions. The ankle and thumb joints are saddle joints, which permit movement in two directions but without rotation.

The ends of the bones forming a joint, such as the knee joint, are covered with a smooth protective layer of cartilage that acts like a shock absorber between bone surfaces. The space between the bones in a joint is filled with a lubricating fluid known as synovial fluid. This fluid works like the oil in an engine; it reduces friction between the moving parts. These joints have strong, nonelastic stabilizing ligaments that bind the joint together.

Muscular System

The muscular system of the human body represents about 35 to 45 percent of the total body weight. It consists of 650 muscles that are grouped in three categories according to their structure and function. Involuntary, or smooth, muscles (about 30) form the muscle portion of the internal organs and function automatically, rather than under the direct control of the brain. The cardiac, or heart, muscle performs its unique function while under the involuntary control of the brain. The voluntary, or skeletal, muscles (about 620) are attached to the bones and are directly controlled by the brain. Both types of muscles, however, operate in the same general way by contracting and relaxing their muscle fibers.

In physical education, we are concerned mainly with the skeletal muscles, although all muscles are indirectly affected through movement. A skeletal muscle is composed of bundles of muscle fibers enclosed in a sheath or fibrous tissue called fascicle (figure 11.3). At the end of the muscle is a

Figure 11.1 The human skeleton.

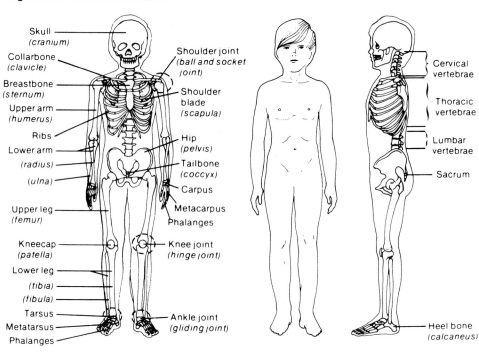

Figure 11.2 Bones forming the knee joint.

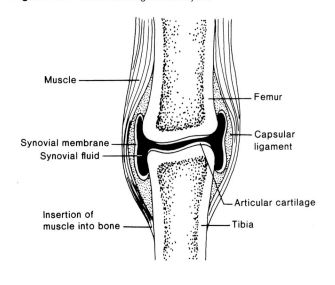

Figure 11.3 Muscle fibers enclosed by the fascicle.

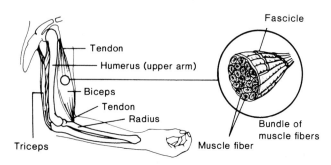

chapter 11

Figure 11.4 Main skeletal muscles.

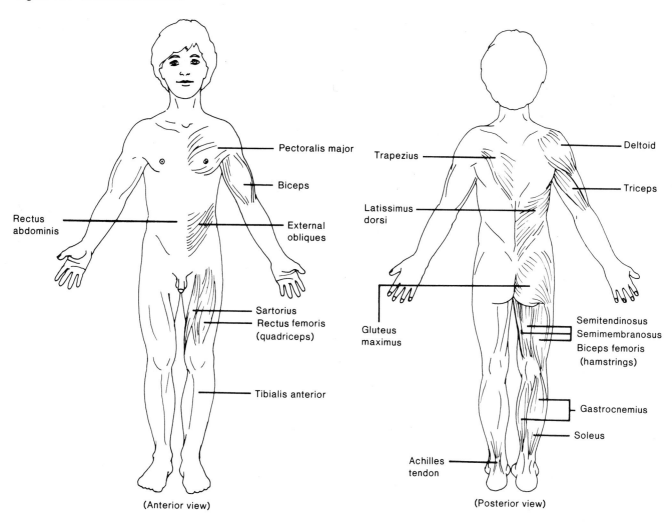

Pectoralis major

Biceps

Rectus abdominis

External obliques

Sartorius
Rectus femoris (quadriceps)

Tibialis anterior

(Anterior view)

Trapezius

Latissimus dorsi

Gluteus maximus

Deltoid

Triceps

Semitendinosus
Semimembranosus
Biceps femoris (hamstrings)

Gastrocnemius

Soleus

Achilles tendon

(Posterior view)

noncontracting fibrous tissue called a tendon. The tendon normally is attached to a bone or ligament. When a nerve impulse is received by a muscle, the fibers contract, causing the muscle to become shorter and thicker. As illustrated in figure 11.3, when the arm is flexed, the biceps become shorter and thicker. Since muscle fibers can only contract, the antagonist (or opposing) tricep muscles relax as the biceps flex. When the arm is extended, the triceps contract and the biceps relax. Figure 11.4 will help you locate the main skeletal muscles. The muscles of the anterior view and posterior view are arranged in pairs. As one (hamstrings) contracts, the antagonist (quadriceps) gradually relaxes to give a smooth and controlled movement. Throughout any movement, however, the antagonist muscle never completely relaxes. The feeling of firmness of a relaxed antagonist muscle is known as muscle tone. When muscle groups, such as the hamstrings and quadriceps or abdominal and lower back muscles, are exercised vigorously and routinely, they show firm muscle tone and good posture.

Cardiorespiratory System

The cardiorespiratory system is primarily made up of the heart, arteries and veins, and lungs (figure 11.5). Blood carrying oxygen and other nutrients leaves the heart through the aorta, which branches into smaller vessels called arteries. Arteries keep branching and getting smaller until they reach every part of the body. The ends of the smallest arteries branch out into a tiny network of vessels called capillaries. Capillary walls are so thin that oxygen and nutrients pass through to the surrounding tissue cells, while carbon dioxide and other waste products move into the capillaries. The capillaries then join small veins, becoming bigger until they reach the upper right chamber of the heart. Blood

Figure 11.5 Blood flow through the body.

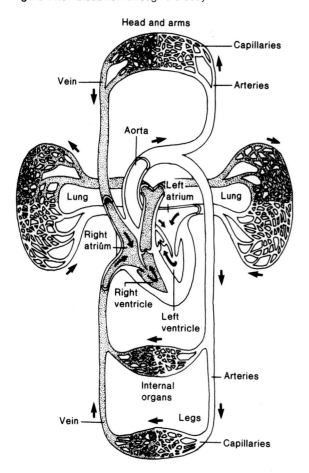

moves down into the lower chamber (right ventricle) and is pumped through the pulmonary artery into the lungs. In the lungs, carbon dioxide is released through the capillary wall into the lung cavity's air sac (figure 11.6). At the same moment this is occurring, oxygen is being moved from the air sac to the capillary to be transported by the blood to the upper left chamber (left atrium) of the heart. During exhalation, the carbon dioxide is moved out of the lungs, through the bronchioles, to the larger bronchi, and finally out through the trachea (windpipe). The oxygen-rich blood that has been transported to the heart is pumped out from the lower left chamber (left ventricle) of the heart through the large aorta to begin the cycle again.

Respiration Rate

Respiration, a chemical process that occurs in every living cell of the body, involves the absorption of oxygen, the release of energy, and the elimination of carbon dioxide. The exchange of these gases in the lungs is the breathing part of respiration. Breathing in is caused by the contraction of the muscular diaphragm, moving it downward (figure 11.7a), and the contraction of the rib muscles, pulling them upward and outward. After the lungs expand and fill with air, the diaphragm and rib muscles relax, allowing the diaphragm to move upward and the ribs to move closer together (figure 11.7b), thus forcing air out of the lungs.

A normal breathing cycle occurs about twelve to sixteen times per minute. However, during vigorous exercise, the demand for oxygen increases in the body tissues, particularly in the muscle cells. When an individual is in good physical condition, his or her breathing rate increases the supply of oxygen to the muscle cells. When oxygen is

Figure 11.6 Circulation of blood through the lungs.

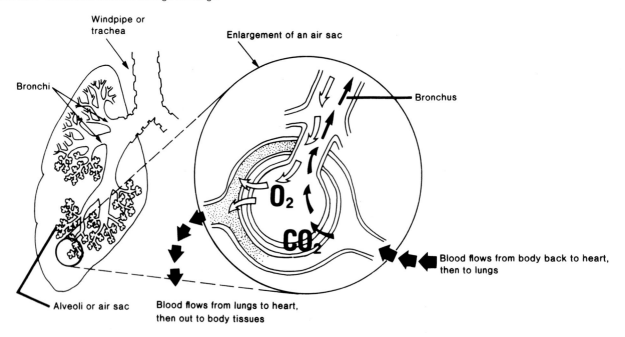

Figure 11.7 Expansion and contraction of the diaphragm during breathing.

a   b

Figure 11.8 Pumping cycle of the heart.

Step 1: heart relaxes

Step 2: upper chambers contract

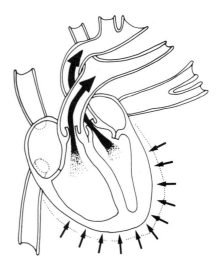

Step 3: lower chambers contract

supplied to the muscle cells and body tissues during a steady state of breathing, energy that is produced with sufficient oxygen supply is termed aerobic. Thus *aerobic exercise* is activity when the cardiorespiratory system is able to meet the demands of the body's muscles and tissues with an adequate supply of oxygen. If the exercise is too strenuous, the muscle cells cannot get enough oxygen from the lungs. When this occurs, the muscle cells begin to produce energy without oxygen, which is called *anaerobic exercise* and can last for a few minutes. During anaerobic exercise, the cells build up an oxygen debt that must be paid back during the recovery or rest period.

Pumping Action of the Heart

The pumping action, or cycle, of the heart is actually a series of very rapid contractions, like squeezes, beginning in the upper chambers and moving in a wavelike action down through the lower chambers (figure 11.8). The cycle includes the following three steps.

Step 1: The heart relaxes. While the heart is relaxed, the valves between the upper and lower chambers are open so blood flows into the upper chamber and down into the lower chamber.

Step 2: The upper chambers contract, forcing more blood into the lower chambers.

Step 3: The thick-walled ventricles contract, causing the valves between the upper and lower chambers to close and the valve in the aorta and pulmonary artery to open, allowing the blood to flow to the lungs and then to the rest of the body. (The heart relaxes again to begin the next cycle.)

Figure 11.9 Heart rate.

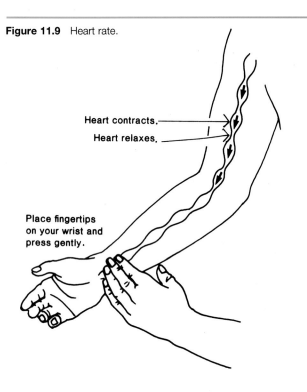

Heart contracts.

Heart relaxes.

Place fingertips on your wrist and press gently.

Heart rate	
220	**Maximum heart rate**
200	
190	
180	
170	**Target heart rate zone** (This is between 70 and 85 percent of a child's maximum heart rate.)
160	
150	
140	
130	
120	
110	
100	
90	
80	**Resting heart rate zone**
70	
60	

Table 11.1 Cardiorespiratory Endurance

How to Measure Heart Rate

First: A person's resting heart rate is the number of times the heart beats per minute while the person is in a quiet resting state. The best time to take this is just before getting out of bed in the morning. In a school situation, have the children take their heart rate in class before going to their physical education class. If this procedure is not possible, have the children take their heart rate after they are sitting down and before they begin to participate in physical activity.

Second: Show children how to place their fingertips gently on the artery on the wrist near the base of the thumb (figure 11.9).

Third: Tell the class they will count their heart rate for ten seconds. You will say "ready," wait a second or two, then say "count." At the tenth second, say "stop" and "record your score."

Fourth: Each child records the number of heart beats. Then tell them to multiply their number by six to give them their heart rate for one minute.

Fifth: Arrange the children in pairs and have them take each other's heart rate. This is to check how accurate each student is in taking his own heart rate.

Resting and Maximum Heart Rate

The best method of determining whether cardiorespiratory endurance is being improved is by monitoring the person's heart rate before and after exercise. Maximum heart rate,

obtained during very strenuous exercise, would reach about 220 beats per minute (table 11.1). To improve cardiorespiratory endurance, children must increase their heart rate to about 160 to 190 beats per minute for about ten to fifteen minutes per day. This training zone heart rate is approximately 70 to 85 percent of an individual's maximum rate. It would be used, therefore, as a very general guideline. Hence, children who have difficulty performing an exercise, such as running or swimming, for a short period of time should adjust their training zone downward to 130 or less. The training zone can be increased to higher levels as the individual gradually improves his or her cardiorespiratory endurance.

How Heart Rate Is Affected

The following cardiovascular activities can be used to illustrate how the heart and circulatory system are affected by a variety of physical and psychological activities.

Experiment 1: Comparative Heart Rates

Have children measure each other's heart rates. Group the results according to age and gender. Compare the heart rates of various children in the class and with that of the teachers. Make further comparisons with parents, grandparents, high school athletes, and so on.

Experiment 2: Heart Rate Recovery

Each child records his resting heart rate, then runs in place for three minutes. Immediately after running, each performer takes his pulse and records it in the appropriate column (see table 11.2). Retake and record heart rates after

chapter 11

Table 11.2 Heart Rate Recovery

Activity	Rate 15 Secs	Rate 1 min
Resting heart rate		× 4 =
Immediately after running on the spot, as fast as possible, for 3 minutes		× 4 =
After 2 minutes		× 4 =
After 4 minutes		× 4 =
After 6 minutes		× 4 =

Table 11.3 Effects of Different Activities

Physical activity	Resting rate	Activity rate	Difference
Resting heart rate	_____	. . . .	. . . .
3 minutes tic-tac-toe	. . . .	_____	_____
Rest and record	_____	. . . .	. . . .
3 minutes playing catch	. . . .	_____	_____
Rest and record	_____	. . . .	. . . .
3 minutes of rope skipping (or run in place)	. . . .	_____	_____
Rest and record	_____	. . . .	. . . .

resting two, four, and six minutes. Use test results to discuss the individual's recovery rate and how cardiovascular fitness can be improved.

Experiment 3: Effects of Different Activities

Divide the class into partners. Partners rotate to each of the three activities listed in table 11.3. Partners cannot start any activity, however, until their heart rates have resumed the resting heart rate. Repeat the experiment at a later date, but change the three activities.

Experiment 4: Excitement and Fear

Divide the class into partners. One partner repeats the rhyme "Peter Piper . . ." twelve times as fast as possible while the other partner attempts to distract him in a fun-like manner. (Make faces, count out loud, . . . maybe tickle.) Use this experiment to discuss the effects of stress and excitement on cardiovascular fitness (table 11.4). Also, design similar experiments involving stressful situations.

Table 11.4 Excitement and Fear

Resting heart rate (take for 15 secs × 4) =	
Heart rate after repeating rhyme (take for 15 secs × 4) =	

Repeat the following rhyme 12 times:
"Peter Piper picked a peck of pickled peppers. How many pecks of pickled peppers did Peter Piper pick?"

Posture

Parents, teachers, and school officials have always been concerned about children's posture, particularly since there appears to be a strong relationship between posture and such factors as perceptual acuity, emotional health, and general fitness. Slanting desks, adjustable chalkboards, and improved lighting have been installed to enhance and maintain correct posture. However, chronic television viewing and inadequate daily exercise for many children have continued to produce numerous postural problems, which are readily detectable and can be corrected by vigorous exercise.

There is no clear definition or standard of "good" posture that can be applied to all children, whether they are standing, sitting, or moving. Standing posture is judged by the alignment of body segments. The child in figures 11.10 and 11.11 has good posture because her body segments are evenly balanced over the base of support. Viewed from the side, the plumb line runs from a little in front of the ankle through the knee, pelvis, shoulders, and ear. In this position, the natural curves of the body are moderate, with the head, shoulders, pelvis, knees, and feet balanced evenly on each side of the line. Viewed from the back, the plumb line runs midway through the head, vertebrae, and hips and equidistant between the feet.

A child with good posture requires a minimum contraction of antigravity muscle groups to keep her body erect and balanced, but, when a child slouches, the upper back muscles must contract to shift the body to the correct posture. If she continues to slouch, her muscles gradually adapt to that position and she might have chronic poor posture if it is not corrected.

Common Posture Problems

Most of the typical posture deviations of young children can be observed and corrected with proper exercise. The following deviations can be observed when the child is standing beside a plumb line.

Figure 11.10 Good posture (side view). Natural curves of the body are moderate.

Figure 11.11 Good posture (back view).

Figure 11.12 Round back (kyphosis).

Figure 11.13 Hollow back (lordosis).

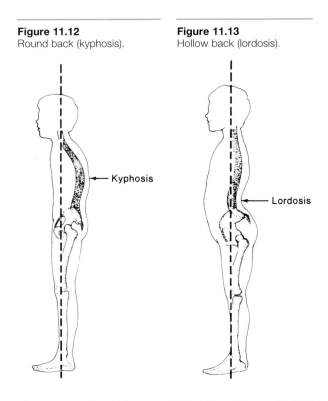

Figure 11.14 Lateral curvature (scoliosis)—(a) c-type curve and (b) s-type curve.

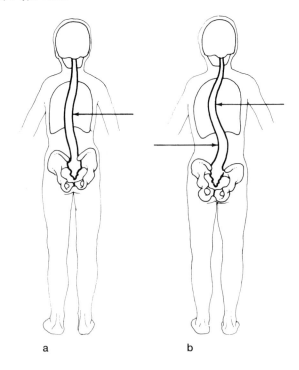

a   b

Round Upper Back (Kyphosis)

Round back, or kyphosis, is a marked increase in the curve of the back (figure 11.12). The head and shoulders are usually held in a forward position, and the backward curve of the upper body causes the pelvis to tilt forward slightly and the knees to bend somewhat. This condition increases the strain on the upper back muscles and shifts the weight of the body to the front of the foot.

Hollow Back (Lordosis)

Hollow back, or lordosis, is an exaggerated forward curve of the lower back (figure 11.13). The most common signs are a protruding abdomen, a swayback, and hyperextension of the knees.

Lateral Curvature (Scoliosis)

Lateral curvature, or scoliosis, can be C-shaped, extending the length of the spinal column, or S-shaped, with a small curve on the upper back and a compensating curve on the lower back (figure 11.14). The C-shaped curve is normally toward the left, since most children are right-handed and tend to lean to the weaker side. This comes from the constant elevation of the right arm and the tendency to lean toward the left side of the desk while writing and performing other sitting activities.

Figure 11.15 Posture chart using the plumb line test.

Name: _____   Date: _____
First evaluation: _____
Second evaluation: _____
Third evaluation: _____

Key to score:
Note: Use figures *a* and *b* as a Normal (0) rating. Children should assume a relaxed, "normal" posture when taking this test.

Normal	0
Slight	1
Moderate	2
Severe	3

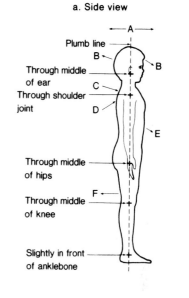

a. Side view

Side View	First Evaluation	Second Evaluation	Third Evaluation
A Body Lean: Forward			
Backward			
B Forward Head			
C Round Shoulders			
D Round Dorsal Curve			
E Protruding Abdomen			
F Hyperextended Knees			
Back View			
G Head Tilt:			
to right			
to left			
H Shoulder:			
lower on right			
lower on left			
I Bow Legs			
J Knock-knees			
K Feet pointing out			
Feet pointing in			
L Curve of Vertebrae:			
C-curve			
S-curve			

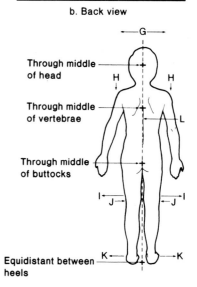

b. Back view

Methods of Assessing Posture

The classroom teacher is generally in the best position to assess her students' postures. Most teachers are genuinely concerned about the way a child sits at his desk and how he moves in his daily activities. For most teachers, the evaluation of posture is primarily one of continual subjective observation. When she notices a major change in a child's posture, the teacher brings in the school nurse or parent to determine whether the change is due to a muscular weakness or to other factors, such as nutrition, eyesight, or an emotional disturbance.

If a teacher wishes to use a simple screening test, she might consider the side- and rear-view plumb line test and the posture chart shown in figure 11.15. The chart can be used in various ways, depending on the interests of the teacher, the ages of the children, and the time available. Most teachers can complete the test in the classroom.

Methods of Improving Posture

The plumb line test is designed as a basic screening device. It can detect major postural problems and, perhaps more important, make the child more conscious of his posture when standing, sitting, or moving through a variety of movement patterns. The foundation of good posture, however, is the possession of optimum levels of muscular strength, endurance, flexibility, and efficient motor skill patterns. If special programs are warranted, the following exercises will assist in correcting functional postural defects and in enhancing general muscular strength endurance and flexibility (see chapter 12).

1. *Exercises for improving head and neck position:*
   Shoulder pull, p. 191

2. *Exercises for improving round shoulders:*
   Hanging, p. 523
   Pull-ups, p. 193
   Push-ups, p. 193
   Arm and shoulder stretch, p. 191

3. *Exercises for improving lower back:*
   Side trunk stretch, p. 191
   Trunk twister, p. 191
   Lower back stretch, p. 192
   Knee to nose touch, p. 196

4. *Exercises for improving abdominal muscles:*
   Curl-ups, p. 194
   Elbow-knee touch, p. 195
   Floor bicycle pump, p. 195
   Reverse curl, p. 195

5. *Exercises for improving functional scoliosis:*
   Hanging, p. 523
   Trunk stretch, p. 195

Nutrition and Wellness

Human wellness as defined in terms of health-related components, must include a concern for the type and amount of food we eat. A well-planned and properly executed exercise program for young children may fail simply because the children lack the basic nutrients or sufficient calories, or they are overweight or obese. These factors, along with high-pressure advertising tactics and questionable diet programs, make it imperative that children understand what constitutes a nutritionally sound diet. The following sections explain what foods must be included in a balanced diet and how to maintain proper weight, and they list a few suggested activities for helping children build and maintain a nutritionally balanced diet.

Table 11.5 Essential Nutrients of a Balanced Diet

Food Class	Function
Protein	Builds and repairs body tissues and provides energy
Carbohydrates	Supply energy and fiber for digestion and elimination
Fats	Supply energy
Minerals (21 essential minerals including calcium, iron, phosphorus, and sodium)	Build and repair body tissues and regulate essential processes
Vitamins (including A, B-complex, C, D, E, and K)	Regulate body processes
Water	Builds and repairs body tissues and regulates essential processes

Balanced Diet

The human body uses more than fifty nutrients to keep its life processes operating effectively and efficiently. These essential nutrients are found in six general food classes listed in table 11.5. They provide the necessary foods for building and repairing body tissues, supplying energy for daily life activities, and regulating body processes.

The task for parents and teachers is to translate knowledge of the nutritional value of various food classes into a balanced daily diet for each child within their care. The U.S. Department of Agriculture designed the Food guide pyramid to help people of different ages and life-styles plan nutritionally balanced diets (figure 11.16). The key to this simple grouping of foods is recognizing that all but fats, oils, and sweets have a high nutritional value. Thus, a balanced diet includes food from all levels of the pyramid. Our task is to teach children to understand the food groups and to consciously select a minimum number of servings from each food group during each day of their lives. The notes on the right side of the pyramid describe the type of foods and their basic functions.

Weight Control

Diet planning based on the food guide pyramid helps every person, regardless of age, receive the essential nutrients. However, the amount of food consumed within each of these groups varies according to age, body structure, metabolism, and daily activities. In addition, the amount and type of food consumed by each member of the family is strongly influenced by the family's cultural and ethnic background. For example, in our multicultural society, children from Hispanic or Asian families eat balanced diets but may not

Figure 11.16 Food guide pyramid.

Food Guide Pyramid
A Guide to Daily Food Choices

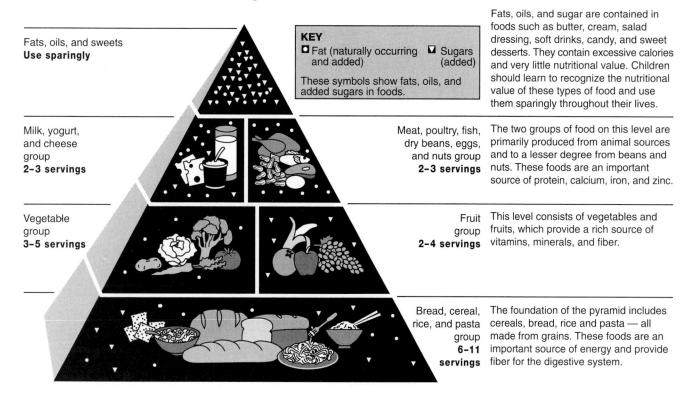

Fats, oils, and sweets
Use sparingly

KEY
☐ Fat (naturally occurring and added) ☑ Sugars (added)

These symbols show fats, oils, and added sugars in foods.

Fats, oils, and sugar are contained in foods such as butter, cream, salad dressing, soft drinks, candy, and sweet desserts. They contain excessive calories and very little nutritional value. Children should learn to recognize the nutritional value of these types of food and use them sparingly throughout their lives.

Milk, yogurt, and cheese group
2–3 servings

Meat, poultry, fish, dry beans, eggs, and nuts group
2–3 servings

The two groups of food on this level are primarily produced from animal sources and to a lesser degree from beans and nuts. These foods are an important source of protein, calcium, iron, and zinc.

Vegetable group
3–5 servings

Fruit group
2–4 servings

This level consists of vegetables and fruits, which provide a rich source of vitamins, minerals, and fiber.

Bread, cereal, rice, and pasta group
6–11 servings

The foundation of the pyramid includes cereals, bread, rice and pasta — all made from grains. These foods are an important source of energy and provide fiber for the digestive system.

appear to follow the typical selection of food from the food groups. Similarly, vegetarians combine rice, grains, and legumes to create the required proteins as well as select other nutrients to complete a balanced diet that is free of meats, eggs, and milk products.

If we take all of the above factors into account, and the child's weight is within the recommended range for his age and height, the food intake (number of calories) is correct. On the other hand, if a child gains excessive weight, he is consuming more calories than he needs. Consequently, his body is converting the excessive food into fat. Taking off excessive body fat and maintaining the proper weight for one's age and life-style require a reduction in daily calorie intake and an increased participation in a regular exercise program. One without the other is not an effective and long-term weight control program. Reducing the amount of food one eats to the point where the body draws on its own stored fat is the first effective part of a weight reduction program.

The daily servings in table 11.6 illustrates how a child who needs to lose body fat would choose foods from the Food Guide Pyramid. It is important to note that table 11.6 can be used by individuals with strong ethnic eating habits or vegetarians in planning their own balanced diets.

Table 11.6 Minimum Daily Servings for Elementary School Children

Food Group	Number of Servings	Sample Serving Size
Meat, nuts	2	2 ounces of lean meat 2 ounces of beans
Milk	3	1 cup of skim milk 1 cup nonfat yogurt
Bread and cereal	6	½ cup cooked pasta 1 slice whole wheat bread
Fruit and vegetables	4	1 orange 2 ounce carrots

When the dietary program is combined with a regular and systematic exercise program, more body fat is used and muscle tone is improved to prevent flabbiness as weight is lost. The end result is a lower percentage of body fat and a general improvement in all body systems.

Teaching Suggestions

Experts in the field of nutrition have clearly indicated that optimum physical fitness and a positive life-style cannot be achieved without a balanced diet. However, what a child

learning about the human body and wellness

eats may be due to the nutritional style of his parents or friends or the availability and cost of food. We have also learned that preaching to children about what and how much they should eat is usually unproductive. Instead, a proven effective approach for leading children toward a positive nutritional life-style is the implementation of activities that allow children to investigate and relate nutritional information to their own immediate needs and life-styles. The following activities and suggestions will help children understand what constitutes a balanced diet and how to maintain proper weight control throughout their lives.

Bulletin Board

The bulletin board can be used to display growth charts of children, energy demands of various physical activities, or comparative nutritional values of various foods.

Measuring Body Fat

Measure each child's body fat with skinfold calipers. This test is included in the AAHPERD Physical Best Test (AAHPERD 1989), along with norms for elementary school children. Inexpensive skinfold calipers may be purchased through several companies listed in appendix C.

Basic Four Food Groups

Use a chart similar to the one shown in table 11.6 and have children make (1) displays, (2) workbooks, or (3) catalogs with pictures from magazines and newspapers.

Daily Food Intake

Use a "Minimum Number of Daily Servings Chart" to have children keep daily records of their food consumption. For older students, include an analysis of their caloric intake and their consumption of junk foods.

Weight Control Programs

Develop a weight control program for all children in the class. Record each child's height and weight. Design daily food and exercise diaries to allow them to see how many calories were used, stored, or needed to meet their daily life activities. This type of activity can lead to effective weight-reducing programs and provide information to parents and health officials concerning children who may need medical attention.

Special Diets and Food Fallacies

Numerous questions relate to food fads, diet pills, and food fallacies. The following questions may develop into interesting class discussions or lead to more extensive individual or group projects:

1. What are three popular fad diets?
2. Should we take vitamin and mineral supplements?
3. Do vegetarians eat a balanced diet?
4. Do fast-food restaurants serve nutritionally valuable foods?
5. Are there special diets for athletes?
6. What happens to the body if we fast for more than three days?

Many outstanding nutrition books and related audiovisual materials suitable for primary and intermediate children are listed in the selected references.

Stress Management

The rapid social-economic changes in our contemporary society have affected children, youths, and adults, regardless of whether they live in cities or rural areas. Problems relating to family break-ups, poor interpersonal relations, and school grades are a few of the current problems that are causing serious stress and anxiety problems among elementary school children.

This stress is the body's response to any demand made on it in order to maintain a state of equilibrium (Corbin and Lindsey 1991). When a person is under stress, he or she may respond in a variety of ways, depending on the problem that is causing the tension or anxiety and the individual's ability to cope with the situation. In most instances, a stressful situation increases the heart rate, blood pressure, and muscle tension. These responses are the body's natural preparations for an activity that may require an extra effort. As soon as the special response has been met, the stress response fades and the body returns to its normal state. If the stress response remains for prolonged periods of time, it leads to serious health problems such as high blood pressure and severe depression.

Stress management is a term used to describe how an individual can reduce high levels of stress. The following guidelines will help each teacher understand and cope with children who may be suffering from excessive tension.

1. Develop a learning environment in which children feel comfortable in your presence and have a sense of trust in you and your judgment.
2. Watch for major changes in each student's general behavior. When serious problems occur, such as excessive aggressive behavior or withdrawal, attempt to find out the cause.
3. Teach children to recognize and cope with stressful situations. This involves discovering how to cope with learning tasks, interpersonal relations, and their own strengths and weaknesses.
4. Provide effective ways to help children cope with stress. This includes teaching children proper breathing techniques, methods of relaxation, and tension-relief techniques through wholesome physical activities.

Substance Abuse

The term *substance abuse* is used to describe the use and effect of alcohol, tobacco, and illegal drugs. According to one article (Kraus 1988), substance abuse is one of the three most popular forms of adult leisure in the United States. In fact, Americans consume 60 percent of the world's illicit mind-altering substances. Although consumption of these substances is predominantly in the adult and upper teen population, there are dangerous signs of a growing number of elementary school children who have experimented with or become users of these substances. Parents, educators, and other leaders in our society look to the school to help educate children about the effects of these substances on health. Although teaching about substance abuse is normally done through health or science courses, there are special "teaching moments" when the adverse effects of alcohol, tobacco, and illicit drugs can be covered effectively in a physical education class. With this in mind, the following key concepts should be emphasized.

1. The use of alcohol and tobacco prevents performers from reaching their greatest potential.

2. Virtually all drugs possess a high potential for addiction. Initially, these drugs are taken because they produce a sense of well-being. However, their continued use leads to dependency and increased levels of stress.

3. Choosing a life-style that involves a dedication to keeping fit and adhering to positive health habits contributes to a productive and happy life.

Exposure to Excessive Sunlight

Many local weather reports now include an ultraviolet index indicating the intensity of the sun's rays. If the index is high on days when children will be outdoors for prolonged periods (sports days, school camping trips, etc.), they should be encouraged to wear protective clothing, such as hats and long sleeve shirts, or use sunscreen lotions.

Selected References

AAHPERD. (1989). *Physical Best Instructor's Guide.* Reston, VA: AAHPERD Publications.

————. (1986). *Physical Activity and Well Being.* Reston, VA: AAHPERD Publications.

Bailey, C. (1984). *The Fit or Fat Target Diet.* Boston: Houghton Mifflin Co.

Corbin, C. B., and Lindsey, R. (1991). *Concepts of Physical Fitness with Laboratories,* Seventh Edition. Dubuque, IA: Wm. C. Brown Publishers.

Greensberg, J. S., and Telljohann, H. S. D. (1992). *Your Personal Stress Profile.* Dubuque, IA: Wm. C. Brown Publishers.

Kraus, R. G. (August 1988). "Changing Views of Tomorrow's Leisure," *JOPERD,* Reston, VA: AAHPERD Publications.

Kuntzleman, C. T. (1990). *Fitness Discovery Activities.* Reston, VA: AAHPERD Publications.

————. (1990). *Instructor's Guide for Feeling Good.* Reston, VA: AAHPERD Publications.

McGlynn, G. (1990). *Dynamics of Fitness: A Practical Approach.* Dubuque, IA: Wm. C. Brown Publishers.

McIntosh, M. (1990). *Lifetime Aerobics.* Dubuque, IA: Wm. C. Brown Publishers.

Maione, J. (1989). *Kids Weigh to Fitness.* Reston, VA: AAHPERD Publications.

Williams, M. (1990). *Lifetime Fitness and Wellness,* Second Edition. Dubuque, IA: Wm. C. Brown Publishers.

12

Assessing and Improving Physical Fitness

According to the most recent National Children and Youth Fitness Study, the general level of health and fitness of elementary school children has not improved over the past few years, when previous studies showed one out of every six American children is so unfit that he or she is classified as physically underdeveloped by the standards of the President's Council on Physical Fitness and Sports. Further, 13 to 20 percent of these children between six and eleven are overweight (Lang 1982). In fact, the proportion of children in the United States who are overweight has increased more than 50 percent over the past two decades. To compound the problem, substantial evidence indicates that children who are unfit and obese show early signs of coronary heart disease, high blood pressure, and high cholesterol levels (Binkhorst, Kemper, and Soris 1983).

It is relatively easy to create positive dietary habits and exercise patterns during the first seven or eight years of life. As children move into puberty and beyond, it becomes increasingly more difficult to change their health habits and routines. Our challenge is to help children develop an active and positive lifestyle from kindergarten on, through each grade in the elementary school. Once children are personally convinced that exercise is important to their well-being, there is a good chance that physical activity will become a permanent part of their daily lives. It also appears that, once a child's lifestyle moves in this direction, he will begin to modify his diet and other health factors to complement this positive and healthy way of living.

The first two sections of this chapter describe ways of assessing and improving the main components of health-related physical fitness. The next section provides information on how children in the primary and intermediate grades can improve their physical fitness and explains how test results are interpreted and used to help children improve their level of physical fitness ∎

Physical Fitness

Since the original Kraus physical fitness survey in 1953, the physical education profession has attempted to define and assess the physical fitness of children, youths, and adults. Although the definition of physical fitness that accompanied each test battery stressed individuals' ability to function according to their own mental, emotional, social, and physical potential, virtually every state and national physical fitness test produced from 1957 to 1978 measured such motor fitness components as strength, muscular endurance, speed, and power. In 1980, with the Health Related Physical Fitness Test developed by AAHPERD, a major change in the philosophy and direction of elementary and secondary school physical fitness programs was established. According to AAHPERD, physical fitness is defined as "a physical state of well being that allows people to: perform daily activities with vigor, reduce their risk of health problems related to lack of exercise, and establish a fitness base for participation in a variety of physical activities" (AAHPERD 1988).

Many elementary education teachers would agree with this definition and would say they contribute to one or more of these general areas of fitness in the classroom. There is general agreement in physical education that "physical fitness" is just one aspect of total fitness. This definition, however, gives little guidance as to what aspects of fitness should be stressed in the physical education program. So we describe a physically fit child as one who possesses adequate strength and endurance to carry out daily activities without undue fatigue and still has energy to enjoy leisure activities and to meet emergencies. This definition, as it applies to each child, must be interpreted on the basis of genetic structure, which sets the optimum level of physical fitness the child is capable of reaching. It must also consider the child's nutritional status and other personal health habits that will determine the potential level of improvement the child is capable of reaching.

Components of Physical Fitness

Although there are differing opinions about which basic components of physical fitness should be measured, the contemporary view is that a health-related test battery should measure muscular strength, muscular endurance, cardiorespiratory endurance, flexibility, and body composition. A low score on a test battery containing the majority of these health-related components would indicate that a child does not possess the strength and vitality to carry out everyday activities and to respond to emergencies. It can also reveal not only a lack of exercise but a possible nutritional need or congenital or temporary illness that could be the cause of low physical fitness.

The following definitions of each component of health-related fitness are generally agreed upon by members of the physical education profession.

Muscular Strength

Strength is defined as the amount of force that a muscle or group of muscles can exert. The importance of developing and maintaining muscular strength cannot be overemphasized. Without sufficient strength, the other components of physical fitness cannot be developed to their full potential.

Muscular Endurance

Muscular endurance is the ability of the muscles to continue to function over a long period of time; it is primarily dependent upon the strength and physiological condition of the muscle groups involved in the movement.

Cardiovascular Fitness

Cardiovascular fitness is the efficiency of the heart, blood vessels, and lungs while performing a continuous movement over a period of time. It is the combined ability of the circulatory and respiratory systems to supply oxygen and nutrients to the muscles, coupled with the ability of the muscles to utilize fuel.

Flexibility

Flexibility is the range and ease of movement of a joint. The amount of flexibility is dependent upon the structure and nature of the joint(s) involved, the nature of the ligaments surrounding the joint, and the extensibility of the muscles relating to the joint. Although flexibility appears to be more of a specific quality relating to one or more joints in a particular movement, it is considered as a general quality in elementary school programs. A child with a relatively high degree of flexibility can absorb an oncoming force or blow through a wider range of movement. Flexibility, or suppleness of movements, is also a prerequisite in performing many gymnastic and creative dance movements.

Body Composition

Body composition is the relative percentage of fat to other tissues (bone, muscle, internal organs) of the body. For example, a child who weighs 90 pounds was tested with skinfold calipers and found to have 15 percent fat (13.50 pounds) and 85 percent (76.50 pounds) of lean body weight. A physically fit child has a relatively low percentage of body fat.

Methods of Assessing Physical Fitness

The Health Related Physical Fitness Test Battery is recommended for use in elementary and secondary schools. The test battery is described in detail in Physical Best: The AAHPERD Guide to Physical Fitness Education and Assessment, AAHPERD Publications, P.O. Box 704, Waldorf, MD, 20601.

Figure 12.1 Skinfold test—triceps.

Figure 12.2 Skinfold test—calf.

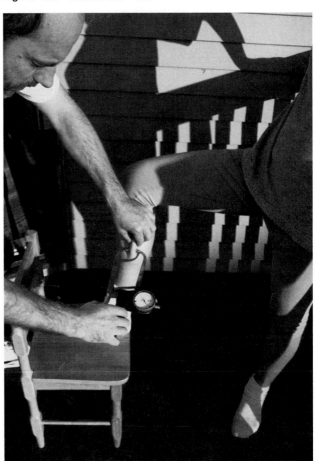

AAHPERD'S Health Related Test

Test No. 1: Aerobic Endurance: One-Mile Run/Walk

Purpose: The purpose of this test is to measure the ability to perform large muscle activity of moderate-to-high intensity over an extended period of time.

Testing area: This test can be conducted on a track or any other flat surface area. Mark off an appropriate area such as a 75×35-yard rectangle. This would require eight laps for a one-mile run/walk.

Equipment: Stopwatch

Description: Students are instructed to move at their fastest pace around the one-mile course. They are permitted to run, walk, or perform combinations of both movements throughout the one-mile distance.

Scoring: Measured in minutes and seconds

Optional tests: Any similar test item that lasts six minutes or longer and where acceptable national standards can be substituted for this one-mile run/walk test. Examples are a one-half-mile run/walk for primary children or a nine-minute run or walk for older children.

Test No. 2: Body Composition: Triceps and Calf Skinfolds

Purpose: The purpose of this test is to measure the degree of body fatness.

Testing area: This test should be conducted away from the main activity area of the class (in a locker room or behind a screen). No other students should be allowed to observe the child being measured.

Equipment: Skinfold calipers; low-cost plastic calipers are acceptable testing equipment

Description: The triceps skinfold is measured on the back of the arm, halfway between the elbow and the shoulder. As the student stands erect with the arm relaxed, grasp the skinfold vertically between your thumb and index finger and approximately ½ inch above the midpoint. While holding the skinfold, place the jaws of the caliper about ½ inch below the index finger (figure 12.1) and allow the caliper to exert its full tension for two seconds before taking a reading. The calf skinfold is measured on the inside of the right lower leg at the point of the greatest calf girth (figure 12.2). Follow the same procedure as the triceps skinfold.

Figure 12.3 Sit-and-reach.

Scoring: Read the scale to the nearest 1.0 mm. Take three separate readings for each skinfold test and record the middle score for each site.

Optional test: Subscapular skinfold

Test No. 3: Flexibility: Sit-and-Reach

Purpose: The purpose of this test is to evaluate the flexibility (range of motion) of the lower back and hamstring muscles (figure 12.3).

Testing area: This test can be administered in any available regular instructional area.

Equipment: Sit-and-reach box or measuring stick substitute

Description: Students are permitted to warm up by a slow stretching of the lower back and hamstring muscles prior to taking this test. The student sits with the knees fully extended, feet about shoulder-width apart, feet flat against the board, and palms down with one hand on top of the other. In one steady movement, the student reaches forward, sliding the fingertips as far forward as possible and holding this position momentarily. Four trials are allowed, with the fourth trial held for at least one second.

Scoring: Each student is permitted four trials. The score is the most distant point reached on the fourth trial.

Optional tests: None

Test No. 4: Muscular Strength and Endurance: Modified Sit-Ups

Purpose: The purpose of this test is to evaluate abdominal muscular strength and endurance.

Testing area: Mats or any other comfortable surface area

Equipment: Mats and stopwatch

Description: The performer lies on his back with knees bent, feet on the floor, and arms crossed and held against the chest, with hands on opposite shoulders and the chin tucked to the chest (figure 12.4). His feet are held down on the floor throughout the

Figure 12.4 Sit-ups.

a

b

exercise. Keeping the elbows against his chest, the performer raises up and touches his elbows to his thighs, then returns until his midback makes contact with the testing surface.

Scoring: Number of sit-ups in sixty seconds; students are permitted to rest between sit-ups

Optional tests: None

Test No. 5: Upper Body Strength and Endurance

Purpose: The purpose of this test is to measure arm and shoulder girdle strength and endurance.

Testing area: A variety of testing areas suitable to mount or construct a horizontal bar

Equipment: Suitable pull-up bar, such as a bar across a doorway, hanging bar, or horizontal ladder

chapter 12

Figure 12.5 Pull-ups.

a

b

Figure 12.6 Modified pull-ups.

a

b

Description: The student assumes a hanging position with an overhand grip (palms facing forward). The feet should not touch the floor. The student raises his body up until his chin is over the bar then returns to a complete hanging position (figure 12.5). The student may take as much time as he desires to complete as many pull-ups as he can.

Scoring: Total number of correctly completed pull-ups

Optional tests: None

Alternate test of upper body strength and endurance

Note: This test is recommended for use with students who scored "0" on the pull-up test. It is not an optional test; it is an adjunct to the pull-up test.

Equipment: Modified pull-up apparatus (see appendix B for detailed plans to construct this apparatus)

Description: The student lies under the bar, back straight and grasping the bar with a forward grip (figure 12.6). The bar is set one to two inches above the student's outstretched arms. An elastic band is placed on a peg seven to eight inches below the bar. The student keeps his body straight and raises up until his chin rises above the elastic band, then returns to the starting position.

assessing and improving physical fitness

Table 12.1 Exercise Zones

Training zone	Cardiorespiratory endurance	Strength	Flexibility
Excessive zone	Runs 10-minute mile first day—feels sick after run and very tired and sore next day	20 curl-ups	Sit-and-reach to 30 cm
Target zone (60–85% of maximum effort)	Runs one mile each day and by end of fifth day runs mile in 10 minutes—feels good each day	10 curl-ups	Sit-and-reach to 13 cm
	Threshold level		
Normal zone	Runs one mile in 12 minutes	7 curl-ups	No exercise
Inactivity zone	No activity beyond getting up, going to school, coming home, etc.	No exercise	No exercise

Scoring: Total number of correctly completed pull-ups; there is no time limit, but the action should be continuous.

Since the development and acceptance of this new physical fitness test, AAHPERD has stopped publishing the former Youth Fitness Test and the Health Related Physical Fitness Test (1984). This was done because of the new direction the profession wishes to take with regard to the emphasis on health-related aspects of physical fitness. However, some teachers, particularly those who have well-established motor fitness testing programs, may wish to continue using these existing motor fitness test batteries, then gradually adopt the new AAHPERD Physical Best Test Battery and accompanying philosophy.

Methods of Improving Physical Fitness

The first part of this section deals with three important principles of exercise that apply to every type of physical fitness activity. The next part discusses the unique characteristics and needs of developmental level I and describes how game, dance, and gymnastic activities can be modified to enhance physical fitness. The latter section, developmental levels II and III, describes how a variety of special physical fitness activities and programs can be integrated into regular physical education.

Principles of Exercise

The activities and special programs in this chapter are designed to improve the health-related components of physical fitness. If the following principles of exercise are adhered to while participating in vigorous physical activities, an individual will improve cardiorespiratory endurance, strength, and flexibility. As children understand and learn to apply these important principles of exercise, they develop the foundation for continuous participation in physical activity.

Principle 1: Overload

The exercise activity should require an overload performance. The systems of the body constantly adapt to a daily routine. For example, if we are inactive, our muscles become smaller (atrophy) and lose strength; our breathing becomes less efficient because we do not force the expansion of the lungs, thus closing off areas of lung tissue where exchange of oxygen and carbon dioxide would otherwise take place. To become stronger or to improve cardiorespiratory efficiency, the performer must increase the intensity (how hard), duration (how long), or frequency (how much) of an activity in accordance with a target zone that sets optimum limits for each individual and for each component of physical fitness. In table 12.1, three components of physical fitness are used to illustrate this overload principle. Under the strength category, if a child performs seven curl-ups (intensity) in one minute (duration) each day (frequency) without causing any "overload" effort, he will not increase his strength. His exercise is below the threshold level. If he begins to perform ten curl-ups each day, without undue strain, he is moving into the target zone and begins to improve his level of strength. If he were to shift immediately to twenty curl-ups each day, he would feel extremely sore and tired, having reached into the excessive zone. Between ten and twenty curl-ups is his optimum training limit. This limit is found by gradually increasing the number of repetitions so there can be an overload performance without excessive soreness and fatigue. This process applies to every component of physical fitness.

Principle 2: Progression

Exercise or activity should provide for progression. This principle is closely associated with principle 1. Any planned exercise program must begin where it is comfortable or within the tolerance level of the child. From there, the program should gradually overload the muscles to increase strength or the demands on the heart and lungs.

Principle 3: Specificity

The principle of specificity described in chapter 5 also applies to developing the components of physical fitness. Simply stated, to increase strength, exercises must be of a strength-building nature such as pull-ups or weight lifting.

However, such exercises may be of little value in improving cardiovascular fitness or flexibility; therefore, other exercises must be included for this part of the program. Specificity of exercise also applies to each part of the body. For example, curl-ups increase the strength of the abdominal muscles but have no effect on increasing the level of strength of the arm and shoulder girdle muscles. The implication of this principle is to develop a balanced physical fitness program that will improve cardiorespiratory endurance, strength, and flexibility.

Developmental Level I

The emphasis of early primary physical education programs should be on exploratory activities in games, dance, and gymnastics. This is a time when children have an opportunity to explore how their bodies work, how to perform a variety of activities, and how to act and react in small- and large-group settings. It is also a time when they form attitudes about themselves and toward physical activities. The following activities can effectively contribute to a child's level of fitness in an enjoyable and positive way. Suggestions are provided to show how to modify these activities in order to enhance one or more elements of health-related physical fitness.

Game Activities

Game activities, such as running, tag, and simple team games, have a minimal effect on improving strength and flexibility. These activities, however, can contribute to cardiorespiratory endurance if the following guidelines are followed.

1. Include rules or modifications that require all children to be moving.
2. Do not eliminate any player from the game.
3. Change the method of moving to enhance the strength and endurance of different parts of the body.

The following games are effective contributors to cardiorespiratory endurance. Suggested modifications are included with each game description.

Name of game	Page
Simple tag	259
Automobiles	259
Traffic lights	256
Dribble tag	262
Crab soccer	265

The creative games approach can be used to design games that enhance cardiorespiratory endurance. For example, posing challenges that require constant movement, moving on all fours, or piggy backing another player meet this goal.

Dance Activities

Dance activities are an enjoyable and integral part of the primary physical education program. With the exception of rhythmics and creative dance, all other dance activities are low contributors to cardiovascular endurance, strength, and flexibility. The rhythmic activities described in chapter 28 can be used to enhance cardiorespiratory endurance, whereas creative dance activities, described in chapter 30, can be used to increase flexibility and strength. The following suggestions illustrate how to use rhythmic activities to enhance physical fitness.

1. Stress rhythmic activities that involve long routines and require running, jumping, hopping, and sliding.
2. Stress rhythmic activities involving rope skipping skills, as well as those that use the rope on the floor for a variety of rhythmic jumping routines.

Gymnastic Activities

Many of the gymnastic activities in the primary program can effectively contribute to strength, flexibility, and, at times, cardiorespiratory endurance. Activities that use the climbing ropes, overhead ladder, and outdoor climbing apparatus are very strong contributors to the strength and endurance of arm and shoulder muscles. Stunts, such as the Bear Walk, Forward Roll, and Wring the Dishrag, enhance a child's flexibility. When the Movement Education approach is used in the medium of gymnastics, teachers can design challenges to enhance one or more health-related components of physical fitness. For example, designing movement challenges that require the child to stretch in a variety of ways enhances range of motion of one or more joints. In a similar way, challenges that stress weight bearing and transfer of weight can be presented so that strength is required in one or more movements involved in the sequence.

Children in the early primary grades enjoy freedom of movement and opportunities to explore different ways of moving and performing game, dance, and gymnastic skills. The previous examples listed in this section illustrate how teachers can modify these activities to enhance physical fitness goals. The more structured activities provided in the next section can be used, at times, with children in developmental level I with some success. Teachers, however, should modify these activities to cope with the unique characteristics of children in the early primary grades.

Developmental Levels II and III

Those who teach children eight years and older face the multiple task of providing vigorous physical activities, of teaching a wide variety of motor skills, and of providing experiences that foster intellectual and social development. No single activity can accomplish all these goals. Furthermore, no single activity can contribute to all of the basic

Table 12.2 Activities for Health-Related Physical Fitness

	Area of contribution									
	Muscular strength		Muscular endurance		Flexibility		Posture		Cardiovascular fitness	
	High	*Low*	*High*	*Low*	*High*	*Low*	*High*	*Low*	*High*	*Low*
Game activities										
Relays		X	X			X	X			X
Tag games		X	X			X		X	X	
Simple team games		X	X			X		X	X	
Individual and team games		X	X			X		X	X	
Dance activities										
Fundamental skills		X		X	X		X			X
Singing games		X		X		X		X		X
Folk dances		X		X		X	X			X
Creative rhythms		X		X	X		X			X
Rhythmics		X	X			X		X		X
Gymnastic activities										
Conditioning exercises	X		X		X		X		X	
Vaulting box	X		X		X			X	X	
Balance beam		X		X	X		X			X
Rope skipping	X		X		X		X		X	
Horizontal bar	X		X		X		X		X	
Climbing rope	X		X		X		X		X	
Stunts and tumbling	X		X		X		X		X	
Swedish gym	X		X		X		X			X
Climbing cube	X		X		X		X			X
Overhead ladder	X		X		X		X			X
Agility apparatus	X		X		X		X			X

Table 12.3 Average Class Scores for Physical Best Fitness Test

Test item	Component	Girls	Health standard	Boys	Health standard
Age		10		10	
One-mile run	Aerobic endurance	12	11	11	9
Skinfold (triceps and calf)	Body composition	30*	16–36	20*	12–25
Sit-and-reach	Flexibility	25	25	25	25
Sit-ups	Abdominal strength and endurance	15*	30	17*	34
Pull-ups	Upper body strength and endurance	0*	1	.5*	1

*Value is below the health standard.

components of health-related fitness described earlier. Table 12.2 shows how various activities contribute to these basic elements.

Let us assume we have tested a fifth-grade class in September and found results similar to those shown in table 12.3. This class needs activities that will increase the strength and endurance of the arm and shoulder girdle and the abdominal muscles. Both boys and girls tend to be overweight, as shown by the high body composition scores. During the first few months of the school year, pleasant weather and student interests indicate that an outdoor activity would be the most suitable choice. The teacher had decided to begin with a four-week unit on soccer activities, but table 12.2 indicates that soccer as a "team game" is a low contributor to strength. Recognizing this inherent weakness of soccer and the need for activities involving strength, the teacher emphasizes pre-game warm-up exercises that develop strength in the arm and shoulder girdle and abdominal and leg muscles.

Because of the high level of overweight children, the teacher emphasizes diet and weight control during her health education program.

Other units of instruction involving game, dance, and gymnastic activities should be analyzed for their potential contribution to health-related fitness (table 12.2). Once the inherent limitations of each activity are known, supplemental activities can be included to meet the special needs of the individual child or the class. The following activities can be used to supplement regular game, dance, or gymnastic lessons or for special programs to enhance one or more components of health-related physical fitness.

Warm-Up Activities

Conditioning, or calisthenic, exercises have traditionally been used as a warm-up activity. The fundamental purposes of these exercises are to develop physical fitness and to prepare the body for the main activities of the lesson. Normally, the warm-up begins with a vigorous activity, such as running around the gymnasium, rope skipping, or playing a vigorous tag game, followed by exercises for flexibility, arm and shoulder girdle, trunk, and legs. The warm-up period normally lasts about three to five minutes; however, time allotments vary from class to class.

The following suggestions can make the conditioning exercises effective and enjoyable:

1. Demonstrate the exercise, then have the class perform it slowly so each child can learn the correct form and cadence.

2. Each exercise should be performed in a steady fashion rather than in quick or ballisticlike motions.

3. Instruct children not to hold their breath during an exercise, but to breathe normally.

4. Once the children know the exercise, let them do the repetitions at their own rates. This is particularly important when performing flexibility exercises, since children's body structures and potential ranges of movement vary.

5. Add variations to each exercise. For example, "trunk bending forward and backward" can be changed on each forward movement by such directions as "through the legs," "to the left side," or "with right foot in front."

6. Change the basic set of exercises on alternate days.

7. Perform exercises to a musical accompaniment. This becomes a "health hustle." Select music with a good 4/4 beat (see chapter 28) and adjust tempo to the class's level of physical fitness.

The exercises described in the following pages are arranged according to: group 1, flexibility; group 2, arm and shoulder girdle; group 3, trunk; and group 4, leg exercises. References to other activities, such as gymnastic stunts and rhythmic skills, are provided within each category.

A typical warm-up activity begins with a general vigorous activity to increase the cardiorespiratory circulation, followed by one or two exercises from each category. The following sample routine illustrates how exercises are selected to complement the main emphasis of the lesson. Once the exercise is demonstrated by a teacher or class leader, the children should perform the exercise at their own speed for the designated period of time.

Lesson Emphasis

Routine No. 1: The general situation involves a fourth-grade class participating in a 30-minute lesson. The main emphasis of the lesson is dribbling the ball with the right and left hand and passing it while on the move.

Performing the "same daily dozen" exercise routine for weeks or months leads to boredom and other class management problems. Hence, change the set of exercises every two weeks, allow children to substitute appropriate exercises from each category, or design a series of color-coded task cards containing a set of warm-up exercises that each child can select and perform according to his own level of physical fitness.

Sample Routine: Games Lesson

Exercise number	Name of exercise	Group	Page	Time
	General vigorous activity—running		404	2 minutes
1	Walk and arm swing	1	190	30 seconds
2	Push-ups	2	193	30 seconds
3	Curl-ups	3	194	30 seconds
4	Alternate leg kneel	4	197	30 seconds
5	Knee to nose touch	3	196	30 seconds

General Vigorous Activities

The following general vigorous activities are used to increase the cardiorespiratory circulation.

Running Begin slowly then increase speed, exaggerate knee lift and other tasks such as "run with hands behind neck, at sides." Add additional challenges, such as change direction and level, and substitute hopping, jumping, or other locomotor skills for running.

Rope Jumping See page 482. Stress different steps performed in a stationary position, as well as while traveling around the gymnasium or outdoor play area.

Rhythmic Activities See page 535. In order to have children begin a vigorous rhythmic warm-up, introduce rhythmic activities in a previous lesson. Once children understand how to develop sequences or routines, the teacher need only say, "Make up a routine that has a run, hop, change of direction," then play a tape with a bouncy tune and a fast tempo.

assessing and improving physical fitness

Vigorous Game Activities Game or tag activities that require all children to keep moving are enjoyable and acceptable vigorous warm-up activities. Following are some examples:

Number game: On signal all children begin to run (or any other locomotor movement called by the teacher). As they are running, she calls out a number, such as three—all must immediately group into threes. The game should move very quickly to improve each child's cardiorespiratory endurance.

Simple tag, page 259

Traffic lights, page 256

Group 1 Exercises: Flexibility

Flexibility or stretching exercises are movements that slowly stretch the muscles to an extended position and are then held for a few seconds before returning to the starting position. The purpose of these exercises is to prepare the muscles for more intensive and complex movements, prevent injuries, and increase the range of motion around the joints (figures 12.7 to 12.15).

Basic Guidelines for Stretching Exercises

The following guidelines should be adhered to when performing stretching exercises.

1. Participate in a general warm-up activity, such as running or rope jumping, before performing any stretching exercises.

2. Perform slow static stretching rather than ballistic stretching that involves stretching by a vigorous force of momentum.

3. Learn to stretch muscles just beyond their normal length but not to the point of pain.

4. Begin stretching muscles in the small joints of the extremities, then progress toward the trunk.

Stunts Stressing Flexibility

Wring the dishrag (arm and shoulder), page 438
Back roller (arm and shoulder), page 426
Camel walk (arm and shoulder), page 436
Gorilla walk (arm and shoulder), page 437
Seal walk (arm and shoulder), page 441
Measuring worm (upper and lower back and legs), page 441
Circle roll (upper and lower back and hamstrings), page 442
Leg wrestling (hamstrings and quadriceps), page 444
Scale stand (quadriceps and hamstrings), page 453

Figure 12.7 Walk and arm swing. Begin walking on the spot or around the instructional area. Swing arms forward and backward and gradually increase the height of the forward and backward swing.

Variations:
1. Walk and swing both arms over head.
2. Repeat (1) to top of swing then rotate one arm, then both arms, toward the right and left.
3. Walk forward and simulate a crawl-stroke swimming action of the arms. Repeat with backstroke action.
4. Walk, clasp hands overhead, then bend alternately toward the right, back, and left side.
5. Walk forward turning head and trunk to right and left sides.
6. Walk and alternately bend trunk toward right side, backward, then left side.
7. Walk with exaggerated high-knee rise. Add hands above head, stretched sideways, or held behind the head.
8. Walk with long stride movement.
9. Walk with extended right leg crossing in front of left, then extended left leg in front of right.
10. Slide toward the left side with a slow extended shift of the left leg followed by a slow follow-up movement of the right leg.

Single leg balance (quadriceps and hamstrings), page 455
Rear support (arm and shoulder and trunk), page 454
Walking down wall (quadriceps and abdominals), page 457
The bridge (quadriceps and abdominals), page 458
Back touch (quadriceps and abdominals), page 494
Thread the needle (upper and lower back), page 495
Twist away (arm and shoulder girdle), page 495

Figure 12.8 Shoulder pull. Extend right hand backward and upward and left hand behind head and downward to grasp hands, hold, pull gently, and release. Reverse hands and repeat movement.

Variation:
Grasp a skipping rope, hold with upper hand, and reach backward and upward with lower hand, hold, and release.

Figure 12.9 Arm and shoulder stretch. Extend arms behind back and grasp hands. Rotate elbows inward, then raise backward and upward.

Figure 12.10 Side trunk stretch. Begin in a cross-legged position, back straight, right arm extended overhead, and left arm reaching as far as possible toward the right. Reverse arms and repeat to opposite side.

Variations:
Repeat exercise from a kneeling or standing position.

Figure 12.11 Trunk twister. Start in a sitting position with right leg extended and left leg bent and crossed over the right leg. The left hand is resting on the floor, and the right arm is resting on the side of the left leg. Simultaneously push against the leg with the right arm and turn the trunk as far as possible toward the left side. Reverse positions and repeat exercise.

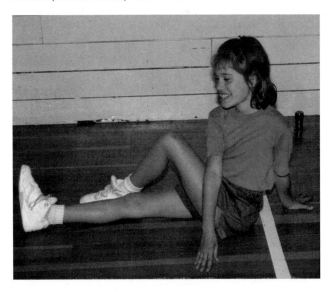

Figure 12.12 Lower back stretch. Begin in a back lying position with knees bent, legs and trunk extended upward, and head and arms on the floor (a). Relax and pull knees to chest and hold for a few seconds (b).

a

b

Figure 12.13 Hip and thigh stretch. Begin with back straight, right knee flexed, and left knee and toe resting on the floor. Keeping both hands resting on the right knee, press the hips forward and downward.

Figure 12.14 Hamstring stretch. Begin in a sitting position, head up, right leg extended forward, left leg flexed with foot near the crotch. Right hand is on the shin, and left hand is on the left knee. Keep head up and bend from the hips toward the right toe and hold. Reverse position of legs and repeat exercise.

a

b

Figure 12.15 Quadriceps stretch. Lie on the right side, left hand behind head, right hand holding top of right foot, and gently pull heel toward the right buttock. Keep the same position, then push the foot against the right hand. Reverse positions and repeat to the opposite side.

Group 2 Exercises: Arm and shoulder girdle muscles

The exercises in this group are designed to exercise the strength and endurance of the arm and shoulder girdle muscles. (See figures 12.16 to 12.20.)

Figure 12.16 Arm rotators. Stand with feet together, back straight, and arms extended sideways, with palms facing forward. Rotate arms forward, upward, and backward in a circular movement. Gradually increase the size of the circle and change direction of arm movement after three or four rotations.

Variations:
1. Swing each arm in the opposite direction.
2. Begin with arms at sides. Alternately swing arms overhead and back to side position.
3. Bend forward and move arms in a breaststroke or crawl action.
4. Swing both arms to the same side or cross them in front.

Figure 12.17 Push-ups. Begin in a front-lying position, with hands approximately shoulder-width apart, fingers pointing forward, and chin a few inches off the floor. Extend arms, keeping the back of the legs straight.

Variations:
1. Rest weight on knees and perform knee push-ups.
2. Instead of lowering the body straight down, lower it to one side.
3. Move hands close together, then farther apart.
4. Repeat original exercise with one leg off the floor.

Figure 12.18 Pull-ups. One partner assumes a back-lying position, with arms up. The other partner stands with feet on opposite sides of partner's shoulders and extends arms down. Both lock hands. The standing partner holds her arms straight while the lower partner pulls her body up.

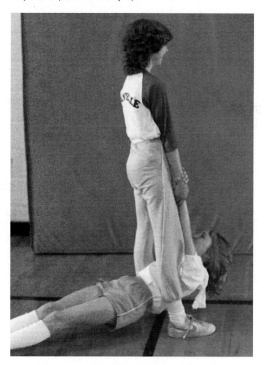

assessing and improving physical fitness

Figure 12.19 Side stretch. Lie on right hip and extend both legs. Place right hand on the floor and extend arm. Place left hand on the hip. Raise the body, keeping the right hand and foot on the floor until the legs and trunk form a straight line. Repeat on opposite side.

Variations:
1. When legs and trunk are straight, stretch top arm and leg forward, then backward.
2. From variation 1, raise top leg upward.
3. From variation 1, place top hand on floor, then twist body toward the ceiling and back.

Figure 12.20 Crab kick. Begin in a crab walk position. Raise left leg up and point toe toward the ceiling.

Variations:
1. From toe pointing position, twist right leg to the left side.
2. From toe pointing position, bend arms and lower shoulders a few inches, and return to the starting position.
3. Repeat with right leg raised.

Stunts Contributing to Arm and Shoulder Girdle Strength and Endurance

Wring the dishrag (arm and shoulder girdle flexibility), page 438

Shoulder wrestling (arm and shoulder girdle strength and endurance), page 444

Lame puppy walk (arm and shoulder girdle strength and endurance), page 437

Crab walk (abdominal strength and endurance), page 439

Seal walk (arm and shoulder girdle strength and endurance), page 441

Measuring worm (arm and shoulder girdle strength and endurance), page 441

Wheelbarrow (arm and shoulder girdle strength and endurance), page 439

Frog stand (arm and shoulder girdle strength and endurance), page 456

Pig walk (arm and shoulder girdle strength and endurance), page 444

Elbow wrestling (arm and shoulder girdle strength and endurance), page 444

Handstand (arm and shoulder girdle strength and endurance), page 458

Forward drop (arm and shoulder girdle strength and endurance), page 446

Group 3 Exercises: Trunk

The exercises in this group are designed to improve the strength and endurance of abdominals, and upper and lower back muscles. Warm-up programs should include one or more exercises from each set of muscle groups. (See figures 12.21 to 12.27.)

Figure 12.21 Curl ups. Begin by lying on back, with hands at sides. Knees should be partially flexed, with heels resting on mat. Raise trunk about thirty degrees and return to starting position.

Variations:
1. Sit up, turning body toward the right. Repeat toward the left.
2. Sit up and wrap arms around knees, then return to starting position.
3. Sit with arms crossed on chest.

Figure 12.22 Elbow-knee touch. Lie on back, with hands placed over ears, elbows forward, knees bent with feet off floor. Raise up, twist body, and touch elbow to opposite knee.

Variations:
1. Touch both elbows to opposite knees.
2. Cross arms and repeat original exercise.
3. From original position, rotate bent legs toward the right, then left.

Figure 12.23 Floor bicycle pump. Sit in a partial back lying position with heels and hands resting on the floor. Lift the left leg slightly off the floor, bend left knee, and move left heel close to buttock. Return to starting position and repeat with the right leg.

Figure 12.24 Reverse curl. Lie on the back with knees bent, feet flat on the floor, and arms placed at the sides with palms down. Raise the knees upward until they are just over the shoulders, then return to the starting position.

Figure 12.25 Trunk stretcher. Begin in a stride-standing position, with hands fully extended over head and knees slightly bent. Bend forward and reach toward the floor with fingertips. Return to original position.

Variations:
1. Repeat original exercise to opposite side.
2. Repeat original exercise and touch right hand to left toe, then repeat to opposite side.
3. Repeat original exercise and grasp left ankle and gently pull body downward. Repeat to opposite ankle.

Figure 12.26 Head and arm raisers. Begin by lying face down, with forehead resting on back of hands. Keeping head in line with body, raise hands, head, and elbows about two inches. Then, keeping hands and head in same position, raise elbows as high as possible.

Variations:
1. Repeat to the two-inch position, then stretch one arm sideways, forward, and back to the starting position.
2. Keep chest on the floor and raise one or both extended legs upward.

Figure 12.27 Cat stretcher. Begin in a partially crouched position. Stretch back upward, hold at the highest point for a few seconds, then return to the starting position.

Variations:
From original position, dip chin to floor and raise right leg upward. Repeat with left leg.

Stunts Contributing to Trunk Strength and Endurance

Backward roll (abdominal strength and endurance), page 429

Rear support (abdominal strength and endurance), page 454

V-sit (abdominal strength and endurance), page 458

Group 4 Exercises: Legs

The exercises in this group are designed to increase strength and endurance of the hip and leg muscles (figures 12.28 to 12.32).

Figure 12.28 Knee to nose touch. Begin in a partially crouched position, right knee on the floor and left knee touching the chest. Simultaneously raise head up and extend left leg backward to a horizontal position. Balance on left knee and repeat exercise.

a

b

Figure 12.29 Treadmill. Lie facedown. Push off the floor, with arms in an elevated push-up position. Keep one leg extended and draw the other leg forward until the knee is under the chest. Reverse leg positions in a continuous and simultaneous motion.

Variations:
1. Begin with both legs together. Draw both legs forward and backward.
2. From variation 1, keep legs together and shift feet toward the right and left sides.

Figure 12.30 Squat jump. Begin in a crouched position, with arms at sides and fingers resting on the floor. Push off floor and extend body until feet are about four to six inches off the mat, with arms remaining at the sides for balance. Return to the starting position and repeat.

Variations:
1. Extend arms over head on each upward movement.
2. Change position of legs while in the air, such as extend sideways, cross, or move forward and backward.

Figure 12.31 Jumping jack. Stand with both legs together and arms at sides. Simultaneously jump to a straddle position and clap hands over head.

Variations:
1. Cross legs instead of bringing feet together.
2. Shift legs to a forward and backward stride position. Jump and alternately move the arms and legs in a forward and backward direction.

a   b

Figure 12.32 Alternate leg kneel. Begin in a standing position with arms at sides and feet together. Step forward with the right foot until the upper and lower leg is at ninety degrees and touch the left knee to the floor. Return to the starting position and repeat movement to the opposite side.

a   b

Figure 12.33 Neck circling.

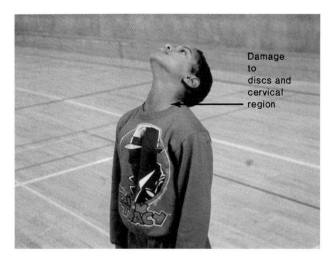

Stunts Contributing to Leg Strength and Endurance

Knee jump (strength and power), page 438
Turk stand (strength and balance), page 453
Heel slap (strength and power), page 439
Bear dance (strength and endurance), page 444
Knee dip (strength and balance), page 456
Leg wrestling (strength and endurance), page 445
Bouncing ball (strength and endurance), page 438

Avoiding Potentially Harmful Exercises

Some conditioning exercises are potentially harmful to the body, particularly to the muscles, tendons, and ligaments. The following exercises are potentially hazardous, especially when performed in unison in a class warm-up or group fitness routine. Young children with immature bone structure may be able to perform some of these activities without much harm; however, from a long-term perspective, it is important to eliminate these exercises from a child's repertoire so he will not use them in the future when his body is fully developed.

Neck Circling

From a standing or sitting position, the head is rotated in circular fashion. This may cause damage to the cervical artery and nerves and may cause depression of the discs in the cervical region (see figure 12.33).

Substitute exercise: Neck stretch

Leg lifts

From a back-lying position, straight legs are raised and lowered. This movement is a hip-flexor strengthening exercise; that is, it strengthens the iliopsoas muscles, which attach to the lumbar vertebrae, ilium, and upper femur;

Figure 12.34 Leg lifts.

Promotes
hyperextension
of
lower
back

Figure 12.35 Toe touch.

Lower back strain
plus
hyperextension
of the
knee

Figure 12.36 Bicycle.

hence, when executed, leg lifts tilt the pelvis forward, arching the body and promoting hyperextension of the lower back (see figure 12.34). The same problem is encountered with the straight leg sit-up; therefore, this exercise should be avoided as well.

Toe Touch

From a standing position with legs straight, the child bends forward and places his hands on the floor. When this movement is performed, particularly in a ballistic way, it may cause lower back strain and hyperextension of the knee, stretching the ligaments and capsule of the joint (see figure 12.35).

Substitute exercises: Sitting stretch

Back Arch

The subject begins by lying face down with hands under shoulders, then raises the body up and arches the head back. This exercise stretches the abdominal muscles, which are usually too weak in young children to act as strong antagonistic muscles, resulting in hyperextension of the lower back. It may also damage the nerves of the neck and the intervertebral discs.

Bicycle

Body weight rests on the head, shoulders, and elbows and the hands are placed under the hips. When the bicycle action is performed, the movement causes hyperflexion of the upper back and neck (kyphosis). It can also cause excessive stretching of the ligaments and nerves in this body region (see figure 12.36). The "plough," which moves legs from this position upward and over the head, causing the same hyperflexion, should also be avoided.

Substitute exercise: Knee-to-chest

Hurdle Stretch

The subject sits on the floor with left leg extended forward and the thigh of the right leg stretched to the side; the knee is bent and stretched toward the rear. She then bends her trunk and reaches toward the foot. This exercise places a heavy stress on the knee of the extended leg and a strain in the groin. It also places heavy stress on the cartilage of the bent knee (see figure 12.37).

Substitute exercise: Lateral straddle stretch

Knee Bends

This exercise begins in a standing position, legs together and arms extended forward. The back is kept straight and the subject squats until the upper and lower leg touch each other (see figure 12.38).

Avoid repeated and excessive knee bends (more than 90 degrees). The knee joints of young children are still maturing and, thus, permit a wide range of movement. To be on the cautious side, and to develop a long-term

chapter 12

Figure 12.37 Hurdle stretch.

Figure 12.39 Sit-ups.

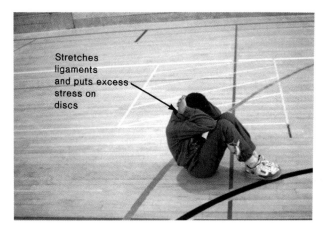

Stretches ligaments and puts excess stress on discs

Figure 12.38 Knee bends.

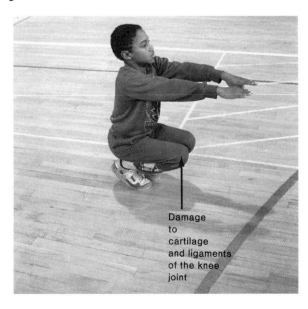

Damage to cartilage and ligaments of the knee joint

attitude, permit half-knee bends for all children. Occasional full-knee bending activities, performed in stunts, animal walks, and some movement challenges are not considered harmful.

Substitute exercise: Wall seat

Sit-Up with Hands Behind Neck

This exercise begins in a back lying position, hands grasped behind the head, knees bent, and feet flat on floor. The upper body is pulled forward to touch the knees. As the person pulls upward and forward, the hands pull on the neck, placing it in a hyperflexion position, which stretches the ligaments and places excess pressure on the intervertebral discs (see figure 12.39).

Substitute exercise: Curl-ups

Other Types of Warm-Up Exercises

Performing the same type of warm-up exercises day after day can be very boring for children. The following exercise programs should be used throughout the school year to provide variety and to cope with individual differences in interest and levels of physical fitness. Modifications can be made to each program to contribute to the unit and lesson emphasis.

Circuit Training

Circuit training is repeating one or more exercises as many times as possible within a time limit. A simple circuit would be doing six push-ups, ten curl-ups, and eighteen toe touches within two minutes. The number and type of exercises are optional and the variations unlimited.

This type of conditioning exercise program has many advantages, particularly for teachers in self-contained classrooms. In the first place, circuit training allows for individual differences. The number of repetitions of each exercise is determined by each child, not by the most physically fit child in the class, and one of the most important administrative advantages is the time limit. The teacher determines how much time she wants to devote to circuit training, then tailors a program to the needs of her class.

An example is provided to show how to develop a circuit for each member of the class.

Step 1: Determine how much time you want to spend on the circuit. Time might range from six to ten minutes; our example is ten minutes.

Step 2: Select appropriate exercises. Let us assume the teacher has administered a physical fitness test and has noted that the majority of students show low strength and endurance in the arm and shoulder girdle (pull-ups), abdominal muscles (sit-ups), and leg muscles (600 yard run). The circuit training program, thus, should contain exercises that improve these weaknesses. The five exercises listed in table 12.4 would meet these needs.

Table 12.4 Circuit Training Program for Increasing Strength and Endurance

Exercise	Page	Maximum number	Training dose no. 1 ($^1/_4$ dose)	Jan. 15	Jan.16	Jan. 17	etc.
1. Jumping jacks (legs)	197	16	4				
2. Push-ups (arms and shoulders)	193	8	2				
3. Head and arm raiser (trunk)	195	6	2				
4. Treadmill	196	20	5				
5. Elbow-knee touch (trunk)	195	11	3				

Step 3: Determine the maximum number of repetitions for each exercise. This is the first day involving exercise. Start with the first exercise, jumping jacks. All children attempt to do the exercise as many times as they can in one minute. Record the number of repetitions under the maximum number column in table 12.4. Let us assume this is the chart of a fifth-grade girl who has performed sixteen jumping jacks repetitions. Immediately following this test, let the children rest for one minute. Next, have them do as many push-ups as possible in one minute. Let them rest for one minute and continue the procedure to the fifth exercise.

Step 4: Set the training dose. The training dose (see table 12.4) is the number of repetitions the child performs when she starts the circuit program. It might be one-quarter, one-half, or three-quarters of the maximum number. As a suggestion, start with one-quarter of the maximum number as the child's first training dose. Place these numbers in the first training dose column. Now the child is ready to perform the circuit without any rest between each exercise. In other words, she must try to complete the following three laps of exercises in ten minutes.

Step 5: Attempt to complete the circuit. Each child has ten minutes to complete the circuit. Let us assume this girl has completed one lap in three minutes. Now, without rest, she starts her second lap. This lap takes her three and one-half minutes, leaving three and one-half minutes to complete the third lap. She immediately starts her third lap and gets to the second exercise, the push-ups, when the whistle blows. Record her results under the appropriate date. She completed two laps and was on exercise 2 of the third lap, so "3-2" would be recorded under the date and opposite push-ups.

Step 6: Continue step 5 until the child performs three laps within the time limit. Then increase each exercise by one repetition. Our girl would now do five jumping jacks, three push-ups, three head raisers, six treadmills, and four elbow-knee touches.

Lap 1	Lap 2	Lap 3
4 jumping jacks	4 jumping jacks	4 jumping jacks
2 push-ups	2 push-ups	2 push-ups
2 head raisers	2 head raisers	2 head raisers
5 treadmills	5 treadmills	5 treadmills
3 elbow-knee touches	3 elbow-knee touches	3 elbow-knee touches

The length of time devoted to a circuit training program depends foremost on the physical fitness needs of the class. If the class scored low on the physical fitness test, it would be wise to require a daily circuit for five to six weeks. The teacher might also design a ten-minute circuit for use in the classroom on those days when her class does not have access to the gymnasium. In this case, she should consider student interest and change the exercises in the circuit each month.

There is a wonderful opportunity here to help the child who scores extremely low on the physical fitness test. First, attempt to determine the reasons for the low fitness, such as obesity or chronic lack of exercise. Design a circuit for the child to do at home. This may involve drawing stick figures to explain the exercises and sending a short note to the parents or interviewing them. Also, the child should set goals for himself in his personal activity log (PAL) as explained in chapter 9. The results may be tremendous if the teacher shows an interest, making periodic checks with the child and the parents.

Obstacle Course

An obstacle course is an arrangement of small equipment and large apparatus designed to improve one or more of the components of physical fitness. Commercial obstacle courses normally include apparatus to climb, balance on, vault over, and crawl through. This type of apparatus is basically for use outdoors and normally is permanently anchored to the ground. Homemade obstacle courses using the natural building materials of a region have become very popular in many elementary schools. They

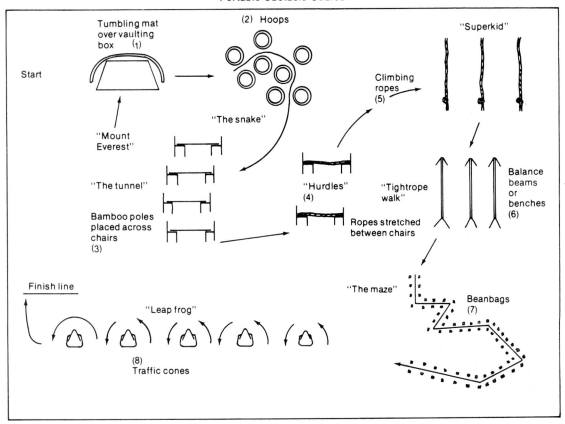

are generally built by parents and usually have a theme, such as a western fort or outpost, space travel, or a jungle trek.

Portable obstacle courses can be made with the equipment and apparatus available in the school. These courses have several advantages: they can be arranged in different patterns and they can be located in a gymnasium or on the playground. The illustrated portable obstacle course requires a minimum amount of small and large apparatus used in an imaginative and constructive way.

Each child tries to complete the course as quickly as possible. The items along this obstacle course contribute to physical fitness in the following ways:

1. *Mount Everest:* Climbing improves strength and power.

2. *The snake:* Running through the hoops, placing alternate feet in them, improves agility.

3. *The tunnel:* Crawling through improves strength and endurance of the arm and shoulder girdle.

4. *Hurdles:* Jumping over them improves leg power.

5. *Superkid:* Climbing the rope as high as possible improves strength of the arm and shoulder girdle.

6. *Tightrope walk:* Walking across balance bench improves balance.

7. *The maze:* Hopping through beanbag course improves strength and power of the legs.

8. *Leapfrog:* Straddle jumping over traffic cones (or milk cartons) improves the power of the legs.

Assign one child to start at each station in order to provide maximum participation and avoid confusion and collisions. On the signal "go," each child tackles the task at his station, then continues through the obstacle course until completing all eight tasks. If possible, duplicate stations two, seven, and eight so that two students can begin at each of these stations.

Children thoroughly enjoy indoor and outdoor obstacle courses. Once the students understand the basic purpose of an obstacle course, they should have an opportunity to plan their own. Their designs are usually very imaginative and more demanding than the "teacher-designed course."

Jogging

Jogging is an easy or relaxed run that does not place undue fatigue on the runner. It is one of the most effective and enjoyable means of improving muscular and cardiovascular endurance. If taught correctly, elementary children—including first graders—can participate in jogging activities in the gymnasium, on the playing field, or in a cross-country setting.

The proper form is like that of a distance runner: body erect and relaxed and arms swinging in an easy manner. The heel of the foot contacts the ground, then rocks forward to a gentle push off the front of the foot.

Before introducing jogging, the teacher should present it to young children as a recreational activity. Jogging should not be seen as a prerequisite to competitive cross-country running; rather, it should be seen as an activity in which children can derive enjoyment and success as they increase the distance they can run without undue fatigue or strain. This means each child should set his own goals (see activity log in chapter 9), and other activities should be interspersed with jogging, since young children may become bored with the same jogging pace and such tracks as "around the gymnasium" or "around the outside of the playing field."

The basic approach used to teach children to jog is to have them begin with a series of stretching exercises, then a walk. When they feel ready, they begin to jog as far as they can without feeling overfatigued or out of breath. Once the children learn to pace themselves to a jog-walk-jog pattern, they will gradually increase the jogging distance as they decrease the walking distance.

After a few days of basic jog-walk-jog activities, introduce the "scout's pace." Have each child jog 110 yards, walk 55 yards, jog 110 yards, continuing the pattern as long as possible. The distances can be adjusted to the child's or the class's ability and condition.

As soon as the majority of the children can jog a reasonable distance, such as a mile, introduce other jogging activities into the program, such as "hash running" (p. 414), orienteering (p. 415), or establishing a 100-mile club, all of which involve enjoyable recreational jogging. The 100-mile club is a program in which each child keeps his own jogging "log" or record sheet. He might receive a certificate when he reaches 100 miles; however, if the jogging program has been introduced correctly, the child should find that completing 100 miles is valuable in itself and he has little need for a badge or certificate.

Rope Jumping

The individual rope jumping steps described in chapter 26 can be incorporated into an excellent program for enhancing cardiorespiratory fitness. The following procedure will help develop a rope jumping program for upper primary or intermediate grades.

1. Set a time limit for rope jumping (duration). This program will last ten minutes.
2. Allow each child to choose three or four steps that can be performed on each turn of the rope (example: two-foot basic, running, one-foot hop, or cross-arm step).
3. Set a heart rate training zone between 160 and 190 beats per minute.
4. Before starting the rope jumping session, have the class perform a series of stretching exercises.

5. For the ten-minute rope jumping program, all children begin jumping rope to a cadence of eighty jumps per minute. (Use a record with a 4/4 beat and adjust the speed to eighty beats per minute.) Each child tries to jump to the pace for ten minutes. If a child stops, say at four and one-half minutes, he should immediately take his heart rate. At the ten-minute mark, have all remaining children take their heart rate. If half of the students' heart rates are less than 160 beats, increase the cadence to 90 beats and instruct each child to include more difficult and demanding steps (intensity).
6. On successive days, each child tries to keep up to the cadence as long as possible. As each child improves, he will continue longer and add more demanding steps. Continue adjusting the cadence upward until all children are performing within the target zone.

Aerobic Dancing

Aerobic dancing is moving rhythmically through a series of movement patterns. It may include simple dance steps, non-locomotor movements, or combined movements involving small equipment such as ropes, wands, or hoops. The musical accompaniment for aerobic dance routines is normally a bouncy even 4/4 rhythm. Most popular rock and roll, disco, marching, folk dance, and western music can be used with equal success.

The success of an aerobic dance program for elementary school children will depend on their ability to keep in time to a musical accompaniment. Teachers should review chapter 28, "Rhythmics and Movement Activities," before designing aerobic routines. Once children understand what even rhythm and accent mean and can design their own rhythmic sequences, they are very close to performing aerobic dance routines.

The following teaching suggestions and sample routines will provide a start toward developing a variety of beneficial cardiorespiratory routines that are thoroughly enjoyed by children from grades two to six. In addition, there are numerous commercial aerobic programs involving written exercises and accompanying records or tapes. Teachers should consult local record stores and talk to local fitness class instructors for additional ideas relating to types of exercises and appropriate music for elementary school children.

Teaching Suggestions

1. Design movement patterns that involve four, eight, or sixteen counts. Stress changing the movement on the first beat of each measure.
2. Teach children a basic aerobic dance vocabulary. The following will provide an example of useful cue words.
   a. Bounce: Perform small jumps on both feet.
   b. Clap: Jump in place, clap hands, and move elbows back, then forward to clap again.

c. Jog: Running with a high knee lift. "Hand jive"—jog and cross and uncross hands in front at a low level. "Wild"—jog and shake hands overhead. "Wiper"—jog and move hands in front like a windshield wiper.

d. Kick: Step on right foot and kick left foot about waist high.

e. Leroy Brown: A variation of jumping jacks that involves feet together and bounce twice while keeping hands at shoulders, then feet astride, bounce twice, and simultaneously raise hands overhead and back to shoulders.

3. Design several aerobic routines involving different steps, exercises, and lengths of time. Change routines when children show boredom or when performance levels dictate more intensity and duration for the children's increased fitness level.

4. Use simple dance steps such as walk, run, jump, hop, slide, and skip.

5. Encourage children to design their own aerobic dance routines and to lead the class through their routines.

6. As soon as the children know a few routines and feel at ease, introduce aerobic dance routines involving small equipment such as individual ropes, elastic bands, or hoops.

Figure 12.40 Jump with feet together.

Figure 12.41 Jump onto left foot.

Figure 12.42 Jump and lunge.

Figure 12.43 Right lunge.

Figure 12.44 Jump and lift left knee to right elbow.

Sample Aerobic Dance Routine   The following aerobic dance routine uses two, four, or eight counts for each movement.

A. Jog
   1. Jog eight steps forward (high knee lift).
   2. Jog eight steps backward (high knee lift).
   3. Hand jive eight steps forward (cross and uncross hands while jogging).
   4. Hand jive eight times backward (cross and uncross hands while jogging)

B. Jump and swing
   1. Jump with feet together (figure 12.40, count 1).
   2. Jump onto left foot and simultaneously lift right foot off floor and swing arms forward and upward (figure 12.41, count 2).
   3. Jump with feet together (figure 12.40, count 3).

4. Jump on right foot and swing arms forward and upward (count 4).
   5. Repeat 1–4 three times.

C. Jump and lunge
   1. Begin with elbows out, fingers on shoulders and feet together. Jump with feet together (figure 12.42, count 1).
   2. Jump to a right lunge (figure 12.43, count 2).
   3. Jump with both feet together (count 3).
   4. Jump to a left lunge (count 4).
   5. Repeat 1–4 three times.

D. Elbow knee jump
   1. Begin with hands clasped behind head. Jump and lift right knee to left elbow (count 1).
   2. Jump and lift left knee to right elbow (figure 12.44, count 2).
   3. Repeat 1–2 sixteen times.

Figure 12.45 Jump with hands on shoulders.

Figure 12.46 Do a modified jumping jack.

E. Leroy Brown (modified jumping jack)
1. Begin with feet together and fingertips touching shoulder. Jump twice with hands on shoulders (figure 12.45, counts 1 and 2).
2. Jump to stride, rebound in this position, and simultaneously raise hands over head (figure 12.46, counts 3 and 4).
3. Repeat three to four times.

Repeat entire sequence of exercises one or more times, depending on each individual's level of cardiorespiratory endurance.

F. Cool down
1. Slow jog on spot (16 counts).
2. Walk slowly around gymnasium for one minute.

Other Appropriate Cardiorespiratory Activities

If the following activities are performed on a continuous basis, they will provide a positive cumulative effect on the child's cardiovascular system.

1. Cross-country running or skiing
2. Distance walking at a brisk rate
3. Bicycling
4. Swimming
5. Rhythmic exercises (chapter 28)
6. Step aerobics

The above examples are individual fitness activities conducted within existing physical education programs. A few school districts have expanded their cardiorespiratory fitness programs to include other important related factors, such as drug education and nutrition. The Sunflower Project[1] in Shawnee Mission, Kansas, is a good example of this type of program. This district initiated a broad-based program for every member of the family. It began with a daily aerobics program before school for family members. Recess became a twenty-minute fitness program for all children and, finally, a special aerobic fitness program was organized for teachers after school.

Helping Children Understand and Improve Their Physical Fitness

The general premise underlying the Physical Best™ test battery is that students who meet the health standards of each test item possess sufficient cardiorespiratory fitness, endurance, strength, and suppleness to meet the demands of their daily life activities. This new test battery provides a health fitness standard for each of the five test items for boys and girls who are between five and eighteen years of age. To illustrate the use of this standard, if a nine-year-old girl can run or walk one mile in eleven minutes or less, she is considered to be at a healthful level of aerobic endurance. A boy of the same age must be able to run or walk the same distance in ten minutes or less. The standard for body leanness is measured in the second skinfold test item. The optimum fat content for this test item for nine-year-old girls is 15 to 27 percent (16 to 36 mm) and 10 to 20 percent for boys of the same age (12 to 25 mm). Children whose scores are higher than the upper limits of these scores are considered overweight or obese, depending on how much excessive body fat they are carrying. Scores falling below these standards would indicate the possibility of undernourished or anorexic children. In the sit-and-reach test for flexibility, 25 cm for boys and girls of all ages is the established standard. Students who fall below this level may develop low back and hamstring disorders; therefore, they should seek stretching exercises that increase range of motion. The last two test items measure abdominal and arm and shoulder girdle strength and endurance. The standard here for nine-year-old girls (28 sit-ups, 1 pull-up) and boys (30 sit-ups, 1 pull-up) is similar. Children who score at or above these standards are considered to possess sufficient muscular strength and endurance to avoid risks of low back disorders and other neuromuscular disorders attributed to low levels of muscular strength and endurance.

The most important factor in determining each child's fitness goals is to assess his initial level of physical fitness. If a child's level of fitness is very low, he has an opportunity to make very large gains. However, children who meet the standard for their age can make only small gains, even with a daily rigorous exercise program. The

1. Contact Instructional Program Center, 6649 Lamar Street, Shawnee Mission, KA 66202 for additional information.

Physical Best™ is protected by trademark and copyright of the Physical Fitness Education and Assessment Program of the American Alliance for Health, Physical Education, Recreation and Dance (AAHPERD).

following example of a nine-year-old girl will illustrate how to use Physical Best's guidelines for setting goals to determine a reasonable target.

In our sample case, nine-year-old Mary Smith is tested initially on September 23, 1992. Her score on the one-mile run/walk is 14.03 minutes. This is a fairly poor performance (the established standard is 11.0 minutes), indicating a need to improve her cardiorespiratory endurance. The Physical Best guideline suggests Mary should start to decrease her time by 1 to 4 minutes. At this point, other factors, such as how many physical education classes she has each week and if she is encouraged by her parents and friends to participate in after-school physical activities, must be considered. Her diet, amount of sleep, and level of stress are also very important considerations when setting this anticipated level of improvement in physical fitness. The next item, skinfold, is 24 mm (the established standard is between 16 and 36), so she does not have excess weight for her age. Similarly, her score of 23 cm (the established standard is 25) on the sit-and-reach test shows she has a good range of motion; hence, she needs little extra stretching activities beyond what she is getting in her regular physical education classes. Her scores of 0 on the pull-up test and 4 on the sit-up test clearly indicate a very low level of strength and endurance of the abdominal and arm and shoulder girdle regions (the established standards suggest 1 and 28, respectively). These low scores suggest a goal-setting figure of five to ten repetitions for sit-ups and one to two for pull-ups. Teachers should use the suggested increases provided in the Physical Best Manual as general guidelines only. As the child improves, new goals can be created to keep the child moving to higher levels of physical fitness. (See activity log in chapter 9.)

Selected References

AAHPERD. (1988). *AAHPERD Technical Manual, Health Related Physical Fitness Test.* Reston, VA: AAHPERD Publications.

———. (1988). *Physical Best Manual.* Reston, VA: AAHPERD Publications.

———. (1976). *AAHPERD Youth Fitness Test Manual,* Revised Edition. Reston, VA: AAHPERD Publications.

Anderson, B. (1980). *Stretching.* Bolinas, CA: Shelter Publications, Inc.

Binkhorst, R. A., Kemper, H. C. G., and Soris, W. H. M. (1985). *Children and Exercise.* Champaign, IL: Human Kinetics Publishers, Inc.

Corbin, C. B., and Linsey, R. (1991). *Concepts of Physical Fitness with Laboratories,* Seventh Edition. Dubuque, IA: Wm. C. Brown Publishers.

Foster, E. R., Hartinger, K., and Smith, K. A. (1990). *Fitness Fun.* Champaign, IL: Human Kenetics Publishers, Inc.

Golding, L. A., Meyers, C. R., and Sinning, W. E. (1989). *Y's Ways to Physical Fitness,* Third Edition. Champaign, IL: Human Kinetics Publishers, Inc.

Kuntzleman, C., and McGlynn, G. (1991). *Aerobics with Fun.* Reston, VA: AAHPERD Publications.

———. (1984). *Fitness for Children.* Spring Arbor, MI: Fitness Finders.

Lang, J. S. (May, 1982). "American Fitness Binge," *U.S. News & World Report.*

Main, S., and Stewart, G. W. (1984). *Fit All Over.* Victoria, B.C.:3 S Fitness Group Ltd.

Pangrazi, R. P., and Hastad, D. H. (1986). *Fitness in the Elementary Schools.* Reston VA: AAHPERD Publications.

Scicchitano, J. (1989). *Super Star Fitness.* Durham, NC: Great Activities Publishing Co.

Seefeldt, V. (1986). *Physical Activity and Well-Being.* Reston, VA: AAHPERD Publications.

Seefeldt, V., and Vogel, P. (1986). *The Value of Physical Activity.* Reston, VA: AAHPERD Publications.

Steen, D. (1982). *Aerobic Fun for Kids.* Toronto: Fitzhenry and Whiteside Ltd.

Stewart, G. W. (1982). *Everybody's Fitness Book.* Santa Barbara, CA: 3 S Publishers.

Stewart, G. W., and Faulkner, R. A. (1984). *Bend and Stretch: Suppleness and Strength Exercises.* Santa Barbara, CA: 3 S Publishers.

Stillwell, J. L., and Stockhard, J. R. (1983). *Fitness Exercises for Children.* New York: Leisure Press.

Williams, M. H. (1990). *Lifetime Fitness and Wellness,* Second Edition. Dubuque, IA: Wm. C. Brown Publishers.

13
Integrating Special Needs Children

One of the major challenges facing public education programs is the reality of inclusion. Originally called mainstreaming, *inclusion* is an educational fact of life that most elementary school teachers will have to deal with at some time during their career.

In the early 1970s more than 1.75 million children with various psychological and physical disabilities were excluded from public education because they were "handicapped." Further, more than one half of the estimated 8 million disabled children throughout the United States were not receiving appropriate educational services. Recognizing this, the federal government passed two laws that substantially affected the educational opportunities of disabled children. Public Law 93–112 (the Rehabilitation Act of 1973, Section 504) made it increasingly difficult for disabled children to be denied an education or excluded from educational institutions receiving federal monies. Subsequently, pressure applied by parents, courts, and legislation resulted in the passage of Public Law 94–142, (Education for All Handicapped Children Act) in 1975 and enacted in 1978. This law, recognized as landmark legislation, entitled school–age disabled children to a free and appropriate public education in the least restrictive environment. Important to our profession is the fact that adapted physical education is written into the law as a required direct service. According to Public Law 94–142, physical therapy does not legally substitute for physical education services.

Throughout the 1970s and 1980s those students classified as mildly handicapped (learning disabled, educable, mentally retarded, socially and emotionally disturbed) began to be integrated into the regular classrooms. Prior to that time, a dual physical education system existed—adapted physical education programs for the "handicapped" children and regular physical education programs for "normal" children. Today, all mildly handicapped children who once received adapted physical education in approved special education schools, inside or outside of their home school district, are taught by elementary school physical education teachers. Today, exceptional children remaining in separate adapted physical education programs are more commonly found to be preschool multihandicapped children, children with severe autism and pervasive developmental delays, or children with such severe social and emotional difficulties that the public school district is not yet ready to address their educational needs.

The implications of Public Law 93–112 and Public Law 94–142 to the elementary school physical education program are basically to integrate all children within instructional and extra class programs and to individualize teaching strategies and activity areas to more successfully address the special needs of disabled children. This chapter provides a general overview of federal and state laws relating to disabled children, a basic description of the various types of disabilities common to public school inclusion, teaching suggestions, and ideas illustrating how children with special needs can be integrated into the regular physical education program ■

Legal Basis for Integrating Disabled Children

Prior to 1971, the responsibility for the education of special needs children lay primarily with state and local governments. This was done with a dual educational system (special versus regular education) serving two types of students (special versus regular). Few quality physical education programs existed. Of those that did, the largest population that was provided with quality physical education were individuals classified as mentally retarded. For others, physical education was not made available. With increased parent pressure, the federal government imposed landmark legislation to more fully equate the civil and education rights of disabled children. As a result, the following two federal laws have brought the disabled child into the mainstream (a more contemporary use today is inclusion) of public education.

Rehabilitation Act of 1973

Section 504 of the Rehabilitation Act (PL 93–112) and the reauthorized PL 99–057 of 1986 state that "no otherwise qualified handicapped individual shall solely by reason of his handicap be excluded from participation or denied benefits of or be subjected to discrimination under any program or activity receiving federal assistance." The implication of this section is that handicapped children are to be provided equal opportunity to participate in regular instructional physical education classes, as well as in intramural and interschool programs. Participation in these programs is based on the premise of "the least restrictive setting." The intention of this definition is not to change the basic way teachers instruct students but to modify teaching strategies and equipment to cope with a variety of handicapped children in the regular instructional program (figure 13.1).

Education for All Handicapped Children Act of 1975

Of all the federal laws enacted, PL 94–142 is the most important to physical education. This law was first enacted in 1975 and has been reauthorized three times. This law now affects the nature and direction of physical education programs in the following areas:

1. Students will be educated in the "least restrictive environment." "Least restrictive environment" is explained on the basis of a cascade of educational placements that should be available within a school district. Accordingly, the least restrictive environment for each student is determined on an individual basis and based on the environment in which the student will gain the most in terms of physical, mental, and social development. The six levels of placement shown in table 13.1 illustrate the variety of environments that should be made available to handicapped children.

Figure 13.1 Planning a physical education program to meet the unique needs of exceptional children is more readily achieved by the combined efforts of physicians, teachers, and parents.

Table 13.1 Placement Cascade for Handicapped Children

Level 1	Full integration in regular physical education classes
Level 2	Full integration, with class size limited (e. g., one handicapped child with fifteen nonhandicapped children)
Level 3	Full integration, with opportunities for handicapped children to have special assistance with an aide as a resource person
Level 4	Partial integration, with handicapped children assigned a number of days a week in regular physical education classes and a number of days in separate adaptive classes
Level 5	Full time in separate adaptive, physical education classes
Level 6	Full time in separate physical education in special schools for handicapped students

The "least restrictive environment" also varies according to the type of disability and the curriculum content and teaching strategies the teacher uses. To illustrate, for a student in a wheelchair, a regular instructional unit of soccer or flag football would be the most restrictive environment for him. However, the same child in an educational gymnastic unit could participate partially or be fully integrated with some special assistance. The same child placed in a swimming class taught with exploratory teaching strategies would be in a least restrictive environment. The essential point is to continually evaluate the teaching unit and teaching strategies used, then place handicapped students into the best situations in which they can develop according to their needs, interests, and levels of ability.

2. Students between the ages of three and twenty-one will receive educational service. According to this age level designation, all elementary schools must provide appropriate physical education programs according to the level system of the placement cascade programs for handicapped children.

3. Each student will have a specially developed program called an Individualized Educational Plan (IEP). This plan must be developed in a meeting with parents, teachers, local administrators, and, where appropriate, the student for whom the plan is intended. The written plan for each child must contain the following (*Federal Register,* August 1977, p. 42490):

   a. A statement of the child's present levels of educational program

   b. A statement of annual goals, including short-term instructional objectives

   c. A statement of the specific education and related services to be provided to the child and the extent to which the child will be able to participate in regular educational programs

   d. The projected dates for the initiation of services and the anticipated duration of the services

   e. Appropriate objective criteria and evaluation procedures and schedules for determining, on at least an annual basis, whether the short-term instructional objectives are being achieved

Figure 13.2, a sample IEP form from Seattle School District, illustrates how each child's program is assessed, incorporated into a short- and long-term program, and evaluated on the basis of established criteria of expected performance. This type of recordkeeping assists all personnel concerned with the child's development to monitor his progress and, where necessary, to make appropriate changes in level of placement, equipment, or teaching strategies.

4. Federal funds will be available to state educational agencies and local educational agencies. The average cost of educating handicapped students is approximately 1,000 dollars more than the cost of educating nonhandicapped children. Part of this extra funding is provided by federal grants awarded to state education agencies. However, these monies must be spent only for the excess cost of special education over the average student costs in regular education.

Generally speaking, the state and local governments raise about 800 dollars for each handicapped child, with the federal government contributing the remaining 200 dollars per student.

5. The subject of physical education is identified as a direct service. Public Law 94–142 clarifies special physical education in the following manner: "If specially designed physical education is prescribed in a child's individualized education program, the public agency responsible for the education of that child shall provide the service directly, or make arrangements for it to be provided through other public or private programs." This definition allows separate or segregated classes of special physical education to be part of physical education rather than part of a separate adapted physical education program (figure 13.3). This interpretation of "specially designed physical education" does not have to be a full-time placement in a separate class; rather, it can be part of the cascade of placements that was outlined in table 13.1.

Regular Education Initiative and Inclusion

Prior to the late 1980s most school-age children having a special education classification were sent to special (segregated) education schools either inside or outside of the home school district. Several factors have resulted in a significant change, including the fact that the majority of these children, unless classified as severely and profoundly multihandicapped, are attending the public school in their home district. In some states, severely disabled children, regardless of school age, are partially or fully integrated across all classes in the public school.

To comprehend today's regular education initiative, it is important that elementary school teachers understand why an increasing number of public school districts are keeping special education children in regular school programs instead of placing them in separate special education programs. The most significant factor in the drive toward inclusion is parents' increasing awareness of their children's educational rights as well as their own rights as parents of disabled children. Second, the weak economy has forced educational administrators at the state level to significantly reduce the amount of money to support special programs that were commonly found outside the public school district. Hence, public education must provide, as best as possible, the appropriate educational staff and programs necessary to successfully address the educational needs of the special child. Finally, the parent awareness movement has become so strong that the importance of elementary school physical education teachers doing the best they can to involve every child in developmentally appropriate and nonrestrictive learning experiences is paramount.

Figure 13.2 Seattle Public Schools IEP form.

The Seattle Public Schools

STUDENT SERVICES DEPARTMENT
Individualized Education Program (IEP)
SPECIAL EDUCATION

Purpose of Meeting	☐ Initial IEP ☐ Annual Review ☐ Develop Exit/Transition Plan ☐ _____

STUDENT: _____ GRADE: ____ UNIT: _____ IEP CONFERENCE DATE: _____

SCHOOL: _____ BIRTHDATE: _____ IEP PROJECTED REVIEW DATE: _____

IEP RESPONSIBLE EDUCATOR: _____ STUDENT ID NO.: _____ MOST CURRENT ASSESSMENT DATE: _____

I. SUMMARY OF PRESENT LEVELS OF PERFORMANCE/SUMMARY OF IEP COMMITTEE MEETING
Description of scholastic, physical and adjustment levels

Wide Range Achievement Test-R Date: _____ Level: _____ Date: _____ Level: _____	Reading Raw Score | Grade Rating _____	Spelling Raw Score | Grade Rating _____	Arithmetic Raw Score | Grade Rating _____	**Slosson Oral Reading Test** Date: _____ Raw Score | Grade Level Date: _____ _____
Woodcock-Johnson Psycho-Educational Battery Date: _____	Reading _____ Standard Score Grade Rating	Math _____ Standard Score Grade Rating		Written Language _____ Standard Score Grade Rating

____ ____ ____ ____ ____ ____ ____ ____ ____ ____ ____ ____ ____

II. ANNUAL GOALS AND SHORT-TERM OBJECTIVES

STUDENT: _____

ANNUAL GOAL

A minimum of one objective is to be written for each grading period. Example: **4** if quarters, **3** if trimesters.

SHORT-TERM OBJECTIVES	Date Initiated	Date Completed

• Each goal statement, related to an assessed deficit area, contains a *measurable* unit of achievement for a school year.
• Each objective states WHO will be doing WHAT and HOW to determine if the objective has been completed (evaluation criteria).

Rev. 04/86   **COMPLIANCE**

Figure 13.2 *(Continued)*

STUDENT: _____

☐ Check if this is an initial placement.

IEP Responsible
Educator: _____

III. PROPOSED EDUCATIONAL PROGRAM AND RELATED SERVICES

		Minutes per Week	Projected Starting Date	Anticipated Duration*
More ← RESTRICTIVE → Less	**Level of Special Education Service** (Please check one only) ☐ 1. Regular Program w/Itinerant Service ☐ 2. Special Education Resource Service ☐ 3. Self-Contained Special Education Service ☐ 4. Specialized Self-Contained Service ☐ 5. Non-District Placement (requires program supervisor approval)	**Description/Areas of Service**		

All non-selected placement options were considered and rejected, at this time, as being too restrictive or for the reasons indicated under "Less Restrictive Environment."

Career/Vocational Education (14 years or older)

☐ Regular Program (list minutes under reg. ed.) Describe: _____

☐ Special Program—Describe: _____ Service Provider: _____

☐ No Vocational Education: Parent Preference ☐ Other _____

Related Services
Services required for the student to benefit from special education.

Service Provider: _____	Speech/Lang. ☐	– – – –
Service Provider: _____	OT ☐	– – – –
Service Provider: _____	PT ☐	– – – –
Service Provider: _____	_____ ☐	– – – –
Service Provider: _____	_____ ☐	– – – –
Service Provider: _____	_____ ☐	– – – –

Evaluation for Service Recommended (Attach referral)

◀ Total Special Education Minutes per Week

Physical Education Program   Regular Program ☐   Special Program ☐

Less Restrictive Environment

Extent of participation in Regular Education (This is the maximum possible for this student):

◀ Total Regular Education Minutes per Week

◀ Total Minutes per Week

Statement of non-academic and extracurricular activities:

Home School: Is student attending school he/she would usually attend if not handicapped? ☐ Yes ☐ No if no, state reason(s):

Less Restrictive Placement rejected for the following reasons: ☐ academic level ☐ behavioral concerns ☐ unique needs
☐ failure to succeed in less restrictive setting ☐ Other _____

Comments (Other tests, information or factors used in making placement decision):

Extended School Year (ESY) Status:

Eligibility for Extended School Year services is determined based on one or more of the following criteria:

Your child will be:	Referred for ESY services	Will be considered at a later date
a) regression/recoupment	☐	☐
b) behavioral regression/recoupment	☐	☐
c) physical/medical	☐	☐
d) new student	☐	☐
e) unexpected growth spurt	☐	☐
f) unique needs	☐	☐

(Rev. 08/89)   **COMPLIANCE**

Figure 13.2 (*Continued*)

STUDENT: _____

IV. GRADUATION STATUS (High School Students Only)

Number of current High School credits _____ . Projected date of High School Completion ____ / ____ .
Comments:

V. ALTERNATIVE DISCIPLINARY PROCEDURES REQUIRED ☐ Yes ☐ No

If yes, document specific agreements (principal or designee must be present). If more space is needed use comments section.

_____

_____

_____

VI. IEP COMMITTEE MEMBERS

We agree the listed programs and related services are necessary to provide an appropriate education in the least restrictive environment for this student.

Present Yes No	Agree Yes No	Name (print or type)	Signature	Position*

*Program Specialists and Supervisors are team members but may not be present at all meetings.

_____   _____
SIGNATURE OF PRINCIPAL   DATE

Comments: _____

_____

_____

_____

_____

_____

_____

VII. PARENTS RIGHTS/AGREEMENT (Copy of Summary of Safeguards and Due Process Procedures on back of form).

I have had the opportunity to participate in the development of this individualized education program. I give my permission for my child/ward to participate in the services and placement listed; this permission can be revoked. I understand that I have the right to request a hearing regarding the identification, evaluation, or educational placement of my child/ward. I also understand that school records will not be released to non-school personnel without my permission. I have received a copy of the Summary of Safeguards and Due Process Procedures and understand my rights and responsibilities in connection with these procedures.

If not parent, please check position below

_____   ☐ Legal Guardian   ☐ Surrogate Parent   _____
SIGNATURE OF PARENT   ☐ Adult Acting as Parent ☐ Adult Student   DATE

(Rev. 08/89)   **COMPLIANCE**

Figure 13.3 Placement in the least restrictive environment.

Integrating Special Needs Children into the Regular Physical Education Program

Federal legislators specified that each disabled child must be afforded the opportunity to participate in the regular physical education program available to nonhandicapped children, unless: (1) the child is enrolled full time in a separate facility or (2) the child needs specially designed physical education, as prescribed in the child's Individualized Education Program (IEP). As described earlier in this chapter, this stipulation brought about the placement of handicapped children into the least restrictive environment. It is a process where disabled children are constantly evaluated, then placed into a new least restrictive environment according to their developmental level. It is also a process within which the teacher adjusts organizational patterns, teaching strategies, and equipment in order to meet the goals and aspirations of fully able students and handicapped children within a regular class setting. Several teaching strategies described earlier in this text are expanded in the following pages to illustrate how handicapped children can be integrated effectively into instructional and extraclass activities.

Terminology

The 1975 Public Law 94–142, "Education for All Handicapped Children Act," which covered students 5–21 years of age, was followed in 1986 with PL 99–457, the "Education for the Handicapped Act," which extended the mandate and services to children below 5 years of age. An additional amendment resulted in PL 101–476 being passed in 1990, that renamed the 1986 law to "Individuals with Disabilities Education Act" (IDEA). These changes reflect both the views of "inclusive" education for all children from birth to adulthood, and the concern for labeling children as "handicapped." Unfortunately, all terms suffer the problem of "label" or "stereotype." Moving toward the global term of "disability" offers some degree of improvement, but even here there are problems. A child who suffers from asthma, or some form of visual impairment, for example, is unlikely to gain through being identified as "disabled." A variety of terms, including "handicapped," "disabled," and "special needs" are used throughout this text, since these terms have been identified in the education literature and refer to certain characteristics and conditions. Knowing there is the potential for "labeling" effects, two important points teachers need to remember are:

1. Care and sensitivity is required at all times to ensure that *all* children, regardless of skill or ability, or any other characteristic, are treated with dignity and respect.

2. Every child is, in fact, "special" and each child has unique "needs."

As educators, teachers must ensure that developmentally appropriate activities are provided for all children in an inclusive environment.

Station Work

The general organization of stations in teaching a variety of physical activities is particularly useful when attempting to individualize the instructional program (see chapter 7). To illustrate this technique, presume a fourth-grade teacher is teaching a gymnastic unit. Three children in her class have moderate limitations (heart, sight, and partially spastic); hence, they cannot participate in vaulting or rope climbing activities. The teacher organizes the class into six groups, with the three moderately handicapped children designated as group IV and assigned to station B along with group II. All children practice the assigned skills at their stations until it is time to rotate. When the groups rotate, group II moves to the vaulting box while groups IV and V shift to small equipment. The teacher has demonstrated her ability to integrate the three exceptional children according to their limitations and without drastically changing the content or emphasis of her gymnastic program.

The organizational structure of station work can be used effectively to teach physical fitness activities, particularly with circuit training and obstacle courses (see chapter 12). This system can also be adopted when teaching a variety of game activities.

Task Cards

Task cards, described in chapter 7, can be predesigned to accommodate a variety of exceptional children. Using the previous station work example, all children, with the exception of the three disabled children, could choose cards representing three levels of performance. (levels 1, 2, and 3). Special task cards for moderately blind (high visibility words or pictures), heart defect, and children with spasticity could be designed to accommodate their expected levels of performance. If the reading level is low, supplementary photographs or drawings with several words identifying the action to be performed or solved could be made. Although task cards present various limitations when working with totally blind or severely mentally disabled children, numerous applications for the task card technique can accommodate the exceptional child in virtually every area of the physical education program.

Figure 13.4 Children with disabilities can achieve a measure of success with guidance and encouragement.

Peer Tutors

Studies of the most accommodating teaching and participation effects for various special needs children who require great amounts of assistance emphasize the use of peer tutors. This strategy is especially helpful for children who have extreme difficulty following directions or when functional mobility and manipulation are very limited. Teachers who have used a peer tutor strategy report more successful results in their ability to attend to the entire class as well as to the special child; this strategy also fosters less teacher dependency. The key to successful peer tutoring is to select mature students, use them on a consistent basis, and rotate them with other tutors so everyone has optimal active learning time. In addition, it is important to train the peer tutors before class time.

Types of Disabilities

In physical education, as in all subjects, it is first necessary to understand the various types of physical, mental, social, and emotional disabilities in order to provide developmentally appropriate activities. A few of the more common disabilities are described below. Once they are understood, it is possible, within the broad range of physical activities and instructional strategies, to provide for the needs of these children (figure 13.4).

Learning Disabilities

This section includes those congenital conditions and disabilities that directly relate to mild and moderate learning difficulties with or without social or emotional disturbances. Children who are classified in this category are described as follows.

chapter 13

Mentally Impaired

This refers to a significantly subaverage intellectual functioning, which exists concurrently with weakness in adaptive behavior and is manifested during the developmental period (Grossman 1984). Other terms, such as "mentally deficient," and "mentally handicapped," are used interchangeably. Although each state has its own classification system, most classify these children as Educable (IQ 50 to 70), Trainable (IQ 30 to 49), and Severely and Profoundly (IQ 29 and below). In the United States, approximately 4 million school-age children are classified as Educable and Trainable and are provided for within the public education system.

Down Syndrome

Down Syndrome is the most recognizable among individuals experiencing mental retardation. This disability comprises less than 50 percent of moderately retarded students educated in today's public schools. While many of these children appear obese, this is not a typical genetic feature accompanying the disability; it is rather more closely linked to poor diet and lack of exercise. What is important for elementary school teachers to recognize is that many of these children may have congenital heart disorders. Consequently, it is imperative for the teacher to review the child's medical record prior to the child's participation in physical education. Depending on the nature of the heart condition, physical restrictions may or may not be advised. However, for legal protection, physical education teachers should have on file current health records indicating what types of activity the child can participate in without undue stress or physical harm.

Another important related disability that may be overlooked is an orthopedic condition called Atlantoaxial instability, which occurs in approximately 17 percent of all children with Down syndrome. Atlantoaxial refers to the joint between the first two cervical vertebrae. The ligaments and muscles surrounding the joint are lax, allowing the vertebrae to slip out of alignment. A forceful forward or backward bending of the neck, which may occur in gymnastic activities or other sport events, may dislocate the vertebrae, causing damage to the spinal cord (Sherrill, 1993). Since Atlantoaxial instability can only be detected through X-rays, it is recommended that teachers of Down syndrome children request the school nurse or parent to provide evidence that this condition is not present in the child.

It should be noted that X-rays are required for persons with Down syndrome to participate in Special Olympics. If the child is an active participant in these activities, check with local Special Olympics officials to see if X-rays have been taken. If medical clearance is not available, the teacher should not allow the child to participate in the above mentioned activities until X-rays are taken.

The physical education program can become a very beneficial medium through which mildly and moderately mentally disabled children can improve their motor proficiency and personal and social skills. It can also be one of the most effective media for improving the child's self-image. The following suggestions relating to these two levels of mental disability provide a general guideline for integrating these children into the regular physical education program.

1. Mentally disabled children tend to be relatively unfit and overweight. Provide a physical fitness program that is individualized and progressive in increasing each child's level of performance.

2. Mentally disabled children tend to be well behind their classmates in performing motor skills. Provide a broad-based program of activities in which children can develop according to their level of ability and speed of learning.

3. Mentally disabled children learn best through direct methods of teaching and demonstrations of skills and movement patterns. Stress direct methods and techniques of instruction wherever possible. When using the problem-solving method, select tasks that are short and have simple solutions, and repeat the same verbal challenge as the child attempts to answer the movement problem.

Learning Disabled

Children classified as learning disabled comprise the greatest number of exceptional children in today's public schools. During the past two decades, there has been considerable debate and discussion about the definition of a learning disabled child. For some parents and educators, the term "learning disabled" is any student who experiences a problem with learning (Dunn and Fait 1989). For others, the term designates a specific brain dysfunction caused by injury or infection. The following definition provided by the Handicapped Act consolidates these concepts into the unified definition that is used as a standard in public schools (*Federal Register,* August 23, 1977, p. 42478):

Specific learning disability [LD] means a disorder in one or more of the basic psychological processes involved in understanding or using language, spoken or written, which may manifest itself in an imperfect ability to listen, think, speak, read, write, spell or do mathematical calculations. The term includes such conditions as perceptual handicaps, brain injury, minimal brain disfunction, dyslexia, and developmental aphasia. The term does not include children who have learning problems which are primarily the result of visual, hearing, or motor handicap, of mental retardation, or of environmental, cultural or economic disadvantage.

Since there is still a general lack of understanding among specialists in medicine, psychology, and education, learning disabled children are often misunderstood. Too often, teachers classify these children as lazy, slow, mentally disabled, or possessing behavioral problems (Horvat 1990). With these factors in mind, teachers should consider the following suggestions when developing physical education programs for these children:

1. Learning disabled children learn best through a learning environment that is structured and routine. Structuring a relatively stable environment allows children to develop a sense of security. Once the children feel comfortable and confident, they acquire motor skills and concepts more rapidly and with a more positive attitude.

2. Learning disabled children may be socially immature and, hence, initially may be afraid to engage in small- and large-group activities. Follow a social-sequence format that begins with children practicing or playing alone, to two students working in a parallel way without interaction, to playing together with small and then gradually larger groups.

The cognitive and motor performance of learning disabled children is delayed when compared with nondisabled children. Difficulties with attentiveness, impulsiveness, ability to sequence (apraxia), and sensory-motor skills are commonly observed by teachers. However, not all learning disabled children demonstrate gross motor difficulty, as their learning disabilities may exist primarily in reading, mathematics, language arts, or any combination of the three subjects. Also, not all learning disabled children have behavior difficulties.

The variation in the classification systems for determining learning disabilities across school districts results in a wide range of learning disabled children manifesting different characteristics. As a group however, children with significant learning difficulties usually have sensory-motor difficulties that result in poor motor performance.

Behavior Disorders

It is not uncommon for physical education teachers to encounter various mildly handicapped students who have behavior difficulties. Quite often, especially at the beginning of the school year or when changes in a routine occur, the behavior becomes the priority to first be addressed, followed by the initiative to improve physical fitness and motor performance. For any teacher, this can be the most difficult task and greatest challenge. The important thing is getting and keeping attention so learning can occur. As long as a student remains in a noncompliance status with the general class management routines and rules established at the beginning of the school year, motor learning will be difficult.

According to Public Law 94–142, the Education for All Handicapped Children Act, behavior disorders mean a condition exhibiting one or more of the following characteristics, over a long period of time, and to a marked degree, which adversely affects educational performance (*Federal Register,* August 23, 1977, p, 42478).

1. An inability to learn that cannot be explained by intellectual, sensory, or health factors

2. An inability to build or maintain satisfactory interpersonal relationships with peers and teachers

3. Inappropriate types of behavior or feelings under normal circumstances

4. A general pervasive mood of unhappiness or depression

5. A tendency to develop physical symptoms or fears associated with personal or school problems

Teachers will observe in regular physical education programs mildly handicapped children who will exhibit behavior patterns related to one or more of the following characteristics: overaggression, direct noncompliance with general rules and basic management routines, and extreme impulsiveness to the point of causing constant interruption and interference with the entire learning process. Any one or combination of these behaviors often results in poor interpersonal skills, ineffective teaching, and less optimal learning opportunities. The following strategies will help teachers become aware of ways to appropriately address behavior disorders to maintain a healthy teaching and learning atmosphere.

1. It is important for the teacher to gain as much information as possible about the child's general behavior. This can be done by talking to other teachers, parents, or any other professional having direct contact with the student. Also, review the child's educational folder to gather information that may help with setting appropriate goals and expectations.

2. Examine the developmental appropriateness of the learning activities presented in class. Many behavior difficulties occur when class content is either too easy or too difficult.

3. Review the medical history of the student. The student may be recovering from a head injury where aggressive behaviors are inherent with post-traumatic head injuries. The student may also be receiving medication for a particular condition that has side effects (e.g., dizziness, aggression, and headaches). This is particularly true for children with seizure disorders that are controlled by medication.

4. Develop an effective method of handling each type of disorder. For example, establish a basic procedure to follow with overaggressive children or use a specific instructional technique to enhance the interpersonal relationships of extremely shy or withdrawn children.

5. Avoid techniques that may weaken appropriate behavior responses. Avoid the use of punishment such as denial, extra exercise, or your own angry expression.

Perceptual-Motor Deficiencies

Throughout the 1960s and 1970s there was a growing awareness of the importance of perceptual-motor development to academic achievement, particularly in such areas as reading, writing, and drawing skills. In 1959, Delacato presented a theory known as neurological organization, which assumed that every individual progressed sequentially through a series of motor skills. He argued that children with perceptual-motor deficiencies missed specific developmental steps along this continuum.

Another theory, proposed by Kephart, holds that a child progresses through a sequence of learning stages (1960). His proposed program for slow learners was based on levels of generalization through which a child is taught. Since the ability to read is based on previously acquired perceptual-motor skills, such as directionality and laterality, these skills are emphasized for children with learning disabilities.

The general conclusion drawn from these investigators is that inadequate preschool motor development could lead to serious perceptual-motor problems. A child who does not possess these prerequisite perceptual motor skills may, in turn, experience serious difficulties in learning to read, write, and perform other academic skills. Hence, over the years a large number of children classified as learning disabled and mentally retarded were placed in perceptual-motor training programs. It was believed that providing gross motor tasks, such as balance beam walking, would assist in reading improvement. Numerous research studies indicate there is not sufficient evidence to substantiate these claims. Teachers considering the use of perceptual-motor training to aid specific academic performance must carefully consider the evidence. Perceptual-motor training programs can improve the performance of the activities worked on, but the transfer link from perceptual-motor training using specific gross motor skills thought to improve academic performance is, at most, weak.

Since all movement is perceptual in nature, the regular physical education program is already providing a variety of activities necessary to enhance perceptual-motor performance. More specifically, a physical education teacher possessing the competence to provide specific perceptual-motor training to a child experiencing serious perceptual-motor deficiencies may provide supplemental activities in addition to the regular physical education program or refer the student to a trained specialist.

Symptoms of Perceptual-Motor Deficiencies

Perceptual-motor competency is a composite of a number of specific motor skills and movement patterns. The following characteristic symptoms are commonly observed in the primary school, particularly in kindergarten and first grade:

1. Body image
   a. Inability to identify and locate body parts, such as the right and left hand, knee, or elbow
   b. Inability to move parts of the body as directed by the teacher, such as raising the right arm or raising the left arm and the left foot
   c. Inability to imitate movements performed by the teacher or another performer

2. Balance
   a. Inability to maintain static balance, such as standing on one foot or standing with the arms folded and eyes closed
   b. Inability to maintain balance while moving, such as walking forward or backward in a straight line
   c. Inability to maintain balance while in flight, such as a simple run, jump, and land or a jump off a low box or balance bench

3. Spatial awareness
   a. Inability to move parts of the body in specified directions, such as crossing the right arm over the left side of the body
   b. Inability to move the body through space, such as moving forward, backward, up, down, and around
   c. Inability to move through space without bumping into objects or other children in the general pathway of movement

4. Hand-eye and foot-eye coordination
   a. Inability to throw a ball into the air and catch it after one bounce
   b. Inability to perform basic locomotor skills, such as running, hopping, jumping, or galloping
   c. Inability to kick a stationary or moving ball
   d. Inability to move to rhythm, such as performing rhythmic hand or foot tapping or walking to rhythmic accompaniment

Guidelines

Once the decision has been made to pursue a perceptual-motor training program in the regular physical education class or in a supplemental remedial program, and the previously mentioned research findings have been taken into consideration, the following guidelines can be applied to help incorporate various types of perceptual-motor activities.

1. A child who is suspected of possessing serious perceptual-motor deficiencies should be referred to competent specialists.

2. The choice of all physical activities should be commensurate with the child's developmental level.

3. Application of individualized instructional techniques, particularly the limitation method, is imperative in coping with individual differences in levels of ability and rate of development.

4. Every movement task that is presented should allow each child to achieve a measure of success.

5. The primary physical education program should stress the following types of activities.

   a. Balance activities—floor work, with small equipment, and on large apparatus

   b. Locomotor skills—moving in different directions, changing speed, and moving to a rhythmic accompaniment

   c. Body awareness—activities and movement challenges stressing shapes (form) and the movement of different parts (unilateral and bilateral movements)

   d. Manipulative activities—stressing hand-eye and foot-eye coordination (ball-handling skills involving throwing, catching, and kicking) and a variety of manipulative skills using beanbags, hoops, and other small equipment

Sensory Impairments

Sensory impairment is a condition in which one or more of the five senses are diminished in their function (Dunn and Fait 1989). From an educational point of view, loss of sight or hearing results in major problems for the learner and teacher. Hence, this section will discuss only visual and auditory disabilities.

Visual Disabilities

According to recent estimates in the United States (Sherrill 1993), approximately 32,000 visually impaired children between the ages of three and twenty-one are receiving special education services. The most common visual disabilities that present several problems for the learner and teacher are myopia, hyperopia, and astigmatism. *Myopia (nearsightedness)* is the result of the anterior-posterior axis of the eye being too long, resulting in the image being focused in front of the retina. Distant objects appear blurred, whereas nearby objects are seen clearly. In *hyperopia (farsightedness)*, the anterior-posterior axis of the eyeball is too short. This causes the image to be focused behind the retina. Distant objects are seen clearly, whereas nearby objects appear blurred. *Astigmatism* is normally caused by an irregularity in the curve of the cornea or lens of the eye. When a child attempts to focus, the object appears blurred.

The following guidelines will help teachers integrate visually impaired students into the regular physical education program.

1. Consult the school nurse and parents of children who have visual disabilities. The teacher's knowledge of each child's deficiency can provide a general guideline for the type of activity and degree of participation appropriate for the child.

2. Refer any child who chronically demonstrates one or more of the following symptoms to the school nurse for further examination.

   a. Excessive squinting

   b. Constant leaning toward or moving close for demonstrations

   c. Inattentiveness and a general lack of interest

   d. Extremely low level of skill; visually impaired children generally show poor catching skills, even with a large utility ball

3. Too often, partially sighted children shy away from vigorous physical activities and, thus, tend to be overweight and generally uncoordinated. Whenever possible, provide a little extra encouragement and praise when these children participate in physical activities.

4. Blind children usually have developed extremely good memories. When teaching physical education, reinforce this strength and increase the child's self-esteem by asking the blind child to review instructions given in previous lessons (Sherrill 1976).

5. Partially sighted children often say they can see more than they actually do in order to act like other children. Teachers should recognize this characteristic and give subtle assistance and encouragement whenever possible.

6. Determine what each partially sighted child is capable of doing in physical education. Within the child's limitations, modify rules, provide special boundary markers, sound sources, peer helpers, and other considerations to help integrate the child into each appropriate physical activity.

Hearing Impairments

In the Educational Handicap Act, both the deaf and the hard of hearing are included in the definition of hearing impairment. Deafness is defined as an impairment so severe that the student is prevented from acquiring linguistic information, even with the use of a hearing aid. On the other hand, an individual who is hard of hearing can, with the assistance of a hearing aid, have sufficient hearing to process linguistic information (Horvat 1990). Approximately 1 million school-age children in the United States are hearing impaired and currently enrolled in regular physical education programs. Of this group, approximately one in every twenty-five has a hearing impairment that requires extensive special education services. The following general guidelines will help the classroom teacher integrate the moderately or mildly hearing impaired child into a regular physical education class.

1. If a child with a hearing loss is in your class, check with his parents on the type of oral, manual, or combined method of communication that is preferred.

2. When giving directions, face in the direction of the deaf child. This is particularly important when writing on a chalkboard. Write the directions first, then face the class and verbally clarify your directions.

3. When giving specific directions to a deaf child, position yourself so the child can see you.

4. If a child is wearing a hearing aid, do not raise your voice when speaking to the child. Also, discuss with the parent and child when the hearing aid will be worn. Rain, wind, mud, sand, or excessive noise may dictate the removal of the hearing aid.

5. When teaching outdoors, try to position yourself so the deaf child does not face the sun.

6. Always permit children with hearing losses to move freely about the instructional space in order to be within seeing or hearing range.

7. Change methods of gaining class attention from audio cues (whistles, yells, and hand claps) to visual cues (raised arms to stop, rolling wrists to continue, and pointing to destinations).

Neurological Disorders

The two most common neurological disorders found among elementary school children are seizures (epilepsy) and cerebral palsy. Both of these impairments affect a child's level of performance in many physical activities. The following definition and characteristics of each impairment, along with a few guidelines, will help teachers determine appropriate adjustments within the physical education program.

Seizure Disorders

Epilepsy is a condition of recurring seizures that is initiated by abnormal electrical discharges in the brain. Seizures affect approximately 3 percent of the general population and may be inherited, or caused by traumatic brain injury (e. g., car or bicycle accidents) or through an infection such as meningitis. It is not unusual for individuals with cerebral palsy to have seizure disorders. Depending on the type of seizure, a loss of consciousness and bladder control may occur. Elementary school children who have a seizure disorder that is controlled through medication may often experience side effects. Teachers should check with the school nurse or parent to determine the nature of the seizure disorder, type of medication, and any physical restrictions that should be noted. Table 13.2 includes the main types of seizures that teachers should be able to recognize and apply appropriate first aid measures for.

The successful medical control of seizure disorders permits the majority of children with these conditions to participate on a restriction-free basis in most or all activities.

Adhere to the following suggestions for children who have seizure disorders and participate in a regular physical education program.

1. A child who has a series of seizures throughout the school year while receiving medication, should not be permitted on large apparatus such as climbing ropes and climbing frames.

2. Adhere to an appropriate procedure for managing a seizure in a large group situation.

3. Review the type of seizure medication a child is receiving and know the side effects.

4. It is possible for a child who has a seizure history to not have a seizure for several years but then suddenly experience one. A reoccurrence may happen during a growth spurt and the medication must be adjusted.

5. Teachers should explain, within the limits of the class's understanding, the nature of the disorder and what should be done when a child has a seizure.

Cerebral Palsy

Cerebral Palsy is a neurological impairment caused by damage to the motor areas of the brain. The majority of such cases occur before or just after birth. Other causes include trauma, infection, and anoxia (lack of oxygen). Many children with cerebral palsy are unable to perform appropriate motor skills because of an interfering reflex behavior that is typically observed in early infancy. The persistence of these primitive reflexes makes it difficult to perform simple neuromuscular skills. In addition, abnormal muscle tone (too high or too low) and skeletal deformities resulting from muscle imbalances all interfere with movement. In cases where both legs are affected, the child wears braces to walk. In extreme cases, mobility is by way of a wheelchair where the hands or, if the hands are affected, the feet are used to propel the wheels. The following guidelines will help teachers make the appropriate adjustment to integrate these children into the regular physical education program.

1. While independence is the goal of all special needs children, develop a peer tutoring strategy to assist with mobility.

2. Review the child's medical file and discuss the child's limitations with the school nurse and a parent.

3. Consult with the school district's occupational therapist for ideas to help provide the most appropriate activities for the child.

4. Most children with cerebral palsy love movement and enjoy participating in physical education. As these students are often slow ambulators, modify the distance they have to travel. For ball activities, a suspended ball can be used to practice throwing, catching, and kicking skills—without the need to retrieve the ball.

Table 13.2 Seizures: Recognition and First Aid

Seizure type	Characteristics	First aid
Convulsive		
Generalized tonic-clonic (also called grand mal)	Sudden cry, fall, rigidity, followed by muscle jerks, shallow breathing or temporarily suspended breathing, bluish skin, possible loss of bladder or bowel control, usually lasts a couple of minutes followed by normal breathing. There may be fatigue, followed by a return to full consciousness	Look for medical identification. Protect from nearby hazards. Loosen ties or shirt collars. Protect head from injury. Turn on side to keep airway clear. Reassure when consciousness returns. If single seizure lasted less than five minutes, ask if hospital evaluation is wanted. If multiple seizures, or if more than five minutes, take to the emergency room.
Nonconvulsive		
Absence (also called petit mal)	A blank stare, beginning and ending abruptly, most common in young students. May be accompanied by rapid blinking, chewing movements of the mouth. Students may be unaware of what's going on during the seizure but quickly return to full awareness once it has stopped. May result in learning difficulties if not recognized and treated.	No first aid necessary, but medical evaluation should be recommended.
Simple partial (also called Jacksonian)	Jerking begins in one area of body, arm, leg, or face and cannot be stopped by patient, but patient stays awake and aware. Jerking may proceed to involve hand, then arm and sometimes spreads to whole body and becomes a convulsive seizure.	No first aid necessary unless seizure becomes convulsive, then first aid as above.
Simple partial (also called sensory)	Preoccupied or blank expression. Student experiences a distorted environment. May see or hear things that are not there, may feel unexplained fear, sadness, anger, or joy. May have nausea, experience odd smells, and have a generally "funny" feeling in the stomach.	No action needed other than reassurance and emotional support.
Complex partial (also called psychomotor or temporal lobe)	Usually starts with blank stare, followed by chewing, followed by random activity. Students appear unaware of surroundings, may seem dazed and mumble. Unresponsive. Actions clumsy and not directed. May pick at clothing, pick up objects, try to take clothes off. May run and appear afraid. May struggle or flail at restraint. Once pattern is established, same set of actions usually occurs with each seizure. Lasts a few minutes, but postseizure confusion can last substantially longer. No memory of what happened during seizure period.	Speak calmly and reassuringly to patient and others. Guide gently away from obvious hazards. Stay with student until completely aware of environment. Provide assistance in getting home.
Atonic seizures (also called drop attacks)	The legs of students between two to five years of age suddenly collapse. After ten seconds to a minute, can recover, regain consciousness, and stand and walk again.	No first aid needed (unless the child is hurt in the fall), but the student should be given a thorough medical evaluation.
Myoclonic seizures	Sudden brief, massive muscle jerks that may involve the whole body or parts of the body. May cause students to spill what they are holding or fall off a chair.	No first aid needed, but should be given a thorough medical evaluation.
Infantile spasms	Starts between three months and two years. If sitting up, the head will fall forward and the arms will flex forward. If lying down, the knees will be drawn up, with arms and head flexed forward as if reaching for support.	No first aid, but prompt medical evaluation is needed.

From *Seizure Recognition and First Aid*, copyright Epilepsy Foundation of America, 4351 Garden City Drive, Landover, MD 20785 (1–800–EFA–1000).

Nutritional Disorders

Two major nutritional disorders are common in the public school system. The first, obesity, will be discussed below. The second, anorexia nervosa, is a disorder that has become prevalent among teenage girls; thus, it is a disorder to be dealt with by high school teachers, rather than by elementary school teachers.

Obesity is a condition in which body weight exceeds the standard weight recommended for the individual on the basis of age, height, and frame size. Approximately 20 percent of elementary school children are obese. The primary causes are overeating, poor diet, and lack of vigorous daily activity. Dysfunction of the endocrine glands, which regulate the fat distribution in the body, accounts for a very small percentage of obese children.

A child who is classified as obese usually has a very low level of physical fitness, lacks coordination and speed, and reveals emotional and social adjustment problems. The following guidelines may help obese children reduce their body weight and help make their participation in physical activities enjoyable and meaningful. These guidelines apply to children whose obesity is the result of overeating.

1. Contact the school nurse and parents and attempt to establish a weight-reduction program for the obese child. Frequent counseling and encouragement by the teacher can help the child stay on a recommended diet.
2. Do not require obese children to perform balance stunts or movements they are incapable of performing.
3. Use extreme care during endurance activities. Set appropriate challenges, such as having all children keep moving until the music stops. This challenge allows each child to run, jog, walk, or perform any type of activity according to his or her own level of physical fitness.
4. Because of serious social and emotional implications, attempt to guide obese children into less demanding playing positions or events. In game activities, the goalie and defense positions are less demanding than a center or forward spot. In track and field, the shot put or tug-of-war would be more appropriate than sprints or distance running.
5. Use techniques of team or group selection that do not make the obese child the last one chosen.
6. Refer to chapter 11 for additional ideas relating to weight-control programs for the overweight child.

Cardiorespiratory Disorders

The major cardiorespiratory disorders found among elementary school children include cardiovascular impairments, such as rheumatic fever, and respiratory impairments, such as asthma. These impairments and suggestions for those who teach physical education to children suffering from such disorders are discussed in the following sections.

Cardiovascular Impairments

The major concern for elementary school teachers is the aftereffects of rheumatic fever. This condition accounts for approximately two-thirds of all cardiovascular problems and, hence, can be dealt with by following these guidelines:

1. The amount and type of physical activity for a child who has had rheumatic fever must be prescribed by a physician.
2. Rheumatic fever flourishes in the northern parts of the United States, particularly during winter and spring. Teachers should watch for early and suspicious signs, such as chronic colds, quick fatigue, and "serious" weight losses.
3. The vast majority of children who have had rheumatic fever can eventually participate in physical activities. Once the family doctor gives the child permission to participate in physical activities, the teacher should allow only moderate and brief participation during the first few weeks. As the child demonstrates the capacity to keep up without showing early signs of fatigue, gradually increase the amount and intensity of exercise. A simple monitoring device can be used to determine the level of exercise tolerance that is appropriate for this type of child. Take the child's pulse rate before the physical activity is started. The pulse rate should rise during exercise, then return to the resting pulse approximately three minutes after stopping the physical activity. If the pulse rate is still excessively high after three minutes, reduce the amount of exercise.

Respiratory Impairments

Two of the most common respiratory disorders are asthma and cystic fibrosis. This discussion will be limited to asthma, since it is the most common respiratory condition that still permits the child to participate in a wide range of physical activities. Teachers interested in a discussion of cystic fibrosis should consult the selected references at the end of this chapter.

Asthma is a disease of the lungs that is characterized by swelling of the mucous membrane lining, excessive secretion of mucous, and spasms of the bronchial tubes. The general symptoms are coughing and heavy wheezing and a constriction, or tightening, of the chest. Approximately 3 percent of the population of the United States are asthmatic. Between 3 and 10 percent of all school-age children are

integrating special needs children

asthmatic, and boys suffer from asthma almost two times as much as girls. If the following guidelines are followed, most asthmatic children can participate in the regular physical education program.

1. Children with asthmatic conditions should, within the limits of their ability, attempt to increase their level of general fitness and health. Planned developmental programs can help asthmatic children reach this goal.
2. Children with asthma should avoid vigorous and sustained activities, particularly in cold and dry climates.
3. Any causative agent (dust on tumbling mats or pollen from flowering trees or plants) should be avoided.
4. A gradual warm-up to vigorous activity may be helpful to some asthmatic children.
5. Teachers should know what to do if a student indicates that an asthmatic attack is starting.

Orthopedic Impairments

The term *orthopedic impairment* includes any congenital or acquired impairment that has produced a motor disability. This category includes birth defects, amputations, spina bifida, and a variety of crippling conditions caused by trauma (acid, fires, or accidents). Each type of physical disability within this broad orthopedic classification must be individually evaluated with respect to the nature and intensity of the activity. If the child is a member of the physical education class, however, the following general guidelines apply:

1. Wherever possible, create tasks that the disabled child is capable of performing; this leads to self-reliance and self-respect.
2. The teacher and children of any class that has a child with an orthopedic disability should treat this child in a normal manner, helping where really necessary, but never pampering him.

Traumatic Brain Injury

This disability is known as the "silent epidemic," as each year hundreds of children suffer traumatic brain injury through accidents involving motor vehicles, bicycles, falls, and projectiles such as softballs, baseballs, and bats. Recently, more attention has been given to children returning to school after these injuries. A teacher who has a child who has recently recovered from a traumatic brain injury needs to be aware of the cognitive, psychomotor, social, and emotional challenges facing the child. Quite often, many previously learned motor skills have to be relearned. Basic cognitive skills such as reading, mathematics, and spelling also have to be relearned. Emotional mood swings paired with episodes of aggressive behavior are not unusual and are part of the rehabilitation expectancy. What the teacher may not observe, depending on the child's trauma background, are periods of mild aggression, a poor memory, lack of coordination, and a poor sense of balance. In addition, there is a need to be sensitive to the fact that when restrictions in an activity are necessary, anger and denial may arise.

Physical Awkwardness

The term *physically awkward* refers to children who do not suffer from a known neurological or physical disability, yet experience difficulty learning and performing basic motor skills. The number of children who could be classified as physically awkward for their age level is unknown, but it may be alarmingly high. Gubbay (1975) suggested as many as 6 to 11 percent of school-age children experience serious difficulties in learning motor skills. Hence, it is important for teachers to understand the general characteristics of physical awkwardness. Unfortunately, there is very little agreement on how physically awkward children can be identified. There is no single measure of physical awkwardness that can be found to identify even one half of the children in a group of clumsy children. It appears the children identified as physically awkward are a heterogeneous group. The following descriptors appear in clinical accounts of physically awkward children.

1. Poor school achievement
2. Confusion and delay in hand dominance
3. Illegible handwriting
4. Immature drawing
5. Reading difficulties
6. Low self-esteem and self-concept
7. Failure in complex motor sequences
8. Difficulty in balance and spatial orientation
9. Low physical fitness

In addition, there appear to be other common warning signs of physical awkwardness, such as: late in walking, poor catching skills, avoidance of ball games and playground equipment, awkward running style, difficulty in learning to ride a bicycle, and a dislike of climbing equipment. The child may also have social problems (few friends) and experience difficulty coping with failure.

Early identification of children with movement problems may allow for remedial help before sensitive periods of development have passed. Consultation with parents, medical practitioners, and other professional groups equipped to offer professional advice on remedial programs is recommended.

Integrating in the Intramural Program

The intramural program provides an excellent opportunity to integrate special needs children. This can be accomplished by modifying games to accommodate children who may possess a variety of physical or mental disabilities.

For example, change the basketball game by adding a slow lane where only walking is permitted. Or include a rule that baskets scored from a sitting position are worth double point value. The latter rule allows the nondisabled children to show off their shooting skill from a seated position. It also permits children in wheelchairs to demonstrate their skill on an equal basis.

A number of other intramural activities are fun and competitive, yet do not require complex motor skill or total body movement. Most children, for example, enjoy chess, checkers, tic-tac-toe, and many other games of this nature. Since all children enjoy these activities, the disabled child needs no special program and is treated during such events as an equal competitor who does not receive any special favors. The latter situation is a healthy example of effective integration of all children regardless of physical abilities.

Another way of accommodating the physically disabled child is through self-directed activities. A child paraplegic can be given a physical fitness program based on movements he can perform and on projected levels of accomplishment. These challenges can be easily translated into points to allow the child to enhance his own self image through contributing to his homeroom or house point total.

Sources of Additional Ideas

A variety of resource centers and associations concerned with exceptional children provide resource materials to the classroom teacher on request. Teachers should write to the appropriate association and indicate the specific type of assistance required. In addition, a number of excellent books dealing with children with special needs are in print. A few examples of the types available are provided in the accompanying selected readings.

Resource Centers

Information and Research Utilization Center in Physical Education and Recreation for the Handicapped (IRUC), c/o AAHPERD, 1900 Association Drive, Reston, VA 22091

National Center on Educational Media and Materials for the Handicapped, Ohio State University, Columbus, OH 43210

The Council for Exceptional Children Information Center, 1920 Association Drive, Reston, VA 22091

Note: In addition, district and state departments of public instruction normally have special education divisions or departments.

Associations

American Alliance for Health, Physical Education, Recreation and Dance, 1900 Association Drive, Reston, VA 22091

American Federation of the Physically Handicapped Inc., 1376 National Press Building, Washington, DC 20004

American Hearing Society, 817 14th Street, NW, Washington, DC 20005

American Heart Association, Inc., 1790 Broadway, New York, NY 10019

Association for the Aid of Crippled Children, 345 East 46th Street, New York, NY 10017

Children's Bureau, Department of Health, Education and Welfare, Washington, DC 20014

Muscular Dystrophy Association of America, Inc., 1790 Broadway, New York, NY 10019

National Association for Mental Health, 10 Columbus Circle, New York, NY 10019

National Epilepsy League, 208 North Wells Street, Chicago, IL 60606

United Cerebral Palsy Association, 50 West 57th Street, New York, NY 10019

United States Office of Education, Department of Health, Education and Welfare, Washington, DC 20202

Selected References

Arnheim, D. D., and Sinclair, W. A. (1985). *Physical Education for Special Populations: A Developmental, Adapted, and Remedial Approach.* Englewood Cliffs, NJ: Prentice-Hall.

Delacato, C. (1959). *The Treatment and Prevention of Reading Problems.* Springfield, IL: Charles E. Thomas.

Dunn, J., and Fait, H. (1989). *Special Physical Education: Adapted, Individualized and Developmental.* Dubuque, IA: Wm. C. Brown Publishers.

Grossman, H. J., Ed. (1984). *Manual on Terminology and Classification in Mental Retardation.* Washington, DC: American Association of Mental Deficiency.

Gubbay, F. (1975). Clumsy Children in Normal Schools. *The Medical Journal of Australia*, Vol. No. 1, 233–36.

Horvat, M. (1990). *Physical Education and Sport for Exceptional Students.* Dubuque, IA: Wm. C. Brown Publishers.

Kavale, K., & Mattson, P. D. (1983). One Jumped Off the Balance Beam: Meta-Analysis of Perceptual Motor Training. *Journal of Learning Disabilities, 16,* 165–73.

Kephart, N. C. (1960). *The Slow Learner in the Classroom.* Columbus, OH: Charles E. Merrill Publishing Co.

Miller, A. G., and Sullivan, J. V. (1982). *Teaching Physical Activities to Impaired Youth: An Approach to Mainstreaming*. New York: John Wiley and Sons.

Morris, L. R., and Schulz, L. (1989). *Creative Play Activities for Children with Disabilities*. Champaign, IL: Human Kinetics Publishers, Inc.

Sherrill, C. (1993). *Adapted Physical Activity, Recreation, and Sport,* Fourth Edition. Dubuque, IA: Wm. C. Brown Publishers.

Stainback, S., Stainback, W., and Forest, M. (1989). *Educating All Students in the Mainstream of Regular Education.* Baltimore: Paul H. Brookes Publishers.

14

Adapting Physical Education Activities to the Classroom

As a general guideline, physical education activities should be taught in the gymnasium or outdoors on designated instructional areas. However, there are situations in many schools where the classroom, hallway, or cafeteria are the only available locations where physical activities can be taught. With a minimum shifting of chairs and desks, and adherence to a few safety rules, numerous physical activities such as active and quiet games, fitness exercises, and rhythmics can be taught in these indoor spaces. There is an additional contribution these physical activities can make to the intellectual and social development of children. Many

of the game, gymnastic, and rhythmic activities provided in this chapter can also be used as an effective medium through which a wide variety of academic concepts and skills can be taught in an exciting and effective manner.

The information provided in this chapter illustrates how many of the game, gymnastic, and dance activities described in other chapters can be modified and taught in the regular classroom, hallway, or cafeteria. A few additional grid activities, which are particularly adaptable to the classroom, are included ■

Teaching Procedures

With minor adjustments and the establishment of a few basic rules and safety procedures, the classroom can be used for many physical activities. Whenever a large, unobstructed space is required for a physical activity, move the desks and chairs in a safe, quiet, and efficient manner. Designating teams (by rows or any other type of classroom grouping), then creating a contest to see which group finishes first greatly speeds up this procedure.

Classrooms, hallways, and cafeterias vary in the amount of free space available, the type of furniture, and acceptable noise levels. The following suggestions, particularly those relating to safety and noise, should be carefully considered before introducing any physical activity to the classroom.

Participation

Provide opportunities for every member of the class to participate in the physical activity. The game activities suggested in the next section present the greatest problem. Break the class into as many separate playing groups as possible—three groups, rather than one, playing charades—or modify the game to increase individual and total class participation.

Safety

Remove pencils and other materials from the tops of desks and keep children away from sharp corners and edges. Other safety procedures, such as permitting running only around alternate rows and only when the noise does not seriously disturb adjacent classrooms, must be translated into simple and clearly understood rules.

Noise

Although classrooms differ with respect to acceptable noise levels, a few basic rules can help keep the noise problem under control. This applies to the noise within the classroom itself as well as the sound that penetrates the walls and ventilation system to other classrooms. In games and contests, modify verbal commands and require hand clapping instead of team or class yells. A lower volume may be called for in dance activities.

Figure 14.1 Classroom games can be quiet.

Classroom Games

Classroom games, or what are commonly known as "rainy day activities," are simple games, relays, and contests that can be played in the classroom, hallway, or cafeteria (figure 14.1). These games usually require little or no adjustment of furniture or elaborate equipment. For classification purposes, these activities are generally designated as either active or quiet, although the dividing line between the two is rather vague. A very enthusiastic class can turn a quiet game into an active one and vice versa. For ease of selection, however, the more vigorous games are listed under active games and the less active under quiet games (table 14.1).

There is no season or time of day that should be set aside for active or quiet games. Their use depends upon such factors as the basic purpose of the game, the weather, and the amount of time and space available. For example, several games listed in table 14.1 provide an effective medium through which children can acquire academic concepts in an exciting and challenging manner. There are other times during the school day, especially after long periods of mental concentration, where an exciting active classroom game provides the needed relaxation for both teacher and students. When selecting classroom games, first decide on the type—active or quiet—you want to use. Second, check the right-hand column of table 14.1 to see whether the game involves guessing, relay, imitation, tag, surprise, small manipulation, and/or academic concepts and skills. Finally, check to see if you have the necessary equipment.

Table 14.1   Classroom Games

Name of game	Developmental level			Type of game						Academic concepts and skills	Page
	I	II	III	Guessing	Relay	Imitation	Tag	Surprise	Small manipulation		
Active Classroom Games											
Fox and Rabbit	x							x	x	Language arts—letter and word recognition Science—living creatures Mathematics—number recognition	228
Beanbag Basket Relay	x	x			x				x	Mathematics—counting	228
Ringmaster	x	x				x					
Squirrel and Nut	x	x		x			x	x		Language arts—word recognition	228
Mirror Mirror	x	x				x		x	x	Language arts—letter recognition Mathematics—whole numbers	228
Water Cycle		x	x		x				x	Science—water cycle Language arts—synonyms, antonyms, homonyms, and consonant blends Mathematics—adding, subtracting, multiplying, and fractions	228
Knots		x	x					x	x		
Beanbag Pile	x	x	x		x				x	Mathematics—counting	229
Poorhouse		x	x					x		Mathematics—subtracting and multiplying	229
Who's Leading?		x	x					x	x		229
Balloon Hit		x	x						x		229
Quiet Classroom Games											
My Ship Is Loaded	x	x						x	x	Language arts—word recognition and memory Social studies—neighborhood and community Health—nutrition	230
Clappers	x	x							x	Language arts—syllables	230
Crambo	x	x		x						Language arts—homonyms	230
Hat Race	x	x	x		x			x	x		230
Rattlesnake and Bumblebee		x	x	x		x		x			230
Human Checkers		x			x				x		230
Puzzled Words		x	x						x	Language arts—letter and word recognition	230
Spell Act		x	x	x		x			x	Language arts—spelling	231
Charades		x	x	x		x			x	Social studies—geographical areas Science—species of animals	231

Active Classroom Games

Fox and Rabbit (Level I)

Formation Single circle or children seated
Equipment Two beanbags
Players Class
Academic concepts Language arts—letter and word recognition; science—living creatures; mathematics—number recognition

One beanbag, the "rabbit," is passed around the circle. A second beanbag, the "fox," is started around the circle. When the fox catches the rabbit, the game ends. Start each game with a new player.

Teaching Suggestions

1. Divide class into two or three groups.
2. Place one child in the center holding a beanbag. The center player calls out "animal," "bird," or "fish," then throws the beanbag to a player. If the word called was "fish," the player must call out the name of a fish as she catches the beanbag. Change positions if the catcher fails to give a name or did not catch the beanbag.
3. The center player has a set of color cards. Smaller color cards are given to opposite circle players. When the caller shows a color card, the two circle players with this color try to exchange places before the caller reaches one of the spots they have vacated. The caller may show two or more color cards at the same time. When he calls "all colors", everyone must attempt to change positions.
4. Substitute numbers, letters, or words for colors in the above variation.

Beanbag Basket Relay (Levels I–II)

Formation Lines facing baskets about six to eight feet in front of first player
Equipment Beanbags, wastepaper baskets, or hoops
Players Class
Academic concepts Mathematics—counting

Arrange pupils in rows facing the baskets. Draw a line across the front of the rows. On command, the first pupil attempts to throw a beanbag into the basket. One point is awarded for each basket. After shooting, each player retrieves his beanbag, gives it to the next player, and tells the teacher his score. Continue until the last player has had a turn. The team with the highest score wins.

Teaching Suggestions

1. Divide teams in half. Turn second half around, place baskets at back of room and play two games.
2. Have children take turns keeping their team's score.

Ringmaster (Levels I–II)

Formation Single circle with one child in the center
Equipment None
Players Class

One child selected as the "ringmaster" stands in the center of the circle. The ringmaster moves about the center of the circle, pretending to crack his whip, and calls out the names of animals. The circle players imitate the animals. If the ringmaster calls out, "All join the parade," the children imitate any animal they wish.

Teaching Suggestions

Call out names of mechanical objects, such as bulldozer, truck, or washing machine.

Squirrel and Nut (Levels I–II)

Formation Rows
Equipment Word cards
Players Class
Academic concepts Language arts—word recognition

The children sit at their desks with their heads resting on one arm. The other arm is held to the side with the hand in an open position. One child, who is chosen to be the "squirrel," carries a word card and moves quietly around the room. When the squirrel drops the "nut" into the hand of a player, that person jumps up, correctly pronounces the word on the card, then tries to tag the squirrel before the squirrel can reach her own seat.

Teaching Suggestions

1. Prepare sets of word cards for current science, social studies, or other subjects.
2. Have players hop, skip, or travel using other locomotor skills.

Mirror Mirror (Levels I–II)

Formation Scattered
Equipment None
Players Class
Academic concepts Language arts—letter recognition; Mathematics—whole numbers

Arrange the class into pairs with players facing each other. Number players one and two. On signal, player one begins to perform a movement, such as winking, moving a finger, or hopping on one foot. Player two must copy the actions of player one until the teacher calls "change." When this occurs, the players exchange roles. When the teacher calls "new mirror," everyone must find a new partner and the game continues.

Teaching Suggestions

1. Have players limit movements to making letters or numbers with their bodies.
2. Add other aspects of movement, such as letters that include moving quickly and slowly or numbers that require the use of a small piece of equipment (e.g., ruler, pencil, etc.).

Water Cycle (Levels II–III)

Formation Rows
Equipment Chalk and ball
Players Class
Academic concepts Science—water cycle; language arts—synonyms, antonyms, homonyms and consonant blends; mathematics—addition, subtraction, multiplication, and fractions

Arrange players into teams of six players, sitting at their desks and facing the front of the room. The first player is assigned water vapor, with the remaining players assigned rain, land, stream, river, and ocean, respectively. The first player calls out "water vapor," passes the ball over his head to the next player, who holds it while "water vapor" runs to the end of the row. The second player calls out "rain," repeats this action, then everyone moves up one seat. The first team to complete two water cycles wins the game.

Teaching Suggestions

1. The teacher calls out a word, such as, "generous," and the first player runs up and writes it on the chalkboard. The second player must write the first letter of a synonym, such as, "B" for bountiful. This procedure is continued with the other players until the word is written.
2. Repeat the above game with antonyms, homonyms, and consonant blends.
3. Repeat above game with addition, subtraction, multiplication, and fraction problems.

Knots (Levels II–III)

Formation   Circle
Equipment   None
Players   Six to eight per group

Players begin standing together in a small circle, with their hands at their sides. On signal, all players move hands forward and grasp other players' hands. Players who are standing next to each other cannot hold hands. When everyone is holding hands, the group, without letting go, begins to undo itself and return to the original circle formation.

Beanbag Pile (Levels I–III)

Formation   Sitting on the floor in rows
Equipment   One beanbag for each member
Players   Five or six in each row
Academic concepts   Mathematics—counting

Players are seated in a single line formation with beanbags placed in a pile in front of the first player in each line. On the signal "go," the first player takes a bag and passes it to the second player. The remaining beanbags are passed back one at a time. The last player lays the first beanbag on the floor. Each succeeding bag must be placed on top of the other, with only the first beanbag touching the floor. The stack must stand without any assistance from the stacker. If the stack falls, it must be restacked. The first team to pile the bags correctly and call out the total number of beanbags, wins the relay.

Teaching Suggestions

1. Change position of players, such as kneeling or standing.
2. Require all players to run on the spot or perform other movements while passing the beanbag.

Poorhouse (Levels II–III)

Formation   Semicircle or horseshoe formation
Equipment   None
Players   Class
Academic concepts   Mathematics—subtraction and multiplication

Players choose partners and sit in chairs placed in a horseshoe pattern. Two chairs representing the "poorhouse" are placed at the open end of the horseshoe. Each couple has a number and must keep their hands joined throughout the game. The game begins with the couple in the poorhouse calling out two numbers, such as "two" and "six." The couples whose numbers are called must change places. During the changeover, the poorhouse couple attempt to reach the chairs of "two" or "six" before the exchanging couples reach these vacated chairs.

Teaching Suggestions

Integrate math skills with this game. For example, saying "16 ÷ 4" and "8 − 6" would require numbers 4 and 2 to exchange positions.

Who's Leading? (Levels II–III)

Formation   Circle formation
Equipment   None
Players   Class

One player chosen to be "it" stands outside the circle with his hands over his eyes. The teacher then selects a player in the circle to be the "leader." The leader starts any motion he chooses (blinking his eyes, waving his arms over his head, etc.). "It" opens his eyes and tries to guess who the leader is. As the game progresses, the leader slyly switches to other movements and "it" tries to find this person. Allow two or three guesses, then change the leader and "it."

Balloon Hit (Levels II–III)

Formation   Desks and chairs moved back against the wall
Equipment   Balloons
Players   Scattered

Every player has a balloon. Each child keeps his balloon in the air by hitting it with his "best" hand. Later add "other hand," "elbows," "hit and turn around," "hit and touch the floor," and so on.

Teaching Suggestions

Play a game with one-half of the class against the other. Sit or kneel in a scattered formation and use five balloons. Use walls for goals and add other rules as necessary.

adapting physical education activities to the classroom

Quiet Classroom Games

My Ship Is Loaded (Levels I–II)

Formation   Seated on floor
Equipment   Utility ball (nine or thirteen inches)
Players   Class divided into groups of three or four players
Academic concepts   Language arts—word recognition and memory; social studies—neighborhood and community; health—nutrition

One child starts by rolling a ball to another and saying "My ship is loaded with cars" (or any cargo he wishes). The player who receives the ball repeats what the first child said and adds a new item as he rolls the ball to another player. He would say, "My ship is loaded with cars and hats." Each player in turn adds a new item. When a child fails to repeat all the "cargo," the ball is given to the player on his right, who starts a new game.

Teaching Suggestions
1. Use one classification, such as clothing, food, or neighborhood.
2. Change to opposites—the first player calls "boy," second calls "girl." The third player starts a new word.
3. Have the first player perform a movement, such as scratching her ear. The second player begins scratching her ear then adds a new movement, such as tapping her knees. This procedure is continued around the circle until someone forgets a movement or performs any movement out of sequence.

Clappers (Levels I–II)

Formation   Circle
Equipment   None
Players   Eight to ten per group
Academic concepts   Language arts—syllables

Arrange groups into small circles around the classroom. The first player in each group claps the number of syllables in her first name, pauses for two seconds then claps the number again. She continues this action and any other player with the same number of syllables in his or her name joins in. Allow each group to clap five times then move to the next player and repeat the game. Repeat for surnames and, finally, a combination of first and last names.

Crambo (Levels I–II)

Formation   Seated
Equipment   None
Players   Class
Academic concept   Language arts—Homonyms

One child chosen to be "it" starts the game by saying "I am thinking of something [inside or outside the room] that rhymes with rain." Other players ask, "Is it a train?" "Is it a drain?" and so on. The child who guesses correctly becomes "it."

Hat Race (Levels I–III)

Formation   Rows
Equipment   Ruler and hat
Players   Class

Every other row participates. All players stand in the aisles with rulers in their right hands. The first player has a hat, which he places on his ruler. On the signal "go," he passes the hat over his right shoulder to the next player, who takes the hat with his ruler and passes it over his shoulder to the next player, and so on. The last player in the row walks down the empty aisle to the front of his line. If a player drops the hat, he must pick it up with the ruler; no hands are allowed. Everyone shifts back one position and the relay continues until all players are back in their original positions.

Teaching Suggestions
Try the game sitting down.

Rattlesnake and Bumblebee (Levels II–III)

Formation   Seated at desks or tables
Equipment   Two small unlike objects
Players   Two equal teams

One player is chosen from each team and sent out of the room. While the two players are out, team captains hide the two articles (team A hides for team B and vice versa). The two players return and begin looking for their articles. Members of either team "buzz" or "hiss" according to how close each player is to his object. Repeat with two new "finders." One point is awarded for the player, and his team, who finds the object first.

Human Checkers (Level III)

Formation   Chairs in a row
Equipment   Seven chairs
Players   Six on each team

Place seven chairs in a row. Three girls sit on the three chairs at one end and three boys sit at the other end. The object is to move the girls to the boys' chairs and the boys to the girls' chairs in fifteen moves. Only one move can be made at a time. Moves are made by sliding into an open chair or "jumping" over one person. Players cannot move backward. For example, girl number three moves to the spare chair; on the second move, boy number four jumps girl number three, who is now in the spare position, and so on.

Puzzled Words (Level III)

Formation   Groups of five to eight players
Equipment   Pieces of paper
Players   Class
Academic concepts   Language arts—letter and word recognition

Organize the class into groups of five to eight children. The teacher gives each group a pile of letters that, after reshuffling, will form a word. On signal from the teacher, each group tries to put its word together. The first team to assemble its word wins the game.

Teaching Suggestions

1. After the group puts the word together, allow it to act out the word for the other children to guess.
2. Add three or four piles to each group. When assembled the words would form a phrase or short sentence.
3. Place a set of twenty-six randomly organized cards (one for each letter) in the front of each group. On signal, the first player runs up, finds letter A, and brings it back to his team. Continue game until all cards have been picked up. First team to finish wins the game.

Spell Act (Levels II–III)

Formation   Two teams on opposite sides of the room
Equipment   None
Players   Class
Academic concepts   Language arts—spelling

Play this game as a regular spelling match. The letters *A* and *T* must not be spoken but must be indicated as follows: *A*, scratch right ear and raise left hand; *T*, scratch left ear and raise right hand.

Teaching Suggestions

1. Change movements for letters *A* and *T*.
2. Use the body to form letters for *A* and *T*.

Charades (Level III)

Formation   Small groups
Equipment   None
Players   Class divided into five or six groups
Academic concepts   Social studies—geographical areas; science—species of animals

Each group is allowed sufficient time to work out a charade. A captain is elected from each group. The word or object chosen by a group should have syllables to make it easier to act out. All dramatizations must be in pantomime. One group acts out its charade in front of the class. The captain of the group asks the class to guess the syllable or complete word. If the word is not guessed within a certain time, the captain tells the class and the next group has its turn.

Teaching Suggestions

Ask the class to decide on a specific category from which all words must be chosen, such as books, cities, famous names, songs.

Grid Activities

A rectangle, square, or specially designed grid, such as the shape of an animal, can become a vigorous and enjoyable activity as well as an effective learning medium for young

Figure 14.2   The first player hops, jumps, or uses part of his body.

children. For classroom use, grids can be drawn on the floor with chalk and easily removed with a rag or brush. However, it is recommended that classroom grids be made on plastic sheets, which allows the teacher to predesign a variety of grids to cope with different levels of academic and physical ability and available floor space. The sheets can be taped to the floor for use, then easily stored until used for subsequent lessons.

The grid activities that follow illustrate how to design and use grids to teach a variety of academic concepts and skills. Each teacher should adapt these grids and accompanying tasks to meet the level of ability and interest of her class. Additional modifications can be made to accommodate children with disabilities; for example, task cards on strings for children in wheelchairs.

Language Arts: Match Letters

Draw or place three or four grids, as shown in figure 14.2, on the floor. The teacher or a child calls out a letter and the first player hops, jumps, or uses part of his body to land on the correct letter. Repeat for every child in the group.

Academic Concepts (including variations below)

Letter recognition—upper and lower case, vocabulary, consonants and vowels, prefixes and suffixes.

Teaching Suggestions

1. Reduce the size of the grid to meet levels of ability.
2. Place upper- and lower-case letters on flash cards or write them on the chalkboard. Use these cards as visual signals.
3. Have children hop and spell words.
4. Have children call out letters or words as they land on them.

Figure 14.3 Using the prefixes combined with words . . .

un	re	mis
ab	dis	ad

5. Have children select three or four letters in a row (e.g., C, D, and E), then have them hop or jump to each letter in the correct sequence.

6. Have children cut out a letter, hop with it to the corresponding letter on the grid, then run and write it on the blackboard.

7. Have the children land on a consonant and sound it out with a word, such as "C in cat." Repeat with vowel sounds.

8. The inventive game approach described in chapter 16, (page 289) can be readily adapted to all grid activities. The following challenge illustrates how to use this approach with children in the primary and intermediate grades.

   For young children. In order to get two children to make up their own game, using words and the letter grid in figure 14.2, pose the following task: "Can you make up a game for two players using the grid? Your game must involve hopping on letters and spelling someone's name."

   For older children. Arrange the class in groups of five around the prefix grid shown in figure 14.3. Pose the following challenge to the groups: "See if you can design a game for five players, using the prefixes combined with words with no more than four letters, and passing a Nerf ball."

Mathematics: Adding Game

Draw or place three or four grids, shown in figure 14.4 around the classroom. The teacher or child calls out an addition question, such as "3 + 2 = ?" The first player must hop or jump on to each number and mathematical symbol to square number 5, then out of the grid.

Academic Concepts (including variations below)

Addition, sign recognition, subtraction, multiplication, division, and fractions.

Teaching Suggestions

1. Repeat above game substituting a subtraction, multiplication, division, or fraction task.

2. Have each child place certain body parts on the squares as she answers the question.

Figure 14.4 "3 + 2 = ?"

3. Use flash cards or chalkboard in the game. For example, one child writes $16 \times 4 =$ on the chalkboard, and his partner must hop on the correct squares to produce the answer.

4. Design inventive game challenges similar to those described under language arts. For example, with four players and a multiplication problem, the challenge would be: "Can your group make up a game for four players using the grid and involving a multiplication problem? The game must be played with partners and you must use a beanbag in your game."

Science, Health, and Social Studies: Name That Thing

Academic Concepts (including variations below)

Science—grouping of living creatures, solar system, and weather; health—nutrition, bones and muscles, safety; social studies—location and size of geographical areas. The teacher prepares three or four grids as shown in figure 14.5 and a set of flash cards for mammals, fish, reptiles, birds, insects, and amphibians. When the teacher holds up "fish" and calls "three," the first player must hop or jump on to three different fish. Repeat game with each child taking a turn.

Teaching Suggestions

1. Have players move to creatures according to a characteristic, such as "a mammal that flies," "a reptile without legs," or "a bird that cannot fly."

2. Repeat the original game, but when a player has landed on a square, she must give a characteristic of the species before jumping to the next square.

3. Design similar grids and tasks for prehistoric animals, flowers, plants, and so on.

Figure 14.5 Name that thing.

Dog	Horsefly	Ant	Lizard	Seagull	Armadillo
Sparrow	Shark	Toad	Butterfly	Bee	Salmon
Snakes	Duck	Seal	Wasp	Hawk	Alligator
Swordfish	Ostrich	Cod	Frog	Dolphin	Cat
Salamander	Elephant	Fly	Turtles	Trout	Mosquito
Crocodile	Buzzard	Pig	Sea Horse	Bat	Penguin

MAMMALS   REPTILES   FISH

INSECTS   BIRDS   AMPHIBIANS

Figure 14.6 Physical fitness testing can be a classroom activity.

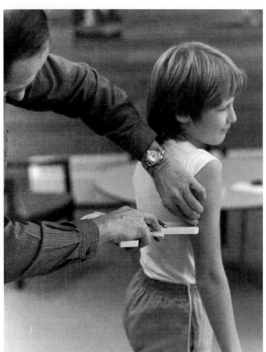

4. Design similar grids for nutrition. For example, flash cards for proteins, carbohydrates, and minerals, and grids containing examples of each food group.

5. Create a grid for capital cities and flash cards for states. Begin with a simple game matching cities with the correct states. Later add, "Which state has the largest population?" "The longest coastline?" "The closest to Asia?" and so on.

Physical Fitness Activities

A variety of physical fitness activities can be performed in the classroom. The following examples illustrate how physical fitness tests and circuit training can be performed within the classroom with a minimum amount of furniture adjustment or noise disturbance to adjacent classrooms.

Physical Fitness Testing

Several test items within the AAHPERD'S *Youth Fitness and Health Related Physical Fitness Test* can be easily administered in the classroom (figure 14.6). These items include sit-ups, standing broad jump, body composition, and sit-and-reach. Other cardiovascular activities, such as

measuring heart rate and blood pressure or conducting the following cardiovascular experiments (see chapter 11), are easily adapted to the classroom.

Experiment 1: Comparative heart rates
Experiment 2: Heart rate recovery
Experiment 3: Effect of different activities
Experiment 4: Excitement and fear

Calisthenics

Simple calisthenics, with or without musical accompaniment, may be among the easiest activities to perform in the classroom (figure 14.7). Once children appreciate the space limitations, they can do the exercises beside their desks or wherever space is available in the classroom. Brief circuit-type activities, described in chapter 12, also can be designed for the classroom. The advantages are that the teacher can develop a basic circuit that does not require any mats or other equipment and that all children begin and stop after a set number of minutes. In addition, where noise is a problem between adjacent classrooms, circuits can be performed in relative silence and without using a whistle or loud voice to give or change directions.

Figure 14.7 Simple calisthenics in the classroom.

Figure 14.8 Performing skills with a beanbag.

Gymnastic and Movement Skills

Gymnastic and movement skills include a large number of activities that can be performed in the classroom with a little planning. Such activities as individual stunts and movement skills (chapter 25), small equipment and partner activities (chapter 26), and a few large apparatus skills (chapter 27) can be adapted to the limited space of the regular classroom. The following stunts do not require a mat and, thus, are more appropriate for classroom use. Other individual movement skills—shapes, weight bearing, and simple sequences—could also be practiced on the available floor space.

Small Equipment

The use of small equipment, such as beanbags, individual ropes, and hoops, in the classroom is growing in popularity (figure 14.8). Schools that have adopted daily physical education programs and have limited gymnasium facilities are using the classroom as an alternate exercise area. Since small equipment can be easily transported, it has many classroom applications.

The following activities can be performed in the aisles or in a cleared area at the back of the room.

Name of stunt	Page
Beanbag activities	478
Individual rope activities	482
Hoop activities	492
Wand activities	493

Juggling Activities

The basic juggling skills described in chapter 26 can be practiced in a classroom or hallway (figure 14.9). Begin with scarves; as skill improves, gradually introduce bags or balls. If the lighting fixtures present a potential hazard, restrict juggling activities to "safe areas" within the classroom or hallway.

Large Apparatus

The use of large apparatus in a typical classroom is limited by the size and weight of the apparatus. There are, however, companies producing large apparatus that is light, collapsible, and capable of numerous arrangements. Agility apparatus provides several different levels to complement the partner movement challenge. See also chapter 27.

Combining Large and Small Equipment

Figure 14.10 illustrates how station work and a rotation system give every child an opportunity to use a variety of small equipment and large apparatus. Since the area is crowded with equipment, the lesson emphasizes matching balance activities. The task for every station is to develop a matching sequence with one piece of equipment. In this case, movement is limited to the space immediately around each piece of equipment.

Rhythmic and Dance Activities

The classroom setting has numerous advantages when teaching rhythmics, singing games, and folk dance activities. For older children, the familiar environment of the classroom can prove to be a stepping-stone for more complex and creative movements in the gymnasium.

Figure 14.9 Juggling skills can be practiced in the classroom.

Figure 14.11 Folk dance.

Figure 14.10 Small equipment and large apparatus.

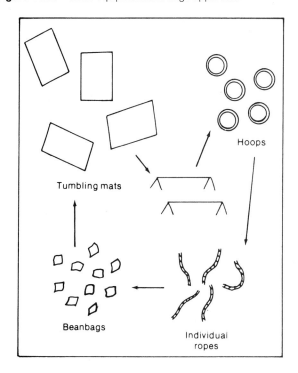

Hoops

Tumbling mats

Beanbags

Individual ropes

Rhythmic Activities

The rhythmic activities described in chapter 28 can easily be performed in the classroom. It is suggested that the same progression—moving from individual to partner to group activities—be followed. Small equipment, such as beanbags, individual ropes, and rhythm sticks, can also be used in the classroom with only minor adjustments. If the noise of a record player or drum is distracting to adjacent classrooms, limit the accompaniment to light drum beats or encourage the children to move in a rhythmic pattern without musical accompaniment. In fact, this will produce some very interesting results.

Singing Games and Folk Dances

Young children, particularly those in kindergarten and first grade, thoroughly enjoy the singing games described in chapter 29. The classroom provides an informal atmosphere in which to learn the words of these games and to practice the basic steps and rhythm patterns. Virtually all singing games can be performed in the space available in a regular classroom.

For older children, folk dance steps, positions, and pathways of movements can be taught in the classroom (figure 14.11). If students have had little exposure to folk dance activities, individual and partner activities involving the basic steps and patterns can be performed in the classroom. This procedure normally breaks the ice for larger group dances that require the larger space of the gymnasium.

Creative Dance

What has been said about the value of an informal classroom atmosphere when teaching folk dance applies even more so to creative dance activities. Students can begin with very simple and "directed" follow-the-leader or matching movements and then gradually be introduced to more creative tasks. In time, more creative challenges involving sound, poetry, or other forms of accompaniment can be introduced to the program. The teacher should review the ideas presented in chapter 30 to determine what other creative dance activities can be adapted to the classroom.

Although many interesting and exciting physical activities can be performed in the regular classroom, such activities are inadequate for the child's normal growth and development. Teachers should use the classroom to supplement rather than to replace the gymnasium. There are times, too, when the mood of the class dictates a change of pace before shifting to another subject area.

Selected References

Haseltine, P. (1988). *Games for All Children.* Oxford, England: Basil Blackwell Ltd.

Humphrey, J. H. (1990). *Integration of Physical Education in the Elementary School Curriculum.* Springfield, IL: Charles C. Thomas Publishers.

Humphrey, J. H., and Humphrey, J. N. (1990). *Mathematics Can Be Child's Play.* Springfield, IL: Charles C. Thomas Publishers.

———. (1991). *Developing Elementary School Science Concepts Through Active Games.* Springfield, IL: Charles C. Thomas Publishers.

Kamiya, A. (1985). *Elementary Teacher's Handbook of Indoor and Outdoor Games.* West Nyack, NY: Parker Publishing Co.

Turner, L. F., and Turner, S. L. (1989). *P. E. Teacher's Skill-by-Skill Activities Program.* West Nyack, NY: Parker Publishing Co.

Wnek, B. (1992). *Holiday Games and Activities.* Champaign, IL: Human Kinetics Publishers, Inc.

15

Designing Extraclass Programs

The extraclass program is an extension of the regular instructional program. Its purposes are to provide opportunities for all children to practice the skills they have learned in their physical education classes, to develop leadership and followership skills, and to enhance personal and social interests through a wide variety of competitive and noncompetitive activities. This is also a program in which students participate on a voluntary basis, where they take on the major responsibility of planning, organizing, and running their own program of activities. It is a program where the teacher starts the process, then gradually shifts to the role of helpful guider.

In order to develop a well-balanced extraclass program, teachers should understand the methods of organizing for competition, when to offer activities, the types of tournaments children enjoy, and special programs such as play days and interschool activities. These topics, along with guidelines and sample programs, are included in this chapter ∎

Intramural Program

The contemporary intramural program in the elementary school should be considered a logical extension of the regular instructional program. As such, it should include all children from kindergarten to grade six. Students participate in this program on a voluntary basis and play a variety of activities learned in the instructional program (figure 15.1). However, the main emphasis of this program should be on playing for fun as well as to experience positive social interactions with fellow students. The following guidelines will provide a basis for developing a student-centered intramural program.

Guidelines

1. All children, including those with special needs, should be free to participate in the program.
2. Boys and girls in the primary and intermediate grades should have equal access to the facilities and activities of the program.
3. Once the intramural program has been established, students should assume the responsibility of planning, organizing, and running their own activities.
4. Since this is a voluntary program, parental consent should be obtained before students are permitted to participate. This is particularly important for afterschool activities.
5. Where facilities and time permit, competition should emphasize continuous participation rather than sudden death or rapid elimination tournaments.
6. Noncompetitive and cooperative activities should be included in the intramural program.
7. Award systems should emphasize group effort and participation on an equal basis with fair competition.

Time Schedules for Participation

The time scheduled for intramural activities usually depends on the nature of the school population and the available facilities. Before school can be an effective time, particularly in districts where many parents work or when children arrive early by bus. The most popular time, of course, is the noon hour; this provides an opportunity for participation by virtually all children. There is, however, a general trend to hold intramural activities after school. In urban areas where many parents work and community recreational facilities are limited, the school playground or gymnasium is used for many afterschool intramural and club activities.

Supervision of Program

The success of any intramural program depends on the support, encouragement, and effective supervision by

Figure 15.1 Intramurals should be a voluntary activity.

teachers, parents, or other adult supervisory staff. The adult's role in this program should be to help children organize themselves and their activities. Through this process, children take on more responsibility for planning and operating their program, while teachers gradually shift from directing the program to the role of interested advisor and supervisor of facilities and student-run activities.

Methods of Grouping Children

Since intramural activities should be voluntary, the procedure used to group children for competition is paramount. Perhaps the success of these programs ultimately depends on equal competition and adequate provision for participation by all children. This must be considered in selecting the method of organization for upper elementary grades, as well as the nature and extent of adult supervision. The following methods are currently being used in elementary schools.

Grade and Homeroom

Organizing teams by homeroom appears to be the most popular method. Sixth graders competing against sixth graders is generally fair competition; sixth graders matched against fifth graders is unfair. Therefore, in team sports, such as volleyball and track, use homerooms within the same grade when possible. Otherwise, competition could be unequal and the children could become disinterested.

Classification Index

By the time children reach the fifth and sixth grades, age alone is an unfair assessment of physical growth and maturation. Another method should be used to arrange players into groups of approximate physical maturation and ability. A classification index can be used to put children into groups according to both size and age. To illustrate, let us suppose 60 fifth- and sixth-grade children register for an afterschool intramural basketball tournament. Here is how the index works.

Player no.	Score
1. 10 × 10 (age) + 70 (weight) =.........................170	
2. 10 × 11 (age) + 86 (weight) =.........................196	
3. 10 × 11 (age) + 92 (weight) =.........................202	
4. 10 × 12 (age) + 123 (weight) =.........................243	

The four examples give an idea of how to divide the sixty players into two leagues of three teams each, with ten players on a team. Assuming that about half of the children had a score of 196 or less, use this score as the dividing line between the two leagues. The actual dividing line, of course, depends on the maturity of the children.

Teacher's Choice

Competition in team and individual sports is often more dependent on skill and desire than on age, height, and weight. Thus, it may be desirable to organize teams and leagues according to the level of skill needed for each intramural activity. However, this method is dependent primarily on the teacher's assessment of the child's performance.

To illustrate, let us assume that, at the end of a four-week instructional unit in volleyball, three sixth-grade classes wish to have a coeducational volleyball tournament after school. Ten boys and ten girls from each class register for the tournament. Since the children are not playing for their homerooms, the intramural director has asked each homeroom teacher to rate the class members as either A or B players and to divide the class into two approximately equal groups. The intramural director could then place all A players in one league and all B players in another. If only one league is desired, the director would place an equal number of A and B players on each team.

Date of Birth

If the school has an average of three classes per grade, the children's birth dates can be the most even and effective way of dividing the whole school into three or more groups. These groups can become permanent from year to year. Subgroups can be organized into leagues on the basis of ability, age, or any other criterion.

To illustrate, assume we have a school of 540 children in grades one to six, with three classes in each grade. The intramural program needs four basic groups. Divide the calendar year into four equal parts and assign the children in the following manner.

Group 1: January 1 to March 31 (approximately 135 children)
Group 2: April 1 to June 30 (approximately 135 children)
Group 3: July 1 to September 30 (approximately 135 children)
Group 4: October 1 to December 31 (approximately 135 children)

Any number of groups can be obtained simply by dividing the calendar year into the desired number of units. It is important to let each group select its own name. Such themes as Indian tribes, colors, and professional sports teams are very popular with elementary school children.

Administrative Organization

The type of administrative organization that a school decides to use depends on its size and the interest of the students. The house system (figure 15.2) provides for maximum student leadership and effective communication to all children.

Children should be elected to the House Council by their own house members. All other committees can be assigned responsibilities by the House Council, and the committee members can be elected, or appointed by the House Council. The roles of the Games and Rules Committee and the Schedule Committee are obvious; the Primary Leaders Committee organizes older children who wish to help primary children. These older students can play a very important role in organizing informal and noncompetitive activities for the boys and girls in the first three grades, such as beanbag bowling, skill instruction during the noon hour, and beanbag basket shooting.

Types of Tournaments

There are numerous ways teams or individuals can compete. The type of tournament selected depends on the activity, the space available, the time, and the number of competitors. An Olympic meet plan is the only feasible type of tournament for track, swimming, and gymnastic activities. Single or double elimination and round-robin tournaments may be used for a variety of team and individual sports. Ladder tournaments are very useful for individual activities that can be played during instruction time, the noon hour, or after school. However, careful consideration should be given to the strengths and weaknesses of the following tournaments on the basis of available time, space, and number of competitors.

Olympic Meet Plan

The Olympic meet tournament is used for contests that include a number of separate events, such as swimming, gymnastics, and track and field activities. The winners of each event are awarded points, with an aggregate individual and team champion determined on the basis of points. In keeping with the idea of wide participation, first- to sixth- or seventh-place winners are awarded points. In an all-school track meet, for instance, the first six places in a fifty-yard dash might be awarded ten, nine, eight, seven, six, and five points, respectively. To encourage participation, relay and tug-of-war contests might be awarded a higher number of points than individual events.

Figure 15.2   Intramural house system.

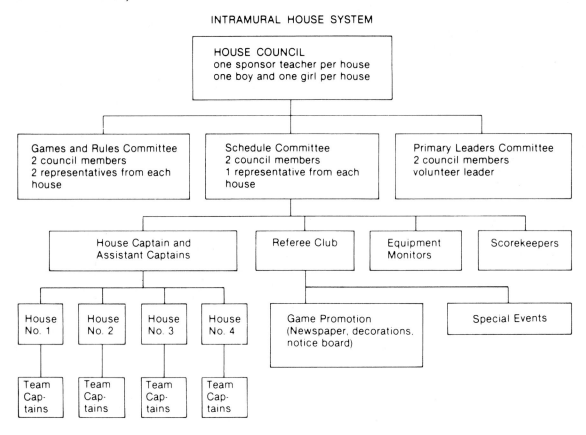

Figure 15.3   Single elimination tournaments.

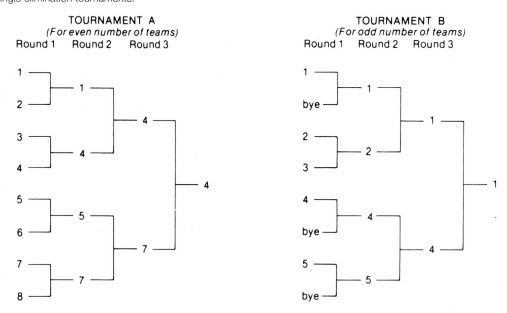

Single Elimination Tournament

The elimination tournament is the easiest to organize and the quickest for determining a winner. Its use, therefore, depends on a large number of teams, limited facilities, and a minimum number of days to complete the tournament. Two examples of a single elimination tournament are shown in figure 15.3.

In the first round of tournament A, the odd-numbered teams played the even-numbered, which eliminated teams 2, 3, 6, and 8 from competition. In the second round, team 4 beat team 1, and team 7 beat team 5. Teams 4 and 7 competed in the last round, and team 4 won the tournament. In tournament B, three teams were given a "bye" in the first round, because there was an odd number of teams.

The single elimination tournament does not require any byes when there is an even number of teams, providing it equals any power of two (2, 4, 8, 16, etc.). With an odd number of teams, or those even-numbered teams not equaling a power of two, it is necessary to give one or more teams a bye in the first round; the number of byes required for specific numbers of teams follows.

Number of teams	Numbers of byes	Number of games
3	1	2
4	0	3
5	3	4
6	2	5
7	1	6
8	0	7
9	7	8
10	6	9
11	5	10
12	4	11

In the single elimination tournament, the number of games required to complete a tournament is always one less than the number of teams.

Double Elimination Tournament

In a single elimination tournament, once a team loses a game, it is eliminated from all further competition. It is also quite possible for the second best team in a league to be defeated in the first round. Since the purpose of intramurals is to provide maximum activity for all competitors, a *consolation bracket* can be added to any single elimination tournament. The added bracket, as shown in figure 15.4, assures each team at least two games.

Round-Robin Tournament

In a round-robin tournament, each team plays every other team in the league. If time and facilities permit, this is the most desirable type of competition for team and individual

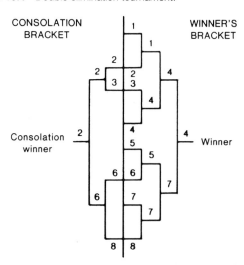

Figure 15.4 Double elimination tournament.

sports. The winner is the player or team that wins the most games. Following is the procedure for organizing a round-robin tournament:

1. Determine the number of games to be played by applying the formula $n(n - 1) \div 2$ (n equals the number of teams). For example, six teams would require $6(6 - 1) \div 2$, or 15, games.

2. Give each team a number and arrange in two columns. For round 1:

   1 plays 6

   2 plays 5

   3 plays 4

3. Keep team number 1 constant and rotate all other teams one place in a counterclockwise direction until fifteen games have been scheduled.

Round 1	Round 2	Round 3	Round 4	Round 5
1 vs. 6	1 vs. 5	1 vs. 4	1 vs. 3	1 vs. 2
2 vs. 5	6 vs. 4	5 vs. 3	4 vs. 2	3 vs. 6
3 vs. 4	2 vs. 3	6 vs. 2	5 vs. 6	4 vs. 5

4. With an odd number of teams, use "bye" in place of a number and follow the same procedure. This example is for five teams, with each bye indicating the team will not play.

1 vs. bye	1 vs. 5	1 vs. 4	1 vs. 3	1 vs. 2
2 vs. 5	bye vs. 4	5 vs. 3	4 vs. 2	3 vs. bye
3 vs. 4	2 vs. 3	bye vs. 2	5 vs. bye	4 vs. 5

Ladder Tournament

A ladder tournament is a continuous competition limited only by the space and time available. Each player or team is placed (arbitrarily, by chance, or by the results of prior competition) on a ladder. The object is to climb to the top

designing extraclass programs

of the ladder and remain there until the end of the tournament. This type of competition is primarily used with individual activities during the instructional period, the noon hour, or after school.

To illustrate how this type of extended tournament can be used, a noon hour tetherball tournament was offered to all children in grades four through six. On the first day, seven children signed up for the tournament. Their names were put into a hat, drawn out, and placed on the ladder (figure 15.5), from the top down. The ladder was made from tongue depressors placed on cup hooks. The rules were explained, posted next to the ladder, then the children were allowed to challenge one another. The next day, thirteen more children wanted to join the tournament, so the teacher simply added two more ladders and gave them a color identification. After placing the new players on the ladders (figure 15.6), she explained to the whole group how players on each ladder may challenge any player one or two rungs above on their own ladder or on either of the other two ladders. This new multiple ladder tournament allowed children to shift back and forth to find other players with similar levels of playing ability.

Pyramid Tournament

The pyramid tournament (figure 15.7), is basically a variation of the ladder tournament. The main difference is that there are always several players sharing the lowest rung, rather than just one player. There are also more opportunities to play a greater number of different players or teams. This factor is increased when the king or crown variation (figure 15.8) is added to a single tournament.

The following procedures illustrate how an eight-team pyramid tournament operates:

1. Construct a pyramid as shown in figure 15.7.
2. Establish a set of rules similar to the ladder tournament.

In this eight-team tournament, all teams begin by challenging any other team. To illustrate, team 7 beat team 5 and so, advances to the lowest row. Similarly, teams 3, 1, 4, and 7 have won their first games. A team on the lowest row may challenge any team on that row only. Winners move up to the next row. If the row immediately above is filled, winners of the lower row simply wait for a space. When all teams are on the pyramid, challenges are made to teams in the above row. The winning team takes the highest position.

The king or crown variation provides many more opportunities to challenge horizontally and vertically.

Figure 15.5 Ladder tournament.

Figure 15.6 Multiple ladder tournament.

Red	White	Blue
Jane	Mark	Frank
Takayo	John	Alfredo
Susan	Surguit	Olga
Pedro	Paula	Sue
Paul	Ping	Brian
Sam	Mary	Diane
Phillip	Louise	

Figure 15.7 Pyramid tournament.

Figure 15.8 King tournament.

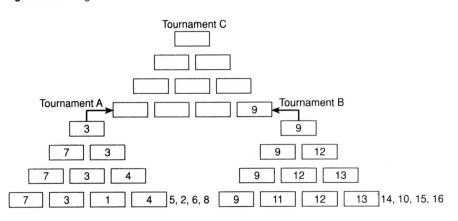

In this example, player number 3 from tournament A has moved to the top of her ladder, then challenged player 9 from tournament B. Player number 9 wins and becomes the first player to reach tournament C. Players from tournament A or B may challenge any player on the opposite side and on the same level. To illustrate, while player number 3 was playing player 9, player 7 from tournament A was playing number 12 from tournament B. Player 7 wins and moves over and takes player 9's position as he, in turn, moves up to tournament C.

Point and Award Systems

Intramural point and award systems are designed to increase participation and to show appreciation for such things as performance, sportsmanship, and leadership. The following suggestions and guidelines will assist in developing a point and award system that will encourage informal participation as well as minimize the importance of winning.

Point Systems

Any point system that places an excessive emphasis on participation tends to place too much pressure on team or house members simply to show up for a game or an event. Similarly, a point system that recognizes only the athletically gifted performers disinterests virtually all other children. The following example provides a balance that reflects participation and achievement.

	Participation	Place in tournament or event				
		1st	2nd	3rd	4th	5th
Team sports	10 points	15	10	8	7	6
Individual sports	5 points	5	4	3	2	1
Olympic meets:						
Individual events	1 point	5	4	3	2	1
Team events	3 points	10	9	8	7	6

This example should be used only as a guideline. Each school should design its own point value system for the various competitive events. Whatever system is decided on should be easy for children to tabulate. The system should also give more weight to activities involving a large number of participants and to those extending over a long period of time.

Award Systems

Ideally, participation in an intramural program should be based on intrinsic values such as enjoyment and friendship. Hence, when presenting awards in the form of cups, ribbons, or other visual recognitions, consideration should be given to the following areas.

1. All awards should reflect the goals of the intramural program. Major awards should represent performance, sportsmanship, leadership, and participation. Special service awards to managers, particularly those who are physically disabled, should be a priority item in any intramural program.

2. Awards should be well earned, rather than a meaningless gesture.

3. Awards should be inexpensive. Exceptions should be perpetual awards, such as the aggregate trophy that is won each year by a classroom or house. These are initially quite expensive; however, yearly winners normally require a simple and inexpensive inscription on the base plate.

4. Intramural awards should be presented at the end of the school year during the school assembly when all other academic and achievement awards are presented to deserving students.

Officiating Intramural Activities

One of the most important factors of any intramural program is the development and performance of student officials. Whether officials are chosen by the intramural director or through the student referees' club, the following suggestions will help contribute to a successful program.

1. Encourage children who have demonstrated good leadership qualities, fair play, and an interest in officiating to join the referees' club. Although age is not a major consideration, fifth and sixth graders tend to command more respect from their peers.

2. A high level of skill should not be a major requirement; thus, disabled children, wherever possible, should be encouraged to become referees, timekeepers, or scorekeepers.

3. The intramural director or an interested staff member should provide special instructions for all officials. This should be done on a weekly basis.

4. A staff member should be present during all competitive events to provide encouragement and support to student officials. Officials' decisions should be respected by all participants and supported by the supervising teacher. If a performer or a team has a legitimate complaint, it should be directed to the referees' club or committee for resolution.

5. All officials should be given recognition for their efforts. This can be accomplished by naming the officials over the loudspeaker, by awarding points to the referee's homeroom or house, or by creating service awards.

Types of Intramural Activities

The intramural activities that children enjoy generally are the activities they have learned in the regular instructional program. Since participation is voluntary, children should be allowed to choose their activities, as well as the type and length of each tournament. The activities listed in tables 15.1 and 15.2 have proven very popular in intramural

Table 15.1 Primary Intramural Activities

Activity	Page	Activity	Page
Simple team games		*Individual activities*	
Squirrel in the Forest (level I)	256	Hopscotch (level I)	265
Simple Tag (level I)	259	Marbles (levels I–III)	266
Beanbag Basket (level I)	263	Beanbag Basket (level I)	263
Two Square (level I)	261	Tetherball (levels I and II)	267
Roll Ball (level I)	266	Jacks (level I)	267
Progressive Dodgeball (level II)	274		
Crab Soccer (level II)	265	*Gymnastic activities*	
Barnyard Golf (level II)	274	Rope Jumping (levels I–III)	482
		Parachute Activities (levels I–III)	496
Cooperative games		Hoop Activities (level I)	492
Doubles Hopscotch (level I)	295		
Perpetual Motion Machine (level I)	296	*Dance activities*	
Recycled Snake Skins (level II)	296	Rhythmic Activities (levels I–III)	539
Twister (level II)	296	Singing Games (level I)	551
Modified Musical Chairs (level II)	297	Folk Dances (levels II–III)	550
Co-op Tag (level I)	298		

Table 15.2 Intermediate Intramural Activities

Activity	Page	Activity	Page
Tournament-type activities			
Basketball games			
Sideline Basketball	381	Tetherball	267
Twenty-One	381	Frisbee	287
Bucket Ball	380	Beanbag Basket	263
Tennis games			
Deck Tennis	287	*Special one-day events*	
Paddleball	288	Cross-Country Meet	416
Field and floor hockey games		Track and Field Meet	412
Line Field Hockey	336	Novelty Track Meet	413
Seven Man Hockey	323	Orienteering Day	415
Football games		Elbow Wrestling Tournament	444
One-Down Football	348	Leg Wrestling Tournament	445
European Handball	284	Punt for Distance Tournament	348
Punt Back	348	Frisbee Tournament	287
Soccer games		Juggling Contests	500
California Kickball	282	Relay Days	115
Sideline Soccer	381		
Seven Man Soccer	323	*Cooperative game activities*	
Softball games		Juggle a Number	296
Five Hundred	398	Cross-over Blanket Volleyball	298
Volleyball games		Nine-Person Skip	298
Newcomb	363	Modified Musical Chairs	297
Blind Newcomb	363	One-Hole Parachute Golf	498
Four-Way Volleyball	364	Tug-o-Peace	298
Goodminton	286	Co-op Tag	298
Sideline Volleyball	364		
Paddle-handball games		*Gymnastic activities*	
Paddleball	288	Rope Jumping	481
Other games		Parachute Activities	496
Shufflecurl	286	Pyramid Activities	463
		Dance activities	
		Folk Dances	550

Figure 15.9 Primary intramural activities.

programs for primary (K–3) and intermediate (4–6) children. Activities selected for any program should be modified to meet the uniqueness of each school.

Primary Intramural Activities

The main emphasis of primary intramural activities should be to develop skills in an enjoyable and informal atmosphere (figure 15.9). Through the assistance of boys and girls in the upper grades, younger children can acquire new skills in addition to a positive attitude toward physical activities.

The following outline of a one-year program of activities reflects instructional program emphases as well as the unique interests of primary children. For example, parachute activities were introduced to the first and second grades in September. The children enjoyed the parachute games so much that they requested more parachute games during their scheduled noon hour in September. The same thing occurred with third grade when it was introduced to sideline soccer in early September. Two new activities, not taught in the regular instructional periods, were introduced to primary children during the intramural program. Volunteer helpers (fifth and sixth graders) taught groups of children in the second and third grades to play Double Hopscotch and Japanese Marbles.

The activities listed under each two-month time schedule follow a similar pattern. Teachers should monitor the interests of children month by month and make adjustments in playing time or, where necessary, delete unpopular activities in favor of newfound interests.

Intermediate Intramural Activities

The main emphasis of intramural activities for the upper elementary grades is on fun, practicing skills, positive social interaction, and competition (figure 15.10). Older children enjoy competing with their peers, just as their older brothers and sisters do in high school. The task for elementary school teachers is to develop a program that has equal competition for all activities; equal playing time for all who wish to play; and, whenever possible, round-robin tournaments to ensure maximum participation of all players and teams. The principles outlined here are reflected in table 15.2. Although interest shifts to more team games, there should be opportunities for individual and dual activities such as sidewalk tennis, kite flying, and slow-motion bicycle racing. Also, the majority of activities outlined in this program should be played as coeducational activities.

Figure 15.10 Having fun, practicing skills, interacting socially, and competing are the primary objectives of an intermediate intramural program.

Club Activities

Club activities should be considered part of the intramural program. Teachers may find a group of children interested in continuing an activity learned in the instructional program that does not lend itself to competition, such as yoga, jogging, or folk dance. Other activities that cannot be offered in the regular instructional program, such as skiing or canoeing, can also be organized as a club activity.

The basic responsibility of the teaching staff is to provide the initial organization. Obviously, if a teacher is interested in sponsoring a skiing or canoeing club, the children will gain by the teacher's efforts and talents. However, club activities can and should reach out into the community for parents and other interested citizens to assist in activities that are beyond the financial, facility, and staff limitations of the school.

Special Programs

Throughout the year, a variety of special activities lasting from one hour to the whole day have become part of most extraclass programs. The following activities, which vary in the length of time to complete, require a lot of planning and voluntary help if they are to be successful.

Play Days

Basketball Play Day

School no. 1 Player no. 1	→	Team A
School no. 2 Player no. 1	→	Team B
School no. 3 Player no. 1	→	Team C
School no. 4 Player no. 1	→	Team D

A play day involves children from two or more schools playing together on the same teams. Consider, for example, a basketball play day involving four schools. Player number 1 from each school is assigned to team A. Player number 2 from each school is assigned to team B, player number 3 to team C, and player number 4 to team D. Player 5 for each school goes to team A, and so on until all children are assigned to a team. Schools lose their identity in this type of competitive event, thus reducing the need to "win for one's school." The emphasis of this type of activity shifts from excessive competition to fun and making new friends from other schools.

Sports Days

Basketball Sports Day

Sports days are similar to play days, except that the teams represent their own schools. For example, each school enters one basketball team in a round-robin tournament. Because one school is eventually declared the winner in sports day events, there is more emphasis on competition and maintaining one's school identity. However, because these are one-day events, the emphasis on winning can be minimized if more effort is given to meeting new friends and sharing ideas about each other's neighborhood, intramural program, or other items of interest to boys and girls of this level.

Field Days

A field day normally involves one school inviting two or more neighboring schools to participate in one activity for an afternoon. A track and field day could involve three schools on a Friday afternoon. Participants from each school participate in activities without keeping an aggregate school score. This type of field day emphasizes fun and meeting new friends. The cooperative activities listed in chapter 17 are particularly suited to field days of this type.

Interschool Sports Program

One of the most longlasting and controversial issues in elementary physical education is the desirability of interschool competition. Proponents of this issue can present numerous facts and opinions to qualify their argument. However, medical authorities and professional organizations have generally opposed highly organized sports for children below the ninth grade because of adverse physical and psychological effects. This point of view was formalized in the 1968 AAHPERD publication *Desirable Athletic Competition for Children of Elementary School Age*. The majority of elementary schools have adhered to the guidelines contained in this publication.

A set of guidelines titled *Guidelines for Children's Sports* (AAHPERD 1979) applies to children thirteen years of age and younger who wish to participate in sports. The intent of this publication is to "encourage and promote the greatest amount of participation in sports under conditions that are safe and enjoyable for children." According to the authors of this book, the philosophy of "child first, winning second"

is easy to endorse for most adults but more difficult to practice in the heat of the game. The experts who wrote this set of guidelines believe that, in order to practice the philosophy of a child's welfare first and winning second, teachers, coaches, and parents must agree to implement the following bill of rights for young athletes (AAHPERD 1979).

Bill of Rights for Young Athletes

1. Right to participate in sports
2. Right to participate at a level commensurate with each child's maturity and ability
3. Right to have qualified adult leadership
4. Right to play as a child and not as an adult
5. Right to share in the leadership and decision making of their sport participation
6. Right to participate in safe and healthy environments
7. Right to proper preparation for participation in sports
8. Right to an equal opportunity to strive for success
9. Right to be treated with dignity
10. Right to have fun in sports

Many of these rights are now being realized through broad-based intramural and extramural or interschool programs. When developing an extramural program of activities, the following points should be incorporated into the operating policies of participating schools.

1. Interschool leagues or events should not interfere with the ongoing instructional or intramural program.
2. Boys and girls should have equal access to the interschool program.
3. Adverse parent or community pressure should not be allowed to interfere with the philosophy and general management of the interschool program.
4. All forms of competition should be minimized, with emphasis placed on participation rather than on winning. Play days and sports days should be given higher priority than organized leagues between schools.
5. Adequate facilities, equipment, and supervision must be available.
6. Interschool activities should usually take place after school. Evening and weekend competition between schools should not be permitted.
7. The health, safety, and general welfare of boys and girls competing in interschool events should be stringently protected. This means medical examinations prior to competition, safe transportation to and from events, and safe facilities and equipment.

Selected References

AAHPERD. (1979). *Guidelines for Children's Sports.* Reston, VA: AAHPERD Publications.

Calgary Board of Education. (1980). *Intramurals in the Elementary School.* Calgary, Alberta: Board of Education.

Micheli, L. J. (1990). *Sportswise: An Essential Guide for Young Athletes, Parents, and Coaches.* Boston: Houghton Mifflin Co.

Orlick, T., and Botterill, C. (1975). *Every Kid Can Win.* Chicago: Nelson-Hall Publishers.

Turner, L. F., and Turner, M. A. (1989). *Alternative Sports and Games for the New Physical Education.* Needham Heights, MA: Ginn Press.

Weiss, M., and Gould, D. (1986). *Sports for Children and Youth.* Champaign, IL: Human Kinetics Publishers, Inc.

Game and Movement Activities

Game activities constitute a major portion of the elementary physical education program. As children progress through the elementary grades, game activities are given more time and emphasis, and gymnastics and dance less. Consequently, the teacher should clearly understand the organization of games so that she can select and emphasize the appropriate skills and practice activities and games without unnecessary repetition. The accompanying introduction to part 5 provides suggestions relating to the use of instructional space, class management techniques, and a variety of teaching strategies. The first chapter of part 5 includes simple team games, tag activities, and individual and partner games. Chapter 17 contains modified traditional games and new cooperative games created by children in the primary and intermediate grades.

Chapters 18 through 24 are primarily designed for boys and girls in developmental levels II and III. However, teachers of children in developmental level I should also refer to these chapters for more advanced practice activities and lead-up games that can be modified to meet the skills and abilities of younger children.

Each chapter of this part contains a variety of approaches that can be used to teach game activities. There are situations in every grade when skills, rules, and games should be presented in a more structured and direct way. At other times, however, the application of problem-solving methods through creative or inventive games is appropriate. These chapters show how each approach can be used separately and how the structured and problem-solving methods and techniques can be blended into a single lesson or unit of instruction ∎

Teaching game activities to elementary school children in large instructional areas, such as the gymnasium or playground, can present unnecessary obstacles. The following suggestions relating to the arrangement of the instructional space and class management and control will help each teacher establish an effective learning environment. The section "Developing Units and Lesson Plans" provides a format for each teacher to develop her own games program.

Arranging the Instructional Space

Most schools have one or more large playground areas that are suitable for running and simple tag games, but usually too large to handle a class in a normal conversational manner. To overcome this problem, assign one or two children to mark off the instructional area just before the class is taken outside; traffic cones or milk cartons are excellent markers.

Use a similar technique in a large gymnasium. Do not use equipment, such as metal volleyball posts, that can cause injury if knocked over.

Many of the running and simple team games described in chapter 16 require a lot of beanbags, balls, milk cartons, and other equipment. To ensure maximum use of instructional and playing time, place the equipment in cardboard boxes or nylon sacks and put them in the corners of the instructional area. Team leaders or monitors can do this job extremely well.

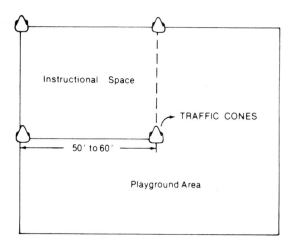

Classroom Management and Control

The following procedures for controlling the class can be used by teachers of any grade. Each teacher, of course, will modify the amount of freedom she allows according to her class's maturity and cooperation.

1. Divide the class into four groups. For primary children, use sections 1, 2, 3, and 4. Intermediate

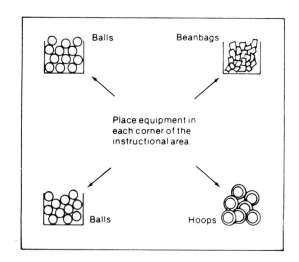

children usually prefer to be called teams 1, 2, 3, and 4, or to be assigned the names of professional ball teams.

2. Select section leaders or team captains and make sure to rotate these positions each week to give every child a chance to be a leader.

3. Choose a place for each group to sit whenever you call "section places"—normally the middle of the instructional area. This is extremely important for good class control. Repeat the procedure until all the children move to their places quickly and efficiently.

4. Follow normal and reasonable safety procedures, paying particular attention to the following:
   a. Tennis shoes should be worn during game activities.
   b. Goal lines should be drawn a reasonable distance from the end or side walls—three to five feet for moderately active games and six to ten feet for vigorously active games.
   c. Require that glasses, if possible, and other personal items, such as chains and baggy sweaters, be removed.

Effective Use of Station Work

To illustrate the station work technique, let us assume that a third-grade class knows how to play chair bowling and four square. The teacher wishes to introduce beanbag horseshoes and barnyard golf in the next lesson. During the first few minutes of this lesson, the teacher assigns each team to a station. Brief demonstrations of beanbag horseshoes and barnyard golf are given before each team is allowed to play its assigned game. Each game is played for a few minutes. The teacher then asks the class to stop, return the equipment to its original position, and rotate to the next station. This procedure continues until all the teams have played the four games. If time does not permit the class to complete the rotation, pick it up in the next lesson.

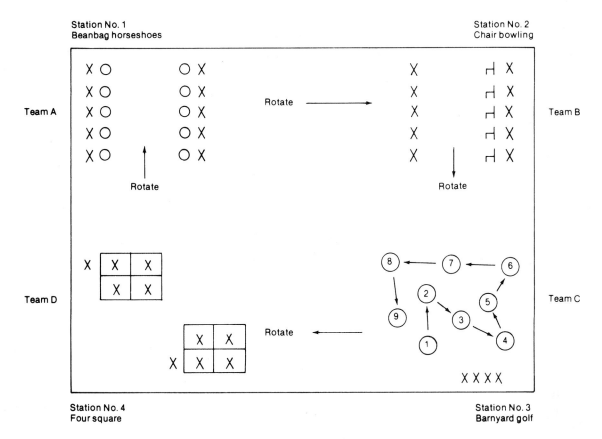

Station No. 1
Beanbag horseshoes

Station No. 2
Chair bowling

Team A

Rotate

Team B

Team D

Team C

Rotate

Rotate

Station No. 4
Four square

Station No. 3
Barnyard golf

Developing Units and Lesson Plans

Three basic types of units can be used to organize and teach game activities (see chapter 6). Primary teachers normally use the multiple unit to cope with the unique characteristics of young children. Intermediate teachers tend to adapt solid or modified units when planning their games program. All teachers, however, should review the advantages and disadvantages of each type of unit before deciding on a particular one. Each unit may also be modified to cope with each local teaching situation.

It is impossible to recommend a standard lesson plan for every teacher to follow rigidly when teaching game activities. Each teacher must adapt to differences in the children's maturity and skill levels, the time allotment, and the supplies available. The Structure of Inventive Games chart provides a basic guideline for teaching individual game lessons.

All game lessons begin with a vigorous warm-up activity such as running, conditioning exercises, or a vigorous tag game (see chapter 16). Acquiring game skills progresses from individual to partner to group activities. This basic

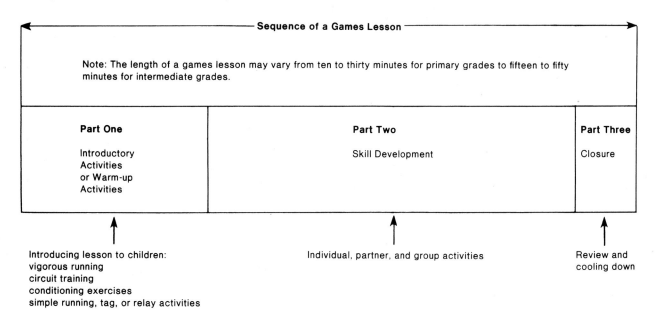

Sequence of a Games Lesson

Note: The length of a games lesson may vary from ten to thirty minutes for primary grades to fifteen to fifty minutes for intermediate grades.

Part One

Introductory
Activities
or Warm-up
Activities

Part Two

Skill Development

Part Three

Closure

Introducing lesson to children:
vigorous running
circuit training
conditioning exercises
simple running, tag, or relay activities

Individual, partner, and group activities

Review and
cooling down

Structure of Inventive Games

Primary level game skills	Areas where limitations can be imposed			
	Number of players	*Playing space*	*Equipment*	*Skills and rules*
Locomotor and nonlocomotor skills	From individual activities	From limited space	From use of simple equipment	From single skills and rules
Walk				
Run				
Skip				
Slide				
Jump				
Hop				
Dodge				
Turn				
Controlling ball with hands	↓ to partner activities	↓ to use of general space		
Bounce				
Throw				
Catch				
Controlling ball with feet	↓ to group activities		↓ to use of more varied and complex equipment	↓ to more complex skills and rules
Kick				
Pass				
Dribble				
Trap				
Projecting ball with hand or equipment				
Striking ball with hand				
Hitting ball with bat, racquet, or stick				

progression allows a child to practice a skill or movement pattern by herself during the initial phase of part two, skill development; she then proceeds to partner activities, which is the next step within part two of the lesson. With two performers, many more challenges and variations can be introduced and dual activities can also provide important lessons in sharing, give and take, and other forms of cooperative behavior. The latter phase of part two is devoted to group activities that stress the skills acquired earlier in the lesson. Finally, closure provides an opportunity to review the main concepts or skills of the lesson. This time is also used as a cooling down period before children return to the classroom.

If a teacher has only fifteen to twenty minutes to teach a games lesson, there may not be sufficient time to complete all parts of the lesson during one class period. A solution to this is as follows. The first lesson starts with warm-up activities, then proceeds with individual and partner activities. Before finishing partner activities, time runs out. The next lesson then begins with a brief warm-up and goes directly to group activities. A similar procedure can be followed with each succeeding lesson as long as the progression is from individual to partner to group activities for each new skill or movement pattern.

Incorporating the Inventive Games Approach

The evolution occurring within the elementary school curriculum is essentially a movement from teacher-directed activities toward a learning environment in which the teacher is an important guider of children who learn by example, practice, and the joy of discovery. In gymnastics and dance, we have witnessed the gradual incorporation of the Movement Education approach, which fosters exploration, experimentation, and discovery—key elements in the creative learning process. This approach also allows children to develop according to their own intellectual and physical ability and readiness. In essence, the style of teaching exemplified by Movement Education is parallel to the current practices in other areas of the elementary school curriculum.

Running, tag, and simple team games have traditionally been organized and taught on the premise that skills, rules, and strategies should be learned in an orderly and progressive manner. It would seem imperative that any new approach should still use the common terms, such as *throw, catch,* and *kick,* and that the skills and knowledge of the games should still be acquired. The approach that follows can be incorporated into any primary or intermediate games program to teach basic skills, as well as to enhance a child's creative development. This approach can be called an inventive, or creative, games approach, but it is essentially the use of the discovery method in the medium of games.

The structure within which an inventive game can be played has four elements: (1) the number of players—a choice among one player, partners, or a group; (2) the area assigned or available for the game; (3) the equipment that is available or chosen by the players; and (4) the rules and skills. Within this structure, teachers and children can develop an infinite number and variety of games. Some of these games lead to the acquisition of standard sport skills, whereas others contribute to fun and the enhancement of creative abilities.

Games for developmental level I should be predominantly creative. Beyond level I, however, children are exposed to more formal games. They enjoy learning the proper form of a specific sport skill, practicing drills, or playing lead-up games that increase their proficiency.

A structured program at any level can, and should, incorporate the inventive games approach within a unit or a specific lesson. This blending of methods neither confuses nor restricts the learner. On the contrary, it enriches the learning environment and stimulates the creative process, and it helps the child acquire specific motor skills or more complex strategies involving perceptual, cognitive, and motor abilities.

Developmental Level I

There are several ways to organize and teach inventive games to primary school children. The approach suggested here begins with simple and fairly structured challenges for this age level, then gradually allows the children to invent or modify games within the limitations imposed by the teacher.

The procedure should be adapted to the ability, maturity, and interests of the class, and the emphasis that the teacher gives to the inventive games approach obviously depends on her philosophy and the nature of the program. However, a major emphasis on creative activity is suggested for primary games programs.

The sample lesson that follows shows how creative games can be incorporated into more formal programs. The lesson plan for creative games is structured similar to plans for other activity areas. The format will vary, of course, according to the children's ages, interests, and prior experiences in creative games.

Example (Developmental Level 1)

Main Emphasis Bouncing a Ball

Part 1: Introductory Activity

If children are used to moving around the floor freely without bumping into each other, have them begin running in different directions. Then have them change speeds, then slide to the right, then to the left. If children are used to warming up by running around the floor and then doing a series of calisthenics, it is not necessary to change the format. After finishing the warm-up, move to the second part of the lesson.

Part 2: Skill Development

Each child should have a ball; any type of utility ball can be used. If the balls are different sizes, give the bigger ones to the children who are less proficient in ball-handling skills.

Ask the children to take their balls and find spaces on the floor. When they are properly spaced, pose the following:

1. "Try to stay in your space and bounce the ball very low, then very high." Do not specify one or two hands—let them experiment.
2. "Can you bounce the ball with one hand?" Allow them to practice, then ask, "Can you bounce it with the other hand?"
3. Ask questions that relate to the following skills:
   a. Bounce in different directions (forward, backward, sideways).
   b. Bounce on the floor, then against the wall.
   c. Bounce around small equipment (beanbags, bowling pins, ropes).

Create a game involving the skill that has been practiced. The Structure of Inventive Games chart lists four areas where limitations can be imposed for the games created. As a general guideline, begin at the top and add more complex challenges as the lessons progress. In this first lesson, you could challenge the children to make up a game with a partner, in their own space, using one ball, and requiring a bounce.

Teaching Suggestions

1. Allow sufficient time to practice.
2. Pick out different ways of performing each task and let the other children watch.
3. Praise the children constantly while they are practicing.
4. Ask the children if they can think of another way of bouncing. A child may suggest that they try sitting down or kneeling while bouncing. Have the class try its own challenges.
5. Give the children time to think up a game and practice it.
6. Have a few children demonstrate the games they have created.
7. If time permits, make up a new game and add beanbags, a chair, or a hoop.

Part 3: Closure

Discuss how the groups made up their games and what suggestions they would like to make for the next lesson.

Note: This is a brief ending to the lesson to allow time to make a few comments or to hear one or two suggestions. Avoid too much talking or talking for long periods of time.

General Comments

1. After the children have had time to create and practice their games, select a few for demonstration to the class.
2. Try other variations, such as in partners, in their own space, using two balls and a hoop, and involving a catch.

3. Allow children to make up games with their own imposed limitations.
4. Keep a creative games notebook. Children will create many exciting games that are worth remembering, so record the best ones for posterity. Next year you could use some of these games to illustrate and motivate children to develop similar ones. This project could also be incorporated into the language arts program by having each child or the whole class make up an illustrated creative games notebook.

Developmental Levels II and III

Incorporating the inventive games approach in developmental levels II and III presents some problems for both the teacher and the children. Running, tag, and simple team games are normally selected from a book and taught according to specific rules and regulations. In essence, these are structured activities taught by the direct teaching method. It is possible, however, to add another dimension to these activities by injecting the creative games approach.

The four areas of limitation in the Structure of Inventive Games chart can be used with intermediate children with equal success. Since most children of this age range know and enjoy running, tag, and simple team games, this is the logical place to introduce creative or student-designed games. The first example that follows illustrates how a teacher can begin with a familiar game and transform it into a different and, in most cases, more enjoyable activity. The second example shows how to use the format to develop a framework for more creative student-designed games.

Example 1 (Developmental Level II)

A fourth-grade class appears apathetic in the middle of the afternoon. The teacher decides to take the children outside for a ten-minute game. After a brief discussion, they decide to play dodgeball using two balls. The game is played for a few minutes, then the teacher asks the class to stop and listen.

The teacher has four elements through which she can introduce a change.

1. *Number of players:* Class divided into equal groups
2. *Playing space:* A large circle
3. *Skills and rules:* Throwing and hitting below the waist
4. *Equipment:* Two inflated balls

She decides to pose a challenge by varying the skills and rules. She says, "Start the game over. However, children in the middle must keep both hands on their knees at all times, and the circle players can only roll the ball." After a few minutes of play, she stops the game again and poses another challenge: "In the game you have just played, I changed the rules. Can you think of another rule change that you would like to try?" Several suggestions are made and the teacher chooses Mary Ann's: "Mrs. Brown, since the players inside

were put out too quickly, how about all circle players rolling only with their left hand?" (Left-handed players must use their right hands.)

The process of introducing creative, or inventive, games has begun. The main tools are the four elements by which the teacher or the children can impose limitations. As the teacher learns to use the challenge method, she gives more freedom of choice to the children, and, with practice, the children appreciate the freedom to modify or create games of their own.

Example 2 (Developmental Level III)

Let us assume that a fifth-grade teacher has experimented with modified tag and simple team games and has noted a positive change in her class's cooperation and enthusiasm. The following suggestions could be tried as part of a regular games lesson or as a ten-minute break:

1. Arrange the class in partners (imposing a limitation on the number of players), give partners a ball and a hoop (limiting the equipment), and tell them to find their own space in the playground area (limiting the playing space). Pose the question, "Can you make up a game with your partner that includes a bounce, a pass, and your hoop (limiting the skills and rules)?"
2. Join two sets of partners together and pose this question: "With four players, two balls, and two hoops, can you make up a new game that involves all the equipment, a bounce pass, and a dribble?"
3. Now join two groups of four and pose this challenge: "See if you can make up a game using two hoops and one ball."

These examples illustrate how the inventive games approach can be used to modify existing games or to provide a basis for children to invent their own. Children adapt to this method of teaching with ease and enthusiasm in a very short time. This approach will be used in later chapters, along with more structured methods and techniques, to teach individual skills, rules, and game strategies.

The emphasis that each teacher gives to the structured or inventive games approach will ultimately depend on her own philosophy. Consideration, however, should be given to her own style of teaching—that is, whether she is comfortable with a formal or exploratory approach. An understanding of the type of physical education program the children had in prior grades is another important factor. Finally, the cultural pressures of the community will determine, in no small measure, whether a structured or exploratory approach to teaching game activities will be successful. In the majority of situations, intermediate children have been taught game activities through a structured approach. Hence, it is wise to begin with what the children are familiar with, then gradually inject a few inventive game ideas or challenges to "test the water." Beyond this point, each teacher will emphasize the approach she and her class feel comfortable with.

16

Locomotor and Manipulative Games

This chapter provides a culturally rich reservoir of locomotor and manipulative games. The purpose and emphasis of these activities vary from level to level. For primary children in developmental level I, particularly those from kindergarten and grade one, these games provide an important and enjoyable means of acquiring locomotor and manipulative skills. Also, if these activities are taught progressively, with a generous application of exploratory teaching methods, such characteristics as sportsmanship, leadership, and creativity can also be developed naturally.

The purpose of these activities remains the same as children reach developmental level II. This is an important transitional period, however. These children still enjoy running and tag games, but they also are beginning to show a much keener interest in learning the more complex team games such as basketball and volleyball. By the time children reach developmental level III, the transition is almost complete. The major goal of an upper elementary school games program is to develop knowledge and skills of the major individual and team sports. The running, tag, and simple team games provided in this chapter still have a place in the upper intermediate grades. They are vigorous and enjoyable activities for a classroom break, recess, or warm-up during regular instructional classes.

Numerous suggestions are provided throughout each developmental level to illustrate how locomotor and manipulative games can be used in an effective way to teach or reinforce academic concepts and skills. These activities can be further adapted or modified to teach other concepts and skills in the elementary school curriculum. The selected references at the end of this chapter provide supporting evidence of the value of these games as a medium through which academic concepts and skills can be acquired. They also are an additional resource of locomotor and manipulative games that can be used to teach a wide variety of academic concepts and skills in language arts, mathematics, science, and social studies.

Also included are a few sample games from an international games project.[*] A few photographs of children playing their traditional games, along with some of their drawings, are provided in each section of this chapter. Teachers and children will note how similar children's games are, regardless of the country or geographical region of the world. Several games, such as Elastic Ropes or Marbles are played in many countries, under different names, but with very similar rules and purposes ■

*The best of these games are included in Kirchner, G. (1991). *Children's Games from Around the World*. Dubuque, IA: Wm. C. Brown Publishers.

Games for Developmental Level I

The running, tag, and simple team games included in this section contribute to two basic types of game skills. The first, locomotor skills, shown in table 16.1, are extensively emphasized throughout this first developmental level. Manipulative skills relating to rolling, throwing, and catching are also emphasized through individual, partner, and small-group games (figure 16.1). The individualistic nature of five- and six-year-olds, as well as their motor skill ability, indicates that striking, dribbling, and kicking skills should be taught in small groups and in an exploratory way.

Toward the upper limit of developmental level I, running and tag games are a little more complicated, and simple team games are more structured and require more skill and team play. Because there is such a spread of interests and abilities throughout developmental level I, teachers should try any game they feel is appropriate in levels I and II. The sample inventive game challenges at the end of this section will illustrate how teachers can design their own challenges to meet the needs, interests, and abilities of their class.

Locomotor Games

Squirrel in the Forest

Motor skills   Running, dodging, swinging
Movement concepts   Personal and general space, traveling
Players   Class
Formation   Scattered
Playing area   Playground, gymnasium, classroom
Equipment   None

One-half of the class members are trees and find their personal space in the playing area. The other half of the children are squirrels who run and dodge around the trees without being touched. When a player is touched, he becomes a tree and the tree becomes a squirrel.

Suggestions and Variations
1. Change method of moving to skip, slide, and so on.
2. Change shape and level of trees—sitting, kneeling, and so on.

Foxes and Squirrels

Motor skills   Running
Movement concepts   Relationships, personal and general space
Players   Class
Formation   Scattered in groups of three
Playing area   Playground or gymnasium
Equipment   None
Academic concepts   Mathematics—sets of three

Choose three children to be the foxes. All other children are arranged in groups of three. Numbers 1 and 2 of the group join hands overhead to form a tree. Number 3 is the squirrel and stands under the tree. On signal from the teacher, squirrels run to find a new tree and foxes try to tag a squirrel before he reaches a new tree. Only one squirrel is

Figure 16.1   Learning manipulative skills.

allowed under a tree. When a fox catches a squirrel, they change positions on the next turn. Repeat game after all squirrels are tagged or under a new tree.

Suggestions and Variations
1. After three turns, have players return to their original positions. Rotate players and continue game.
2. Change method of moving, to skipping, walking, or sliding.

Traffic Lights

Motor skills   Run, walk, stop
Movement concepts   Traveling, change of direction and speed
Players   Class
Formation   Scattered
Playing area   Playground, gymnasium
Equipment   None
Academic concepts   Social studies—community safety

Ask children to find their own space. Teach signals. Red means stop, yellow means walk, and green means run. On signal, all children begin to move according to the teacher's signals.

Suggestions and Variations
1. Have children change direction after each signal.
2. Change locomotor skills for yellow and green.

Fragile Rock

Motor skills   Run
Movement concepts   Relationships—sharing
Players   Class
Formation   Scattered
Playing area   Playground, gymnasium
Equipment   Beanbags

Every player places a beanbag on the floor, then places one finger on the beanbag. On signal from the teacher, who is a rock collector, all children begin to run in different directions. While children are running, the rock collector

Table 16.1 Locomotor and Manipulative Games (Developmental Level I)

Name of game	Type of game	Players	Motor concepts and skills	Movement concepts and skills	Academic concepts and skills	Page
Locomotor Games						
Squirrel in the Forest	Tag	Half class vs. other half	Run, dodge	Personal and general space, change of direction, change of speed		256
Foxes and Squirrels	Tag	Groups of 3+ taggers	Run, dodge, stop	Personal and general space, change of direction and speed	Mathematics—sets of three	256
Traffic Lights	Run	Class and teacher signals	Walk, run, stop	General space, change of direction, change of speed	Social studies—community safety	256
Fragile Rock	Run	Class and teacher signals	Run, slide	Relationships—sharing		256
Simple Tag	Tag	Class and tagger(s)	Run, dodge	General space, change of direction and speed		259
Automobiles	Run	Class and teacher signals	Run, stop	General space, pathways	Social studies—community safety	259
Red Light	Run	Class and player(s) signals	Run, stop	Change of direction and speed	Mathematics—ordinal numbers and counting	259
Mousetrap	Tag	Circle of players and 5 runners	Run	High and low, change of speed	Mathematics—counting, subtracting, greater and less than	259
Do As I Do	Run	Circle of players and 1 in the middle	Run, jump, hop, etc.	Matching	Language arts—word recognition and following directions	260
Crows and Cranes	Tag	Half class vs. the other half	Run, dodge	Change of direction and speed	Language arts—auditory directions Mathematics—counting, adding, and subtracting	260
Find Your Letter	Run	Class	Run, slide	General and personal space, change of direction and speed	Language arts—letter and word recognition, vocabulary Mathematics—whole numbers	260
Hot Spot	Run	Class	Run, stop	Change of direction and speed	Language arts—letter recognition Mathematics—whole numbers	260
Manipulative games						
Roll Ball	Roll	1 vs. 1	Roll, catch	Near and far, transfer of weight	Mathematics—adding, cardinal numbers, greater and less than Language arts—drawing numbers	260
Three Down	Roll	4	Roll	Transfer of weight, strong and light	Mathematics—sets of two, counting, squares and circles	261
Hot Ball	Roll	6–8	Roll, catch	Transfer of weight, change of speed	Mathematics—cardinal numbers and counting	261
Hoop Bounce	Bounce	1 vs. 1	Bounce, catch, slide	Change of direction and speed, transfer of weight	Mathematics—counting Social studies—social interactions; common goal	261
Two Square	Bounce	1 vs. 1	Bounce, slide	Change of direction and speed	Mathematics—counting Social studies—taking turns	261
Pirates	Dribble	Class	Run, walk, dribble, dodge	General space, transfer of weight, levels, change of direction and speed		262
Dribble Tag	Dribble	Class	Run, walk, dribble, dodge	General space, transfer of weight, levels, change of direction and speed		262

locomotor and manipulative games

Table 16.1 Continued

Name of game	Type of game	Players	Motor concepts and skills	Movement concepts and skills	Academic concepts and skills	Page
Butterflies	Throw	1 vs. 1	Throw, catch	Personal space, strong and light, transfer of weight	Mathematics—near and far Social studies—social interaction; taking turns	262 262
Throw, Catch, Run	Throw	1 vs. 1	Throw, catch, run	Personal and general space, change of direction and speed		
Quoit Tennis	Throw	1 vs. 1	Throw, catch, run	Change of direction and speed	Social studies—social interaction; sharing a common goal	262
Simple Dodgeball	Throw	Class	Throw, catch	General space, transfer of weight, change of direction and speed	Mathematics—counting Social studies—social interaction; working together	263
Steal the Crowns	Retrieve	One-half of class vs. the other half	Run, retrieve	General and personal space, change of direction and speed	Mathematics—subtraction and greater and less than Language arts—listening; remembering directions	263
Jump the Shot	Jump	5–6	Jump, turn	Levels, strong and light	Mathematics—radius of a circle and quick and slow	263
Snowball	Throw	Class	Throw, run, dodge	General space, transfer of weight, change of direction and speed	Mathematics—subtraction and sets	263
Beanbag Basket	Throw	1 vs. 1	Throw	Transfer of weight, strong and light	Mathematics—counting, adding, greater and less than, and near and far	263
Name It	Hop	5–6	Hop	Personal and general space, pathways	Language arts—letter recognition	264
Queenie I.O.	Throw	5–6	Hop, run, throw, catch	Near and far, change of direction and speed	Social studies—social interaction; working together	264
Call Ball	Throw	6	Throw, catch	Transfer of weight, change of direction	Mathematics—whole numbers, adding and subtracting	264
Soap Box Soccer	Dribble	3	Dribble, run	General and personal space, change of direction and speed	Mathematics—sets	265
Crab Soccer	Kick	Class	Kick	Balance, general space, change of direction and speed		265
American Hopscotch	Throw	1 vs. 1	Throw, hop	Personal space, transfer of weight	Mathematics—counting and greater and less than	265
Marbles	Dribble	2–4	Dribble	Personal space, strong and light, change of direction	Mathematics—adding, subtracting, greater and less than, and diameter and radius of a circle	266
Jacks	Throw	2–4	Throw, catch, balance	Strong and light, personal space, levels	Mathematics—counting and sets	267
Tetherball	Hit	2	Hit	Strong and light, transfer of weight, change of direction and speed		267
Inventive Games	All skills	Individual to group	All skills	All movement concepts		267

picks up three or four beanbags, then calls out, "Go home." All children run and place one finger on a beanbag. Two or more players may place one of their fingers on a rock (beanbag). Continue game until only three or four "rocks" are left.

Suggestions and Variations

1. Use hoops instead of beanbags and have players stand inside hoop.
2. Repeat game with different parts touching the rock.

Simple Tag

Motor skills   Running, dodging
Movement concepts   General space, change of direction
Players   Class
Formation   Scattered
Playing area   Playground, gymnasium
Equipment   None

One child is chosen to be "it." All players are scattered within a designated playing area. "It" tries to tag another player. When a player is tagged, he must call out, "I'm it," and the game continues.

Suggestions and Variations

1. Vary the locomotor skill, such as requiring all to hop or skip, or require animal walking movements such as crab walk or bear walk.
2. "It" tags a particular part of the body such as the side, back, or leg.
3. Any player is safe who assumes a particular position such as balancing on one foot, crouching, or standing back to back with another child.
4. Add one or more taggers.

Two or three players are assigned to be "it." They remain "it" for a set period of time (teacher sets time limit). Taggers try to tag other players. When a player is tagged he forms a bridge with his body. When another "free" player can crawl under the "bridge" without being tagged, the "bridged" player can join the game again.

Automobiles

Motor skills   Run, stop
Movement concepts   General space, pathways
Players   Class
Formation   Scattered
Playing area   Playground, gymnasium
Equipment   None
Academic concepts   Social studies—community safety

The teacher stands in the middle of the circle. On "go," the children run around the circle, pretending to be automobiles. A child may move out to "pass" another but must then move back into the circle. No one may reverse directions. When the teacher calls "stop" or blows a whistle, everyone must come to a full stop. A player who fails to stop or who bumps into another player must run and touch the teacher, then return to his place in the circle.

Suggestions and Variations

1. Play the same game moving in a reverse direction.
2. Substitute hand signals or flash cards for "go" and "stop."
3. Change game to "animal pass." Children move like crabs, monkeys, and so on, and follow same rules as automobiles.

Red Light

Motor skills   Run, stop
Movement concepts   Change of direction and speed
Players   Class
Formation   Two lines drawn across ends of playing area
Playing area   Playground, gymnasium
Equipment   None
Academic concepts   Mathematics—ordinal numbers and counting

One player chosen to be "it" stands on one line with his back to the opposite line. All other players stand on the opposite line. As "it" begins to count to ten, all players begin running toward his line. At any time before reaching ten, "it" may call out, "Red light," and turn around. If "it" sees anyone moving, he sends him back to the opposite line. The game continues until a player crosses the line. That player becomes "it" and the game starts over.

Suggestions and Variations

1. Use a variety of locomotor movements.
2. Use letters or children's names instead of numbers.
3. Change to counting by two's, four's, ten's, etc.

Mousetrap

Motor skills   Run, dodge
Movement concepts   High and low, change of speed
Players   Class
Formation   Circle
Playing area   Playground, gymnasium
Equipment   None
Academic concepts   Mathematics—counting, subtracting, greater and less than

Five children are chosen to be "mice," while the remaining children form a large circle called the "trap." The teacher starts the game with the mice outside the circle and the circle players holding hands. When she says, "Open trap," the circle players raise their hands as high as their heads and hold them in this position. The teacher then calls, "Run, little mice, run!" and the mice run freely in and out of the circle. When she says, "Snap," the circle players lower their joined hands. Any mice caught inside the circle must join the circle players. Continue until all mice are caught. Choose new mice and repeat the game.

Suggestions and Variations

1. Always have five "mice" playing; if two are caught, immediately replace with two new "mice" before the next "call."
2. Change name to other animals and move in that fashion (crab trap with a crab walk).

Do As I Do

Motor skills Locomotor, inventive movements
Movement concepts Matching
Players Class
Formation Circle
Playing area Playground, gymnasium
Equipment None
Academic concepts Language arts—word recognition and following directions

The teacher stands at the front of the class with two flash cards. One child is chosen to be the first leader and stands in front of the teacher facing the class. The leader begins to perform a movement, such as hopping, running, or walking like a lame puppy. The class does not move until the teacher flashes one of the two cards. If the card "Do This" appears, the class must copy the movements of the leader. When "Do That" is flashed, the class must stop moving while the leader continues to perform his movements. As the game continues, the leader continues to change to other movements and the teacher continues to randomly flash the two cards. Change leaders after two or three different movements.

Suggestions and Variations

1. Have the leader display written directions on flash cards.
2. Limit the game to animal or mechanical movements.

Crows and Cranes

Motor skills Run, dodge
Movement concepts Quick and slow, change of direction
Players Class
Formation Line
Playing area Playground, gymnasium
Equipment None
Academic concepts Language arts—auditory directions; Mathematics—counting, adding, and subtracting

Divide class in half and call one group "crows" and the other "cranes." Each team lines up on its centerline, facing the other. When the teacher calls, "Crr—ow," the crows turn and run toward their goal line and the cranes try to tag them before they cross it. If a player is tagged, he joins the opposite team. The game continues until the last player is caught.

Suggestions and Variations

1. Draw out the beginning of both words to keep the children in suspense as long as possible.
2. Use other words from the language arts program.
3. Add a third "neutral" word such as *creep*. If players move when a neutral word is called, they make a funny face or perform a special trick.

Find Your Letter

Motor skills Run, slide
Movement concepts General and personal space, change of direction and speed
Players Class
Playing area Playground, gymnasium
Equipment Letter cards
Academic concepts Language arts—Letter and word recognition, vocabulary; Mathematics—whole numbers

Construct a duplicate set of upper case letter cards. If there are twenty-six children, randomly hand out thirteen sets of letters, giving one card to each player. On signal, the children begin to run around the playing area. When the teacher calls "stop," everyone changes to a fast walk, then tries to find the other player with the same letter. As soon as they reach each other, they form the letter with their bodies. When everyone has formed their letter, the teacher calls, "New Letter," signaling partners to separate and begin fast walking until the teacher calls, "Exchange." Each child must exchange their cards with the nearest player, and the game continues.

Suggestions and Variations

1. Play same game with words, numbers, colors, or physical objects.
2. Change locomotive skills to hop, jump, etc.
3. Play above games in threes or fours.

Hot Spot

Motor skills Run and stop
Movement concepts Change of direction and speed
Players Class
Formation Scattered
Playing area Playground, gymnasium
Equipment Posters and cardboard cards
Academic concepts Language arts—letter recognition; Mathematics—whole numbers

The teacher scatters three or four cardboard cards for each number from 0 to 9 around the playing area. She holds ten posters with collections of objects, such as four dogs or seven flowers, representing the numbers 0 to 9. When the teacher displays a poster that has five chickens, she asks, "How many?" Each child calls out the name and number of objects and then runs and places one foot on that numeral on the floor. Three or four children may share each card. Continue the game, changing the posters.

Suggestions and Variations

1. Change posters to include sets of objects, such as nine pairs of rabbits, to indicate they must recognize sets of two and run and touch a card displaying a "2."
2. Change cardboard cards to lowercase letters and change posters to display capital letters.

Manipulative Games

Roll Ball

Motor skills Roll, catch
Movement concepts Near and far, transfer of weight
Players Class—play in pairs
Formation Scattered
Playing area Playground, gymnasium
Equipment Three balls and one chair for each set of partners
Academic concepts Mathematics—adding, cardinal numbers greater and less than; Language arts—drawing numbers

Partner 1 stands behind one line with a ball and partner 2 stands directly opposite, behind the chair. The chair's backrest faces partner 2. The score sheet and a pencil are placed on the seat of the chair. Partner 1 rolls three balls, then changes places with partner 2. Award five points for each ball that rolls through the legs of the chair. The game may be played to any score, selected on the basis of skill and available time.

Suggestions and Variations
1. Hit a milk carton or draw a target on the wall at floor level, rather than using a chair.
2. Substitute beanbags for balls.
3. Bowl backward through outstretched legs.
4. Hit a milk carton placed on other side of chair.

Three Down

Motor skills Rolling
Movement concepts Transfer of weight, strong and light
Players Four per game
Formation Circle
Playing area Playground, gymnasium
Equipment Four clubs, two balls
Academic concepts Mathematics—sets of two, counting, squares and circles

Four clubs are arranged in a square about three feet apart in the middle of an eight-foot circle. Two players are pinsetters. Circle players roll the two balls at the clubs, attempting to knock them down, while the pinsetters keep setting up the clubs. When three clubs are down, the circle players call, "Three down." Change positions and start a new game.

Suggestions and Variations
1. If pinsetters are too good, reduce to only one pinsetter.
2. Throw or kick the ball.

Hot Ball

Motor skills Roll, catch
Movement concepts Transfer of weight, change of speed
Players Six to eight
Formation Circle
Playing area Playground, gymnasium, classroom
Equipment Ball
Academic concepts Mathematics—cardinal numbers and counting

One child chosen to start the game pretends to set a fire under the ball. He then rolls it and says, "The ball's hot." Circle players try to roll the ball away from them to keep from getting "burned." If the ball goes out of the circle, the person who last touched it becomes "it" and pretends to set the ball on fire again.

Suggestions and Variations
1. Play the same game using feet.
2. Allow circle players to use only the left or right hand to roll the ball.
3. Have children count the number of hits before the ball goes out.

Hoop Bounce

Motor skills Bounce, catch, slide
Movement concepts Change of direction and speed, transfer of weight
Players Two for each game
Formation None
Playing area Playground, gymnasium
Equipment Hoop and ball
Academic concepts Mathematics—counting; Social studies—social interaction; common goal.

Two players face each other across the hoop. One player bounces the ball into the hoop so his partner can catch the rebound. Make this a cooperative game by counting one point each time a player catches the rebound. As children become more proficient, have them both move constantly around the hoop as they bounce the ball to each other.

Suggestions and Variations
Have partners add a movement after they have released the ball, such as make a full turn, slide to left and back, and so on.

Two Square

Motor skills Bounce, slide
Movement concepts Change of direction and speed
Players Two per game
Formation Two five-foot squares drawn side-by-side, with one player in each
Playing area Playground, gymnasium
Equipment Ball
Academic concepts Mathematics—counting: Social studies—taking turns

One player stands in each square while the remaining players stand just outside the squares. Player in one square bounce-serves the ball into the other square. (It may be wise to let players throw the ball at first instead of bounce-serving it. As skill increases, require a bounce-serve.) After the ball bounces in the opposing player's square, that player returns it into the server's square by batting it upward with one or both hands. Continue play until one of the following violations occurs:

1. The ball lands out of the square (liners are good).
2. The ball is hit with the fist.
3. The player holds the ball (catches it).
4. The ball is hit downward.

A player committing a violation leaves the game and the next waiting player takes his place.

Suggestions and Variations
1. Play same game with different types and sizes of balls (Nerf, tennis, etc.).
2. Add a trick, such as a bounce hit, then turn around or jump in the air and clap hands.
3. Have waiting players count the number of hits.

Pirates

Motor skills Run, walk, dribble, dodge
Movement concepts General space, transfer of weight, levels, change of direction and speed
Players Class
Formation Scattered
Playing area Playground, gymnasium
Equipment Balls

Give about two-thirds of the students a ball and tell them to start bouncing the ball anywhere in the playing area. Scatter the remaining third of the class throughout the playing area. On signal, those without a ball ("pirates") try to steal the ball away from a player who is bouncing a ball. When a player loses his ball, he becomes a pirate.

Suggestions and Variations

Players are safe if they kneel down and dribble.

Dribble Tag

Motor skills Run, walk, dribble, dodge
Movement concepts General space, transfer of weight, levels, change of direction and speed
Players Class
Formation Scattered
Playing area Playground, gymnasium
Equipment Balls

Players are given their own balls and told to find their own space. Two or three players are designated to be "it." On signal, every player starts to dribble the ball with their hands, then "it" attempts while dribbling, to tag another player. Players change positions when tagged.

Suggestions and Variations
1. Players can be safe if they kneel and dribble or are in any other special dribbling position.
2. Play game with series of obstacles (cones, mats, etc.) placed in the playing area.

Butterflies

Motor skills Throw, catch
Movement concepts Personal space, strong and light, transferring weight
Players Two per game
Formation None
Playing area Playground, gymnasium
Equipment One ball and one small container for each set of partners
Academic concepts Mathematics—near and far; Social studies—social interaction, taking turns

Children sit on floor, legs spread (hence, the name "Butterflies"). Player 1 throws a ball to player 2. If player 2 catches the ball, she has a chance to throw it into the container and score a point. If player 2 fails to catch the ball, she throws it back to player 1, who has the chance to throw it into the can (figure 16.2). Retake any poor throws.

Figure 16.2 Butterflies.

NUNA, AGE 7

Suggestions and Variations
1. Move farther apart as skill increases.
2. Use beanbags or different-sized balls.

Throw, Catch, Run

Motor skills Throw, catch, run
Movement concepts Personal and general space, change of direction and speed
Players Two per game
Formation None
Playing area Playground, gymnasium
Equipment Post, box, and balls

Arrange post, box, and throwing distance according to the children's level of skill. Player A must hold on to the post and player B holds a ball and stands behind the throwing line. Player B throws the ball; if it lands and remains in the box, he gets one point and another try. Player A must remain at the post until the ball has landed in the box or on the ground. Player B throws the ball again; if it does not land and remain in the box, player B must fetch it and return it to the box before player A can run around the box and back to the post. If player A gets back first, they exchange positions. If player B gets back first, he gets another turn.

Quoit Tennis

Motor skills Throw, catch, run
Movement concepts Change of direction and speed
Players Two per game
Formation None
Playing area Playground, gymnasium
Equipment Quoit, rope, two chairs
Academic concepts Social studies—social interaction, sharing a common goal

Place a skipping rope over backs of two chairs placed about three feet apart. Draw boundary lines on either side of rope. Players throw quoit back and forth over the rope. Emphasize throwing to each other by awarding each player a point each time either player catches a quoit.

Suggestions and Variations

Once skill level is good enough, play competitive game—one tries to throw quoit where opponent cannot catch it.

Simple Dodgeball

Motor skills Throw, catch
Movement concepts General space, transfer of weight, change of direction and speed
Players Class
Formation Circle
Playing area Playground, gymnasium
Equipment Ball
Academic concepts Mathematics—counting; Social studies—social interaction, working together

Divide class into two teams and place on either side of a line. Players must remain on their side of the line. Players then try to hit each other with a Nerf ball. If a person is hit, he must run to the marker and back before joining the game again.

Suggestions and Variations

Rescue Dodgeball. When a player is hit, he must lie down (or kneel with elbows bent so rescuers can lift and carry him) until another player can pull him to the end line, and both resume playing. However, if the rescuer(s) is hit while trying to rescue his teammate, he must stop and wait to be rescued.

Steal the Crowns

Motor skills Run, retrieve
Movement concepts General and personal space, change of direction and speed
Players Class
Formation None
Playing area Playground, gymnasium, classroom
Equipment Ten to twelve quoits or beanbags
Academic concepts Mathematics—subtraction and greater and less than; Language arts—listening; remembering directions

Draw one center and two endlines approximately thirty feet and place ten to twelve beanbags or quoits ("crowns") on each endline. Draw a small dungeon on the side of each endline. Divide class in half and place each team behind its own endline. On signal, players from either team try to cross over the center line and steal a "crown." A player cannot be tagged on his own side; however, once he crosses over the line and is tagged, he must go to the dungeon. Players who are tagged while running with a stolen crown must return it before going to the dungeon. Only one prisoner is allowed in a dungeon; hence, when a second prisoner arrives, the "old" prisoner must walk back to his endline before he can enter the game again.

Suggestions and Variations

Place one or two hoops on each side as safe houses. Players may stay at a safe house for ten seconds, then must leave.

Jump the Shot

Motor skills Jump, turn
Movement concepts Strong and light, levels
Players Five to six per game
Formation Circle
Playing area Playground, gymnasium
Equipment Rope
Academic concepts Mathematics—radius of a circle, quick and slow

Center player holds the rope by one end and swings it in a circle, keeping it about one foot off the ground. Circle players try to jump the rope as it approaches. If hit, they are charged with one shot. The game continues for a designated period. The winner, who is the player with the least number of shots charged against him, becomes the "turner" in the next game.

Suggestions and Variations

1. Vary the length and speed of the rope according to level of skill.
2. Have circle players join hands with a partner.
3. Have circle players bounce a ball as the rope is turned; start with a two-hand bounce.

Snowball

Motor skills Throw, run, dodge
Movement concepts General space, transfer of weight, change in direction and speed
Players Class
Formation Two endlines and one center line, with each team scattered on its side of center line
Equipment Balls
Academic concepts Mathematics—subtraction and sets

Divide the class into two equal teams and give each team an equal number of balls (about five or six each). On signal, players attempt to hit opposing players with the balls. Any player who is hit must move to the sideline. Sideline players may retrieve balls and throw them to teammates, but they may not throw them at opponents. The game ends when one player remains.

Suggestions and Variations

Play the same game with both teams grouped in "twos" or "threes."

Beanbag Basket

Motor skills Throw
Movement concepts Transfer of weight, strong and light
Players Two per game
Formation Line—five feet from basket
Playing area Playground, gymnasium, classroom
Equipment Beanbags and box or basket
Academic concepts Mathematics—counting, adding, greater and less than, near and far

locomotor and manipulative games

Each child is given three consecutive throws at the basket. Award five points if the beanbag goes into the basket, three points if it hits the basket, and one point if it lands within two feet of the basket. After each player completes his throw, he adds his score, collects the beanbags, and gives them to the next player, then waits for his next turn. Add both scores together at the end of the game.

Suggestions and Variations

1. As skill improves, use small baskets or increase the throwing distance.
2. Use Nerf or other soft balls.
3. Change target; for example, to line on floor or square on wall.

Name It

Motor skills Hopping
Movement concepts Personal and general space, pathways
Players Five to six per group
Formation Groups scattered
Equipment Chalk or plastic sheets
Academic concepts Language arts—letter recognition

Draw three or four identical grids on the blacktop or on plastic sheets. (Plastic sheets can easily be stored, and they provide a means of predesigning a series of grids to emphasize a variety of concepts and skills.) Assign five or six children to each grid and give each child a number. The teacher then calls a number and flashes a letter. The child whose number is called must hop to the letter, call it out, then hop out of the grid.

Suggestions and Variations

The following suggestions will assist teachers in using grids to teach children a variety of academic concepts and skills.

1. Change the size and shape of the grid to suit the ages and interests of the children.
2. Flash word cards and have children hop to each letter of the word.
3. Change grid to pictures and flash words corresponding to the picture on the grid.
4. Change grid to home and neighborhood themes and create games involving the recognition of buildings, people, and places.
5. Change grid to a health theme and create games involving hygiene and safety.

Queenie I.O.

Motor skills Hop, run, throw, catch
Movement concepts Near and far, change of direction and speed
Players Five to six per game
Formation Scattered
Playing area Playground, gymnasium
Equipment Beanbag
Academic concepts Social studies—social interaction, working together

Figure 16.3 Queenie I.O.

"QUEENIE IO"

Player A throws the ball (beanbag) backward over his head in the direction of other players (figure 16.3). After throwing, A remains facing away from them. When the ball has been caught[†] and hidden away, usually in the hands behind the back, they begin to chant:

Queenie I.O.
Who's got the ball I.O.
It isn't in my pocket
It isn't between my legs
Hop Scotch. (They hop from one foot to the other.)

When chanting begins, player A turns around to guess who has the ball. To further this aim, A may ask each player in turn to turn around, which they must do, carefully hiding the ball if they have it or pretending to hide it if they haven't. Player A must also run through the group. If A does so, the other players turn, as she passes through the group to keep the ball concealed. After that, A must make a guess. If A guesses correctly, another turn is taken. If not, the person who has successfully concealed the ball takes A's place in front.

Call Ball

Motor skills Throw, catch
Movement concepts Transfer of weight, change of direction
Players Six per game
Formation Circle
Playing area Playground, gymnasium
Equipment Ball
Academic concepts Mathematics—whole number recognition, adding and subtracting

Five children form a circle. The center player tosses the ball into the air and calls out a number(s), such as 3, 3 + 2, or 8 − 5 (depending on the age and concepts to be reinforced).

[†] If the ball is actually caught and doesn't touch the floor first, that player takes A's place right away without completing the game. The game then starts again.

The leader then bounces the ball to any player, who must try to catch the ball and give the correct answer before the leader counts to five. Award one point for every correct answer. Keep one group score and change leaders when the group score reaches five.

Suggestions and Variations

1. If skill level is very low, allow one bounce before attempting to catch the ball.
2. Use different types and sizes of balls.
3. Assign each player a consonant blend, such as, "bl," "cl," "gr," etc. The leader throws the ball and calls out a word that contains an initial consonant blend. Players with consonant blends must call out a word using the consonant, then catch the ball.

Soap Box Soccer

Motor skills   Dribble, run
Movement concepts   Personal and general space, change of direction and speed
Players   Three
Formation   None
Playing area   Playground, gymnasium
Equipment   Ball, traffic cones
Academic concepts   Mathematics—sets

A soccer ball is placed on the starting line. Three players hold hands and form a triangle around the ball. They must keep the ball inside the triangle and dribble the ball to the traffic cones and back to starting line.

Suggestions and Variations

Repeat game in groups of two or four.

Crab Soccer

Motor skills   Kick
Movement concepts   Balance, general space, change of direction and speed
Players   Class
Formation   Playing area divided into two equal sections, with goals placed on endlines
Playing area   Playground, gymnasium
Equipment   One ball and two goals

Players from both teams start in a crab walk position and move anywhere in the court area. All players except one goalie for each team remain in a crab walk position. The goalies may use their hands; however, all other players must move the ball with their feet. A foul occurs when a player catches the ball or strikes it with his hands. The teacher should stop the game when a foul occurs and give the ball to the nearest opponent. Award one point for each goal scored.

Suggestions and Variations

1. Practice the crab walk first.
2. After the game is well understood, require striking with hands only or allow a combination of hands and feet.
3. Change to moving on all fours and facing down, and repeat game.
4. Play crab soccer on all "threes."

American Hopscotch

Motor skills   Throw, hop
Movement concepts   Personal space, transfer of weight
Players   Two per game
Formation   See diagram
Playing area   Playground, gymnasium
Equipment   Buttons, beads, or small objects
Academic concepts   Mathematics—counting, and greater and less than

The first player stands on his right foot (this is his declared "hopping" foot and must be used throughout his turn) outside area 1, holding the "puck" (beanbag, button, etc.) in his hand. He tosses the puck into area 1, hops into this area, picks up the puck while balancing on his right leg, then hops out. He next throws the puck into area 2. He then hops into area 1, straddles ("spread eagle") areas 2 and 3, picks up the puck, hopping and landing with one foot in single spaces and with both feet in adjacent areas. Two hops are permitted in area 10 in order to turn around. A player is out if he steps on a line, tosses the puck onto a line or into the wrong area, changes feet on single hops, or touches his hand or other foot during any hopping or retrieving movement. When a child commits an error, he goes to the back of the line.

Suggestions and Variations

1. French Hopscotch. The game follows the basic rules of the American hopscotch with the player hopping on one foot in single squares and landing with both feet in adjacent squares. However, when a player lands with one foot in area 7 and the other in area 8, he must jump up, turn around in the air, and land in the same areas.
2. Italian Hopscotch. The first player stands on one foot outside square 1, holding a "puck" (beanbag, etc.) in his hand. He throws the puck into square 1 and then hops into this area. Still standing on one foot, he kicks the puck into square 2, then hops into that square. He continues this pattern to square 8. When he reaches square 8, he places both feet on the ground, picks up the puck, and hops backward through all squares to the starting position. A player is out if he steps on a line, if his puck stops on a line, if he puts both feet down in any square except 8, or if he changes feet. When a child commits an error, he goes to the back of the line.
3. Ask children to design their own pattern (zigzag, circle, etc.) and also make up their own rules.

American Hopscotch

French Hopscotch

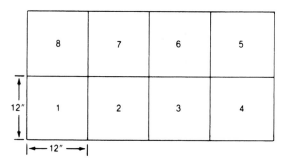

Italian Hopscotch

Motor skills Dribble
Movement concepts Personal space, strong and light, change of direction
Players Two to four
Formation Circle
Playing area Playground, gymnasium
Equipment Marbles
Academic concepts Mathematics—adding, subtracting, greater and less than, and diameter and radius of a circle

Each player places one or two marbles in the center of the circle. The playing order is determined by each player throwing his shooting marble (called the taw) toward a line six to ten feet away. The player whose marble is closest to the line shoots first; the player whose marble is next closest shoots second, and so on. A player may shoot from anywhere outside the circle, trying to knock the marbles out of the circle. His taw must remain inside the circle. If successful, he continues from where his taw has stopped (figure 16.4). After all players have had a

Figure 16.4 Playing marbles.

turn, they remove their taws from the circle. At the end of the game, all marbles should be returned to their owners.

Suggestions and Variations

1. Play doubles. Player 1 of team A shoots until he misses. Player 2 of team A shoots next, followed by player 1 of team B.
2. Exchange taws. Same as marbles except opponents exchange taws.
3. Marble Golf. Sink five or six small cans in a golf course pattern. Use same rules as for Barnyard Golf in the next section.

Jacks

Motor skills Throw, catch, balance
Movement concepts Strong and light, personal space, levels
Players Two to four
Formation None
Playing area Playground, gymnasium
Equipment Jacks and balls
Academic concepts Mathematics—counting and sets

The first player tosses the jacks on the ground. He then throws the ball into the air. With the same hand, he picks up one jack and tries to catch the ball before it lands. If successful, he places the jack in his other hand and continues playing until he picks up all the jacks. If unsuccessful, the next player takes a turn. If a player picks up all the jacks, one at a time, he repeats the game, picking up two at a time. Continue with three at a time, and so on.

Suggestions and Variations

1. Pigs in the Pen. Jacks are brushed into the other hand, which is held in a cupped position.
2. Eggs in the Basket. Jacks are picked up and transferred to the opposite hand before the ball is caught.
3. Lazy Susan. The ball is allowed to bounce twice before the jacks are picked up.

Tetherball

Motor skills Hit
Movement concepts Strong and light, transfer of weight, change of direction and speed
Players Two per game
Formation None
Playing area Playground, gymnasium
Equipment See diagram

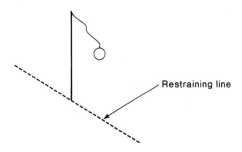

Players stand on opposite sides of the restraining line. One player starts the game by throwing the ball into the air and hitting it in any direction with his hand or fist. The opposing player strikes the ball in the opposite direction only after the ball passes him on the second swing around the pole. The player who winds the ball around the pole first is the winner.

A foul occurs when a player:

1. Hits the ball with any part of his body other than his hands
2. Touches the rope or pole
3. Catches the ball
4. Throws the ball

The penalty for a foul is to forfeit the game to the opponent.

Suggestions and Variations

1. Play "doubles." Players of each team alternate hitting the ball.
2. Play the same game using a paddle.

Inventive Games

The following sample challenges illustrate how each of the locomotor and manipulative game skills can be emphasized in small- and large-group games. These challenges are appropriate for children who are closer to the upper end of developmental level I. One of the most important uses of the inventive games approach is to design challenges that emphasize game skills that need extra attention or that help teachers cope with children who may have special talents or needs that are not met by the list of games in this chapter.

Locomotor Game

Two players "See if you can make up a game with your partner that must include a run, chasing your partner and using two hoops."

Manipulative Games

Rolling "Can you make up a game for four players where everyone must roll the ball? You can use any four small pieces of equipment in your new game."

Bouncing "Try to invent a new game for three players. You must have a bounce and catch and use one hoop."

Hand dribble "Is it possible to create a game all by yourself where you dribble the ball with one hand and keep your other hand on top of your head?"

Throw and catch "Make up a game for ten players that has a throw and a catch and uses only one goal."

Dribble and kick "Invent a new game for the whole class that includes dribbling the ball with your feet and using ten milk cartons scattered in your playing area."

Hit with small implement "See if you can make up a game with your partner that uses a bat [small paddle or bat made from coat hanger and panty hose—see appendix B] and a small ball."

Games for Developmental Level II

Children in developmental level II are at a transitional stage with regard to game activities (figure 16.5). They still enjoy running, tag, and simple team games. However, during the latter phase of this developmental level, their proficiency in throwing, catching, dribbling, kicking, and hitting shows a marked increase. These changes, along with this age group's psychological and social needs, begin to show a major shift to more organized and challenging team games. Use table 16.2 to select the appropriate games. When the skill and maturity levels are low, review the games and suggestions for developmental level I. Conversely, if the skill level and interest are high, do not hesitate to draw from the games listed in table 16.3 or from the lead-up games provided in chapters 18 to 23.

Locomotor Games

Loose Caboose

Motor skills Run, dodge
Movement concepts General space, change of direction and speed
Players Class
Formation Scattered
Playing area Playground, gymnasium
Equipment None
Academic concepts Mathematics—sets

Each group of three forms a line with each member holding on to the waist of the player in front. The first player is the "engine," the second the "baggage car," and the last the "caboose." Choose two players to be "loose cabooses." On signal, each train tries to prevent a loose caboose from attaching onto its own caboose. When this occurs, the engine becomes a new loose caboose, and each player moves up one place on the train. If a train pulls apart trying to avoid a loose caboose, this constitutes being caught.

Suggestions and Variations
1. Change size of groups to four, five, or six.
2. Change method of moving, such as hopping, sliding, or jumping.

Back Pass the Beanbag (Australia)

Motor skills Run, dodge
Movement concepts Change of direction and speed
Players Five
Formation Scattered
Playing area Playground, gymnasium
Equipment Beanbag
Academic concepts Mathematics—counting and multiplying

Figure 16.5 The transition stage.

Table 16.2 Locomotor and Manipulative Games (Developmental Level II)

Name of game	Type of game	Players	Motor concepts and skills	Movement concepts	Academic concepts and skills	Page
Locomotor games						
Loose Caboose	Tag	Groups of 3+ taggers	Run, dodge	General space, change of direction and speed	Mathematics—sets	268
Back Pass the Beanbag	Tag	Groups of 5	Run, dodge	Change of direction and speed	Mathematics—counting and multiplying	268
Without Hands	Run	Class	Balance, walk, run	General and personal space, change of direction and speed		271
Stick Touch Tag	Tag	Class + taggers	Run, dodge	General space, change of direction and speed	Mathematics—sets	271
Running Steps	Tag	6–8 players	Run, jump	Personal space, levels, change of speed	Language arts—word recognition and following directions	271
					Mathematics—adding, subtracting, and dividing	
Numbers	Run	Class	Run, dodge, stop	General space, change of direction and speed, relationships	Mathematics—sets, multiplying, and dividing	272
Steal the Bacon	Tag	12–14 players	Run, dodge, stop	Near and far, change of direction and speed	Language arts—word recognition and parts of speech Mathematics—whole numbers, adding, subtracting, multiplying, geometrical forms, and dividing Science—planets, animals, and mechanical objects	272
Red Stop, Green Go	Tag	Class + taggers	Run, stop, dodge	General space, levels, change of direction and speed	Mathematics—sets	273
Crazy Circle	Tag	8–10	Push, pull	Change of direction and speed, strength		273
Mouse and Cheese	Tag	Class	Run, tag, dodge	Change of direction and speed	Language Arts—auditory directions, consonant digraphs, word recognition, prefixes, and suffixes	273
Manipulative games						
Four Square	Bounce	2 to 4	Bounce, catch	Change of direction and speed		273
Progressive Dodgeball	Throw	Class	Throw, catch, dodge	General space, change of direction and speed	Mathematics—counting and subtracting	274
Ricochet	Throw	Half class vs. other half	Throw	Change of direction and speed		274
Bombardment	Throw	Half class vs. other half	Throw, catch, guard	Change of direction and speed		274
Barnyard Golf	Throw	4	Throw	General space, change of direction		274
Tail of the Rat	Run	Class	Run, manipulative movements	General and personal space, shapes, change of direction and speed	Mathematics—adding, subtracting, and averaging	274
Ball Pass	Throw	5–7	Throw, catch, run, dodge	Transfer of weight, change of direction and speed		275

locomotor and manipulative games

Table 16.2 *Continued*

Name of game	Type of game	Players	Motor concepts and skills	Movement concepts	Academic concepts and skills	Page
Guard Ball	Throw	Class	Throw, catch, guard	Change of direction and speed	Mathematics—adding and subtracting	275
Keep Away	Throw	8–10	Pass, catch, guard	Near and far, change of direction, speed, and levels	Science—electricity	275
Four Goal Soccer	Kick	Class	Kick, dribble, pass, trap	General and personal space, change of direction and speed	Mathematics—adding and subtracting	276
Goal	Dribble	3	Dribble, shoot, guard	Near and far, change of direction and speed		276
Instant Goal	Dribble	3	Dribble, shoot	Personal and general space, change of direction and speed		276
Trick the Guard	Dribble	2	Dribble, dodge, throw, catch	Change of direction and speed		276
Mimic the Word	Tag	Class	Run, manipulative movements	General and personal space, shapes, change of direction and speed	Language arts—word recognition and suffixes	276
Magic Carpet	Run	Class	Run, dodge	Change of direction and speed	Language arts—word recognition, vocabulary, and sentence structure	277
Place Kickball	Kick	10–20	Run, kick, catch	General space, change of direction and speed	Mathematics—adding, subtracting, averaging, and percentages	277
Boundary Ball	Kick	Half class vs. other half	Kick, trap	General space, change of direction and speed	Mathematics—adding and subtracting	277
Battle Ball	Kick	Half class vs. other half	Kick, trap	General space, change of direction and speed	Mathematics—adding and subtracting	277
Elastic Ropes	Jump	4	Jump	Personal space, change of direction and speed	Mathematics—sets, adding, subtracting, and multiplying	278
Alphabet Game	Jump	1 vs. 1	Jump	Personal space, transfer of weight	Language arts—spelling, prefixes, and suffixes	278
Five-Hole Marbles	Dribble	2–4	Dribble	General and personal space, change of direction, strong and light	Mathematics—counting	278
Softball Croquet	Hit	1 vs. 1	Hit	General space, change of direction, strong and light	Mathematics—counting	279
Long Ball	Hit	10–20	Hit, throw, pitch, catch, run	General space, strong and light, change of direction and speed	Mathematics—counting and averaging	279
Bounce Netball	Volley	12–18	Volley	General space, change of direction, levels		280
Bat Ball	Hit	18–20	Hit, run, throw	General space, change of direction and speed, levels	Mathematics—counting and averaging	280
Inventive Games	All skills	Individual to group	All skills	All movement concepts		280

Figure 16.6 Back passing the beanbag.

One person is "it" and stands about twenty feet away from the other four players. She now faces the opposite direction and counts to twenty. The other players stand with their hands behind their backs, passing the beanbag between each other until "it" calls out "20" (figure 16.6). On that cue, "it" tries to tag one of the players as they all run away, keeping their hands behind their backs, concealing which one of them has the beanbag. "It" must try to catch the player who has the beanbag. Players may secretly pass the beanbag to each other during the game. Once the player with the beanbag is caught, she becomes "it." If a player is caught and doesn't have the beanbag, she can then rejoin the game.

Suggestions and Variations
1. Have players hop or jump or move backward.
2. Have "it" repeat multiplication table instead of counting.

Without Hands (Zimbabwe)

Motor skills Balancing, walking, running, and sliding
Movement concepts Personal and general space, change of direction and speed
Players Class
Formation Line
Playing area Playground, gymnasium

Children stand behind a line with two stones placed on any part of their body. On signal, the children move to a place designated by the teacher. Once children start moving, they cannot touch the stones with their hands until they reach the designated place. Any player who drops one or both stones must turn around three times, place the stones back on their body and continue the game. First player to reach the designated place is declared the winner. Repeat game with a new designated place.

Suggestions and Variations
1. Have children hop, skip, or slide while carrying the stone.
2. Have children carry the stone on different parts of their body, such as on their shoulder, elbow, or foot.
3. Play game in twos with partners holding the two stones between parts of their bodies, such as hips, elbows, or seats.

Stick Touch Tag

Motor skills Run, dodge
Movement concepts General space, change of direction and speed
Players Class
Formation Scattered
Playing area Playground, gymnasium
Equipment Sticks
Academic concepts Mathematics—sets

The game begins with three taggers holding onto a stick. They cannot release their hold as they try to tag another player. When a player is tagged, he holds onto the outside tagger. However, as soon as three players are caught, they pick up the second stick and form a new tagging team. The game continues until the last player is caught.

Suggestions and Variations
1. Substitute a short rope for the stick.
2. As soon as a player is tagged, he must pick up the second stick, hold it over his head, and keep running on the spot until three players are caught.
3. Change the number of taggers to two or four.

Running Steps (South Africa)

Motor skills Run, jump
Movement concepts Personal space, levels, change of direction
Players Six to eight
Formation See diagram.
Playing area Playground, gymnasium
Equipment Steps
Academic concepts Language arts—word recognition and following directions; Mathematics—adding, subtracting, and dividing.

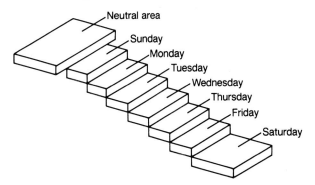

Modify game according to the number of steps that are available. Each step is given a day of the week. The caller stands on the flat surface at the bottom of the stairs and calls out the name of a day. Players must move to the step that was called out (figure 16.7). If they move to the wrong step, they become taggers. If the caller says, "Saturday," all players must touch the bottom area with one foot, then run back to neutral area. The caller tries to tag a player as soon as she touches Saturday. However, the caller or taggers are not permitted to climb the stairs in pursuit of the player. Change the caller every few minutes.

Suggestions and Variations
Change steps to numbers, verbs, nouns, etc., and repeat game.

locomotor and manipulative games

Figure 16.7 Running steps.

Figure 16.8 Steal the bacon.

Numbers

Motor skills   Run, dodge, stop
Movement concepts   Change of direction, speed
Players   Class
Formation   Scattered
Playing area   Playground, gymnasium
Equipment   None
Academic concepts   Mathematics—sets, multiplying, and dividing

Class begins in a scattered formation. On "go" signal, players run in different directions, and when the teacher calls out a number such as "three," all players must form groups of three. Children who do not make the required group number must make a funny face or sing a rhyme—but no push-ups or the like as punishment.

Suggestions and Variations

1. Have each new group balance on one foot, form a pyramid, or do an additional stunt.
2. Add a ball-bouncing skill to the game—for example, bounce ball at all times, running and forming groups.
3. Change number to a multiplication or division exercise.

Steal the Bacon

Motor skills   Run, dodge, stop
Movement concepts   Near and far, change of direction and speed
Players   Twelve to fourteen
Formation   Two lines
Playing area   Playground, gymnasium
Equipment   Beanbag
Academic concepts   Language arts—word recognition and parts of speech; Mathematics—whole numbers, adding, subtracting, multiplying, geometrical forms, and dividing; Science—planets, animals, and mechanical objects

Two teams line up behind their own endline. Each player has a number and the beanbag is placed in the middle of the playing area. The teacher calls out a number, such as four, and the "fours" from each team race for the beanbag (figure 16.8). When a player picks up the beanbag, he must run back across his own endline without being tagged by the opposing number four player. If the player is touched by the opposing player before reaching his endline, the opponent receives one point. On the other hand, if the player reaches his endline without being tagged, his team is awarded one point.

Suggestions and Variations

1. Two teams are numbered and stand on a line facing the teacher, who is holding a flag in each hand. The teacher calls a number, such as "five," then two players race for their flag, run around their own team, return the flag, and go back to their starting position. The player who returns to his own place first wins one point for his team.
2. Change numbers to adverbs. Teacher would call out, "He drives safely," and the two players who are designated as "safely" run out to pick up the beanbag.

1	carefully	5	safely
2	daily	4	early
3	dangerously	3	dangerously
4	early	2	daily
5	safely	1	carefully

3. Change numbers to pronouns, vowels, prepositions, and so on, and repeat the game.
4. Change numbers to family names (grandfather, grandmother, son, etc.) and use in an English as a second language program.
5. Give opposing players on each team a word card with a mathematical definition, such as, "four equal sides," "center to circumference," etc. The teacher holds up a word card with the word "radius" signaling the two opposing players with "center to circumference" to run to the teacher.
6. Repeat number 4 with language arts or science words and definitions.
7. Give opposing players opposite words, with the teacher calling out one of these words.

Red Stop, Green Go

Motor skills Run, stop, dodge
Movement concepts General space, levels, change of direction and speed
Players Class
Formation Scattered
Playing area Playground, gymnasium, classroom
Equipment Bands
Academic concepts Mathematics—sets

Three players are designated as "catchers" and wear a red band. Three players are designated as "releasers" and wear a green band. The remaining players scatter in the playing area. On signal, catchers try to tag as many players (other than releasers) as possible. When a player is tagged, he stands still until a releaser can tag him free to move again. The game continues for a few minutes; then change players.

Suggestions and Variations

1. Have tagged players perform a special movement while they are waiting to be released.
2. Play the game in pairs, including the taggers and releasers.

Crazy Circle (Spain)

Motor skills Pushing and pulling
Movement concepts Change of direction, speed, and strength
Players Eight to ten per game
Formation Circle
Playing area Playground, gymnasium
Equipment None

Eight players hold hands and form a circle. One child is chosen to be "it" and stands in the middle of the circle and does not move from this position. On signal, circle players must keep holding hands, then try to maneuver any circle player so the player touches "it." Once a player touches "it," they change positions and the game starts over.

Mouse and Cheese

Motor skills Run, tag, and dodge
Movement concepts Change of direction and speed
Players Class
Formation Circle
Playing area Playground, gymnasium
Equipment Ball and word cards
Academic concepts Language arts—auditory directions, consonant digraphs, word recognition, prefixes, and suffixes

Arrange players in a large circle and facing the center. Walk around the circle and assign "ch," "sh," "th," and "ph" to each successive group of four children. Continue assigning digraphs until all children have one. Place a small ball (cheese) in the middle of the circle. When the teacher calls out a word such as, "shift," all players who were given the "sh" consonant digraph run around the circle, through their own space toward the cheese. The first player to touch the cheese is the winner. Repeat game with another word and beginning with a new consonant digraph.

Suggestions and Variations

1. Hold up word cards instead of calling out the words.
2. Repeat above game with prefixes. Assign "ad" for vance, "in" for come, "sub" for tract, and "ob" for serve.

Manipulative Games

Four Square

Motor skills Bounce, catch
Movement concepts Change of direction and speed
Players Two to four per game
Formation Sixteen-foot square divided into four four-foot squares designated as squares A, B, C, and D
Playing area Playground, gymnasium
Equipment Utility ball

One player stands in each square. The player in square D starts the game by bouncing the ball, then hitting it with one or both hands so that it bounces into one of the other squares. The player receiving the ball hits it after one bounce to any of the other squares. The game proceeds until a player fails to return the ball properly or commits a foul. When this happens, the offending player goes to the end of the waiting line. All players move one square toward D and the waiting player moves to square A.

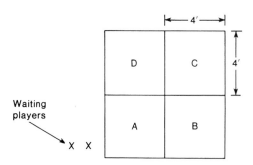

Basic Rules

1. The ball must arch before landing; it cannot be struck downward.
2. Service always begins from square D.
3. A player may go anywhere to return a fair ball, even out of his own square.
4. The ball may not be held.

Fouls occur when—

1. A ball hits any line.
2. A ball is struck with closed fists.
3. A ball hits a player who is standing in his own square.

Suggestions and Variations

1. Two Square. Play same game with two squares, and three or four players.
2. Team Two Square. Same as variation 1, except teammates take alternative turns.

Progressive Dodgeball

Motor skills   Throw, catch, dodge
Movement concepts   General space, change of direction and speed
Players   Class
Formation   Three parallel twenty-foot squares designated as A, B, and C
Playing area   Playground, gymnasium, classroom
Equipment   Ball
Academic concepts   Mathematics—counting and subtracting

This game is played in three periods of three to five minutes each. Teams rotate playing areas (A, B, and C) after each period. On signal, a player in one square tries to hit players with the ball (below the waist) in either of the two squares. No player is eliminated, so a player who is hit should try to get the ball and throw it at an opponent as soon as he is hit. Scores are made by hitting players on another team. The teacher or leader keeps the score for each team, and the team with the highest score after three periods wins. Players may not cross boundary lines.

Suggestions and Variations

Require every player to be constantly on the move.

Ricochet

Motor skills   Throw
Movement concepts   Change of direction and speed
Players   Class
Formation   Two endlines approximately three feet from each wall and a line drawn across the center of the playing area
Playing area   Playground, gymnasium
Equipment   One large utility ball (twenty-four inches) and approximately twenty small play balls (six inches)

Divide the class in half and arrange students along the endlines, facing each other. Give ten play balls to each team and place the large utility ball in the center of the playing area. On signal, both teams begin throwing the small balls at the large utility ball, attempting to force it over the opponent's goal line. Players may retrieve the play balls from their own half of the playing area; however, they must go back over their own endline before they attempt another throw. The team that forces the ball over its opponent's goal line wins the game.

Suggestions and Variations

1. Have players use different types of throws.
2. Introduce two to four large "throwing" balls.

Bombardment

Motor skills   Throw, catch, guard
Movement concepts   Change of direction and speed
Players   Class
Formation   Players scattered in playing area divided in half, with a four-foot restraining line next to each team's endline
Playing area   Playground, gymnasium
Equipment   Twelve to twenty milk cartons or Indian clubs, ten balls

Place equal numbers of milk carton or Indian clubs in these four-foot sections. Each team starts with five balls and tries to knock down the cartons or clubs in the opponents' goal area. Players may use their hands or legs to prevent the cartons or clubs from being knocked over. All players must stay on their own half of the playing area. Defending players must also stay in front of the four-foot restraining line. The team that first knocks down all of its opponents' milk cartons or Indian clubs wins. If the game is played in time periods, the team knocking down the most pins wins.

Suggestions and Variations

1. Require one or two passes before attempting to score a goal.
2. Use different types of balls.

Barnyard Golf

Motor skills   Throw
Movement concepts   General space, change of direction
Players   Four per game
Formation   Nine hoops or old bicycle tires (or circles drawn on blacktop), scattered and numbered as "holes"
Playing area   Playground, gymnasium
Equipment   One beanbag for each player, nine hoops
Academic concepts   Mathematics—adding, subtracting, and averaging

Allow each group of four to arrange its own "golf course," scattering the hoops in the space allocated. Player 1 begins from behind the starting line and attempts to throw his beanbag into the first hoop. If it lands inside or on the rim, he is awarded one point. He then picks up his beanbag and moves to the side of the first hoop and throws his beanbag into the second hoop. As soon as player 1 starts his second throw, player 2 begins his first throw. The game continues until every player has completed the course. The player with the most points wins the game.

Suggestions and Variations

1. This version is more similar to golf. Each player attempts to throw his beanbag into the first hoop. If he fails, he fetches it and tries again. No player can advance to the next "hole" until his beanbag lands in the hoop. This pattern continues around the course. The winner is the player with the lowest score.
2. Tin Can Golf. Sink tin cans into the ground and use old tennis balls and hockey sticks. Play according to the rules of variation 1.
3. Play the above game with partners.

Tail of the Rat (Switzerland)

Motor skills   Locomotor and nonlocomotor
Movement concepts   Personal and general space, shapes, change of direction and speed
Players   Class
Formation   Scattered
Playing area   Playground, gymnasium
Equipment   Tape recorder

Figure 16.9 Tail of the rat.

Figure 16.10 Children's drawing of "tail of the rat."

This game begins with the players scattered in the playing area. Everyone closes their eyes while the teacher moves through the area and silently touches one of the players to become the "rat." On signal, everyone opens their eyes and begins to move to the rhythm of the music. Suddenly, the "rat" begins to perform a special movement, such as jumping with both hands held overhead. As the "rat" continues to perform this movement, other players who detect she is the "rat," run behind her and mimic her movements. When the "rat" has six or more players behind her, she stops, spreads her legs, and every player in line must follow her movements. All other players must crawl through their legs. The game starts over with the teacher finding a new "rat" (figures 16.9 and 16.10).

Ball Pass

Motor skills Throw, run, catch, dodge
Movement concepts Transfer of weight, change of direction and speed
Players Five or six
Formation Circle
Playing area Playground, gymnasium
Equipment Ball

Four players form a circle and the fifth player stands in the middle. One player in the circle has a ball and says, "Go." Circle players begin to run counterclockwise and at any time the player with the ball may try to hit the middle player below the waist with it. The middle player may dodge, jump, or use any other movement to avoid being hit. When the middle player is hit, he exchanges position with the player who hit him.

Suggestions and Variations

1. Vary method of throwing ball.
2. Allow center player to prevent ball from hitting him by using hands.

Guard Ball

Motor skills Throw, catch, guard
Movement concepts Change of direction and speed
Players Class
Formation A large rectangle (thirty by ninety feet) divided into three equal sections, A, B, and C, with team 1 scattered in section B and team 2 scattered equally in sections A and C
Playing area Playground, gymnasium
Equipment Ball
Academic concepts Mathematics—adding and subtracting

Players on team 2, using a roll or a bounce pass, try to pass the ball to teammates in the opposite section. The ball must be passed below head level. Players on team 1 attempt to block the passes with their hands. Award one point for each successful pass, and subtract one point when a player on team 1 blocks a pass. Rotate teams every two or three minutes.

Suggestions and Variations

Vary the type of pass.

Keep Away

Motor skills Pass, catch, guard
Movement concepts Near and far, change of direction and speed, levels
Players Eight to ten on each team
Formation Scattered
Playing area Playground, gymnasium, classroom
Equipment Ball
Academic concepts Science—electricity; Mathematics—adding and subtracting

The teacher gives the ball to a player on one team, who then passes it to a teammate. The opposing players attempt to intercept the ball or break up the pass. If successful, they pass the ball to each other. Fouls are called whenever a defensive player grabs or holds onto an offensive player.

Suggestions and Variations

1. Do not let players run with the ball.
2. If adequate space is available, play two games by dividing the class into four teams.
3. If the teams are large and the playing area is limited, rotate in fours or fives every few minutes.
4. For science project, ball becomes "electricity." Players in possession of the ball are "conductors" and opponents are "nonconductors."

Four Goal Soccer

Motor skills Kick, dribble, pass, trap
Movement concepts Personal and general space, change of direction and speed
Players Class
Formation See figure 16.11
Playing area Playground, gymnasium
Equipment None

Figure 16.11 Four goal soccer.

The playing area is bounded by four lines. Place four goals (traffic cones or sticks) in the center of each line. Team A's goals are on the north and west side of the field. Team B's are on the east and south side. The game is played without goalies and each team attacks and defends two goals. Soccer rules apply with the exception of the off-side and corner kick rules.

Goal

Motor skills Dribble, shoot, guard
Movement concepts Near and far, change of direction and speed
Players Three per game
Formation See figure 16.12.
Playing area Playground, gymnasium
Equipment Ball

Figure 16.12 Goal.

The "goal" is at one end of the playing area and "home" is at the other end. One player is goalkeeper and the other two players start from "home," dribbling and passing the ball. The player who is in the act of dribbling may not score; however, when he feels his partner is in a good position to score he shouts "Goal," just before he passes the ball (figure 16.12). The player receiving the pass must shoot at the goal without any further dribbling. If the ball goes into the goal, each of the two field players gets one point. If the ball misses or if the goalkeeper prevents it from going in, the goalkeeper rushes out and tries to tag one of the players. If the player is tagged before he can reach "home," they exchange positions. If the goalkeeper is unsuccessful, he goes back into goal and the game starts over.

Instant Goal

Motor skills Dribble, shoot
Movement concepts Personal and general space, change of direction and speed
Players Three per game
Formation None
Playing area Playground, gymnasium
Equipment Ball

Three players begin dribbling and passing the ball to each other. Suddenly, player A moves away from the other two and spreads his legs to make a goal. The other two players must dribble and pass the ball at least two times before one of them tries to kick the ball between player A's legs. The game continues, with players B and C taking their turn at making a goal.

Trick the Guard (New Zealand)

Motor skills Dribble, dodge, throw, catch, guard
Movement concepts Change of direction and speed
Players Two per game
Formation None
Playing area Playground, gymnasium
Equipment Ball

One player is the attacker and the other is the defender. The attacker dribbles the ball with his hand within his own half of the playing area until, with a dodge or feinting action to fool the defender, he throws the ball high into the opponent's half. He then runs and tries to catch the ball before it lands on the ground. The defender cannot cross the line but can try to block the throw or intercept it before his opponent can retrieve it. If the attacker catches the ball, he is given a free throw at the goal. Each player has five turns before exchanging positions. The winner is the player with the highest number of points at the end of the game.

Mimic the Word

Motor skills Locomotor and manipulative skills
Movement concepts Personal and general space, shapes, change of direction and speed
Players Class
Playing area Playground, gymnasium
Equipment None
Academic concepts Language arts—word recognition and suffixes

Draw two lines approximately thirty feet apart and place "it" on one line and the remainder of the class on the other line. The group on the line decides on a word, such as "twisting," and all children mimic this word when they move in this manner as they run toward "it." As soon as "it" guesses the word, he tries to tag as many players as he can before they cross over the opposite endline. Any player who is tagged must stand beside "it" and help him catch players on each successive turn. The last player to be caught wins the game and becomes the new "it."

Suggestions and Variations

1. Use different parts of speech and change word endings.
2. Have the class work in groups of two or three.

Magic Carpet

Motor skills   Run, dodge
Movement concepts   Change of direction and speed
Players   Class in groups of five or six
Formation   Scattered
Playing area   Playground, gymnasium
Equipment   Word cards and wall charts
Academic concepts   Language arts—word recognition, vocabulary, and sentence structure

Five one-foot squares are numbered and randomly placed on the playing area. Five charts with corresponding numbers are placed on the wall. Each chart contains new words from current language arts, mathematics, science, social studies, or health units. Charts may include words from separate subjects or a mixture of all subject areas. Five groups of children each form a chain by holding hands. On signal (or with music), the groups run around and through the five squares on the ground. When the teacher calls "stop," everyone stops. The player in each group who is the closest to the square touches it, then identifies any word from the corresponding number listed on the word chart. After each team has had a turn, the teacher erases each word, if correctly answered, and the game continues. One point is scored for each correct answer. The team with the highest score wins the game.

Suggestions and Variations

1. Have each child make up a sentence with the chosen word.
2. Change the method of moving, such as hopping, sliding, etc.

Place Kickball

Motor skills   Run, kick, catch
Movement concepts   General space, change of direction and speed
Players   Class
Formation   Softball diamond with thirty feet between bases; one team in the field and one in a line formation behind home plate
Playing area   Playground, gymnasium
Equipment   One ball
Academic concepts   Mathematics—adding, subtracting, averaging, and percentages

Place the fielding team in the playing area outside the baselines. Each player on the kicking team is given one stationary kick from home plate. If the kick is fair (inside the boundary lines), the kicker tries to run around the bases before a member of the fielding team can get the ball and beat him to home plate. The kicker is out if a fly ball is caught.

Suggestions and Variations

1. After the stationary kick is learned, introduce a "dribble and kick." Draw a line ten to fifteen feet behind home plate and require the kicker to dribble to the plate and then kick the ball.
2. Require that the kick be made with the opposite foot the second time "up to bat."
3. If only a few players make it around the bases, have players run to first base and back.

Boundary Ball

Motor skills   Kick, trap
Movement concepts   General space, change of direction and speed
Players   Class
Formation   Three parallel lines drawn twenty to thirty feet apart, and each team scattered on each side of the centerline
Playing area   Playground, gymnasium, classroom
Equipment   One ball
Academic concepts   Mathematics—adding and subtracting

Each team has a ball, which it kicks toward the opponent's goal line. Players on both teams move about freely in their own half of the playing area, trying to prevent the opponent's ball from crossing the goal line. Players cannot touch the ball with their hands. One point is scored each time the ball crosses the opponent's goal line. One point is deducted each time the ball is touched with the hand.

Suggestions and Variations

1. Once children understand the game, play two games by dividing class into four teams.
2. Change to a throwing game.

Battle Ball

Motor skills   Kick, trap
Movement concepts   General space, change of direction and speed, levels
Players   Class
Formation   Two parallel lines twenty feet apart, with one team on each line and the players holding hands
Playing area   Playground, gymnasium
Equipment   Ball
Academic concepts   Mathematics—adding and subtracting

Side A tries to kick the soccer ball over side B's goal line. Side B tries to stop the ball and kick it back over side A's line, and so on. The team that kicks the ball over the opponent's line receives two points. The first side to reach a score decided by the teacher wins the game. A team loses a point if one of its players touches the ball with his hands, or if the ball is kicked too high—over the heads of the other team.

Suggestions and Variations

1. Have players pass the ball from teammate to teammate before kicking it toward the opponent's line.
2. Allow children to use their hands to prevent the ball from hitting their faces.

locomotor and manipulative games

Elastic Ropes**

Motor skills Jump
Movement concepts Personal space, change of direction and speed
Players Four per game
Formation None
Playing area Playground, gymnasium
Equipment Long elastic ropes (pantyhose tied in long strips can be an effective substitute)
Academic concepts Mathematics—sets, adding, subtracting, and multiplying

Players 1 and 2 hold the elastic rope with their legs. Player 3 performs various jumping movements inside the ropes or "in and out of the ropes" (figure 16.13). Player 1 exchanges position with player 3 and must repeat exactly what player 3 performed. If she makes a mistake or fails to perform a movement, she exchanges position with player 2. Game continues until player 2 makes a mistake or forgets a movement. Each player has a turn creating her own movements.

Suggestions and Variations

1. Raise the rope and/or change positions of the outside players' feet.
2. Outside players pose movement problems for player number 3. For example, jump in sets of two when you are inside the ropes and in sets of three when outside the ropes.

Figure 16.13 Elastic ropes.

Alphabet Game

Motor skills Jump
Movement concepts Personal space, transfer of weight
Players Two per game
Formation Pattern drawn as in diagram on dirt, gravel, or blacktop surface, with the size of the squares adjusted according to level of ability
Playing area Playground, gymnasium
Equipment None
Academic concepts Language arts—spelling, prefixes, and suffixes

**This game is played in the same way in Germany (called "Gummitwist"), South Africa (called "Coca Coke"), and Peru (called "The Garter").

Player 1 begins in square A, and attempts to move from square A to Z, in alphabetical order, without touching any lines. As soon as player 1 touches a line, he is out and player 2 begins. The winner is the player who progresses to the highest letter in the alphabet.

Suggestions and Variations

1. Have each child "touch" a four-letter word (or a longer word) before touching Z.
2. Change letters to numbers, then make up challenges involving adding, subtracting, multiplying, and dividing.
3. Add prefixes and suffixes to the game.

Z		
Y	P	G	O
F	X	R	C
L	J	T	N
S	Q	B	H
W	E	M	D
K	I	V	U
	A	

Five-Hole Marbles

Motor skills Dribble
Movement concepts General and personal space, change of direction, strong and light
Players Three or four per game
Formation See figure 16.14
Playing area Playground, gymnasium, classroom
Equipment Marbles
Academic concepts Mathematics—counting

The playing area has five small holes about three feet apart (see figure 16.14). Player 1 shoots from beside hole one and tries to roll his marble into hole two. If player 1's marble goes into the hole, he leaves it there until his next turn. If his marble does not go into the hole, it remains where it stops. The second player takes his turn. If he hits player 1's marble, player 1 is eliminated from the game. This rule applies to all future plays. If the marble rolls into the hole, player 3 takes his turn. Each player keeps taking his turn, provided he is not eliminated by being struck by an opponent's marble. The player who returns to hole number one first wins the game (figure 16.15).

Figure 16.14 Five-hole marbles formation.

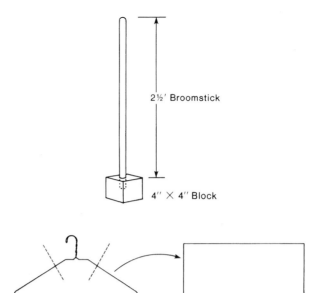

2½' Broomstick

4" × 4" Block

Figure 16.15 Five-hole marbles.

Softball Croquet

Motor skills Hit
Movement concepts General space, change of direction, strong and light
Players Two per game
Formation See diagram
Playing area Playground, gymnasium
Equipment Stick, block, coat hanger, and ball
Academic concepts Mathematics—counting

Player A hits the ball from behind the starting line. If the ball goes through both arches, A is given another hit. Player B hits the ball. Players alternate hitting throughout the game. Whenever a player hits the ball through an arch, he is given another hit. If a player's ball travels and hits his opponent's ball, no infraction occurs. The first person to hit his ball across the starting line wins the game.

Suggestions and Variations

1. Change the pattern of the arches.
2. Play "doubles" croquet and make up your own rotation rules.
3. Play the same game with different-sized balls such as field hockey, tennis, or Nerf balls.

Long Ball

Motor skills Hit, throw, pitch, catch, run
Movement concepts General space, strong and light, change of direction and speed
Players Class
Formation Softball diamond with thirty to thirty-five feet between each base, one team in the field and the other in a file formation behind a restraining line drawn ten feet back and to the right of home plate
Playing area Playground, gymnasium
Equipment Bat, ball, bases
Academic concepts Mathematics—counting and averaging

Divide players into two teams and number each player. Each team selects a pitcher and a catcher; other players are fielders or batters. When a ball is hit, the batter runs to first base and, if possible, returns home. The runner may stop on first base, and any number of runners may be on base at the same time. Runners may not steal home. Any hit is good; there are no fouls in this game. Batter is out when he strikes out, is touched with the ball off base, steals home, or throws the bat or when a fly ball is caught. One point is awarded for each run to the base and back.

Suggestions and Variations

1. Alternate pitchers and catchers.
2. Move pitcher closer as skill indicates.
3. Use a batting tee if skill level is too low.
4. Use a Nerf ball and hit ball with arm.
5. Shorten bases if necessary

locomotor and manipulative games

Bounce Netball

Motor skills Volley
Movement concepts General space, change of direction, levels
Players Six to nine per team
Formation Drop the volleyball net to about six feet or string a rope between two standards. Place one team on each side of the net in rows or in scattered formation.
Playing area Playground, gymnasium
Equipment Net and ball

Play is started by one player hitting the ball over the net. The ball must bounce before being returned. Any number of players can hit the ball any number of times; however, the ball must bounce once between each player. The team that loses the point starts the ball the next time. Fouls occur when the ball is (1) thrown, (2) caught and held, (3) allowed to bounce more than once, or (4) hit out of bounds. When a team commits a foul, the opposite team gets one point.

Suggestions and Variations

1. Instead of requiring one bounce between players, make them hit the ball directly from a volley pass.
2. Change the type of ball; try beach or Nerf balls.

Bat Ball

Motor skills Bat, run, throw
Movement concepts General space, change of direction and speed, levels
Players Nine per team
Formation Softball diamond with thirty to thirty-five feet between each base, one team in the field and the other in a file formation behind a restraining line drawn ten feet back and to the right of home plate
Playing area Playground, gymnasium
Equipment None
Academic concepts Mathematics—counting and averaging

One team is in the field and the other is at bat. Players at bat try to hit the ball into the field and run to first base and back home in one complete trip. The batter may not stop on base. A player who makes a complete trip without being put out scores one run. The batter is out if (1) a fielder catches a fly ball or (2) a fielder touches the runner with the ball before he reaches home. When the team at bat has three outs, it goes into the field and the team in the field comes to bat. The team with the most points at the end of the playing period is the winner. (Teams must have the same number of times at bat.)

Suggestions and Variations

1. Alternate pitchers and catchers.
2. Alternate boy and girl in the batting order. Try two outs if one team stays up too long.
4. Vary the distance between bases according to the level of skill.
5. Use a batting tee if the skill level is too low.

Inventive Games

As boys and girls progress through developmental level II, they become increasingly interested in playing in larger group games with more complexity and social interaction. The inventive game challenges can produce more complexity and social interaction. The inventive game challenges presented to children in this age range should

reflect these changing characteristics and interests. The following sample challenges are designed for larger groups and emphasize the locomotor and manipulative game skills of developmental level II.

Locomotor Games

Class "Can you design a tag game for the whole class to play? Your game must use five hoops and no player can be eliminated from the game."
Group of eight "See if you can make up a game for eight players that does not involve tagging someone and that also does not use any equipment."

Manipulative Games

Bounce "Invent a game for five players that uses three hoops, a change of direction, and a bounce pass."
Throw and catch "Make up a game for twelve players that includes a throw and catch, a line or wall, and every player always on the move."
Hand dribble "Design a game for the whole class where every player has a basketball (or substitute). Your game must include dribbling the ball with one hand, and four goals."
Foot dribbling "Can you add three new rules to the game Pig in the Middle? Your game will be played with six players."
Hitting "See if you can make up a hitting game for twelve players. You may use a volleyball, beachball, or Nerf Ball and you must hit the ball with your hand."

Games for Developmental Level III

Running, tag, and simple team games become less important when children reach developmental level III (figure 16.16). Their dominant interest, of course, is team sports. Chapters 18 to 25 include skill charts and appropriate lead-up games for each major team sport. However, boys and girls of this age range occasionally enjoy a vigorous running game or a simple team game such as California Kickball or Borden Ball. Listed in table 16.3 are a few of the more popular games these children enjoy playing. Other cooperative games are provided in chapter 17.

Teachers should also review the games listed in the previous developmental level for possible additions to their program of activities. Later in this section, several suggestions will illustrate how the inventive games approach can be applied to children in this age range.

Figure 16.16 Without hands.

Table 16.3 Locomotor and Manipulative Skills (Developmental Level III)

Name of game	Type of game	Players	Motor concepts and skills	Movement concepts	Academic concepts and skills	Page
Locomotor and manipulative games						
Dandy Shandy	Throw	Half class vs. other half	Throw, dodge	General space, change of direction and speed		282
King	Tag	Class	Run, throw, dodge	General space, change of direction and speed		282
Tug-of-War	Pull/push	10–12	Push, pull	Strong and light, transfer of weight	Science—inertia	282
California Kickball	Throw/kick	18–20	Run, throw, catch, kick	General space, transfer of weight, change of direction and speed		282
Chain Tag	Tag	Class	Run, tag	General and personal space, change of direction and speed	Mathematics—sets	283
Solids, Liquids, and Gases	Throw	6–7	Throw, catch	Change of direction and speed	Science—solids, liquids, and gases	283
Borden Ball	Throw	Half class vs. other half	Throw, catch	General space, change of direction and speed		283
Geometrical Shapes	Run	Class	Run	General and personal space; pathways, change of direction	Mathematics—geometrical shapes	284
European Handball	Throw	Half class vs. other half	Throw, run, catch, check	General space, change of direction and speed		284
Open the Window	Tag	7–9	Run, dodge	General and personal space, change of direction and speed	Mathematics—sets	285
Goodminton	Hit	16–18	Hit	Transfer of weight, levels, change of direction and speed		286
Shufflecurl	Shoot	2–4	Shoot	Transfer of weight, strong and light	Mathematics—geometrical forms; Science—friction	286
Frisbee	Throw	2	Throw	General space, strong and light, change of direction	Science—force and friction	287
Deck Tennis	Throw	2–4	Throw	Change of direction and speed		287
Paddleball	Hit	2–4	Hit	Change of direction and speed		288
Inventive Games	All skills	Individual to group	All skills	All movement concepts		289

locomotor and manipulative games

Locomotor and Manipulative Games

Dandy Shandy (Jamaica)

Motor skills Throw, dodge
Movement concepts General space, change of direction and speed
Players Class
Formation See diagram
Playing area Playground, gymnasium
Equipment Utility or Nerf Ball

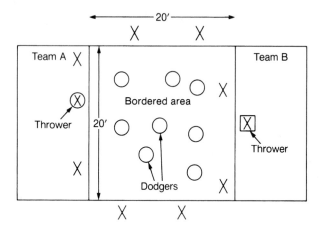

Divide the class into two equal teams and toss a coin to decide which team will be in the bordered area first (the dodgers). The other team spreads around the bordered area to retrieve balls for the two players chosen to be the "throwers." The throwers stand opposite each other and try to hit the players inside the area with the ball(s). The outside players can pick up and pass the ball, but only the two throwers can hit the other team's players. Any player hit with a ball is required to stand outside the bordered area and becomes a member of the thrower's team. After all the players are hit, the other team goes inside the bordered area, and the game is repeated. If the last player from any team dodges ten consecutive balls, his team is allowed to return to the bordered area and dodge the balls again.

King (India)

Motor skills Throw, dodge
Movement concepts General space, change of direction and speed
Players Class
Formation Scattered inside a fifty-foot square
Playing area Playground, gymnasium
Equipment Ball

One player is chosen to start the game. She throws the ball and tries to hit another player. Players must remain inside the square and use their fists to prevent their bodies from being hit. They also use their fists to hit the ball toward another player. Any player hit must move outside the square. Once a player is outside the square, she continues to play; however, she may not enter the square. If the ball goes out of the square, any player who is on the outside

Figure 16.17 King.

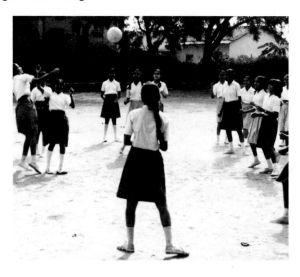

of the square may retrieve it and hit it back into the square (figure 16.17). Game continues until one player, the "king," remains.

Suggestions and Variations
Require players to use their nondominant hand to hit the ball.

Tug-of-War

Motor skills Pull, push
Movement concepts Strong and light, transfer of weight
Players Ten to twelve per game
Formation Line
Playing area Playground, gymnasium
Equipment None
Academic concepts Science—inertia

Divide class into two equal teams on the basis of the children's weight and strength. Stretch a tug-of-war rope across a centerline and place two tags on each side of the rope about five to six feet from the centerline. On signal, each team tries to pull the other until the opponent's marker crosses the centerline.

Suggestions and Variations
Have players pull from different positions, such as on seat or facing the reverse direction.

California Kickball

Motor skills Run, throw, catch, kick
Movement concepts General space, transfer of weight, change of direction and speed
Players Nine per team
Formation Arrange the playing area the same as in a softball game. Modify the length of bases and other rules according to space and other conditions
Playing area Playground, gymnasium
Equipment Utility ball

chapter 16

Figure 16.18 California kickball.

Figure 16.19 Chain tag.

The game is played like softball with the following modifications: (a) use a utility ball or old volleyball; (b) the pitcher rolls the ball and the "batter" kicks it; (c) the batter runs whether the ball is kicked fair or foul; (d) first base is the only base that the fielding team can touch to get a batter out—on all other bases, the fielder must tag the runner or throw the ball and hit him to get him out; (e) any number on the batting team may get on a base and stay, run when they think it is safe to try for another base; (f) on any hit balls, if the fielding team throws the ball to the pitcher, any runner who is between bases must go back to the previous base; (g) any runner caught between bases on a caught fly ball is automatically out; (h) change teams after three to six outs, or when everyone on the batting team has had a turn at bat (figure 16.18).

Suggestions and Variations
Use a Nerf ball and bat the ball with the arm.

Chain Tag (Czechoslovakia)

Motor skills   Run, tag
Movement concepts   General and personal space, change of direction and speed
Players   Class
Formation   Scattered
Playing area   Playground, gymnasium
Equipment   None
Academic concepts   Mathematics—sets

Mark off a designated playing area. The teacher selects four players to be "it." On signal, "it" players try to tag the other players. When a player is tagged, he joins hands with "it," then "it" continues to tag other players. The first "it" to tag five players calls out "five caught." When this occurs, the "six-member train" now tries to tag any other train or individual players. The winner is the last train or individual player to be tagged. (See figure 16.19.)

Suggestions and Variations
Split trains when three players are caught. Last individual player wins the game.

Solids, Liquids, and Gases

Motor skills   Passing
Movement concepts   Change of direction and speed
Players   Six to seven per team
Playing area   Playground, gymnasium
Equipment   Basketballs
Academic concepts   Science—solids, liquids, and gases

Divide class into four teams and have each team form a circle with approximately six feet between each player. One player on each team is given a ball. When the teacher calls "solids," players must stretch toward each other to receive and transfer the ball. "Liquids" would require players to bounce pass the ball and "gases" to throw the ball. As soon as the class understands the directions, call out each word in random order. If a player drops the ball, he must retrieve it, return to his place in the circle, then continue the game. The first team to move the ball twice around the circle wins the game.

Suggestions and Variations
1. Place a player in the middle and require alternate passes to go to the center player.
2. Have all players moving according to the speed of the molecules—solids move slowly, liquids move fast, and gases move very fast.

Borden Ball

Motor skills   Throw, catch
Movement concepts   General space, change of direction and speed
Players   Class
Formation   Playing areas divided into two equal sections, with each team scattered in each section
Playing area   Playground, gymnasium
Equipment   Football, two posts or traffic cones

Place one goalie from each team in an eight-foot goal area in the center of each endline (use two posts or traffic cones as goalposts). The object is to throw the ball through the opponent's goal. The game begins with a jump ball

locomotor and manipulative games

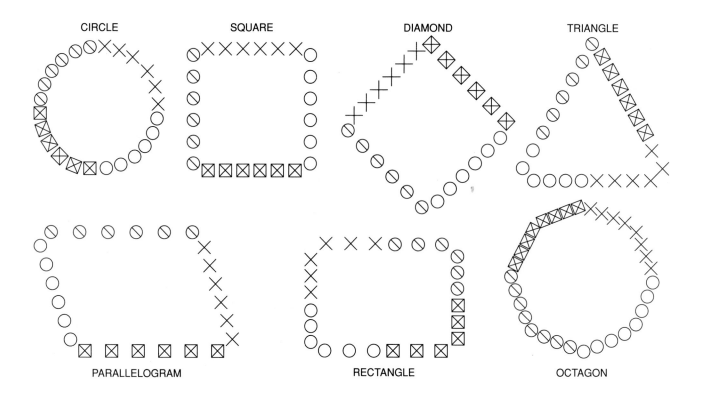

CIRCLE SQUARE DIAMOND TRIANGLE

PARALLELOGRAM RECTANGLE OCTAGON

between two opposing players at the centerline. The ball may be thrown in any direction, but it may not be hit or kicked. A player may take a maximum of three steps while holding the ball no longer than three seconds. On penalties, the ball is given to the nearest opponent. Members of the team that does not have possession of the ball may check the player with the ball, but they may not touch, hold, or push him. One point is awarded for each goal. After a point is scored, at halftime, or at any official stopping of play, restart play with a jump ball at the center. If the ball goes over the sidelines, a player on the opposing team throws it into the field of play.

Suggestions and Variations
1. Use different types and sizes of balls.
2. Change the three-second rule or number of steps to meet skill level of the class.

Motor skills Running
Movement concepts General and personal space, pathways, and change of direction
Players Four equal teams
Playing area See diagram above
Equipment None
Academic concepts Mathematics—Geometrical shapes

Divide the class into four equal teams and number each team 1, 2, 3, and 4. Each team forms a line, hold hands, then begins to run anywhere within the playing area. When the teacher calls, "Two, Diamond, and Clockwise,"

all players must keep moving, and team 2 runs to a place in the playing area where a large diamond could be formed, makes the first part of the diamond and continues to run in place. Since the teacher has called "clockwise," team 3, who is next in this direction, forms the next part of the diamond, followed by teams 4 and 1. When the last player on team 1 is running in place, the teacher calls out "scatter," signaling each team to return to running through the playing area. If the next call was "Four, Octagon, and Counterclockwise," team 4 forms the first part of the eight-sided figure, followed by teams 3, 2, and 1. The four groups can also form a triangle or rectangle by placing fewer players on one side of each form as shown in the diagrams.

Motor skills Throw, run, catch, check
Movement concepts General space, change of direction and speed
Players Six to eight per team
Formation See diagram on top of page 285
Playing area Playground, gymnasium, classroom
Equipment Four goalposts

The object of the game is to throw the ball through the goalposts. The game begins with a jump ball between two opposing forward players. Once the ball is tapped out of the center circle, any player may attempt to retrieve it. A player who has possession of the ball may take one to three steps, bounce it, take three more steps, and so on, or attempt to throw it through the goalposts. A player has three seconds

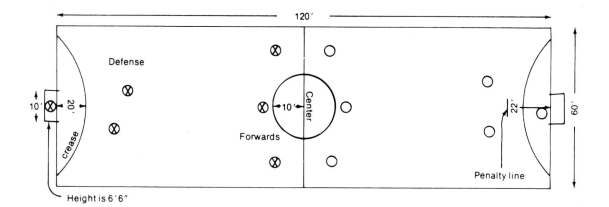

to get rid of the ball. A player may check on an opponent in the same way as in basketball. If a defensive player fouls his opponent, the opponent is given a free throw at the point of infraction. All defensive players must stay ten yards away until the throw is made. If the ball goes over the sidelines or endlines, the nonoffending team throws the ball back into play (one- or two-hand throw, according to age and ability). The goalie must stay within the crease (the semicircle around the goalposts); however, no other player may enter this area. One point is awarded for each goal scored from outside the crease area.

Suggestions and Variations

1. Play the game without allowing a bounce.
2. Add "nonscoring" sideline player similar to sideline soccer.
3. Play same game with a Nerf ball, but allow no dribbling or holding.

Open the Window (Denmark)

Motor skills Running, dodging
Movement concepts General and personal space, change of direction and speed
Players Groups of seven
Formation Line
Playing area Playground, gymnasium
Equipment None
Academic concepts Mathematics—sets

Arrange class into groups of seven within a designated playing area. Three sets of partners line up behind a starting line. One player, the "window," stands ten feet in front of the first set and facing away from the group. When the "window" calls, "Open the window," the two partners at the end of the line run up each side of the line and in front of the "window." Once the runners pass the "window," he tries to tag one of them before they can join together. If the "window" tags a player, they exchange positions, with the new set of partners returning to the front of the line. The game continues until everyone has had a turn. (See figures 16.20 and 16.21.)

Figure 16.20 Open the window.

Figure 16.21 Children's drawing of "open the window."

Goodminton

Motor skills Hit

Movement concepts Transfer of weight, change of direction and speed, levels

Players Six or fewer per team

Formation Two equal teams across a rope or net

Playing area Playground, gymnasium, classroom

Equipment Volleyball net (or rope), bats (see diagram in appendix B), badminton bird (used ones are quite suitable) or yarn ball (covered with tape or cloth)

This game is played like volleyball with the following basic rules. The server has only one serve to get the bird over the net, and the bird must clear the net on each serve. The server continues to serve as long as his team wins points. After the first serve has been taken by each team, and after each succeeding "side out," the team receiving the serve rotates one position clockwise. (The front row players move to the right, the back row players to the left, and the left back moves to the left forward position.) Teams change sides after each game (figure 16.22)

The bird may be batted in any direction, but scooping, lifting, and any form of holding are not permitted. The bird, except on service, may be recovered from the net, provided the player avoids touching the net. The bird may be batted only three times by one team before being returned over the net. A player may not hit the bird twice in succession, but he may give it the first and third hits.

If any player on the serving team commits any of the following acts, it shall be "side out." If any player on the receiving team commits any of the acts, the serving team is awarded a point. The illegal acts are serving illegally; catching or holding the bird; touching the net with any part of the body or bat (if two opponents touch the net simultaneously, the bird shall be re-served); reaching over the net; playing out of position, touching the floor on the opposite side of the centerline; allowing hands or bats over the centerline; "spiking" or "killing" the bird when playing a back position.

Figure 16.22 Goodminton.

Suggestions and Variations

1. Play the same game with a Nerf ball. Try eliminating the bat and use the flat of the hand.
2. Limit game and nondominant hand.

Shufflecurl

Motor skills Shooting

Movement concepts Transfer of weight, strong and light

Players Two to four

Formation See diagram below

Playing area Playground, gymnasium

Equipment Shuffleboard cues and disks

Academic concepts Science—friction; Mathematics—geometrical forms

The rules are the same as in shuffleboard, but the object is to slide the disks as close to the center of the circle as possible. Players in this game also try to knock the opponent's disks out of scoring position. When each player has used his four disks by sliding them to the opposite

Shufflecurl

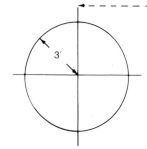
30'
or vary distance according to skill level and available space

3'

circle, one "end" has been completed. Two "ends" make one round, and a game may be five, ten, or any other number of rounds. To score, award one point for each disk that a player has placed closer to the center of the circle than the closest disk of his opponent. (In the diagram, the player with the black disks would score three points.)

Suggestions and Variations

Play same game with different disks, such as beanbags, quoits, or deflated balls.

Frisbee

Motor skills Throw, catch, run
Movement concepts General space, strong and light, change of direction
Players Two
Formation None
Playing area Playground, gymnasium
Equipment Frisbee
Academic concepts Science—force and friction

Frisbee activities, whether throwing the disk for distance, catching it in a variety of unusual ways, or playing new types of Frisbee games, have become very popular with elementary school children. It involves a new way of throwing an object and a flight pattern different from that of a thrown or hit ball. More important, Frisbee activities provide a reservoir within which children can invent unlimited numbers of creative and cooperative game activities.

The backhand throw is the easiest and most popular way of throwing the Frisbee. Stand with feet about shoulder-width apart and weight evenly distributed over both feet. The right foot points toward the target. The disk is held with the thumb on top, index finger on the rim, and the remaining fingers curved under the rim of the disk (figure 16.23a). Shift the weight to the rear foot, then simultaneously twist the trunk toward the target and pull the right arm forward (figure 16.23b). Continue forward and release the disk with a snap of the wrist when the disk is parallel to the ground (figure 16.23c).

Suggestions and Variations

The following activities are simple modifications of partner or team games. Teachers and children are encouraged to invent other variations as well as entirely new Frisbee games.

Figure 16.23 Throwing a frisbee.

a   b   c

1. Throw and Catch with Partner. Throw and catch at different levels using a variety of catches. Other variations, such as increasing the distance, using either hand, or performing a trick when catching the Frisbee, can be added to partner activities.
2. Frisbee Golf. Play the same game as barnyard golf, except expand the distance between "holes."
3. Frisbee Tennis. Play the same game as deck tennis, and add or modify any rule to accommodate levels of skill and interest.
4. Frisbee Soccer. Play the same game as soccer and add or modify rules to accommodate levels of skill and interest.
5. Frisbee Softball. Play the same game as softball, and add to or modify the rules to accommodate the level of skill and interest.

Deck Tennis

Motor skills Throw, run
Movement concepts Change of direction and speed
Players Two to four
Formation Court drawn as in the diagram below, or use any existing volleyball or badminton court
Playing area Playground, gymnasium, classroom
Equipment Deck tennis ring made of rope or plastic tubing, which can be purchased through local sports stores

Deck tennis ring

locomotor and manipulative games

Singles

The server, standing outside the baseline and on the right half of the court, delivers the ring in a forehand fashion. The ring must rise to an arch before it begins to descend into the opponent's right court outside the neutral area. After the serve, the ring may land anywhere in the court. The server must serve into alternate courts each time. The receiver must catch the ring with one hand and immediately return it. The server scores a point if the receiver fails to return the ring or commits one of the following fouls:

1. Catching the ring with both hands
2. Changing the ring to his other hand before returning it
3. Holding the ring too long before returning it (count three seconds)
4. Stepping over the net line
5. Failing to make the ring arc before it begins to descend into the opponent's court

If the server faults or misses the return throw, his opponent then serves. However, no point is scored by the opponent. Game may be played to eleven, fifteen, or twenty-one points.

Doubles

The game is played according to singles rules with some modifications. Each team has two serves in succession. After the receiver has returned the server's toss, any player may return a toss. For example, player A from team 1 serves, and player C of team 2 catches the ring and returns it to player A. It is legal for player A to catch the ring and return it.

Suggestions and Variations

1. Nerf Ball Deck Tennis. Play the same game with a Nerf Ball. Allow one bounce, and hit with an open palm.
2. Paddle Tennis. Play variation 1 with a paddle.

Paddleball

Motor skills   Serve, hit, run
Movement concepts   Change of direction and speed
Players   Two to four
Formation   Court drawn as in diagram using any available wall and floor space. Use chalk or plastic tape to mark court dimensions.
Playing area   Playground, gymnasium, classroom
Equipment   Bats, tennis or sponge balls

Singles

The server, standing anywhere between the wall and the serving line, bounces the ball and hits it toward the front wall. The ball must hit the wall above the two-foot line and land behind the serving line inside the court. If it does not, the next player serves. After the ball has bounced once, the receiver hits it back to the wall. All returned balls by either player must hit above the two-foot line, but they may land anywhere inside the full court area (sixteen by twenty-six feet). The players alternate hitting the ball. If the server hits the ball above the line and back over the serving line, and the receiver fails to return the ball, the server receives one point. One player continues serving until he faults or

misses the ball. Any player may go outside the court to return a ball. Game may be played to eleven, fifteen, or twenty-one points.

Doubles

The game is played according to singles rules with a few modifications. On the serve, the server's teammate stands outside the court to prevent any hindrance to the opponents who are trying to return the service. When the server loses his serve, his teammate takes a turn. Each team, therefore, has two serves in succession. On the serve, either opponent may return the ball. Thereafter, players on each team alternate hitting the ball.

Triples

This game is played according to singles rules with the following modifications. The server represents one team and, therefore, is playing against the other two players as a team. When the server loses his service, he moves to the right back court. The right back court player shifts to the left, and the left back court player becomes the new server. After the serve, the server hits every other ball. For example, the server hits, then player A of the opposing team, then the server, then player B. Each player keeps his own score.

Suggestions and Variations

1. Handball. Game is played the same as paddleball, except the ball is hit with the hand. Use tennis, sponge, or Nerf balls.
2. Allow two bounces for either paddleball or handball.
3. Adjust serving and restraining line to meet level of ability.

Paddleball

By the time children reach developmental level III, team sports are the order of the day. However, inventive games can be used to complement many lead-up games. If children in developmental level III have not been exposed to the inventive games approach, begin by modifying one or two of their favorite lead-up games. When these children become used to modifying these games, shift to a more exploratory method of posing more open-ended challenges, as illustrated in the following examples.

Throw and dodge   The class has played Dandy Shandy in a previous lesson. Arrange the class to play the game in the same way as the previous lesson. After a few minutes, have both teams sit down in opposite areas and pose the following: "Can you add a new rule to your game?" After a few minutes, ask each group to explain its rule, then play the game with two new rules. Repeat the procedure two more times, then move on to another game.

Throw and catch   Select Borden Ball and repeat the procedure used to modify Dandy Shandy.

Shooting   "Can you invent a shooting game for eight players that uses paddles, one Nerf ball (or sponge ball), and three goals (hoops or wastepaper baskets?"

Hand dribbling   "Create a game for twelve players who have twelve basketballs. Your game must include a dribble, pass, and pivot, and no goals."

Frisbee   "Can you invent a Frisbee game for four players, using a volleyball net and court?"

Using Inventive Games to Teach Academic Concepts and Skills

During the past few years, the inventive game approach has become very popular in the elementary school physical education program (figure 16.24). This problem-solving method, however, has been used almost exclusively to guide children to create their own running, tag, and simple ball games.

Figure 16.24   Using inventive games to teach academic concepts and skills.

The following examples will illustrate how this approach can be adapted to teach a wide variety of academic concepts and skills in exciting and challenging ways.

Before adapting this approach to teaching language arts, mathematics, or other academic concepts and skills, each teacher should learn how to pose simple inventive game challenges described in the introduction of part V and at the conclusion of each developmental level of this chapter. As soon as you feel confident in using this approach, begin to adapt it to teach a variety of language arts, mathematics, science, and other subject areas, academic concepts and skills. The examples that follow illustrate how to pose inventive game challenges that include language arts and mathematics concepts and skills.

Language Arts

Challenge No. 1: Word Recognition

Make up sets of cards as shown.

Set 1: | apples | | pears | | grapes |

Set 2: | potatoes | | carrots | | beans |

Sets 3–15:   create other sets as required

Two players have one set of cards between them. Pose the following challenge.

Challenge   Can you make up a hopping game with your partner that uses three word cards? You must call out one or more words in your game.

Challenge No. 2: Prefixes and Suffixes

Three children draw a word grid on a gymnasium mat or outside on the blacktop. The grid has sixteen squares with prefixes as shown. When everyone is ready, pose the following challenge.

Challenge   See if you can design a game for three players using the prefix grid. You must use a hop, a jump, and a change of direction in your game?

ab	pro	pre	mis
ex	sub	de	ad
com	un	dis	ob
in	non	re	trans

Suggestions and Variations
1. Repeat game with suffixes.
2. Add flash cards to the above games.
3. Design new grids that can be used to emphasize one or more language arts skills.

Mathematics

Since set concepts are taught throughout the elementary school grades, two examples are provided to illustrate how to use the inventive game approach with young and older children. In the first example, sets of twos, threes, and fours are taught to a group of eight-year-olds. The second example, for older children, illustrates how a large group can be broken down into subsets on the basis of a variety of features and properties.

Sets for Younger Children

A third-grade class is learning the concepts of sets in a mathematics unit. The teacher has also planned a games unit that will include Snowball (sets of two), Loose Caboose (sets of three), and Numbers (sets of three). As the children begin to understand the concept of sets and have played the three games, the teacher begins to pose several inventive game challenges, described below.

Challenge No. 1: Sets of Two

This first game involves one child, eight beanbags, and a limited space to play the game.

> **Challenge** Can you arrange your equipment in sets of two and make up a game that involves jumping over sets and a change of direction?

After each child has designed and played the first game, the teacher adds other related challenges, described in the next three challenges.

Challenge No. 2: Sets of Three

Repeat the above challenge and substitute sets of three or four.

Challenge No. 3: Change Requiring Physical Skill

Repeat the above challenge and change way of moving to running, hopping, leaping, etc.

Challenge No. 4: Change Quantity of Equipment

Arrange class into groups of four children with twelve pieces of equipment for each group. Pose the challenge:

> **Challenge** "Can your group design a new game, in your own space, and use twelve pieces of equipment? Your game must arrange the equipment in sets of two, three, or four."

Sets for Older Children

Prior to giving this group of eleven-year-olds a challenge, the teacher noted the gender and eye color of the children. She found there were fifteen boys with brown eyes and nine girls with blue eyes. The teacher assigned six brown-eyed boys and six blue-eyed girls to group A. This composition provided a potential for different arrangements by gender as well as possible subsets by eye color. The second group, composed of nine brown-eyed boys and three blue-eyed girls, held a similar potential if they were grouped in sets of three. The teacher then gave each group twelve pieces of small equipment. The twelve pieces of equipment provided a structure to create sets of six, four, three, or two. These

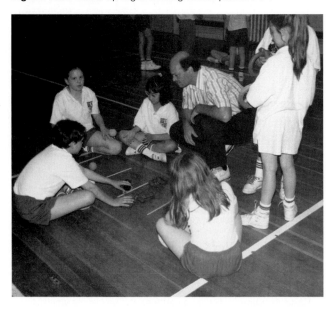

Figure 16.25 Make up a game using twelve pieces . . .

sets could also involve players grouped in similar numbers. The next four challenges illustrate how the teacher used this basic structure to teach sets in a very interesting and challenging way (figure 16.25).

Challenge No. 1: Sets

> **Challenge** See if your group of four can make up a game using twelve pieces of equipment and stay in your own space. Somewhere in your game you must use sets of two, three, or four.

Challenge No. 2: Change Quantity of Equipment

Repeat the above challenge, but change the number of equipment to twenty-four pieces. This provides for sets of eight or twelve.

Challenge No. 3: Increase The Size of the Group

Repeat the above challenge and consolidate the two groups into one group of twenty-four children. Now there is an increased potential for different sets and groupings by eye color.

Challenge No. 4: Change Method of Moving

Repeat any of the challenges and change the method of moving to running, hopping, or jumping.

Mathematics, like every other subject in the elementary school curriculum, should be fun and exciting to learn. The inventive game challenges presented under each age level provide a physical medium to learn mathematical concepts and skills. These games also provide a creative avenue to express ideas and to experience a sense of joy and success while children play their own games.

Selected References

Ashlock, R. B., and Humphrey, J. H. (1976). *Teaching Elementary School Mathematics Through Motor Learning*. Springfield, IL: Charles C. Thomas.

Blatt, G. T., and Cunningham, J. (1981). *It's Your Move: Expressive Movement Activities for the Language Arts Class*. New York: Teacher College Press.

CAHPER. (1986). *K-3 Games*. Ottawa, Ontario: CAHPER Publications.

Doray, M. (1982). *J Is for Jumping: Moving into Language Arts*. Belmont, CA: Pitman Learning Inc.

Draper, M., Rosenthel, S., Stillwell, J., and Fahrman, L. (1989). *The Gym Dandies Series: Volume 4*. Durham, NC: Great Activities Publishing Co.

Gable, S. (1988). *The Gym Dandies Quarterly: Games Games Games*. Durham, NC: Great Activities Publishing Co.

Gilbert, A. G. (1977). *Teaching the Three R's Through Movement Experiences*. Minneapolis: Burgess Publishing Co.

Hall, T. (1981). *Academic Ropes*. Bryon, CA: Front Row Experiences.

Haseltine, P. (1987). *Games for All Children*. Oxford, England: Basil Blackwell Ltd.

Humphrey, J. H. (1990). *Integration of Physical Education in the Elementary School Curriculum*. Springfield, IL: Charles C. Thomas Publishers.

Humphrey, J. H., and Humphrey, J. N. (1990). *Mathematics Can Be Child's Play*. Springfield, IL: Charles C. Thomas Publishers.

———. (1991). *Developing Elementary School Science Concepts Through Active Games*. Springfield, IL: Charles C. Thomas Publishers

Kamiya, A. (1985). *Elementary Teacher's Handbook of Indoor and Outdoor Games*. West Nyack, NY: Parker Publishing Co.

Kirchner, G. (1991). *Children's Games from Around the World*. Dubuque, IA: Wm. C. Brown Publishers.

Mauldon, E., and Redfern, H. B. (1981). *Games Teaching*, Second Edition. London: Macdonald and Evans Ltd.

Morris, B., and Stiehl, J. (1989). *Changing Kids' Games*. Champaign, IL: Human Kinetics Publishers, Inc.

Turner, L. F., and Turner, S. L. (1989). *Alternate Sports and Games for the New Physical Education*. Needham Heights, MA: Ginn Press.

Werner, P. H., and Burton, E. C. (1979). *Learning Through Movement: Teaching Cognitive Content Through Physical Activities*. St. Louis: C. V. Mosby Co.

17

Cooperative Games

Since the publication of Terry Orlick's *The Second Cooperative Sports and Games Book* and Andrew Fluegelman's *More New Games Book,* many children have been introduced to a delightful cooperative and nonthreatening games program. Cooperative games may be new, borrowed from other cultures, or modified versions of team games that children have played for generations.

The first part of this chapter describes the basic elements of a cooperative game. The next section includes examples of several cooperative games that have become very popular with elementary school children. The third area describes how teachers can guide children toward creating their own cooperative games. The latter two sections describe how cooperative games are used to teach academic concepts and skills ∎

Elements of a Cooperative Game

Webster's Dictionary defines *cooperation* as the association of persons for common benefit.* On the basis of this definition, any competitive game, such as volleyball, basketball, or dodgeball, would meet this criterion, since a measure of cooperation is required if a team is to win a contest. The contemporary meaning of "cooperative games," however, goes beyond Webster's definition. The cooperative games described in this chapter are essentially noncompetitive activities that emphasize the interaction of people rather than the game or the final score. They normally stress the elements of fun, cooperation, equality, participation, success, and trust. Each of these distinguishing characteristics or elements of cooperative behavior are described below. The game of Cross-Over Blanket Volleyball (page 298) is used to illustrate how and where each element is emphasized in the rules and the way the game is played. Other games, such as Doubles Hopscotch (page 295), Modified Musical Chairs (page 297), and Juggle a Number (page 296), could serve the same function.

Figure 17.1 Working together.

Fun

Everyone must receive a measure of enjoyment from playing the game. The game encourages the players to laugh with, not at, others as they play. And, when finished playing, all players leave the "magic circle" of play with a sense of joy and happiness (figure 17.1).

Volleyball has been a favorite game of elementary school children for many years; but it is a competitive game with winners and losers. Cross-Over Blanket Volleyball (figure 17.2), with players constantly changing sides, and total group scoring rather than individual team scoring, eliminates the pressure of winning. The new rules encourage children to play because the game is not only fun and exciting to play, but it also encourages positive social interaction among all players.

Cooperation

Everyone must work together to achieve a common goal. Cooperation involves helping each other and sharing each task as the group moves toward its common goal.

Cross-Over Blanket Volleyball is a very cooperative game. For example, every player must cooperate or the ball

Figure 17.2 Cross-over blanket volleyball.

can not be caught or propelled over the net. The new rotation system ensures that each player has a chance to share each task and to learn to help in different group efforts as he or she crosses under the net to join a new group.

Equality

Everyone has an equal role in the game; that is, each player "hits the ball" roughly the same number of times as any other player, "rotates" to every other position, and, in part of the game, assumes the leadership role on a rotational basis. The rules of this modified version of volleyball require every player to rotate his or her position on the blanket as well as from one blanket to the other. This ensures equality of all players throughout the game.

*By permission. From Webster's Ninth New Collegiate Dictionary © 1984 by Merriam-Webster Inc., publisher of the Merriam-Webster® Dictionaries.

chapter 17

Participation

Everyone is actively involved in the game. The rules of the game cannot eliminate any player from playing. If a player is "hit," "touched," or misses a "hit" or "catch," he continues to play.

Requiring a team effort every time the ball is flipped or caught ensures everyone has an active and continuous role to play throughout the game. Rotation of players to the opposite side guarantees additional movement on the part of all players. This rule also stresses participating in a total group, rather than on an individual team.

Success

Everyone experiences a sense of accomplishment. Cooperative games have no losers. Success must be personally defined rather than determined by a score or group standard.

Since the score is kept for the whole group, there are no losers in this game. Also, the act of flipping or catching is also a measure of how well the group cooperatively performs. The individual's measure of success centers on how the individual player felt about his contribution as he helped perform each of the collective movements.

Trust

Everyone must be able to place a measure of trust in other players. This means that situations within the game require a player to rely on another player to "miss him," "hold him," "balance him," or perform a movement that considers his safety and well-being.

There is a slight measure of trust in this game. It is the part of the game that requires all players to hold the blanket and execute the required movement in unison. This is, by comparison to all others, a relatively weak game to illustrate the element of trust. However, the reader will be able to find games in this chapter where trust is clearly illustrated.

These six elements of a cooperative game were selected on the basis of a review of articles and books dealing with cooperative games, plus information obtained from field studies with elementary school children. During the past several years, teachers and children from many countries have suggested that other elements, such as "sharing" and "fairness" or "sportsmanship," be added to the list. Each teacher should modify or expand this list of elements to meet the needs, ability, and cultural background of the children in her class.

Popular Cooperative Games

All the games described in this section (table 17.1) are cooperative in nature. Some of these games, such as Doubles Hopscotch and Modified Musical Chairs, are modified versions of competitive games children have played for years. These modified versions, however, stress the elements of fun, cooperation, equality, participation, success, and trust rather than "winners and losers."

Doubles Hopscotch (Levels I, II)

Partners hold inside hands. Follow the rules of Hopscotch (p. 265), except hop on inside feet in squares 1, 4, 7, and 10, and on outside feet in the other squares. Use one puck between partners and modify any other rule to accommodate Doubles Hopscotch.

Suggestions and Variations
1. Change methods of holding, moving, and throwing the puck.
2. Adapt Doubles Hopscotch to other games such as Marbles, and Jacks.
3. Change partners after every game.

Table 17.1 Cooperative Games

Name of game	Number of players	Developmental level			Main cooperative elements						Page
		I	II	III	Fun	Cooperation	Equality	Participation	Success	Trust	
Doubles Hopscotch	2	→			X	X	—	—	—	X	295
Perpetual Motion Machine	3–4		→		X	X	—	X	—	—	296
Recycled Snake Skins	4		→		X	X	X	—	—	—	296
Juggle a Number	5		→		X	X	X	—	—	X	296
Twister	5–6		→		X	X	X	X	—	—	296
Eight-Legged Caterpillar	class		→		—	X	—	X	—	X	297
Modified Musical Chairs	class		→		X	X	X	X	—	X	297
Pass-a-Person	class		→		—	X	—	X	—	X	298
Tug-o-Peace	class		→		X	X	X	X	—	—	298
Co-op Tag	class		→		X	X	—	X	—	—	298
Airplanes	5			→	X	X	—	—	—	X	298
Cross-Over Blanket Volleyball	12–14			→	X	X	X	X	—	—	298
Nine-Person Skip	11			→	—	X	—	—	—	X	298

cooperative games

Perpetual Motion Machine (Levels II, III)

This game should start with about three or four players. Add more players as their timing and cooperative behavior improve. To begin, the first player starts to move in any way and in any direction. The second player joins on behind and copies the exact motions of the first player. Repeat with each remaining player (figure 17.3).

Suggestions and Variations
1. As soon as the class understands the nature of the game, add the following variation. The first player starts as usual; the second player attaches, copying the movements of the first player, and adds a new movement. Continue with each player adding a new movement.
2. Repeat variation 1, keeping in time to a musical accompaniment.
3. Change the leader after each game.
4. Repeat game with a beanbag on each person's head. If any player drops the beanbag, the game starts over.
5. Add small equipment, such as hoops, balls, or wands, to the game.

Figure 17.3 Perpetual motion machine.

Recycled Snake Skins (Levels II, III)

This modified version of Skin the Snake is played with the following variations. Four players per team stand and place left hands back through legs and grasp right hands of teammates. Keeping grip, all players lie down. As soon as all players on a team are lying down, the player at the front of the team releases his grip and runs to find a new group of "threes." Taking the front position, he signals the rear player to stand and move forward. The game continues until there is a complete change, or "a new skin."

Juggle a Number (Levels II, III)

Begin with five players in a circle formation. Number each player in a random fashion rather than sequentially around the circle. Place five balls behind player 1. Player 1 throws a ball to 2, 2 to 3, and so forth until the ball is returned to player 1. Repeat two or three times, or until all players know the rotation pattern. Members of each group decide how many balls they can keep moving, then player 1 starts throwing the first ball to player 2, and then picks up a second ball and repeats until the selected number of balls are all moving from player to player. If a ball drops, any player may pick it up and try to get it back into the throwing sequence.

Suggestions and Variations
1. Have each group try to keep all five balls moving.
2. Play same game, but with players using one hand.
3. Play the game with a balloon instead of a ball and have each player keep a beanbag on her head, elbow, or lower back.

Twister (Levels II, III)

Begin with five or six players in a circle formation. Each player joins each hand with a different person. When all hands are joined, the group tries to untwist itself without letting go of any handgrip (figure 17.4).

Suggestions and Variations
1. Start with three players, then gradually increase the number.
2. Play same game, but with each player balancing a beanbag on his head.

Figure 17.4 Twister.

Eight-Legged Caterpillar (Levels II, III)

This game illustrates how a competitive relay (caterpillar race) can be changed into a cooperative activity. Arrange class into partners. One player stands behind the other, bends forward, and grasps the ankles of her partner. On signal (voice or musical), all partners move in a caterpillarlike fashion (figure 17.5). When the teacher calls "fours," two partners join and keep moving like a caterpillar. Continue to "eight" or "ten," then start over.

Suggestions and Variations
1. Play same game in wicket or crab walk positions.
2. Start with partners of the same sex. When you call fours, sixes, and so on, each new set added must be of the opposite sex.

Figure 17.5 Eight-legged caterpillar.

Modified Musical Chairs (Levels, II, III)

This game is played like Musical Chairs, except no one is eliminated. Start with the whole class and fifteen chairs. When the music stops, players rush to sit down. Instead of eliminating the remaining players, they sit on the knees of seated players, placing their own knees together so that the next players can sit down. Start music again, remove one or more chairs, and continue playing until one chair remains. Allow children to use their hands to help balance other players.

Suggestions and Variations
1. Aerial Musical Hoops. Start with every player in a "hula-hoop" position. Say "go" and everyone runs. When you call "twos," players join up in twos and keep moving. When you call "fours," all join up in fours and continue moving. Continue to eight, then start the game over (figure 17.6).

2. Floor Musical Hoops. Similar to variation 1, except everyone places his hoop on the floor. Start music, all run, remove three hoops, and stop music. Everyone runs and stands inside a hoop. Instead of eliminating players, any number of players may stand inside a hoop. Continue playing music and removing hoops. Game gets very exciting and fun when only two or three hoops remain (figure 17.7).

Figure 17.6 Aerial musical hoops.

Figure 17.7 Floor musical hoops.

Pass-a-Person (Levels II, III)

Divide class into two groups. Two groups lie on their backs, with heads touching and arms extending upward. One player starts from one end and is moved to opposite end of line. The next player stands up and repeats action. As each player finishes, she joins the end of the line.

Suggestions and Variations

Roll a person. All class members lie side by side, facing downward. One player lies across the backs of players, then all players begin to roll toward the opposite end. As each player is rolled "off," she joins the end of the "rolling line."

Tug-o-Peace (Levels II, III)

Begin with class members standing equal distance apart along the side of a rope. Class members count off in "twos," then turn and face each other. On signal "pull," 1s pull against 2s—usually with no winner, but a lot of fun.

Suggestions and Variations

1. Arrange class in the same fashion as the first game, except have an extra 1 and 2 player stand next to their own teammates. On signal, extra players tickle the opposing player, who is attempting to pull.
2. "Ones" face "twos" and sit. On signal "pull," each pulls and stands up.

Co-op Tag (Levels II, III)

The following co-op tag games are similar to other tag activities, except a player is safe when involved in a designated type of cooperative behavior.

1. Back-to-Back Tag. One person designated as "it" tries to tag the other players, who run to avoid him. A player is safe when in a back-to-back position with another player. Back-to-back players keep moving, and then separate after five seconds.
2. Elbow-Linked Tag. Same as variation 1, except players are safe when they link elbows.
3. Hug Tag. Same as variation 1, except players are safe when they are hugging. Set special rules, such as "partners may hug for a maximum of five seconds," "fours for seven seconds," "sixes for eight seconds," and so forth. Let players keep their own count.
4. Ball Balance Tag. Arrange class into partners. Partners hold a ball (utility or Nerf) between their heads, sides, backs, or any other specified part of their bodies. Designate one set of partners to be "it." All, including "it" partners, move in the designated contact position.

Airplanes (Level III)

Arrange groups of five players behind a starting line. One player in each group lies face down with arms and legs stretched sideways. The four carriers grasp the "airplane's" elbows and ankles and carry him to a turning line then back to the starting line. Repeat for each player on the team.

Suggestions and Variations

1. Since this is not a relay race, team members carry their airplane back and forth at their own speed.
2. Do not play this game on rough gravel or other dangerous surfaces.
3. For safety, have the airplane land first with feet, then hands.

Cross-Over Blanket Volleyball (Level III)

Arrange two teams of six or seven players on each side of a volleyball net (rope will do). Each team holds a blanket, keeping the net side open. One team starts with the ball on the blanket and tries to flip it over the net to the other team. As soon as the ball leaves the blanket, one player from the "sending team" crosses under the net and joins the other team. Receiving team tries to catch the ball in the blanket and return it to the other team. Each time the ball is returned, a player crosses under the net. One "collective" point is awarded to the group each time the ball crosses over the net and is successfully caught (figure 17.8).

Suggestions and Variations

1. Try same game with two or three players crossing under the net after each toss.
2. Play same game with different types and sizes of balls.
3. Play same game with two or more balls—all balls must be tossed together.

Figure 17.8 Cross-over blanket volleyball.

Nine-Person Skip (Level III)

Three to nine players stand next to a rope. On signal, outside players turn the rope and all players jump rope.

Suggestions and Variations

1. Start game with three or four players, then gradually increase the number.
2. Have each jumper enter one by one.
3. Have jumpers hold or bounce a ball.

Name of activity	Developmental level			Page
	I	II	III	
Partner Rope Skipping			→	489
Partner Balance Stunts	→			451
Leap Frog	→			438
Wheelbarrow	→			439
Elephant Walk	→			443
Chinese Get-Up	→			440
Twister	→			443
Pig Walk		→		444
Partner and Group Pyramid		→		464
Wand Activities		→		493
Juggling Activities		→		500
Rhythmic Activities		→		539
Creative Folk Dance Activities		→		552

Numerous cooperative activities are included in the gymnastic and dance sections of this book. The activities in the above table include cooperative movements between partners, small groups, or the whole class. Many of these activities can be incorporated into a variety of cooperative games.

Cooperative Games Created by Children

The process used in guiding children to create their own cooperative games is a simple extension of the approach used when teaching creative games. To illustrate, the first four columns of table 17.2 are used to set limitations for children to create their own games. Hence, if we pose a challenge, such as "make up a game with your partner, in your own space, using one ball and two hoops and a dribble," children may or may not create a cooperative game. Their game might become a dribbling contest around the hoops or a cooperative game, such as dribbling and passing as they each dribble around their own hoop. By adding the fifth column, "cooperative elements," we lead children to develop a creative game that possesses one or more of the elements of fun, cooperation, equality, participation, success, and trust.

There is one general comment we have received from numerous teachers who have used the cooperative games approach. They have consistently found if children do not understand the meaning of these elements, there is, in almost every instance, little chance of a cooperative game being produced. Hence, before posing any challenge involving one or more of these elements, teach the children the meaning of these words. This can be accomplished by discussing each element in class and by illustrating them by playing several cooperative games, such as Cross-Over Blanket Volleyball or Modified Musical Chairs.

When children understand these terms, pose a cooperative game challenge that stresses one or more of the cooperative elements listed in the last column. The following are cooperative games children created after the challenge described under each game was presented to them. Each game usually stresses nearly all six cooperative elements. The important aspect of the challenge is to get children to think consciously about one or two key cooperative elements and to stress them in their game.

Several of the games listed in table 17.3 were invented by children in other countries. These games are examples of more than 1,000 games one of the authors received as part of an international game exchange project. In the forty-six countries that participated in this study, all children, regardless of geographical area or cultural background, were capable of creating cooperative games. Many games arising from the same challenges were remarkably similar from country to country. The only major difference in these games was the type and amount of equipment that was used in each geographical location.

Table 17.2 Elements of a Cooperative Game

Game elements				Cooperative elements
Players	*Space*	*Equipment*	*Skills and rules*	
From two to all class members	From limited to all available space	From no equipment to many types and pieces of equipment	From no required skills and rules to many skills and rules	Fun, cooperation, equality, participation, success, and trust

Table 17.3   New Cooperative Games Invented by Children

Name of game	Country	Type of game	Developmental level			Main cooperative elements						Page
			I	II	III	Fun	Cooperation	Equality	Participation	Success	Trust	
Passing in the Square	Israel	Ball	⟶			X	X	X	—	X	—	300
Give And Take	Zimbabwe	Manipulation	⟶			—	X	X	X	X	—	300
Stick Exchange	Japan	Manipulation		⟶		X	X	X	—	—	X	301
Tallia	Greece	Ball		⟶		—	—	X	X	X	X	301
Blind Flight	Luxembourg	Manipulation			⟶	—	X	X	X	X	X	302
Geometry Class	Argentina	Manipulation			⟶	—	X	X	X	X	X	302
Jump Ball	Botswana	Ball			⟶	X	X	X	X	—	—	302
Clock	Czechoslovakia	Ball			⟶	X	X	X	X	—	—	302
Paga-Ajuda	Brazil	Tag			⟶	X	—	X	X	X	—	303

Passing in the Square (Israel) (Levels I, II)

Challenge   See if you can make up a game with four players, using two balloons, two nylon balls, and four plastic strips (approximately four feet long). Your game must involve the *cooperation* of all players.

The children build a square with the four plastic strips. Each player stands on one corner holding a balloon or nylon ball (figure 17.9). Player number 1 calls out the name of another player and throws her ball up into the center of the square. The child whose name was called must quickly call another player's name, throw her balloon into the center, then try to catch player number 1's ball. If a ball is dropped or goes out of reach, everyone stops and returns to the starting position. The game continues until all four names are called out. Player number 2 begins the next game.

Figure 17.9   Passing in the square.

Give And Take (Zimbabwe) (Levels I, II)

Challenge   Make up a game that involves ten children per group. Each player must have a ball (or some small object). Players must pass their balls at the same moment so that, at any time, each player is passing and receiving a ball.

Ten players form a circle, kneel, and hold the ball in their right hand (figure 17.10). On signal from a player, all players pass the ball along the ground and in front of the player on his right side. As the ball is passed, all players call out "one." Passing and counting continues until the group calls out "ten." Repeat game in the opposite direction.

Figure 17.10   Give and take.

Figure 17.11 Stick exchange.

Stick Exchange (Japan) (Levels II, III)

Challenge Can you design a cooperative game with your partner using any available equipment? Your game must stress that each player has an *equal role* in the game and must, in some way, place *trust* in the other player.

Two players assume a crawling position and face each other. One player places a stick on his right shoulder while the other places the other end on his left shoulder. Without using their hands, they try to help each other move the stick to their other shoulder while gradually shifting to a standing position (figure 17.11). After reaching a standing position, they try to reverse directions and return the stick to the original position. If either player uses his hands or if the stick drops off either player's shoulder, they must start over from the beginning.

Tallia (Greece) (Levels II, III)

Challenge See if you can make up a game for the whole class, using all the available space and no equipment. Your game must stress *participation* and *equality*.

Arrange the class into groups of twelve players. One half of each group forms a line and the first player holds onto a tree or other stable object (figure 17.12). Each player then places his head between the legs of the player directly in front of him. The remaining six players climb on their backs and stay there until the leader counts to a certain number. If the six players stay on for the full count, they score one point. If any player touches the ground during the counting, they start over. Reverse roles and repeat the game.

Figure 17.12 Tallia.

cooperative games

Blind Flight (Luxembourg) (Levels II, III)

Challenge See if you can make up a game for ten players, using all the available space and equipment. Your game must *stress equality, participation, success,* and *trust.*

The first nine players hold the rope at the sides of their bodies, then place a paper bag over their heads. The last player (guide) arranges the four traffic cones, comes back to his group, and teaches it three nonverbal commands (figure 17.13). These are (1) "pull right," meaning front player turns right; (2) "pull left," meaning front player turns left; and (3) "pull on both," meaning front player moves straight ahead. The guide then tries to lead the group to the first traffic cone. When the front player touches the first traffic cone, he places the cone in another spot, then exchanges positions with the guide. The old guide takes the paper bag and moves to the back of the group to become the last player. The group continues to the next cone, changes players, and continues this pattern to the last player.

Figure 17.13 Blind flight.

Geometry Class (Argentina) (Levels II, III)

Challenge See if you can make up a game for the whole class, using all of the available space and no equipment. Your game must stress *participation* and *equality.*

Form geometrical shapes with groups of children. Divide the class into two teams. Each team writes the names of five different shapes on separate pieces of paper and places them face down in the middle of the playing area. By turns, one member from each team selects one piece of paper and announces the geometric shape they have to form. The other team tries to guess the name of the shape before they exchange positions (figure 17.14).

Figure 17.14 Geometry class.

Jump Ball (Botswana) (Levels II, III)

Challenge Can you make up a game with three players, one ball, and a drop and a catch?

Three players stand in a straight line. Player 1 bounces the ball in front of player 2. As soon as the ball leaves player 1's hands, players 1 and 2 exchange positions, while player 3 catches the ball. Player 3 returns to his original position, then bounces the ball in front of player 1, who is now in the middle position (figure 17.15). The game continues for five or six rotations.

Figure 17.15 Jump ball.

Clock (Czechoslovakia) (Levels II, III)

Challenge Develop a game where you divide the class into four equal groups. Each group has one ball and each player must move according to some rule. The game should also stress *fun, equality,* and *cooperation* (figure 17.16).

Figure 17.16 The clock.

Figure 17.17 Movement of the clock.

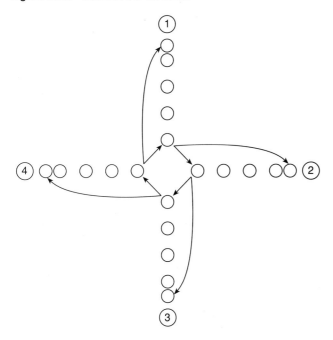

Figure 17.19 Children's drawing of "Paga-ajuda."

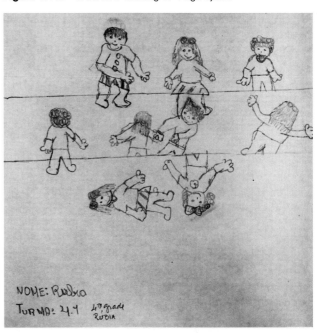

Arrange the four groups as shown in figure 17.17. The first player in each group holds the ball in both hands. When the teacher says, "Go," the first player in each group passes the ball clockwise, then moves clockwise to the back of the next line. The game continues until all players return to their starting positions.

Paga-Ajuda (Tag and Help) (Brazil) (Levels II, III)

Challenge   Invent a new tag game for the whole class using all the available space and no equipment. Your game must stress *participation* and *equality* (figure 17.18).

One player is chosen to be "it" and all other players scatter in the playing area. On signal from the teacher, "it" tries to tag another player. When a player is tagged, she holds "its" hand and both try to tag another player. As each player is tagged, he holds on to the last player until every player is tagged (figure 17.19).

Figure 17.18   Paga-ajuda.

Using Cooperative Games to Teach Academic Concepts and Skills

The cooperative games listed in table 17.4 are used to teach a variety of academic concepts and skills. They are used in a similar way to the running, tag, and simple team games described in chapter 16. However, since these games also stress one or more elements of cooperative behavior, they provide effective avenues for children to share in the solution of academic problems. They also provide a noncompetitive learning environment in which children with different levels of academic ability or with physical disabilities can be integrated with high achievers and nondisabled children.

Using Cooperative Game Challenges to Teach Academic Concepts and Skills

In chapter 16, several examples were provided to illustrate how inventive games are used to teach a wide variety of academic concepts and skills. The examples that follow represent a simple but important extension of this approach, in that it adds one or more cooperative elements to the inventive game challenge.

Involving children in cooperative learning tasks has academic and social value. For example, it provides an effective medium through which children learn to share in the solution of a problem. A collective answer can, in many instances, be more exciting and enriching than an individual's response to the same task. And, when specific cooperative elements, such as cooperation and trust, are added to the challenge, cooperative behavior becomes a mandatory dimension of the game.

Table 17.4 Cooperative Games Stressing Academic Concepts

Name of game	Number of players	Developmental level			Academic concepts and skills	Page
		I	*II*	*III*		
Doubles Hopscotch	2	X	X		Sets of two, one less than	295
Juggle A Number	5	—	X	X	Adding, subtracting, dividing	296
Cross-Over Blanket Volleyball	12	—	—	X	Adding	298
Nine-Person Skip	11	—	—	X	Adding, subtracting, dividing	298
Eight-Legged Caterpillar	8	—	X	X	Sets of two or more	297
Modified Musical Chairs	Class	—	X	X	Subtracting	297
Co-op Tag	Class	—	X	X	Sets	298
Tug-o-Peace	Class	—	X	X	Force	298
Geometry Class	Class	—	X	X	Geometry shapes	302

The next three challenges illustrate how to gradually progress from a simple inventive game challenge to the addition of one or more elements of cooperative behavior. Similar sets of challenges could be designed to enhance academic concepts and skills in langauge arts, science, and other academic subjects.

Challenge No. 1: Counting, Partners, and No Equipment

Challenge no. 1 is the beginning of a set of three tasks involving partners, without any equipment, and requiring a fairly structured series of movements. No mention is made of the use of space; hence, partners can decide for themselves whether to stay in one location or to make up a game using all the available space. It should also be noted that this challenge lays the groundwork for the next two tasks, which involve cooperative elements described earlier in this chapter.

> **Challenge** Can you make up a counting game with your partner where you face each other, stand side by side, and in one other position you make up yourself?

Challenge No. 2: Counting, Partners, Equipment, and Trust

In challenge no. 2, the addition of two pieces of equipment has a general influence on the nature of the game the two players will create. For example, the ball was included to help players find a medium for counting. The wand was added to encourage some form of trust to develop between the two players. This could be one player holding or moving the wand while the other player bounced the ball under, over, or around the wand. The last sentence in the challenge makes the cooperative element of trust a requirement rather than an incidental aspect of the game.

> **Challenge** Is it possible to invent a game with your partner using one ball and one wand? Somewhere in your game you must trust your partner to do something with the wand.

Challenge No. 3: Counting, Partners, More Equipment, and Cooperation

There is a subtle attempt in challenge no. 3 to guide players to work together. This is accomplished by asking them to exchange balls and to keep one score between the two players. Partners may decide to throw the ball into the air, and hold and maneuver it in various ways. The choice, however, is theirs.

> **Challenge** Design a counting game with your partner using two balls and one rope. Somewhere in your game you must exchange balls. Also, just keep one score between the two of you.

The process of teaching cooperative games as outlined in this chapter should be considered a flexible guideline. This approach is successful when challenges begin with two or three players and involve one or two cooperative elements. Gradually increase the size of the group and add more elements as children demonstrate an understanding and acceptance of these elements of cooperative behavior.

Selected References

Fluegelman, A. (1981). *More New Games*. New York: Doubleday and Co., Inc.

Kirchner, G. (1991). *Children's Games from Around the World*. Dubuque, IA: Wm. C. Brown Publishers.

Morris, D. (1976). *How to Change the Games Children Play*. Minneapolis: Burgess Publishing Co.

Orlick, T. (1982). *The Second Cooperative Games Book*. New York: Pantheon Books.

18

Soccer Activities

Of all the major sports played in the United States and Canada, soccer has shown the most rapid increase in participation in recent years. It requires a great deal of skill in kicking, running, and dribbling. However, it is an inexpensive sport—only requiring a ball and two goalposts—and involves total body movement, making it an excellent activity for upper elementary children. Furthermore, only a few basic skills and rules need to be learned to enjoy the game.

This chapter provides sufficient information to develop a major soccer unit. The central purpose is to give children an opportunity to acquire the basic soccer skills, rules, and playing strategies through as many enjoyable, gamelike situations as possible. Modification of practice activities and lead-up games, coupled with the application of the inventive games approach, should be the rule rather than the exception when teaching soccer ∎

Emphasis and Progression

Children have usually learned to kick a stationary or moving ball by the end of third grade. Their ability to stop the ball is normally limited to a simple foot or leg trap. They understand dribbling but are not very proficient at it, as they tend to use their toes and to "kick and chase."

As outlined in table 18.1, a systematic presentation of the basic soccer skills and rules should begin in fourth grade. These children should learn to kick and pass with either foot, to control the ball with the side of the foot, and to increase their control while dribbling. A few of the basic rules relating to kicking, handling the ball, and checking should also be introduced in this grade. Lead-up games, such as Circle

Table 18.1 Suggested Sequence of Presenting Soccer Skills and Rules

	Developmental level II	Developmental level III
Kicking		
Instep Kick	Pass with either foot	Increase distance and accuracy
Inside-of-Foot Kick	Pass with either foot	Increase distance and accuracy
Outside-of-Foot Kick	Introduce	Increase distance and accuracy
Punting		Introduce
Volley Kick		Introduce
Rules: Kickoff	Introduce	
Free Kick		Introduce
Corner Kick	Introduce	
Goal Kick	Introduce	
Penalty Kick		Introduce
Trapping		
Foot Trap	Acquired or introduce	Refine
Side-of-Foot Trap	Introduce	Refine
Leg Trap		Introduce
Body Trap		Introduce
Rules: Handling the Ball	Introduce	
Dribbling		
Inside of Feet	Acquired or introduce	Increase accuracy and speed
Outside of Feet	Acquired or introduce	Increase accuracy and speed
Heading		
Stationary Heading		Introduce
Feet Off Ground		Introduce
Throw-in		
From Behind Head	Introduce	Increase distance and accuracy
Rules: Throw-in	Introduce	
Tackling		
With Feet	Introduce	Refine
Rules: Charging	Introduce	
Other rules		
Team Positions	Introduce	
Goalkeeper Privileges		Introduce
Rules: Offside		Introduce

30-Minute Lesson

10–15%	15–80%	2–5%
3–5 minutes	5–20 minutes	1–3 minutes
Introductory Activities	*Skill Development*	*Closure*
Vigorous running, dodging, and conditioning exercises	Demonstrations Individual practice Partner and practice activities Exploratory activities Lead-up games modified or official game of soccer	Review and cool down

Soccer and Soccer Dodgeball, should be emphasized, rather than playing the official game or a modified version.

Throughout fifth grade, improved passing, trapping, and dribbling skills should be emphasized. After these basic skills are acquired, the children should be introduced to a few of the more specialized kicking skills, the side-of-leg trap, and heading the ball. More advanced lead-up games, such as Forwards and Backs and Mini- or Seven-Person Soccer with more specific rules and playing positions, are also indicated.

Although children in this age group should play mini- or eleven-person soccer, their skill level still calls for a lot of individual and small-group practice and lead-up activities. Therefore, balancing the time spent on these two types of activities with the regulation soccer game is very important. Minisoccer, which uses half the field, is also more desirable for the intramural program than the official eleven-person game because it allows more children to participate.

Teaching Procedures

The general instructional procedures discussed in previous chapters also apply to teaching soccer activities. Of particular importance are the development of a unit of instruction discussed on pages 101–106 and the illustrated lessons on page 107. In addition, the inventive games approach (p. 252) can be applied successfully when teaching soccer and all other team game activities.

Developing a Soccer Unit

Since each teaching situation varies according to the length of the unit and lesson and the available facilities and equipment, the following approach should be considered as only a basic guideline. Soccer is a relatively new sport to many teachers and children, so this outline should be modified to meet each situation.

Step 1: Determine the length of the unit. Since a class may have from one to five physical education lessons a week, the units should be expressed in terms of the number of lessons.

Step 2: Assess the class's level of ability. The evaluative techniques at the end of this chapter can be used. Having the class play one or two lead-up games also provides an overview of its ability.

Step 3: List sequentially the skills, rules, and playing strategies that will be emphasized.

Step 4: Choose the appropriate practice activities and lead-up games. Later in this chapter, the practice activities, listed by skill, are organized into individual, partner, and group activities. The lead-up games are appropriate for developmental levels II and III.

Structure of a Lesson

The following approach is a basic guideline for planning and teaching a lesson. Each lesson should include a vigorous introductory activity that is related to the general theme of the lesson. The second part of the lesson should be devoted to acquiring and practicing one or more skills and playing a variety of lead-up games. Finally, closure allows time to review the key points of the lesson and to relax.

Adjust shorter or longer lessons on the basis of time allocation. Introductory activities and closure should always be included in each lesson. The length of time devoted to part two of the lesson depends on the stage of development of the unit and the ability of the students.

Each soccer lesson should begin with running, dodging, and general conditioning activities to increase the children's cardiorespiratory endurance and to prepare them for the next part of the lesson. During the first few lessons, the demonstration and practice activities should be given a considerable amount of time in order to introduce and practice skills and playing strategies. After a skill is explained and demonstrated, each child should have an opportunity to practice it without excessive pressure and to test and explore other ways of performing a movement pattern. Once the children understand the skill and can perform it, they should practice with partners. Since most classes are coeducational, partner activities are an excellent way to cope with varying levels of ability and to mix boys and girls subtly.

Partner activities also provide a springboard for introducing inventive games. For example, in lessons emphasizing passing and trapping, partners can be challenged to "make up a game with your partner that involves a pass and a trap . . . and a hoop" (or any other piece of small equipment). Refer to chapter 26 for more ideas. The more structured practice activities that are used in this part of the lesson can be presented initially in a more formal or direct manner. After the class has practiced the activity, the teacher can introduce variations by presenting simple challenges to each group. For example, if the class is practicing the game Keep Away, a challenge, such as "see if you can play the same game but add a hoop" (or three beanbags), gives each group a chance to create a new version of the game.

During the latter phase of part two, lead-up games provide a low-key means of practicing skills in a gamelike situation. Playing space should be used to maximum capacity. Divide the playing field into halves or quarters so that two or four games can be played. The inventive games approach also works extremely well with lead-up games. Limit these games in a small way at first; later, challenge each group to design its own game or to choose any equipment it wants. This will open the door to many new and exciting soccertype games. Use closure to emphasize one or two key points of your lesson and to provide praise and constructive comments.

As the soccer unit progresses, more time should be devoted to lead-up and modified games and less time to practice activities. Group activities should include a wide variety of lead-up games, inventive games, and to a lesser degree mini- or official soccer. The more competitive aspects of soccer and other team games should be reserved for the junior and senior high school physical education program.

The following suggestions can also help in developing a safe and effective program of activities:

1. Limit the playing field to a small, manageable instructional area. Mark off a 100-foot square section of the field with traffic cones or milk cartons (p. 250) for demonstrations and practice activities. Enlarge the area as needed.

2. Soccer requires a great deal of endurance, particularly of the heart and lungs and the leg muscles. Increase running and other endurance activities gradually and systematically. Watch for overfatigued children and switch them to less demanding positions.

3. Although soccer rules do not allow any players except the goalie to use their hands, adjustments should be made for the children's safety. They should be taught to protect their faces against oncoming balls, and, in addition, girls should be instructed to fold their arms across their chests to prevent injury.

4. One of the cardinal principles of good teaching is total participation by all children. Whenever possible, keep each team small and divide the playing area so two or more games can be played.

Description of Skills

Soccer is basically a kicking and running game; however, when played correctly, such skills as dribbling, trapping, heading, and throwing are also necessary for maximum success and enjoyment. Each of these skills will be described, along with the more common faults to observe and correct.

Kicking

In soccer, the ball may be kicked with either foot from a stationary, running, or volley (while in the air) position. Certain fundamentals should be stressed in every practice and game situation. First, players should keep their eye on the ball as it approaches them or as they approach the ball. Second, players should kick the ball with their instep (top side of the foot)—never with their toes. Finally, after the ball has been kicked, players should follow through with their

Figure 18.1 Instep kick.

kicking foot for a short distance in the direction of the kick. Each of these fundamentals applies to the following five basic kicking skills.

Instep Kick

The instep kick (figure 18.1), used for passing and for shooting at the goal, is the most common skill in soccer. Just before the ball is kicked, the nonkicking foot is slightly flexed and even with the ball. The head and trunk lean slightly forward, with the arms extended sideways, and the kicking leg is well back, with the knee slightly bent (figure 18.1a). As the kicking leg moves downward and forward, the knee moves forward and over the ball. The ankle extends downward to allow the top of the instep to contact the ball (figure 18.1b). Follow through by continuing the forward movement of the kicking leg (figure 18.1c).

Key Teaching Points

1. Look at the target, then at the ball.
2. Keep toe of kicking foot pointing down.
3. Contact center of ball with instep.
4. Use arms to maintain balance.
5. Follow through with an upward swing of the leg.

Inside-of-Foot Kick

This is a variation of the instep kick and is used for short, accurate passes or for shooting at the goal (figure 18.2). The body is bent slightly forward, with the weight evenly distributed on both feet. The front of the ball should be even with the toes and about six inches to the side of the kicking foot. Shift weight to the nonkicking foot and swing the kicking foot outward, with knee slightly bent (figure 18.2a). Swing the foot down and toward the ball, contacting it with the inside of the foot (figure 18.2b). Follow through with the kicking foot crossing in front of the opposite leg (figure 18.2c).

Figure 18.2 Kicking with inside of foot.

a   b   c

Key Teaching Points

1. Look at the target, then at the ball.
2. Keep a slight forward body lean throughout the kicking action.
3. Turn the toe of the kicking foot outward to allow inside of foot to contact the ball.
4. Follow through upward and in front of the opposite leg.

Outside-of-Foot Kick

This kick requires a pushing or jabbing action with the outer part of the foot. It is used for short passes or dribbling without breaking the running movement. The player stands slightly to the side of the ball. Bend the nonkicking leg and shift weight onto it (figure 18.3a). Bend knee of kicking leg with toe pointing down, then swing leg toward the ball (figure 18.3b). Contact the ball with the outer edge of the foot and follow through in the direction of the kick (figure 18.3c).

Key Teaching Points

1. Begin with the body at a slight angle to the ball.
2. Look at the target, then at the ball.
3. Snap the lower leg quickly to the side contacting the ball with the outside edge of the foot.
4. Follow through in the direction of the ball.

Figure 18.3 Kicking with outside of foot.

a   b   c

Volley Kick

The volley is performed when the ball is in flight. This is a difficult kick, so elementary school children should not be expected to do it with a high degree of accuracy. However, because this kick is a time-saver and because it generates much force, children will attempt to perform it. The player stands with the nonkicking foot in front and weight evenly distributed on both feet. The head and body face the ball and the body tilts forward slightly (figure 18.4a). As the ball approaches, the player shifts weight to the nonkicking foot and raises the kicking leg, with the knee slightly bent and the toes pointing down (figure 18.4b). The player contacts the ball with the top of the instep and follows through in a forward and upward direction (figure 18.4c).

Figure 18.4 Volley kick.

a   b   c

soccer activities

Figure 18.5   Punting.

a. Hold ball chest high.   b. Swing kicking leg forward.   c. Contact ball with top of foot.   d. Follow through to an extended leg position.

Key Teaching Points

1. Take a quick look at the target, then quickly focus on the oncoming ball.
2. Keep body lean slightly forward.
3. Contact the ball with instep and toe down.
4. Follow through in the direction of the ball.

Punting

The goalkeeper is the only player allowed to punt. The ball is held about chest high (figure 18.5a). The kicking leg swings forward and upward as the ball is dropped (figure 18.5b). As the leg moves in a forward and upward direction, the ball contacts the instep (figure 18.5c). Follow through into an extended leg position (figure 18.5d).

Key Teaching Points

1. Take a quick look at the target, then look at the ball.
2. Hold the ball with two hands.
3. Drop the ball, rather than throwing it downward.
4. Contact the ball high on the instep.
5. Follow through in the direction of the ball.

Trapping

Trapping is stopping the ball while it is moving through the air or on the ground. Any part of the body except the hands and arms may be used. The type of trap a player uses depends on the flight of the ball, the position of opponents, and the amount of time the trapper has. Upper elementary school children should be able to perform the following four trapping skills.

Figure 18.6   Front foot trap.

a   b

Front Foot Trap

The front foot trap is used to trap a rolling or bouncing ball. As the ball approaches, the player raises her foot about six inches off the ground, with her toes up, forming a **V** between the ground and the sole of the foot (figure 18.6a). When the ball contacts the sole, the foot relaxes to let the ball lose its recoil action and remain beneath the foot (figure 18.6b).

Key Teaching Points

1. Keep eyes on the ball.
2. Move into position and directly face the oncoming ball.
3. Raise leg from the hip, keeping knee slightly bent.
4. As the ball is contacted, apply pressure to the top of the ball.

Figure 18.7 Side-of-foot trap. The foot gives slightly.

Side-of-Foot Trap

The side-of-foot trap is used in the same manner as the front foot trap; the main difference is the direction from which the ball approaches. The player raises her trapping leg four to five inches off the ground, with the inside of the foot toward the ball. As the ball strikes, the foot relaxes to absorb the force of the ball, allowing it to drop rather than to recoil forward (figure 18.7).

Key Teaching Points

1. Keep eyes on the ball.
2. Move into position and directly face the oncoming ball.
3. Lean the body in the direction of the oncoming ball.
4. When the ball contacts the inside of the foot, allow the foot to move slightly backward to slow down the ball.

Leg Trap

The leg trap is used when the ball is approaching from a high volley or a low bounce. As the ball approaches, the player shifts his weight to the nontrapping foot nearest the oncoming ball. His trapping leg bends at almost a right angle and his foot is well off the ground (figure 18.8a). When the ball makes contact, the leg gives a little to prevent the ball from rebounding too far forward (figure 18.8b).

Key Teaching Points

1. Keep eyes on the ball.
2. Move into position and directly face the oncoming ball.
3. Contact the ball halfway between knee and hip.
4. When the ball contacts the thigh, draw the leg back to allow ball to drop to the ground.

Body Trap

The body trap is used when the ball is descending from a high volley or when a player wants to prevent a high-rising ball from getting past him. To perform this type of trap, the player brings arms forward but does not touch the ball with his hands or arms. Legs should be shoulder-width apart, with knees slightly bent. Lean backward, tuck chin in, and contact ball on the chest (figure 18.9a). As the ball

Figure 18.8 Leg trap.

a   b

Figure 18.9 Body trap.

a   b

contacts the chest, draw slightly back to allow the ball to drop to the ground (figure 18.9b). Girls should fold their arms across the chest and press elbows snugly against the body when attempting this trapping skill (figure 18.10).

Key Teaching Points

1. Keep eyes on the ball.
2. Move into position and directly face the oncoming ball.
3. Give with the ball as it contacts the chest.

Figure 18.10 Chest protected body trap.

Dribbling

Dribbling in soccer is moving the ball with short pushes by the inside or outside of either foot. These pushes permit the player to control the ball, whether dribbling forward or sideward. Although dribbling with the inside of the foot is quite easy, good ball control requires use of the outside of either foot. Dribbling backward is bad practice, as it only helps the opponent.

The body should be bent forward slightly, with the head over the ball. Gently push or "persuade" the ball, keeping the head up high enough to make an offensive move and to watch oncoming opponents (figure 18.11).

Figure 18.11 Dribbling. Push, or "persuade," the ball.

a   b   c

Key Teaching Points

1. Dribble with short, controlled steps.
2. Keep the ball close to the feet when near opponents.
3. Keep looking around while dribbling to know where opponents and teammates are positioned.
4. Push, rather than kick, the ball.

Heading

Heading is hitting or bunting the soccer ball with the front of the forehead. As the ball approaches, the player bends her knees and leans back from the hips. Arms are raised, and slightly to the side (figure 18.12a). She then shifts her body weight forward and upward and brings her head forward to meet the ball (figure 18.12b). The ball must contact the front of the forehead, with a continuous forward movement of the body in the direction of the intended flight of the ball (figure 18.12c). The key to good heading lies in correctly judging the speed and height of the oncoming ball.

Key Teaching Points

1. Keep eyes on the ball.
2. Bend from the hips.
3. Just before contact, thrust the head and trunk forward.
4. Follow through in the direction of the ball.

Figure 18.12 Heading.

a   b   c

Throw-in

Whenever the ball goes over the sidelines, it is put back into play by a throw-in. The ball is thrown from behind the head with both hands. Parts of both feet remain on the ground until the ball leaves the player's hands, although any position of the feet is permissible. Begin with one foot in front of the other or with the feet parallel. Hold the ball with fingers at the side and thumbs behind (figure 18.13a). Simultaneously raise the ball up and behind the head, lean backward, and bend the knees (figure 18.13b). Shift the trunk forward and upward and bring the ball over the head, extending the arms toward the direction of the throw. Release the ball and follow through with hands and arms (figure 18.13c).

Figure 18.13 Throw-in.

a   b   c

Figure 18.14 Tackling.

a. Watch feet for clues.

b. Tackle when opponent is off balance.

Key Teaching Points

1. Keep both hands behind the ball.
2. Keep both feet in contact with the ground.
3. Make one move backward followed by one move forward.
4. Learn to follow through and step into the playing field.

Tackling

In soccer the team in possession of the ball is known as the *offensive,* or *attacking,* team. Any defensive player may legally tackle a player who has possession of the ball, but only from the front or side, with the feet or shoulders. Using the hands or tackling from behind is against the rules. When tackling, the defensive player watches the ball and the opponent's feet for clues to the direction she may take (figure 18.14a). The body weight should also be evenly distributed on both feet in order to shift right or left. The tackle should be made when the opponent is slightly off balance, which is just before she begins to dribble or pass the ball (figure 18.14b).

Key Teaching Points

1. Be quick and decisive when approaching an opponent who has possession of the ball.
2. Tackle the opponent when she is in control of the ball but is slightly off balance, usually when she pushes the ball forward a little.
3. Be ready to pass the ball as soon as you gain possession.

Goalkeeping

The primary responsibility of the goalkeeper is to keep the ball from crossing over the goal line and between the goalposts. To accomplish this task, the goalkeeper can catch or deflect the ball away from the goal.

The technique used to catch a ball depends on the location of the oncoming ball. The first move is to get in line with the oncoming ball (figure 18.15). Next, catch it with both hands and pull the ball toward the chest. When a ball is approaching along the ground, slightly flex the knees, bend forward and down, and place both hands behind the ball with fingers pointing down (figure 18.16). Scoop the ball upward into the arms and chest (figure 18.17). A ball approaching from below the waist should be caught with hands down similar to the stance position, then draw ball back into chest. For balls approaching above the waist, the arms are up, elbows sideways, and the ball is caught with the

Figure 18.15 Get in line with the oncoming ball.

Figure 18.16 Both hands behind the ball, with fingers pointing down.

Figure 18.17 Draw the ball into the chest.

Figure 18.18 Hands behind the ball.

hands behind the ball, fingers pointing up and thumbs close together (figure 18.18).

The technique used to deflect a ball that cannot be caught is a punch or push shot. The punch shot is made with clenched fists (figure 18.19) and players may hit the ball with one or both hands.

Figure 18.19 Punch shot.

Key Teaching Points

1. Keep the body between the goal and the ball.
2. Move out from the goal to cut down the angle of the approaching ball.
3. Watch the ball, not the player.
4. Keep fingers spread and always pull a caught ball toward the chest.

Practice Activities and Lead-Up Games

Table 18.2 includes practice activities and lead-up games for developmental levels II and III. As children move from level II to III, there should be an increase in their level of skill and general playing ability. The majority of practice activities relating to kicking and trapping skills involve two or more players. However, the few individual activities that follow give each child opportunities to get used to the bounce of the ball and to control the ball with the feet. Partner and small-group activities provide more realistic ball-handling situations including one or more skills. The procedure used to teach passing and trapping can also be followed when teaching dribbling skills. Begin with individual activities, add small equipment, move on to partner activities, and then perform group activities. Heading and throw-in skills are normally practiced together in partner or group activities. However, individual activities can be practiced if a wall is available. Tackling is normally practiced in combination with another skill, and two or more players are involved. The lead-up games in table 18.2 allow children to practice the skills learned in each section.

Table 18.2   Practice Activities and Lead-Up Games

Name of activity	Type of activity	Players	Developmental level		Soccer concepts and skills	Movement concepts	Page
			II	III			
Practice activities							
Throw, Bounce, Trap	Trap	Individual	———————➤		Throw, bounce, trap	Moving ball into space, use of space	316
Wall Kicking	Kick, trap	Individual	———————➤		Kick, trap	Use of space, change of of direction, strong and light	316
Juggle the Ball	Kick	Individual	———————➤		Kick	Strong and light, personal space	317
Individual Dribbling	Dribble, trap	Individual	———————➤		Dribble, trap	Moving into space, change of direction	317
Throw and Head	Throw, head	Individual	———————➤		Throw, head	Moving into space, change of direction	317
Stop, Go, Turn	Dribble, stop, turn	Individual	———————➤		Dribble, stop, turn	Moving into space, change of direction, pathway, and speed	317
Passing and Trapping	Pass, trap	2	———————➤		Pass, trap	Moving into space, changing direction and pathway	318
Wall Passing and Trapping	Pass, trap	2	———————➤		Pass, trap	Use of space, change of direction	318
Target Shooting	Pass, trap	2	———————➤		Pass, trap	Moving into space, change of direction and speed	318
Circle Passing	Pass, trap	2	———————➤		Pass, trap	Moving into space, change of direction and speed	318
Follow the Leader	Dribble	2	——————➤		Dribble	Moving into space, change of direction and pathway	318
Dribble and Pass	Dribble, pass, offensive play	2	——————➤		Dribble, pass	Moving into space, change of direction, pathway, and speed	319
Throw and Head	Throw, head	2	——————➤		Throw, head	Moving into space, change of direction, pathway, and speed	319
Partner Keep Away	Dribble, dodge, stop	2	——————➤		Dribble, dodge, stop	Moving into space, change of direction, pathway, and speed	319
Triangle Pass	Pass, trap	3	——————➤		Pass, trap	Change of direction	319
Kicking for Distance	Kick	4–5	——————➤		Kick	Moving into space, strong and light	319
Goal Kicking	Kick, trap	4–6	——————➤		Kick, trap	Moving into space	320
Goal Heading	Head, throw	4–6	——————➤		Head, throw	Moving into space, use of space, change of direction and speed	320
Shuttle Dribble and Tackle	Dribble, tackle	4	——————➤		Dribble, tackle	Moving through space, change of direction and speed	320
One vs. Two Players	Dribble, pass, tackle	3	——————➤		Dribble, pass, tackle	Moving into space, change of direction and speed	320

Table 18.2   *Continued*

Name of activity	Type of activity	Players	Developmental level		Soccer concepts and skills	Movement concepts	Page
			II	*III*			
Lead-up games							
Circle Soccer	Kick, trap	4 or 5 per team	——————————▶		Kick, trap	Personal space, moving into space	320
Soccer Dodgeball	Kick, trap	Class	——————————▶		Kick, trap	Moving into space, change of direction and speed	321
Boundary Ball	Kick, trap	20–30	——————————▶		Kick, trap	Moving into space, change of direction and speed	321
Change Soccer	All skills	6 per game	——————————▶		All soccer skills	Use of available space, change of direction, pathway, and speed	321
Marble Soccer	Shoot, trap	3–4 per game	——————————▶		Shoot, trap	Moving into space, strong and light	321
Circle of Fun	Dribble, shoot	6 per game	——————————▶		Dribble, pass, shoot, tackle	Moving through space, change of direction and speed	321
Punt Back	Kick, trap	4–20	——————————▶		Kick, trap	Use of available space, moving into space	322
Alley Soccer	Pass, trap, kick	20–24	——————————▶		Pass, trap, kick	Personal space, moving into space, change of direction and speed	322
Forwards and Backs	Pass, dribble, trap	20–24	——————————▶		Pass, dribble, trap	Personal space, moving into space, change of direction and speed	322
Four-Goal Soccer	All skills	8–10	——————————▶		All soccer skills	Use of available space, moving into space, change of direction and speed	322
Seven-Person Soccer	All skills	14	——————————▶		All soccer skills	Use of available space, moving into space, change of direction, pathway, and speed	323

Practice Activities

The following practice activities are arranged to allow students to progress from individual, to partner, to group activities.

Throw, Bounce, Trap

Motor skills   Throw, bounce, trap
Movement concepts   Moving into space, use of space
Players   Individual
Formation   Scattered
Playing area   Playground, gymnasium
Equipment   Ball

Each child has a ball (any inflated ball can be used) and finds his own space in the playing area. Have the child throw his ball into the air, allow it to bounce once, and then try to trap it with one foot. Add other limitations, such as trapping with the left foot, the side of the leg, or the chest.

Wall Kicking

Motor skills   Kick, trap
Movement concepts   Use of space, change of direction, strong and light
Players   Individual
Formation   Line
Playing area   Playground, gymnasium
Equipment   Ball

Arrange children in a line formation along available wall surface. Each player stands about six feet from the wall, kicks the ball to the wall, and retrieves his own rebound with a foot or leg trap.

Suggestions and Variations
1. Allow each child to kick the ball as it rebounds (no trap required).
2. Start several yards back from the ball, run up and kick it, and trap the rebound.
3. Start several yards back, dribble to a line, kick the ball to the wall, and trap the rebound.
4. Place a target on the wall (a circle or square) and repeat previous activities.
5. Repeat previous activities with the opposite foot.

Motor skills Kick
Movement concepts Strong and light, personal space
Players Individual
Formation Scattered
Playing area Playground, gymnasium
Equipment Soccer ball

Juggling a ball is not part of playing soccer; nevertheless, this is an excellent practice activity for a small space and for learning to control the ball. This practice activity should be introduced in steps. First, the player drops the ball toward his instep (figure 18.20). Then he softly kicks it back up and catches it. Next, he drops the ball onto the thigh (figure 18.21), rebounds it, and catches it. Then he repeats the drop to the instep, kicks the ball up two times, and catches it on the second kick. He repeats with the thigh. As skill improves, allow players to combine the kick with instep to thigh, to instep to other foot, to head then back to foot, and so on.

Figure 18.20 Drop ball toward the instep.

Figure 18.21 Drop ball onto the thigh.

Individual Dribbling

Motor skills Dribble, trap
Movement concepts Moving into space, change of direction
Players Individual
Formation Scattered
Playing area Playground, gymnasium
Equipment Soccer ball

Each child has a ball (any inflated ball) and finds her own space in the playing area. Allow children to dribble anywhere within the playing area, as long as they do not bump into other players.

Suggestions and Variations

1. Dribble and stop on whistle or voice command (figure 18.22).
2. Dribble in different directions on voice command (right, forward, left, right).
3. Dribble with the outside of the foot.
4. Give each player two or more pieces of small equipment (beanbags, hoops) and have her dribble around them.
5. Add other skills, such as dribbling, stopping, trapping, and then shooting at the wall.

Figure 18.22 Dribble and stop.

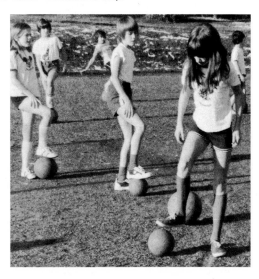

Throw and Head

Motor skills Throw, head
Movement concepts Moving into space, change of direction
Players Individual
Formation Scattered
Playing area Playground, gymnasium
Equipment Soccer ball

Each player has a ball and stands about five or six feet from the wall. Practice the throw-in, then do a throw-in and head the rebound back to the wall. Repeat the throw-in, then turn sideways and attempt to head the ball back to the wall.

Stop, Go, Turn

Motor skills Dribble, stop, turn
Movement concepts Moving into space, change of direction, pathway, and speed
Players Individual
Formation Scattered
Playing area Playground, gymnasium
Equipment Soccer balls

Mark off a square of about twenty by twenty yards. Every player has a ball. On "go" signal, all players dribble the ball in different directions, avoiding other players as they move through the playing area. On "stop" signal, players must stop the ball with their feet and be ready for the next signal. On "go" signal, they all start dribbling again. As they continue dribbling, the teacher calls, "Turn," signaling every player to turn in any direction in which there is space to move.

Suggestions and Variations

1. Change method of signaling by hand signals (hand overhead—"go," hand forward—"stop," hands sideways—"turn"). This requires all players to watch both ball and teacher as they move through space.
2. Add obstacles to the playing space.

Passing and Trapping

Motor skills Pass, trap
Movement concepts Moving into space, change of direction and pathway
Players Two
Formation Scattered
Playing area Playground, gymnasium
Equipment Soccer ball

Partners sharing one ball find a space in the playing area. They stand about ten to fifteen feet apart. One player passes to the other, who traps the ball and returns the pass.

Suggestions and Variations

1. Change the type of pass and trap.
2. Repeat with one player stationary and the receiving players on the move.
3. Repeat above with both players on the move.
4. One player tries to kick the ball through the outstretched legs of his partner.

Wall Passing and Trapping

Motor skills Pass, trap
Movement concepts Use of space, change of direction
Players Two
Formation None
Playing area Playground, gymnasium
Equipment Soccer ball

This drill is essentially the same as wall kicking. One player kicks the ball to the wall and his partner traps it and returns the kick. All other variations can be adapted to partner activities.

Target Shooting

Motor skills Pass, trap
Movement concepts Moving into space, change of direction and speed
Players Two
Formation See diagram
Playing area Playground, gymnasium
Equipment Soccer ball and traffic cones

Partners share one ball and two traffic cones (or milk cartons). Arrange partners and equipment as shown. One partner kicks the ball through the goals (cones) and the other partner traps the ball and repeats the kicking skill.

Player 1 ⊗ ○ ball   traffic cones   5′ ←— 10-15′ —→ ⊗ Player 2

Suggestions and Variations

1. Change the type of kicking and trapping skills.
2. Change the angle of shooting.
3. Change the distance between goals.
4. Change the distance from the goals.

Circle Passing

Motor skills Pass, trap
Movement concepts Moving into space, change of direction and speed
Players Two
Formation Circle
Playing area Playground, gymnasium
Equipment Soccer ball

One player turns around a stationary partner. Stationary partner passes and traps the ball while circling player dribbles and passes.

Suggestions and Variations

1. Change the type of pass and trap.
2. Reverse directions.
3. Repeat activity without involving a trap.
4. This is an opportune time to introduce the problem-solving method. For example, after practicing several variations of the previous activity, pose a question such as, "Can you change the position of your traffic cones and make up a drill that involves an inside-of-foot pass and a leg trap?" If children have experienced the inventive games approach, a challenge, such as "Using two cones and a ball, create your own passing and trapping drill," will produce a wide variety of responses.

Follow the Leader

Motor skills Dribble
Movement concepts Moving into space, change of direction and pathway
Players Two
Formation Line
Playing area Playground, gymnasium
Equipment Balls

This is an excellent activity to teach ball control and keeping an eye on another player. Each player has a ball. One partner dribbles in any direction and her partner follows (figure 18.23).

Figure 18.23 Follow the leader.

Suggestions and Variations

1. Partners dribble side by side.
2. Add one or more obstacles to dribble around.

Dribble and Pass

Motor skills Dribble, pass, offensive play
Movement concepts Moving into space, change of direction, pathway, and speed
Players Two
Formation None
Playing area Playground, gymnasium
Equipment Soccer ball

Partners dribble and pass a ball back and forth.

Suggestions and Variations

1. Add two or more obstacles to dribble around.
2. Repeat earlier drills with outside of feet.
3. Add other skills such as dribble, pass, and trap.

Throw and Head

Motor Skills Throw, head
Movement concepts Moving into space, change of direction, pathway, and speed
Players Two
Formation Line
Playing area Playground, gymnasium
Equipment Soccer balls

Partners stand about eight to twelve feet apart, facing each other. One partner, using a throw-in pass, throws the ball high into the air so that it descends just in front of his partner. That partner attempts to head the ball forward and downward toward the first partner's feet. Repeat several times, then change positions.

Suggestions and Variations

1. Tie a rope between two posts; the height may vary from four to six feet. Repeat the original activity but with the throw-in going over the rope and the headed ball returning under the rope.
2. Place a hoop on the floor between the players. Repeat the original drill, requiring the headed ball to hit the center of the hoop.

Partner Keep Away

Motor skills Dribble, dodge, stop
Movement concepts Moving into space, change of direction, pathway, and speed
Players Two
Formation Scattered
Playing area Playground, gymnasium
Equipment Soccer balls

One player is given a ball and tries to keep it by dribbling, dodging, stopping, and pivoting away from his partner. As soon as the defensive partner touches the ball, players exchange positions and repeat the drill.

Suggestions and Variations

Partners stand about twenty feet apart, facing each other. On signal, each approaches the other. The player with the ball tries to dribble past his opponent, while the defensive player attempts to gain possession of the ball.

Triangle Pass

Motor skills Pass, trap
Movement concepts Change of direction
Players Three
Formation Triangle
Playing area Playground, gymnasium
Equipment Ball

Arrange three players in a triangle (eight to ten feet apart). First player passes ball to the right. Second player traps and passes ball to the next player. Continue pattern for a few minutes, then call, "Change," signaling players to reverse directions.

Kicking for Distance

Motor skills Kick
Movement concepts Moving into space, strong and light
Players Four to five per group
Formation Scattered
Playing area Playground, gymnasium
Equipment Soccer balls

Divide the class into squads of four or five players. One squad lines up to kick, while the other scatters in the field to retrieve the ball. The field can be marked with lines every five yards or the retrievers can simply mark the kick. Each child on the kicking squad kicks the ball three or four times, depending on the number of balls available. Mark where the ball lands, not where it rolls. After each player on the kicking squad has had a turn, change squad positions.

Suggestions and Variations

The kicking squad may vary the type of kick—a stationary kick, a punt, or a kick while the ball is rolling forward.

Goal Kicking

Motor skills Kick, trap
Movement concepts Moving into space
Players Four to six per group
Formation Semicircle
Playing area Playground, gymnasium
Equipment Soccer balls

Divide the class into squads of four to six players and arrange them in semicircles on each side of the goalposts (traffic cones or milk cartons). Player on team A kicks the ball through the goal, and any player on the opposite team traps the ball and returns the kick. If the ball goes through the retrieving team, allow the player who was closest to the ball as it passed by to retrieve it.

Suggestions and Variations

1. Vary the type of kick—a stationary kick, kicking a moving ball, using the inside and outside of the instep. (Move closer to the goal when practicing this type of kick.)
2. Place a player in the center of the goalpost to practice goaltending (guarding the goal).
3. Practice volley kicking. Players on team A must throw the ball over the goalposts. Any player on team B may attempt to kick the ball through the goalposts before it lands.

Goal Heading

Motor skills Head, throw
Movement concepts Moving into space, use of space, change of direction and speed
Players Four to six per group
Formation Line
Playing area Playground, gymnasium
Equipment Soccer balls

Divide the class into as many squads as you have goals. (Wire backstops or any substitute goal area will work for this drill.) Arrange squads in a line ten feet in front of and parallel to the goal. Player A in each squad moves fifteen feet in front of his team beyond the goal, turns, and faces the second player in the line. Player A throws to B, who attempts to head the ball through the goal. Player B chases his own ball, throws it to A, and then returns to the end of the line.

Suggestions and Variations

Make two lines facing the goal, with A standing on the goal line and the front players of the two lines standing ten feet away. A throws the ball up between the first two players. Both attempt to head the ball back to A.

Shuttle Dribble and Tackle

Motor skills Dribble, tackle
Movement concepts Use of space, moving into space, change of direction and speed
Players Four per group
Formation See diagram
Playing area Playground, gymnasium
Equipment Soccer balls

This is a basic shuttle relay formation, with the following modifications. Player 1 dribbles the ball toward the other line, while player 2 moves out to tackle player 1. Player 1 tries to reach the opposite line without being tackled, and player 2 attempts to touch the ball. Allow about twenty seconds of play, then blow the whistle and start the next two players.

One vs. Two Players

Motor skills Dribble, pass, tackle
Movement concepts Use of space, moving into space, change of direction and speed
Players Three per group
Formation Scattered
Playing area Playground, gymnasium
Equipment Soccer balls

Two players attempt to keep the ball away from the third player. If player 3 touches the ball, the opposing player who last touched it changes position with him.

Suggestions and Variations

1. Add a goal behind the defensive player and require the two offensive players to move in and attempt to score.
2. Repeat the previous activities and change the combination to one of the following:
   a. One defensive player vs. three offensive players
   b. Two defensive players vs. two offensive players
   c. Two defensive players vs. three offensive players

Lead-Up Games

The lead-up games described in this section can be used for developmental levels II and III. Numerous suggestions are provided to illustrate how these activities can be modified to cope with facilities, equipment, and levels of playing ability. Teacher are also encouraged to use the inventive games approach to modify these games or to help the children invent their own lead-up games.

Circle Soccer

Motor skills Kick, trap
Movement concepts Personal space, moving into space
Players Four or five per team
Formation Circle
Playing area Playground, gymnasium
Equipment Ball

The captain of one team begins play by kicking the ball toward the opponents. The players on each team attempt to kick the ball past the opposing players, below their waists. They also must try to prevent the ball from going out of the circle on their own side. Every player remains at his place in the circle while the ball is in play. One point is awarded each time the ball is kicked out of the circle.

Suggestions and Variations

1. Introduce a second ball to the game.
2. Restrict kicking to the right foot, then to the left foot.
3. Expand the size of the circle.

Soccer Dodgeball

Motor skills   Kick, trap
Movement concepts   Moving into space, change of direction and speed
Players   Class
Formation   Circle
Playing area   Playground, gymnasium
Equipment   Soccer ball

The circle players attempt to hit the players inside by kicking the ball at them. Inside players cannot use their hands to stop the ball, except for a pass that may strike the face. When a player is hit below the waist, he joins the circle. The winners are the last three players remaining inside the circle.

Suggestions and Variations

1. Introduce a second ball to the game.
2. Add a new rule, such as every player must be constantly moving or inside players must hop while circle players use only a side-of-foot kick.
3. Ask each team to make up a new rule for the opposing side.

Boundary Ball

Motor skills   Kick, trap
Movement concepts   Moving into space, change of direction and speed
Players   Ten to fifteen on each team
Formation   Playing area divided by a centerline, with players scattered on their own side of the centerline
Playing area   Playground, gymnasium
Equipment   Soccer balls

Each team has a ball, which it kicks toward the opponent's goal line. Players may move about freely in their own half of the field to prevent the opponent's ball from crossing the goal. However, they cannot touch the ball with their hands. One point is scored each time a ball crosses a goal line.

Suggestions and Variations

1. Restrict players to one type of kick and one type of trapping skill.
2. Give each team an additional ball.
3. Ask children to suggest a new rule.

Change Soccer

Motor skills   All soccer skills
Movement concepts   Use of available space, change of direction, pathway, and speed
Players   Six per game
Formation   See diagram
Playing area   Playground, gymnasium
Equipment   Ball and four goalposts

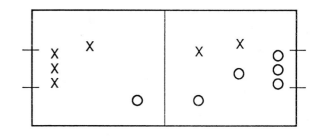

Three players on each team are goalies and cannot use their hands to stop a ball. The remaining three players may move anywhere within the playing area. Game begins with a kick-off in the center of the field. When the teacher calls, "Change," everyone must immediately exchange positions with the goalies, then return to playing the game. Use soccer rules as they apply to this game.

Marble Soccer

Motor skills   Shoot, trap
Movement concepts   Moving into space, strong and light
Players   Three or four per game
Formation   Scattered around circle
Playing area   Playground, gymnasium
Equipment   Soccer balls

Draw a circle (six to ten feet in diameter) and place a ball in the center. Three players stand outside the circle and one player is given a ball. The player with the ball kicks it, trying to hit it into the center of the circle. If he hits it, he receives one point; if it is knocked out of the circle, he receives five points. Players may enter the circle to retrieve their own ball but may not kick their ball while in the circle. First player to score 21 points wins the game.

Circle of Fun

Motor skills   Dribble, pass, shoot, tackle
Movement concepts   Moving through space, change of direction and speed
Players   Three per team
Formation   Circle
Playing area   Playground, gymnasium
Equipment   Soccer balls and traffic cones

Draw a large circle in the playing area and place a traffic cone in the center. All players start outside of the circle. The object of the game is to shoot from outside the circle and knock down the traffic cone. Once the game begins, each team tries to keep possession of the ball and score goals. All players are permitted to run through the circle, but no player is allowed to touch the ball while it is in the circle. If the ball remains in the circle without the traffic cone being knocked down, the player who last kicked it may run in, pick it up, run out of the circle, and place it on the ground to continue the game.

Motor skills   Kick, trap
Movement concepts   Use of available space, moving into space
Players   Four to twenty
Formation   Scattered on each side of a playing area
Playing area   Playground, gymnasium
Equipment   Soccer ball

A captain is chosen for each team. The ball is placed in the middle of the field and the captain of the kicking team kicks the ball to start the game. Once the game has started, opposing teams stay at least fifteen feet apart. Any member of the receiving team may trap the ball. The player who traps the ball kicks it toward the opponent's goal. If a player kicks the ball over the opponent's goal, his team receives one point. The team that did not score starts the ball from the center of the field. Any player who contacts another player who is attempting to kick the ball commits a foul. A free kick is then awarded to the other team.

Suggestions and Variations

1. Add two or more balls.
2. Limit kicks to either an instep, side-of-foot, or punt kick.
3. Ask each team to suggest a new rule.

Alley Soccer

Motor skills   Pass, trap, kick
Movement concepts   Personal space, moving into space, change of direction and speed
Players   Ten to twelve per team
Formation   See diagram
Playing area   Playground, gymnasium
Equipment   Soccer ball

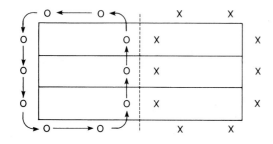

Each team has three forwards, who may move anywhere within their own alley. All remaining players on each team remain on the sideline and goal line of their own half of the field. No player may touch the ball with his hands. The player in the middle alley starts the game by passing the ball to another forward player. Forwards pass the ball back and forth to other forwards or to sideline players as they attempt to move it forward and kick it over the opponent's goal line below the waist of the opposing players. One point is awarded for each goal. If the ball goes over the sideline, it is thrown in by the nearest player on the team that did not allow it to go over the line. Only forwards may score a goal. Rotate players after a set time and according to the rotation pattern shown in the diagram.

Suggestions and Variations

1. Add one free forward, who may roam anywhere.
2. Limit skills to one type of pass and one type of trap.
3. Allow sideline players to score a goal.

Forwards and Backs

Motor skills   Pass, dribble, trap
Movement concepts   Personal space, moving into space, change of direction and speed
Players   Ten to twelve per team
Formation   See diagram
Playing area   Playground, gymnasium
Equipment   Soccer balls

The center forward of team A starts the game with a kickoff. Team A forwards try to kick the ball over the opponent's goal line. Players on team B try to gain possession of the ball and kick it over their opponent's goal line. Forwards may not cross back over their own center zone line, and backs may not cross the center zone line. Only forwards can score a goal. Each goal counts one point. If the ball goes over the endline or sideline, it is thrown in by the nearest player on the opposite team.

Suggestions and Variations

1. Change forwards and backs every few minutes.
2. Add sideline players with rules similar to Sideline Soccer.
3. Vary the type of kick and trap.

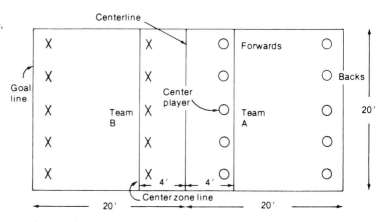

Four-Goal Soccer

Motor skills   All soccer skills
Movement concepts   Use of available space, moving into space, change of direction and speed
Players   Four or five per team
Formation   See figure 18.24
Playing area   Playground, gymnasium
Equipment   Soccer ball and four goals

A field has four goals marked with the flags (figure 18.24). These are located in the center of each line. Two teams of five players are formed, all wearing a uniform. The number of players can be increased to seven or eight per team. The game is played without goalkeepers and each team attacks and defends two goals (see markers). Soccer rules are applied, with the exception of using no offside or corner kicks (original description of game).

chapter 18

Figure 18.24 Four goal soccer.

Teacher

Seven-Person or Mini-Soccer

Motor skills All soccer skills
Movement concepts Use of available space, moving into space, change of direction, pathway, and speed
Players Seven per team
Formation See diagram
Playing area Playground, gymnasium
Equipment Soccer ball

See the official rules of soccer in the following section. Since there are seven players on each team, this is an ideal game to accommodate an average-sized physical education class. The playing field is normally divided in half to allow two games to be played at the same time. Modify any rule to cope with local conditions.

Suggestions and Variations

Young players tend to "follow the ball" rather than play their positions. Too often the fullback and halfbacks are "caught" too far in front of their forwards. To prevent this, play seven-person soccer, but after the kickoff, require:

1. Forwards must remain in their opponent's half of the field.
2. Backs must remain in their own half of the playing field.

Soccer Rules and Regulations

By the time children reach fifth grade, they should have learned the majority of skills necessary to play soccer. This does not imply, however, that time should not be devoted to practice activities and lead-up games. With some basic modifications, the game of soccer should be played in its entirety periodically during an instructional unit. This will help children understand that practice sessions and lead-up activities are designed to improve the speed and accuracy of the required skills.

I. Field of play
  A. Length of field—not more than 120 yards and not less than 110 yards
  B. Width of field—not more than 75 yards and not less than 65 yards

II. Names of players and line-up positions (positions of players at the start of the game, after a goal is scored, and after halftime): Over the years, soccer's playing positions have evolved to four general positions. The goalie represents the first defensive position. Immediately in front are four defenders, who are most often near their own goal. The outside defenders are called wing fullbacks and the inside players fullbacks. The middle line is the midfielders, who play between the defenders and forwards. These players are the workhorses of the team, as they move back to help the defenders when in trouble and forward to help the forward line when on the offense. Forwards or strikers are normally nearest the opponent's goal line. *Playing system* is a term that describes how the players on a team are positioned. The general starting system for elementary school children is the one described. It is known as the 4–3–3 system. A 4–2–4 system would include four defenders, two mid-fielders and four forwards.

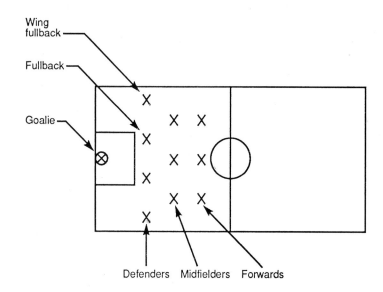

Wing fullback

Fullback

Goalie

Defenders Midfielders Forwards

Side or touch line

18 yds.

44 yds.

Goalposts
(8' high and
24' wide)

20 yds.

6 yds.

Goal line

Center circle
(radius = 10 yds.)

III. Penalty kick: If a defensive player other than the goalie touches the ball with his hands in the eighteen-by-forty-four-yard penalty area, a penalty kick is awarded to the offensive team. This kick is made from the twelve-yard penalty mark by any member of the offensive team. The goalie stands on the line between the goalposts, and all other players stand outside the penalty area until the ball is kicked. After the ball is kicked, any player from either team may enter the penalty area.

IV. Free kicks: The direct free kick and the indirect free kick

A. Direct free kick: This is a kick from which a goal may be scored directly. In other words, the ball can be kicked from where an infraction occurred and travel directly through the goal. Defenders must stay ten yards away from the ball until it is kicked. This kick is awarded to a team when any opposing player commits any of

the following infractions outside the penalty area (a direct free kick awarded inside the penalty area automatically results in a penalty kick, taken from the penalty mark).

1. Kicking an opponent
2. Charging in a violent and dangerous manner
3. Tripping an opponent
4. Handling the ball. (The goalkeeper may handle the ball only when he is inside the penalty area. If he handles the ball when he is outside the penalty area, a direct free kick is awarded to the opposing team.)
5. Pushing with the hands or arms. The ball is placed on the spot where the infraction happened. Any player on the team awarded the kick lines up three or four yards behind the ball and players from both teams stand anywhere in front of him, providing they are at least ten yards away. The whistle sounds, the ball is kicked, and play resumes.

B. Indirect free kick: This is a kick from which a goal cannot be scored, unless the ball is touched by another player before it enters the goal. This kick is awarded to a team when any opposing player commits any of the following infractions.

1. A player kicks the ball a second consecutive time after a kickoff, a free kick, a goal kick, or a corner kick.
2. A ball is not kicked forward from a penalty kick.
3. The goalie carries the ball more than four steps.
4. Misconduct—improper language, unnecessary arguing, and so on
5. Offside
6. Obstruction other than holding
7. The ball is passed (by kicking the ball) to the goalkeeper by a player on the goalkeeper's own team. (Note: The ball can be headed, thrown directly from a throw-in, or chest-passed to the goalkeeper.)

V. Throw-in: When the ball is kicked, headed, or legally forced over the sideline by a player, the opposing team is awarded a throw-in. The ball is put back into play from behind the sideline at the point where the ball went out. The player who makes the throw-in must have both hands on the ball and throw it from behind his head. He must also have parts of both feet in contact with the ground until the ball is released. If the ball is not thrown in properly, the opposing team is awarded the second throw-in.

VI. Corner kick: When the ball is kicked, headed, or legally forced over the goal line (but not between the goalposts) by a defensive player, the opposing team is awarded a corner kick. The ball is placed on the corner of the field (where the sideline meets the goal line) on the side the ball went out. Usually a wing player kicks the ball into play. All other players stand anywhere on the field, providing they are at least ten yards from the ball.

VII. Goal kick: When the ball is kicked, headed, or legally forced over the goal line by a player on the attacking team, a goal kick is awarded to the defensive team. The ball is placed anywhere in the goal area. Any defensive player may kick the ball back into play; however, it must leave the penalty area for it to be in play. If it does not, the kick is repeated. The offensive team remains outside the penalty area until the ball crosses over the penalty area boundary.

VIII. Offside: A player is offside if the ball is kicked forward toward a player, by one of his own team players, and he does not have two opponents in front of him at the moment the ball is played. He is not offside, however, if (1) he is in his own half of the field; (2) two opponents are nearer their goal than he is at the moment the ball is played; (3) he receives a ball directly from a corner kick, a throw-in, or a goal kick; or (4) the ball is passed back to the player.

A. Offside: The right winger is offside because he does not have two defensive players in front of him at the moment the ball is kicked.

B. Not offside: In this case, "at the moment" the inside right kicks the ball, the right winger has two defensive players in front of him. Now the right winger may dribble in and attempt a shot at the goal.

IX. Scoring: A goal is awarded to the attacking team if any player kicks, heads, or legally causes the ball to cross over the goal line between the goalposts and under the crossbar. A ball accidentally kicked through the goal by a defensive player, therefore, would count for the attacking team.

Evaluative Techniques

The evaluative checklist in figure 18.25 is an example of a teacher-made formative evaluative tool to assess the general progress of the class. A simple rating of 1, 2, and 3 can be used to provide a quick evaluation of each student's level of soccer ability, as well as how well each child understands and uses the five key movement concepts.

Although a number of standardized tests measure soccer skills, they generally are designed for secondary and college-level students. These tests, however, can be modified to meet the ability of upper elementary children. The following test battery is an example of a "teacher-made" test that can be administered without elaborate equipment and in a short period of time (see table 18.3). Keep scores from year to year in order to develop appropriate norms for your school.

Table 18.3 Soccer Skill Test						
Name	Kick and trap (total pts.)	Dribbling	Shooting	Subjective evaluation	Total score	Grade
1 2 3 4 5		Rank total scores for the class, then convert to letter grades or ratings (superior, good, etc.).				

Figure 18.25

Evaluation Checklist

Rating

1	Needs practice
2	Shows progress
3	Has acquired skill or concept

1st evaluation _____

2nd evaluation _____

3rd evaluation _____

Name	Pass	Trap	Dribble	Shoot	Tackle	Use of space	Move through space	Change of direction	Change of pathway	Change of speed

Test 1: Kick and Trap

Draw a line five feet from the wall. The ball is placed on the line. Each player attempts to kick the ball and hit the front wall as many times as possible within thirty seconds. All kicks must be taken from behind the five-foot line. If a player loses control of the ball, he may retrieve it with his feet and continue kicking. Award one point for each successful hit. Allow two trials and record the highest score.

Test 2: Dribbling

Arrange four chairs as shown in the diagram. Place a ball on the starting line. Each player starts behind the starting line, with both hands resting on his knees. On the signal "go," he dribbles the ball around the chairs in a zigzag pattern. One point is awarded for each time he passes a chair as he moves forward and as he returns to the starting line. Allow thirty seconds for the test. Allow two trials and record the highest score.

Test 3: Shooting

Arrange the field markings in front of the goalposts as shown. A player may use the right or left approach. The player starts dribbling the ball in the approach area and continues moving into the shooting zone. While in the shooting zone, the player attempts to kick the ball through the goalposts. Ten trials are given, with five points awarded for each successful goal.

Starting line

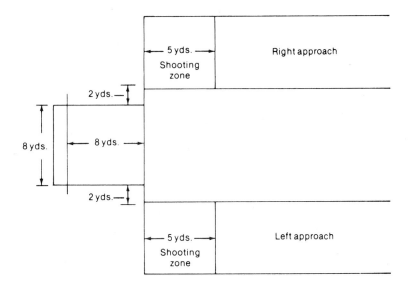

Test 4: Subjective Evaluation

Establish criteria that represent the skills and playing ability required in soccer. For example, using such skills as passing, dribbling, team play, and defensive ability, the teacher awards each player a total score from zero to fifty points. Three players can be used as judges, with the average score recorded.

Selected References

Caerver, W. (1983). *Soccer Fundamentals for Players and Coaches.* Englewood Cliffs, NJ: Prentice-Hall Inc.

CAHPER. (1985). *Soccer Type Games.* Ottawa, Ontario: CAHPER Publications.

Hooper, C. A., and Davis, M. S. (1985). *Coaching Soccer Effectively.* Champaign, IL: Human Kinetics Publishers, Inc.

Simon, J. M., and Reeves, J. A. (1982). *The Soccer Games Book.* Champaign, IL: Leisure Press.

Turner, L. F., and Turner, S. L. (1989). *P.E. Teacher's Skill-by-Skill Activities Program.* West Nyack, NY: Parker Publishing Co., Inc.

Waiters, T., and Howe, B. (1988). *Coaching 6, 7, and 8 Year Olds.* Vancouver, B.C.: World of Soccer Ltd.

19

Hockey Activities

Field hockey is a relatively new game to many North Americans. Its origins, however, date back over 2,000 years to ancient Greece and Egypt. During the Middle Ages, field hockey was known as "hurling" in Ireland, as "shinty" in Scotland, and as "hoquet" in France. The modern version of hockey started in England around the middle of the nineteenth century. Today, the game is played in more than one hundred countries and is enjoyed equally by men and women.

Field hockey has also become very popular with elementary school children. Because it is relatively new, it provides an enjoyable medium for boys and girls to learn to play together on an "even skill" basis. Improvised equipment, along with numerous modified lead-up hockey type games has made field hockey one of the fastest growing activities in the elementary physical education program ■

Emphasis and Progression

Many of the basic skills and simple playing strategies of hockey are introduced in developmental level II through street hockey and organized floor hockey during school hours. Although field hockey is similar to these games, it has several unique skills and rules (table 19.1) that should be learned correctly and in an organized manner in level III.

During level II, the main emphasis is learning the correct way to dribble, pass, and shoot a ball. Children of this age range should also learn how to stop a ball and a few basic rules of the game. The major portion of any unit of instruction should be devoted to practice activities and lead-up games.

The basic dribbling, passing, and shooting skills continue to be emphasized through level III. Teachers should expect a general increase in the accuracy, speed, and control of these skills. New skills, such as the scoop shot, tackling, and dodging, should be introduced in this level. More time should also be devoted to seven-person hockey, and occasionally time should be allowed for playing eleven-person field hockey. The latter is important in order to give each child an opportunity to understand and appreciate the importance of good ball control and positional play.

Teaching Procedures

Throughout this chapter, numerous references are made to various sections in chapter 18, "Soccer Activities." The reason for this is that both soccer and field hockey may be relatively new to many elementary school children and the same approach can be used to teach both activities. In addition, many of the practice activities and lead-up games described in chapter 18 can be easily adapted to field hockey skills. Teachers should also adapt the procedures for teaching soccer when organizing and planning a hockey unit.

The following suggestions will assist teachers in coping with several problems that are unique to hockey:

1. Hockey can be a dangerous sport if children are not taught proper stick handling and legal checking methods. Since boys and girls play this activity together, it is especially important that the proper skills be taught and enforced.

2. Since sticks may not be available for every member of the class, station work (p. 114 and 250) and a rotation system should be used.

3. Hockey, like soccer, requires a high level of strength and endurance. Teachers should plan practice activities and lead-up games so the children gradually build up their cardiorespiratory endurance. Station work can be used for alternating vigorous running drills with less tiring shooting activities.

4. During all hockey type activities, the goalkeeper should wear a protective face mask, chest pads, and leg protectors. Shin guards for field players are also recommended.

Description of Skills

Field hockey skills are classified as dribbling, passing, hitting, and receiving. The following skills should be taught to elementary school children in a systematic and progressive way. Special attention must be given to proper stick handling, reinforcing it throughout every lesson.

Table 19.1 Suggested Sequence of Presenting Hockey Skills and Rules

Skills and rules	Developmental level II	Developmental level III
Dribbling	Introduce	Increase speed and accuracy
Rules: Dribbling with the flat side of the stick	Introduce	
Passing	Introduce	Increase speed, distance, and accuracy
Receiving	Introduce	Increase speed of the ball
Hitting: Forward, right, left	Introduce	Increase distance and accuracy
Scoop shot	Introduce	Increase accuracy
Rules: Hit with flat side of stick		Introduce
Tackling		Introduce
Rules		
Fouls		Introduce
Dodging		Introduce
Rules		
Offside		Introduce
Pass ball	Introduce	
Rules: Player positions		Introduce

Figure 19.1 Grip.

Figure 19.2 Dribbling and stopping.

a   b

Grip

The basic hockey grip is fundamental to all shooting, dribbling, and fielding skills. The left hand stays at the top of the stick while the right hand slides up or down the stick according to how the ball should be moved. To begin, grasp the stick in the middle with the right hand and hold it parallel to the ground. The toe of the blade should be sticking up, with the flat side of the blade facing left. Grasp the top of the stick with the left hand, with the V of the hand pointing down toward the blade. Lower the stick to the ground and turn the blade so that it faces outward. Keeping the same grip with the left hand, reposition the right hand eight to twelve inches below the left hand. The result is that the hands grip the handle from opposite sides (figure 19.1). Players will want to experiment to find the most suitable distance between their hands. Players should carry the stick ahead and to the right of their feet, with the body leaning forward slightly and head over the ball.

Key Teaching Points

1. Keep a firm grip with the left hand and allow the stick to rotate in your right hand.
2. Left hand up, right hand down.
3. Maintain a slight forward body lean.

Dribbling and Stopping

Dribbling in hockey is a controlled means of propelling the ball along the ground with the hockey stick. The ball is dribbled in the front and slightly to the right of the feet by making short taps with the flat side of the blade (figure 19.2a). The movement is from the shoulder, forearm, and wrist. In open field play and when the opponent is not near, the ball may be tapped ten to fifteen feet ahead, followed by short running steps, then another tap of the ball. The flat side of the blade should always be to the ball, and the blade should be close to the ground. To stop the ball, rotate the wrist to bring the flat side of the stick over the ball (figure 19.2b).

Key Teaching Points

1. Keep a firm grip.
2. Rotate from shoulders.
3. Think "tap" . . . "stop" . . . "look."

Controlled Dribbling

For more controlled dribbling, spread the hands farther apart (figure 19.3a). To push the ball right, rotate the stick with the left wrist so that the flat side of the stick taps the left side of the ball (figure 19.3b). Keep the ball and stick in front of the body, then rotate the stick back to the right side of the ball (figure 19.3c).

Key Teaching Points

1. Hold arms in front of body.
2. Reach for the ball in front of the body.
3. Push, rather than strike, the ball.
4. Watch where you are going and where teammates and opponents are positioned.

Figure 19.3 Controlled dribbling.

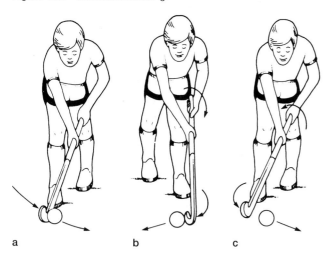

a   b   c

Figure 19.4 Push pass.

a

b

Push Pass

The push pass is used for short passes or to shoot at the goal. Dribble the ball in a forward direction and, when ready, place that side of the stick against the ball, look at the target, then look down (figure 19.4a). Sweep the ball toward the target (figure 19.4b).

Key Teaching Points

1. Keep the ball close to the stick prior to making the pass.
2. Sweep the ball—don't hit it.
3. Follow through in the direction of the pass.

Receiving

Receiving a hockey ball or puck (figure 19.5) is very similar to fielding a grounder in softball. The face of the stick is at a right angle to the direction of the oncoming ball. As the ball contacts the stick, loosen the grip slightly to absorb the impact of the ball. Contact the ball as far away from the body as possible to allow the force to be absorbed over the greatest distance.

Figure 19.5 Receiving.

Key Teaching Points

1. Meet the ball in front and to the right of the body.
2. As the ball is contacted, give slightly to stop the ball.
3. Move quickly into the next playing position.

Hitting

Hitting is forcefully hitting the ball along the ground. The left drive is the most common driving stroke, used for long and medium passes, shots on goal, and free and corner hits. When moving into position to hit the ball, the right hand shifts next to the left hand. The left shoulder points in the direction of the drive, and the head is over the ball. The arms swing back, keeping the stick below shoulder level (figure 19.6a). Then bring the arms forward and downward and contact the ball just off the lead foot (figure 19.6b). Follow through low and in the direction of the hit.

Figure 19.6 Hitting.

a   b

Figure 19.7 Scoop shot.

a   b

Key Teaching Points

1. Keep hands close together.
2. Use a short back swing and a quick hit.
3. Follow-through should be low to the ground.

Scoop Shot

The scoop shot is used to lift the ball slightly off the ground in order to dodge an opponent, to pass, or to shoot the ball into the corner of the goal. Contact the ball in front, with the stick tilted back as it is placed under the ball (figure 19.7a). Then make a strong lifting and shovellike action with the right arm, but using no follow-through (figure 19.7b).

Key Teaching Points

1. The stick should contact and lift the ball without any sound.
2. The scoop is a controlled lifting action.
3. There is no follow-through action.

Tackling

A tackle is a legal means of taking the ball away from an opponent. Move in toward the opponent with eyes on the ball, body well forward, with weight evenly distributed over both feet. Hold the blade of the stick close to the ground (figure 19.8a). Make the tackle when the ball is farthest from the opponent's stick. At that moment, place the face of the blade on the ball perpendicular to the ground (figure 19.8b). As soon as you have possession of the ball, immediately pass it to another player or quickly dribble it away from the opponent.

Key Teaching Points

1. Keep your eyes on the ball and the opponent's stick.
2. Keep both hands on your stick.
3. When ready to move, make your action quick and direct; do not swing your stick toward the ball.

Figure 19.8 Tackling.

a. Approach with blade close to the ground.

b. Blade is on the ball and perpendicular to the ground.

Dodging

A dodge is an evasive movement that an offensive player uses to move the ball past an opponent. It is essentially a controlled pass to oneself. In figure 19.9, the dribbler pushes the ball to the right, then runs around the other side to pick up her own pass. Timing is the most important part of this movement. The ball must be pushed late enough to prevent the opponent from backing up to gain possession of the ball.

Key Teaching Points

1. Keep the ball close to your stick.
2. Do not give away your move by an early shift or look to where you intend to pass the ball.
3. Move very quickly after your dodge to regain possession of the ball.

Figure 19.9 Dodging.

 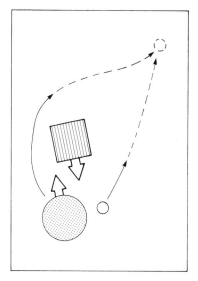

Figure 19.10 Stand in a ready position, with the stick in the right hand.

Goalkeeping

In most instances, proper goalkeeping equipment is not available in small enough sizes for elementary school children. If lighter balls such as tennis or perforated plastic balls are used, goalkeepers should wear shin guards and a face mask for protection.

The goalkeeper should stand about one yard in front of the goal and move in a semicircle from post to post. He should stand in a ready position, with the stick held in the right hand and the flat side of the stick facing forward (figure 19.10). The left hand is positioned with the palm facing forward, body leaning slightly forward, knees partially flexed, and feet in a comfortable stride position.

The goalkeeper is permitted to stop the ball with any part of the body and the ball is permitted to rebound off the body or hand. The goalkeeper is not allowed to hold the ball or throw it into the field of play. He can, however, clear the ball with the stick or kick it clear with his foot.

Practice Activities and Lead-Up Games

The following practice activities are, in many respects, modifications of soccer drills and relay activities. A few hockey type activities are also included in this section (table 19.2). Since field hockey may be a new game to many children, these practice activities are extremely important in developing basic skills. Also, many of the lead-up games are adaptations of soccer lead-up games. Teachers should modify these games to meet the class's general level of ability and the limitations of facilities and equipment.

Most of the practice activities and lead-up games provided in this section are appropriate for developmental levels II and III. As children move from level II to level III, there should be an increase in their level of skill and general playing ability.

Practice Activities

Push Pass

Motor skills   Pass, receive
Movement concepts   Moving into space, change of direction
Players   Three per activity
Formation   See diagram
Playing area   Playground, gymnasium
Equipment   Sticks and ball

Arrange three players as in diagram. Player 1 passes to player 2. Player 2 returns to player 1, who then passes to player 3. Player 3 returns the ball to 1, and the sequence begins again.

Suggestions and Variations
1. Pass from player 1 to 2 to 3 to 1 and continue in the same pattern.
2. Repeat number 1, with every player moving one position to the left. Player 1 dribbles to 2's position and passes to 2, who has shifted to 3's position.

Table 19.2 Practice Activities and Lead-Up Games

Name of activity	Type of activity	Players	Developmental level (II — III)	Hockey concepts and skills	Movement concepts	Page
Practice Activities (Adapted from soccer activities)						
Wall Kicking	Shoot	Individual	II →→→ III	Shoot, receive	Moving ball into space	316
Individual Dribbling	Shoot	Individual	II →→→ III	Dribble	Moving into space, change of direction	317
Stop, Go, Turn	Dribble, stop	Individual	II →→→ III	Dribble, stop	Moving through space, change of direction	317
Passing and Trapping	Dribble, pass, stop	2	II →→→ III	Dribble, pass, receive	Moving into space, change of direction, pathway, and speed	318
Wall Passing and Trapping	Shoot, receive	2	II →→→ III	Pass, trap	Use of space, change of direction	318
Target Shooting	Shoot, receive	2	II →→→ III	Shoot, receive	Moving into space, change of direction and speed	318
Circle Passing	Pass, receive	2	II →→→ III	Pass, receive	Use of available space, change of direction and pathway	318
Follow the Leader	Dribble	2	II →→→ III	Dribble	Moving into space, change of direction, pathway, and speed	318
Dribble and Pass	Dribble, pass	2	II →→→ III	Dribble, offensive play	Moving into space, change of direction, pathway, and speed	319
Partner Keep Away	Dribble, dodge	3	II →→→ III	Dribble, dodge, stop	Moving into space, change of direction, pathway, and speed	319
Triangle Pass	Pass, receive	3	→→ III	Pass, receive	Moving into space, change of direction	319
Goal Heading	Shoot, receive	4–5	II →→→ III	Shoot, receive	Moving into space, change of direction and speed	320
One vs. Two	Dribble, pass	3	II →→→ III	Dribble, pass, tackle	Moving into space, change of direction, pathway, and speed	320
Push Pass	Pass, receive	3	II →→→ III	Pass, receive	Moving through space, change of direction	334
Lead-Up Games (Adapted from soccer activities)						
Circle Hockey	Shoot, receive	8–10	II →→→ III	Shoot, receive	Moving through space, change of direction	320
Change Hockey	All skills	12	II →→→ III	All hockey skills	Moving into space, change of direction, pathway, and speed	335
Zone Field Hockey	All hockey skills	10–12 per team	II →→→ III	All hockey skills	Moving into space, change of direction and speed	336
Line Field Hockey	Pass, receive	6–8 per team	II →→→ III	Shoot, pass, receive	Moving into space, change of direction, pathway, and speed	336
Hockey Golf	Shoot, receive	2 per game	II →→→ III	Shoot, receive	Moving into space, change of direction and speed	336
Circle of Fun	Dribble, shoot	6 per game	II →→→ III	Dribble, pass, shoot, tackle	Moving through space, change of direction and speed	335
Partner Keep Away	Dribble, dodge	3	II →→→ III	Dribble, pass, dodge, tackle	Moving into space, change of direction and speed	319

Lead-Up Games

Motor skills   All hockey skills
Movement concepts   Moving into space, change of direction and speed
Players   Ten to twelve per team
Formation   See diagram
Playing area   Playground, gymnasium
Equipment   Hockey sticks and balls

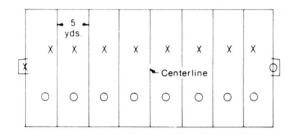

The game starts with a face-off between two opposing players at the center of the field. All players must remain in their own five-yard zone. The game is played like regular field hockey. After each goal is scored, the player in the zone closest to the centerline becomes the new goalie, and all the other players move forward into the next zone.

Line Field Hockey

Motor skills   Shoot, pass, receive
Movement concepts   Moving into space, change of direction, pathway, and speed
Players   Six to eight per team
Formation   See diagram
Playing area   Playground, gymnasium
Equipment   Sticks and ball

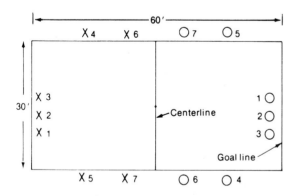

The ball is placed in the middle of the field. On signal, player 1 from each team runs out and tries to gain possession of the ball. Once the ball is in possession, a player may pass to any side player or try to shoot the ball over his opponent's goal line. No other player on his team may enter the field of play or score a goal. After each goal, rotate players and start the game again.

Suggestions and Variations
1. Allow two players to come out each time.
2. Shorten the distance between goals as skill improves.

Hockey Golf

Motor skills   Shoot, receive
Movement concepts   Moving into space, change of direction and speed
Players   Two per game
Formation   See diagram
Playing area   Playground, gymnasium
Equipment   Eight traffic cones, sticks, and ball

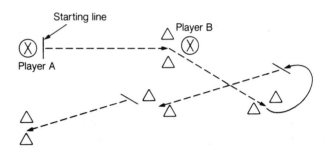

The playing positions for field hockey are shown in the diagram. Also, the same field dimensions for soccer can be used for hockey. Inclusion of the semicircle (or penalty area) is the only difference in the general layout of the field. Player A attempts to drive the ball through the traffic cones. If successful, he is awarded one point. Player B retrieves the ball and changes places with player A. Player B takes his turn, and the game continues around the four sets of traffic cones. Vary the distance and size of the goal according to the ability of players.

Suggestions and Variations

Play same game in teams. Each player on team A takes his turn before changing positions with the other team.

Field Hockey Rules and Regulations

The following basic rules of field hockey are essentially a modification of regulation field hockey. By dividing a playing field in half, two games with seven players on a team can be played (one goalie, one fullback, two halfbacks, and three forwards). Since the game is similar to soccer, it is wise to introduce it after the class has been exposed to a unit of soccer.

The playing positions for field hockey are the same as for soccer (chapter 18). Also, the same field dimensions can be used for both games. Inclusion of the semicircle (or penalty area) is the only difference in the general layout of the field.

I. Field of play: Field is 60 by 100 yards. Adjust to available space.
II. Time: Two periods of thirty minutes (divide your available time in two). Teams change ends at halftime.

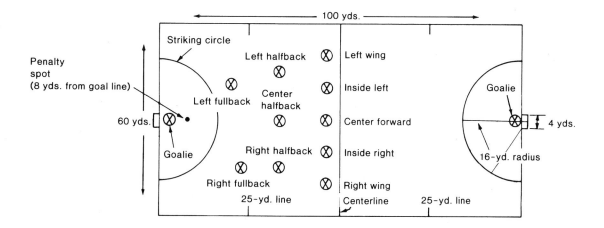

III. The pass-back is a pass from the center backward to another player. (Bully is no longer used.) This is taken at the center of the field at the start of the game, after each goal, and after halftime. During the pass-back, all other players stand on their own side of the face-off line until the ball is played.

IV. Ball rolls over sideline: When a ball is forced over a sideline, a hit is awarded to the opposing team. A hit must be performed with the stick in contact with the ball throughout the stroke. All other defending players must be five yards away.

V. Ball sent over endline:
  A. If by the attacking team, the defending team is awarded a free hit sixteen yards from the end-line, opposite the spot where the ball crossed.
  B. If by the defending team, the attacking team is awarded a corner hit. The hit must be taken from a point on the endline within 15 feet from the corner of the field.

VI. Fouls committed outside the penalty area (the semicircles in front of goals): A free hit is awarded to the opposing team. All players must be five yards away from the player taking the hit. Fouls are
  A. Using any part of the stick except the *flat surface of the blade*
  B. Raising the stick above the shoulder
  C. Using any part of the body to propel the ball
  D. Hitting another player, or hooking, slashing, or interfering with opponent's stick
  E. Being offside, which means that an offensive player who is in his opponent's half of the field and does not have possession of the ball must have two opponents between him and the goal line.

VII. Fouls committed inside the penalty area:
  A. If by the attacking team, the defending team is awarded a free hit from anywhere inside the semicircle.

B. If by the defending team, any player on the attacking team is given a free hit on a spot seven yards in front of the center of the goal. All other players, except the goalie, must remain behind the twenty-five-yard line until the penalty hit is taken.

Evaluative Techniques

Very few standardized hockey tests are available for elementary school children, so the teacher must develop her own. Since hockey is a relatively new activity, several of the basic skills can be easily developed into objective test items, and most classroom teachers can make reasonably accurate subjective ratings of the child's general playing ability.

If a teacher wishes to develop a simple test battery, tests 2, 3, and 4 from the previous chapter on soccer activities can be modified for hockey. Other items should be added at the teacher's discretion.

Selected References

CAHPER. (1985). *Floor Hockey Type Games.* Ottawa, Ontario: CAHPER Publications.

Falla, J. (1987). *Hockey: Learn to Play the Modern Way.* New York: Sports Illustrated Winner's Circle Books.

Field Hockey Canada. (1993). *Level I, II, III, Coaching Manuals.* Ottawa, Ontario: CAHPER Publications.

John, J. (1980). *Field Hockey Handbook.* North Vancouver, B.C.: Hancock House Publishers Ltd.

Wein, H. (1985). *The Science of Hockey,* Third Edition. London: Pelham Books.

20

Flag or Touch Football Activities

When football is suggested as an activity for elementary school children, parents and teachers usually think of it in terms of the competitive game involving expensive equipment, elaborate coaching, and the problems associated with a contact sport. These are valid points that should be taken into consideration. However, this does not mean that modified games involving many of the skills of football should not be taught to children in the upper intermediate grades. Appropriate football skills and rules can be taught through modified games such as field ball, flag football, and touch football. None of the practice activities or lead-up games suggested in this chapter involve tackling or any other form of body contact. Thus, the nature of these activities, coupled with such instructional techniques as station work and inventive games, provides an opportunity for boys and girls to participate in a cooperative and enjoyable way.

This chapter has been arranged to help teachers develop an instructional unit that takes into consideration such factors as coeducational classes, variable levels of instruction, and available equipment. It is strongly suggested that flag rather than touch football be emphasized in the regular instructional period. Flag football is the same as touch football, except two flags located on the seat of each player are removed. Pulling off these flags avoids disputes over whether a player was actually touched with two hands ■

Emphasis and Progression

The problems of teaching football skills are very similar to those found in teaching basketball and softball. Many boys, even ten- and eleven-year-olds, can throw a spiral pass, punt a ball, and elucidate the advantages of a single- or double-wing formation. Others may not have even thrown or kicked a football. Although girls enjoy throwing and catching a football and playing many of the lead-up games described in this chapter, cultural patterns have generally denied them equal opportunity to play football. Consequently, their understanding and skill are generally much less developed than that of boys.

Although major differences in skill level appear within each grade, the following suggested sequence of presenting skills provides a basic guideline for most elementary school situations (table 20.1).

Basic throwing and catching skills have normally been learned in the primary grades, so the main task for developmental level II is to learn to throw and catch an oblong ball. These children should also be introduced to punting.

The major skills and playing strategies should be taught at level III. Children in these grades should learn the various stances and how to throw a ball to a moving receiver. They should also learn other ways of passing the ball and a few simple play patterns.

Teaching Procedures

Teaching flag or touch football activities presents a few major problems for most upper elementary school classes. As stated earlier, football has been mainly an activity for boys. Even with coeducational classes, girls were usually given other games to play while the boys enjoyed touch or flag football. However, most girls enjoy football activities and, therefore, should participate in many practice activities and lead-up games, with a few modifications to cope with differences in skill level and previous football experience. An inadequate number of footballs also is often a major problem for teachers planning partner and small-group practice activities. The following suggestions are intended to assist the teacher in developing an integrated and meaningful football unit.

Station Work

Station work is basically organizing the field into stations where specific skills are practiced by small groups. Each group practices the skill assigned to a station for several minutes, then rotates to the next station. Boys and girls may be mixed at each station, or they may be separated if their level of skill varies widely or they prefer to work with their own gender. If only a few footballs are available, use them at stations 3 and 5 and use a soccer, Nerf, or utility ball for the other stations.

Table 20.1 Suggested Sequence of Presenting Football Skills and Rules

Skills and rules	Developmental level II	Developmental level III
Passing		
Forward pass	Introduce	Increase accuracy and distance
Lateral pass		Introduce
Centering	Introduce	Increase accuracy
Rules: Passing and receiving	Introduce	
Scoring	Introduce	
Catching		
Pass receiving	Introduce	Refine
Receiving a kicked ball	Introduce	Refine
Stance		
Three-point stance		Introduce
Four-point stance		Introduce
Rules: Line of scrimmage		Introduce
Punting		Introduce
Rules: Kickoff	Introduce	
Safety		Introduce
Blocking		Introduce
Rules: Use of hands and shoulders		Introduce
Other rules		
Downs		Introduce
Position and plays		Introduce

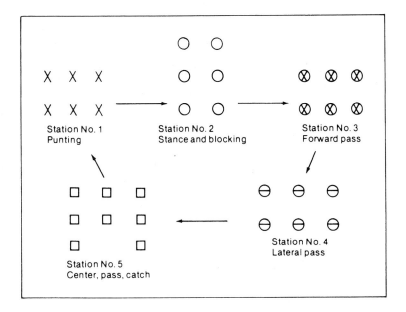

Station No. 1
Punting

Station No. 2
Stance and blocking

Station No. 3
Forward pass

Station No. 4
Lateral pass

Station No. 5
Center, pass, catch

In addition, the following considerations and safety procedures should be included in a football instruction unit.

1. Use junior-size footballs.
2. Play flag rather than touch football. If commercial flags are not available, strips of plastic or cloth may be used.
3. All positions should be rotated frequently to permit each player to experience and enjoy the skills required for each position.

Inventive Games Approach

It has been stated in previous chapters that the inventive games approach can be used to teach skills as well as to nurture children's creative abilities. This approach can be applied to football, too. If two boys and two girls are assigned a drill, such as "center, throw, and catch," the boys will normally show more skill and, thus, will dominate the practice session. However, a challenge such as "In groups of four, make up a drill in which the ball must be alternately passed from a boy to a girl" encourages cooperative planning and copes with the problem of one gender dominating.

Adding small equipment, such as milk cartons or traffic cones, can also break down the rigidity of many football drills and make the practice activity less competitive and more enjoyable. The teacher could add, "Use four milk cartons in your drill" to the earlier challenge. Passing is still emphasized in the drill, but the additional equipment adds to the challenge and encourages everyone in the group to suggest ways of incorporating it.

Description of Skills

Touch or flag football requires the same skills as the competitive game, with the exception of tackling and blocking. For elementary school children, the emphasis should be on passing, catching, and kicking skills, team positions, and simple play formations.

Passing

Three types of passing are used in touch football. The forward pass is similar to the baseball throw; however, it requires a different hand grip and release so that the ball spirals. Lateral passing is a sideward throw of the ball and is an effective technique virtually anywhere in the field of play. Hiking or centering the ball is a throw used solely by the center to start each play from the line of scrimmage.

Forward Pass

When executing a forward pass, the player stands with the foot opposite his throwing arm forward and pointing in the direction of the throw. His weight is evenly distributed on both feet, and he holds the ball with both hands. The fingers of his throwing hand grip the lace behind the center of the ball, and the other hand holds the front and side of the ball. The ball is shifted back past the ear and the body is rotated away from the throw. The elbow of the throwing arm should be kept high (figure 20.1a). Young children with proportionately smaller hands find this difficult and tend to drop the elbow in order to hold the ball in this position. The ball is then rotated toward the target, the forearm and wrist are thrust forward, and the wrist is dropped to allow the ball to roll off the fingers (figure 20.1b and c). This "roll-off" gives the ball the spiral action. Follow through in the direction of the ball.

Figure 20.1 Forward pass.

a   b   c

flag or touch football activities

Figure 20.2 Lateral pass.

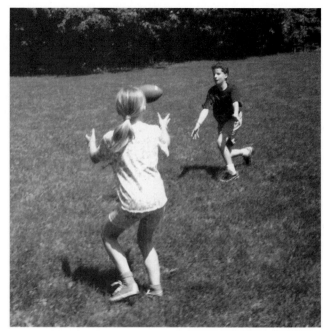

a
b

Key Teaching Points

1. Grip ball with fingers spread over laces.
2. Just prior to throwing, the nonthrowing side should be pointing toward the pass receiver.
3. Keep ball above shoulder as throwing arm moves back.
4. Throw ball from behind the ear with a strong shoulder and wrist snapping action. Follow through with fingers pointing toward receiver.

Lateral Pass

The lateral pass is basically a sideways throw of the ball. The ball is shifted from a one-arm carry to two hands. Once the ball is firmly held in both hands, shift it to the opposite side of the intended throw (figure 20.2a). Then bring the ball across the body and release it about waist high (figure 20.2b).

Key Teaching Points

1. Shift weight and ball to opposite side prior to throwing the ball.
2. Swing the ball across the body.
3. Release and follow through toward the receiver.

Centering the Ball

Once the ball is placed into position for the next play, it cannot be removed from the ground until a pass, or hike, is made by the center player. The center player positions his body in a wide stride position, with her knees bent and her body weight well forward over her shoulders and arms. She then grasps the ball with the fingers of her right hand spread over the lace, and the left hand on the side and near the back of the ball. On signal from the quarterback, the center extends her arms and hands backward through her legs and releases the ball off her fingertips (figure 20.3a and b).

Key Teaching Points

1. Spread legs and point toes forward.
2. Reach forward and place hands on the ball.
3. Thrust the ball backward with both hands.
4. Immediately after releasing ball, shift forward and upward.

Catching

A ball thrown from a quarterback or a lateral pass is normally caught with an underhand catch. However, a forward pass is usually caught while on the run, requiring balance, timing, and a cradling action of the hands. This skill requires an accurate pass and lots of practice on the part of the receiver.

At the moment the receiver is ready to catch the ball, he turns slightly toward the passer, with his hands held forward and upward (figure 20.4a). His elbows are slightly flexed and his fingers spread. He reaches for the ball (figure 20.4b), immediately pulls it toward his body (figure 20.4c), then shifts it to a carrying position. The ball is carried with one hand

Figure 20.3 Centering the ball.

a

b

Figure 20.4 Catching.

a. Elbows flexed
   and fingers spread.

b. Reaches for the ball.

c. Pulls it toward the body.

under and around the front end of the ball. The other end of the ball is held close to the body by the inside of the forearm and elbow.

Key Teaching Points

1. Keep your eye on the ball.
2. Move into position to reach and receive the ball.
3. Quickly shift ball into proper carrying position.

Carrying the Ball

The ball is carried with the arm farthest away from the opposing player. It is cradled on the inner surface of the arm with the end tucked into the notch formed by the elbow and forearm (figure 20.5).

Figure 20.5 Carrying the ball.

Figure 20.7 Offensive position: three-point stance.

Key Teaching Points

1. Always keep the body between the ball and the defender.
2. Carry the ball close to the body.
3. Keep a firm grip on the ball.

Handoff

The handoff is an elusive exchange of the ball from one player to another. This skill should be executed in such a way that, at the moment of exchange, the ball may be given to a teammate or faked to allow the ball carrier to run with or pass the ball. When the handoff is executed, the ball carrier shifts the ball to the hand closest to the approaching receiver.

The receiver moves forward with his nearest arm flexed and in front of his chest and palm down (figure 20.6). The lower arm is just below with arm bent and palm facing up. At the moment the two players pass each other, the ball is either handed to the receiver or faked (known as a bootleg) by the ball carrier in order to continue to run or to pass the ball.

Figure 20.6 Handoff.

Figure 20.8 Defensive position: four-point stance.

Key Teaching Points

1. Stress handing rather than throwing the ball to the on-coming receiver.
2. Practice alternating the handoff and the bootleg maneuvers until both moves appear to be the same.

Stance

The type of starting position a player takes depends on whether he is in an offensive or a defensive situation and whether he is playing on the line or in the backfield. The following stances are typical positions for defensive or offensive playing situations.

Three-Point Stance (Offensive Player)

Assume a crouched position, feet approximately shoulder width apart, and the weight of the body shifted slightly forward and lightly resting on the forward arm and knuckle. The head is up, trunk parallel to the ground, feet even or with one foot slightly in front of the other. If one foot is slightly back, it should be on the same side as the hand that is resting on the ground (figure 20.7).

Key Teaching Points

1. Keep the head up and parallel to the ground.
2. Keep most of the weight over the legs.

Four-Point Stance (Defensive Player)

Assume a crouched position with both hands on the ground. The head is up, back parallel to the ground, and feet about shoulder width apart. The weight is evenly distributed over the balls of both feet (figure 20.8).

chapter 20

Figure 20.9 Punting.

a. Hold ball in front. b. Release ball. c. Contact ball on top and outer side of foot. d. Follow-through.

Key Teaching Points

1. Keep head up and eyes focused on the play.
2. Keep an even balanced position over both legs.
3. Be ready to shift toward either side.

Punting

The player stands with his right foot slightly forward and his weight evenly distributed over both feet. He holds the ball with his right hand on the right side near the front of the ball. His left hand holds the left side of the ball (figure 20.9a). He steps right, then left, and simultaneously drops the ball as he brings his kicking leg forward (figure 20.9b). The ball should be contacted with the top and slightly outer side of the foot (figure 20.9c). He then continues the forward and upward movement of his kicking leg (figure 20.9d). His arms should extend sideways to assist balance.

Key Teaching Points

1. Keep eyes on ball until it is kicked.
2. Release rather than throw the ball toward the kicking foot.
3. Straighten the kicking leg forward and upward with a high follow-through.

Placekick

The ball holder should hold the ball for a right-footed player with his right hand and on the opposite side with his left hand for a left-footed kicker. The ball should be held with one or two fingers and slanting slightly backward toward the kicker (figure 20.10a). Laces of the ball face away from the kicker. The kicker runs toward the ball, places the nonkicking foot to the side and slightly behind the ball (figure 20.10b). The kicking leg swings forward, contacting the ball with the top of the foot (figure 20.10c), and continues forward and upward in the direction of the ball.

Key Teaching Points

1. Practice the approach until the nonkicking foot is consistently placed just behind the ball and slightly to the side.
2. Just prior to beginning the downward swing, bend the kicking leg backward (hyperextended) at the hip and flex the knee.
3. Follow through in the direction of the ball.
4. Keep eyes on the ball until it is kicked.

Figure 20.10 Placekick.

a b c

flag or touch football activities

Blocking

A player in flag or touch football may block by simply placing his body in the way of an opponent. When an offensive player blocks, he must have both feet on the ground and his forearms must be held against his chest when he contacts the defensive player. The defensive player may use her hands to protect herself but is limited to touching the shoulders and body of the blocker (figure 20.11). Do not permit players to drop to their knees to improve their blocking stance.

Figure 20.11 Act as an obstruction.

Key Teaching Points

1. Keep a slightly forward body lean.
2. Keep elbows out and forearms close to the chest.

Practice Activities and Lead-Up Games

Football activities normally require two or more players in practice situations. Normally, two or more skills are practiced in the same drill. The lead-up games described in this section may be played by boys and girls together or separately, depending on the children's ability (table 20.2). If their skill and experience vary widely, girls and boys are normally much happier playing separate games. This is particularly true for children who have reached the middle to upper limits of skill proficiency of developmental level III.

Practice Activities

Partner Passing

Motor skills Pass, catch
Movement concepts Moving into space, change of direction, pathway, and speed
Players Two
Formation None
Playing area Playground, gymnasium
Equipment Football

Players begin fifteen to twenty feet apart. Require them to throw with a spiral pass and catch with an underhand or overhand catch.

Suggestions and Variations

1. One partner runs and tries to catch the other's pass.
2. One partner centers, then runs forward to catch the other's pass.

3. Both run and pass back and forth, using a lateral pass.
4. Partners punt and catch.
5. One partner runs with (or without) the ball and the other partner tries to block, as in basketball.
6. Repeat above with one partner trying to tag the other.

Blocking Practice

Motor skills Feint, dodge
Movement concepts Moving into space, change of direction and speed
Players Ten to twelve per group
Formation See diagram
Playing area Playground, gymnasium
Equipment None

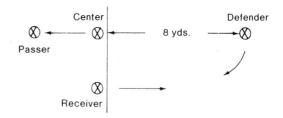

Arrange the field and players as shown in the diagram. One player is designated as the offense, the other as defense. Both assume a football stance position. On signal "hike," the offensive player attempts to get past the defensive player. The offensive player must stay within the eight-foot line and may feint, dodge, or do any movement to get around the defensive player.

Suggestions and Variations

Repeat the drill with a ball.

Pass and Defend

Motor skills Pass, catch, defensive move
Movement concepts Moving into space, change of direction, pathway, and speed
Players Four per group
Formation See diagram
Playing area Playground, gymnasium
Equipment Football

Arrange field and players as shown in diagram. The center snaps the ball to the passer. As soon as the passer has the ball, the receiver runs forward and tries to catch the pass. The defender moves at the same time and tries to prevent the receiver from catching the pass or tries to intercept it. If the skill level is high enough, allow the receiver and defender to move at the moment the snap is made.

Table 20.2 Practice Activities and Lead-Up Games

Name of activity	Type of activity	Players	Developmental level		Hockey concepts and skills	Movement concepts	Page
			II	III			
Practice activities							
Partner Passing	Pass, catch	2	⟶		Pass, catch	Moving into space, change of direction, pathway, and speed	346
Blocking Practice	Feint, dodge	10–12	⟶		Feint, dodge	Moving into space, change of direction and speed	346
Pass and Defend	Pass, catch	4	⟶		Pass, catch, defensive moves	Moving into space, change of direction, pathway, and speed	346
Punt and Catch	Punt, catch	6–10	⟶		Punt, catch	Moving into space, change of direction and speed	347
Adapted from soccer activities							
Circle Passing	Pass, catch	2	⟶		Pass, catch	Moving into space, change of direction and speed	318
Triangle Pass	Pass, catch	3	⟶		Pass, catch	Moving into space, change of direction	319
Kicking for Distance	Kick	4–5	⟶		Kick	Moving into space, strong and light	319
Lead-up games							
Football End Ball	Pass, catch	6–8	⟶		Pass, catch	Moving into space, change of direction and speed	348
Punt Back	Punt, catch	Class	⟶		Punt, catch	Moving into space, change of direction and speed	348
One-Down Football	Pass, catch	16–20	⟶		Throw, catch, tag	Moving into space, change of direction and speed	348
Grab It	Run, tag	Class	⟶		Run, tag	Moving into space, change of direction and speed	349
Keep Away and Score	Pass, catch	8–10 per team	⟶		Pass, catch	Moving into space, change of direction and speed	349

Motor skills Punt, catch
Movement concepts Moving into space, change of direction and speed
Players Six to ten per team
Formation See diagram
Playing area Playground, gymnasium
Equipment Football

A player from one team punts the ball over the neutral zone into the opponent's area. The opponent closest to the ball tries to catch it. If successful, he punts the ball back and the game continues. If an opponent misses a catch (it must be in the air), the kicking side is awarded one point. If the ball does not pass out of the neutral zone, the captain of the opposite team may enter the zone to retrieve it. No score is awarded if the ball lands outside the playing area.

Suggestions and Variations

1. Rotate the lines on each team after a number of points have been scored or at set intervals.
2. Play the same game using a forward pass.

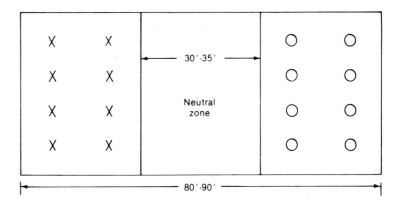

flag or touch football activities

Lead-Up Games

Football End Ball

Motor skills Pass, catch
Movement concepts Moving into space, change of speed and direction
Players Six to eight per group
Formation See diagram
Playing area Playground
Equipment One football per game

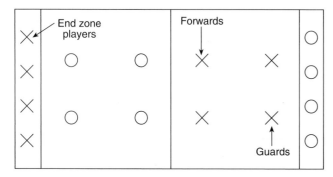

Arrange the field and players as shown in the diagram. The objective of the game is for a forward player to pass the ball to an end zone player. Players must remain in their own zones, and guards can only pass to forwards and forwards to end zone players. The game begins with a jump ball between two opposing forwards. The team that gets the ball tries to throw the ball to an end zone player, who must catch it while in the end zone area. Balls crossing end or side lines are put into play by the nearest player who did not cause the ball to go out of bounds. The ball is put into play by a throw from behind the line and closest to where the ball went out of bounds. Players may not hold the ball longer than five seconds, cross over into an opponent's territory, or push or hold an opponent. If a penalty occurs, the ball is given to the nearest opponent and the game continues. Award one point for each successful catch by an end zone player. Resume play with a jump ball at the center.

Punt Back

Motor skills Punt, catch
Movement concepts Moving into space, change of direction and speed
Players Class
Formation Half of a regular playing field, with each team scattered on its own side of the field
Playing area Playground, gymnasium, classroom
Equipment Football

The object of this game is to punt the ball over the opponent's goal line. One player begins the game by punting the ball from his own twenty-five-yard line. Once the game is started, opposing players must stay at least ten yards apart. If the ball is caught by a player on the opposite team and he calls "mark" and remains motionless for two seconds, he then has two options: (1) he may take five steps and then punt the ball, or (2) he may pass it to any

teammate. All players on his team, however, may be checked (as in basketball) as they try to catch the pass. If a player catches the ball, he must kick it from the point of the catch. If the catcher moves his feet while he is catching the ball or fails to call "mark," he is allowed only three steps before kicking the ball. If the ball is not caught, the player who secures the ball must punt it from the point where it was stopped.

A ball that goes over the sideline is punted back from the point where it went over the line. A ball that is caught in the air behind the goal line does not count as a point; it is put back into play by a punt from the goal line. One point is awarded for a successful punt over the goal line, provided it is not caught. The ball is put into play again at the twenty-five-yard line.

Suggestions and Variations
Use a placekick or a forward pass instead of a punt.

One-Down Football

Motor skills Throw, catch, tag
Movement concepts Moving into space, change of direction and speed
Players Eight to ten per team
Formation See diagram
Playing area Playground, gymnasium
Equipment Football

To start the game, both teams line up on opposite sides of the centerline. One team is designated as the offense and is given one down to score a touchdown. After the hike, the ball may be run or passed any number of times in any direction from any position on the field. The defensive team attempts to tag the ball carrier below the waist with two hands. If a player is tagged before he reaches the opponent's goal line, the ball is downed and the other team takes its down at this point. If a ball is intercepted, the game continues, with the defensive team becoming the offensive team.

Suggestions and Variations
1. When introducing this game, have all players play "man-to-man," that is, linemen checking linemen and backs checking backs. Later, variations can be made to meet the wishes of the defensive team.
2. Play same game using only the lateral pass.

Motor skills Run, tag
Movement concepts Moving into space, change of direction and speed
Players Class
Formation Large rectangular field
Playing area Playground, gymnasium
Equipment Flag football tags

Place one-half of class on one endline and the other half on the opposite line. Every player has a tag tucked into the back of his shorts. On signal, everyone runs to the appropriate line and tries to protect his own tag from being stolen while stealing as many as he can before reaching the opposite line.

Motor skills Pass, catch
Movement concepts Moving into space, change of direction and speed
Players Eight to ten per team
Formation Large rectangular field with centerline
Playing area Playground, gymnasium
Equipment Football

Each team stands on its own endline. One player is given the ball and his team begins to run, pass, and catch toward the opposite endline. The opposing team runs out to intercept the ball. When a player is tagged, he must immediately drop the ball, and he and his teammates must wait until an opponent has picked up the ball before anyone can resume running and tagging. Loose balls may be picked up by any player from either team.
Score one point for each touchdown.

Touch Football Rules and Regulations

It is recommended that upper elementary school children play seven-person touch or flag football. Commercial flags may be purchased from local sports stores, or you may improvise your own. (Flags are sometimes called tags.)

I. Field layout and lineups: See field layout and team positions in the accompanying diagram.
II. Start of game: The game is started with a kickoff (punt or placekick) from the goal line. The ball must be kicked past the centerline and must land within the field of play. If the first ball is kicked out-of-bounds, it is kicked again. If the second kick goes out-of-bounds, the other team starts play at its twenty-yard line. The kickoff team may recover the ball only after the other team touches and fumbles it.

III. Offensive play:
   A. Once a player who is returning the kickoff is touched, the ball is placed on the spot where he was tagged. The line drawn through this spot is known as the *scrimmage line*. In all cases, the ball must be placed five paces in from the sideline.
   B. The offensive team has four downs to move the ball into the next twenty-yard zone or to score a touchdown. Always start a new series of downs whenever a team crosses a zone line.
   C. The offensive team must have at least three players on the scrimmage line when a play begins. The center player must pass the ball backward through his legs. A backfield player who receives the ball may run with it, hand off, or throw a lateral or forward pass from behind the line of scrimmage. Any player except the center may receive the forward pass. The offensive team may punt on any down, providing it calls for a punt formation. When this occurs, neither team may cross the scrimmage line until the punt receiver has caught the ball.
IV. Defensive play:
   A. The defending team must remain behind the scrimmage line until the ball has left the opposing center's hands. A special rule applies to a punt, as previously described.

Field layout:

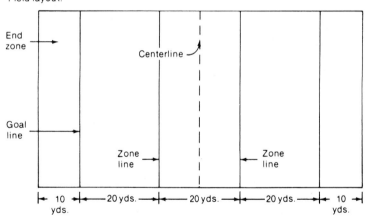

Offensive and defensive lineup positions:

flag or touch football activities

B. A defensive player may stop the ball carrier if he places two hands on or below his opponent's waist.

V. Blocking: A player may block only by placing his body in the way of an opponent. Review the description of blocking earlier in this chapter.

VI. Scoring: Points are awarded for the following:
A. Touchdown: Six points. Following the *touchdown,* one play or down is given to the scoring team from the three-yard line, and one more point is awarded if the team crosses the goal line.
B. Safety: Two points. The defensive team is awarded two points if the team in possession of the ball is tagged behind its own goal line. Immediately following the *safety,* the ball is put into play by the team scored against by a kickoff from behind the goal line.

VII. Touchback: A *touchback* occurs when a defensive player intercepts a ball behind his own goal line and does not run it out, or when the ball is kicked over the goal line by the offensive team. The ball is taken to the twenty-yard line and given to the defending team.

VIII. Penalties: Award five yards to the nonoffending team for the following infractions:
A. Pushing, holding, or tripping
B. Unsportsmanlike conduct
C. Interfering with the pass receiver
D. Offside

IX. Length of game: Two eight-minute periods

Evaluative Techniques

A few standardized tests are designed to measure the basic football skills. The majority of these tests, however, are designed for high school or college-level players, so they must be modified for elementary school players (table 20.3). This "teacher-made" test battery can be administered without elaborate equipment and in a short period of time. Use students to assist in testing, and keep scores from year to year in order to develop appropriate norms for your school.

Test 1: Accuracy Pass

Place a target on the wall as shown in the diagram. Each player is given ten consecutive throws from behind the starting line. He must use a forward pass. Score six, four, and two points for hits within each respective circle. If the ball hits a line, award the higher score. Record the total score.

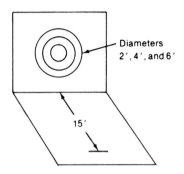

Test 2: Punting

Place lines on the field as shown in the diagram. Stakes can be used as a substitute for gypsum lines. Each player must punt a regulation-size football from behind the starting line. Mark where the ball lands with a stick or small object. Allow a total of three kicks and record the highest score. Yards are equivalent to points.

Test 3: Ball Carrying

Arrange four chairs as shown in the diagram. Place a ball on the starting line. Each player stands behind the starting line, with both hands resting on his knees. On signal, he picks up the football and runs around the left side of the first

Table 20.3	Touch Football Skill Test					
Name	**Accuracy pass (total pts.)**	**Punting (total pts.)**	**Ball carrying (total pts.)**	**Subjective evaluation (50 pts.)**	**Total score**	**Grade**
1 2 3 4 5			Rank total scores for the class, then convert to letter grades or ratings (superior, good, etc.).			

chair, and continues the zigzag running pattern around each chair. Allow thirty seconds for the test. One point is awarded for each chair he passes correctly. Two trials are allowed, with the highest score recorded.

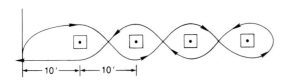

Test 4: Subjective Evaluation

Establish criteria that represent the skills and playing ability required in touch football, such as passing, feinting, kicking, and defensive ability. The teacher or a group of three players awards each player a total score ranging from zero to fifty points. When three players are judging, take an average of their scores.

Selected References

CAHPER. (1985). *Football Type Games.* Ottawa, Ontario: CAHPER Publications.

Fooss, D. (1984). *Complete Handbook of Winning Football Drills.* Newton, MA: Allyn and Bacon, Inc.

Kamiya, D. (1985). *Elementary Teacher's Handbook of Indoor and Outdoor Games.* West Nyack, NY: Parker Publishing Co., Inc.

Phillip, J. A., and Wilkerson, J. D. (1990). *Teaching Team Sports: A Coeducational Approach.* Champaign, IL: Human Kinetics Publishers, Inc.

Torba, E. M. (1983). *The Boys Club Guide to Youth Football.* New York: Leisure Press.

Turner, L. F., and Turner, L. S. (1989). *P. E. Teacher's Skill-by-Skill Activity Program.* West Nyack, NY: Parker Publishing Co., Inc.

Volleyball Activities

Volleyball was originated by William G. Morgan in 1895 while he was teaching at the YMCA in Holyoke, Massachusetts. Although the rules, number of players, and size of the ball have changed since that first game, volleyball can be classified as an American contribution to the world of sports. Today it is played by millions of people in more than sixty countries each year. This phenomenal growth in such a short time is probably due to the game's simplicity, enjoyment, and contributions to physical fitness.

Because volleyball can be adapted to the available facilities and varying levels of proficiency, it is a particularly good activity for the upper elementary physical education program ■

Emphasis and Progression

One of the most difficult tasks in teaching physical education is determining whether the children are familiar with the activity you wish to teach and whether they have the potential to develop the required skills. Volleyball is no exception. Some children already understand the rules of the game and have acquired a few of the basic skills. Others may not have seen a volleyball game or even have hit the ball correctly. With these factors in mind, the following suggested sequence for presenting skills and rules should be considered as a basic guideline.

Prior to the beginning of developmental level II, most children have learned to hit a utility ball from a bounce (two square and four square) or to hit a volleyball with a two-hand overhand hit. The main skills and playing strategies of volleyball are normally taught in the upper elementary grades. In developmental level II, as indicated in table 21.1, the overhand pass and underhand serve should be introduced with a beach ball. Once the skill level is high enough, a volleyball training ball or regular volleyball should be used. Serving distances, as well as the height of the net, should be adjusted to each class's ability.

The major emphasis throughout level III should be on refining the underhand serve and overhand pass and to learn the more advanced skills of the game. The latter skills include the forearm or bump pass, overhand serve, set-up, and net recovery. Although children in this age range enjoy playing regulation volleyball, such play should be limited. Such games as modified volleyball and sideline volleyball are more appropriate, as they contribute to skill development yet allow for greater participation and success by every player.

Teaching Procedures

A general format for planning a unit of instruction has been discussed extensively in previous chapters. Teachers should review the teaching procedures discussed in chapter 18 prior to developing a volleyball unit. In addition, the sample lesson plans in chapter 18 and the suggestions about incorporating the creative games approach can be applied to volleyball activities.

The following suggestions may help the teacher with some of the problems that are unique to teaching volleyball activities.

1. When there is only one instructional area, such as a gymnasium, choose or modify activities to be played on smaller courts (divide the volleyball court in half) and require fewer players (six or fewer) on a team.

2. During the initial stages of a volleyball unit, use beach, foam, or lightweight volleyball training balls. Young children, particularly third graders, normally lack sufficient arm and wrist strength to hit a heavy ball. Lighter balls are also slower, allowing children more time to get into position.

3. Adjust the height of the net to the ability of the class. As a general guideline, the net should be six feet high for level II children and seven feet high for level III children. Ropes with a few ribbons spaced every few feet can be substituted for a net.

4. Require the ball to be rolled to the server in all lead-up games or any type of modified volleyball activity that involves two teams on opposite sides of the net. Experienced teachers can verify the amount of time this simple procedure saves.

Table 21.1 Suggested Sequence of Presenting Volleyball Skills and Rules

Skills and rules	Developmental level II	Developmental level III
Volleying		
Overhand pass	Introduce	Refine
Forearm pass (bumping)		Introduce
Rules: Number of hits	Introduce	
Rotation	Introduce	
Line violations	Introduce	
Personal fouls		Introduce
Serving		
Underhand serve	Introduce	Refine
Overhand serve		Introduce
Rules: Serving positions		Introduce
Side out and points		Introduce
Setup		Introduce
Recovery from net		Introduce
All other official rules		Introduce

Description of Skills

There are two basic skills in volleyball, passing (or volleying) and serving a ball. Each of these skills, however, can be modified such as the two-hand underhand volley, requiring use of the forearms. Basic skills for intermediate grades—passing, serving, the set, and net recovery—are described and illustrated in this section.

Passing, or Volleying

The ball may be passed, or volleyed, to another player or over the net by an underhand or overhand hit. Both hands must be used in the overhand pass, whereas the forearms are normally used in the underhand pass. Children should be taught to watch the ball, not their hands or opponents. Body weight should be evenly distributed on both feet before the ball reaches the player. Finally, stress follow-through with the hands and arms after the ball has been hit.

Two-Hand Overhand Pass

The two-hand overhand pass is the most important volleyball skill for elementary school children to learn. It is virtually the prerequisite to playing volleyball; therefore, it requires a great deal of practice and constant correction by the teacher. The feet are in a forward stride position, with knees bent, back straight, and weight evenly distributed over both feet. Arms are extended upward and forward, with elbows rotated outward. The wrists are hyperextended, thumbs pointing toward each other, fingers relaxed and pointing diagonally upward (figure 21.1a). As the ball approaches, the player should be able to see through the window created by her thumbs and fingers. As the ball drops, the player extends her body upward and slightly forward, flexing the wrist and fingers, and contacts the ball with the fingers (figure 21.1b). After the ball is hit, follow-through is in the direction of the ball (figure 21.1c).

Key Teaching Points

1. Move into correct position, with hands and elbows up prior to hitting the ball.
2. Look through the "window" made by thumbs and spread fingers.
3. Contact the ball close to the forehead.
4. Contact the ball with the fingers and thumbs.
5. Snap the wrists forward and upward and follow through in the direction of the ball.

Forearm Pass

The forearm pass, also known as a "bump" or "bounce" pass, is used to receive a serve and to handle a ball that is too low or too far from the midline of the body to use an overhand pass.

As the ball approaches, the player moves into a position in which the midline of the body is in line with the ball. In

Figure 21.1 Two-hand overhand pass.

a   b   c

Figure 21.2 Forearm pass.

a   b   c

the ready position (figure 21.2a), feet are in a forward stride position, with the back straight, seat down, knees bent, and weight evenly distributed over both feet. The arms are held at a forty-five-degree angle forward and away from the body, with elbows straight, palms up, and fingers together. Simultaneously, one hand is placed diagonally onto the fingers of the other hand, and legs are extended to lift body and arms upward. As the ball is contacted just above the waist, the arms are straight and the thumbs are pointing downward (figure 21.2b). Follow-through is a continuation of the upward extension of the legs and a very slight upward movement of the arms (figure 21.2c).

Key Teaching Points

1. Move into correct position prior to executing the pass.
2. The ball should be contacted when it is between the knees and waist.
3. Contact the ball on the forearms between the wrists and elbows.
4. Upon contact, "lift" the body upward by straightening the legs. Do not swing forearms upward to hit the ball.
5. Do not follow-through.

Serving

It is permissible to serve the ball from either an underhand or overhand position. The hand may be open or closed. Boys and girls in the intermediate grades are capable of developing a high level of skill in both serves. Begin with the underhand serve and, after sufficient skill has been developed, introduce the overhand "float" serve.

Underhand Serve

The underhand serve is performed with the left foot (right foot for left-handed players) slightly in front of the right foot. The weight is on the rear foot and the body is bent forward slightly (figure 21.3a). The ball is held with the palm of the left hand in a "ready" position in front of the right knee. The right arm is extended backward and upward. As the right arm swings down and forward, a small step is taken as the weight shifts to the front foot. The ball is hit with the heel of the right hand (figure 21.3b) or the side of the fist. Immediately before the hand contacts the ball, the ball is released out of the left hand. Continue the follow-through action of the right arm (figure 21.3c).

Key Teaching Points

1. Opposite foot to striking hand should be in forward position.
2. Draw striking hand directly backward with straight arm.
3. Simultaneously, take a short step and swing arm downward and forward.
4. Follow through to about shoulder level.

Overhand Serve

The overhand serve should be learned only after a player has mastered the underhand serve. The advantages of the overhand, or "float," serve are that it can place the ball accurately and it has an element of deception caused by its floating and wobbling action.

The server stands with hips and shoulders square to the net, ball held chest high and in line with the right shoulder. Feet are in a stride position with the left foot pointing toward the net and the right foot pointing diagonally toward the right.

Figure 21.3 Serving.

a b c

Figure 21.4 Overhand serve.

a b c

Weight is evenly distributed over both feet. The server's right hand is held in a ready position just above the right foot. The ball is tossed up with the left hand two or three feet above the right shoulder (figure 21.4a). As the toss is made, the weight shifts to the back foot. As the ball begins to descend, the weight is shifted to the front foot and the striking arm snaps forward (figure 21.4b). Contact is made near the center of the ball with the heel of the hand and palm and the ball is hit through the midline. The wrist remains rigid as contact is made (figure 21.4c).

Key Teaching Points

1. Opposite foot to striking hand should be in a forward position.
2. Hold the ball about eye level.
3. Simultaneously, shift weight to rear foot as toss is made, then to front foot as striking hand moves forward.
4. Snap the wrist as contact is made and do not follow through with the extended arm.

The Set

The set is a two-hand overhand hit, normally the second hit in the series of three that is allowed each team. This overhand hit is used to pass the ball about fifteen feet above the receiver and approximately one foot away from the net. Since the ball moves in the direction the body is facing, it is extremely important for the setter to get into position under the ball and facing the intended receiver just before the pass is made.

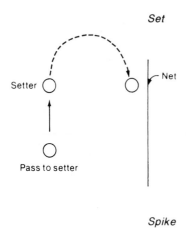

Set

Spike

Key Teaching Points

1. Move into correct position just before passing the ball.
2. Watch the ball through the triangle made by fingers and thumb.
3. Pass the ball in a high arc so it floats down to the intended receiver.
4. Quickly move back to playing position.

Net Recovery

The one- or two-hand forearm pass is used to recover a mispassed ball from the net. The player stands with her side to the net in order to move quickly toward or away from the net, or to pass in any direction. Whenever possible, use a two-hand forearm pass (figure 21.5) and contact the ball as low as possible. Normally, the lower the ball, the farther it is away from the net; thus, the easier it is to pass to another player or directly over the net. The one-hand forearm pass (dig) should only be used when poor position or lack of time prevents application of the two-hand pass (figure 21.6).

Key Teaching Points

1. Move quickly into the correct position.
2. Hit the ball upward and slightly away from the net.
3. Quickly move back to playing position.

Figure 21.5 Two-hand forearm pass.

Figure 21.6 One-hand forearm pass.

Practice Activities and Lead-Up Games

The following activities are designed to allow students to practice one or more volleyball skills in an enjoyable, gamelike situation (table 21.2). Each skill should begin with individual activities so that children develop a basic understanding of the skill and can explore the limits of their ability. Partner activities should follow, stressing ball control and positional play. Finally, group activities involving three or more players provide a gamelike experience while concentrating on one or two basic skills. There is ample opportunity in each type of activity for teachers to inject the inventive games approach by modifying existing drills or creating student-designed practice activities.

The lead-up games described in this section are popular in both developmental levels. However, children in level II require the greatest number of modifications to the rules and court dimensions in order to provide a game that is within their general level of ability. Teachers should modify any of these games to meet the level of ability and interest of each class.

Table 21.2 Practice Activities and Lead-Up Games

Name of activity	Type of activity	Players	Developmental level		Volleyball concepts and skills	Movement concepts	Page
			II	III			
Practice activities							
Individual Volleying	Throw, volley	Individual	———→		Throw, overhead volley	Personal space, transfer of weight	360
Partner Passing	Volley	2	———→		Volley, catch	Moving into space, change of direction and speed	360
Partner Serving	Volley, serve	2	———→		Serve, volley, set	Moving into space, change of direction and speed	360
Triangle Passing	Pass	3	———→		Pass	Moving into space, change of direction	360
Volley and Backset	Volley	3	———→		Volley, set	Moving into space, change of direction	360
Hit the Square	Volley	3	———→		Throw, volley	Moving into space, change of direction	361
Set Up the Ball	Set	4	———→		Volley, set	Moving into space, change of direction and speed	361
Shuttle Volley	Volley	5–6	———→		Throw, volley	Moving into space, change of direction and speed	361
Circle Volley	Volley	5–6	———→		Throw, volley	Personal space, moving into space	361
Zigzag Volley	Volley	6–8	———→		Throw, volley	Personal space, moving into space, change of direction	361
Baseline Serving	Serve	Class	———→		Serve	Use of available space, serving into empty space	362
Circuit Volleying	All skills	Class	———→		All skills	Use of available space, moving into space, change of direction, speed, and pathway	362
Lead-up games							
Nebraska Ball	Serve, volley	9 per team	—→		Serve, volley	Personal and general space, change of direction	362
Bound Ball	Serve, volley	6–10 per team	—→		Serve, volley	Moving into space, change of direction	362
Mass Volleyball	Serve, volley	6–9 per team	—→		Serve, volley	Moving into space, change of direction	362
Newcomb	Serve, volley	6–9 per team	—→		Serve, volley	Moving into space, change of direction	363
Keep It Up	Volley, bump	6–9 per team	———→		Volley, bump	Personal space, levels, change of direction	363
Donkey	Volley, bump	5–6 per team	———→		Volley, bump	Moving into space, levels, change of direction and speed	363
Modified Volleyball	Serve, volley	6–9 per team	———→		Serve, volley, rotate	Personal space, moving into space, change of direction and speed	363
Volleyball Keep Away	Volley	5–6 per team	———→		Volley	Moving into space, change of direction and speed	364
Four-Way Volleyball	Volley, serve	4–5 per team	———→		Serve, volley, bump	Change of direction and speed	364
Sideline Volleyball	Ball skills	8–10 per team	———→		Serve, volley, bump	Moving into space, change of direction and speed	364
Cross-Over Blanket Volleyball	Running	8–10 per team	———→		Running	Moving into space, change of direction	294

Practice Activities

Individual Volleying

Motor skills   Throw, overhand volley
Movement concepts   Personal space, transfer of weight
Players   Individual
Formation   Scattered
Playing area   Playground, gymnasium
Equipment   Volleyballs, Nerf balls, or beach balls

Arrange players in a scattered formation. This drill requires one ball for each child; however, any type of inflated ball can be used. Begin with each player throwing the ball into the air and catching it close to his forehead after one bounce. He should be in a semicrouched position. Gradually introduce the following individual variations.

1. Throw the ball up, perform an overhand volley on the returning ball, then catch it.
2. Throw . . . set . . . set . . . catch.
3. Throw . . . set . . . set . . . continue.
4. Throw . . . set . . . allow one bounce . . . set . . . catch.
5. Throw . . . kneel and set . . . stand and set . . . catch.
6. Repeat variations 1 to 3 while sitting.
7. Arrange the class in a line formation around the gymnasium approximately six feet from the wall. Have the children
   a. Throw the ball against the wall, set, and catch
   b. Throw against the wall, set, set, and catch
   c. Throw against the wall and continuously set the ball back to the wall
   d. Throw against the wall, allow one bounce, set, and catch

Partner Passing

Motor skills   Passing
Movement concepts   Moving into space, change of direction and speed
Players   Two
Formation   Scattered
Playing area   Playground, gymnasium
Equipment   Volleyball

Partners standing about ten feet apart are arranged in a scattered formation. One partner throws a high pass and the other catches it. Stress moving into position to receive the ball. Player 1 throws to player 2. Player 2 sets back to 1, who catches the ball. Player 1 throws to 2. They continue to set to each other. Player 1 throws to 2. As soon as player 1 has thrown, he moves to a new position. Player 2 then sets to 1, then moves to his new position. Continue pattern.

Suggestions and Variations

1. Partners are arranged around the gymnasium about ten feet from the wall. Player 1 throws against the wall and player 2 sets the ball above player 1. Player 1 catches. Partners change positions and repeat. Player 1 throws against the wall, player 2 sets back to wall. Continue drill, alternating sets. Repeat above variation, but require a bounce before the return set is attempted.

2. Arrange partners on opposite sides of a net or rope. Player 1 throws over the net and player 2 sets back over the net to 1, who catches the ball. Repeat above variation, but continue setting back and forth.

Partner Serving

Motor skills   Serve, volley, set
Movement concepts   Moving into space, change of direction and speed
Players   Two
Formation   Scattered
Playing area   Playground, gymnasium
Equipment   Volleyball

Arrange partners on opposite sides of the net. Adjust the distance to the class's level of ability. Have partners free serve back and forth. Move partners closer together. Player 1 serves to player 2, who sets the ball back to player 1. Change positions and repeat. One partner serves to the wall, the other catches the ball and repeats the serve. One partner serves and the other sets back to the wall. Continue setting until one partner misses a return.

Triangle Passing

Motor skills   Passing
Movement concepts   Moving into space, change of direction
Players   Three
Formation   Triangle
Playing area   Playground, gymnasium
Equipment   Volleyball

Arrange groups of three in a triangle pattern with about fifteen feet between players. Player 1 volleys to 2, 2 volleys to 3, and 3 volleys to 1.

Suggestions and Variations

1. Player 1 volleys to 2, then moves forward to take player 2's position. Player 2 volleys to 3 and moves to his position. Continue pattern.
2. Repeat first practice activity and introduce a bump on alternate hits.

Volley and Backset

Motor skills   Volley, set
Movement concepts   Moving into space, change of direction
Players   Three
Formation   Line
Playing area   Playground, gymnasium
Equipment   Volleyball

Player 1 volleys to 2, 2 backsets to 3; player 2 turns and faces 3, 3 volleys to 2, and 2 backsets to 1. Repeat movement.

Suggestions and Variations

Player 1 volleys to 2; 2 volleys to 1; 1 volleys to 2; 2 backsets to 3.

Hit the Square

Motor skills Throw, volley
Movement concepts Moving into space, change of direction
Players Three
Formation See diagram
Playing area Playground, gymnasium
Equipment Volleyball

The leader tosses the ball to the first player, who tries to return a high arc set into the square. Each player is given three turns before going to the back of the line. The leader rotates after every player has had a turn.

Suggestions and Variations

The leader throws, the first player returns a set and then goes to the back of the line, and the leader returns a set to the second player in the line.

Set Up the Ball

Motor skills Volley, set
Movement concepts Moving into space, change of direction and speed
Players Four
Formation See diagram
Playing area Playground, gymnasium, classroom
Equipment Volleyball, net

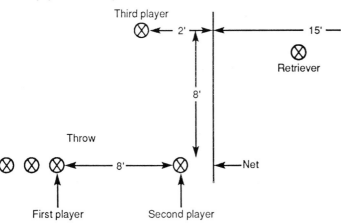

Player 1 throws a high arc pass to player 2, who sets up the ball for player 3. Player 3 attempts to pass the ball over the net to the retriever. After each play, the retriever goes to the back of the line and all other players move up one position.

Suggestions and Variations

1. Player 1 throws the ball up to himself, then volleys it to player 2. The drill continues as previously described.

2. Repeat original drill with retriever attempting to pass the ball to the next thrower.

Shuttle Volley

Motor skills Throw, volley
Movement concepts Moving into space, change of direction and speed
Players Five or six per group
Formation Shuttle
Playing area Playground, gymnasium
Equipment Volleyball

Divide class into squads of five or six players. Arrange squads in a shuttle formation with about six feet between players. Player 1 throws the ball to player 2. Player 2 volleys it to player 3, who has taken player 1's position. Each player goes to the end of the line after volleying the ball. Reverse the direction of the throw after everyone has had a turn.

Suggestions and Variations

1. Same formation with net between lines.
2. Volley with one or two hands.
3. As proficiency develops, increase the distance between the lines.

Circle Volley

Motor skills Throw, volley
Movement concepts Personal space, moving into space
Players Five or six per group
Formation Circle
Playing area Playground, gymnasium
Equipment Volleyball

Divide class into squads of five or six players. Arrange each squad in a circle formation with about five feet between each player. Player 1 throws the ball up and toward player 2, who volleys it to player 1. Player 1 then throws to player 3 and so on until every circle player has volleyed the ball back to player 1.

Suggestions and Variations

1. As proficiency increases, have player 1 throw to player 2, who volleys to player 3. Player 3 volleys to player 4, and so on around the circle.
2. Keep It Up. After the first player has started the drill, allow anyone to hit the ball and see how long the squad can keep it up.

Zigzag Volley

Motor skills Throw, volley
Movement concepts Personal space, moving into space, change of direction
Players Six to eight per group
Formation Zigzag
Playing area Playground, gymnasium
Equipment Volleyball

Divide the class into squads of six to eight players. Arrange squads in a zigzag formation, with about ten feet between each line. Player 1 throws the ball across to player 2, who volleys the ball to player 3. Continue the zigzag volleying pattern.

Baseline Serving

Motor skills Serve
Movement concepts Use of available space, serving into empty space
Players Class
Formation Line
Playing area Playground, gymnasium
Equipment Volleyballs

Divide class into two squads, with each evenly distributed along its baseline. One player from each team is assigned to the retriever position. Use as many balls as you have available. Any child on the baseline may begin by serving the ball over the net. The ball is then served back by the child who retrieves it. No serving order need be kept. The retriever's job is to catch and pass the ball back to anyone on his team.

Suggestions and Variations

1. Raise or lower height of net according to skill level of class.
2. Place one or more large mats on each side of net and near the middle of the court. Direct players to try to hit the mat.

Circuit Volleying

Motor skills All skills
Movement concepts Use of available space, moving into space, change of direction, pathway, and speed
Players Class
Formation See diagram
Playing area Playground, gymnasium
Equipment Volleyballs

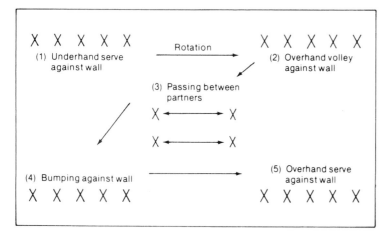

Divide the class into five teams and arrange as in the diagram. On "go," each team practices its respective skill for a set period of time (ranging from one to several minutes). At the end of each practice period, each team places the ball on the floor and rotates to the next station. Continue rotation.

Lead-Up Games

Nebraska Ball

Motor skills Serve, volley
Movement concepts Personal and general space, change of direction
Players Nine on each team
Formation Scattered on each side of the net (or rope)
Playing area Playground, gymnasium, classroom
Equipment Volleyball court, net or rope, beach ball or large utility ball

Establish a serving line approximately ten to fifteen feet from the net. One player serves the ball over the net. Any number of players may hit the ball before it returns over the net. A point is scored when the ball hits the floor. Start play on the side where the ball hits the floor.

Suggestions and Variations

1. Lengthen the distance of the serving line.
2. Limit the number of passes to five, four, then three.
3. Limit passing to forearm passes.

Bound Ball

Motor skills Serve, volley
Movement concepts Moving into space, change of direction
Players Six to ten per team
Formation Scattered on each side of net
Playing area Playground, gymnasium
Equipment Volleyball

The server, standing anywhere behind the endline, bounces the ball once and then hits it over the centerline. The ball must bounce once before an opposing player is allowed to return it over the line. Each team is allowed three hits; however, the ball must bounce between each hit. No player is allowed to hit the ball twice in succession. If the ball hits the centerline, it is considered dead and the play is retaken. Balls hitting boundary lines are still in play. If the nonserving team fails to return the ball within three bounces, the serving team is awarded one point. If the serving team fails to get the serve over the centerline or fails to return a played ball, no point is scored and the ball is given to the other team. Game continues to fifteen points.

Suggestions and Variations

1. Have server begin from behind a fifteen-foot serving line.
2. Add a net or rope and require players to pass the ball over it.

Mass Volleyball

Motor skills Serve, volley
Movement concepts Moving into space, change of direction
Players Six to nine per team
Formation Players of each team arranged in equal rows on each side of the net
Playing area Playground, gymnasium
Equipment Volleyball

Any player may serve the ball from anywhere in his court. Teams volley the ball back and forth across the net. Anyone may hit the ball as many times as he wishes; however, only three players may touch the ball before returning it over the net. Change the serve after a team fails to return the ball. The serving team scores one point whenever the opposing team commits one of the following fouls: (1) failing to return the ball, (2) catching the ball, (3) knocking the ball out-of-bounds, (4) allowing the ball to touch the floor, or (5) touching the net. A game may be played to any number of points (eleven or fifteen is desirable).

Suggestions and Variations

1. Have players serve from behind a serving line.
2. Allow any number of players to hit the ball as many times as they wish before returning it over the net.
3. Limit passing to either overhand or forearm passes.

Newcomb

Motor skills Serve, volley
Movement concepts Moving into space, change of direction
Players Six to nine per team
Formation Volleyball court with teams arranged in equal rows on each side of net
Playing area Playground, gymnasium
Equipment Volleyball court, net, volleyball or large utility ball

Server serves the ball over the net. The other team tries to return the ball after the serve, with any number of players allowed to hit the ball. The server continues until his team loses the ball. Only the serving team scores. A predetermined time limit or score is set. Fouls are (1) hitting the ball out-of-bounds, (2) holding the ball, (3) touching the net, (4) walking with the ball, (5) throwing the ball out-of-bounds, or (6) letting the ball hit the floor.

Suggestions and Variations

1. If skill level is too low, allow the ball to bounce once before it is hit. Also, adjust the position of the serving line to the level of skill.
2. Blind Newcomb. Play the same game with a blanket draped over the net to restrict visibility, which provides an element of fun and excitement.

Keep It Up

Motor skills Volley, bump
Movement concepts Personal space, levels, change of direction
Players Six to nine per team
Formation Circle
Playing area Playground, gymnasium
Equipment Volleyball

Each circle tries to keep its ball in the air by volleying it from player to player. The ball may be hit to any player in the circle. The team that keeps the ball up the longest wins.

Suggestions and Variations

1. Simplify the game by allowing one bounce between each hit.
2. Place a player in the middle of the circle.
3. As skill improves, allow only one type of pass.

Donkey

Motor skills Volley, bump
Movement concepts Moving into space, levels, change of direction and speed
Players Five or six per team
Formation Groups
Playing area Playground, gymnasium
Equipment Volleyball

Arrange class into groups of five players. Players form a line facing a wall, with the first player standing about four feet from the wall and holding a ball. The first player throws the ball up, then volleys it above a line drawn seven feet up the wall. The next player must move forward and volley the ball above the seven-foot line. A player who misses a volley gets the first letter and so on until he reaches D-O-N-K-E-Y. Once a player reaches "Donkey," he continues to play until three players have reached "Donkey." When this happens, change positions of players and begin a new game.

Modified Volleyball

Motor skills Serve, volley, rotate
Movement concepts Personal space, moving into space, change of direction and speed
Players Six to nine per team
Formation See diagram
Playing area Playground, gymnasium
Equipment Volleyball

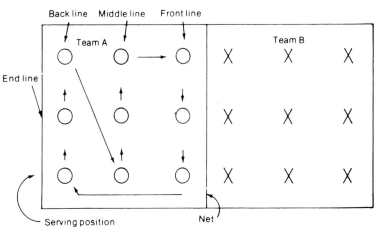

The server stands behind the endline and serves the ball over the net. If the level of skill is too low, allow any player in the front line to assist the ball over the net. The opposing team attempts to get the ball back over the net before it touches the ground. The ball can be volleyed by as many players on either team as is necessary to return the ball over the net. All other volleyball rules and scoring apply to this game.

Suggestions Variations

1. Allow the server two tries to get the ball over the net.
2. Use only one type of pass.
3. Fanny Ball. Play the same game using a beach ball and with all players remaining in a sitting position.

Motor skills   Volley
Movement concepts   Moving into space, change of direction and speed
Players   Five or six per team
Formation   Teams scattered with a designated play area
Playing area   Playground, gymnasium
Equipment   Volleyball

By volleying the ball from one team member to another, the team with the ball tries to keep the ball away from the other team. Members of the other team try to intercept the ball. It can be intercepted only when it is dropping (on the downward arc). After the ball has been intercepted, the team in possession volleys the ball. The team volleying the ball the highest number of times wins. A time limit also may be used.

Suggestions and Variations
1. Limit playing area to enhance ball control.
2. Limit game to one type of pass.

Four-Way Volleyball

Motor skills   Serve, volley, bump
Movement concepts   Moving into space, change of direction and speed
Players   Four or six per team
Formation   See diagram
Playing area   Playground, gymnasium
Equipment   Volleyball and two nets or ropes

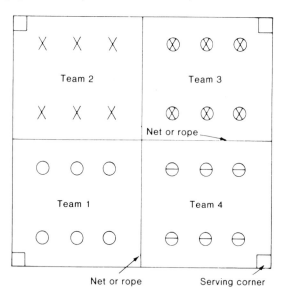

There are four separate teams in this game. Players in courts 1 and 2 may serve only into courts 3 and 4. Similarly, players in courts 3 and 4 may serve only into courts 1 and 2. However, after the serve, a team may hit the ball into any of the other three courts. When a fair serve is made and the ball touches the floor or fails to get out of the receiver's court within the allotted three hits, the serving team scores one point and continues serving as in regular volleyball. However, when a receiving team hits the ball into another court fairly, this team becomes the serving team the moment the ball leaves its court. If the new receiving team fails to pass the ball out of its court, the new serving team is awarded one point. All other regular volleyball rules apply.

Suggestions and Variation
Limit any receiving team to only one pass.

Sideline Volleyball

Motor skills   All volleyball skills
Movement concepts   Moving into space, change of direction and speed
Players   Eight to ten per team
Formation   See diagram
Playing area   Playground, gymnasium
Equipment   Volleyball

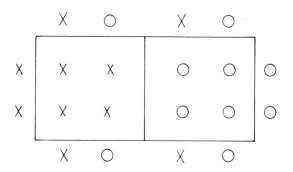

This game is played like regular volleyball, with the addition of active sideline players. Sideline players stay in their assigned positions; they cannot enter the court area, but they are permitted to pass any loose balls from either team, providing the balls have not touched the ground. Sideline players cannot pass to each other. A hit made by a sideline player is a free hit for his team and does not count as one of the team's hits. Rotate the court and sideline players after six points are scored and continue the game to fifteen points.

Suggestions and Variations
1. Count sideline hits.
2. Restrict sideline hits to one type of volley.

Volleyball Rules and Regulations

Although there are fewer skills to learn in volleyball than the other major sports, it is one of the more difficult games for boys and girls in developmental levels II and III. The difficulty, in most cases, is the result of inadequate arm and shoulder girdle strength and inaccuracy in serving and volleying. Nevertheless, fifth and sixth graders should be exposed to the complete game of volleyball early in the instructional unit. Modify the rules to meet the level of skill, available facilities, and number of children. Consider modifying the length of the game, the number of players, the height of the net, type and size of ball, and the size of the playing court.

I. Field of play: See the diagram.

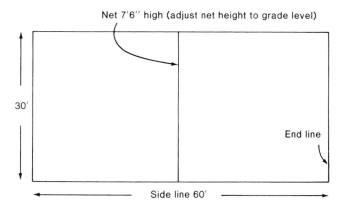

Net 7′6″ high (adjust net height to grade level)

30′

End line

Side line 60′

II. Recommended net heights:
Grade four—six feet
Grade five—seven feet
Grade six—seven feet

III. Positions and Rotation Pattern (after opponents lose their serve): See the diagram.

LB Left back   LF Left forward

CB Center back   CF Center forward

RB Right back   RF Right forward

IV. To start the game: The right back player starts the game by serving the ball from behind the endline. He is allowed only one serve.

V. To return the ball: After the ball has been served, players on both sides must abide by the following rules:
   A. Any player who receives the ball is allowed one volley (hit) over the net or to another teammate.
   B. The ball may not be volleyed (hit) more than three times by a team before it is sent over the net.
   C. A ball that hits the net on the return volley and falls into the opponent's court is a fair ball.
   D. A ball that hits the net on the return volley and falls back into the court from which it was sent may be played before it hits the ground, provided (1) it is not volleyed by the player who hit it into the net and (2) it was not volleyed by more than two players before it hit the net.

VI. To play: The server hits the ball over the net. If the opposing team fails to return it over the net, one point is awarded to the serving team. However, if the ball is returned to the serving team and it fails to return again, the serving team loses the serve. No point is awarded on the loss of serve. Player rotation should be made only by the team receiving the serve.

VII. Violations: If any of the following violations is committed by the serving team, the serve is lost. This is called *side out.* If one is committed by the receiving team, the serving team is awarded one point.
   A. Failing to make a fair or legal serve
   B. Returning the ball in any way other than by hitting it. Balls may not be caught and thrown over the net.
   C. Volleying the ball more than three times before it goes over the net
   D. Letting the ball touch the floor outside the court lines. Note: A ball may be played from outside the court area if it has not touched the ground.
   E. Failing to return the ball over the net
   F. Failing to rotate in the proper order

VIII. Scoring:
   A. Only the serving team can score.
   B. Eleven, fifteen, or twenty-one points constitutes a game. A team must win by two points; thus, if the score is ten-all in an eleven-point game, one team must score two successive points to win.

Evaluative Techniques

There are numerous methods of measuring volleyball skills and knowledge. The majority of tests used by classroom teachers are of an objective nature and usually are modifications of existing standardized test batteries. Teachers should be encouraged to develop their own test batteries and keep scores of each test in order to develop appropriate norms for their teaching situations. The test battery in table 21.3 is an example of a "teacher-made" test that can be administered to the children in a short period of time.

Test 1: Wall Volley

Draw one line on the wall six feet up from the floor and a second line on the floor three feet from the wall. The player must stand behind this line, toss the ball in the air, and volley it against the wall above the six-foot line. One point is awarded for each hit above the line. Score the number of hits made in twenty seconds. A player who drops the ball within this period may pick it up and continue volleying. Allow two trials and record the highest score.

Table 21.3 Volleyball Skill Test

Name	Wall volley (total pts.)	Service over net (20 pts.)	Forearm pass (20 pts.)	Subjective evaluation (50 pts.)	Total score	Grade
1 2 3 4		Rank all total scores for the class, then convert to letter grades or ratings (superior, good, etc.).				

Test 2: Serving over the Net

Each player is given ten consecutive serves, with each successful serve awarded five points. This test can be modified by dividing the opposite court into zones, with each given a different point value. For example, make three equal zones running perpendicular to the net; the zone farthest from the server would equal five points; the next one, three points; and the nearest zone, one point.

Test 3: Forearm Pass

One student, who will throw the ball over the net, stands behind a line drawn six feet away from the net. Adjust the height of the net according to grade level. The student taking the test stands in the opposite court behind a line drawn six feet away from the net. The first student throws the ball in a high arc over the net. The second student (testing) must pass the ball back over the net with a forearm pass. Repeat four times and award five points for each successful pass. If the throw was too low and poorly thrown, allow the player another try.

Test 4: Subjective Evaluation of Playing Ability

Establish criteria that represent the skills and playing ability required in volleyball. For example, using such factors as positional play, alertness, volleying ability, and team play, the teacher awards each player a score from zero to fifty points. Three players can be used as judges, with the average score recorded.

Selected References

CAHPER. (1985). *Volleyball-Type Games.* Ottawa, Ontario: CAHPER Publications.

Kamiya, A. (1985). *Elementary Teacher's Handbook of Indoor and Outdoor Games.* West Nyack, NY: Parker Publishing Co., Inc.

Kluka, D. A., and Dunn, P. J. (1989). *Volleyball.* Dubuque, IA: Wm. C. Brown Publishers.

NAGUS. (1989). *Volleyball Guide.* Reston, VA: AAHPERD.

Philipp, J. A., and Wilkerson J. D. (1990). *Teaching Team Sports: A Coeducational Approach,* Champaign, IL: Human Kinetics Publishers, Inc.

Samula, L., and Valeriote, T. (1984). *Volleyball Development Model.* Vanier, Ontario: Coaching Association of Canada, Canadian Volleyball Association.

Scates, B. L., and Ferguson, B. J. (1989). *Winning Volleyball Drills.* Dubuque, IA: Wm. C. Brown Publishers.

Turner, L. F., and Turner, S. L. (1989). *P.E. Teacher's Skill-by-Skill Activities Program.* West Nyack, NY: Parker Publishing Co., Inc.

Viera, B. C., and Ferguson, B. J. (1989). *Teaching Volleyball: Steps To Success.* Champaign, IL: Leisure Press.

22

Basketball Activities

Basketball, like volleyball, originated in the United States and has since become a sport that is played in nearly every country in the world. There is no single reason for its popularity as both a participant and spectator sport. Children, youths, and adults enjoy the game because it is fun and challenging, and it contributes to many important components of physical fitness. Since the game can be modified to meet court size limitations and varying levels of skill, it should be considered a basic activity for the upper elementary physical education program. This chapter has been organized to provide a format for teaching basketball skills and knowledge to these children ■

Emphasis and Progression

Many basketball skills have been learned in earlier grades or out of school. The many backyard basketball courts not only attest to the popularity of the sport, but they also provide the opportunity for elementary school children to learn basketball skills from their older brothers and sisters and parents. Consequently, there is a wide variation in the level of basketball skill in virtually every intermediate grade in the elementary school. With these considerations in mind, the suggested sequence of presenting skills and rules in table 22.1 is provided as a basic guide.

By the time children have reached developmental level II, most of them have learned several of the basic skills involved in passing, catching, dribbling, and shooting. However, the acquisition of these skills prior to developmental level III should not result in a conscious extension of the basketball program down to the primary grades. Rather, developmental levels I and II should continue to emphasize low-organization games, with some of the specialized skills of basketball and other sports being acquired in the process.

The main emphasis throughout developmental level III should be to continue practicing the basic passing, catching, dribbling, and shooting skills to improve accuracy and proficiency. Children should also be introduced to a few new shooting skills and several main rules of basketball. More emphasis is placed on using both hands, pivoting and weaving, and general playing ability. It is a period of refining playing skills and team strategies.

Teaching Procedures

Teaching the skills and team strategies of basketball to children in developmental levels II and III presents several problems. A main one, as stated earlier, is that the skill level and playing ability of these children vary widely. Some children have played on out-of-school teams or have their own backyard hoops, whereas others have not had any experience with the game. The challenge to the teacher is to cope with these major differences in the design and presentation of an instructional unit.

Developing a Basketball Unit

The general instructional procedures discussed in previous chapters also apply to basketball activities. Of particular importance is the process of developing units of instruction in chapter 18 and the structure of a lesson on page 307. In addition, the inventive games approach described on page 252 can be applied to the teaching of basketball activities.

Table 22.1 Suggested Sequence of Presenting Basketball Skills and Rules

Skills and rules	Developmental level II	Developmental level III
Passing		
Chest pass	Acquired or introduce	Increase proficiency and accuracy
Bounce pass	Acquired or introduce	Increase proficiency and accuracy
Two-hand overhead pass		Introduce
One-hand bounce pass	Acquired or introduce	Increase proficiency and accuracy
Baseball pass	Acquired or introduce	Increase distance and accuracy
Catching		
From below the waist	Acquired or introduce	Catch while moving
From above the waist	Acquired or introduce	Catch while moving
Rules: Line violations	Introduce	
Out-of-bounds	Introduce	
Dribbling		
While standing and moving	Acquired or introduce	Dribble, weave, and pivot
Rule: Traveling		Introduce
Shooting		
One-hand push	Introduce	Increase distance and accuracy
Lay-up	Introduce	With either hand
Free throw		Introduce
Rules: Scoring	Introduce	
Key positions		Introduce
Related skills		
Pivoting	Introduce	Refine
Feinting		Introduce
Guarding	Introduce	Refine
Rebounding		Introduce
Rules: Personal fouls		Introduce

Figure 22.1 Two-hand chest pass.

a   b   c

Since the length of the unit and the lesson, as well as the facilities and equipment available, will vary in each teaching situation, the following suggested approach should be considered a basic guideline. Modify it to cope with your individual situation.

Step 1: Determine the length of your basketball unit. Express this in the number of lessons rather than weeks.

Step 2: Assess the general level of ability of your class (see the evaluative techniques at the end of the chapter).

Step 3: Select the skills and rules you wish to emphasize in your unit (see table 22.1).

Step 4: Choose the appropriate practice activities and lead-up games.

Structure of a Lesson

The detailed explanation of how to plan a lesson described in chapter 18, "Soccer Activities," should be followed when preparing and presenting basketball activities. The procedure of moving from individual to partner to group activities can be adapted successfully to each basketball lesson.

Description of Skills

Basketball skills can be broadly classified as passing, catching, dribbling, shooting, guarding, and feinting. Each skill, in turn, can be subdivided, such as the chest pass, two-hand overhead pass, and baseball pass. Each of these skills is described in this section, accompanied by a list of the more common faults.

Passing

Passing is transferring the ball from one player to another, from a stationary position or while in motion. A player may pass the ball with one or both hands and from a variety of positions. The basic fundamentals of all passes are (1) accuracy—avoiding "wild throws," (2) following through with every pass, and (3) shifting the ball as quickly as possible from a receiving position to a passing position.

Two-Hand Chest Pass

The two-hand chest, or push, pass is one of the most useful and effective passes in basketball. Since its main advantages are ease and speed of delivery, it is the pass used most often, particularly for short distances.

Assume a forward-stride position, with weight evenly distributed over both feet. Grip the ball with both hands, fingers spread around the sides of the ball, with thumbs behind and close together (figure 22.1a). Simultaneously shift weight to rear foot and the ball toward the chest, keeping elbows comfortably at the side of the body, waist high and pointing toward the floor (figure 22.1b). Step forward, extend arms, and turn thumbs downward. Release the ball with a quick wrist snap downward and outward, giving the ball a slight backspin (figure 22.1c).

Key Teaching Points

1. Hold the ball on tips of fingers and thumbs.
2. Keep elbows reasonably close to sides of body and pointing down.
3. Step forward with the dominant foot.
4. Extend arms and push thumbs downward.

Figure 22.2 Two-hand bounce pass.

Two-Hand Bounce Pass

The two-hand bounce pass is performed by bouncing the ball on the floor before it rebounds to the receiver (figure 22.2). This type of pass provides a deceptive action to get the ball past an opponent to another teammate. In order for a teammate to receive the ball about waist high, the ball should strike the floor two-thirds the distance between the two players and nearer the receiver.

Key Teaching Points

1. Begin with weight distributed evenly over both feet.
2. Keep ball close to chest and elbows reasonably close to sides of body.
3. Take a quick step, extend arms, and release ball with a quick snap of the wrists.
4. Catcher should receive the ball about waist high.

Two-Hand Overhead Pass

The two-hand overhead pass is extremely effective for short passes and when a player wishes to throw the ball to a teammate above the reach of an opponent. In addition, when the ball is held overhead, it is very easy to "fake" or pretend to pass, thus putting the opponent off guard before the ball actually is released. Start the pass with feet apart and weight evenly distributed over both feet. Hold the ball

Figure 22.3 Overhead pass.

a   b

above the head, elbows slightly flexed, hands on the side of the ball, and wrists extended (figure 22.3a). Shift the arms forward, release the ball, and follow through in the direction of the ball (figure 22.3b).

Key Teaching Points

1. Begin with one foot in front of the other.
2. Hold the ball just above the head, with wrist cocked.
3. Simultaneously take a short step forward, extend arms, and snap the wrist.
4. Follow through in the direction of the pass.

chapter 22

Figure 22.4 Pass around a defensive player. **Figure 22.5** Baseball pass.

a   b   c

One-Hand Bounce Pass

This pass is particularly effective when a player is closely guarded. It is used to pass the ball quickly around a defender directly from a dribble (figure 22.4). As the offensive player is bouncing the ball close to a defender, she pivots on her right foot, turns the left side of her body in the direction of the pass, steps on her left foot, then releases a bounce pass with her right hand. The pivot action allows the offensive player to step around the defender and protect her pass with her body.

Key Teaching Points

1. Keep the body low in approaching the defender.
2. Use the body to protect the pass.
3. Release the pass with the hand slightly behind the ball rather than on top of it.

Baseball Pass

The baseball pass is used when a player wishes to throw the ball a long distance. Care must be exercised in using this pass, particularly with beginners, as it may lead to inaccurate passing. Begin the pass with one foot slightly forward and weight evenly distributed over both feet. Hold the ball in front of the body, with elbows bent and fingers spread around the sides of the ball. Bring arms back and transfer the ball to the right hand when it is above the shoulder and behind the ear (figure 22.5a). Shift body weight to the right foot as the hands shift backward. Extend right arm forward, rotate body toward the left, and shift weight to forward foot (figure 22.5b). Release the ball with a final snap of the wrists and fingers (figure 22.5c).

Key Teaching Points

1. Simultaneously shift weight to right foot as the right arm is drawn backward.

2. Simultaneously shift weight to front foot as throwing arm moves forward.
3. Release ball with a snap of the wrist and follow through in the direction of the throw.

Catching

Basic catching skills have been described in an earlier section of this book (see chapter 4). In basketball, the overhand catch (figure 22.6) is used when the ball is caught above the waist. The fingers point up for this catch. The underhand catch (figure 22.7) is used to catch a ball below the waist. The fingers point down. In both types of catches, the receiver reaches out and catches the ball on his fingertips, then gradually relaxes his arms to reduce the speed of the oncoming ball. However, because young children often do not have adequate strength to catch the basketball in this manner, allow them to catch the ball with their palms, then quickly shift to a fingertip grip.

Figure 22.6 Overhand catch.

Figure 22.7 Underhand catch.

basketball activities

Figure 22.8 Dribbling.

a   b   c

Key Teaching Points

1. Keep your eyes on the ball and quickly move into position to catch it.
2. Catch the ball on the tips of the fingers and thumb.
3. Relax arms as ball is caught.
4. Quickly shift ball into offensive passing position.

Dribbling

Dribbling is controlled bouncing in any direction and at varying speeds. The basic fundamentals to stress in teaching this skill are (1) do not slap the ball downward—push it toward the floor; (2) learn to dribble with either hand; and (3) when not being guarded, bring the ball in front of the body and raise the height of the dribble to increase running speed.

The dribbler's body leans forward slightly, with knees partially flexed, and head up. The wrist of the dribbling hand is relaxed, with fingers cupped and spaced apart (figure 22.8a). "Push" the ball toward the floor off the fingertips (figure 22.8b). As the ball rebounds, fingers, wrist, and arm "ride" back with the ball (figure 22.8c).

When being checked, place the body between the opponent and the ball. When dribbling, keep an eye on the opponent to watch for sudden moves and to shift the ball to a more advantageous position. Also, when being guarded, keep the ball close to the body and lower the bounce to between the waist and the knees.

Key Teaching Points

1. Keep head up and eyes on target.
2. Push the ball toward the floor.
3. Allow fingers, wrist, and arm to ride back with the ball.
4. Keep knees slightly bent and trunk leaning slightly forward.

Shooting

While all the skills of basketball are important, none is as important as shooting. When teaching the following basic shooting skills, stress two fundamental principles: (1) watch the target instead of the ball and (2) follow through after every shot.

If elementary school children are to learn shooting skills correctly and efficiently, the height of the basket rim should be lowered from the official ten feet to a height that allows the children to shoot without undue strain. The appropriate height for upper elementary school children should be between eight and nine feet, depending on the children's age and ability.

One-Hand Set Shot (Push Shot)

The one-hand set shot is performed by placing the same foot as the shooting hand slightly in front of the body. The ball is held with both hands opposite the chin and above the lead foot (figure 22.9a). The back is straight with knees partially bent. In a simultaneous action, straighten the knees, release the nonshooting hand, extend the shooting arm forward and upward, and push the ball toward the basket (figure 22.9b). Release the ball with a slight snap of the wrist and fingers (figure 22.9c).

Key Teaching Points

1. Keep eyes focused on rim of basket.
2. Extend elbow toward basket and release ball with a high arc.
3. Release ball with a slight snap of the wrist.

Lay-Up Shot

The lay-up, which involves dribbling, leaping, and the ability to judge distance, can be learned by boys and girls in the

Figure 22.9 One-hand set shot.

a b c

Figure 22.10 Lay-up shot.

a b c

intermediate grades. In fact, most children are more successful at this skill than at the one-hand set shot. The reason is the short distance between the hand and the rim of the basket when the ball is released.

Approach the basket at a forty-five-degree angle (figure 22.10a). Just prior to shooting, shift the weight to the foot opposite the shooting hand, and raise the ball as far as possible with both hands (figure 22.10b). Release the non-shooting hand as the shooting arm carries the ball up. Then release it off the fingertips (figure 22.10c). The ball should

bounce against the backboard about eighteen inches above the hoop, then drop into the hoop.

Key Teaching Points

1. Keep eyes focused about eighteen inches above the rim and on the backboard.
2. Take-off foot is opposite the shooting hand.
3. Lay the ball against the backboard.
4. Land on both feet and flex knees to absorb shock.

basketball activities

Free Throw (Two-Hand Underhand)

The one-hand set shot is normally used for free throws. However, some children may not have sufficient strength to throw the ball with one hand from the foul line. Allow them to use this shot.

Stand with the back straight, knees slightly bent, arms straight, and weight equally distributed over both feet. Hold the ball with the fingertips of both hands slightly under the ball (figure 22.11a). In a simultaneous action, swing arms forward and upward and straighten the knees (figure 22.11b). It is important to keep the back straight throughout this movement and to release the ball off the tips of the fingers (figure 22.11c).

Figure 22.11 Free throw.

a   b   c

Key Teaching Points

1. Keep eyes focused on rim of basket.
2. Keep back and arms straight.
3. Release ball off fingertips.
4. Follow through in the direction of the ball.

Pivoting

Footwork in basketball involves stopping, starting, pivoting, and turning in all directions and at varying speeds. When teaching the pivot and turn, stress the importance of gaining body control before attempting the pivot or turn. Also, teach pupils not to change the pivot foot once it is declared; otherwise, traveling will be charged. Finally, emphasize the need to maintain fingertip control of the ball for quick release after the pivot is made.

Prior to performing a pivot, make sure the weight is evenly distributed on both feet (figure 22.12a). Hold the ball firmly with the fingertips of both hands and keep the elbows out to protect the ball. As soon as one foot becomes the pivot foot, it must remain on the floor. The player may turn in any direction on her pivot foot (figures 22.12b and c); however, she may not drag it away from the original pivot spot. The opposite foot is permitted to step in any direction.

Figure 22.12 Pivoting.

a   b   c

Key Teaching Points

1. Make sure weight is evenly distributed on both feet before declaring your pivot foot.
2. Trunk is bent slightly forward with elbows out.
3. Pivot in any direction, but don't drag the pivot foot.

Defensive Skills

It is essential that elementary children first learn to move the ball by dribbling and passing, and then learn the basic skills of defense. It is important to stress the fact that legally

chapter 22

Figure 22.13 Defensive skills.

a. Body bent slightly forward, knees flexed, and weight evenly distributed over both feet.

b. Stance to guard opponent, who is within shooting range.

stopping an opponent from scoring is just as important as scoring itself. The following basic defense techniques should be emphasized, particularly in the fifth and sixth grades.

Approach an offensive player, keeping body bent slightly forward, and stop with one foot slightly in front of the other. Weight is equally distributed over both feet, seat down, back straight, and arm flexed and slightly away from the body (figure 22.13a). If the opponent is within shooting range, hold the hand that is opposite the opponent's shooting hand high and at face level (figure 22.13b). Move by shuffling the feet—never cross one foot over the other.

Key Teaching Points

1. Never cross the feet when guarding an opponent—use a sliding step.
2. Keep the buttocks low and the back upright.
3. When checking, keep one hand up at all times.
4. Do not reach across for a ball; move the body to a position in front of the offensive player and then attempt to take the ball.
5. Always try to get the body in front of the offensive player.
6. Guard with one hand toward the ball and the other hand toward the opponent.

Practice Activities and Lead-Up Games

The following practice activities will assist in developing passing, shooting, dribbling, and pivoting skills (table 22.2). Modify any of them to overcome the limitations of the playing area and variations in the children's level of skill and interest.

All activities described in this section are designed to give each student the maximum amount of practice. If there are not enough basketballs, use soccer balls, volleyballs, or utility balls. Also, it is important for the teacher to circulate among the students during practice activities in order to correct errors or to provide encouragement and praise where needed.

Many of the low-organization games and relays described in chapter 16 can be modified and used as passing, catching, and other basketball skills.

The lead-up games described in this section are designed to give children practice in playing games that require one or more basketball skills. Each game can be modified to meet the class's ability and the available facilities and equipment. Whenever possible, divide the playing area into two, three, or four sections to allow two or more games to be played at the same time.

Table 22.2 Practice Activities and Lead-Up Games

Name of activity	Type of activity	Players	Developmental level II	Developmental level III	Basketball concepts and skills	Movement concepts	Page
Practice activities adapted from soccer activities							
Circle Passing	Pass	2	———————→		Dribble	Moving into space, change of direction and speed	318
Follow the Leader	Dribble	2	———————→		Dribble	Using available space, moving into space, change of direction and speed	318
Triangle Pass	Pass	3	———————→		Pass	Moving into space, change of direction	319
Practice Activities							
One-Knee Dribble	Dribble	Individual	———————→		Dribble	Personal space, levels, change of direction and speed	377
Wall Passing	Pass	Individual	———————→		Pass, catch	Moving into space, change of direction and speed	378
Movement Drill	Dribble	Individual	———————→		Dribble	Moving into space, change of direction and speed	378
One on One	Dodge, check	2	———————→		Run, dodge, check	Moving into space, change of direction and speed	378
Partner Passing	Pass, catch	2	———————→		Pass, catch	Moving into space, change of direction and speed	378
Pig in the Middle	Pass, check	3	———————→		Pass, catch, check	Moving into space, change of direction and speed	378
Circle Passing	Pass, catch	5–6	———————→		Pass, catch	Moving into space, change of direction and speed	378
Weave Dribble	Dribble	4–5	———————→		Dribble	Moving into space, change of direction and pathway.	379
Whistle Dribble	Dribble	3–4	———————→		Dribble, stop, pivot	Moving into space, change of direction and space	379
Basket Shooting	Dribble, shoot	5–6	———————→		Shoot, dribble, guard	Moving into space, change of direction and speed	379
Dribble and Shoot	Dribble, shoot	3–4	———————→		Dribble, shoot	Moving into space, change of direction, pathway, and levels	379
Set Shot Shooting	Shoot, dribble	6–8	———————→		Shoot, pass	Shooting into space, levels	380
Pass, Post, Shoot	Dribble, pass	3		————→	Dribble, pass, pivot, shoot	Moving into space, change of direction	380
Pivot and Pass	Pivot, pass	6–8		————→	Pivot, pass	Personal space, change of direction	380
Lay-Up Shooting	Shoot, dribble	10 per group		————→	Dribble, shoot, catch	Moving into space, change of direction	380
Modified Lead-Up Games from Other Chapters							
Change Basketball	All skills	6 per team	———————→		All basketball skills	Moving into space, change of direction, pathway, and speed	321
Circle of Fun	Dribble, shoot	6 per team	———————→		Dribble, pass, shoot, guard	Moving into space, change of direction and speed	321
Alley Basketball	Pass, shoot	20–24	———————→		Pass, check, shoot	Personal space, moving into space, change of direction and speed	322
Donkey	Pass	5–6 per team	———————→		Pass, catch	Moving into space, change of direction and speed	366

Table 22.2 *Continued*

Name of activity	Type of activity	Players	Developmental level		Basketball concepts and skills	Movement concepts	Page
			II	III			
Lead-Up Games							
Bucket Ball	Pass	5–6 per team	⟶		Pass, catch, dribble, shoot, guard	Moving into space, change of direction and speed	380
Keep Away	Pass	3–4 per team	⟶		Pass, catch, pivot, dribble	Moving into space, change of direction and speed	381
Basketball Touch	Pass, catch	4–5 per team	⟶		Pass, catch, guard	Moving into space, change of direction and speed	381
Sideline Basketball	All skills	10–12 per team	⟶		All basketball skills	Moving into space, change of direction and speed	381
Twenty-One	Shoot, catch	3–4 per game	⟶		Shoot, catch	Shooting into space, levels	381
Basketball Snatch Ball	Dribble, shoot	5–6 per team	⟶		Dribble, shoot	Moving into space, change of direction	381
In-and-Out Basketball	Shoot	5 per team	⟶		All basketball skills	Moving into space, change of direction and speed	382
Captain Ball	Dribble, pass	8–10 per team	⟶		Dribble, pass, guard	Personal space, moving into space, change of direction and speed	382

Figure 22.14 One-knee dribble activity.

Figure 22.15 Move the ball under the leg to the other hand.

Practice Activities

One-Knee Dribble

Motor skills Dribble
Movement concepts Personal space, levels, change of direction and speed
Players Individual
Formation Scattered
Playing area Playground, gymnasium
Equipment Basketball or other inflated balls

All players are scattered. They kneel on one knee and begin bouncing the ball with the same hand as the kneeling knee (figure 22.14). This drill eliminates unnecessary arm action. Players should keep their eyes on the teacher and "feel" for the ball.

Suggestions and Variations
1. Dribble the ball, with the elbow of the opposite arm at the side.
2. Move the ball backward and forward.
3. Move the ball around the front of the opposite leg and change hands.
4. Move the ball under the leg to the other hand (figure 22.15).
5. Bounce the ball in rhythm set by the teacher.
6. Play follow the leader while kneeling. This makes everyone look at the leader and not the ball.
7. Repeat these drills while standing.

basketball activities

Wall Passing

Motor skills Pass, catch
Movement concepts Moving into space, change of direction and speed
Players Individual
Formation Scattered along wall
Playing area Playground, gymnasium
Equipment Basketball

Players should stand approximately five feet from the wall and gradually move back as their skill increases. This wall drill can be used to practice all types of passing and catching skills.

Suggestions and Variations

1. Put lines or targets on the wall to increase accuracy.
2. Add timing contests—for example, the number of hits in ten seconds.

Movement Drill

Motor skills Dribble
Movement concepts Moving into space, change of direction and speed
Players Individual
Formation Scattered
Playing area Playground, gymnasium
Equipment Basketball

The teacher or a leader stands in front of the group, then dribbles to the right, left, forward, or any other direction. All players move in the same direction as the leader but with a mirror image, bouncing the ball with the appropriate hand.

Suggestions and Variations

The leader may use hand directions instead of actually shifting positions.

One on One

Motor skills Run, dodge, check
Movement concepts Moving into space, change of direction and speed
Players Two
Formation Scattered
Playing area Playground, gymnasium
Equipment Basketball

Partners, facing each other, are scattered around the gymnasium. Without a ball, one player attempts to run past the other. The defensive player moves his body into position to stop the offensive player. He may not use his arms and feet to stop the player or lean into him. Players are not allowed to touch each other.

Suggestions and Variations

1. Repeat drill with a ball.
2. Repeat variation 1 and dribble toward a basket.

3. The following combinations can be used in a variety of ways. Begin each with passing only, then add dribbling, and finally add a target. (Improvise according to available backboards.)
   Two on one
   Two on two
   Two on three
   Three on one
   Three on three

Partner Passing

Motor skills Pass, catch
Movement concepts Moving into space, change of direction and speed
Players Two
Formation Circle
Playing area Playground, gymnasium
Equipment Basketball

Partners scattered around playing area stand about ten to fifteen feet apart, depending on skill. Each player remains in a stationary position. After a few minutes of practice, have one player remain stationary and the other move around him. After a few more minutes of practice, have both players move, pass, and catch.

Suggestions and Variations

1. Use different types of passes—two-hand bounce, one-hand bounce, baseball.
2. Add obstacles between players.

Pig in the Middle

Motor skills Pass, catch, check
Movement concepts Moving into space, change of direction and speed
Players Three
Formation Line
Playing area Playground, gymnasium
Equipment Basketball

Arrange three players in a line, with approximately six feet between each. The two outside players are the end players, while the middle player is designated as the "pig." Allow the end players to move to the right or left. They attempt to pass the ball to each other without the "pig" touching the ball. If the "pig" touches the ball, he replaces the person who threw it. The ball may not be thrown above the reach of the middle player, who must always advance toward the ball.

Circle Passing

Motor skills Pass, catch
Movement concepts Moving into space, change of direction and speed
Players Five or six
Formation Circle
Playing area Playground, gymnasium
Equipment Basketball

Divide the class into squads of five or six players. Arrange the children in circles, with approximately six feet between them. Player 1 turns toward player 2 and passes the ball to him; player 2 catches the ball, turns toward player 3, and passes to him; and so on. If the ball is dropped, it is retrieved by the receiver, who returns to his place in the circle and continues the drill.

Suggestions and Variations

1. Five Against One. One player goes to the center of the circle. The five outside players pass the ball to each other, always skipping a person, while the center player tries to intercept the pass. When the center player intercepts a pass, he switches positions with the player who threw the ball.
2. One player goes to the center of the circle with the ball and passes to each player in the circle.
3. Double Passing. This is similar to variation 2, with the addition of one more ball. Require the center player to make a bounce pass, while the circle players make direct passes.

Weave Dribble

Motor skills Dribble
Movement concepts Moving into space, change of direction and pathway
Players Four or five
Formation Line
Playing area Playground, gymnasium
Equipment Basketball

Divide the class into squads of about four or five players. Arrange each squad in a straight line formation, with about ten feet between each player. Player 1 dribbles around player 2 and back and around the opposite side of each successive player until he is back in his original position. Everyone moves up one position and player 1 goes to the rear of the line.

Suggestions and Variations
Use chairs or pins instead of players for obstacles.

Whistle Dribble

Motor skills Dribble, stop, pivot
Movement concepts Moving into space, change of direction and speed
Players Three or four per group
Formation Line
Playing area Playground, gymnasium
Equipment Basketballs

Divide class into squads of about three or four players. Line up the squads at one end of the floor. The teacher stands in the center of the playing area. When you blow the whistle, the first player from each squad dribbles forward. When you blow the whistle again, all players stop immediately and hold the ball ready for the next move. As soon as any player reaches a line parallel to you, he turns and dribbles back to his team.

Suggestions and Variations

1. Use hand signals rather than the whistle for stopping and starting; this encourages the "head-up" dribble. A hand over the head means dribble; a hand straight down means stop.
2. Extend arms sideward (right or left) as a signal to pivot right or left. The signals then would be hand over head (dribble forward), hand down (stop), arm out to right (pivot right, then back and ready for the next command).

Basket Shooting

Motor skills Dribble, shoot, guard
Movement concepts Moving into space, change of direction and speed
Players Five or six per group
Formation Line
Playing area Playground, gymnasium
Equipment Basketball

Divide the class into as many squads as you have baskets. Arrange each squad in a file formation behind the free throw line. One player remains on the endline behind the basket. The first player dribbles forward, and the player on the endline comes forward to guard the basket. The player with the ball attempts a shot, and then both players try to recover the rebound. Whoever retrieves it passes it on to the next player. The two rebound players exchange positions; that is, the player who took the shot moves behind the endline and the guarding player goes to the end of the line behind the free throw line.

Suggestions and Variations

1. Have two offensive players team up and try to get by the guard and shoot.
2. Do the same with two guards and two offensive players.
3. Repeat with two guards and three offensive players.

Dribble and Shoot

Motor skills Dribble, shoot
Movement concepts Moving into space, change of direction, pathway, and levels
Players Three or four per group
Formation Line
Playing area Playground, gymnasium
Equipment Basketball and chairs

This drill follows three stages, with the last stage arranged as shown in the diagram.

1. Each player stands three to four feet away from the basket, takes one step with the left foot (if shooting with the right hand), and shoots.
2. Same as stage 1, but begin with the right foot.
3. Place chairs in a line at approximately a forty-five-degree angle. Chairs should be about three to four feet apart. Players dribble around the chairs and shoot.

Motor skills Shoot, pass
Movement concepts Shooting into space, levels
Players Six to eight per group
Formation Semicircle
Playing area Playground, gymnasium
Equipment Basketball

Arrange six to eight players in a semicircle near a basket. One player, the leader, is stationed under the basket with a ball. The leader passes the ball to the first player in the semicircle, who attempts a set shot. The leader recovers each ball and passes it to each player in sequence. Adjust the distance from the basket according to the group's level of skill.

Suggestions and Variations
Use two or more balls and have the leader return the balls to any player.

Pass, Post, Shoot

Motor skills Dribble, pass, pivot, shoot
Movement concepts Moving into space, change of direction
Players Three per group
Formation See diagram
Playing area Playground, gymnasium
Equipment Basketball

The post player remains stationary throughout the drill. The ball is given to the offensive player, who tries to maneuver past the defensive player and take a shot at the basket. The ball may be passed back and forth between the offensive player and the post player until the offensive player is ready to move toward the basket and attempt a shot. Allow about thirty seconds to complete the drill, then blow the whistle and rotate players to the next position.

X Defensive player

⊗ Post player

◯ Offensive player

Suggestions and Variations
Set up two drills on each side of the key. If facilities and equipment are limited, draw circles on the wall and place traffic cones or other markers on the floor and restrict players to their assigned areas.

Pivot and Pass

Motor skills Pivot, pass
Movement concepts Personal space, change of direction
Players Six to eight per group
Formation Circle
Playing area Playground, gymnasium
Equipment Basketball

Circle formation, with six to eight players standing about ten feet apart. Each player faces the center of the circle. A player on each side of the circle is given a ball. On signal, each player with a ball keeps his left foot on the ground and pivots a quarter-turn away from the center of the circle, then steps forward on his right foot and passes to the next player. Continue the drill around the circle, then repeat reversing directions.

Lay-Up Shooting

Motor skills Shoot, dribble, catch
Movement concepts Moving into space, change of direction
Players Ten per group
Formation Lines
Playing area Playground, gymnasium
Equipment Basketball

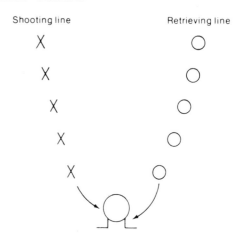

Arrange two lines of players at a forty-five-degree angle to the basket. The first player in each line should be about twenty feet from the basket. The first player in the shooting line dribbles toward the basket and attempts a lay-up shot, then goes to the end of the retrieving line. The first player in the retrieving line leaves his line at the same time as the shooting player to retrieve the ball and pass it to the next player in the shooting line. The retriever then goes to the end of the shooting line. Continue the drill to the last shooting player; then reverse lines and repeat drill.

Lead-Up Games

Bucket Ball

Motor skills Pass, catch, dribble, shoot, guard
Movement concepts Moving into space, change of direction and speed
Players Five or six per team
Formation A rectangle drawn approximately thirty by forty feet or the gymnasium divided into two playing courts
Playing area Playground, gymnasium, classroom
Equipment Two wastepaper baskets and one ball for each game

Place wastepaper baskets on the floor at the center of the endlines. If desired, a player may stand on a chair and hold the basket. Players on team A pair off with players on team B, and each checks the other. The game begins with a jump ball between two opposing players. The game continues until one team makes a basket. The general rules of basketball are followed; however, modify any rule as desired.

Suggestions and Variations

1. Play the same game, but use two hoops suspended from the ceiling or walls as goals.
2. Play the same game, but require one type of locomotor movement such as jumping, hopping, or sliding.

Keep Away

Motor skills Pass, catch, pivot, dribble
Movement concepts Moving into space, change of direction and speed
Players Three or four per team
Formation Scattered within a designated playing area
Playing area Playground, gymnasium, classroom
Equipment Basketball

On signal, the teacher gives the ball to one team, which passes it among themselves, trying to keep it away from the other team. Players on the opposing team check as in regular basketball. If teams are large and space is limited, rotate in fours or fives every few minutes.

Suggestions and Variations

1. Limit person in possession of the ball to three steps before passing the ball.
2. Require every player to pivot before passing the ball.

Basketball Touch

Motor skills Pass, catch, guard
Movement concepts Moving into space, change of direction and speed
Players Four or five per team
Formation Two teams scattered within a designated playing area, with one goalie standing on the baseline
Playing area Playground, gymnasium
Equipment Basketball

Arrange two teams in scattered positions within the court area. Goalies stand on opposite lines and may move up and down their own line. Court players are allowed to pass the ball any number of times as they try to pass it to their goalie. Players may check but are not allowed to dribble the ball. Start game with one player throwing in the ball from the middle of the sideline.

Suggestions and Variations

Add limitations, such as only use an overhand pass or every player must dribble three steps, pivot, then pass the ball.

Sideline Basketball

Motor skills Pass, catch, shoot, dribble, pivot
Movement concepts Moving into space, change of direction and speed
Players Ten to twelve per team

Formation Five players from each team play in the court area, while the remaining players from both teams are placed alternately along the sidelines and endlines. Leave equal spaces between line players.
Playing area Playground, gymnasium, classroom
Equipment Basketballs

Basketball rules are followed, except the ball may be passed to a sideline player. Sideline players cannot enter the court, dribble, or pass to another sideline player. Start the game with a jump ball in the center of the playing area. The team that gains possession is designated as the offensive team. If the defensive team intercepts the ball, it must pass to one of its sideline players before it becomes the offensive team. Stepping over the sideline gives the ball to opponents on their sideline. Players on the sidelines rotate with players on the floor. Field goals score two points and free throws one point.

Suggestions and Variations

1. Require every third pass to go to a sideline player.
2. Limit number of steps court players may travel before passing or shooting the ball.
3. Ask each team to suggest a new rule.

Twenty-One

Motor skills Shoot, catch
Movement concepts Shooting into empty space, levels
Players Three or four per game
Formation Players of each group scattered around one basket
Playing area Playground, gymnasium, classroom
Equipment Basketball

The object of this game is for any player to score twenty-one points by a combination of field shots and free throws. Player 1 shoots from the free throw line, while the other players stand wherever they wish in the playing area. Player 1 continues shooting from the free throw line until he misses, with each successful basket counting one point. When he misses, any player who can get possession of the ball may try for a field goal; if successful, it counts two points. If the try for a field goal fails, any player who can get the ball may try for a field goal. This procedure continues until a field goal is made. After a field goal is made, the ball is given to player 2, who takes his turn at the free throw line. Continue until one player has twenty-one points.

Suggestions and Variations

1. Reduce game point to nine or eleven.
2. Allow field goal attempts to be a lay-up shot from the closest side to the basket.

Basketball Snatch Ball

Motor skills Dribble, shoot
Movement concepts Moving into space, change of direction
Players Five or six per team
Formation Divide class into two equal groups. Each team on opposite lines. Place two basketballs on a line midway between two opposing teams.
Playing area Playground, gymnasium
Equipment Basketballs

Players are numbered consecutively and must stand in this order on the sideline of the playing area. When the teacher or leader calls a number, that player from each team runs to one of the balls, picks it up, dribbles it to the basket, and shoots until he makes a basket. When he succeeds, he dribbles back and replaces the ball. The first player to make a basket and return the ball scores one point for his team.

Suggestions and Variations

1. Players may run by pairs, with two players from each team having the same number. In this case, the ball must be passed between the players three times before and after the shot is made.
2. Require specific types of shooting skills.
3. Add a math challenge for fun, such as "8 – 5" or "¼ of 12," instead of the simple number.

In-and-Out Basketball

Motor skills Shoot, catch, dribble, pivot
Movement concepts Moving into space, change of direction and speed
Players Five per team
Formation Two teams playing in half of the basketball court, and a third "waiting" team on the sideline
Playing area Playground, gymnasium, classroom
Equipment Basketball

Regular basketball rules apply, with the following modifications: (1) three teams play in half the court; (2) two teams play, while the third team remains on the side line; (3) when a field goal or free throw is made, the third team takes the loser's place; and (4) each player is allowed only two dribbles.

Suggestions and Variations

1. If goals are not being scored, use a time limit instead.
2. Have waiting team practice passing or dribbling skills.

Captain Ball

Motor skills Dribble, pass, guard
Movement concepts Personal space, moving into space, change of direction and speed
Players Eight to ten per team
Formation See diagram (Note: two games can be played in each half of a typical elementary school gymnasium.)
Playing area Playground, gymnasium
Equipment Two basketballs, eight hoops

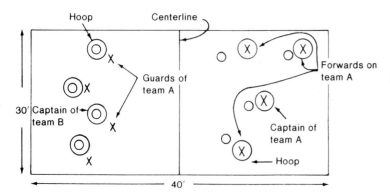

The captain and three forward players of team A must keep one foot inside their hoops. Four guards from team A may roam anywhere in team B's side of the playing area; however, they cannot enter the hoop of any opposing player. The object of this game is for the guards to get the ball to any of their forward players. The forward players, in turn, try to get the ball to their captain. Start the game with a jump ball between two opposing guards. Award two points each time the captain receives the ball from one of his forwards.

Fouls occur when-

1. A guard steps into an opposing player's hoop, steps over the centerline or boundary line, or throws the ball directly to the captain (ball is given to the nearest forward player on opposing team).
2. A forward steps out of his circle, holds the ball longer than five seconds, or commits unnecessary rough play (ball is given to the nearest guard on the opposing team).

Suggestions and Variations

1. Add more circle or guard players. Even numbers make the game more difficult.
2. Require only one type of pass.
3. Add any rule or modification as desired.

Basketball Rules and Regulations

Basketball is probably the most popular team sport in the upper elementary grades. Although skill development, especially ball handling and shooting skills, necessitates that the majority of the time be spent on practice activities and lead-up games, the full game should be played several times during a unit of instruction. Modify the rules, such as lowering the height of the basket and limiting the number of dribbles, to encourage the development of specific skills. Care should be taken, however, not to play the full game too often, perhaps neglecting needed skill development.

I. Field of play: Adjust court and key dimensions to available space.

II. Positions:

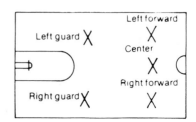

Name	Passing (total pts.)	Dribbling (total pts.)	Shooting (50 pts.)	Subjective evaluation (50 pts.)	Total score	Grade
1 2 3			Rank total scores for the class, then convert to letter grades or ratings (superior, good, etc.).			

Table 22.3 Basketball Skill Test

III. To start game: The game is started at the center circle. The referee tosses the ball in the air between the two opposing centers, who attempt to tap it to one of their teammates. This jump ball is also used when the ball goes out of bounds and the referee is uncertain which team caused it to go out and to start the second half of the game.

IV. After a successful free throw: The ball is put into play at the end of the court by the defending team.

V. After a ball goes out of bounds: The ball is put into play from behind the line and immediately in front of the place where it went out. Any player from the team that did not cause it to go out may put it into play.

VI. Game time: The game is divided into four quarters of six minutes each.

VII. Points: Two points are awarded for every field goal and one point for every successful free throw.

VIII. Substitution: One or all substitutes may enter the game whenever the ball is not in play (out of bounds, before a jump ball, etc.).

IX. Violations: A violation is charged against a player if he:
   A. Travels—takes more than one step with the ball without dribbling
   B. Double dribbles—dribbles the ball, stops, then dribbles again without another player handling the ball or palms the ball (that is, does not clearly dribble or dribbles with two hands)
   C. Steps on or over a boundary line while in possession of the ball
   D. Kicks the ball
   E. Stays longer than three seconds in the key area under the offensive basket, in which case play is stopped and the referee awards a throw from the sideline to the other team near the point where the infraction occurred

X. Fouls: A foul is charged against a player if he:
   A. Kicks, trips, or pushes another player
   B. Holds or charges another player
   C. Commits unsportsmanlike conduct

XI. The penalty: Play is stopped and the referee awards one or two free throws to the nonoffending team from the free throw line.
   A. One free throw is awarded to a player who is fouled while participating in an activity other than shooting. If the free throw is successful, the defending team puts the ball into play from behind the endline. If the free throw is unsuccessful, the ball continues in play.
   B. Two free throws are awarded to a player who is fouled when he is shooting. If the second free throw is successful, the defending team puts the ball into play from behind the endline. If the second free throw is unsuccessful, the ball continues in play.

Evaluative Techniques

Several tests can be used to measure the basic passing, dribbling, and shooting skills. The following test items are reliable and quite easy to administer. Modify any of them to meet your own teaching situation and add additional ones if desired. Also keep scores from each year in order to build appropriate norms for your school (table 22.3).

Test 1: Passing

Place a target on the wall as shown in the following diagram. The player must stand and pass from behind the ten-foot line. He has thirty seconds to hit the target as many times as possible. If a player drops the ball within the time period, he may pick it up, return to the ten-foot line, and continue adding to his cumulative score. One point is scored for each pass that lands on the target area. Allow two trials and record the highest score.

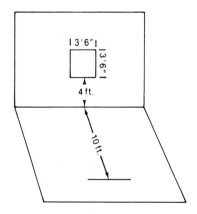

Test 2: Dribbling

Arrange four chairs in a line at ten-foot intervals from the starting line. A ball is placed on the starting line. Each player stands behind the starting line, with both hands resting on his knees. On signal "go," he picks up the ball and dribbles around the chairs in a zigzag pattern. One point is awarded each time he passes a chair. Allow twenty seconds for the test. Two trials are allowed, with the highest score recorded.

Basketball test no. 2

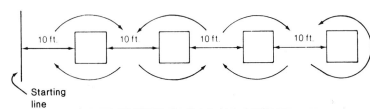

Starting line

Test 3: Shooting

Draw a line at a forty-five-degree angle thirty feet from the basket. Each student attempts ten lay-up shots. He must begin dribbling from the thirty-foot line and attempt a shot when he reaches the basket. Award five points for each successful basket. Other shooting tests, such as free throws or one- or two-hand sets, may be substituted for the lay-up test.

Test 4: Subjective Evaluation

Establish criteria that represent the skills and playing ability required in basketball. Using shooting ability, dribbling, defensive skill, and passing, the teacher can award each player a total score from zero to fifty points. Three players can be used as judges, with the average score recorded.

Selected References

CAHPER. (1985). *Basketball-Type Games.* Ottawa, Ontario: CAHPER Publications.

Garchow, K., and Dickinson, A. (1992). *Youth Basketball: A Complete Handbook.* Dubuque, IA: Wm. C. Brown Publishers

Johnson, C. (1989). *Practical Basketball for Teacher and Coach.* Champaign, IL: Stipes Publishing Co.

Kamiya, A. (1985). *Elementary Teacher's Handbook of Indoor and Outdoor Games.* West Nyack, NY: Parker Publishing Co., Inc.

Krause, J. V. (1991). *Basketball Skills and Drills.* Champaign, IL: Leisure Press.

Philipp, J. A., and Wilkerson, J. D. (1990). *Teaching Team Sports: A Coeducational Approach.* Champaign, IL: Human Kinetics Publishers, Inc.

Turner, L. F., and Turner, S. L. (1989). *P.E. Teacher's Skill-by-Skill Activities Program.* West Nyack, NY: Parker Publishing Co., Inc.

Wilkes, G. (1990). *Basketball,* Fifth Edition. Dubuque, IA: Wm. C. Brown Publishers.

Softball Activities

Softball is an extremely popular recreational activity throughout Canada and the United States and in many other countries. Its popularity is probably due in part to the game's relative ease and safety. In addition, softball requires only a minimum amount of protective equipment and a smaller playing field than is required for baseball.

If softball is to be played as a competitive recreational game, every participant must know the rules and be reasonably proficient in the basic throwing, catching, and batting skills. Furthermore, each child should be given an opportunity to play every position. Assigning only the more proficient players to the catcher, pitcher, and first base positions is educationally unsound.

This chapter has been organized to provide a basic approach to teaching softball to upper elementary school children. Although lead-up games should be emphasized more than regulation softball during the instructional period, the official game or a modified version should be played occasionally to provide an opportunity for the class to understand the skills and playing strategies and, of course, for the teacher to test the children's abilities as batters and fielders ■

Emphasis and Progression

The problems of selecting and teaching softball skills and rules are very similar to those found in teaching basketball activities. Through television, organized leagues, and "sandlot" games, most children of this age level are already acquainted with many of the skills and rules of softball. Thus, there will be a very wide variation in the development of softball skills in virtually every grade and within each class. The suggested sequence of presenting skills and rules in table 23.1, therefore, should be used as a basic guideline.

Table 23.1 indicates that children normally have been introduced to most throwing and catching skills prior to developmental level II. During level II, continued emphasis should be given to improving the throwing, catching, and batting skills, and to acquiring the basic rules and strategies of the game.

Developmental level III should be seen as continuous periods of refining the basic softball skills. More experienced players will also develop a reasonable level of skill in the sidearm throw and bunting. Most of these children should also show major improvement in general positional play. It is not uncommon for these children to be able to steal a base, sacrifice, or make a double play.

Teaching Procedures

The approaches used to teach softball and basketball are very similar. Many elementary school children have played modified versions of softball such as scrub and two-person softball; their skill and general understanding of the game are well beyond the beginner stage. However, children who have not had this advantage are far behind in skill development and general playing ability. Since the teaching approach suggested for soccer can apply equally to softball, review chapter 18 to see how a unit of instruction and individual lessons can be developed.

Table 23.1 Suggested Sequence of Presenting Softball Skills and Rules

Skills and rules	Developmental level II	Developmental level III
Throwing		
Overhand throw	Acquired or introduce	Increase distance and accuracy
Underhand throw	Acquired or introduce	Increase speed and accuracy
Pitching	Acquired or introduce	Increase speed and accuracy
Sidearm throw		Introduce
Rules: Safe and out	Introduce	
Fair and foul ball	Introduce	
Strike zone	Introduce	
Pitching rule	Introduce	
Catching and fielding		
Catching low and high throws	Acquired or introduce	Increase proficiency
Catching fly balls	Acquired or introduce	Increase proficiency
Fielding grounders	Acquired or introduce	Increase proficiency
Rules: Fielding positions	Acquired or introduce	
Foul tip	Introduce	
Bunt rule		Introduce
Batting		
Batting	Acquired or introduce	Increase distance and accuracy
Fungo hitting	Introduce	Increase distance and accuracy
Bunting		Introduce
Rules: Balls and strikes	Introduce	
Base running		
To first base	Acquired or introduce	Increase speed
Around bases	Introduce	Increase speed
Rules: Touching base	Introduce	
Off base on caught fly	Introduce	
Related skills		
Positional play		Introduce
Stealing bases		Introduce
Double play		Introduce
Sacrifice		Introduce

The inventive games approach suggested in previous chapters can also be applied with equal success to softball activities. Presenting such challenges as "Make up a four-person drill emphasizing grounding and a sidearm throw" provides freedom for a group to develop an activity that is challenging and enjoyable yet concentrates on one or two important skills. You can also cope with problems associated with gender and peer performances through this problem-solving approach.

The following suggestions apply more specifically to problems associated with teaching softball activities.

1. Softball is too inactive for most of the players. To help overcome this problem:
   a. Rotate positions as often as possible.
   b. Use a batting tee if pitching and batting abilities are generally low.
   c. Select lead-up games that require smaller playing areas and fewer players.
   d. Modify the official game, such as two outs before changing positions or all players hitting before changing sides, or shorten the distance between bases.
2. Several safety precautions should be considered during every instructional and recreational period involving softball activities.
   a. All waiting batters should stay behind a designated safety line located to the rear and on the first base side of the catcher.
   b. Every player should be taught how to release the bat after hitting the ball. Stringent enforcement of this rule is extremely important for everyone's safety.
   c. Proper-fitting face masks should be provided for the catcher.
   d. Sliding should be prohibited, since it can cause unnecessary injury and tear street clothes.
   e. All bases should be made of soft material.
3. An umpire should be used in the more complex lead-up games and in every modified or regulation softball game. Establish a procedure for rotating the umpire as the teams change positions.
4. Modify every game to cope with the class's general level of ability and interest.
5. If softball gloves are available, they should be in good condition. Infielders should have priority for use.
6. Some children will ask if they can wear their own gloves during the softball unit. The teacher and her class should discuss this situation and reach a group decision about wearing personally owned gloves.

Station System for Softball

Station 1: Base running (group)

Station 2: Pitching practice (partners)

Station 3: Bunting practice (partners)

Station 4: Fly ball catching (group)

Station 5: Grounders (partners)

Station 6: Pepper (group)

Available field space

7. One of the most common complaints by elementary school teachers is the insufficient number of balls and bats for practice activities. This can be overcome by using a station system and rotating groups. The accompanying illustration shows several partner and group activities involving a variety of skills going on simultaneously. Each group rotates to the next station after a set period of time. If the groups do not have time to rotate through all the stations in one lesson, simply continue in the next lesson.

Description of Skills

Softball skills for elementary school children can be classified as hitting and fielding skills. All throwing and catching skills are appropriate for this age range. As for batting skills, most children have little difficulty learning to hit a ball with a full swing, although bunting and fungo batting present some problems.

Throwing

The major part of all fielding and defensive play depends on how fast and how accurately a player can throw the ball. Although the skill and style of performance vary from child to child, each is capable of throwing an overhand, sidearm, and underhand toss or pitch with relative ease and accuracy.

Gripping the Ball

The softball can be gripped in two basic ways. If the hand is large enough, the ball can be held between the thumb and first two fingers, with the third and fourth fingers

Figure 23.1 Gripping the ball.

a. Thumb and   b. See daylight.
   four-finger grip.

resting against the side of the ball. Elementary school children's smaller hands make it necessary for them to grip the ball with the thumb, and all four fingers spread around the side and bottom of the ball (figure 23.1a). However, only the top surface of the fingers should touch the ball. The grip is correct if the young thrower can see daylight between the ball and his hands (figure 23.1b).

Overhand Throw

This is the basic throw for all players, except the pitcher. Begin in a staggered stride position with the weight on the back foot, throwing arm extended backward, wrist cocked, and ball facing the rear. At this point, the left side faces the direction of the throw and the left arm extends forward (figure 23.2a). In a simultaneous movement, the upper right arm moves upward and forward and the left arm moves down and back as the weight shifts to the front foot (figure 23.2b). With a snap of the wrist, the ball is released off the fingers and toward the target (figure 23.2c). In the follow-through action, the throwing-side shoulder moves forward and downward as the weight shifts to the front foot (figure 23.2d).

Key Teaching Points

1. Keep eyes focused on the target.
2. Begin in a staggered stride position with the weight on the rear foot.

3. Rotate hips and shoulders as throwing arm moves backward.
4. Throwing arm moves forward and upward with the elbow leading.
5. Release ball slightly above and in front of the head.
6. Follow through toward the target and finish with the throwing-side foot even with the opposite foot and weight evenly distributed over both feet.

Sidearm Throw

The sidearm throw is used when the ball is thrown a short distance and in a hurry; thus, it is the most effective throw for infielders. As the ball is received, keep the body low and shift weight to the rear foot (figure 23.3a). Move the throwing arm to a horizontal position with the elbow bent and the ball in a throwing position (figure 23.3b). The opposite elbow should face the target. Simultaneously shift weight to the front foot as the throwing arm moves across and parallel to the ground (figure 23.3c). The ball is released with a snap of the wrist. In the follow-through action, the throwing arm moves horizontally toward the target as the elbow of the opposite arm moves backward.

Key Teaching Points

1. Keep eyes focused on the target.
2. Keep throwing arm below shoulder level.
3. Swing the throwing arm parallel to the ground.
4. Follow through in the direction of the throw.

Underhand Toss

The underhand toss is used for short, quick throws, most often around the infield area. The player extends his upper arm and forearm backward as his weight shifts to his rear foot. On the forward movement, his arm swings down and forward and his weight is shifted to the front foot (figure 23.4). As the ball is released, the player follows through with his upper arm and hand in the direction of the throw.

Figure 23.2 Overhand throw.

a   b   c   d

chapter 23

Figure 23.3 Sidearm throw.

a b c

Figure 23.4 Forward pendulum action of the arm.

Key Teaching Points (for underhand toss)

1. Keep eyes focused on the target.
2. Grip ball with fingers and thumb.
3. Simultaneously swing arm downward and forward.
4. Release ball off fingers and point in the direction of the throw.

Pitching

The pitcher stands with feet parallel, holding the ball in front with both hands, and facing the batter (figure 23.5a). He moves both hands forward until his arms are extended to about waist high and releases his left hand from the ball as he brings his throwing arm down and back. At the top of the backswing, his body twists slightly toward his pitching arm and his weight is on his right foot (figure 23.5b). In a simultaneous action, he swings his left arm forward close to the body, rotates his shoulders toward the right, and steps forward on his left foot (figure 23.5c). As the ball is released off the fingers, he follows through with the pitching arm.

Figure 23.5 Pitching.

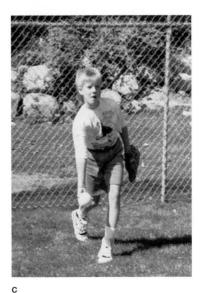

a b c

Key Teaching Points

1. Keep eyes focused on the target.
2. Keep pivot foot in contact with pitcher plate.
3. Simultaneously step forward as arm rotates forward and downward.
4. Follow through in the direction of the batter.

Catching and Fielding

Good fielding ability requires the player to be able to catch a high fly ball and a variety of throws and to stop a ball hit along the ground. In all types of fielding it is important to be in a ready position, with the feet spread apart comfortably and the weight on both feet. The trunk leans forward slightly and the knees are flexed. The hands are in front of the body about knee high. The eyes are on the ball (figure 23.6).

Figure 23.6
Fielding—ready position.

Key Teaching Points

1. Keep eyes focused on the oncoming ball.
2. Stand with trunk bent slightly forward, knees partially bent, and weight evenly distributed over both feet.
3. Put hands in front of knees, with fingers spread apart.

Catching

If the ball approaches below the waist, the fingers point with the little fingers together (figure 23.7a). When the ball approaches above the waist, the thumbs are together and the fingers point upward (figure 23.7b). As the ball is caught, the hands recoil toward the body to deaden or soften the force of the oncoming ball (figure 23.7c).

Key Teaching Points

1. Keep eyes focused on the oncoming ball.
2. Move quickly into position to catch the ball.
3. Extend arms toward the ball, then recoil and shift ball to throwing hand.

Fielding Grounders

The first important move in grounding a ball is to shift the body toward the direction of the oncoming ball. As the fielder moves toward the ball, he shifts his weight forward, holding his arms low and in front of his body (figure 23.8a). Just before grounding the ball, he stops, with his left foot in front of his right foot, his knees bent, and his trunk well forward (figure 23.8b). He contacts the ball just inside his front foot with his left hand, then covers or traps it with his throwing hand (figure 23.8c). The eyes should be kept on the ball until it is firmly held. Once the ball is caught, the fielder begins to straighten up and takes a step in the direction of the throw.

Fielding a ground ball requires good fielding position and split-second timing to catch the ball on a good bounce. Because of these factors, plus the use of poor and uneven

Figure 23.7 Catching.

a

b

c

Figure 23.8 Fielding grounders.

a

b

c

Figure 23.9 "Sure-stop" grounding.

playing fields, the "sure-stop" grounding skill should be used, particularly by outfielders. This is similar to the regular grounding skill, except that the fielder makes a half turn toward the direction in which the ball is approaching, then lowers and rests on the back knee. The thigh and lower leg provide a good rebound surface for a ball that is missed (figure 23.9).

Key Teaching Points

1. Keep eyes focused on the oncoming ball.
2. Move quickly into position to field the ball.
3. Stop the ball with the nonthrowing hand and cover it with the throwing hand.
4. Once the ball is caught, quickly shift into a throwing position.

Hitting the Ball

A softball can be hit in three ways. The first, and most important, is hitting a pitched ball with maximum force and follow-through. *Bunting* is a form of hitting a pitched ball; however, it requires a different grip, force, and follow-through. *Fungo batting* is simply throwing the ball up with one hand, regrasping the bat, and hitting the ball before it hits the ground.

The bat may be gripped in one of three positions, depending on the batter's strength and the type of hit desired. In the long grip (figure 23.10a), the hands are placed close to the bottom of the bat. For the medium grip (figure 23.10b), the hands are moved up one to two inches. For the choke grip (figure 23.10c), the hands are three to four inches from the knob of the bat. In each grip, the bat is held with the hands together and the fingers and thumbs wrapped around the handle. For right-handed batters, the right hand grips the handle above the left hand.

Batting

The batter stands with his feet parallel and about shoulder-width apart and weight evenly distributed over both feet. The left side of the body faces the pitcher. The bat is held at the back of the head about shoulder high. The arms are bent at the elbows and held away from the body. As the ball leaves the pitcher's hand, the batter shifts his weight to the rear foot (figure 23.11a). He then swings the bat forward as his weight shifts to the lead foot (figure 23.11b). After the ball is contacted, the batter continues to swing the bat around in a wide arc, ending over the left shoulder (figure 23.11c).

Key Teaching Points

1. Keep eyes focused on the pitched ball.
2. Begin with weight evenly distributed over both feet.
3. Turn head and look at the pitcher's throwing hand.
4. As bat swings downward and forward, rotate hips, trunk, and shoulders toward the pitcher.
5. Contact ball in front of front hip and follow through around the body.

Figure 23.10 Gripping the bat.

a

b

c

Figure 23.11 Batting.

a

b

c

Bunting

In bunting, the bat is placed in the way of the oncoming pitch, then allowed to "give" as the ball contacts the bat. Begin in a normal batting position (figure 23.12a). As the ball moves toward the strike zone, the batter draws his rear foot forward and squares his body to the pitcher. At the same time, he slides his top hand up the bat. The bat is held with the thumb on top and the fingers underneath (figure 23.12b). When the ball is hit, the bat slips back toward the palm of the hand as the arms recoil back toward the chest. The bat is angled in the direction of the intended bunt.

Key Teaching Points

1. Always begin in a normal batting position.
2. Keep in mind that slow pitches are easiest to bunt.
3. Emphasize "giving" or "catching with the bat" as the ball makes contact with the bat.
4. Do not follow through.

Figure 23.12 Bunting.

a

b

chapter 23

Figure 23.13 Fungo batting.

a   b   c

Fungo Batting

Fungo batting is useful for hitting the ball during fielding practice and in many lead-up games. Start with the feet parallel and comfortably spread apart, with the weight evenly distributed on both feet. Suspend the bat over the right shoulder while holding the ball in the left hand (figure 23.13a). Simultaneously toss the ball up and swing the bat down and forward, grasping it with the left hand (figure 23.13b). Continue forward, transferring the weight to the front foot and twisting the body toward the left. Hit the ball approximately in front of the left foot (figure 23.13c) and follow through with a swing around the left shoulder.

Key Teaching Points

1. Keep eyes on the ball until it is hit.
2. Grip the bat about ten inches up the grip.
3. Toss the ball about three feet above shoulder.
4. Simultaneously swing from shoulder, regrasp with left hand, contact ball, and continue forward swing around body.

Base Running

As soon as a ball is hit, the batter drops the bat and runs as fast as possible to and through first base. If she decides to

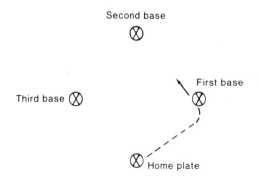

Second base
⊗

Third base ⊗   First base
                     ⊗

⊗ Home plate

try to run to second base, she begins curving to the right a few feet before reaching first base, touches the inside corner of the bag, and continues running to second base (figure 23.14).

Key Teaching Points

1. Hold onto the bat until the follow-through is completed.
2. Drop the bat and run as fast as possible toward first base.
3. Keep eyes focused on the base.
4. Touch and run through the base.

Figure 23.14 Running bases.

Practice Activities and Lead-Up Games

Most practice activities for softball involve partners or small groups. Each of the following drills and practice activities should be modified to cope with the available space, time, and equipment (table 23.2).

The following lead-up games are designed to provide maximum participation and practice in one or more softball skills. As a general guideline, use these games extensively in level II and proportionately less in level III. Playing the official game of softball can be a challenging and enjoyable experience for upper elementary school children, but only when the majority of players have developed adequate throwing, catching, and batting skills. These lead-up games can be played in smaller areas and require fewer players than the regulation game.

Table 23.2 Practice Activities and Lead-Up Games

Name of activity	Type of activity	Players	Developmental level		Softball concepts and skills	Movement concepts	Page
			II	III			
Practice activities							
Throwing and Catching	Throw, catch	2	———————▶		Throw, catch grounders	Moving into space, change of direction and speed	395
Partner Batting	Bat, catch, throw	2	———————▶		Throw, hit, catch	Hitting into empty space, strong and light	395
Overtake the Base	Throw, catch, run	8–10 per squad	———————▶		Throw, catch, run	Moving into space, change of direction, pathway, and speed	395
Fly Ball Catching	Hit, catch, throw	6–8 per squad	———————▶		Hit, catch, run	Hitting into empty space, levels, change of direction	395
Swing at Four	Hit, catch, throw	10–12 per squad	———————▶		Pitch, hit, catch, throw	Moving into space, change of direction and speed, strong and light	396
Pepper	Hit, catch, throw	5–6 per squad	———————▶		Hit, catch, throw	Moving into space, change of direction and speed	396
Lead-up games							
Flies and Grounders	Hit, catch	6 per group	———————▶		Throw, hit, field	Hitting into empty space, levels, change of direction and speed	396
One Old Cat	Throw, hit, catch	9 per team	———————▶		Throw, catch, hit	Hitting into empty space, moving into space, change of direction and speed	396
Long Ball	Throw, hit	9 per team	———————▶		Throw, catch, hit	Hitting into empty space, moving into space, change of direction and speed	396
Tee Ball	All skills	9 per team	———————▶		All softball skills	Moving into space, strong and light, change of direction and speed	397
Twenty-One Softball	Throw, catch	9–10 per team	———————▶		Throw, catch, hit	Moving into space, change of direction and speed, strong and light	397
Overtake the Ball	Catch, throw	5–7 per team	———▶		Throw, catch	Change of direction and speed	397
Roll at the Bat	Hit, catch, throw	4–5 per group	———▶		Fungo hit, catch, throw	Moving into space, hitting into empty space, change of direction and speed	397
Beatball Softball	Hit, catch, throw	9 per team	———————▶		Throw, catch, hit	Moving into space, hitting into empty space, change of direction and speed	397
Scrub	All skills	7–9 per team	———————▶		All softball skills	Moving into space, hitting into empty space, change of direction and speed	398
Five Hundred	Fungo hit, catch, throw	4–6 per group	———▶		All softball skills	Moving into space, change of direction and speed	398

Practice Activities

Throwing and Catching

Motor skills Throw, catch grounders
Movement concepts Moving into space, change of direction and speed
Players Two
Formation None
Playing area Playground
Equipment Softball

Perhaps the most common type of softball practice activity involves two players. Some of the most useful partner activities are described.

1. Have the partners throw and catch. Have both partners remain stationary, varying the distances; then have one remain stationary while the other moves, practicing grounders.
2. Have the pitcher and catcher alternate positions.
3. Practice hitting a target. Set up a target on a wall or the ground for pitching or accurate throwing practice.
4. Partners throw to each other but make the ball bounce before it reaches the receiver.
5. One partner throws a grounder while other partner throws ball directly back.

The inventive games approach can be used quite effectively in partner activities to increase skill and to provide an avenue for unique and enjoyable practice activities. The following example should provide a general idea:

Situation: Divide the class into partners. Give the partners a ball and one piece of small equipment (bat, hoop, traffic cone).

Challenge: "Can you make up a practice activity (or drill) with your partner that includes a sidearm throw, a grounder, and one piece of small equipment?" Allow the class several minutes to make up their games, then select one or two partner groups and have them demonstrate their games.

Partner Batting

Motor skills Throw, hit, catch
Movement concepts Hitting into empty space, strong and light
Players Two
Playing area Playground
Equipment Ball and bat

The success of any softball game centers on each player's ability to hit the ball. Too often, however, batting practice is one player hitting the ball to ten or more very inactive fielders. The following partner activities are very effective in developing batting skills.

1. One player hits the ball off a tee to his partner. Use a traffic cone mounted on a cardboard box as a substitute tee.
2. One player fungo hits to his partner.

3. Add a third player. One player pitches, another bats, and the third player fields the ball. Rotate after three hits.
4. Practice close-range bunting. One player pitches, while the batter attempts to bunt the ball back.

Overtake the Base

Motor skills Throw, catch, run
Movement concepts Moving into space, change of direction, pathway, and speed
Players Eight to ten per squad
Formation Diamond
Playing area Playground
Equipment Ball

Divide the class into squads of eight to ten players. Arrange the squads around the bases, with player A at the pitcher's line, B on home plate, C on first base, D on second, and E on third. The remaining players form a line near home plate. When the whistle blows, player A throws to B, B throws to C, and so on around the diamond to home plate. At the same time A throws the ball, F takes off for first base and continues around the bases, attempting to reach home plate before the ball. Two rules apply: (1) The base runner must touch all bases and (2) the players rotate after each run. A takes B's position, B goes to C's, F takes A's. Everyone shifts one place to the right, with player E on third going to the back of the line.

Suggestions and Variations

1. Make two diamonds, with the smaller one for runners and the larger one for throwers.
2. Add one or more fielders.

Fly Ball Catching

Motor skills Hit, catch, throw
Movement concepts Hitting into empty space, levels, change of direction and speed
Players Six to eight per squad
Formation Scattered
Playing area Playground
Equipment Softball and bat

Place one batter at home plate and scatter the remaining players in the field. The batter, using fungo batting, hits fly balls into the field. When a fielder catches a fly ball, he becomes the batter.

Suggestions and Variations

1. Place all fielders in a large semicircle and require the batter to hit two balls to each player in turn. Rotate after the last player has received his second fly.
2. Add a pitcher and a catcher.

Motor skills   Pitch, hit, throw, catch
Movement concepts   Moving into space, change of direction and speed, strong and light
Players   Ten to twelve per squad
Formation   Squads
Playing area   Playground
Equipment   Baseballs, bats, bases

Divide the class into two or three squads of ten to twelve players. Arrange squads in infield positions, with spare players in a line behind home plate. The pitcher throws four balls to each batter, who attempts to hit them into the infield. Infield players retrieve the balls and throw them to first base. The first baseman returns the balls to the pitcher. Rotate players after each player has had four hits. The batter takes the third baseman's position and everyone shifts one place to the left. The catcher goes to the back of the "waiting" line, and the pitcher becomes the catcher.

Suggestions and Variations

Add outfielders and allow batters to hit anywhere.

Pepper

Motor skills   Hit, catch, throw
Movement concepts   Moving into space, change of direction and speed
Players   Five or six per squad
Formation   Line
Playing area   Playground
Equipment   Softball, bat

Divide the class into groups of five or six. Place five players in a line, with about ten feet between each player. One player, the "leader," stands about twenty feet in front of the line with his bat. The first player in the line pitches the ball to the leader, who hits it to the next player in line. The second player fields the ball and pitches it back to the leader. Continue the drill to the last player, then rotate the leader.

Suggestions and Variations

If a line player misses the ball, he goes to the end of the line. If a batter misses a fair pitch, he changes places with the player at the end of the line.

Lead-Up Games

Flies and Grounders

Motor skills   Throw, hit, fielding
Movement concepts   Hitting into empty space, levels, change of direction and speed
Players   Six per group
Formation   Scattered
Playing area   Playground
Equipment   Softball and bat

The batter hits the ball into the field off the tee or fungo-style. The player in a position to catch the ball calls "Mine"

and attempts to catch it. A player receives five points for catching a fly ball, three points for a ball caught after one bounce, and one point for a grounder. The first player to reach fifteen points becomes the new batter.

Suggestions and Variations

1. Substitute a pitcher for fungo hitting.
2. Require only one type of throw.

One Old Cat

Motor skills   Throw, catch, hit
Movement concepts   Hitting into empty space, moving into space, change of direction and speed
Players   Nine per team
Formation   Players divided into two teams of nine each, with one team in the field and one at bat
Playing area   Playground
Equipment   Softball, bat, bases

The first player on the batting team hits the ball into the field and tries to run to first base and home in one complete trip. He may not stop on the base. If he makes a complete trip without being put out, he scores one run for his team. The runner is out if (a) a fielder catches a fly ball or (b) a fielder touches the runner with the ball before he reaches home. When the team at bat makes three outs, it goes into the field and the team in the field comes to bat. The team with the highest score at the end of the playing period wins. (Teams must have the same number of times at bat.)

Suggestions and Variations

1. Alternate pitchers and catchers. Alternate boy and girl in batting order.
2. Try two outs if one team stays up too long.
3. Vary the distance to the base according to the level of skill.
4. Use batting tee if skill level is too low.

Long Ball

Motor skills   Throw, catch, hit
Movement concepts   Hitting into empty space, moving into space, change of direction and speed
Players   Nine per team
Formation   Class divided into two equal teams. The fielding team consists of a pitcher and a catcher, with the remaining players scattered in the field.
Playing area   Playground
Equipment   Softball, bat, bases

Each team selects a pitcher and a catcher. Other players are fielders or batters. When a batter hits the ball, he runs to the base and, if possible, returns home to score a point. Any hit is good and there are no fouls. The base runner may stop on first base, and any number of runners may be on base at the same time. Runners may not steal home. The batter is out when he strikes out, is touched off base, steals a base, throws the bat, or hits a fly ball that is caught. One point is awarded for each run.

Suggestions and Variations

1. Substitute a batting tee if skill level is too low.
2. Change any rule or add new ones as need or interest dictates.

Tee Ball

Motor skills All softball skills except pitching and stealing bases
Movement concepts Moving into space, strong and light, change of direction and speed
Players Nine per team
Formation Regulation softball field
Playing area Playground
Equipment Softball, tee, bases

This game is played in the same way as softball, with the following modifications.

1. The batter is allowed one hit off the tee.
2. Since there is no pitcher, no one is permitted to steal a base. A runner must stay on base until the ball is hit by a teammate.

Twenty-One Softball

Motor skills Throw, catch, hit
Movement concepts Moving into space, change of direction and speed, strong and light
Players Nine or ten per team
Formation Regulation softball field
Playing area Playground
Equipment Softball, bat, bases

Play according to regular softball rules, with the following exceptions: The batter gets three swings to hit the ball. When he hits the ball, he runs the bases in order until he is put out. A runner safe at first scores one point; at second, two points; at third, three points; and at home, four points. Teams exchange places after three outs. The first team to score twenty-one points wins.

Suggestions and Variations

1. Change pitcher and catcher each time the teams change positions.
2. Use fungo or hit off a tee.
3. Change scoring to eleven or fifteen points rather than twenty-one.

Overtake the Ball

Motor skills Throw, catch
Movement concepts Change of direction and speed
Players Five to seven per team
Formation Circle
Playing area Playground
Equipment Softball

The players stand in a circle and count off by twos. The ones are members of one team and the twos, the other. Each team selects a captain, who stands in the center of the circle. Both captains have a ball. On signal, each captain tosses his ball to any team member, who tosses it back to the captain. The captain tosses it to the next team member (in a clockwise direction), who also tosses it back to the captain. The ball is tossed in this manner clockwise around the circle by both teams until each ball has been thrown to all members of the team and is back in the captain's hands. One team "overtakes" the other when its ball passes that of the other team as the balls are tossed around the circle. The team that tosses the ball completely around the circle first scores one point. When a team overtakes and finishes first, it scores two points. The first team to score five points wins the game.

Suggestions and Variations

1. Play the game with various kinds of balls and different throws and passes.
2. Vary the distance according to the level of skill.

Roll at the Bat

Motor skills Fungo hit, catch, throw
Movement concepts Moving into space, hitting into empty space, change of direction and speed
Players Four or five per group
Formation Outdoor playing area, with fielders scattered, facing the batter
Playing area Playground
Equipment Softball, bat

One player chosen to be the first batter hits the ball anywhere into the field of play. If a player catches a fly ball, he rolls it back and tries to hit the bat, which has been placed on the ground. The length of the bat must face each "roller." If the ball is not caught, it is thrown back to the batter again. A fielder becomes the new batter when (a) he successfully rolls a ball back and hits the bat, (b) he catches two fly balls, or (c) he successfully retrieves three grounders. All players start at zero when a new batter takes a turn.

Beatball Softball

Motor skills Throw, catch, hit
Movement concepts Moving into space, hitting into empty space, change of direction and speed
Players Nine per team
Formation Regular softball field
Playing area Playground
Equipment Softball, bat, bases

Play according to regular softball rules, with the following exceptions: Any fielder who gets the ball must throw it to the first baseman, who must touch the base with the ball in his hand, then throw from first to second, second to third, and third to home. If the ball gets home ahead of the runner, he is out. If the runner beats the ball home, he scores a run for his team. After three outs, the teams exchange places.

Suggestions and Variations

1. Use fungo or tee hitting.
2. Move the bases closer together.
3. Require one type of throw, such as a sidearm or underhand toss.

Motor skills   All softball skills
Movement concepts   Moving into space, hitting into empty space, change of direction and speed
Players   Seven to nine on each team
Formation   Regular softball field
Playing area   Playground
Equipment   Softball, bat, bases

One player (the "scrub") stands at bat. All other players are numbered: the catcher is one; pitcher, two; first baseman, three; and fielders, four and up. The batter hits a pitched ball and must run to first base and back. He is out if he is tagged at first or home, strikes out, slings his bat, or hits a fly ball that is caught. If he gets home, he bats again. The batter is allowed only three times at bat; then he becomes the last fielder. If the batter is put out, every player moves up one position.

Suggestions and Variations

1. If a player catches a fly ball, he exchanges positions with the batter.
2. Two players may be up at the same time. In this situation, the first batter is permitted to stop on first base and be hit home by the other batter.
3. Use tee or fungo hitting.

Five Hundred

Motor skills   Fungo hit, throw, catch, field
Movement concepts   Moving into space, change of direction and speed
Players   Four to six per team
Formation   Scattered
Playing area   Playground
Equipment   Softball, bat

One player is chosen to be the first batter. The object of the game is for each fielder to try to be the first to reach 500 points. Points are scored as follows: 100 for catching a ball on the fly, 75 for a ball caught on the first bounce, and 50 for fielding a grounder. The same number of points is deducted from a player's score if he commits an error. As soon as a player has reached 500 or more points, he exchanges positions with the batter.

Suggestions and Variations

1. Use a pitcher.
2. Require only one type of throw.
3. Add a roll at the bat and award another 100 points for hitting it.

Softball Rules and Regulations

Although skill development varies for each grade and class, the complete game of softball should be played periodically throughout a softball unit. By playing the game according to the basic rules, children learn to appreciate the value of practice and team play. Modifications might include shortening the length between bases and substituting a batting tee for a pitcher. While children are playing the full game, the teacher should note their major weaknesses so she can select appropriate drills and lead-up games that can be used to improve these deficiencies.

I. Field of play and positions: See illustration.

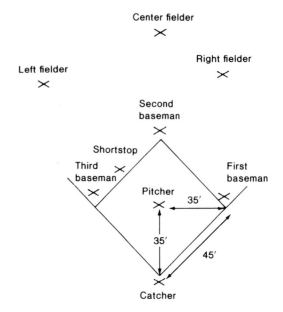

II. Batting order: Players are permitted to hit in any order; however, it is wise to have players bat according to their positions. Once an order is established, it cannot be changed, even if players change their positions.

III. The batter advances to first base when he:
   A. Hits a fair ball and reaches base before the ball does
   B. Is walked (receives four called balls)
   C. Is hit by a pitched ball
   D. Is interfered with by the catcher when batting

IV. The batter is out when he:
   A. Has three strikes
   B. Is thrown out at first
   C. Is tagged before reaching first base
   D. Hits a fair or foul ball that is caught on the fly
   E. Hits the third strike and the catcher catches the ball
   F. Bunts a foul on the third strike
   G. Throws the bat more than ten feet
   H. Steps on home plate when batting
   I. Interferes with the catcher when he is catching a fly or putting out a runner coming home
   J. Fouls any ball to the catcher that rises above the batter's head and is caught

V. When traveling the bases, the base runner:
   A. May advance to the next base after a fly is caught

Table 23.3 Softball Skill Test

Name	Accuracy throw (total pts.)	Distance throw (total pts.)	Fielding (total pts.)	Subjective evaluation (50 pts.)	Total score	Grade
1 2 3 4		Rank total scores for the class, then convert to letter grades or ratings (superior, good, etc.).				

B. Must advance to the next base when forced to do so by another base runner

C. May advance one base on an overthrow at first or third base

D. May advance two bases when overthrows are in the field of play

E. May attempt to steal a base as soon as the ball leaves the pitcher's hand

F. May advance to the next base on a fair hit that is not caught on the fly

VI. The base runner is out when he:

    A. Leaves the base before the ball leaves the pitcher's hand

    B. Is forced to run to the next base and does not arrive before the fielder touches the base with the ball in his possession

    C. Leaves the base before a fly ball is caught and a fielder tags him or that base before he returns

    D. Is hit by a batted ball when off base

    E. Intentionally interferes with a member of the fielding team

    F. Is tagged when off base

    G. Fails to touch a base and the fielder tags him or the base before he returns

    H. Passes another base runner

    I. Touches a base that is occupied by another base runner

VII. The pitcher:

    A. Must stand with both feet on the rubber, face the batter, and hold the ball in front with both hands

    B. Is allowed one step forward and must deliver the ball while taking that step

    C. Must deliver the ball with an underhand throw

    D. Cannot fake or make any motion toward the plate without delivering the ball

    E. Cannot deliberately roll or bounce the ball

    F. Cannot deliver the ball until the batter is ready

VIII. If there is an illegal pitch, the batter is entitled to take a base.

IX. The game is five to seven innings, as agreed by both teams. When there is not sufficient time to complete the game, the score reverts to the even innings score (the score after both squads have been up to bat the same number of times).

X. One point is scored each time a batter touches home base after touching each base sequentially.

Evaluative Techniques

Several tests can be used to measure the basic softball skills. The following tests are quite reliable and can be administered with student help in a short period of time. Modify any test item to meet your own teaching situation and add items if desired. Also, keep scores from year to year in order to build appropriate norms for your school (table 23.3).

Test 1: Accuracy Throw

Place a target on the wall as shown in the diagram. Use a regulation softball. A player is given ten consecutive throws from behind the throwing line. He must use the overhand throw. Score six, four, and two for hits within each respective circle. If a ball hits a line, award the higher value. Allow only one trial and record the total score.

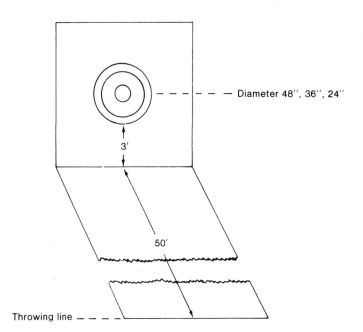

Diameter 48", 36", 24"

3'

50'

Throwing line

Test 2: Distance Throw

Place lines on the field as shown. Stakes can be used as a substitute for white gypsum lines. Use a regulation softball. Award points according to where the ball lands.

Test 3: Fielding

Place lines on a field as shown. Stakes or other "corner" markers can be substituted for lines. The teacher (or a student who is proficient at fungo batting) bats a grounder into the field area. As soon as the ball is batted, the player runs from the starting line, picks up the ball inside the field area, and throws it to the catcher. Ten trials are given, with five points awarded for each successfully fielded ball. Since it is difficult to hit grounders with reasonable consistency, use your discretion to allow retrials on any ball you feel was unfair to the contestant. Also, if batting skill is too poor, substitute a throw for the fungo batting.

Test 4: Subjective Evaluation

Establish criteria that represent the skills and playing ability required in softball. Since it is difficult to construct a fair and reliable test for batting, include this skill as part of your subjective evaluation. Consider other skills such as base running, catching, and team play. Award a total point score (zero to fifty points) and use three players as judges. Take an average of the three ratings.

Selected References

Athletic Institute. (1991). *Youth League Baseball: Coaching and Planning Edition.* North Palm Beach, FL: The Athletic Institute.

CAHPER. (1985). *Fastball-Type Games.* Ottawa, Ontario: CAHPER Publications.

Elliott, J., and Ewing, M. (1991). *Youth Softball: A Complete Handbook.* Dubuque, IA: Brown and Benchmark Publishers.

Houseworth, S. D., and Rivkin, F. V. (1985). *Coaching Softball Effectively.* Champaign, IL: Human Kinetics Publishers, Inc.

Kneer, M. E., and McCord, C. L. (1987). *Softball Slow and Fast Pitch.* Dubuque, IA: Wm. C. Brown Publishers.

Polter, D. L., and Breckmeyer, G. A. (1989). *Softball Steps to Success.* Champaign, IL: Leisure Press.

Track and Field and Cross-Country Activities

Upper elementary school children have a keen interest in track and field activities. They can participate in these events according to their ability and motivation. Furthermore, track and field activities are relatively easy to teach, require little expense, and provide vigorous competitive experience for all children. The inherent values of this activity, coupled with the feasibility of modifying facilities, make it one that should be considered a basic requirement in the elementary physical education program.

This chapter describes the basic track and field events and presents some methods of organizing and teaching these activities. Special attention has been given to developing improvised equipment and planning track meets ∎

Emphasis and Progression

Skill development in any of the official track and field events depends on the performer's potential or inherent ability and the amount and type of previous training. Taking these factors into consideration, the suggested sequence of skills shown in table 24.1 provides a rough guideline. In this type of activity, the improvement in individual events is not simply the accumulation of new skills; it is the sequential addition of skills plus improvement in form and general conditioning.

The early phase of level II is an important starting point for many track and field skills. Correct starting positions, sprints, and distance running should be introduced to these children. They also should develop reasonable skill in the standing and running long jumps, as well as the high jump using the scissors method.

Most of the remaining track and field skills are introduced in level III. These youngsters are interested in and capable of learning baton passing, hurdling, high jumping using the straddle method, putting the shot, and triple jumping. They display a major increase in skill and performance levels in track and field events.

Expected Proficiencies

Proficiency in track and field events is measured in time or distance; table 24.2 provides a rough estimate of what can be expected of elementary school children. If teachers are introducing track and field activities similar to those listed,

it is wise to establish school records. Use the suggested high and low records as a guide in establishing "expected" records within your school.

Teaching Procedures

Several important factors must be considered when planning a track and field unit. Although it is important for all children to experience the enjoyment and challenge of all the events, they should be allowed to concentrate on a few events that they enjoy and do well. This means the teacher should introduce the children early to as many track and field events as possible. Each child can then select a certain number of events for more extensive practice.

A second major consideration is how to cope with available space and equipment. Since there is never enough equipment for all children to practice the same event at the same time, station work should be used. The track and field circuit provides a basic guideline.

It is important to locate each event in a relatively permanent place on the field. Jumping pits are normally in the corners of the field. A temporary track can be made by placing traffic cones or milk cartons filled with sand or earth in an oval pattern. Placing the shot put circles inside the oval provides a safe, restricted area for this event. Sprints and hurdles can be located near each other for dual instruction purposes.

Once the general layout is established, the teacher can divide her class into squads and assign each to a station. Give brief demonstrations at each station, then allow time for practice before the squads are rotated to the next station. Rotation should be from a track event to a field event.

The following general considerations and safety procedures should be included in every track and field unit of instruction.

1. All facilities and equipment should be checked before the class begins. In particular, look for broken glass or other hazardous materials in jumping pits and field areas.

2. Each lesson should begin with a comprehensive warm-up or conditioning period involving running, jogging, and conditioning exercises designed to increase strength, endurance, and flexibility.

3. Whenever possible, provide instruction to mixed groups rather than separating boys and girls. The difference in performance levels of boys and girls at this age is more often due to motivation and prior experience than to physiological differences.

Track and Field Circuit

Table 24.1 Suggested Sequence of Presenting Track and Field Skills and Rules

Skills and rules	Developmental level II	Developmental level III
Starting		
For distance runs	Introduce	Refine
For sprints	Introduce	Refine
Rules: False start	Introduce	
Running		
Sprints	40- to 60-yard dashes	50- to 80-yard dashes
Relay running		Introduce
Hurdling		Introduce
Distance running	500- to 600-yard run	Increase distance and speed
Jogging	1 to 2 miles	1 to 3 miles
Rules: Lane position		Introduce
Passing rule		Introduce
High jumping		
Scissors method	Introduce	Increase height and form
Straddle method		Introduce
Rules: Number of jumps	Introduce	
Broad jump		
Standing long jump	Introduce	Increase distance and form
Long jump	Introduce	Increase distance and form
Rules: Foot fault	Introduce	
Triple jump		
Rules: Foot fault		Introduce
Shot put		
Rules: Foot fault		Introduce
Other rules		
General track meet rules	Introduce	

Table 24.2 Proficiency Levels for Track and Field (Combined Scores for Girls and Boys)

Events	Minimum to optimum records							
	Age 9		Age 10		Age 11		Age 12	
	Low	High	Low	High	Low	High	Low	High
50-yard dash (sec)	11.0	7.0	10.0	6.0	9.5	6.0	9.0	6.0
220-yard run (sec)	43.0	33.0	42.0	31.0	40.0	32.5	38.0	30.5
150-yard run (sec)	29.0	23.0	27.0	22.0	25.0	19.1	23.0	18.2
High jump	2'7"	3'	2'11"	3'4"	3'0"	3'10"	3'6"	4'2"
Standing long jump	3'7"	6'4"	4'0"	6'4"	4'8"	6'8"	4'10"	6'11"
Running long jump	10'5"	11'8"	11'0"	12'2"	12'0"	13'2"	13'0"	14'2"
Triple jump	11'6"	14'3"	12'	15'	13'	16'	14'	17'
Softball throw	35'	165'	45'	175'	70'	205'	76'	207'
Shot put	8'6"	13'	9'	15'	10'	16'	12'	17'

track and field and cross-country activities

4. Require all children to wear running shoes. Do not allow any child to participate in bare feet or with spiked track shoes.

5. Provide special considerations and support for children with weight problems. This includes setting realistic goals and providing ongoing support, especially to children who are excessively overweight.

6. Provide special consideration and events for disabled children.

Description of Skills

There are two basic types of events in track and field: (1) running events, which include sprints, hurdles, and longer endurance runs, and (2) field events, which include the high jump, long jump, triple jump, and shot put. These skills should be taught to all students regardless of their inherent ability. Once the children have been exposed to these skills, allow them to select and concentrate on the events that are best suited to their potential capabilities.

Starting

The starting position for running events is determined by the length of the race. For short races, such as twenty- and thirty-yard dashes, the "kneeling start" or "sprint start" is best. For longer races, the "standing start" is more acceptable.

Standing Start

In the standing start (figure 24.1), one foot is close to the starting line and the other foot is slightly to the rear. The head is up, the trunk is bent forward, the knees are slightly flexed, and the weight is on the front foot. The opposite arm to the lead foot is held forward, with the elbow flexed, while the other arm is down and slightly back.

Figure 24.1 Standing start. Body leans forward slightly.

Sprint Start

The sprint start is important to the success of any beginning sprinter. The form and techniques of this skill are quite easy to master, even for fourth graders.

On the "on your mark" command, the runner kneels and places the toe of her front foot six to twelve inches behind the starting line (figure 24.2a). The front foot is normally the opposite foot to the "kicking foot." She extends her arms straight down, with the weight on the fingertips. (If children do not have adequate arm and shoulder girdle strength, allow them to support their weight on their knuckles.) The runner squeezes her fingers together to make a "bridge" with the thumb. On "set" she raises her lower knee and buttocks until her back is straight and parallel to the ground (figure 24.2b). Her weight should be evenly distributed between her hands and her front foot. Her head is not raised, as she should be looking at a spot on the ground a few feet in front of the starting line. On "go" she drives forward with her lead leg and, at the same instant, brings her rear leg forward (figure 24.2c).

Key Teaching Points

1. At the starting position, keep head looking at a spot a few feet in front of the hands.
2. Teach children to react to a starting signal rather than trying to anticipate it.
3. Keep body low and exaggerate forward lean during the first steps off the mark.

Running

There are several types of running positions, each with its own body lean, arm action, and foot contact. The elementary school track program, however, involves only two types, sprinting form and distance running form. In the sprinting form (figure 24.3), the runner's body leans well forward and contact is made with the ball or front of the foot. The arms are bent at the elbows and swing vigorously from the shoulders. In distance running (figure 24.4), the body is

Figure 24.2 Sprint start.

a   b   c

Figure 24.3 Sprinting form.

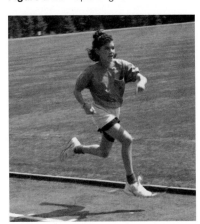

Figure 24.4 Distance running form.

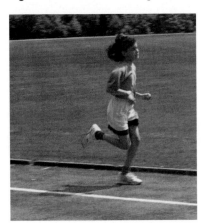

Figure 24.5 Relay receiver forms a V.

more erect and the weight is taken on the heel, then rocked forward. The elbows are bent slightly and the arm action is less vigorous than in sprinting.

Key Teaching Points

Teach runners to run in a straight line—arms straight forward and backward.

Relay Running

There are two types of baton passes. The visual pass allows the receiver to look back at the moment of the pass. The blind pass requires the receiver to keep looking straight ahead as she receives the baton. Although the visual pass is slower, it is recommended for elementary school children.

Visual Pass

The runner who is to receive the baton draws his right hand straight back toward the approaching runner. He holds his fingers together, pointing to the side, while he points his thumb toward his body. This forms a V into which the approaching runner places the baton (figure 24.5). The approaching runner brings the baton up into the receiving runner's hand (figure 24.6). As soon as the front runner receives the baton, he brings it forward into his left hand in preparation for the next pass.

When students are ready to practice baton passing at full speed, it is important that they establish their own check marks—when they should start to run. As a general rule, have the runner place a mark on the ground five yards back of his starting point.

The incoming runner starts fifty yards back of the passing zone and runs as fast as possible. When he passes the check mark, the outgoing runner turns and runs as fast as possible. When the outgoing runner reaches the passing zone, he puts his hand back for the baton. He must be inside the passing zone before he receives the baton or his team is

Figure 24.6 Passing the baton upward into the hand.

disqualified. If the incoming runner cannot catch up to the outgoing runner, the check mark should be moved closer to the outgoing runner's starting point. If the incoming runner runs past the outgoing runner, the check mark should be moved farther back from the outgoing runner's starting point.

Key Teaching Points

1. As the runner with the baton gets close to the exchange zone, the baton should be in his left hand.
2. Receiver should have his right hand back as he begins to run in the exchange zone.
3. Receiver looks back to make sure the baton is placed in his extended right hand.

Standing Long Jump

The performer stands with his toes just behind the starting line, his feet comfortably spread, his knees bent, and his trunk well forward (figure 24.7a). After several preliminary swings with the arms, he swings his arms forward and upward vigorously and extends his legs. As soon as his feet leave the ground, he begins to flex his knees, keeping his arms forward (figure 24.7b). He lands with his feet parallel and his trunk and arms extended forward (figure 24.7c).

Key Teaching Points

1. In the starting position, the weight is well forward in an almost overbalanced position.
2. Simultaneously push off from both feet and swing arms forward and upward.
3. Flex at the waist as the arms move forward and upward.

Long Jump

A successful long jumper must be able to combine jumping and speed. Elementary school children have sufficient speed for this event and can execute the approach flight and landing relatively well. The performer begins several yards back from the takeoff board, runs forward, and places her takeoff foot on the board (figure 24.8a). As soon as she leaves the board, she brings her rear leg and both arms forward and upward (figure 24.8b). Her heels contact the ground and she immediately thrusts both arms back (figure 24.8c), forcing her body well forward.

An effective technique to help students gain height in the jump is to suspend a hat from a crossbar or on the end of a rope attached to a stick (figure 24.9). The height of the hat should be adjusted so that the student jumps to maximum height in order to put the hat on his head. The distance from the takeoff point varies, but it should be a little more than half of the total jump.

Key Teaching Points

1. Have each child pace out the correct number of strides, then practice the approach until the takeoff becomes consistent.
2. After the takeoff, keep head up and reach upward and forward.
3. Vigorously thrust arms backward upon landing.

Figure 24.7 Standing long jump.

a b c

Figure 24.8 Long jump.

a b c

Figure 24.9 Technique for gaining height.

chapter 24

Figure 24.10 Jumping hurdles.

a   b   c

Hurdles

Elementary school children can run the hurdles with speed and efficiency. The main reason they usually do not learn the proper form is because the hurdles are set too high, too far apart, or both.

When the runner is approximately seven feet from the hurdle, she lifts her lead leg and extends it forward (figure 24.10a). The arm opposite to the lead leg should also extend forward (figure 24.10b). She continues moving her lead leg forward and upward until it clears the hurdle. The rear leg then starts forward, with the toes turned up. Note the important forward body lean as the runner prepares for the next stage. She draws her lead leg down and thrusts her trailing leg forward (figure 24.10c). Throughout this whole movement, the shoulders should be parallel to the finish line.

The following stages should be followed when introducing hurdles:

1. Begin by having the children sprint about twenty-five yards.

2. Place an obstacle (a cane or an old broom handle) on the ground approximately halfway or between thirty to forty-five feet from the starting line. Again, the children sprint the full length; however, they should make no attempt to hurdle the obstacle.

3. Place a second obstacle on the ground so that it is midway between the third and fourth strides (figure 24.11). The teacher can check whether runners are taking the correct three strides between hurdles by observing if they are taking very short steps (usually five) or if they land on a different foot after each hurdle (usually four steps). In order to assist the

Figure 24.11 Introducing hurdles.

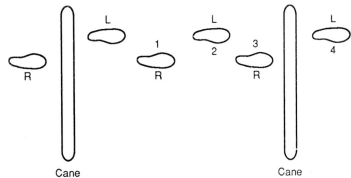

runner in developing the three-step sequence between hurdles, set up numerous courses (see diagram) so that each runner can select the one that fits his step pattern.

4. The obstacles should now be raised nine to twelve inches. Use shoe boxes, bricks, small stands, or adjustable hurdles. Let the children practice and then gradually raise the hurdle height to thirty inches. When the obstacle approaches twenty-four inches, the children should be taught what to do with the trailing leg. Have them walk down beside the hurdle. As they approach it, have them step in front and slightly to the side of the hurdle with their lead leg

track and field and cross-country activities

Table 24.3   Recommended Competitive Hurdles (12 and Under)*

Height of hurdles	Number of hurdles	Start to first hurdle	Between hurdles	Last hurdle to finish line	Total distance
20″ to 30″	6	33′4″	22′3″	35′5″	60 yards

*Adjust the height of the hurdle to meet the performer's level of ability.

Figure 24.12 High jump—scissors style.

a   b   c

and then take the trailing leg over the hurdle. The thigh of the trailing leg should be parallel to the top of the hurdle; then it should be brought through quickly into the next stride. Once the correct technique is acquired, the children should jog down beside the hurdles doing the same drill. Finally, have them run from the starting position and hurdle in the center of each hurdle (table 24.3).

Key Teaching Points

1. The takeoff must be between five and seven feet from the hurdle. The actual distance depends on the child's size and strength. This seems like a long way when standing and looking at it, but it is very easy to negotiate the hurdle from this distance when in motion.
2. Take off from the ball of one foot and land on the opposite foot.
3. Bring the knee of the lead leg up quickly toward the hurdle.
4. Bring the lead leg down quickly. Snap the trailing leg through quickly into the next running stride.
5. Keep shoulders parallel to the finish line throughout the whole movement.
6. Keep the same number of strides between each hurdle and lead with the same foot.

High Jump

Two types of jumping styles are described here. The "scissors style" is the easier of the two and should be learned first. The "straddle roll," although more difficult to learn, is the better of the two in terms of heights that can be reached. Regardless of the method taught, it is imperative that a good landing surface be provided. Children will not learn to jump correctly if they are afraid to land in the pit. Although foam rubber is more acceptable, shavings or an improvised rubber tube pit provide a satisfactory landing surface.

A very inexpensive jumping pit can be constructed by using discarded automobile tire inner tubes. Place tubes on the ground, as shown in appendix B, and tie them together. Then place a tumbling mat on top of the tubes. This provides a safe and comfortable landing surface that can be used both indoors and outdoors.

Scissors Method

The jumper approaches from the left at a slight angle to the bar—fifteen to twenty degrees (figure 24.12a). He takes a few steps, plants his right ("takeoff") foot, then swings his left foot high into the air. The left leg continues over the bar (figure 24.12b), followed by the right in a scissors action. At the same time, the arms swing forward and upward, assisting the upward lift of the body (figure 24.12c). The left foot lands first, followed by the right, completing the scissors action.

Figure 24.13 Straddle roll.

a   b   c   d

Key Teaching Points

1. Practice the run of the approach until the takeoff foot hits the same spot every time.
2. Stress a vigorous upward thrust of the front leg and both arms.
3. Land on the lead foot.

Straddle Method

Proper technique must be stressed when introducing this method of jumping. Poor technique leads to little or no improvement and a disillusioned jumper. The jumper approaches from the left side approximately forty-five degrees to the bar. He takes a few steps, plants his left ("takeoff") foot, swings his right leg forward and upward, and raises his arms (figure 24.13a). He continues the upward and forward movement, extending his body and lifting his leg upward (figure 24.13b). At the height of the jump, his body is parallel to the bar (figure 24.13c). He continues "rolling" over the bar, landing on his hands and right leg (figure 24.13d).

Key Teaching Points

1. Practice the run of the approach until the takeoff foot hits the same spot every time.
2. Make sure the last three steps are fast, with the body leaning slightly backward.
3. At the top of the jump, the jumper should "lay out" and roll across the top of the bar with a twist of the body.

Triple Jump: Hop, Step, and Jump

This event is a very popular event among boys and girls alike. The appeal seems to be both the distance that is traveled and the immediate improvement once the proper techniques are learned. The runner starts thirty to forty yards back to gain maximum speed at the takeoff mark. The first stage is a hop on the right foot from the takeoff board (figure 24.14a). To maintain forward speed, the hop is kept low. The left leg drives forward and the jumper lands on her right foot (figure 24.14b). She continues forward with a thrust of the left leg (figure 24.14c), lands on the heel of her left foot, and rocks forward toward the toe. She continues the forward action by pushing off from her left foot (figure 24.14d) and landing on both feet in the pit.

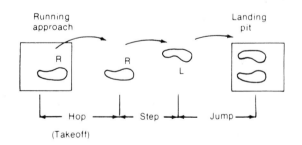

Key Teaching Points

1. Have each child pace out the correct number of steps, then practice the approach until the takeoff foot hits the board every time.
2. Keep the hop low and, upon landing on the right foot, drive the left leg forward.

Figure 24.14 Hop, step, and jump.

a. Hop right. b. Land right. c. Step left. d. Jump.

3. Continue forward thrust of left leg and land on heel of the left foot.

4. Immediately following the step, reach forward and upward.

Shot Put

The six-pound shot put event has proved to be an extremely safe and enjoyable activity for boys and girls in the upper elementary school. The performer stands near the back of the circle, with his weight on his right leg and his left toe touching the ground. He holds the shot in a "cradled" position on the side of his neck (figure 24.15a). He extends his left arm upward for balance (figures 24.15b and 24.16a). He then lowers his trunk over his right leg and raises his left leg upward and toward the front of the circle (figure 24.16b). In a simultaneous action, he drives his right leg toward the front of the circle and shifts his left leg in the same direction. Throughout this shifting movement, the body should be kept low (figure 24.16c). At the end of this shifting movement, he begins to extend his right leg upward, rotates his trunk toward the front, and extends his right arm forward and upward. The shot is released with a final push off the fingertips (figure 24.16d). The body continues to move around to the left side.

To construct a throwing area for shot putting, take a piece of rope approximately five feet long and tape the ends. Drive two nails through the rope exactly three and a half feet apart. Hold one nail stationary and scribe an arc with the other end.

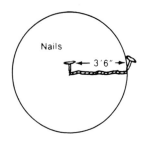

Nails

3' 6"

Figure 24.15 Holding the shot.

a b

Key Teaching Points

1. Learn to push, rather than throw, the shot.
2. Begin near the back of the circle, flex the knee, and lower the body.
3. Once in the lowered position, immediately thrust the left leg forward and upward and shift the right leg in the same direction.
4. Keep low through the shifting movement.
5. Rotate and extend the body, then push the shot off the fingertips toward the landing area.

Practice Activities

Track and field skills require a great deal of individual attention by the teacher and extensive practice by the student. The following practice activities should be used throughout

chapter 24

Figure 24.16 Putting the shot.

a   b   c   d

the track and field unit to supplement individualized instruction and to encourage a competitive spirit among all members of the class.

Continuous Running

A set distance is established. For example, the children could be asked to run one mile on the track or to run from the school to a point one mile away. Each child runs as far as he can, then walks the rest of the mile. With practice, the children should gradually increase the distance they run. Enjoyable courses can be set up on the school ground or in a nearby park or wilderness area.

Interval Training

This is the most commonly used training method among track and field athletes. This form of training has three components: (1) the distance covered on each interval, (2) the recovery period between intervals, and (3) the number of repetitions performed. The following example illustrates this form of training.

A group of children are training for a 440-yard race. The best time for the group is seventy seconds. Since the length of the interval is 220 yards, the time is reduced to thirty-five seconds expected for each 220-yard run. Each child attempts to run the first 220 yards within thirty-five seconds, rests or walks for three minutes, then attempts to run the next 220 yards within thirty-five seconds. This procedure continues to the end of the fifth 220-yard run. When a runner can complete the five 220-yard runs in the time allotment, the training can be increased in three different ways: (1) reduce the running time, (2) reduce the recovery period, or (3) require more repetitions (increase to six or seven 220-yard runs).

Walk, Jog, Run

Make a small track out of traffic cones or any other type of markers. Teach the children the difference between walking, jogging, and running. A jog is about half speed and a run is full speed. To start, students are allowed to walk at their own speed around the markers. The first blow of the whistle means that everyone jogs. The second blow means that everyone runs at top speed. The third blow means that everyone jogs, and the fourth blow means everyone walks. Continue this sequence.

Teaching Suggestions

At the beginning of the unit, allow more time between the walk and jog phases and short periods at top speed. Gradually increase the time at full speed.

Start and Pass

Arrange class into a line formation, with six to eight on each team. Put half the team behind each of two starting lines twenty-five feet apart. This is essentially a starting drill. The teacher should use the following commands: "Take your marks," "Set," and "Go," or blow a whistle. On the whistle, two runners on each team behind opposite lines make fast starts and run until they pass each other. At the passing point, each player slows to a walk and goes to the rear of the line.

Teaching Suggestions

1. Each player runs all the way over the opposite line, then slows down to a walk back to the rear of the line.
2. Use standing and kneeling starts.

track and field and cross-country activities

Call Race

Arrange two teams of five to ten runners on a starting line. Draw a turning line thirty feet in front of the starting line. Line up each team along the starting line. Number the players on each team. The teacher calls out any number, such as "four." Both number four players run to the turning line and back across the starting line. Continue calling numbers at random until all runners have had a turn.

Teaching Suggestions

Call out "Take your mark," "Set," and then the number. Only players whose numbers are called should run. The remaining players stand up and wait. This is an excellent starting drill.

Number of Jumps

Arrange class in a long line formation, with the children's toes touching the starting line. Draw a finish line twenty to thirty feet in front of the starting line. Each child begins on the starting line and makes a standing broad jump as far as possible. His subsequent jumps start from where his heels touched. The object is to see who can make it across the finish line in the fewest number of jumps.

Teaching Suggestions

Use partners to mark landing positions and to count jumps.

Over the Rope

Arrange teams of five to eight in a line formation, facing a mat. This high jumping activity can be used outside on grass or indoors on mats. Two players hold a long skipping rope at various heights while the remainder of the squad practices the scissors or straddle roll over the rope.

Baton Passing

The class is divided into groups of four to eight runners placed in a single line approximately four feet apart as shown in the diagram. From a stationary position, the children start passing the baton from the end of each line. The first runner passes with his left hand to the runner in front, who takes the baton in his right hand. He immediately brings it forward into his left hand in preparation for the next pass. The baton should be brought up into the receiving runner's right hand. When the baton reaches the front of the line, everyone turns around and the drill is repeated.

After the students have the feel of passing the baton in a stationary position, have them do it in a slow jog. Therefore, the distance between runners will have to be increased. Repeat the drill, gradually increasing the speed and the distance between runners.

Track and Field Meet Rules and Regulations

The organization and general rules and regulations of any elementary school track and field meet will depend on the children's general interest, the available time, and the facilities. The following information, although not complete, will assist in developing the facilities, meet rules, and order of events for most elementary school track meets.

I. Track dimensions: The 220-yard running track illustrated in figure 24.17 can be constructed on most outdoor playing areas.

II. High jump pit: The pit should be twelve feet long and ten feet wide. Sawdust or shavings should be used to fill the pit, which should be boarded with straw bales. (Also see appendix B for an improvised pit constructed of rubber tubes.)

III. Long jump pit: The runway to the pit should be approximately thirty yards long, with an eight-inch takeoff mark five feet from the pit. The pit should be ten feet wide and twenty feet long. It should be filled with fine sand.

IV. Order and number of events: Each school may vary the length of dashes and include additional events. The following order of events should provide a format for scheduling:

A. 50-yard dash	G. 220-yard run
B. Shot put	H. Triple jump
C. Standing long jump	I. Softball throw
D. Long jump	J. Hurdles
E. 220-yard relay	K. Obstacle race
F. High jump	L. Tug-of-war

X Baton ⟶ X ⟶ X ⟶ X ⟶ X

Pass with left	Take with right and pass with left			
X Baton	X	X	X	X
X Baton	X	X	X	X
X Baton	X	X	X	X

Figure 24.17 Plan for a 220-yard running track.

V. Track and field officials: The following jobs should be allocated to teachers or dependable students:
A. Meet director
B. Starters, same for all track events
C. Finish judges—head finish judge, first-, second-, and third-place judges, and additional place judges, if desired
D. Field judges—one judge and one helper for the high jump, standing long jump, triple jump, and running long jump
E. Announcer and head recorder with assistants for running messages and obtaining results of the events
VI. Meet requirements: Each school should establish its own eligibility requirements for the following situations:
A. Number of events each participant may enter. For example, perhaps each child could enter two track events and one field event.
B. Classification of participants. Several methods can be used to classify participants such as age, grade, or a classification index.
C. Number of places and point awards. For example, the first four places could be recorded with five, four, three, and two points, respectively.

Many other questions need to be answered if the track meet is to be successful. Give some thought to types of awards, methods of keeping school records, and required practice before a participant is eligible for the track and field meet. Once you and the students agree on the basic rules and regulations of the track meet, take time to explain them to the students and post rules in the classroom and gymnasium.

Novelty Track and Field Meet

A novelty or mock track and field day is composed of a variety of enjoyable novelty events. This type of special day provides an avenue for young and older children to work together, and to emphasize fun and cooperation, rather than competing in traditional track and field events.

In the accompanying illustration, the meet begins with all children of each house participating in a round robin tug-of-war, followed by each house dividing into four groups of mixed partners (one primary level child with one intermediate level child). This provides an opportunity for young children to participate with older children in a fun-type activity. After this event, boys and girls from each house separate into primary and intermediate groups, then rotate through four individual activities. The final slow motion bicycle race brings all children back to their four houses. Primary children from each house first compete in a slow-motion bicycle race, followed by a similar race among intermediate children.

The events in the novelty track meet are provided as sample events. Since the underlying purpose is fun and cooperation, design a scoring system that will reflect this goal—lots of points for participation and sportsmanship. One final suggestion: station a parent or teacher at four locations in the general playing area. Whenever one of these observers notices something special, such as good sportsmanship or a special effort on the part of an individual or team to cooperate, the observer blows a horn or whistle and awards the player(s) with bonus points for their house. This special award mechanism can also be used, in a subtle way, to keep the running house scores fairly even. It is also an effective means of rewarding disabled children for their efforts as participants or meet helpers.

Begin: Tug-of-War. Primary and intermediate children of each house all pull on the same rope.

Mixed Partner Activities: One primary and one intermediate child
Partners rotate through:
(1) 3-legged race—partners with tied ankles
(2) Egg and spoon race—partners hold hands with primary child holding spoon and egg
(3) Partner ball toss—partners stand behind a line, hold inside hands and the ball. Five joint throws into the basket.

Primary Children
Individual Activities

Groups of three children per house rotate through:
(1) Sack race—12 per heat
(2) Obstacle race—6 courses
(3) Chin pass relay—12 per heat
(4) Chair ring toss—4 chairs and 12 quoits

Intermediate Children
Individual Activities

Groups of three children per house rotate through:
(1) Nerf shot put
(2) Frisbee throw
(3) Obstacle race
(4) Juggle a number

Final Event: Slow-Motion Bicycle Race
(1) Primary children's bicycle race
(2) Intermediate children's bicycle race

Cross-Country Activities

The following cross-country activities may be taught as part of a track and field unit or as separate events throughout the school year.

Hash Running

Hash running is a team race in which markers are located along the route, hidden directions are located near the markers, and a total team effort is required in order to finish the race in the shortest period of time. The following example provides a basic format that can be used in any rural or urban school.

Before the class arrives for physical education, set up your "hash course." In the sample course, the starting position is in front of the school. Each team (the size is optional) starts

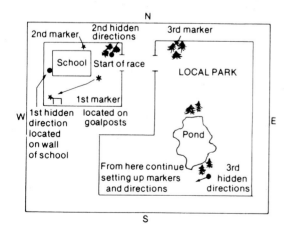

here (stagger the starting times) and is told it will find the first marker—a red ribbon placed on a goalpost—within fifty yards of the starting position. As soon as the marker is found by any member of the team, he calls to his teammates and they all come to the marker. They know that the first hidden directions will be somewhere within fifty yards (keep this distance constant) of the marker. The teammates move in different directions until one finds the directions, located on the school wall. This pattern continues throughout the course. The team that returns in the shortest time wins the race. Following are some considerations in hash running:

1. Since most physical education periods last approximately thirty minutes, begin with three or four markers, then increase the number and difficulty as experience dictates.

2. Make a rule that markers must be located before the directions, because some children may find directions first.

3. Although teams are staggered, one team may catch up to another and "give away" vital information. Encourage teams to make up diversionary signals if this occurs.

4. If you have taught orienteering and compass directions, use these skills in hash running.

5. Since schools in urban areas have problems with traffic and restrictive park areas, take care in planning hash courses to ensure the children's safety and the protection of public gardens.

Table 24.4   Word Description Chart

Name: John Smith

Time allowed: 10 minutes
Start time:
Finish time:
Penalty points: (at 5 points a minute)

No.	Description of landmark (checkpoint)	Value	Insert code letter
1	On the east end of softball backstop	15	T
2	On the north side of flower garden	10	B
3	On the south goalpost of field B	5	C
4	On the northwest side of an old stump	10	F
5	On the northeast end of the softball stands	15	R
6	On the bench near three pine trees	15	U
7	On the southwest side of field A	10	A
8	On the west corner of statue	25	Y

Total points _____
Penalty points _____
Final score _____

Figure 24.18   Map of the area.

Score Orienteering

Each player is given a hand-drawn map of the area, including all necessary landmarks—buildings, statues, trees, paths, and so on. Figure 24.18 shows a school and the immediate major landmarks. Each player is also given a "word description chart." Note in table 24.4 that each description is simple, and that the farthest sites are awarded the highest points. Players leave the starting point at a designated time and, with the aid of their maps and charts, try to find the various landmarks or checkpoints.

General Procedure and Instructions

Each student writes his name on his chart and leaves everything else blank. Four or five runners leave the starting point at the same time; to avoid congestion, allow thirty seconds between groups. The teacher marks the starting time on each chart, and the runners have ten minutes (or whatever time the teacher sets) to go to as many checkpoints as possible before returning to the recorder's desk. The teacher has placed a code letter on each landmark, or checkpoint, before the orienteering lesson and, when a

Figure 24.19 Score orienteering.

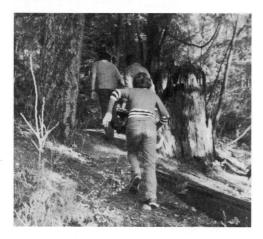

runner arrives at the checkpoint, he places that code letter in the appropriate space on the recording sheet. Runners may choose their own order of reaching checkpoints. A runner is penalized five points for each minute he exceeds the ten-minute time limit.

Teaching Suggestions

Competitions can be developed on the basis of one type of landmark such as trees, flowers, or buildings. If a school is near a park or wilderness area, the possibilities are almost unlimited (figure 24.19). Also, the addition of compasses and authentic maps of the area open the door to an enjoyable and constructive recreational pursuit. Finally, if a teacher is not skillful at reading a compass or a geographical map, she can find many people in the community, such as scout leaders and surveyors, more than willing to donate their services.

Cross-Country Running

Cross-country or long-distance running activities for elementary school children must be based on sound medical evidence and good training principles. A brief review of the medical evidence, along with statements made by qualified experts, provides a basis for selecting appropriate long-distance running activities for children in the primary and intermediate grades. Proper jogging form and appropriate cross-country activities are also described for a variety of instructional and extraclass programs.

Physical and Psychological Effects

According to the American Academy of Pediatrics, medical evidence of injury to children running long distances is limited and largely anecdotal (American Academy of Pediatrics 1982). The main concern about long-distance running and children relates to the immediate and long-term physiological and psychological effects of this activity. Physiologically, there is general concern about possible damage to the epiphyseal or growth plates at the ends of long bones. Other considerations relate to overtaxing the

heart and respiratory systems and to damaging the tendons of the knees and ankles. Long-distance runs, such as ten to fifteen kilometers, under extreme competitive pressure and high temperatures may cause children to overextend themselves (Olson 1982). With respect to psychological effects, the evidence is still very limited. The main concern expressed by psychologists, parents, and educators is the undue stress to win and the negative aftereffects on the loser. Also, long-distance running or racing is not seen by most children as an inherently enjoyable activity. Children, if given the opportunity, would rather play a game than train for long hours in an activity that is essentially void of fun and social interaction.

The conclusion to be drawn from scientific evidence is that long-distance competitive running events primarily designed for adults are not recommended for children prior to physical maturation (American Academy of Pediatrics 1982). This does not mean that elementary school children do not enjoy or need to participate in recreational running activities such as cross-country running, hash running, or orienteering events. The following activities are designed to provide fun and variety in a very beneficial form of physical activity.

Running Activities

Cross-country running is a recreational run through a course marked on the school grounds or adjacent park area. The length of the course will depend on the age and condition of the participants and the type of terrain (blacktop, grass, etc.). The following chart provides a rough guideline for upper primary and intermediate grades.

Age	Distance
8–9	1 to 1½ miles
10–11	1 to 2 miles
12–13	1½ to 3 miles

Prior to puberty there are essentially no major physiological reasons boys and girls cannot run, jump, or do any other physical activity with equal ability. Hence, set the same standards for both sexes. If girls are slower, the reasons are attributed to social or cultural factors. With time and equal opportunities, girls perform as well, and at times, better than boys of similar ages.

Cross-country running requires good training methods and lots of variety in the course. The following suggestions and activities help make this activity fun for all participants.

1. Teach children the proper long-distance form of running.

2. Begin this program with such activities as Interval Training or Walk, Jog, Run.

3. Organize cross-country activities for partners. Children normally pair up on the basis of friendship and ability.

4. Provide variety in cross-country activities by introducing the following tasks while the children are running.
   a. Dribbling and passing a ball
   b. Skipping
   c. Balancing an object
   d. Maneuvering over obstacle courses
   e. Running a certain distance, then hopping, jumping, or performing any other skill for a set number of repetitions, then running again

Guidelines for Long-Distance Running

The following suggestions help establish an enjoyable, beneficial, and educationally sound long-distance running program for elementary school children.

1. Run with arms relaxed—elbows bent—and swinging in a slight arc across the body. The hands should not cross the center line of the body.
2. Tilt hips slightly backward to flatten the curve of the lower back.
3. Land on the heel and rock forward and off the front of the foot. Bouncing is caused by pushing up on the toes and thus should be eliminated.
4. Knees should be bent on landing.
5. Breathing should be relaxed, emphasizing the exhale phase to ensure an adequate exchange of air.
6. Wear proper shoes. Shoes that are too short or too long are damaging to the runner's feet.
7. Cool down after long runs with walking and stretching exercises.

Evaluative Techniques

Although performance in track and field and cross-country events appears to be easy to evaluate, quite the contrary is true. Each event is scored on the basis of either distance or time. The problem lies in placing a value on improvement rather than merely awarding an arbitrary number of points for the student's ranking in each event. This is further complicated by the philosophy underlying a track and field unit. At this age level, boys and girls should be free from excessive competitive pressure and should not have to judge themselves against the standards set by exceptional athletes.

The solution is to allow students to select a certain number of events and then record their initial and final scores. This approach to evaluating performance and improvement, thus, becomes a personal assessment. A child who is a low achiever can set a realistic goal without worrying about who is the best in each event. Similarly, the outstanding performer can set a high standard, which motivates him to work at maximum capacity.

Selected References

American Academy of Pediatrics. (1982). "Risks in Long-Distance Running for Children," *The Physician and Sportsman* 10:8.

CAHPER. (1985). *Track and Field in the Elementary School.* Ottawa, Ontario: CAHPER Publications.

Foreman, K. (1982). *Coaching Track and Field Techniques,* Fourth Edition. Dubuque, IA: Wm. C. Brown Publishers.

Gambetta, V. (Ed.). (1989). *The Athletic Congress's Track and Field Coaching Manual.* Champaign, IL: Leisure Press.

Olson, E. (1982, November). "Kid Stuff," *The Runner.*

Powell, J. (1987). *Track and Field Fundamentals for Teacher and Coach.* Champaign, IL: Stipes Publishing Co.

Gymnastic and Movement Activities

art 6 has been organized to meet the conditions existing in the majority of elementary schools. Many classroom teachers are still teaching gymnastic activities through a reasonably structured approach. At the same time, however, they are attempting to apply Movement Education concepts and skills to various parts of their gymnastic programs.

The three chapters in part 6 attempt to bridge the gap between the structured and the Movement Education approaches to teaching gymnastic activities. Chapter 25 provides the basic stunts and tumbling activities. At the end of this chapter, the concepts and skills of Movement Education are introduced systematically. Numerous examples show how to incorporate these movement ideas into stunt and tumbling lessons or units of instruction. Similarly, chapters 26 and 27 present the structured skills that are performed with small equipment and large apparatus and provide additional suggestions for applying movement concepts and skills.

Each elementary grade presents unique organization and teaching problems. The children's age and maturity dictate the amount of material that can be covered within the allocated time in the gymnasium or activity room. The number of mats available may be the reason for organizing a class in a particular way, and the teacher's ability and confidence in handling this type of physical activity may be the central reasons for organizing a class in a certain fashion and for selecting particular activities. Regardless of such individual conditions, the following general teaching suggestions apply to all grade levels:

1. Children should be taught to listen to your normal conversational voice for all directions and commands. Once they learn to move and listen to your voice, there is no need to rely on a loud whistle.

2. Teach children standard procedures for (a) changing into their clothes and entering the gymnasium, (b) using their free time before the lesson begins, and (c) lining up in a specific way or place before the lesson begins or at any time you want to speak to all of the class.

3. Try to provide maximum participation and movement for each child during the instructional period. If a limited number of mats and other equipment means that the children must wait in

Chapter 25
Stunts, Tumbling, and Movement Skills

Chapter 26
Stunts and Manipulative Skills with
 Small Equipment

Chapter 27
Large Apparatus Activities

long lines, the program should be changed. Techniques such as station work, task cards, and rotation procedures can be adapted to any grade level.

4. Establish a stunts and tumbling program based on the children's individual abilities and progress. Do not establish a set number of skills for every child to accomplish. Some children simply are physically incapable of performing certain stunts. A wide variety of activities should be presented to each grade level.

5. Establish and consistently maintain a basic list of safety rules and regulations. These should include the following:
   a. If children are permitted to wear street clothes during an activity, do not allow bulky sweaters or jewelry.
   b. Children should not be allowed to practice any stunt or tumbling activity unless the teacher is in the gymnasium.
   c. When a stunt requires a spotter, children should be taught the proper spotting techniques. Once the techniques are learned, children should be permitted to perform stunts with the assistance of the required number of spotters.

Purposes and Techniques of Spotting

In stunts and tumbling or other gymnastic movements, spotting is defined as providing assistance in the performance of a skill. Spotting is both a teaching technique and a safety device. The teaching aspect is accomplished by the teacher or classmate holding the performer or positioning himself to assist the performer. For example, the spotter helps the performer maintain balance while performing a headstand. In an agility move, the spotter gently pushes or lifts at the strategic moment, helping her get the "feel" of the movement before she attempts it on her own. The safety aspect of spotting involves positioning one or two helpers near the performer to provide additional support and to prevent a loss of balance, a fall, or an accident.

It is difficult to say which stunts and gymnastic skills require the use of spotters. Furthermore, the teacher and the child must judge when to remove close spotting so the child can attempt the skill alone. As a general guideline for elementary school children, be overcautious until you are completely sure the performer can execute the skill with relative ease.

The following suggestions may also help you find a safe procedure and environment for teaching the more difficult and challenging stunts and tumbling and gymnastic skills:

1. Analyze each stunt's points of difficulty and teach spotters the correct position and movements.
2. Teach spotters to stay close to the performer but not to hamper movement.
3. Use the strongest and most reliable children for the most difficult stunts.
4. Teach children not to "overspot." Instruct spotters to help only when the performer needs an extra lift or push so he does not come to rely too much on the assistance.

Developing Units and Lesson Plans

There are several methods of organizing units and teaching individual or sequential lesson plans involving stunts and tumbling, small equipment, or large apparatus activities. The approach you decide to use will depend on such factors as the children's age, the time and equipment available, and the emphasis the teacher wishes to give to one or more activities or movement skills. Thus, a standard unit or lesson plan suitable for any developmental level would be of little value. The sample lessons in the next three chapters illustrate how teachers can use the structured skills and Movement Education concepts and skills in a variety of lesson formats ■

25

Stunts, Tumbling, and Movement Skills

The gymnastic activities most familiar to elementary school children are probably stunts and tumbling. For generations, children have learned to mimic animal walks; to balance on their heads, hands, and other parts of their bodies; and to perform a variety of agile tumbling skills. The purposes of these activities have remained the same. Children learn to move their bodies safely and gracefully. They improve their strength, agility, balance, and other important aspects of physical fitness, and they learn the importance of safety and perseverance when attempting a difficult stunt or tumbling skill.

One of the most exciting additions to this program has been the introduction of movement concepts and skills developed in the Movement Education approach. These unstructured skills and movement concepts, coupled with the use of exploratory teaching methods and techniques, have provided an effective way for every child to experience success and enjoyment, regardless of physical ability or prior gymnastic experience.

This chapter has been organized to help teachers cope with the varying programs and conditions that exist in elementary schools. The main instructional emphasis for the three developmental levels is described to provide a guideline for selecting appropriate skills and movement concepts. The sample lesson plans in the next section illustrate how teachers can select from four skill areas when developing lesson plans. All stunts and tumbling activities have been organized under four general sections for ease of use. Tumbling activities include all movements that involve a rotation of the body, such as a Forward Roll and Cartwheel. These skills are listed in their approximate order of difficulty. The sequential lead-up skills for several key tumbling movements are listed immediately below each skill. The next section, "Agility Activities," includes skills that involve transferring weight, springing, or moving with a partner in different ways. Balance activities include holding an upright or inverted position while stationary or moving. The next section, "Movement Education Concepts and Skills," describes the four main elements of Movement Education. Sample lesson plans illustrate how teachers can develop lessons that emphasize movement concepts or a combination of movement concepts with tumbling, agility, or balance skills. The last section describes and illustrates how a variety of academic concepts and skills are learned through performing and analyzing tumbling, agility, and movement skills ∎

Developmental Level I

The stunts and tumbling activities contained in this section include numerous animal movements, balance stunts, simple partner activities, and tumbling and safety skills. These activities are the foundations on which the more advanced stunts and tumbling skills are built. As in a later section of this chapter, there is a very close relationship between the activities described and many Movement Education skills. Each naturally complements the other.

If an individual or a class's skill level is high, move on to more advanced skills. As children progress into the next developmental level, they become ready for more challenging skills.

Developmental Level II

As children progress to developmental level II, the tumbling, agility, and balance skills become increasingly more difficult. Also, teachers should begin to place more emphasis on the quality and form of each movement. Boys and girls in this developmental level thoroughly enjoy partner and group agility and balance activities. These children also are capable of developing fairly complex movement sequences individually, in partners, or in small groups.

Developmental Level III

The stunts and tumbling program for level III is essentially a continuation of the level II program. As children progress to the more advanced tumbling, agility, and balance stunts, more strength, power, and control are required. More spotters are needed because of the difficulty and potential hazards of performing several balance and tumbling movements. Pyramid building, particularly involving two or more students, requires strength, balance, and teamwork. If the children in this developmental level have been taught the Movement Education concepts and skills, they will develop complex sequences that show a high level of quality and creativity.

Sample Lesson Plans

There are several methods of organizing individual or sequential lesson plans involving tumbling, agility, and balance activities. The approach you decide to use will depend on such factors as the children's age, the time and equipment available, and the emphasis you wish to give to one or more activities or movement skills. Thus, a standard unit or lesson plan suitable for any grade level would be of little value.

The sample lesson plans in this section can be used as models or basic guidelines to design lessons from the four resource sections in this chapter. As a general rule, begin each lesson with a vigorous warm-up activity, such as running, jumping, and landing, followed by exercises designed to increase general strength and fitness (see chapter 12). Circuit training and vigorous tag and team games are also

appropriate warm-up activities. The rest of the lesson should include a mixture of tumbling, agility, balance, and movement concepts and skills.

Sample lesson plan no. 1 considers lack of equipment, the attention span of five-year-olds, and a need to provide variation in movement skills within the context of a single lesson. The lesson emphasizes tumbling, balance, and agility skills. A chasing game from chapter 16 fulfills cardiorespiratory fitness needs, along with other personal and social needs. This type of lesson is very popular with kindergarten and first-grade teachers.

Lesson no. 2 illustrates how to cope with a minimum amount of equipment and how to use station work. The rotation pattern allows the child to practice a balance stunt, then shift to skill involving agility or climbing. Emphasis throughout the lesson, however, is on individual balance and agility skills. The same equipment layout could be used for several lessons, with variations in skills and sequence development.

The previous two lessons emphasize the acquisition of individual balance or agility skills. Once children have acquired a repertoire of agility and balance stunts and can practice them independently and safely, a further challenge can be presented. The next task is to encourage children to perform two or more stunts or movement skills in a sequence. The following examples illustrate the types of challenges that can be presented to children of this age range during the second part of the lesson. As a basic guideline, begin with simple, structured challenges involving known and previously practiced stunts and progress to more creative challenges that allow maximum freedom to interpret and create individual or partner routines.

Example Challenges for Individual Agility Sequences

Developmental Level I

"Can you start with a Log Roll (p. 425), change to a Crab Walk (p. 439), then go back to a Log Roll?

"You know how to perform a Forward Roll (p. 426), a Side Roll (p. 425), and a Backward Diagonal Roll (p. 428). Can you perform all these stunts, one after the other?"

"Select three agility stunts that can be performed on the floor. Arrange your own sequence of these stunts and practice until you can move smoothly from one movement to the other."

Developmental Level II

Partners have one mat to share. "Make up a matching routine (facing each other, side by side, or follow the leader) that includes a balance, a roll, and a new balance stunt."

"In partners, design a matching routine on the floor that has a cartwheel and at least three other agility stunts."

Developmental level I
Length of lesson Twenty minutes
Equipment Gymnasium—no available mats
Emphasis Balance and agility skills

Part 1	Part 2	Part 3
Warm-up (3 to 5 minutes): Run, stop, change direction	Tumbling activities (10 to 15 minutes): Log Roll Agility activities: Wicker Walk Balance activities: Stork Stand Game: Simple Tag	Closure (2 minutes): Sitting and discussing how to balance on different parts of the body

Developmental level II
Length of lesson Thirty minutes
Equipment Three large mats, eight individual ropes, four benches, three climbing ropes
Emphasis Balance and agility skills

Part 1	Part 2	Part 3
Warm-up (3 to 5 minutes): Run, change direction; tag game	Station work (20 to 25 minutes): Rotating to next station every four minutes	Closure (2 minutes): Sitting and discussing how to build a sequence

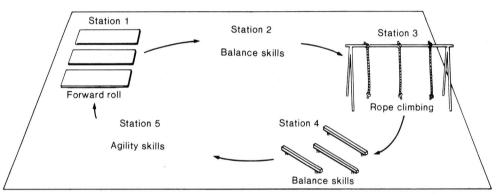

Tumbling:
Station 1: Forward and Backward Rolls
Station 2: Frog Stand, Knee Dip, Swing Turn
Station 3: Strengthening exercises, making shapes while holding on to rope
Station 4: Walking, Swing Turn
Station 5: Agility skills: Egg Roll, Heel Click

Developmental Level III

"Make up a routine beginning with Rolling the Log (p. 440), shift to a Seal Slap (p. 447), and finish with a Jump Through (p. 448)."

"Can you make up a routine that combines a Kip (p. 450), a Forward Drop (p. 446), and a Judo Roll (p. 430)?"

Example Challenges for Individual Balance Sequences

Developmental Level I

"Remember the Tightrope Walk and how you balanced on one leg? Can you show me how you can start with balancing on one leg, then Tightrope Walk for three steps, then balance on the other leg?"

"Show me a Turk Stand, a One-Leg Balance, and another Turk Stand all in a row."

Developmental Level II

"Using the mat, make up a sequence that has a Headstand and two other balance stunts."

Developmental Level III

"Make up a sequence using the following stunts: The Bridge (p. 458), V-Sit (p. 458), and Headstand (p. 457)."

"Using a mat, make up a sequence that has a Headstand and two other balance stunts."

stunts, tumbling, and movement skills

Tumbling Activities

The tumbling activities listed in this section include skills that involve a rolling action of the body (see figures 25.1 through 25.33). Each rotational skill is listed in table 25.1 according to its level of difficulty. Teachers should recognize that some children will lack the physical maturity or ability needed to perform the more difficult skills. Special considerations should be given to children who have low levels of physical fitness and motor skill ability. Children who are overweight or obese should also be given special care and attention as they perform Forward or Backward Rolls and other skills that require the weight of the body to be taken by the arms.

Table 25.1 Tumbling Skills

Name of stunt	Developmental level			Movement concepts	Page
	I	II	III		
Log Roll	→			Transfer of weight, change of direction, low level	425
Side Roll	→			Transfer of weight, curled shape, change of direction, medium level	425
Forward Roll:					
Looking Back Through Legs	→			Transfer of weight, medium level	425
Back Roller	→			Transfer of weight, curled shape, change of direction	426
Tip Over	→			Transfer of weight, curled shape, change of direction	426
Forward Roll	→→			Transfer of weight, curled shape	426
Forward Roll to One-Leg Stand		→		Transfer of weight, curled and stretched shape	427
Forward Roll to Jump Tuck		→		Transfer of weight, curled and stretched shapes, force	427
Consecutive Rolls		→		Transfer of weight, curled shape	427
Reach over Roll			→	Transfer of weight, curled shape, relationship to partner	427
Dive Forward Roll			→	Transfer of weight, curled shape, force, speed	427
Eskimo Roll			→	Transfer of weight, curled shape, levels	427
Backward Diagonal Roll	→→			Transfer of weight, curled shape, levels, force	428
Egg Roll		→		Transfer of weight, curled shape	428
Backward Roll:					
Back Rocker	→			Transfer of weight, curled shape	429
Finger Touch	→			Transfer of weight, curled shape	429
Toe Touch	→			Transfer of weight, curled shape	429
Back Shoulder Roll		→		Transfer of weight, curled shape, change of direction	429
Backward Roll		→		Transfer of weight, curled shape	429
Backward Roll to Knee Scale		→		Transfer of weight, curled shape, levels	430
Backward Straddle Roll			→	Transfer of weight, wide shape	430
Judo Roll		→		Transfer of weight, curled shape, levels	430
Triple Roll		→		Transfer of weight, force, change of direction, levels	431
Backward Extension			→	Transfer of weight, stretch and curled shapes	431
Cartwheel:					
Single Mule Kick	→			Transfer of weight, force, levels	431
Mule Kick	→			Transfer of weight, force, levels	432
Side Kick	→			Transfer of weight, force, change of direction, levels	432
Half Cartwheel		→		Transfer of weight, force, change of direction	433
Cartwheel		→		Transfer of weight, force, change of direction	433
Round-Off			→	Transfer of weight, force, change of direction and speed	434

Figure 25.1 Log roll. This is the easiest roll to perform. Lie on the back, with the arms extended over the head and the hands locked together. Keep the body in a straight line and roll to the side and then around to the starting position.

Variations:
1. Children should also learn to roll toward either side, stop halfway through, and change directions.
2. Change position of arms.
3. Combine log rolls with other stunts, such as from a long roll, change to a crab walk, to a long roll, to a bear walk.

Figure 25.2 Side roll. Begin in a back-lying position. Perform the roll with elbows, knees, and nose "hidden" or tucked in. Explain to young children that hiding these parts of the body helps them roll in a ball-like fashion and protects vulnerable parts.

Variations:
1. Roll toward either side.
2. "See if you can roll from a log to a side to a log roll."
3. "See if you can combine a side roll, a log roll, and a balance stunt."

Figure 25.3 Looking back through legs. Begin in a squat position, with hands on the floor. Lean forward, raise hips, and look back through the legs.

Figure 25.4 Back roller. Crouch down at one end of the mat and place fingertips on the floor. Slowly roll backward, tuck chin in, bring knees to chest, and wrap arms around knees. Continue rolling backward until head touches the mat. Roll forward to starting position.

Figure 25.5 Tip over. Begin in a squat position, with hands on mat and knees between arms. Lean forward, raise seat, look back through legs; then place top of shoulders on mat and roll over to a sitting position.

Figure 25.6 Forward roll. Most children have already learned the forward roll before the first grade and can usually demonstrate many variations involving different leg and arm positions. Begin in a squat position, with the head up, the arms extended forward slightly, and the fingers pointing straight ahead. Push off from the toes, raise the seat, and tuck the chin to the chest. Continue forward movement, landing on the base of the neck and the top of the shoulders. Push off with the hands and continue forward motion to a crouching or standing position.

Variations:
1. Start from a standing position and end in a standing position.
2. "Try three different ways to change your leg position as you perform the roll."
3. Try supine and straddle sit.
4. "See if you can perform a forward, log, and side roll in any order you like."

a   b   c

Figure 25.7 Forward roll spotting.

Figure 25.8 Forward roll to one-leg stand. Begin in a partially crouched position. Roll forward and end in a one-leg stand, with arms forward.

Figure 25.9 Forward roll to jump tuck. Begin in a partially crouched position. Roll forward to crouched position. Jump forward and upward to a tucked position, then land.

Figure 25.10 Reach-over roll. One partner assumes a low crouch position across the end of the mat. The other partner bends and reaches over the partner, then performs a forward roll.

Figure 25.11 Dive forward roll. Begin in a partially crouched position in front of the mat. Spring forward, slightly arch the back, and push off with both feet. There is a moment when the body is totally off the floor; then the hands touch as the body makes a forward roll.

Variations:
1. Perform movement from a standing start or from a run, jump, and dive roll.
2. Perform a dive roll over partner in a low crouched position.

Figure 25.12 Eskimo roll. One partner lies on his back and the other partner stands, facing forward and near her partner's head. The partner on the floor grasps his partner's ankles and raises his own legs in order to allow his partner to grasp each leg above the ankles. Top partner leans forward, places partner's feet on the floor, and then performs a forward roll. Lower partner follows, and both continue performing a series of forward rolls.

stunts, tumbling, and movement skills

Figure 25.13 Backward diagonal roll. This is one of the most important safety rolls. It is a means of rolling backward with a gradual dissipation of speed, thus preventing injury as well as providing an effective and graceful means of shifting from one movement to another. The roll is performed by rolling backward and bringing both legs to the side of one ear. This takes the weight off the neck and allows the child to roll off the shoulder. It is an appropriate skill for children who are not strong enough to perform the backward roll.

Variations:
1. Roll to both sides.
2. "Can you combine a log, side, and backward diagonal roll?"

a   b   c

Figure 25.14 Backward diagonal roll spotting. Kneel on the performer's left side and face in the direction of the backward diagonal roll. Place the right hand under the left shoulder with fingers spread and hold the left hand near the performer's seat and ready to assist the performer in the backward movement.

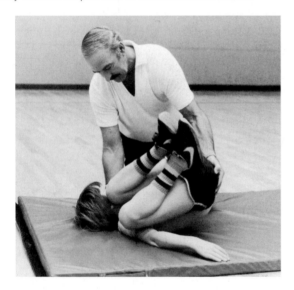

Figure 25.15 Egg roll. Begin in a squat position. Place the arms on the inside of the knees, then stretch the hands around the lower legs and overlap them over the feet. Roll sideways, on the shoulder, to the back, to the shoulder, and then back to a sitting position. Continue the action around the circle to the starting position.

Variations:
1. Roll toward right, then left side.
2. "See if you can vary your leg and hand position and repeat this stunt."

Figure 25.16 Back rocker. Start in a squat position at the edge of the mat, facing away. Grasp the shins with the hands and rock back until the head touches the mat. Then return and repeat movement.

Figure 25.18 Toe touch. Begin in a squat position at the edge of the mat, facing away. Place the hands by the ears, with palms facing forward. Keeping chin tucked, roll back, touch the mat with the fingertips, and extend the legs overhead until the toes of both feet touch the mat. Return to starting position and repeat movement.

Figure 25.17 Finger touch. Start in a squat position at the edge of the mat, facing away. Raise the hands by the ears, with palms facing forward and chin tucked. Roll back until both hands touch the mat. Then return to starting position.

Figure 25.19 Back shoulder roll. Begin in a squat position. Roll back, turn head to left, and roll over right shoulder.

Figure 25.20 Backward roll. This is the most difficult roll to perform because it requires the weight to be taken on the arms during the roll. Begin in a squat position, with the body weight evenly distributed on the fingers and toes. The back should be toward the mat. Push off the hands and roll backward, keeping the knees to the chest and the chin down (a). Continue backward roll until the body weight is well over the shoulders (b). At this point, push off with the hands, and land on the knees and toes (c).

Variations:
1. Perform backward roll with legs straight.
2. "Change position of legs as you perform a backward roll."

a   b   c

stunts, tumbling, and movement skills

Figure 25.21 Backward roll spotting. Stand on the right side of the performer (a). As she rolls onto her shoulders (b), gently lift performer upward and backward.

a

b

Figure 25.22 Backward roll to knee scale. Start in a standing position, with hands at sides. Roll backward, and end in a knee scale position.

Figure 25.23 Backward straddle roll. Begin in a straddle support position. Keep knees straight and roll backward, ending in a straddle support position.

Figure 25.24 Judo roll. Start this roll from a standing position. Bend forward, extend the right arm, and turn the head toward the left side. As the body moves forward and downward, swing the right arm toward the left and contact the mat with the top of the right shoulder. Continue the forward rolling action over the back and side, then move forward and upward.

Variations:
1. Perform roll to opposite side.
2. Run, then perform a judo roll from a one-foot takeoff.

a

b

c

d

Figure 25.25 Triple roll. This is a continuous log roll involving three performers. As the center performer (#3) begins to roll to his right, the outside performer (#1) begins to thrust himself upward, over, and toward the center performer's previous position. The new center performer (#1) continues to roll toward the other side. As soon as he starts his roll, performer (#2) thrusts himself up, over, and toward the center position. This action is then continued for several rotations. The important aspects of this triple stunt are the timing of each performer and the quick recovery of the outside performer.

Figure 25.26 Backward extension. This roll starts with the same backward rolling action as the backward roll. As soon as the hands begin to press against the mat, the legs begin to extend upward. At the moment the legs are vertical, vigorously push off from the hands and snap the feet downward toward the mat, landing in a partially crouched position.

Spotting:
Use the same spotting technique described for the backward diagonal roll.

Figure 25.27 Single mule kick. Begin standing, with arms raised overhead and facing the mat; one foot is slightly in front of the other. Bend forward, head up; place hands on mat, then kick back leg upward.

a

b

a

b

c

d

stunts, tumbling, and movement skills

Figure 25.28 Mule kick. Begin in a semicrouched position, with hands about shoulder-width apart, knees bent, and feet together. In a simultaneous movement, shift weight over hands, and vigorously thrust legs upward and backward.

Variations:
1. Thrust backward, upward, and apart.
2. Twist body to side as legs extend backward and upward.
3. "Can you add your own variation to this stunt?"

a

b

c

Figure 25.29 Side kick. Begin standing, with arms raised overhead and facing the mat, with the right foot slightly in front of the left. Bend forward, keeping head up. Place hands on the mat, kick left leg upward, and swing hips toward the left side. Land on both feet, facing the side, and return to starting position.

a

b

chapter 25

Figure 25.30 Half cartwheel. Start with the right foot slightly in front of the left and arms overhead. Bend forward and toward the right foot. Place right hand, then left hand on the mat and swing around and land in a partially crouched position.

Figure 25.32 Cartwheel spotting. Stand opposite the spot where the performer's hands will be placed. Cross the right arm over the left, then place both hands on the performer's hips as she pushes off from her lead foot. Aid the performer in her sideward motion and vertical balance position when indicated.

Figure 25.31 Cartwheel. Begin with the back straight, the arms extended sideward, and the legs approximately shoulder-width apart. Bend toward the left, placing the left hand, then the right, on the mat and, at the same time, raising the side. Note: In the middle of this stunt, the legs and arms should be fully extended and the body in a straight line. Continue sideways, placing right, then left leg on the mat and ending in the starting position.

a

b

c

stunts, tumbling, and movement skills

Figure 25.33 Round-off. The first part of the round-off is the same as the cartwheel. As soon as both feet are off the ground, bring them together, then make a half turn toward the left (counterclockwise). Bend at the hips, and land on both feet, facing the opposite direction.

Spotting:
Stand on the left side of the performer and opposite the spot where his hands will be placed. As the performer places his right hand on the mat, place your left hand under his right shoulder. Lift as he pushes off from his hands when indicated.

a

b

c

Agility Activities

Agility activities are movements that involve body action (figures 25.34 through 25.88). The simplest type of agility activity is the animal walks that primary children enjoy performing. Elementary school children also enjoy agility skills involving partners, provided their partners have about the same level of ability. Other types of agility skills are movements that involve a springing action such as a Heel Click or Neckspring. These skills are arranged in table 25.2 according to their approximate order of difficulty.

Table 25.2   Agility Skills

Name of skill	Developmental level			Movement concepts	Page
	I	*II*	*III*		
Alligator Crawl	→			Transfer of weight	436
Wicket Walk	→			Transfer of weight, change of direction	436
Camel Walk	→			Transfer of weight, change of direction	436
Puppy Dog Walk	→			Transfer of weight, change of direction, force	436
Jump Turn	→			Transfer of weight, change of direction	437
Gorilla Walk	→			Transfer of weight, wide shapes, change of direction	437
Two-Foot Jumps	→			Transfer of weight, force	437
Lame Puppy Walk	→			Transfer of weight, change of direction, balance	437
Wring the Dishrag (partner)	→			Transfer of weight, change of direction, relationships	438
Bouncing Ball	→			Change of direction and levels	438
Leap Frog (partner)	→			Transfer of weight, change of direction, relationships	438
Knee Jump	→			Force, levels	438
Rocking Chair (partner)	→			Transfer of weight, change of direction, force, relationships	439
Crab Walk	→			Transfer of weight, change of direction	439
Heel Slap	→			Transfer of weight, force	439
Wheelbarrow (partner)	→			Transfer of weight, force, balance, relationships	439
Chinese Get-Up	→			Transfer of weight, force, balance, relationships	440
One-Foot Jump	→			Transfer of weight, force, balance	440
Rabbit Jump	→			Transfer of weight, force, balance	440
Rolling the Log	→			Transfer of weight, change of direction	440
Elbow Crawl	→			Transfer of weight, force	441
Seal Walk	→			Transfer of weight, force	441
Frog Jump	→			Transfer of weight, force, balance	441
Measuring Worm	→			Transfer of weight, levels, balance	441
Circle Roll (partners)	→			Transfer of weight, change of direction	442
Coffee Grinder	→			Transfer of weight, change of direction	442
Front Support to Stand		→		Transfer of weight, force, change of direction, levels	442
Rooster Fight (partner)	→			Balance, force, change of direction, relationships	442
Crab Fight (partner)	→			Transfer of weight, balance, force, relationships	443
Twister (partner)	→			Transfer of weight, balance, change of direction	443
Prone Knee Fall	→			Transfer of weight, levels	443
Elephant Walk (partner)	→			Transfer of weight, force, change of direction	443
Bear Dance		→		Transfer of weight, balance, force	444
Pig Walk (partner)		→		Transfer of weight, change of direction, relationships	444
Elbow Wrestling		→		Transfer of weight, force, relationships	444
Shoulder Wrestling (partner)		→		Transfer of weight, force, relationships	444
Leg Wrestling		→		Transfer of weight, force, relationships	445
Going Down		→		Force, levels, relationships	445
Push War		→		Force, relationships	445
Double Wheelbarrow (triple)		→		Transfer of weight, balance, relationships	445
Upswing		→		Transfer of weight, force, levels	446
Forward Drop		→		Transfer of weight, force	446
Centipede		→		Transfer of weight, force	447
Seal Slap			→	Transfer of weight, force	447
Jackknife			→	Transfer of weight, force	447
Heel Click			→	Transfer of weight, force	447
Jump Through			→	Transfer of weight, force	448
Handspring over Partner (partner)			→	Transfer of weight, force, relationships	448
Knee Handspring (partner)			→	Transfer of weight, force, relationships	448
Handspring			→	Transfer of weight, force, levels, change of speed	448
Neckspring			→	Transfer of weight, force, levels, change of speed	449
Headspring			→	Transfer of weight, force, levels, change of speed	449
Kip			→	Transfer of weight, force, levels, change of speed	450

stunts, tumbling, and movement skills

Figure 25.34 Alligator crawl. Begin lying facedown on the floor, with elbows slightly bent. Move along the floor by moving right arm and right leg. Later, try moving with right arm and left leg, then left arm and right leg, and so on.

Figure 25.35 Wicket walk. Bend forward and grasp the legs just above the ankles. Take short steps without releasing the grip.

Variations:
1. Walk backwards, sideways, and in a circle.
2. Place hands on opposite ankles and repeat.
3. Keep legs straight and repeat.
4. "Can you hold your ankles and find a new way to move your feet?" (jump, hop, etc.)

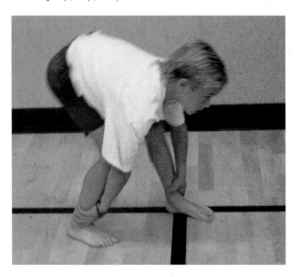

Figure 25.36 Camel walk. Place one foot in front of the other, bend over from the waist, and lock hands behind back to represent the camel's hump. Walk slowly, raising the head and chest with each step.

Variations:
1. Walk backwards or sideways.
2. "See if you can keep your arms in the same position and sit down . . . then stand up."
3. "Can a camel run or gallop?"

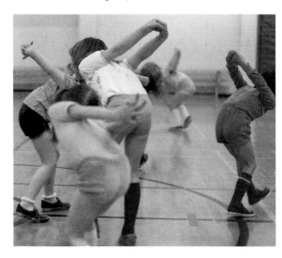

Figure 25.37 Puppy dog walk. Begin in a crouched position, with weight on hands and feet. Keep head up and move on all fours.

Variations:
1. Move in different directions—backwards, sideways, and so forth.
2. "Can you show me how a pussy cat . . . squirrel . . . or monkey would walk?"

chapter 25

Figure 25.38 Jump turns. Begin with knees slightly bent, feet about twelve inches apart, and arms close to body. Jump up and make a half turn to the left.

Variations:
1. Jump and make a three-quarter or full turn.
2. Jump, turn, and clap hands.
3. "Can you jump, turn, and do something in the air before you land?"
4. "See if you can jump and turn, then land and roll."

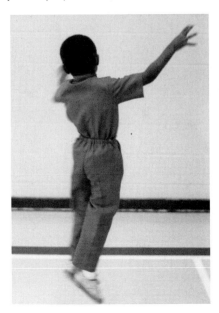

Figure 25.40 Two-foot jumps. Start with feet together and arms at the side of the body. Bend knees, then extend body upward and forward. Bend the knees on landing, and spread arms sideways for balance.

Variations:
1. Jump, land, and roll.
2. Jump, tuck, and land.
3. Jump, straddle, and land.

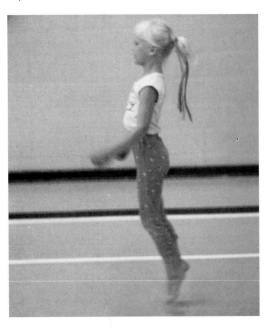

Figure 25.39 Gorilla walk. Start with knees bent and trunk forward. The arms should "hang" loosely at the sides. Walk like a gorilla and gradually lower trunk until fingers touch the floor as you walk.

Variations:
1. "Can you move like an angry gorilla . . . a sad . . . happy one?"
2. Move in different directions—backward, sideways, etc.

Figure 25.41 Lame puppy walk. Begin with both hands and one foot on the floor. Keep the head up and walk or run "on all threes" like a lame puppy.

Variations:
1. Move in different directions—sideways, backward, and so on.
2. Change the position of the hands—farther apart, facing inward like a monkey, and so on.
3. Do a double lame puppy walk, with one hand and one foot on the floor.
4. "Show me how you can lie down, roll over right back to the same lame puppy position."

stunts, tumbling, and movement skills

Figure 25.42 Wring the dishrag. Partners face each other and join hands. With hands joined, each partner raises one arm (right for one partner and left for the other), and they turn back-to-back. Repeat with the other arms to return to the original position.

Variations:
1. When in a back-to-back position, both raise one leg as high as possible.
2. "When in this back-to-back position, can you do something different?" (bend down, twist to one side, etc.)

Figure 25.43 Bouncing ball. Stand erect, with arms at the sides and feet approximately shoulder-width apart. Take short jumps and gradually lower the body. Continue jumping and lowering the body until the hands touch the floor. This should simulate a ball coming to rest. Repeat action upward until the standing position is again reached.

Variations:
1. Repeat stunt, turning body as stunt is performed.
2. "Try to change the position of your hands or feet as you perform your stunt."

Figure 25.44 Leap frog. One partner squats, keeping her head down. The other partner assumes a semicrouched position about two feet behind, with his hands resting on his partner's shoulders. Back partner spreads his legs and leaps over his partner. Continue sequence for several jumps.

Variations:
1. Raise the height of lower performer.
2. After performing a vault, land and roll.
3. Add two or more performers. Last performer in the row leap frogs over all performers before next person begins the sequence.

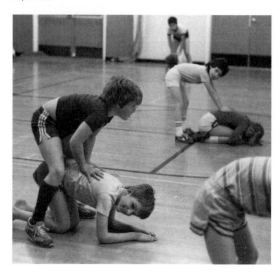

Figure 25.45 Knee jump. Stand with the feet about shoulder-width apart, the knees slightly bent, and the arms raised forward and sideways. Jump up, pull the knees up to the chest, wrap the hands around the lower legs, release grip, and land on the toes. Landing should be made with the knees bent.

Variations:
1. Jump up, straddle legs.
2. Jump up and slap seat, feet, or other parts.
3. "Invent a new position in the air."

chapter 25

Figure 25.46 Rocking chair. One partner lies on the floor on her back, with her knees bent and her arms extended upward. The other partner stands at her feet, bends forward, and grabs her hands. One partner rocks back, pulling the other up and forward until they have changed positions.

Variation:
"Try the same stunt with both performers keeping one foot off the ground at all times."

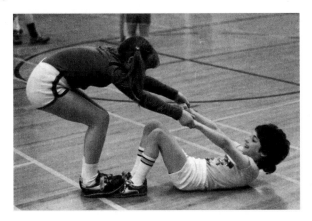

Figure 25.48 Heel slap. Stand with the feet about shoulder-width apart. Jump up, slap heels, and return to starting position.

Variations:
1. Jump and make a half or full turn in the air.
2. Jump, slap heels, and clap hands over head.
3. Jump and slap heels twice.
4. "Find a new way to jump up and a new part of your body to slap."

Figure 25.47 Crab walk. Start with the hands and feet on the ground. The back should be fairly straight to keep the seat off the ground. Walk forward by lifting the left hand and right leg up and forward.

Variations:
1. Walk backwards and sideways.
2. Walk with one foot in the air.
3. Balance a ball (or small object) on your tummy and walk.
4. "Can you hold one hand on your head, or tummy, and walk?"

Figure 25.49 Wheelbarrow. One partner lies on the floor, with legs spread and arms extended. The other partner stands between the extended legs and grasps her partner's lower legs. The lead partner takes short steps with her hands while the other player follows with short walking steps.

Variations:
1. Walk backwards or sideways.
2. Standing partner remains stationary while lower partner begins to move in a circle.
3. "How can you change the wheelbarrow to make it more fun?"

stunts, tumbling, and movement skills

Figure 25.50 Chinese get-up. Partners sit back-to-back, with their elbows locked, knees bent and together, and feet flat on the floor. Both rise off the floor by pushing against each other and, if necessary, taking short backward steps.

Variations:
1. Stop when halfway up and walk forward, sideways, and backward.
2. When all the way up, one pulls partner off floor. Repeat to other side.
3. "Can you think of a way to add or change this stunt?" (add a third person, etc.)

Figure 25.51 One-foot jumps. Begin standing on right leg, with arms extended forward and sideways. Keep arms forward, then swing left leg backward, then forward, and push off toe. Land on right toe. Continue movement in a forward direction.

Variations:
1. Change legs.
2. Jump, and perform same movement in a backward direction.
3. "Can you jump and extend your leg in other directions?"

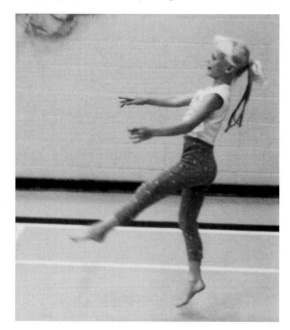

Figure 25.52 Rabbit jump. Begin in a squat position, with the body weight over the toes. Leap forward and land on the hands and then the feet to simulate a rabbit hop.

Variations:
1. Hop backward.
2. "Try to kick your feet high as you land on your hands."
3. "How many different directions can a rabbit hop?" (examples—circle, zigzag)

Figure 25.53 Rolling the log. Begin in a front-leaning position. Keeping the right hand on the floor and the legs, feet, and back straight, swing the left arm up and over the turning body. When the left hand returns to the floor, swing the right arm up and toward the left side, turning the body back to the original position.

Variations:
1. Perform stunt toward right and left sides.
2. "Can you change a part of this stunt to make it more challenging?"

Figure 25.54 Elbow crawl. Begin in a front-lying position, with elbows on the mat. Crawl forward on the elbows.

Variations:
1. "Can you crawl forward and change the position of your legs?"
2. "Can you crawl to a balance position?"

Figure 25.55 Seal walk. Begin in a prone position, with the belly down, the body and legs straight, and the toes pointed. Keep the arms straight to support the body and move the right hand forward. Shift the left hand forward and drag the legs, simulating the walking action of a seal.

Variations:
1. Use elbows instead of hands.
2. Crawl holding one leg in the air.
3. "See if you can find another part of your body to drag you forward."

Figure 25.56 Frog jump. Begin in a squat position, with hands on the floor. Jump forward and land on the hands, followed by the toes touching the floor. Gradually increase height and distance.

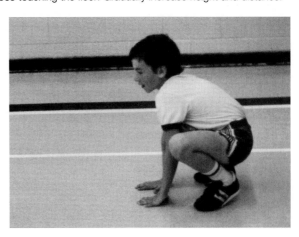

Figure 25.57 Measuring worm. Begin in a squat position, with the arms shoulder-width apart and the hands on the floor. Without moving the feet, take short steps with the hands until the legs and the back are straight. Now, without moving the arms, take short steps with the feet until the toes touch the backs of the hands.

Variations:
1. Keep one leg in the air at all times and repeat measuring worm.
2. "Can you perform the measuring worm with a partner or in threes?"

Figure 25.58 Circle roll. Partners join hands, keep legs straight, and turn in a circle.

Figure 25.60 Front support to stand. Begin in a front support position. Shift body to a squat position, then jump to a standing position.

Figure 25.59 Coffee grinder. Begin in a side-leaning rest position, with free hand extended upward. Keep the body straight and slowly walk forward and around to make a full circle.

Variations:
1. Repeat stunt backward.
2. Change position of free arm, and repeat stunt.

Figure 25.61 Rooster fight. Stand on one leg, with the arms folded across the chest. On "go" command, attempt to push opponent off balance; do not hit. As soon as one player touches the floor with her free foot, the other player is declared the winner.

Variations:
1. Place hands behind back and repeat stunt.
2. Place beanbag on head. If one player drops the beanbag, opposite player is declared the winner.
3. "Can you find another part of your body to rest the beanbag on and repeat your stunt?"

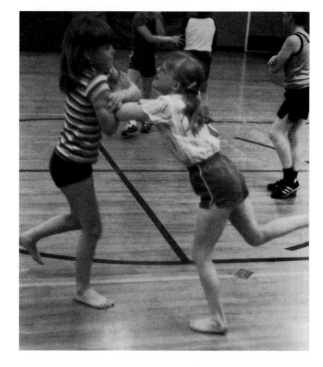

Figure 25.62 Crab fight. Partners assume a crab walk position, with hands and feet on the floor and seats off the floor. On signal "go," each attempts to push the other off balance. As soon as one player touches the floor with her seat or falls over, the other is declared the winner.

Variations:
1. Keep outside foot off ground.
2. Place utility ball on stomach. If a player drops the ball, the other is declared the winner.
3. "Invent a new rule for this game."

Figure 25.64 Prone knee fall. Start on knees, with body erect and arms at side. Fall forward and land on hands, with a gradual bending of the arms to break the fall.

Figure 25.63 Twister. Partners stand back to back, with legs apart and left hand on left knee. Each partner reaches through his legs with his right hand and grasps his partner's hand. Keeping the hand grip, one partner swings to the right and lifts his left leg over his partner's back. They return to the original position by reversing the movement.

Variations:
1. When both face each other, switch hands and return to a back-to-back position.
2. "Place a beanbag on your head and repeat the twister."

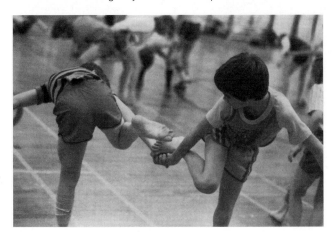

Figure 25.65 Elephant walk. One partner sits on the floor, with her legs extended sideward, while the upper partner bends down and places his hands between her legs (his feet are opposite the sitting partner's shoulders). The lower partner wraps her legs around the upper partner's trunk and places her hands over his seat. The lower partner rises off the floor and the upper partner takes short, "elephantlike" steps while the lower partner holds on.

Variations:
1. Walk backward and sideways.
2. "Can you and your partner make up a new animal walk? Give it a name!"

Figure 25.66 Bear dance. Squat on the right foot and extend the left leg forward. Extend arms from the sides. Simultaneously jump forward, draw the right leg back, and extend the left leg forward.

Variations:
1. Change position of arms—folded across chest, behind back, on head, and so on.
2. Turn body toward right or left on each leg exchange.
3. "See if you can wrap inside arm around partner's waist and perform a double bear dance."

Figure 25.67 Pig walk. One partner assumes a partial push-up position, with his legs apart and his seat up. The lower partner faces the opposite direction and shifts backward until his arms are opposite his partner's ankles. The lower partner wraps his legs around his partner's trunk and grasps his partner's ankles. The upper partner takes short, "piglike" steps.

Variations:
1. Keep in pig walk position, lower toward mat, roll sideways, and return to original position.
2. "Try to modify this stunt in any way possible."
3. "Is it possible to design a three-person pig walk?"

Figure 25.68 Elbow wrestling. Partners lie with their right elbows on the floor and holding hands. Their left forearms should be in contact with the floor. On signal, and without taking their elbows off the floor, partners attempt to push each other's hands to the floor.

Variations:
1. Change hands.
2. Repeat stunt; allow players to use both hands.
3. Repeat elbow wrestling; however, players must have knees off the mat (or one leg in the air, etc.).

Figure 25.69 Shoulder wrestling. Partners kneel side-by-side, facing in opposite directions, with their hands locked behind their backs and their shoulders touching. On signal, and without losing shoulder contact, partners attempt to push each other off balance.

Variations:
1. Change position of hands—extend overhead, hold knees, and so on.
2. Repeat shoulder wrestling; however, back must be parallel to the floor.
3. Repeat shoulder wrestling, with both players holding a large utility ball or basketball.

Figure 25.70 Leg wrestling. Partners lie side-by-side on their backs, facing opposite directions. On the signal "go," both raise their inside legs so that their knees are crossed. From this position, each partner tries to force her opponent's leg down to the mat.

Variations:
1. Repeat stunt, keeping outside leg off the mat.
2. "Modify any part of this stunt to make it more difficult and more fun for each performer."

Figure 25.71 Going down. Players sit side-by-side, with their arms linked. On the signal "go," each player tries to force the other to roll backward. Players are not allowed to touch the floor with their free hands.

Variations:
1. Keep outside leg off the mat and repeat stunt.
2. Place outside hand on head (or grasp partner's hand above head) and repeat stunt.
3. "Think of a new way to hold inside hands and repeat stunt."

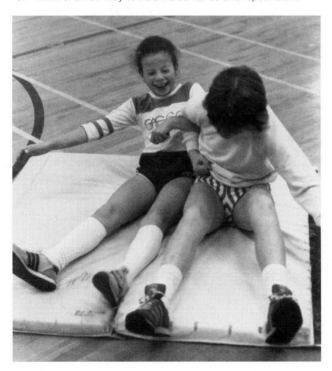

Figure 25.72 Push war. Draw three lines twenty to thirty feet apart. Players stand at the center line and place their hands on each other's shoulders. On the signal "go," each player attempts to push his opponent back over the endlines.

Variations:
1. Start in push-war position, then, on command, try to pull partner over line.
2. Grasp knee of partner with both hands. On command, try to pull opponent over the line.
3. "Make up your own variation of this stunt."

Figure 25.73 Double wheelbarrow. The first performer gets down on his hands and knees. Second performer places her hands about two feet in front of the first performer, then she places her legs on top of the first performer. The third performer then grasps the first performer's ankles and raises upward. On command from standing performer, "wheelbarrow" moves forward, with right hands, then left hands, moving together.

Figure 25.74 Upswing. Kneel with arms extended sideward and backward. Swing arms forward and upward vigorously; at the same time, push off from the feet. Finish in a partially crouched position.

Variations:
1. Repeat stunt, with a quarter or half turn in the air.
2. "Can you modify this stunt in any way?"

a   b   c

Figure 25.75 Forward drop. Stand with the arms extended downward beside the body. In a simultaneous action, begin to fall forward, allowing the hands and arms to gradually absorb the downward momentum.

Variations:
1. Knee Drop: Begin in a kneeling position, with arms extended over the head. Fall forward in a similar manner as the forward drop.
2. Repeat forward drop but raise one leg and keep it off the ground as you drop.

a   b   c

chapter 25

Figure 25.76 Centipede. This stunt should be performed by three children of equal size and strength. First performer gets down on his hands and knees. Second performer places his hands about two feet in front of the first performer, then his legs and hips on top of the first performer. Third performer repeats the same steps as the second performer. The centipede now walks with the first performer using hands and feet while the other two use only their hands.

Variations:
1. Walk backward and sideways.
2. Try turning around.

Figure 25.77 Seal slap. Begin in a front-lying position, with the toes on the floor and the hands directly under the shoulders. Simultaneously push off from the hands and toes, clap the hands in the air, and return to the starting position.

Variations:
1. Attempt a double clap before returning to the starting position.
2. Instead of pushing off, see how far you can extend arms forward without touching the floor with your stomach (long bridge).
3. "Repeat seal slap and invent a new position of the arms and head when in the air."

Figure 25.78 Jackknife. Begin in a partially crouched position, with arms extended forward and sideways. Jump upward and raise legs, touching toes with hands, and return to starting position.

Variations:
1. Repeat stunt with a run and a two-foot takeoff.
2. Run; jump; perform a tuck, straddle, twisted or other shapes; and land.

Figure 25.79 Heel click. Start in a partially crouched position, with arms sideways and slightly backward. Jump up, click heels together, and return to the starting position.

Variations:
1. Start on one foot, jump up, click heels, and return to starting position.
2. Run, jump, click heels, and land on both feet.
3. Make up a sequence of three heel clicks, each starting from a different position.

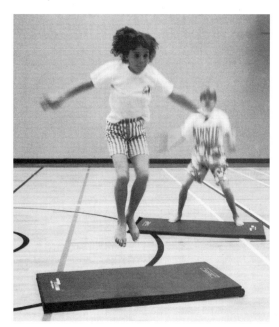

stunts, tumbling, and movement skills

Figure 25.80 Jump through. Begin in a front-leaning support position, with the hands about shoulder-width apart. In one continuous movement, shift the legs forward between the arms to a back-leaning support position.

Variations:
1. Walk Through: Same as above but walk through the movement.
2. Side Shift: Same as the walk through, except that, as the performer moves forward, he tilts slightly to one side, raises the opposite arm off the floor, and brings his legs through.

a

b

c

Figure 25.81 Handspring over partner. This is a lead-up stunt to the handspring. One partner kneels on the mat, places his hands well apart, and tucks his head toward his chest. The standing partner places his hands opposite the trunk of the kneeling partner, keeping his arms straight, and raises one leg off the mat. Still keeping his arms straight, he kicks upward with his free leg, pushes off with his back leg, and rolls over the kneeling partner.

Figure 25.82 Knee handspring. The knee handspring can also serve as a lead-up stunt to the handspring. One partner lies on his back, with his knees bent and together and his arms extended forward. The standing partner places his hands on his partner's knees, lowers his body forward, and raises one leg slightly off the mat. The top partner then swings his top leg up, pushes off his lower leg, and continues the forward movement, placing his shoulders against the lower partner's hands. The lower partner keeps his arms extended to assist the top partner's forward motion.

Figure 25.83 Handspring. Begin in a standing position. Run forward, skip on the left foot, place the right foot on the mat and then the hands, with the arms extended. Continue the upward and forward thrust of the right leg, followed by the left leg. When the body is in front of the head, push off from the hands and land on both feet, with the knees partially bent.

a

b

c

Figure 25.84 Handspring spotting. Kneel on the right side of the performer at the spot where his hands will land. Place your left hand on his right upper arm near the shoulder. As the performer shifts forward and upward, lift with the right hand and guide the forward action with your left hand. A second spotter may be required on the other side of the performer.

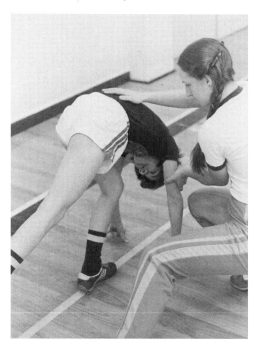

Figure 25.85 Neckspring. This stunt should be taught from a stationary position over a rolled mat. Once the performer can execute the kipping action, he should be allowed to attempt the skill with a running approach to the rolled mat. Run toward the rolled mat, take off with both feet, place the hands on the mat, bend the arms, and place the back of head on the mat. Roll forward, dropping the legs, then extend the legs forward and upward vigorously and push off the hands.

Spotting:
Use same technique as for the kip.

Figure 25.86 Headspring. This stunt is similar to the neckspring and should also be taught from a stationary position over a rolled mat. Once the performer can execute a kipping action, he should be allowed to attempt the headspring with a running approach. Run toward the rolled mat, take off with both feet, place the hands, then the top of the head, on the rolled mat. Keep the head and hands on the mat and bring the extended legs forward until an "overbalanced" position is reached. Then extend the legs up and forward vigorously and push off with the hands. Land on both feet, swing the arms forward, and bend the knees to regain a forward balanced position.

Spotting:
Use the same spotting technique described for the forward handspring.

stunts, tumbling, and movement skills

Figure 25.87 Kip. Begin in a back-lying position, with arms at sides and legs extended. From this position, raise the legs and rock back until the knees are above the head (a). Note: The fingers should be pointing toward the body. Vigorously thrust the legs forward and upward and push off with both hands (b). Continue raising trunk forward and upward (c), and land in a partially crouched position (d).

a   b   c   d

Figure 25.88 Kip spotting. Kneel on the right knee at the performer's left side. Place the left hand on the performer's left upper arm and the right hand around the performer's lower arm. As the performer kips, pull with your left hand and lift upward with the right hand.

Balance Activities and Pyramid Building

Balance activities include a wide variety of individual, partner, and group stunts (figures 25.89 through 25.129). The simple individual balance activities, such as One-Foot Balance and Stork Stand, are enjoyed by virtually all children in developmental level I. In developmental level II, balance activities, such as the Headstand and partner balance stunts, require more strength and balance ability. The same challenge is provided to older children in developmental level III, as they attempt to master the Handstand or a difficult Pyramid involving six or seven participants (table 25.3).

Table 25.3 Balance Skills

Name of skill	Developmental Level			Movement concepts	Page
	I	II	III		
Front Support	→			Balance, levels	452
Tuck V-Sit	→			Balance	452
Tightrope Walk	→			Balance, transfer of weight	452
Knee Walk	→			Balance, transfer of weight	452
Stork Stand	→			Balance, transfer of weight	453
Thread the Needle	→			Balance, transfer of weight	453
Scale Stand (partner)	→			Balance, transfer of weight, relationships	453
Turk Stand	→			Balance, force	453
Single-Leg Balance	→			Balance, wide shape, transfer of weight	454
Hand-Knee Balance	→			Balance, transfer of weight	454
Twin Balance (partner)	→			Balance, force, relationships	454
Rear Support	→			Balance	454
Single-Knee Balance	→			Balance, transfer of weight	455
Seat Stand (partners)	→			Balance, force, levels, relationships	455
Teddy Bear Stand		→		Balance, levels	455
Ankle Stand		→		Balance, relationships	455
Push-Up Stand		→		Balance, relationships	455
Wheel Stunt		→		Balance, levels, relationships	456
Knee Dip		→		Balance, levels	456
Frog Stand		→		Balance, force	456
Headstand		→		Balance, levels	457
Swing Turn		→		Balance, change of direction	457
Walking Down Wall			→	Balance, transfer of weight	457
V-Sit			→	Balance	458
The Bridge			→	Balance	458
Headstand Variations			→	Balance	458
Handstand			→	Balance, transfer of weight, force	458
Handstand Roll Out to Jump			→	Balance, transfer of weight	459
Handstand to Bridge			→	Balance, transfer of weight	459
Forearm Stand			→	Balance, transfer of weight	459
Elbow Balance			→	Balance, transfer of weight	460
L-Support			→	Balance, transfer of weight	460
Side Stand (partner)			→	Balance, relationships	460
Table (partner)			→	Balance, relationships	461
Back Layout (partner)			→	Balance, levels, relationships	461
Flying Dutchman (partner)			→	Balance, levels, relationships	461
Knee and Shoulder Stand (partner)			→	Balance, levels, relationships	462
Knee Stand (partner)			→	Balance, levels, relationships	462
Individual Pyramid			→	Balance, levels, relationships	464
Double Pyramid			→	Balance, levels	464
Triple Pyramid			→	Balance, levels, relationships	465
Quadruple Pyramid			→	Balance, levels, relationships	465
Group Pyramid			→	Balance, levels, relationships	465

stunts, tumbling, and movement skills

Figure 25.89 Front support. This is the traditional push-up position. Arms are shoulder-width apart, head up, with back and legs forming a straight line.

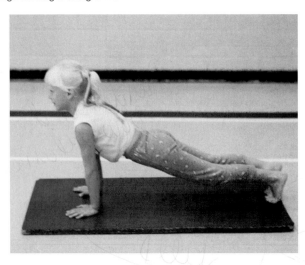

Figure 25.90 Tuck V-sit. Begin in a crouched position, with hands wrapped around knees. Raise feet off floor, and balance on seat.

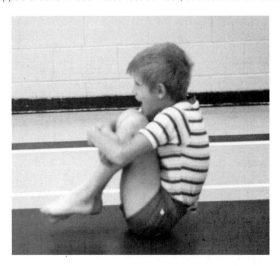

Figure 25.91 Tightrope walk. Draw a line on the floor. Stand with arms extended sideward, head up, and both feet on the line. Walk forward, placing the toe, then the heel, on the floor.

Variations:
1. Change position of arms.
2. Walk backward.
3. Make a half knee-bend and repeat.
4. "Can you walk on just part of your foot—heels, toes, side?"

Figure 25.92 Knee walk. Start with the hands and knees on the mat. Reach back and grasp the feet or ankles. Shift the weight to the left side and take a short step with the right knee. Continue movement with short steps forward.

Variations:
1. Walk backward and sideways.
2. "See if you can balance on one knee for three seconds."

Figure 25.93 Stork stand. Stand on one leg, with arms extended sideways. Raise right leg and rest bottom of foot against the knee.

Variations:
1. Change position of arms.
2. Repeat stunt and try to bend left leg.

Figure 25.95 Scale stand. One partner stands with feet together and arms extended forward. The other partner holds the partner's hands, then balances on one leg and extends free leg back to a front scale position.

Figure 25.94 Thread the needle. Begin in a standing position, arms straight in front, with hands grasping. Keeping hands touching, bend forward, raise right foot up and through arms. Return to starting position.

Variations:
1. Repeat with opposite foot.
2. Change hand position (interlocking fingers, grasping wrists, etc.) and repeat.
3. "Can you add your own variation to this stunt?"

Figure 25.96 Turk stand. Begin in a cross-legged sitting position, with the arms folded across the chest and the body leaning forward slightly. Without releasing the grip, lean forward and extend the legs to a standing position. Return to the cross-legged sitting position.

Variation:
Lower yourself all the way down; roll onto your back without uncrossing your arms. Return to a standing position.

stunts, tumbling, and movement skills

Figure 25.97 Single leg balance. Stand on one leg, with the knee slightly bent, lower the trunk, and raise the arms and other leg until they are parallel to the floor.

Variations:
1. Extend the elevated leg to the side.
2. Place the arms in different directions—pointing forward or downward or holding against the sides.
3. Place sole of elevated foot against side of other leg (stork stand).
4. "Can you balance on one leg and twist your body?"
5. "See if you can swing your free leg forward and turn around and face the other way."
6. "Can you balance on one leg, jump, and change to balancing on the opposite leg?"

Figure 25.98 Hand-knee balance. Begin with hands and knees on the mat. Simultaneously raise arms and left leg off the mat.

Variations:
1. Try raising the same arm and leg off the mat.
2. "Can you perform the hand-knee balance, then show me a twist in your body?"

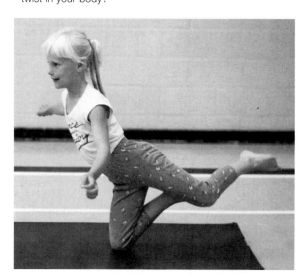

Figure 25.99 Twin balance. One partner assumes a hand-knee balance position. The other performer places his knees on the lower partner's seat, with his hands on his shoulders.

Figure 25.100 Rear support. Start in a sitting position. Gradually raise seat off mat until body forms a straight line.

Variations:
1. "Can you balance on one foot and twist your body when you get into the rear support position?"
2. Turn over to a front support position.

Figure 25.101 Single-knee balance. Begin in a partial crouched position, with hands and knees on the mat. Simultaneously raise body up and move arms sideward while left leg gradually extends backward.

Variations:
1. Change position of arms after reaching balance position.
2. Change balance leg.

Figure 25.103 Teddy bear stand. Begin this stunt with forehead and hands making a triangle. The feet should be on the mat. Gradually "walk" forward on the toes until the knees are near the elbows. At this point, slowly shift knees to rest on elbows.

Figure 25.104 Ankle stand. Lower partner sits on mat. Upper partner stands with feet on each side of lower partner's knees. Upper partner grasps lower partner's ankles while upper partner raises lower partner's legs above her head.

Figure 25.102 Seat stand. One partner assumes a hand-knee balance positon. The other partner stands and balances on the lower partner's seat.

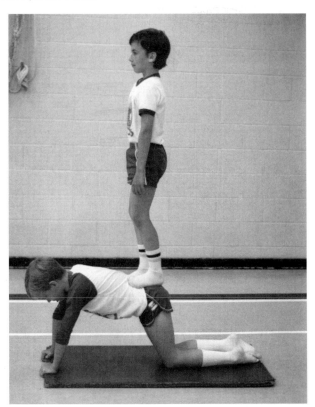

Figure 25.105 Push-up stand. Back partner assumes a hand-knee balance position. Front partner raises right leg and places it on his partner's right shoulder. Repeat with opposite leg.

Figure 25.106 Wheel stunt. Center performer stands with legs apart and arms extended sideward. Outside performers place feet near center's foot, grasp hands, then lean outward.

Figure 25.107 Knee dip. Stand on the left foot and bend the right leg back and up, grasping the foot with the right hand. Gradually bend the left leg until the right knee touches the mat. Return to the starting position without releasing the grip.

Variations:
1. Place hands on hips, extend right leg forward, bend, and return.
2. "Can you invent a new way to perform the knee dip?"

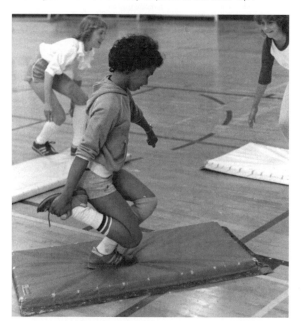

Figure 25.108 Frog stand. Squat with the arms straight, hands resting on the floor and knees outside the elbows. The fingers should be pointing forward and spread apart for balance. Lean forward slowly, pressing the inside of the thighs against the elbows. As the feet rise off the ground, lower the head and trunk. Return to the starting position.

Variations:
1. Shift forward and perform a forward roll.
2. Shift forward, place head on mat, and perform a headstand.

Figure 25.109 Headstand. Form a triangle with the hands and forehead. Push off the mat with the toes of both feet, flex the knees, and raise the body to a halfway position. Once the body is in a stable, balanced position, continue raising the legs until the body forms a straight line. Note: Too much arch in the back tends to cause the body to fall forward.

Suggested progression in learning this stunt:
1. Begin in position (a), walk forward on toes, shift to position (b), and return.
2. Repeat (a) to full headstand.
3. Kick up from position (a).
4. Perform stunt as shown.

a   b   c

Figure 25.111 Swing turn. Begin balancing on left leg, with arms extended sideways. Swing right leg backward, then forward. As leg moves forward, rise up on toes and pivot toward the left side, making a half turn.

Variations:
1. Change balance leg.
2. Reverse direction of free leg.

Figure 25.110 Headstand spotting. Kneel on the left side of the performer and place left hand under performer's shoulder. As she lifts her legs, grasp the shin of the left leg with right hand. Once she is in the headstand position, gradually release the hands, but keep them a few inches away and ready for support. A second spotter can be added to the other side.

Figure 25.112 Walking down wall. Stand facing away from the wall, with the feet about two feet away from the wall, the elbows high, and the palms facing up and toward the wall. Arch the head and shoulders back and place the hands on the wall. Walk the hands down the wall and touch the head to the mat. This movement should be performed without moving the feet; however, most children will have to move their feet a little farther away from the wall as they reach the lower phase of the arched position. Use a spotter when a performer first tries this stunt.

Variations:
1. Keep one foot in the air throughout movement.
2. Walk up the wall. Start in push-up position with heels touching the wall. Gradually move backward to a handstand position, with feet resting on wall.

Figure 25.113 V-sit. Sit with the knees bent, feet flat on the floor, and the hands grasping the sides of the ankles. Still grasping the ankles, extend the knees and balance on the seat.

Variations:
1. Repeat stunt holding toes.
2. When in the V-sit position, release grip and extend arms and legs sideways.
3. "Can you modify this stunt while still emphasizing a balance on the seat?"

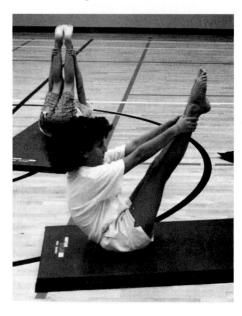

Figure 25.115 Handstand. Begin this stunt with the arms approximately shoulder-width apart, hands on the mat, and the fingers slightly bent (this aids in maintaining balance). Both feet should also be on the mat in the starting position, with the right knee slightly bent. With the body weight well forward on the arms, kick the right leg up and follow with the left. Continue the upward movement of the legs, ending with the legs, body, and arms in a nearly straight line. The head should be well forward to assist in maintaining balance.

Variations:
1. Handstand against the wall, then bend elbows (about halfway) and straighten to original position.
2. Walk on hands.

a   b   c

Figure 25.114 The bridge. Sit on the edge of the mat, holding the elbows high and the palms of hands facing up. Lower the back and place the palms on the mat, then arch the body.

Variations:
1. When in the arched position, raise and extend one leg.
2. Lower body, place head on mat, and extend arms sideways (wrestler's bridge).
3. "Can you perform a bridge with a variation in the arm, leg, or trunk position?"

Figure 25.116 Headstand variations: Review headstand before attempting the following variations.

Variations:
1. Change the position of the legs, such as straddle, one forward and one backward, and so on.
2. Hold a ball or beanbag between legs.
3. "See if you can balance on your head and change the position of any other part of your body."

chapter 25

Figure 25.117 Handstand spotting. This is similar to the spotting technique described for the headstand. Both spotters kneel on the sides of the performer and place their hands under her shoulders. As the performer lifts her legs, each spotter grasps the thigh of the nearest leg. Once the performer is in the handstand position, the spotter should gradually release the hands but keep them a few inches away and ready to give support.

Figure 25.119 (a) Handstand roll out to jump. From the handstand position, bend arms, tuck body, roll to a squat, and continue forward and upward to a lunge position. Land with knees bent. (b) Handstand to bridge. From the handstand position, lower and arch body, and land with head up and body in a full arched position.

a

b

Figure 25.118 Handstand spotting. Use the same spotting technique described for the headstand. An alternate method is to stand just in front of the spot where the performer's hands will be placed. The spotter's left leg should be extended back to provide a firmly balanced position. As the performer shifts her legs upward, the spotter should brace the performer's right shoulder against his own left leg and catch her legs as they come up.

Figure 25.120 Forearm stand. Kneel with the elbows, hands, and forehead on the mat. Gradually begin to rise upward until the legs are fully extended and the toes are pointed.

Variations:
1. Change position of legs after balance has been achieved.
2. "Can you change the position of your legs and twist your body?"

Spotting:
Use the same spotting technique described for the headstand.

stunts, tumbling, and movement skills

Figure 25.121 Elbow balance. Begin this stunt in a partially front-lying position, with the elbows bent and touching the sides of the body, and the fingers spread apart. Keep the elbows close to the sides and shift the trunk slightly downward and forward as the legs are raised.

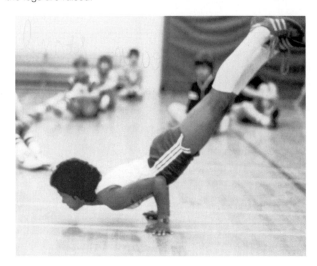

Figure 25.122 L-support. Sit on the floor, with the legs together and pointing straight ahead. Rest the hands on the floor below the shoulders. Keep the shoulders slightly forward of the hips, press down, and raise the hips and legs off the floor.

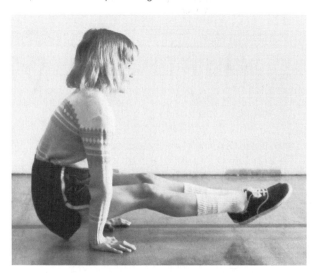

Figure 25.123 Side stand. Base partner assumes a wide kneeling position, with his weight evenly distributed on his arms and legs. Top performer stands on the side and curls his arm around his partner's trunk. The palms of both hands face up. The top performer leans across his partner and gradually raises his knees to a partially bent position above his partner's back. Then he extends his legs fully.

Variations:
1. "See how many ways the top performer can change the position of his legs."
2. "Is it possible for one or both performers to add a twist to their balanced position?"

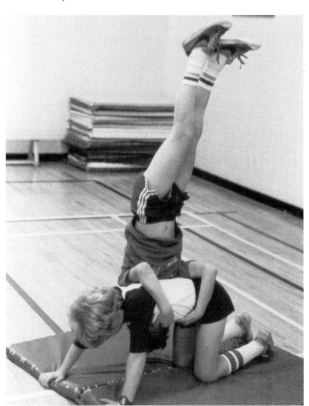

Figure 25.124 Table. Base partner assumes a crab-walk position, with her thighs and trunk in a straight line. Top partner straddles base, places her hands on base's shoulders and feet on her knees. Top performer then raises seat until thighs and trunk are in a straight line. Both heads are facing the ceiling.

Variations:
1. When balance is reached, base partner raises right foot and top partner raises left foot into the air.
2. "Try to invent a new double balance stunt, with both facing the ceiling."

Figure 25.125 Back layout. The base partner lies on her back, extends her arms up, and bends both knees. The soles of her feet should face her partner's back. The top partner rests the small of her back against her partner's feet and slowly extends back as her partner straightens her legs. The base partner can give support to the top partner by holding her arms just above the wrists.

Variation:
Repeat stunt and release hand grip as balance is achieved.

Figure 25.126 Back layout spotting. Stand near the top of the base performer's right shoulder, assist in placing the feet, and maintain balance when indicated.

Figure 25.127 Flying Dutchman. Base performer lies on her back, extends her arms up, and bends both knees. Top performer faces the base performer, grasps her hands, and places her stomach against the support's feet. Base performer extends her legs; then the top performer arches her back, releases her hands, and extends her arms sideways. Note: Begin with a spotter to find balance position and as a standby safety person.

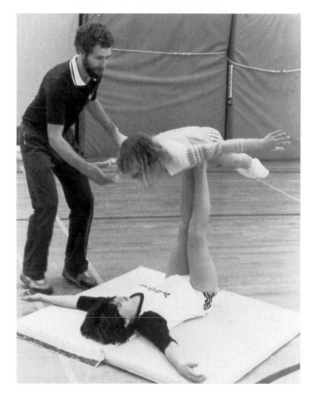

stunts, tumbling, and movement skills

Figure 25.128 Knee and shoulder stand. The base partner lies on her back, with her knees bent and her arms up. The top performer stands facing her partner and places her hands on her partner's knees as she brings her shoulders forward. The base partner places her hands on the top performer's shoulders. As soon as the top performer's shoulders are held in a fixed position, she begins to raise her legs until they are in a vertical position.

Variations:
1. Top performer places one leg forward and one extending backward.
2. "Find a new position for your legs." (sideways, knees flexed, etc.)
3. "What other way can you modify this stunt?"

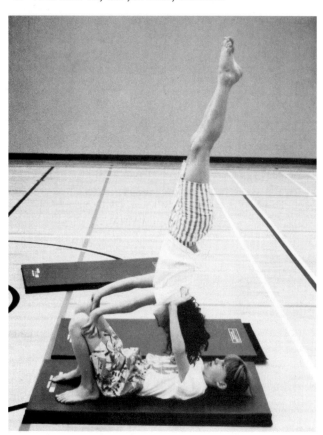

Figure 25.129 Knee stand. Base partner stands with his legs about shoulder-width apart, bends forward, and places his head between his partner's legs. Top partner places her hands on base partner's shoulders, and base partner grasps upper partner's thighs. Base partner begins to stand up, while top partner places her feet on base partner's thighs, releases her hands from her partner's shoulders, and begins to arch forward.

Variation:
"Can you redesign this stunt so that the final balance position of the top performer is facing the reversed direction?"

A human pyramid is usually considered to be a group of students forming a pyramidlike structure, with one child at the top and the others gradually tapering to the sides. This is known as a true pyramid; however, other kinds of pyramids have high points somewhere within the pyramid or even at the ends. The block illustrations may be used as basic guides in constructing pyramids with two or more students.

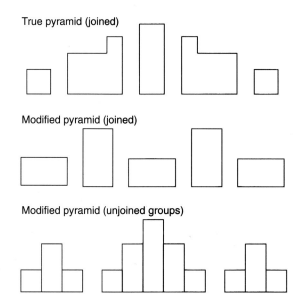

True pyramid (joined)

Modified pyramid (joined)

Modified pyramid (unjoined groups)

The first stage of pyramid building is to learn to create individual poses that can be used for the center, side, and end position. Many balance stunts, such as the Headstand and the V-Sit, can be used. Other poses can be added (figure 25.130). It is also important to allow the class to design its own individual positions.

The next stage in pyramid building is the development of dual stunts. Again, many dual balance stunts can become the nucleus of a pyramid. Require the heaviest and strongest students to form the base of the pyramid and lighter students to be on top (figure 25.131).

Once the dual stunts are learned, combine these positions. A symmetrical, six-person pyramid can be formed, with two facing base stands and one individual pose, such as the Dog Stand—on each end—facing the center. Beyond this point, the teacher and students can use their imaginations to design and construct an unlimited variety of pyramids. Examples are shown in figures 25.132 and 25.133.

Since pyramid building involves teamwork and timing, the teacher should develop a standard procedure or set of whistle cues. The first cue could mean that all students stand at attention and face one direction. The second cue could signal all participants to move into the ready or primary position. A third blow might be necessary in two- and three-person pyramids for the upper participants to shift into final position. A similar procedure should then be followed when dismounting.

Movement Concepts and Skills

Introducing movement concepts and skills is more difficult for intermediate teachers than for primary teachers. By the time boys and girls reach the fourth or fifth grade, they have learned many stunts and tumbling skills, normally through a process of explanation, demonstration, and practice. It would be difficult and unwise to change this process completely and adopt a new movement vocabulary and a new way of learning. A more profitable approach is for the intermediate teacher to acquire an understanding of the basic movement concepts and skills described in this section, then to introduce them gradually into the regular stunts and tumbling program. If the class is receptive to these ideas and demonstrates the ability to work independently and safely, greater emphasis can be put on the movement concepts and skills.

The four Movement Education elements—body awareness, qualities, space awareness, and relationships—are described on the following pages. Wherever possible, suggestions are offered for teaching the movement skills of each element, along with ideas for relating or incorporating

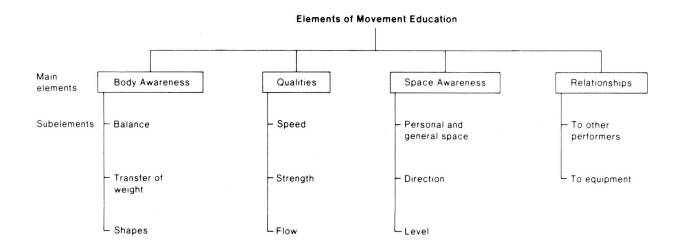

Elements of Movement Education

stunts, tumbling, and movement skills

Figure 25.130 Individual balance and poses.

a   b   c

d   e   f

Figure 25.131 Dual balance and poses.

a   b   c

d   e   f

Figure 25.132 Triple and quadruple balance poses.

a   b

Figure 25.133 Group pyramids.

a

b

stunts, tumbling, and movement skills

them into the stunts and tumbling activities of the primary or intermediate program. The sample unit and lesson in this section provide a general format for teachers to follow when developing their own themes and lesson plans.

The stunts and tumbling skills described in the previous sections are classified as structured skills or movement patterns. Each skill is performed in a standard way; however, variations are allowed in the position of the hands or legs. In order to overcome the structured limitations of formal stunts and tumbling activities, many of the movement concepts and skills developed in the Movement Education approach are being incorporated into stunts and tumbling and into activities with small equipment and large apparatus. These movement concepts and skills allow children to perform movements according to their own levels of physical and creative ability.

However, the problems encountered when introducing unstructured movement concepts and skills to stunts and tumbling activities are similar to those encountered when introducing the problem-solving method in games programs. Introducing the movement concepts and skills to primary children, particularly those in the first two grades, is relatively easy because primary children do not have a wide background of stunts and tumbling skills. Instead, many of their skills involve imitative movements rather than the complex skills of balance and agility taught in later grades. Also, primary children are normally taught through more informal methods, both in the classroom and in the gymnasium. As a consequence, primary teachers have little difficulty incorporating movement concepts and skills into their stunts and tumbling programs. Once the teacher understands this movement vocabulary, she usually gives more emphasis to movement concepts and skills and less to structured stunt activities.

Body Awareness (What the Body Can Do)

Body awareness describes the ways in which the body or its parts can be controlled, balanced on, or moved from one position to another. Skills involved in body awareness fall into the following three groups.

Balancing, or Weight Bearing

A child is capable of balancing, or taking the weight, on different parts of the body. He can balance on one foot, on his head, or on all "threes" such as in the Lame Puppy Walk. In order to help the child learn what parts of the body he can balance on, it is necessary to present a challenge in the form of a movement problem and then let him answer the challenge in his own way. The question should begin with such phrases as "See if you can. . . ," "How many ways . . . ," "Can you . . . ," or "Try to discover . . ."—rather than a direct command such as "I want you to . . ." The following questions show how to use the problem-solving method to assist the child in finding his own way of balancing on one or more parts of the body.

Figure 25.134 "Can you balance on two or three parts?"

1. "Can you show me the One-Leg Balance?" Children may have already learned this balance stunt.
2. "See if you can balance on your seat." This is still somewhat structured, yet the question allows each child to put his arms and legs in any position he wishes. A series of similar questions directing the child to balance on other parts—side, back, stomach—could follow.
3. Present a series of questions involving two or more parts of the body (figure 25.134)—"Can you balance on one foot and two other parts of your body?" "Can you balance on three (or four) different parts of your body?" "Can you find another way of balancing on three parts of your body?"

The main task within this subelement of body awareness is to help children become aware of the many different ways in which they can balance their bodies. The movement challenges begin with a familiar stunt (the One-Leg Balance), then shift to specific parts of the body. The final challenge mentions only a certain number of "points of contact," thus providing more freedom for the child to discover other ways that the body or its parts can be balanced.

Transfer of Weight

Transfer of weight, the second subelement of body awareness, is the ability to shift from one balanced position to another. This skill can be developed as a logical extension of balancing on different parts of the body (figure 26.135). The following illustrate how this progression can occur:

1. From one known skill to another: "Can you show me the Measuring Worm Stunt, then change to a Headstand?" (This is shifting from one three-point balance to another three-point balance.)

Figure 25.135 Transfer of weight.

a

b

c

2. From a known part to three unknown parts: "See if you can balance on your seat, then shift to balancing on three different parts of your body." (This is shifting from a one-point balance to a three-point balance.)
3. From unknown parts to unknown parts: "Can you show me a three-point balance, then shift to a two-point balance?"

Shapes

Shapes, the third subelement of body awareness, includes the ways the human body can make stretched, curled, wide, narrow, and twisted shapes. The task is similar to balancing or weight bearing in that questions must be presented to help the children discover what shapes they can perform.

Stretched and curled shapes should involve the whole body first, then progress to individual parts. Questions should encourage the children to make the following shapes from various starting positions.

1. *Curled shapes* (figure 25.136)
   a. From a sitting position
   b. From a standing position
   c. While in flight
   d. From a front, back, or side lying position
   e. From a curled position to another curled position
2. *Stretched shapes* (figure 25.137)
   a. From a standing position
   b. While in flight
   c. From a sitting position
   d. From a front, back, or side lying position
   e. From a stretched position to another stretched position

Progression should be from a stationary position into a curled or stretched shape. Begin with questions or

Figure 25.136 "Can you make a curled shape?"

Figure 25.137 "See if you can show me a stretched shape."

statements directed at curled shapes (from a-e), then try the same with stretched shapes (a–e), or switch from one to the other. Following are samples:

"Can you curl up and make a very small, ball-like shape?"

"Can you make a stretched shape from a standing position?"

Figure 25.138 Wide shapes.

Figure 25.139 Twisting—body stabilized.

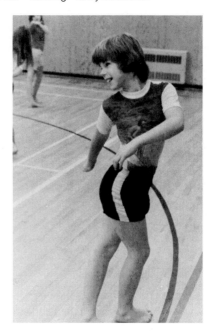

"See if you can repeat your stretched shape or find a new one and then change into a curled shape."

"See if you can start with the Turk Stand and, when you are low to the ground, roll to a very curled-up shape."

Allow the class sufficient time for experimentation. During this time, look for unusual shapes and provide encouragement and praise wherever necessary. Choose one or two shapes and let the children show them to the rest of the class; don't always choose the same children.

Once the class has a general understanding of stretch and curl, introduce wide and narrow and twisted shapes in a similar way. Wide and narrow shapes, like curled and stretched shapes, are contrasting. A wide shape (figure 25.138) requires the legs, arms, or both to be away from the trunk. In contrast, a narrow shape is characterized by its thinness, which means the arms or legs must be close together or in line with the trunk.

A twisted shape can be performed in two ways. The first is by holding one part of the body in a fixed, or stabilized, position, such as on the floor, and then turning the body or any part of it away from the fixed base. In figure 25.139, the body is stabilized as the feet restrict the degree of twisting. A twisted shape can also be made when the body is in flight. In this case, one part of the body is held in a fixed position while the other part turns away from the *fixed* part, producing a twisted shape. Although it could be argued that the latter is a *turn* (usually defined as rotation of the body and loss of a fixed contact), with younger children the synonymous use of *twist* and *turn* is quite acceptable. The meaning can be refined later.

At this stage in the introduction of movement skills and concepts, children should learn the meaning of balance and shape. They should also be able to develop simple sequences involving a variety of shapes and balance skills.

Qualities (How the Body Moves)

The element of qualities describes how the body moves from one position to another in relation to speed, force, and flow. Speed is the ability to move quickly or slowly from one position to another (figure 25.140). Force is the effort involved in a single movement or throughout a series of related movements. A child may leap high into the air, demonstrating a strong, forceful movement of the leg muscles (figure 25.141). In contrast, a gentle shift from a high stretch to a low curl illustrates a light or gentle movement. Flow is the smooth transition or linking of one movement pattern to another (figure 25.142).

These aspects of qualities can be integrated into previously learned stunts, tumbling and safety skills, and the three components of body awareness. The following examples show a few of the many applications of speed, force, and flow to a single skill or a sequence of skills:

1. *Stunts:* Ask the class to perform the Measuring Worm Stunt. After one or two practices, ask the class to perform part of the stunt very slowly and part very quickly (figure 25.143).
2. *Tumbling skills:* Pose a challenge such as "See if you can move slowly from a Log Roll to a Side Roll, then quickly from a Side Roll back to a Log Roll."
3. *Shapes:* Ask the class to make up a sequence of stretched, curled, and wide shapes. After each child knows his sequence, pose the following suggestion: "As you practice your sequence, try very hard to make each movement link smoothly to the next

chapter 25

Figure 25.140 Speed—quick and slow.

Figure 25.141 A strong, forceful movement.

Figure 25.142 Flow.

a. A smooth transition from one position . . .   b. . . . to another position . . .   c. . . . and to another position.

Figure 25.143 Measuring worm stunt.

Figure 25.144 General space.

with no sudden stops or jerky movements between each skill." The stress here is on flow, or the ease and efficiency of moving from one shape or position to another.

Space Awareness (Where the Body Moves)

The third element, space awareness, includes movement skills relating to use of general or limited space, direction, and levels of movement.

All the space in a gymnasium that can be used by a child constitutes his *general space* (figure 25.144). In contrast, *limited,* or *personal, space* is the immediate area a child can use around him to perform a movement or series of movements. When a child is challenged to perform a series of different balance positions while remaining inside his hoop, he is using his personal, or limited, space (figure 25.145). Direction is the ability to move safely and purposely in a variety of pathways, such as forward, backward, or sideways, and to trace out pathways such as over, under, around, and through. Levels concerns the ability to perform

stunts, tumbling, and movement skills

Figure 25.145 Limited space.

Figure 25.146 Matching shapes.

a

b

c

a movement or series of movements that requires the body to be low to the ground, as when performing a series of rolls, at a medium level, as in moving on all fours, or at a high level, as when performing a cartwheel or a leap from the floor.

Many of these aspects of space awareness have been stressed in teaching stunts and tumbling and, to a lesser degree, when teaching the movement skills of body awareness and qualities. For example, when each of the tumbling skills is introduced, each child begins on his own mat. This is his personal, or limited, space. Gradually, his space is expanded to two mats, then to three, and finally to all the mats available in the general space of the gymnasium. Each child is also asked to move to an open space on the mat. His rolling movement may be forward, sideways, or diagonal.

Relationships

The fourth element of Movement Education is the relationship of the individual or group to other performers or objects.

Partner Relationships

Movements with a partner can involve matching shapes (figure 25.146), contrasting shapes (figure 25.147), or one child acting as the leader while the other acts as the follower through a sequence of movements.

Many useful and enjoyable partner activities can be applied to a stunts and tumbling program. All of the partner activities described under the stunts sections for primary and intermediate children are essentially dual balance stunts or tandemtype agility walks. With "matching," "contrasting," and "following" challenges, partner activities can be greatly enriched. Following are examples of the many ways that partners can develop structured and unstructured movement sequences.

1. *Matching movements using structured skills:* "See if you can make up a sequence (or routine) with your

Figure 25.147 Contrasting shapes.

partner that begins with a Headstand, includes a Roll, and ends with both in a balancing position (figure 25.148)."

2. *Contrasting movements using unstructured skills:* "One partner makes a stretched shape and the other partner makes a contrasting curled shape. Next, the first partner makes another stretched shape and his partner makes a contrasting curled shape."

Figure 25.148 Partner relationships.

a. Begin with a headstand.

b. Include a roll.

c. End in a balance position.

Figure 25.149 *Performing a movement in a manipulative way.*

Figure 25.150 *Performing a movement in a nonmanipulative way.*

Repeat with two new stretched and curled shapes. Allow time to practice the contrasting shapes in a smooth sequence.

3. *Follow the leader:* One partner leads and the other copies each movement. Challenges can be "Make a shape, change direction, make another shape, change direction," and so on. "Develop a sequence of balancing and rolling, with one following the other" or "Make up a sequence with your partner that includes a change of direction and a change in speed."

Equipment Relationships

Equipment relationships involve the ability to perform a movement in a manipulative way, such as balancing or rolling with a hoop (figure 25.149), or in a nonmanipulative manner, such as leaping over a hoop (figure 25.150). Numerous examples of these types of relationships are described in the next two chapters.

This introduction to the four movement elements has simply opened the door to a range of movement skills. Each of the skills within body awareness, qualities, space

Figure 25.151 Developing Movement Education units and lessons.

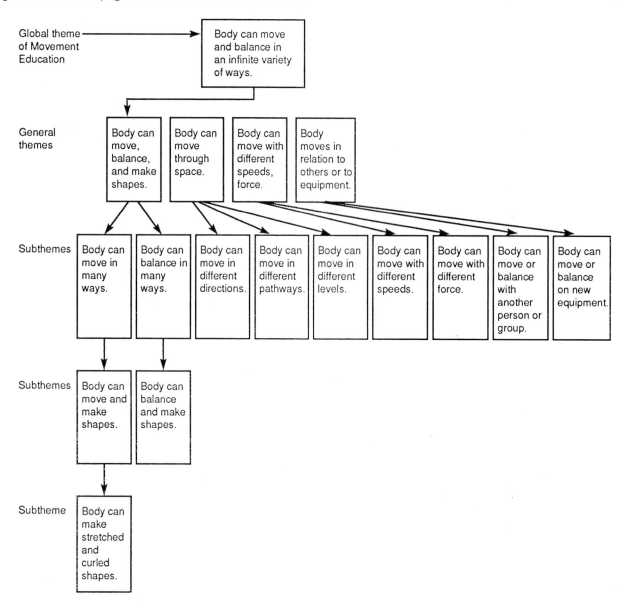

awareness, and relationships is unstructured and, thus, allows children to perform each movement in their own unique ways. Since these movement skills can be mixed with stunts or tumbling skills, they enrich a child's movement experience.

Developing Units and Lesson Plans

Units and lesson plans in Movement Education are developed from a central theme, or idea. As shown in figure 25.151, the global theme of gymnastics is exploring how the body can move and balance in an infinite variety of ways. At the next level are the general themes, which represent the four elements of Movement Education. These are normally too broad to develop teachable themes or units. The subthemes,

such as "Body can balance in many ways," could be developed into a short theme involving four to six lessons. A single lesson theme of balancing on different parts of the body could then be developed for a thirty-minute lesson. An outline of this unit and a sample lesson plan follow, as a format for developing similar units and lessons.

Developmental Level I

Theme Body can balance in many ways
Number of lessons Six
Main theme Balancing in different ways
Subthemes Change of direction and level, change of speed

Main theme content

1. Balance on different parts of the body—seat, knees, elbows, one foot, and so on.

---

2. Balance on large and small parts of the body.
3. Balance on flat and sharp parts of the body.
4. Balance on upper and lower parts of the body.
5. Combine subthemes, such as change of speed, with balancing on different parts.
6. Design and perform simple sequences with ease, efficiency, and form.

Lesson No. 1: Balancing on Different Parts of the Body

Part 1: Introductory activity (3–4 minutes)

—Run, change directions.

—Run, change directions, and on signal "stop" touch floor with fingers of both hands.

—Run, "stop" (touch floor), and balance on one foot . . . next time "seat," and so on.

Part 2: Skill development (10–12 minutes)

This is the part of the lesson where the main theme is developed. The first two or three challenges will normally take up the alloted ten to twelve minutes. If time permits, complete #4 or add one or more similar challenges.

Find a Space—all move to scattered positions.

Challenges:

1. "Show me how you can balance on . . . 'your seat' . . . [wait a few moments] . . . 'your side'. . . 'knees and one elbow,' " and so on.
2. "Can you show me how you can balance on a big 'patch'? . . . Now a 'patch and one point.' " Continue asking for different patches and points.
3. Introduce "take the weight on" for the word "balance." "See if you can take the weight on three parts of your body. . . four parts, 'a new three parts' " and so on.
4. Repeat challenge no. 3, introducing the subtheme "speed." "Can you balance on three parts and move very slowly to four parts? . . . Now, try it again and balance on three, slowly to four parts, then quickly back to three."

Part 3: Closure—discuss various ways of balancing

During the next lesson, introduce or repeat any of the previous challenges. At the end of the last challenge, ask the children to get a hoop and find a new space. Pose the following challenges involving a hoop.

1. "Place your hoop on the floor. Can you balance on your seat on the inside of the hoop? . . . one part inside the hoop? . . . one part inside and two parts outside?" . . . Continue.
2. "Show me how you can hold onto the hoop with both hands and balance on one foot . . . one foot and the hoop must touch the floor." . . . Continue.
3. Continue adding "quick and slow" to one or more challenges. Subsequent lessons would continue to stress balance but would add subelements, such as change of direction and levels, and using other small equipment.

Teachers and children in developmental levels II and III normally modify this theme approach to cope with the backgrounds and interests of older children. The following suggestions can help these teachers incorporate some of the movement concepts and skills of Movement Education.

1. Continue to organize units and lessons in the same general way.
2. As you teach routines involving balance, tumbling, and agility skills, begin to use some of the movement concepts, for example, "Develop a routine that has one tumbling and two balance skills." After a few minutes add, "Can you move quickly from a balance to the next balance, then slowly back to the first balance?"

Such phrases as "balance on four," "change of direction and level," and "moving quickly and slowly" are understandable and acceptable to older children. As the children demonstrate their ability to create routines, gradually use more movement concepts and skills.

Using Stunts and Movement Skills to Teach Academic Concepts and Skills

In previous chapters, locomotor, manipulative, and cooperative games were used to teach academic concepts and skills in a variety of subjects. Stunts, tumbling, and movement skills can be used in a similar way to teach or reinforce a variety of academic skills. In addition, more complex scientific concepts relating to gravity, motion, and force, can be explained and demonstrated through performing and analyzing individual stunts and movement sequences. The following examples are provided to illustrate how performing and analyzing stunts can help children understand academic concepts through an active and enjoyable medium.

Language Arts

1. Make letters of the alphabet—individually, with a partner, or with three or more children.
2. Spell words with parts of the body (finger or leg tracing the word), with whole body, or with a partner or small group. (In groups of three, make the letters of the words cat, Bruce, and Mississippi; choose words according to the appropriate grade level.)

Mathematics

1. Make whole numbers with your body or with a partner (figure 25.152).
2. Make different geometrical shapes (line, circle, asymmetrical, concave, etc.) with your body, with a partner, or with a small group.
3. Illustrate quantitative concepts, such as high/low, small/large, with your body, with a partner, or with a small group.
4. Perform movement sequences in sets of two or three.

Figure 25.152 Forming numbers and geometrical shapes.

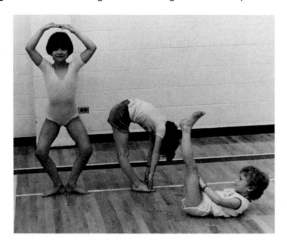

Science

1. Gravity: Select a variety of gymnastic stunts, such as the Headstand or balancing on one or two feet. Show how a wide base of support and a low center of gravity provide a stable base of support.

2. Third-class lever: This is sometimes called the human lever, since most physical skills involve third-class levers. Examples to study are the Handstand, Single Leg Balance, and Elbow Crawl.

3. Motion: Inertia (Newton's first law) can be illustrated by performing a series of forward rolls; run, change of speed and stop; and performing individual stunts, such as Seal Walk, Neckspring, and Handspring.

4. Motion: The Law of Acceleration (Newton's second law) can be explained by arranging partners in different sizes and heights, then have them perform Push War, Leg Pull, and Chinese Get-Up.

5. Motion: The Law of Action-Reaction (Newton's third law) can be illustrated by performing and analyzing the Heel Click, Cartwheel, and Round-off.

6. Force: Application of force. Select a series of stunts that illustrate the importance of applying muscular force sequentially and in the direction of the movement. Example stunts include Forward Roll, Cartwheel, and Heel Slap.

7. Force: Direction of force. Select a few agility stunts to illustrate the importance of directing the force of a movement through the center of the weight and in the direction intended. Example stunts are Jump Turn, Knee Jump, Push War, and Kip.

8. Force: Absorption of force. Select a series of stunts to illustrate how force should be dissipated through the widest surface and the greatest distance. Example movements are run, jump, land, and roll; Judo Roll; and the Triple Roll.

Figure 25.153 Integrating scientific areas of study with physical education.

a

b

Other Scientific Areas

Numerous other scientific principles and concepts can be illustrated through human movement activities. The following are a few examples of integrating scientific areas of study with physical education (figure 25.153a and b).

1. Matter: Design movement challenges to illustrate the movement of molecules, the solar system, and the expansion and contraction of gases. For example, divide the class into two even groups. When the groups are sitting on the floor, pose a challenge, such as "See if your group can design a series of

chapter 25

movements that illustrate how molecules move in solids, liquids, and gases." After a few minutes of planning, let each group perform its series of movements.

2. Biology: Pantomime activities to illustrate plant growth, animal movements and behavior, and human growth and development stages.

3. Physical science: Design movements and challenges to explain pendulum action, wind, temperature, magnetism, and sound. These examples provide a basic idea of the tremendous potential that physical education has to offer other subject areas. Integration however, is not a one-way process. If integration is to work, academic subject areas should also attempt, where possible, to fortify the principles, concepts, and values inherent in the content areas of physical education.

Selected References

Blatt, G. T., and Cunningham, J. (1981). *It's Your Move: Expressive Movement Activities for the Language Arts Class.* New York: Teachers College Press.

CAHPER. (1985). *Gymnastics: A Movement Approach.* Ottawa, Ontario: CAHPER Publications.

Graham, G., Holt-Hale, S. A., and Parker, M. (1987). *Children Moving.* Mountain View, CA: Mayfield Publishing Co.

Kirchner, G., Cunningham, C., and Warrell, E. (1978). *Introduction to Movement Education,* Second Edition. Dubuque, IA: Wm. C. Brown Publishers.

Ryser, O., and Brown, J. (1990). *A Manual for Tumbling and Apparatus Stunts.* Dubuque, IA: Wm. C. Brown Publishers.

Wall, J., and Murray, N. (1994). *Children and Movement,* Second Edition. Dubuque, IA: Wm. C. Brown Publishers.

Werner, P. H., and Burton, T. C. (1979). *Learning Through Movement: Teaching Cognitive Content Through Physical Activities.* St. Louis: C. V. Mosby Co.

Stunts and Manipulative Skills with Small Equipment

The material in this chapter provides two basic services. The first, and perhaps more common, is to teach children how to manipulate small objects with different parts of the body. The second is to provide a logical extension of the Movement Education approach, which was begun in the previous section. For example, small equipment, such as beanbags, individual ropes, and wands, is used to provide more difficult challenges involving one or more of Laban's elements of movement.

The material in this chapter has been organized to provide primary and intermediate teachers with sufficient information to teach a wide variety of manipulative skills, to expand a child's understanding of movement concepts, and to provide examples of how to use small equipment to teach academic concepts and skills ■

Teaching Procedures

The addition of small equipment activities to a gymnastic lesson presents several organizational and instructional problems. The following suggestions will assist you in incorporating small equipment into your gymnastic program.

Routine Procedures

Perhaps the most frustrating aspect of using small equipment is getting it out and putting it away in an orderly manner. One of the most successful and efficient ways of handling equipment is to have each type to be used in a lesson placed in boxes or containers near the instructional area. The teacher can then give instructions about who will be using what type of equipment and where their working areas will be (figure 26.1). When the equipment is not being used, it is returned to the appropriate container. Suggestions for carrying and placing such equipment as wands and hoops are given in the sections on each type of equipment.

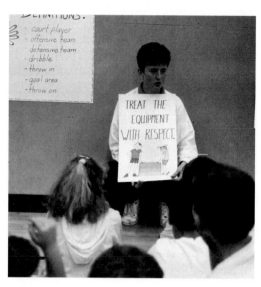

Figure 26.1 The teacher can give instructions about the equipment.

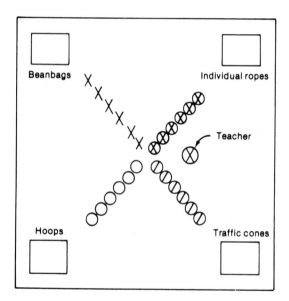

Using Small Equipment

It was stated in the previous chapter that small equipment should be used to provide additional challenges to movement skills. Since each class and grade level varies according to the time and equipment available and the students' background of skill, no standard application of this equipment can be recommended.

Activities and Developmental Levels

The nature and variety of small equipment makes it difficult to arrange skills in the exact order of difficulty. Table 26.1 provides a basic guideline that teachers can use when selecting and emphasizing small equipment activities.

Beanbag Activities

Beanbags are the most common type of small equipment and are available to virtually every classroom teacher. Beanbags should be at least six inches square for the activities suggested in this program. Cloth covers, rather than smooth plastic or nylon ones, are preferred for homemade beanbags.

Although beanbags traditionally have been used by primary teachers for simple games and manipulative activities, they have many applications at the intermediate level. The more familiar, structured beanbag activities are presented first to illustrate contemporary beanbag use in the gymnastic program. Following that is a section on how the beanbag can be used as an obstacle or focus point in developing movement concepts and skills.

Individual Activities

The beanbag can be used to increase the difficulty of many previously acquired stunts and tumbling skills, as well as with many new balance and stunt activities. The following examples illustrate the beanbag's versatility:

1. *Stunts and tumbling skills:*
   a. Wicket Walk (p. 436), beanbag behind neck
   b. Tightrope Walk (p. 452), beanbag on head
   c. Bouncing Ball (p. 438), beanbag on head
   d. Single-Knee Balance (p. 455), beanbag on head or arm
   e. Forward Roll (p. 426) and Side Roll (p. 425), beanbag under chin
   f. Knee Dip (p. 456), beanbag on head
   g. L-Support (p. 460), beanbag between knees

Table 26.1 Small Equipment Activities

Activity	Developmental Level			Page
	I	*II*	*III*	
Beanbag Activities				
Individual Activities	——▶	——▶		478
Partner Activities	——▶			480
Movement Skills	——▶	——▶	——▶	480
Rope-Jumping Activities				
Individual Activities	some ——▶	——▶	——▶	482
Partner Activities		——▶	——▶	489
Long Rope Activities	some ——▶	——▶	——▶	489
Movement Skills	——▶	——▶	——▶	491
Hoop Activities				
Individual Activities	——▶	——▶	——▶	492
Partner Activities	——▶	——▶	——▶	493
Movement Skills	——▶	——▶	——▶	493
Wand Activities				
Individual Activities	——▶	——▶	——▶	493
Partner Activities	——▶	——▶	——▶	493
Movement Skills	——▶	——▶	——▶	496
Parachute Activities				
Exercises	——▶	——▶	——▶	497
Games	——▶	——▶	——▶	498
Dances	——▶	——▶	——▶	498
Movement Skills	——▶	——▶	——▶	498
Indian Clubs, Milk Cartons and Traffic Cones	——▶	——▶	——▶	*499*
Juggling Activities		——▶	——▶	*500*

2. *Throwing and catching skills:* The wide surface and lack of rebound property make the beanbag a valuable tool in helping young children learn how to throw and catch. Following are a few examples of how primary teachers can use the beanbag to develop hand-eye coordination:

   a. Toss the beanbag into the air and catch it with both hands, with the left hand, then with the right.
   b. Toss the beanbag into the air, change direction or perform a hand movement (clap hands, touch the floor), and then catch the beanbag.
   c. Place targets on the floor (hoops, milk cartons) and throw the beanbag into the target. Change throwing skill and distance.
   d. Move, throw, and catch. Use a variety of locomotor skills (running, skipping, and so on) and throw and catch beanbags, moving around the instructional area.

3. *Balance the beanbag on different parts of the body* (figure 26.2): Designate specific parts of the body—head, elbow, and so on. Change body position and

Figure 26.2 Balance the beanbag on your head.

stunts and manipulative skills with small equipment

Figure 26.3 Throw and catch the beanbag.

Figure 26.4 Balance on one part of the body on the beanbag.

continue. For example, "Put the beanbag on your back and balance on one foot."

4. *Move the beanbag with different parts of the body:* Ask the class to propel the beanbags with their knees and catch them; then designate other parts of the body such as the head, foot, elbow, and shoulder.

Partner Activities

Many of the previous individual skills can be performed with two performers:

1. *Throwing and catching:*
   a. Throw the beanbag back and forth, changing the distance and the type, position, and angle of throw to create variable practices (figure 26.3).
   b. Throw and catch with two beanbags.
   c. Throw and catch with one or both performers on the move.

2. *Pass and catch the beanbag with different parts of the body:* Propel it with the feet and catch it with the hands or feet. Propel it with the head and catch it with the stomach or another part of the body.

Applying Movement Skills

The individual and partner activities previously described indicate the value and potential of beanbag activities in developing throwing, catching, balancing, and agility skills. If children have been taught through the problem-solving method and understand movement concepts and skills, the next step is to use beanbag activities in a much more creative and challenging way. The following examples illustrate how the beanbag can be used as an obstacle to balance on or with and as an object to maneuver on or over. By posing tasks or challenges using movement skills, children explore and discover the various ways their bodies or body parts can manipulate and control small obstacles.

Although the same challenge can be presented to primary and intermediate children, the movement response should be different. As children progress through the grades, they acquire more skill and movement understanding, which is revealed in the complexity and quality of their movement patterns. Following are examples of the types of questions or instructions that should be given. Each teacher, however, should present challenges according to her class's gymnastic background and receptiveness to this exploratory approach.

1. *Balance and transfer of weight:*
   a. "How many different parts of your body can you balance the beanbag on?"
   b. "Place the beanbag on the floor. Can you balance with one part of your body on the beanbag (figure 26.4)?"
   c. "Place the beanbag on your seat and see how many ways you can balance on three different parts of your body.
   d. "Place a beanbag on the floor. How many different ways can you balance over the beanbag (figure 26.5)?"
   e. "How many different ways can you cross the beanbag?"

2. *Direction and speed:* Scatter beanbags around the floor area and pose these challenge activities illustrating how the beanbag acts as an obstacle or focus point in the development of directional movements and the quality of speed.
   a. "Move around as many beanbags as possible, but do not jump over any."
   b. "Run in any direction and when you come to a beanbag, run completely around it; then move to another beanbag."

Figure 26.5 *"How many different ways can you balance over the beanbag?"*

Figure 26.6 Jump over a beanbag, change directions, and jump over another beanbag.

Figure 26.7 Follow your partner.

a. Place the beanbag on your head.

b. One child leads.

c. The other child must match her movements.

   c. "Move in any direction and, as you approach a beanbag, jump over it, land, and then change direction to find another beanbag (figure 26.6)."
   d. "Can you run in different directions, showing a change of speed every time you jump over a beanbag?"
   e. "Run and jump over a beanbag."

3. *Shapes*
   a. "Can you make a stretched shape, with the beanbag on the highest part of your body?"
   b. "See if you can keep the beanbag on one part of your body while you try to make two different curled shapes."

4. *Relationships:* Each partner has a beanbag.
   a. "Place the beanbags on the floor and make up a matching sequence that shows a change of direction and a change of speed."

   b. "Keep the beanbag between your feet and make up a matching sequence that includes moving forward, backward, and sideways."
   c. "Place the beanbags on your head. One child leads and the other must match her movements (figure 26.7)."

Rope-Jumping Activities

Children perform three basic types of rope-jumping activities in the primary and intermediate grades (figure 26.8). One is rope jumping that involves light, graceful leaps over a rope turned by an individual or with a partner. The second is long rope jumping, which involves jumping over a long rope turned by two performers. Finally, ropes are used in a variety of ways to enhance movement concepts and skills.

   Children of all ages enjoy performing individual rope-jumping skills with or without musical accompaniment. In

stunts and manipulative skills with small equipment

Figure 26.8 Rope jumping.

Figure 26.9 Having the correct length of rope is important for the child to jump properly.

Figure 26.10 Correct jumping form.

the primary grades, the level of interest or skill varies little between boys and girls. For many years, the trend has been for girls to continue this activity through the intermediate grades and for boys to shift their interests to other types of activities. However, recent physical fitness programs, such as "Jump Rope for Heart," have created a very positive change in boys' attitudes toward all types of rope-jumping activities. Today this activity is enjoyed equally by boys and girls and with virtually no difference in skill level.

Individual Activities

Several kinds and thicknesses of rope can be used for individual rope jumping. A 3/8-inch sash cord is probably the best; however, any rope, sash or plastic, up to 1/2-inch thick is acceptable. It is equally important to have the proper length of rope for each child. To determine the correct length, have the child stand in the center of the rope; it should extend from armpit to armpit (figure 26.9). An incorrect length adversely affects performance.

The correct rope-jumping form is to hold the ends of the rope loosely in the fingers, with the thumbs placed on top of the rope and pointing to the sides. The elbows are held close to the sides, with the forearms and hands pointing slightly forward and away from the body (figure 26.10). To start the rope turning, swing the arms and shoulders in a circular motion; once the rope begins to follow the circular motion, all further action should be initiated from the wrists and fingers. The jumping action should be a slight push off the toes, just high enough to allow the rope to pass under the feet.

The following rope-jumping skills are listed in approximate order of difficulty. It is helpful to begin each new step without a rope. Once the child can execute the foot movements, let him try with a rope. At this stage, a musical background helps the child keep up a steady rhythm. Any folk-dance record, with a 4/4 rhythm, such as "Shoo Fly" or "Pop Goes the Weasel," works very well. All popular tunes with a similar beat work as well and, in fact, are enjoyed more than folk-dance records by upper elementary school children.

Many of the basic steps shown in figures 26.11 to 26.22 can be performed in slow or fast time and with the rope turned forward or backward. With slow rhythm, the performer jumps over the rope, takes a rebound jump in place as the rope passes overhead, and then performs the original step or shifts to a new movement. The pattern is jump-rebound-jump. With slow musical accompaniment, the performer jumps over the rope on every other beat. With a fast rhythm, the rope is turned twice as fast, so the performer executes a step only as the rope passes under her feet. With fast musical accompaniment, the performer jumps over the rope on every beat.

Once the children have learned two or more basic steps, they can begin to create many interesting and enjoyable routines. A few suggestions follow; however, each child should have an opportunity to develop his own routine.

1. Combine a change of speed with the alternate step.
2. Make up a sequence involving three different steps.
3. Make up a sequence involving a hop, an alternate step, and a change of direction.
4. Perform three different steps in a cross-arm position.
5. Move in different directions, using hopping, jumping, and rocking-step skills.
6. Make up a sequence, with the rope turning backward.

chapter 26

Figure 26.11 Two-foot basic. The two-foot basic step includes two jumps for each complete turn of the rope. Pull the rope around and jump over it, and take a second "rebound" jump as the rope passes backward and upward.

a. Jump.   b. Rebound.   c. Jump.

Figure 26.12 Skier. A double-foot jump represents the leg actions of a skier. (a) Stand with feet together and straddling a line. (b) Use a two-foot basic action, jump over rope, and land about one and one-half feet on the other side of the line. (c) Take a rebound jump, then jump and shift both feet back to the other side of the line. Once the skill is learned, try shifting feet forward and backward.

a   b   c

stunts and manipulative skills with small equipment

Figure 26.13 Alternate step. Jump over rope with the right foot (jump), hop on same foot (rebound), jump over rope with left foot (jump), and hop on the same foot (rebound). Pass the rope overhead.

a. Jump right. b. Rebound right. c. Jump left. d. Rebound left.

Figure 26.14 Swing step. This is basically the same as the alternate step, except swing the "free leg" forward, backward, or to the side during the rebound step.

a. Jump. b. Rebound. c. Jump.

Figure 26.15 Heel toe. This is a combination of the "heel to heel" and "toe to toe" steps. Begin by standing on left foot, then jump on left foot, simultaneously placing heel of right foot forward (a). Take a rebound jump (b) on the left foot. Jump and land on left foot and place right toe to back of left heel (c). Jump and land on right foot and place heel of left foot forward (d). Continue pattern.

a. Jump and heel.　　b. Rebound.　　c. Jump and toe.　　d. Jump and heel.

Figure 26.16 Can can. Stand on the left foot. Jump on left foot and bring right knee up, pointing toe down (a). Rebound on left foot (b). Jump on left and kick right leg as high as you can (c). Jump on right foot and bring left knee up (d). Continue pattern.

a. Jump and knee.　　b. Rebound left.　　c. Jump and kick.　　d. Rebound right.

Figure 26.17 One-foot hop. Perform the one-foot hop with each turn of the rope or with a rebound step after each jump over the rope. However, continue hopping on one foot for several rotations of the rope before transferring to hopping on the opposite foot.

a. Hop left.

b. Rebound left.

Figure 26.18 Rocker. When performing the rocker step, one leg is always forward and the weight shifts from the back to the front, or lead, foot. As the rope passes under the front foot, transfer the weight forward, allowing the back foot to raise and the rope to pass under it. After the rope passes under the back foot and begins its upward and forward arch, "rock" back, transferring the weight to the back foot.

a. Pass rope under front foot.

b. Rock forward.

c. Pass rope under back foot.

d. Rock backward.

chapter 26

Figure 26.19 Spread legs. Begin the spread-legs step in a front stride position, with the weight evenly distributed on both feet. Pull the rope around, jump, and as it passes under change the position of the feet. Continue pattern.

a. Begin in a stride position. b. Jump and change. c. Land in a stride position.

Figure 26.20 Crossed legs. Begin the cross-leg step with the right leg crossed in front of the left leg and the weight evenly distributed on both feet. Pull the rope around, jump, and as it passes under cross the left leg over the right. Continue the pattern, alternating the front leg position.

a. Begin in a cross-legged position. b. Jump and cross. c. Cross left leg over right.

stunts and manipulative skills with small equipment

Figure.1 Crossed arms. Crossing arms should take place during an ongoing rope-jumping movement. As the rope begins its forward and downward movement, cross the left arm over the right and bring the right hand up and under the left armpit. Make the next jump in this position. Continue in the crossed-arm position or alternate the crossed-arm position on each turn of the rope.

a. From a regular rope-skipping position . . .   b. . . . to cross left over right . . .   c. . . . right hand up under left armpit.

Figure 26.22 Pepper. The pepper step is two full turns of the rope while the performer's feet are off the ground.

a. Jump.   b. Turn—turn.   c. Jump.

chapter 26

Figure 26.23 Begin with a two-foot basic step.

Figure 26.24 Partner enters front.

Figure 26.25 One partner moves in.

Partner Activities

Children can perform several enjoyable partner activities with an individual rope. Many variations and routines can be developed from the following basic starting positions. One partner begins with a two-foot basic step. As the rope comes forward and down, the outside partner enters and places his hands on his partner's waist (figures 26.23 and 26.24). Some variations follow:

1. Partners perform mirror images, hopping, jumping, or other basic rope-jumping steps.
2. Outside partner turns his back to his partner and they continue jumping.
3. Outside partner keeps the same jumping cadence as his partner but begins to make a quarter or a half turn, then jumps back to his original position.

Partners stand facing each other with the rope held in the same hand. Some variations follow:

1. One partner moves in, then out (figure 26.25).
2. One partner moves in, followed by her partner.
3. When both are inside, they make up a sequence of matching steps.

Long Rope-Jumping Activities

Long rope jumping is performed with one or more children jumping over a rope turned by two other children. The rope can be turned two different ways for jumping activities. Teach the Front Door first, then introduce the Back Door skill

Figure 26.26 Front door. The children turn the rope toward the jumper (clockwise), and the jumper waits until the rope is moving away from her before she runs in. Back door: The turners turn the rope away from the jumper (counter-clockwise), and the jumper waits until the rope has passed its highest peak and is moving downward before she runs in.

(figure 26.26). To assist in teaching both types of jumping skills, use the suggested list of rope-jumping rhymes in the next section.

The following progression of rope-jumping activities can be performed by entering through either the front or back door.

1. Run under the rope.
2. Run in, jump once, run out.
3. Run in, jump several times, run out.

Figure 26.27 Arms over partner's shoulders.

4. Run in, jump once on one foot, run out.

5. Run in, jump several times on one foot, run out.

6. Run in, jump making quarter, half, three-quarter, or full turns with each jump, run out.

7. Run in, jump on alternate feet, run out.

8. Run in, touch the floor with the hands on every other jump, run out.

9. Run in, squat (on all fours), jump in this position, run out.

10. Run in, jump up and touch toes, land, run out.

11. Run in, turners gradually increase speed to "hot pepper," slow down, run out.

12. Run in, turners gradually raise rope off the ground ("high water").

13. Run in with a ball, bounce the ball several times, run out.

14. Repeat these skills with a partner.

15. Place arm over partner's shoulder, run in, jump several times, run out (figure 26.27).

16. With partner, run in, stand back to back, jump several times, run out.

17. With partner, run in, face partner, hold partner's right leg, jump several times, run out.

18. Follow the leader with four or five players and one chosen to be the leader. The leader runs in and performs any skill or stunt, then runs out. Each player follows and repeats the leader's stunt.

Rope-Jumping Rhymes

Rope-jumping rhymes, like singing games, are centuries old and belong to people of many nations. The first four rhymes are perhaps the most popular in North America. Each region may also have slight variations. Encourage children to use their own version.

Down by the Meadow

Down by the meadow where the green grass grows,
There sits (call the name of jumper) sweet as a rose.
She sang, she sang, she sang, she sang so sweet,
And along came (jumper's sweetheart's name), and
Kissed her on the cheek.
How many kisses did she get?
1, 2, 3, 4, etc.
(Child keeps jumping until she misses.)

Teddy Bear, Teddy Bear

Teddy Bear, Teddy Bear, turn around.
Teddy Bear, Teddy Bear, touch the ground.
Teddy Bear, Teddy Bear, shine your shoes.
Teddy Bear, Teddy Bear, that will do.
Teddy Bear, Teddy Bear, go upstairs.
Teddy Bear, Teddy Bear, say your prayers.
Teddy Bear, Teddy Bear, turn out the light.
Teddy Bear, Teddy Bear, say good night.
Teddy Bear, hop on one foot, one foot.
Teddy Bear, hop on two feet, two feet.
Teddy Bear, hop on three feet, three feet.
Teddy Bear, hop right out.

Johnny on the Ocean

Johnny on the ocean,
Johnny on the sea,
Johnny broke a bottle,
And blamed it on me.
I told ma,
Ma told pa.
Johnny got a whipping
And a ha! ha! ha!
How many whippings did he get?
1, 2, 3, etc. (Child keeps jumping until she misses.)

I'm a Little Dutch Girl

Charlie Chaplin went to France
To teach the pretty girls
The hula dance.
First on the heel,
Then the toe,
Do the splits,
And around you go.
Salute to the Captain,
Curtsey the Queen,
Touch the bottom of the submarine.

All in Together

All in together, this fine weather,
January, February, March, etc.
(Jumper runs in on the month of his birthday.)
All out together, this fine weather,
Jaunary, February, March, etc.
(Jumper runs out on the month of his birthday.)

I Love Coffee

I love coffee, I love tea, I love (name).
I dislike coffee, I dislike tea, I dislike (name).
So go away from me.
(Child who is jumping calls the name of another child, who comes in, then goes out.)

Mabel, Mabel

Mabel, Mabel, set the table,
Don't forget the salt, vinegar, pepper. . . .
(Turners turn "pepper" on the last word.)

Fudge, Fudge

Fudge, Fudge, tell the judge,
Mama's got a newborn baby.
Wrap it up in tissue paper,
Send it down the elevator,
Elevator one, splits . . . elevator two . . . splits, (and so
on until the jumper misses. Jumper performs the splits on
the word "splits.")

Apple, Apple

Apple, Apple, up in the tree,
Tell me who my lover shall be,
A, B, C, D, E, etc. (Jump to each letter until the jumper
reaches his sweetheart's first initial.)

Mama, Mama

Mama, Mama, I am sick,
Send for the doctor, quick, quick, quick.
Mama, Mama, turn around,
Mama, Mama, touch the ground.
Mama, Mama, are you through?
Mama, Mama, spell your name.
(Child performs actions indicated in the verse.)

Playground Ideas with Long Ropes

Long ropes have traditionally been used for jumping activities. The following examples illustrate other enjoyable uses of one or two long ropes:

1. *Jumping over one rope:* Two performers hold a long
   rope approximately two feet off the ground (vary the
   height according to the ability of the group).
   Activities may include:
   a. High jumping (figure 26.28)
   b. Jumping and making shapes in the air
   c. Jumping and turning in the air
   d. Crossing the rope with a cartwheel movement
      (figure 26.29)
   e. Follow-the-leader activities
2. *Jumping over two ropes:* Two performers hold two
   ropes about two feet off the ground. Repeat the same
   skills (figure 26.30). Then have the rope holders hold
   one rope low and the other high; repeat the skills.

These few examples should provide the teacher with a starting point. The creative teacher and class will come up with other ideas, such as jumping over one rope, then crawling under the other or hopping, jumping, or performing another locomotor movement from one end to the other.

Applying Movement Skills

Several basic rope-jumping skills that can be performed by an individual or with a partner have been described. A

Figure 26.28 High jumping.

Figure 26.29 Crossing with a cartwheel.

Figure 26.30 Jumping over two ropes.

rope can also be used in many other interesting and challenging ways. For example, it can become an obstacle to manipulate, as when tying a knot using only the feet (figure 26.31). It can also become an obstacle to maneuver around or over, such as finding many ways of crossing a rope.

It is possible to apply the problem-solving method and the movement skills described in the previous chapter to individual rope activities. The rope, thus, becomes a means of further challenging the physical and creative abilities of the child. The

Figure 26.31 Tie a knot with your feet.

Figure 26.32 "How many ways can you cross the rope?"

Figure 26.33 Hula hooping.

Figure 26.34 Jump over it.

four movement concepts and the various movement skills become the framework for developing a series of tasks or challenges. Following are some examples:

1. *Balance or weight bearing:* "See if you can hold the rope with both hands and balance on both knees and one elbow." This is a manipulating activity.

2. *Shapes:* "Can you make a twisted shape with your rope?" This is another manipulating activity.

3. *Direction:* "Place the rope on the floor in any pattern you like and make up a sequence that involves three changes in direction (figure 26.32)." This is a maneuvering activity.

4. *Force and rolling:* "Place the rope on the floor, then move a few steps away from it. See if you can run, leap over the rope, land, and roll."

5. *Relationships and force:* "With your partner and one rope, make up a sequence that has three different pulling actions."

6. *Relationships and shapes:* "Can you make up a sequence of matching shapes with your partner? You may use one or two ropes any way you like."

Hoop Activities

The introduction of hoop activities adds challenge and variety to any gymnastic program. Hoops are inexpensive, easily stored, and, most important, a very versatile piece of equipment. It is strongly recommended that a class set, plus six to eight extra hoops, be purchased. A mixture of the standard 42-inch hoops and the smaller 36-inch hoops is adequate for any elementary grade.

Since hoops can be extremely noisy, establish a strict routine for getting them out of the equipment room and carrying them to instructional areas. Require the children to place their hoops on the floor gently and to sit inside them while listening to instructions.

A few of the more common activities will be presented, followed by several suggestions for applying movement skills to hoop activities. The following hoop individual and partner activities can be presented as a direct challenge. However, variations occur in the way the children attempt to perform the skills.

Individual Activities

1. Hula Hooping: This skill is normally performed around the waist; however, other areas of the body, such as the arm, leg, wrist, and ankles, can also be used (figure 26.33).

2. Hula Jumping: The hoop can be used as a jumping rope. This is an effective rope jumping substitute, particularly for primary children.

3. Place the hoop on the floor, then jump over it (figure 26.34), or jump across it.

chapter 26

Figure 26.35 Jump over and through.

Figure 26.36 Balance over your hoop.

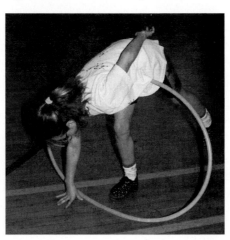

Figure 26.37 Make up a sequence, with one holding.

4. Roll the hoop with a reverse spin and jump over it as it returns.

5. Spin the hoop. While it is spinning, try to run around it or jump over it before it falls.

6. Place the hoop on the floor. Walk around the edge of the hoop or run and jump into the center and then out.

Partner Activities

1. Play catch with one or two hoops.

2. Target throwing with partner: One partner throws the hoop at a designated part of his partner, such as his arm, right leg, or head. Vary the distance according to the level of skill.

3. One partner holds the hoop in a horizontal position while the other tries to run and jump over it or crawl under it or through it (figure 26.35).

4. One partner rolls the hoop while the other partner attempts to crawl through it.

Applying Movement Skills

The hoop has become one of the most popular pieces of small equipment for use with movement skills. The following challenges illustrate the scope and versatility of this piece of equipment.

1. *Balance or weight bearing* (figure 26.36): "Can you balance over the hoop?" "Can you balance with three parts on the hoop?" "See if you can balance on four parts and hold the hoop off the ground." "On how many different parts of your body can you balance the hoop?"

2. *Shapes and flow:* "Make up a sequence of three different shapes while holding your hoop."

3. *Rolling and flow:* "Can you roll while holding onto your hoop?"

4. *Direction:* "Place four hoops on the floor in any pattern you wish, then make up a sequence that shows four changes in direction." After the sequence is developed, "Now add a change of speed or level to your sequence."

5. *Relationships and shapes* (figure 26.37): "Make up a sequence with your partner in which one partner holds the hoop and the other moves from shape to shape."

Wand Activities

Initially, a lack of commercial equipment in many elementary schools forced teachers to improvise with what was available or to make their own equipment. The wand is an example of the latter. Discarded broom handles or ¾-inch to 1½-inch doweling cut into 36-inch or 42-inch lengths are adequate for elementary school children. Wands present the same noise problem as hoops, so establish a similar handling procedure as suggested for hoops.

Numerous structured stunts can be performed with a wand. In addition, a wide variety of movement tasks or challenges can be designed to use the wand in a manipulative way or as an obstacle to maneuver around or over. The following activities should begin in the second or third grade. However, movement challenges using the wand can begin in the first grade.

Individual and Partner Activities

The stunts in figures 26.38 to 26.46 are some of the many individual and partner activities children can perform with wands.

Figure 26.38 Finger balance. Hold wand with one hand, then place the index finger of the opposite hand under the end of the wand. Release grip and balance the wand on the end of the finger. After practice, try balancing wand while walking forward and backward and then running.

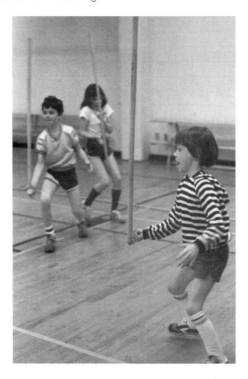

Figure 26.40 Back touch. Begin with the legs straight and the feet approximately shoulder-width apart. Grasp the wand close to one end. Arch back, place the end of the wand on the mat, and continue arching back and down.

Figure 26.39 Foot balance. Place wand near the big toe, raise the foot off the floor, release grip, and try to balance the wand on the foot.

Figure 26.41 Double foot balance. Begin in a back-lying position, hold the wand above the head and place the feet under the wand. Release hands and extend the legs upward, keeping the wand balanced across the feet.

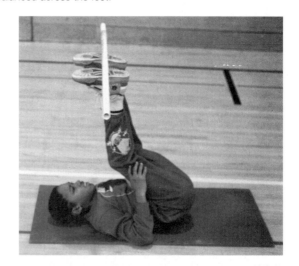

chapter 26

Figure 26.42 Jump through stick. Stand with the knees partially bent and the feet about twelve inches apart. Hold the wand with the palms face down and the arms spread apart and the fingers grasping it. While keeping the arms straight, jump up and over the wand, landing in front, with the knees slightly bent.

Figure 26.43 Thread the needle. Begin in a back-lying position, knees bent, and hold the wand in front of the body. Without losing balance or touching the wand, bend the knees, pass the feet up and under the wand, and return to the original position.

Figure 26.44 Twist away. Partners stand with their feet about shoulder-width apart. They grasp the wand with palms facing down. Each partner attempts to twist to her right. As soon as one partner releases her grip, the other is declared the winner.

Figure 26.45 Floor touch. Partners sit on the floor in a cross-legged position. They grasp the wand, with their palms facing down and their arms partially flexed. The wand must be parallel to the floor. On a signal from the teacher, each child tries to touch the wand to the floor on her right side. Change sides after each contest.

Figure 26.46 Dishrag. This is similar to Wring the Dishrag. Both partners must maintain their grips throughout the movement.

Figure 26.47 Matching shapes.

Figure 26.48 Circle sitting.

Figure 26.49 Fruit basket. Children begin with feet about shoulder-width apart, arms downward, and hands grasping parachute with an overhand grip.

Applying Movement Skills

The wand can be as useful as a hoop or rope in developing movement concepts and skills. The following examples illustrate how balance, levels, and relationships can be further enhanced by a wand:

1. *Balance or weight bearing:* If the class has had prior experience with a wand, try these: "See how many different parts of your body you can balance the wand on." "Is it possible to balance the wand on your elbow (knee, stomach, and so on)?"

2. *Transfer of weight and flow:* "Can you hold the wand with both hands and roll along the floor?" "Place the wand on the floor and see how many ways you can cross it using your hands and feet."

3. *Levels and shapes:* "See if you can show me three stretched shapes—one low, one halfway up, and a high stretch—while holding a wand with both hands." "Can you make a twisted shape over your wand? Now under your wand?"

4. *Relationships:* Each partner has a wand. "Make up a sequence of matching (or contrasting) shapes with your partner (figure 26.47)."

Parachute Activities

Parachute activities have become an integral part of many elementary physical education programs. Children from grades two through six enjoy performing a variety of stunts, games, and rhythmic activities while holding a parachute and moving in a variety of ways. The following sections outline the basic teaching procedures and illustrate how parachute

activities can contribute to fitness, skill development, and cooperative behavior. This type of activity is one of the most "fun" group experiences for all children—from the highly skilled to the severely disabled.

Circle Sitting

During the first lesson, have the children sit in a circle, with each child about two feet from the edge (skirt) of the parachute (canopy) (figure 26.48). Gradually introduce the following positions and turns:

1. *Overhand grip:* Grip the edge of the parachute with the palms facing down.

2. *Underhand grip:* Grip the edge of the parachute with the palms facing up.

3. *Mixed grip:* Grip the edge of the parachute with the palm of one hand facing up and the palm of the opposite hand facing down.

4. *Fruit basket:* This is a resting position. Begin with feet about shoulder-width apart, arms downward, and hands grasping the parachute with an overhand grip (figure 26.49). To coordinate all future group movements, begin with a preparatory signal, such as "ready," then a command such as "go" or "begin."

5. *Making waves:* Begin in the fruit basket position. All children begin to gently shake the parachute

Figure 26.50 Making waves.

Figure 26.51 Umbrella.

Figure 26.52 Mushroom.

(small waves) up and down (figure 26.50). An increase in arm movements and speed increases the wave action. Other variations, such as odd numbers moving up while even numbers move down, or half the class up and the other half down, produce different wave effects.

6. *Umbrella:* Begin in the fruit basket position. On command, lift the chute overhead (figure 26.51). A slow count of 1, 2, 3 is normally needed to lift the chute into an umbrella position.

7. *Mushroom:* Begin in the fruit basket position. On signal, lift the chute to an umbrella position, then quickly take one step in and pull the chute down, holding the edge firmly to the floor (figure 26.52).

Exercise Activities

The ultimate value of the following exercises is derived when the child is required to hold the chute taut and stretch, pull, or twist with an "overload" effort. Repetitions within exercises should be adjusted to the number that is appropriate for each child.

Side Stretcher

All students hold the chute taut with the left hand. The left knee is on the floor, and the right leg extends sideways, with the right hand resting on the right leg. On command, the chute is pulled toward the right side. Repeat to opposite leg.

Row the Boat

All children sit with legs extended under the chute. The canopy is held with an overhand grip, arms bent, and chute touching the chest. On command, bend forward, extend arms, and touch hands to toes. Return to an upright position. Continue rowing action. Some variations follow:

1. Place right arm backward and repeat exercise.
2. Cross arm in front of chest and repeat exercise.

Curl-Ups

Begin with the body under the parachute in a curl-up position. In this position, the chute is held with an overhand grip and held taut under the chin. Hold this grip and sit up to an upright position, then return to starting position.

Push-Ups

Children first make a mushroom, keeping their hands and knees on the edge of the chute. Extend legs backward, perform one or more push-ups, then return to a starting position.

Chest Raiser

Children begin in a front lying position, facing the parachute, arms extended forward, and grasping chute with an overhand grip. Have all move backward until the chute is taut. On signal, raise arm upward, hold for a few seconds, then return to starting position. Some variations follow:

1. Raise arms and legs at the same time.
2. Hold chute with one hand and repeat exercise.
3. Begin lying on your side with a mixed grip and repeat exercise.

V-Sit

Children begin in a back lying position, top of head facing the chute, and palms facing upward, grasping the chute. Keep the chute taut, then raise chest and straighten legs to a V-sit position. Return to starting position.

stunts and manipulative skills with small equipment

Figure 26.53 Circus tent. From an umbrella position, all move under, turn around, kneel down, and hold chute to floor, then scramble out before chute falls on them.

Game Activities

Number Exchange

Children are numbered from one to five around the circle. When the parachute is in the umbrella position, the leader calls one or two numbers. Players with these numbers exchange positions.

Snatch Club

Divide class into two groups, then number each player in each group. Place a pin in the middle of the circle. When the chute is in an umbrella position, call a number. Each player then tries to snatch the club and return to his position before the other tags him.

Circus Tent

From an umbrella position, all move under, turn around, kneel down, and hold the chute to the floor; then they scramble out before the chute falls on them (figure 26.53).

Parachute Golf

Place five or six balls on the chute. All players try to get the balls to drop through the holes (figure 26.54).

Dance Activities

The parachute is extremely useful in teaching a variety of dance activities (figure 26.55). All locomotor steps can be taught to children while they are holding the chute in the fruit basket, umbrella, or other position. Changing directions, such as forward, sideways, and backward, as well as position exchanges can also be done while performing movements with the parachute. Rhythmic activities described in chapter 28 can be performed with the parachute. Marches, Dixieland tunes, and many current hits can be used as

Figure 26.54 Parachute golf. Place five or six balls on the chute. All players try to get the balls to drop through the hole.

Variations:
1. On and Off: Designate two teams on each half of the circle. Each team has three balls (three white and three red balls). On signal, each team tries to get opponents' balls off the chute.
2. Repeat game, but try to get your own balls through the hole first. If a ball rolls over outer edge, it is placed back on the chute.

Figure 26.55 Dance with the parachute.

musical accompaniments for these rhythmic activities. Several folk dances, such as Pop Goes the Weasel, Seven Jumps, and Cshebogar, can also be performed with modification while holding the parachute.

Applying Movement Skills

Several movement skills, creative games, and inventive rhythmic sequences can be performed with a parachute. The following suggested challenges provide a basic starting point:

Movement Skills

1. "Hold the chute in the fruit basket position and make a stretched, curled, and twisted shape." Hold in the same position and balance on two parts, three parts, one knee and one elbow, and so on.

2. Hold chute with one hand and change direction and level.

Creative Games

Divide the class into four working groups. Each group invents a game, then teaches the whole class.

1. "Design a game that starts with the parachute in the fruit basket position and uses one ball and four beanbags."
2. "Can you make up a game for the class that uses the parachute, one ball, and four bowling pins?"

Rhythmic Skills

1. Use same approach as in creative games.
2. "Make up a sequence that has a run, hop, and jump while holding onto the parachute."
3. "Can you design a routine that has a skip, slide, change in direction, and change in level?"

Indian Club, Milk Carton, and Traffic Cone Activities

The success of any gymnastic program is very closely related to the number and variety of small equipment available to each child. Since most elementary schools lack sets of the previously described equipment, the following "bits and pieces" can be useful. Discarded bowling pins from local bowling alleys make excellent substitutes for Indian clubs. Plastic-coated milk cartons are also readily available. Traffic cones, which are used extensively in the games program as field markers and goals, are also a valuable addition to the gymnastic program.

These types of small equipment are basically used as obstacles to maneuver around or over. They are also used in combination with other small equipment, such as individual ropes, hoops, and wands, to provide more complex and creative challenges. Following are examples of their use:

1. *Direction, speed, and force:* Scatter all available Indian clubs, milk cartons, and traffic cones around the floor area. The following challenges can be used to develop directional movements and a change of speed:
   a. "Run in different directions around the equipment."
   b. "Repeat with a change in speed."
   c. "Run sideways, diagonally, and backward around the equipment."
   d. "Run, jump over any piece of equipment, land, move to a new piece of equipment, and repeat (figure 26.56)."
   e. "Repeat with a land and roll."

Figure 26.56   Run and jump over a cone, then over a hoop.

Figure 26.57   Make shapes over your equipment.

2. *Shape and balance:*
   a. "How many ways can you balance over your equipment?"
   b. "Can you balance with one part of your body on the equipment and one part on the floor?"
   c. "Make three different shapes over your equipment (figure 26.57)."
   d. "Run, jump, and make a shape over your equipment."
3. *Relationships:* Each partner has one piece of equipment.
   a. "Make three matching shapes over your equipment.
   b. "Develop a matching sequence that includes a balance, a shape, and a change of direction (figure 26.58)."

stunts and manipulative skills with small equipment

Figure 26.58 Develop a matching sequence.

a. Make up a sequence that includes balance, . . .

b. . . . a shape, and . . .

c. . . . a change of direction.

Juggling Activities

Juggling with scarves, bags, balls, and clubs has become another very popular activity within the elementary physical education program. Boys and girls can learn this activity within a short period of time and can become equally adept at it. It is an excellent hand-eye coordination skill, it allows every child to be active, and it is inexpensive. Perhaps its real value lies in its noncompetitive and life-long recreational use. Once the basic cascade, or figure eight, pattern is learned, a child's juggling repertoire can be expanded to include different throwing items and an unlimited number of exciting and challenging routines.

When introducing a juggling program, make sure every child has three items to juggle (figure 26.59). Light scarves are extremely useful in demonstrating the basic cascade pattern. Juggling bags, which are easier to use than balls, may be purchased commercially or made by children. Balls of various sizes and weights are the third choice when teaching basic juggling. Once children have acquired the basic juggling skill, they will seek more challenging routines using disks, clubs, or other objects.

The basic juggling skill is performed in a figure eight pattern in an area roughly between the waist and top of the head (figure 26.60). Once proficiency has been acquired in this basic skill, a performer may throw high, to the side, or under one leg, but the basic figure eight movement is always maintained. Follow the next four steps to learn how to juggle with three bags. Master each step before moving on to the next one.

Step 1: One-bag throw. Hold the bag with the fingertips and thumb of your dominant hand (figure 26.61a). Scoop right hand toward the left and release bag at about the middle of your body. Let the bag rise, then catch it as it descends down the left side

Figure 26.59 Juggling.

Figure 26.60 Figure eight pattern.

chapter 26

Figure 26.61 Step 1: one-bag throwing.

a

b

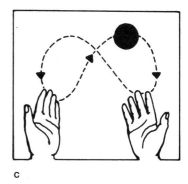c

Figure 26.62 Step 2: hold and throw.

a

b

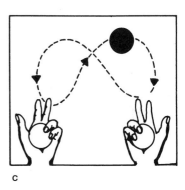c

Figure 26.63 Step 3: exchange two bags.

a

b

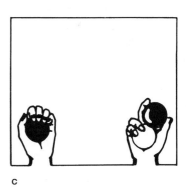c

(figure 26.61b). Scoop left hand toward the middle and throw the bag upward toward the right side (figure 26.61c). Continue practicing this figure eight pattern until it is a smooth wrist and fingerlike action.

Step 2: Hold and throw. Pick up two bags and hold them on the heels of your hands. Pick up the third bag and hold it with fingertips and thumb (figure 26.62a). Throw the third bag from hand to hand in the figure eight pattern (figures 26.62b and 26.62c).

Step 3: Exchange two bags. Hold two bags in your dominant hand and one in the other hand. Throw the bag from the fingertips of your dominant hand and call "1" (figure 26.63a). When the bag reaches its highest point, call "2," then scoop the bag from your less dominant hand upward and under the other bag (figure 26.63b). The bag coming to the less dominant hand should land on the palm. The bag coming to the dominant hand should be caught with the fingertips and thumb (figure 26.63c).

stunts and manipulative skills with small equipment

Figure 26.64 Step 4: three-bag juggling.

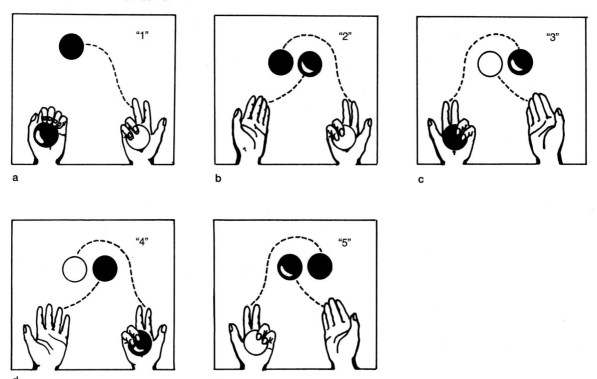

Step 4: Three-bag juggling. Throw the bag from your dominant hand and call "1" (figure 26.64a). When bag 1 peaks, scoop the bag from the less dominant hand and call "2" (figure 26.64b). When bag 2 peaks, scoop the bag from your dominant hand and call "3" (figure 26.64c). When bag 3 peaks, throw the bag from your less dominant hand and call "4" (figure 26.64d). When bag 4 peaks, throw the bag from your dominant hand and call "5" (figure 26.64e). Keep throwing and counting in this figure eight pattern.

If children have difficulty, have them repeat to the end of figure 26.64c, ending with two bags in the left hand and one in the right. Repeat figures 26.64a, b, and c several times, then start from the first figure and continue on through figure 26.64e. Once children master to the end of figure 26.64e, they have learned to juggle.

Using Small Equipment To Teach Academic Concepts and Skills

The ideas and suggestions provided below illustrate how small equipment is used to enhance or teach academic concepts in language arts, mathematics, and health. These examples are similar to those found in previous chapters in that concepts are learned while a child participates in an active and enjoyable activity.

Language Arts

1. Make letters of the alphabet or words with an individual rope and using different parts of the body, such as hands, elbows, or feet.
2. Perform rope-jumping steps while singing or chanting rhymes and songs.
3. Make upper- and lower-case letters with a wand.

Mathematics

1. Make whole numbers with an individual rope or wand.
2. Make different geometrical shapes with individual and long ropes.
3. Perform individual or long rope jumping and call out numbers according to a counting, subtracting, or multiplying challenge.
4. Use symbols < (less than) and > (more than) in rope-jumping challenges. For example, "Using the alternate step, jump > fifty times."

Health

Circulation of the Blood: Some of the more common ways of learning how the blood circulates through the body is by watching a film, using a model of the heart, or drawing the body then tracing the blood through the heart, lungs, and blood vascular system. The following method has been used to teach children how the blood circulates through the body in a physically active, exciting, and enjoyable way.

The first thing to do is create a giant lying on his back (figure 26.65). Use individual ropes to form the head, arms, and legs. Lungs and the four chambers of the heart are large mats or plastic sheets. Next, arrange the class in a long line behind you. Explain that the giant is lying on his back and point to the lungs, heart, arms, and legs. Tell the class to follow you and, as you cross over the right atrium, call out "right atrium." Each child, in turn, calls out "right atrium" as he or she crosses this part of the body. Continue crossing the right ventricle, lungs, left atrium, and so on, calling out each part (figure 26.66). After several "journeys" through the body, have one or more children act as leaders and repeat the procedure.

Once everyone understands how the blood flows through the body, place a pile of red cards (or beanbags) on the lungs and a pile of blue cards on the right foot. Repeat the running procedure with the children picking up red cards (oxygenated blood) from the lungs, carrying them to the right foot, and exchanging red for blue (deoxygenated) cards. The deoxygenated blood is carried back through the heart to the lungs to be reoxygenated.

The central theme of this chapter has been to provide as many ideas as possible for using small equipment in both structured and exploratory ways. The next chapter continues this theme with large apparatus.

Figure 26.65 Circulation of the blood.

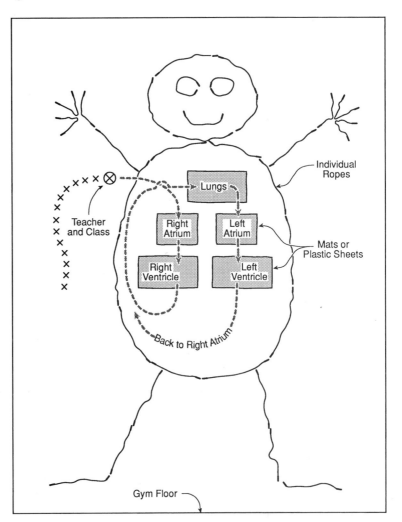

Selected References

American Heart Association. (1984). *Jump for the Health of It: Basic Skills.* Dallas, TX: American Heart Association.

Doray, M. (1982). *J Is for Jumping.* Belmont, CA: Pitman Learning, Inc.

Melson, B., and Wornell, V. (1986). *Rope Skipping for Fun and Fitness.* Wichita, KS: Woodlawn Publishers.

Prentup, F. B. (1980). *Skipping the Rope.* Boulder, CO: Pruett Publishing Co.

Skolnik, P. S. (1974). *Jump Rope.* New York: Workman Publishing Co.

Solis, K. M. and Budris, B. (1991). *The Jump Rope Primer.* Champaign, IL: Human Kinetics Publishers, Inc.

Figure 26.66 Right ventricle.

stunts and manipulative skills with small equipment

Walker, D. A., and Haskin, J. (1986). *Double Dutch.* Hillside, NJ: Enslow Publishing Co.

Wasserman, S. (1990). *Serious Players in the Primary Classroom.* New York: Teacher College Press.

Werner, P. H., and Burton, T. C. (1979). *Learning Through Movement: Teaching Cognitive Content Through Physical Activities.* St. Louis: C. V. Mosby Co.

Video

Solis, K. M., and Budris, B. (1991). *Jump Rope Primer Video* (35 min). Champaign, IL: Human Kinetics Publishers, Inc.

27

Large Apparatus Activities

The fundamental purpose of large apparatus in any gymnastic program is to provide an opportunity for children to test their ability on more challenging equipment and to improve physical fitness. This chapter continues the central theme of the previous chapter. The basic skills that can be performed on such apparatus as the balance beam, vaulting box, and climbing rope are described and illustrated. Then numerous suggestions are given for applying movement skills to this apparatus or integrating them with many of the traditional climbing, balancing, and vaulting movements performed on or over large apparatus. The last part of this chapter describes how language arts skills can be integrated with large apparatus activities ∎

Teaching Procedures

The following suggestions will assist the teacher in organizing and teaching both structured and movement skills with a variety of large apparatus:

1. Children of all ages should learn to carry and arrange apparatus—the position of the body when lifting a heavy piece of equipment—with a concern for their own safety and that of the class (figure 27.1).

2. The arrangement of individual and multiple pieces of equipment and apparatus should complement the main theme of the lesson. For example, if the theme is "change of direction" and four benches are used, they should be scattered to encourage movements in a variety of directions. If the benches are placed in a row, the children will usually follow one or two classmates around each bench.

3. Since there is never enough large apparatus, adopt station work, using both small and large apparatus, coupled with a rotation system. In the following diagram, the lesson stresses force (jumping and landing) and change of direction. The hoops, benches, traffic cones, and vaulting boxes are arranged to complement this theme. Each group practices at a station for a few minutes and then rotates to the next station. This gives each child an opportunity to use both small and large apparatus during an average lesson.

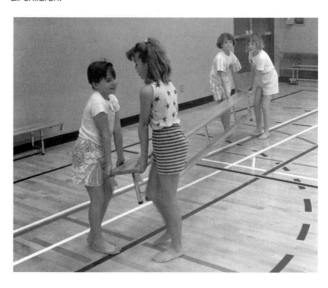

Figure 27.1 Carry the apparatus with concern and safety for all children.

4. Whenever a stunt or movement pattern requires a spotter or spotters, proper instruction should be given to the children prior to and during the time they act as spotters. This is particularly important with vaulting skills over a box or bench.

5. Task or challenge cards can be used effectively with large apparatus activities.

6. Mats should be used with large apparatus according to school district policy. Several illustrations appear in this chapter of children performing stunts and movement skills without mats under the apparatus. These children have been taught a series of safety skills and only to attempt skills according to their level of skill and ability.

Developmental Level I

Three types of large apparatus contained in this chapter stress balance, agility, or arm and shoulder strength and endurance. Many of the skills listed for this developmental level have been learned as stunts and tumbling activities or as movement skills and sequences. This is particularly true of balance beam and some vaulting activities. Activities on the climbing rope, horizontal bar, and ladder require a great deal of arm and shoulder girdle strength and endurance. Hence, it is important to begin with simple movements with minimum repetitions, as well as to use movement challenges that stress these key components of fitness. As children gain strength, proficiency, and confidence, they will be ready to attempt more challenging stunts, listed in the next developmental level.

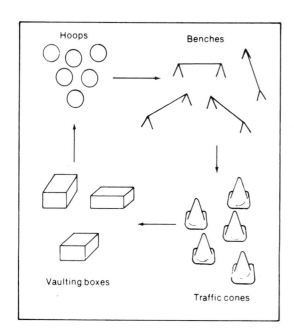

Figure 27.2 Performing stunts across the long axis of the balance beam.

Figure 27.3 Locomotor skills. Begin by walking forward and backward, with arms extended sideways. Repeat with other locomotor skills—running, hopping, and so on.

Variations to each locomotor skill:
1. Change position of hands.
2. Place a beanbag on head or other part of body while performing locomotor skill.
3. Repeat skills with narrow surface or with bench on an incline.
4. Walk, run, or hop to middle, pick up beanbag, walk forward and off.
5. Perform animal walks across the bench.

Developmental Level II

Children in developmental level II have gained sufficient strength, endurance, and proficiency to perform many of the more complex apparatus skills and movement patterns. They are also at the stage in development where they feel it is important to test the limits of their physical ability. As a consequence, teachers should make sure children do not attempt skills beyond their capability.

Developmental Level III

As children in this developmental level progress to the more complex stunts, more strength, endurance, and control are required. Like the more advanced tumbling stunts, more spotters are needed because of the potential hazards of performing many balance, vaulting, and climbing stunts. Children who have been exposed to movement education will be able to apply movement concepts and skills to large apparatus in very creative and challenging ways.

Balance Beam and Bench

The balance beam and bench have been used in gymnastic programs for a number of years. However, they have been used in a very limited way, usually flat on the ground, with children performing stunts on or across the long axis (figure 27.2). When the balance beam—fitted with a hook or connector on one end—is placed at different angles or used in combination with other apparatus, the variety of movements and challenges becomes infinitely greater. This applies to teaching structured skills as well the movement concepts and skills described in the previous two chapters. A wide variety of structured skills is presented in the relative order of difficulty, followed by suggestions for applying movement skills to the balance beam and bench.

Individual Activities

Activities performed on the balance beam and bench require two types of balance skill: (1) static balance and (2) dynamic balance. *Static balance* is the ability to maintain a fixed position, such as in the foot and knee balance. *Dynamic balance* is the ability to maintain correct body position while moving, as when walking forward and backward or when performing the one-foot hop. Most developmental level I balance skills are basically dynamic. As the children's strength and skill increase, the more advanced static balance activities can be introduced. Each of the suggested skills can be made more challenging by narrowing the space, raising the height, or by varying the angle of the beam or bench.

The skills listed in table 27.1 and shown in figures 27.3–27.10 can be performed on the broad surface of the bench or on the narrow beam. To assist in learning, have the children practice all the stunts on the floor, then move to the broad surface of the bench, and finally advance to the narrow surface of a beam. Any fixed line on the floor can serve as an imaginary balance beam or bench.

Table 27.1   Balance Beam Skills

Name of Stunt	Developmental Level			Movement Concepts	Page
	I	*II*	*III*		
Locomotor Skills (Chapter 4)	→			Balance, transfer of weight, change of speed	48
Turk Stand (Chapter 25)	→			Balance, levels	453
Swing Turn	→			Balance, transfer of weight	457
Front Dismount	→			Balance, transfer of weight	509
Rear Support (Chapter 25)	→			Balance, transfer of weight	454
Camel Walk (Chapter 25)	→			Balance, transfer of weight	436
Jump Turn (Chapter 25)	→			Balance, transfer of weight, force	435
Bouncing Ball (Chapter 25)	→			Balance, transfer of weight, levels	438
Foot and Knee Balance	→			Balance, transfer of weight, levels	509
Side Balance	→			Balance, transfer of weight	509
Stork Stand (Chapter 25)	→			Balance, transfer of weight	453
Squat Mount		→		Balance, transfer of weight	509
Foreward Roll (Chapter 25)		→		Balance, transfer of weight	426
Lame Puppy Walk (Chapter 25)		→		Balance, transfer of weight	437
Crab Walk (Chapter 25)		→		Balance, transfer of weight	439
Knee Dip (Chapter 25)		→		Balance, transfer of weight, levels	456
Rabbit Jump (Chapter 25)		→		Balance, transfer of weight	440
Seal Walk (Chapter 25)		→		Balance, transfer of weight	441
Measuring Worm (Chapter 25)		→		Balance, transfer of weight, levels	441
One Foot Jump (Chapter 25)		→		Balance, transfer of weight, force	440
Jackknife			→	Balance, transfer of weight	510
Squat On One Leg			→	Balance, transfer of weight, levels	510
Backward Roll (Chapter 25)			→	Balance, transfer of weight	429
Frog Stand (Chapter 25)			→	Balance, transfer of weight	456
Heal Click (Chapter 25)			→	Balance, transfer of weight	447
Cartwheel (Chapter 25)			→	Balance, transfer of weight	433
Bridge (Chapter 25)			→	Balance, transfer of weight	459
L Support (Chapter 25)			→	Balance, transfer of weight	460

Figure 27.4   Swing turn. Walk to the center of the beam. Shift weight to the left foot and swing the right leg forward. Continue swinging the right leg forward, lift up on the ball of the left foot, and make a half turn, facing the opposite direction.

Variations:
1. Hop forward and repeat stunt.
2. Combine the swing turn with a side balance and a squat on one leg.
3. Make up your own routine with a swing turn and two other stunts.

a

b

c

Figure 27.5 Front dismount. Begin in a crouched position, with the arms straight and the hands grasping the outside edges of the balance beam. Extend the legs back until the head, trunk, and legs form a straight line. Lift the legs up and sideways, push off with the hands, and land on both feet beside the balance beam.

Figure 27.6 Foot and knee balance. Begin with the right foot well in front of the left, the knees bent, and the arms extended sideways. Bend the knees until the left knee rests on the beam. Hold this position for a few seconds, then extend and return to the starting position.

Variations:
1. "Can you repeat this stunt with a change in arm position?"
2. "Can you add another variation to the stunt?"

Figure 27.7 Side balance. Walk to the center of the balance beam and stop, with the left foot in front of the right. Turn the left foot sideways, shift weight to the ball of the foot, and lift the right foot off the beam, arch the back, and raise the right leg.

Variations:
1. Hop to center, then perform the side balance.
2. Repeat stunt, turn sideways, and change the position of your right leg.
3. See if you can perform a front knee balance, shift to a side balance, then back to a front knee balance facing the opposite direction.

Figure 27.8 Squat mount. Stand with the feet about shoulder-width apart, the body erect, and the hands resting on the balance beam. While keeping the hands on the beam, jump up slightly forward, placing the feet on the beam.

Variations:
1. Straddle Mount: Mount, placing feet outside of hands.
2. Squat Mount: Perform a balance stunt, leap off, and land with flexed knees.
3. Leap off, make a tuck shape, and land with flexed knees.

large apparatus activities

Figure 27.9 Jackknife. Sit on the beam, with the legs extended, the heels of both feet resting on the beam, and the hands holding the top edge of the beam. Bend the knees and raise the feet off the beam. Continue the upward movement of the feet, lower the trunk backward, and straighten the legs. After practice, raise the legs without bending the knees and touch the feet with the fingertips.

Variations:
1. Repeat stunt, raising right leg and left arm.
2. "Can you repeat this stunt and twist your body in some way?"
3. "See if you can add your own variation to this stunt."

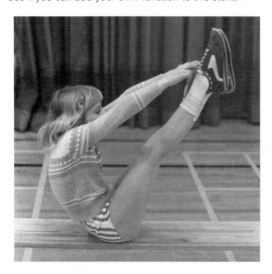

Figure 27.10 Squat on one leg. Stand on the right foot, with the arms extended sideways and the left foot off the beam. Bend the right knee and raise the extended left leg forward and upward. Lower the body until the right knee is fully flexed.

Variations:
1. Repeat on opposite leg.
2. "In how many positions can you place the right leg while balancing on your left foot?"
3. "Can you shift from your balance position to the same position, facing the opposite direction?"
4. "Can you shift from a squat on one leg to a side-balance position?"

Figure 27.11   Small equipment activities on the balance beam.

Several small equipment activities described in the previous chapter also can be performed on the beam or bench (figure 27.11). It may be wise to require students to perform the skill on the bench before they attempt it on the narrower surface of the balance beam.

1. *Beanbag activities:*
   a. Throw and catch to self.
   b. Balance beanbags on different parts of the body and perform a series of balance stunts.
2. *Rope-skipping activities:* Basic skills, particularly the two-foot basic, one-foot hop, and rocker step
3. *Hoop activities:*
   a. Hula Hooping
   b. Hula Jumping
4. *Wand activities:*
   a. Foot Balance
   b. Thread the Needle

Applying Movement Skills

One of the teacher's first tasks is to help children use the balance beam or bench in a variety of ways when performing a single movement skill or a sequence of movements. A movement task such as "See if you can make a twisted shape on the balance bench (or beam)" usually produces something like the shape illustrated in figure 27.12. The parallel arrangement of the benches lacks imagination. Also, the use of the word *on* encourages all children to begin their movements from the same starting position. Questions should be presented in such a way that children begin to see the apparatus in a much wider perspective. Rephrasing the question to "Can you make a series of twisted shapes using various parts of the balance bench?" allows for greater scope, as illustrated in figure 27.13. Thus, when applying movement ideas to the balance beam or bench, think of the apparatus as

Figure 27.12 Twisted shapes on the balance beam.

Figure 27.14 Combining the balance beam with other apparatus.

Figure 27.13 "Can you make a series of twisted shapes?"

Figure 27.15 Flight and rolling.

either a point of contact or an obstacle to move around, across, or over (in flight). The following movement challenges illustrate this application:

1. *Direction and speed:* Move around the benches, showing a quick change of direction.
2. *Balance and transfer of weight:* Travel across the benches by changing from two to three to two points of balance (figure 27.14).
3. *Balance, shape, and direction:* Develop a sequence traveling across the bench, including a twisted shape, balancing on the side, and a change of direction.
4. *Flight and rolling:* Beginning anywhere on the floor, run, jump onto a bench, leap off, land, and perform a safety roll. The roll may be a sideways, diagonal, or forward roll (figure 27.15). Repeat and perform a stretched, twisted, or curled shape before landing.
5. *Relationships:* The balance beam or bench can be one of the most effective and versatile apparatus for

developing the concept of relationships. The following examples illustrate how matching and contrasting can be integrated with other concepts and skills such as levels, direction, and speed:

a. "Develop a sequence of matching shapes with your partner on the top surface of your bench." "Repeat with one partner on the bench and the other on the floor (figure 27.16)." "Repeat with both touching the bench."
b. "With one partner leading and the other following, make up a sequence of balance positions as you move from one end of the bench to the other."

At this stage in the development of movement concepts and skills, the angle of the bench or its combination with other types of apparatus adds to the challenge. These variations provide a greater opportunity for the children to test and expand their physical and creative abilities. A challenge such as "Make up a sequence that shows a change in level" is

large apparatus activities

Figure 27.16 Patterns on and off the floor.

a. Matching shapes . . .   b. . . . with one on the floor . . .   c. . . . and one on the bench.

Figure 27.17 Climbing ropes.

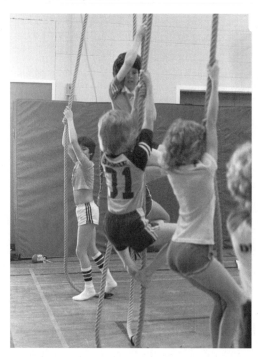

complemented by the angle of the bench. Also, adding chairs to the same challenge creates new dimensions for partners as they develop a matching sequence.

Climbing Rope

A variety of climbing, swinging, and movement skills can be performed with a climbing rope (figure 27.17). With proper instruction, including strengthening exercises for the arm and shoulder muscles, as well as following a sequential progression of skills, children can develop a high level of skill on the hanging ropes.

Suggestions for safety procedures and conditioning exercises are presented, followed by a description of the basic climbing skills and ideas for applying movement skills to this apparatus.

Safety Procedures

Many school districts require that a mat be placed under the climbing rope when a child is performing a climbing or swinging skill. It must be recognized, however, that the mat has very little resilience and thus may have little value in preventing an injury. The following suggestions and procedures contribute far more to a child's safety than a mat:

1. Teach the proper hand and foot grip techniques for climbing and descending the rope.
2. Set individual goals rather than an arbitrary standard for every child to accomplish.
3. Use spotters for difficult stunts, particularly those involving inverted hangs.
4. Establish safe and sensible rules for children, including the following:
   a. Never use ropes when a teacher is not present.
   b. Always climb down a rope; never slide.
   c. Never leave a rope swinging when you have finished with it.
   d. Never touch other performers on the rope unless you are spotting.
   e. Never climb a swinging rope.

Conditioning Exercises

Climbing skills require sufficient arm and shoulder strength to raise and support the full weight of the body. The abdominal muscles also play a very important role in both climbing and descending skills. The exercises listed in table 27.2 help increase the general strength and endurance of these muscle groups:

Table 27.2 Conditioning Exercises For Rope Climbing Skills

Exercise	Region of Body	Page
Single Mule Kick	Arm and shoulder girdle	431
Mule Kick	Arm and shoulder girdle	432
Cartwheel	Arm and shoulder girdle	433
Wheelbarrow	Arm and shoulder girdle	440
Rabbit Jump	Arm and shoulder girdle	441
Seal Walk	Arm and shoulder girdle	441
Measuring Worm	Arm and shoulder girdle	441
Frog Jump	Arm and shoulder girdle	441
Frog Stand	Arm and shoulder girdle	456
Pull-Ups	Arm and shoulder girdle	525
Push-Ups	Arm and shoulder girdle	193
Coffee Grinder	Arm and shoulder girdle	442
Curl-Ups	Abdominals	194
V-Sit	Abdominals	458

Figure 27.18 Pull-ups. Lie under the rope, with the hands grasping it. Gradually raise the body upward. As strength increases, repeat exercise, but keep the body straight throughout the movement.

Individual Activities

The individual skills in table 27.3, some of which are shown in figures 27.18–27.28, are listed in their approximate order of difficulty. Since many elementary school children lack sufficient arm and shoulder girdle strength, time should be spent on the preliminary conditioning exercises and the simpler climbing and swinging skills before attempting the more advanced skills. Success leads to success; this is extremely important with rope-climbing activities.

Figure 27.19 Reach and pull. Sitting under the rope with the arms extended over the head and grasping the rope, pull body up. As strength increases, keep the legs extended and parallel to the floor.

Figure 27.20 Letters. Hang between two ropes and make shapes of letters (Y, X, L, etc.).

Table 27.3 Rope Climbing Skills

Exercise	Developmental Level			Movement Concepts	Page
	I	*II*	*III*		
Rope Pull-Ups	——▶			Force, level, shapes	513
Reach and Pull	——▶			Force, level, shapes	513
Letters	——▶			Force, shapes	513
Backward Roll	——▶			Force, change of direction, shapes	514
Jump and Tuck		——▶		Force, shapes	514
Hands and Leg Hold		——▶		Force, transfer of weight	515
Skin the Cat		——▶		Force, transfer of weight, change of direction	515
Bench Swing and Drop		——▶		Force, transfer of weight, change of direction, shapes	515
Scissors Climb			——▶	Force, levels, transfer of weight	516
Foot and Leg Lock Climb			——▶	Force, levels, transfer of weight	516
Stirrup Climb			——▶	Force, levels, transfer of weight	516

Figure 27.21 Backward roll. Lie on back and grasp ropes with arms extended. Perform a backward roll with legs tucked, straddled, or in other positions.

Figure 27.22 Jump and tuck. Begin in a standing position facing the rope. Jump up, grasp the rope and draw the knees up to the chest.

Variations:
1. Repeat, but this time draw legs up above the head.
2. Repeat and draw legs up and over the head so that toes point towards the floor.
3. Repeat and draw the legs up, then spread them sideways above the head.

Figure 27.23 Hands and leg hold. Begin in a standing position, jump up, grasp the rope, wrap legs around the rope, and hold for several seconds.

Variations:
1. From hands and leg hold, release right then left hand.
2. From hands and leg hold, release right hand and right leg and hold for several seconds.

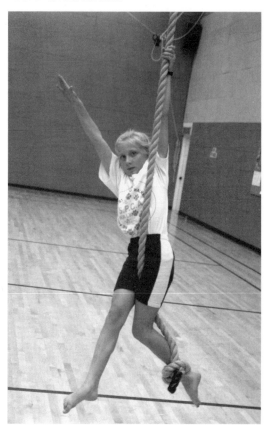

Figure 27.25 Bench swing and drop. Place a bench several feet away from the rope. Carry the rope back to the bench and hold it with a bent arm position and facing forward. Swing forward and drop off at the upper end of the swing.

Variations:
1. Swing forward and backward and land on the bench.
2. Swing forward and raise the knees to the chest.
3. Swing, make a half or full turn and land.

Figure 27.24 Skin the cat. Reach up and grasp the rope. Pull legs up and over the head to a back hang position and return to original position.

large apparatus activities

Figure 27.26 Scissors climb. Grasp the rope with one hand slightly above the other. Pull the body up, with the right leg slightly in front of the left. Place rope inside the right knee and around the outside of the left foot. Cross the left leg over the back of the right leg, and press the inside of the left foot against the rope (a). Release the pressure on the rope with the feet, then raise knees toward the chest (b). Lock the feet firmly against the rope, straighten legs, and reset hands (moving hand over hand) above the head (c). To descend, keep pressure against feet and lower body in hand-under-hand position until knees are bent. Hold hands firmly and lower legs to new position, then lock feet again. Continue pattern.

Figure 27.28 Stirrup climb. Grasp the rope with one hand slightly above the other. Pull the body up and let the rope rest against the left side of the body. The rope then passes under the left foot and over the right foot (a). Release pressure of feet and raise body (b). Lock grip of feet, raise hand to higher position, and continue action (c). To descend, move hand under hand and control pressure against the feet.

a   b   c

Applying Movement Skills

The hanging rope can be used to develop movement skills in three basic ways: (1) movement challenges relating to shapes and weight bearing with a stationary rope, (2) movement challenges while the rope is swinging, and (3) movement challenges with the rope associated with another type of large apparatus.

The following movement tasks illustrate each type of challenge: "Can you balance with one part of your body on the floor and three parts on the rope (figure 27.29)?" "How many different shapes can you make while holding the rope?" "Can you make different shapes while holding the rope and with both feet off the ground?" "Repeat previous challenge while the rope is swinging." Place one bench near both ends of the rope swing. "Swing and land on each bench." "Swing, make a half turn, and land on the opposite bench."

Figure 27.27 Front and leg lock climbs. Grasp the rope with one hand slightly above the other. Pull the body up and loop the rope over the top of the right foot. Place the left foot on top of the rope, thus "locking" the foot position (a). Pull the body up to a new position (b). Repeat upward movement (c). Descend by maintaining the locked position of the legs, then move the hands down in a "hand-under-hand" fashion until the knees are against the chest. Hold the hand grip and slowly lower the legs to an extended position. Continue action to the floor.

a   b   c

Figure 27.29 Balance three parts on the rope.

Springboard, Beatboard, Mini-tramp, and Vaulting Box

The springboard and vaulting box are two of the oldest apparatus in the gymnastic program. In this chapter, the term *vaulting box* includes other similar apparatus, such as the vaulting bench, the jumping box, and the long horse, since they are used in much the same way. Teachers who do not have a vaulting box should refer to the diagrams of inexpensive equipment in appendix B.

The majority of vaulting stunts are usually performed from the springboard or mini-tramp onto a mat. Once children have developed sufficient skill in using the springboard and controlling their bodies while in flight, the vaulting box can be added to provide greater challenge and versatility of movements. The approach, takeoff, and landing are essentially the same for all vaulting activities, so children should practice these movements until they become automatic (figure 27.30). A well-executed and consistent takeoff allows the child to concentrate on height and the execution of a specific vault.

Individual Activities

The first few stunts listed in table 27.4 help performers develop a consistent takeoff and execute aerial and landing movements with control and efficacy. The remaining vaults listed can be performed over a box or long horse with a takeoff from the floor, or off a springboard or mini-tramp. Some of the stunts are shown in figures 27.31–27.42.

Figure 27.30 Approach and takeoff. The hurdle step is used to change running speed into a two-foot takeoff roll. Begin with a few short running steps, then take off with the right foot and (a) swing the opposite leg and arms forward and upward. Land with arms swinging downward and backward and knees slightly bent (b). When the performer's toes touch the board (or mini-tramp), the body should be just behind a vertical line drawn through the performer's toes. This position allows the performer to gain maximum height and control (c) rather than a rapid and uncontrolled low forward shifting action. Land with knees bent and continue into a forward roll.

Variations:
1. After takeoff, make a tuck, straddle, or twisted shape, land and roll.
2. After takeoff, perform a quarter, half, or full turn, land and roll.

a   b   c

Figure 27.31 Knee mount. Stand on the springboard with hands resting on the box. Jump upward and forward and land on lower legs. Repeat mount with a run and a two-foot takeoff. Stand up, leap off, land, and roll. Use the same spotting as for the squat vault.

Variations:
1. After leaping off, make a tuck, straddle, or twisted shape, land and roll.
2. After leaping off, perform a half turn, land, and execute a backward diagonal roll.

Table 27.4 Springboard and Vaulting Box Skills

Name of Stunt	Developmental Level			Movement Concepts	Page
	I	*II*	*III*		
Movement Skills	⟶			Force, transfer of weight, shapes, levels	552
Approach and Takeoff	⟶			Force, transfer of weight, shapes, levels	517
Knee Mount	⟶			Force, transfer of weight, shapes, levels	517
Squat Mount	⟶			Force, transfer of weight, shapes, levels	518
Flank Mount	⟶			Force, transfer of weight, shapes, levels	518
Straddle Mount	⟶			Force, transfer of weight, shapes, levels	519
Squat Vault		⟶		Force, transfer of weight, shapes, levels	519
Flank Vault		⟶		Force, transfer of weight, shapes, levels	520
Straddle Vault		⟶		Force, transfer of weight, shapes, levels	520
Headspring		⟶		Force, transfer of weight, shapes, levels	521
Handspring		⟶		Force, transfer of weight, shapes, levels	521

Figure 27.32 Squat mount. Stand on the springboard with hands resting on the box. Jump upward and forward, and land in a squat position. Repeat mount with a run and a two-foot takeoff. Stand up, leap off, land, and roll. Use the same spotting as for the Squat Vault.

Variations:
Repeat variations for knee mount.

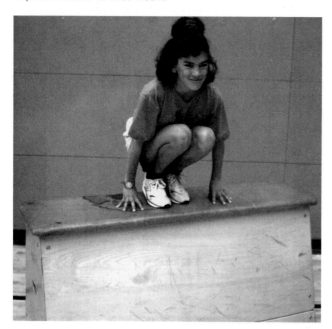

Figure 27.33 Flank mount. Stand on the springboard with hands resting on the box. Jump upward and forward, swing both straight legs to the right side and release the right hand. Land on the top of the box with right leg on top of the left leg and the right hand resting on the right thigh. Repeat mount with a run and a two foot takeoff. Stand up, leap off, land and roll. Use the same spotting as for the squat vault.

Variations:
Repeat variations for the knee mount.

Figure 27.34 Straddle mount. Stand on the springboard with hands resting on the box. Jump upward, spread legs sideways, and land on the top of the box in a straddle position. Repeat mount with a run and a two foot takeoff. Stand up, leap off, land, and roll. Use the same spotting as for straddle vault.

Variations:
Repeat variations from knee mount.

a   b   c

Figure 27.35 Squat vault. From a two-foot takeoff (a) reach up, leaning slightly forward, and touch hands on top of the box (b). Simultaneously tuck the knees close to the chest (c) and continue forward and upward. Land with a gradual bending of the knees (d).

a   b   c   d

Figure 27.36 Spotting. Stand on the opposite side of the vaulting box and to the right of the oncoming performer. As she moves over the box, grasp her right wrist with your right hand. As she shifts forward, supply additional support to her upper body with your left hand.

large apparatus activities

Figure 27.37 Flank vault. From a two foot takeoff, (a) reach forward with straight arms and extend both legs to the right side, (b) continue forward releasing the right hand as straight legs pass over box, (c) continue forward and downward, and (d) land with a gradual bending of the knees.

a   b   c   d

Figure 27.38 Straddle vault. From a two-foot takeoff (a), reach forward with straight arms and extend legs sideward (b). Continue forward and upward, raising chest upward, bringing legs together (c). Land with a gradual bending of the knees (d).

a   b

c   d

Figure 27.39 Spotting. Stand close to the box directly in front of the oncoming performer. If she catches her toes or has too much forward momentum, place your hands on her shoulders to break the fall. If the performer clears the box and does not have too much forward momentum, step to the side quickly.

Figure 27.40 Headspring. From a two-foot takeoff, place the hands and then the head on top of the box as the body extends upward and over. When the body is in a forward "overbalanced" position, push off from the fingertips and land with a gradual bending of the knees. Note: Most children tend to push off before they reach the overbalanced position, which causes them to "drop" onto the box rather than gradually arch and land.

a   b   c   d

Figure 27.41 Spotting. Use one spotter. As the performer's hands contact the top of the horse, place your left hand on the performer's neck and support her through the movement to a safe landing position.

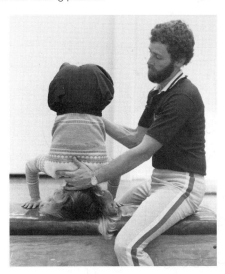

Figure 27.42 Handspring. From a two-foot takeoff (a), extend body upward and touch hands on top of horse (b). Keeping body straight, continue forward and push off as body loses point of balance (c). Continue arching forward and land with knees slightly bent (d). Note: Beginners bend at the hips as they touch the top of the horse, then "flip" and arch as they leave the horse. With practice, a full body extension is maintained throughout the movement. Use two spotters similar to the squat vault position.

a   b

c   d

large apparatus activities

Figure 27.43 Make a shape in the air.

Figure 27.44 Move from one side to the other side of the apparatus.

Applying Movement Skills

The springboard, beatboard, mini-tramp, and vaulting box can be used individually or in combination with other apparatus to provide interesting and challenging movement tasks involving body awareness, qualities, space awareness, and relationships. For example, all the individual shapes performed in flight from the floor can be applied to the springboard, beatboard, or mini-tramp. These provide additional height and time necessary for executing curled or stretched, wide or narrow, and twisted shapes. In addition, since children have learned safety rolls—sideward, backward, and forward—they should be able to land and roll with grace and ease. The movement task shown in figure 27.43 illustrates the additional challenge and increased quality of movements performed from the springboard, beatboard, or mini-tramp. Similar movements can also be performed from the vaulting box.

The vaulting box should also be used as an additional challenge for the development of other movement concepts and skills. It is important to present challenges in such a way that all surfaces—particularly the sides and ends—are used when answering movement tasks. The following examples illustrate the variable use of the vaulting box:

1. *Shapes and balance:*
   a. "Make a stretched (or wide or twisted) shape on the side, end, and top of the box."
   b. "Can you balance with one part on the apparatus and two parts off?"
   c. "See if you can balance with part of your body on top of the apparatus and part on the side or end of the apparatus."
   d. "Move from one side of the apparatus to the other (figure 27.44)."
2. *Relationships:*
   a. "Make up a matching (or contrasting) sequence of shapes, with one partner on top of the apparatus and the other on the floor."
   b. "How many different balance positions can you make with your partner on the side or top of the apparatus?"

   c. "Make up a sequence with your partner on the apparatus and show a change in balance."

Sequences involving body awareness, qualities, space awareness, and relationships can be designed to include the springboard and vaulting box individually or in combination with other small and large apparatus. The selection and arrangement of the apparatus should complement the movements of the sequence. Excessive rearrangement of apparatus serves little purpose in the development of movement skills, so teachers should caution children if they tend to waste time in arranging apparatus. One arrangement of apparatus should last for several lessons.

Horizontal Bar

In comparison with stunts on other indoor apparatus, stunts performed on the horizontal bar are extremely difficult for elementary school children. Thus, teachers must give a great deal of encouragement. In most cases, the initial disinterest in this apparatus is the result of insufficient arm and shoulder strength rather than an inherent absence of skill. The following suggestions will help maintain enthusiasm and prevent unnecessary accidents:

1. Check equipment before allowing children to perform any stunt.
2. Make sure you are in the proper position to spot for safety.
3. Begin with simple stunts and progress to more difficult ones.
4. Stress forward grip with fingers over top of bar and facing forward, with thumbs under the bar and facing the fingers.

Individual Activities

The stunts in table 27.5 are listed according to their approximate order of difficulty. Figures 27.45–27.60 illustrate some of the stunts.

Table 27.5   Horizontal Bar Skills

Name of Stunt	Developmental Level			Movement Concepts	Page
	I	*II*	*III*		
Two Arm Hang	→			Force, shapes, relationships	523
Body Swing	→			Force, shapes, transfer of weight, relationships	523
Hand Walk	→			Force, shapes, transfer of weight, relationships	524
Hang Like a Monkey		→		Force, shapes, transfer of weight, relationships	524
Arm and Leg Hang		→		Force, transfer of weight, relationships	524
Double Leg Hang		→		Force, transfer of weight, relationships	524
Skin the Cat		→		Force, transfer of weight, relationships	525
Pull-Ups		→		Force, shapes, transfer of weight, relationships	525
Front Support			→	Force, transfer of weight, relationships	525
Roll Over Barrel			→	Force, transfer of weight, relationships	525
Scramble Over Fence			→	Force, transfer of weight, relationships	526
Single Knee Swing			→	Force, transfer of weight, relationships	526
Inverted Hang			→	Force, transfer of weight, relationships	526
Knee Circle			→	Force, transfer of weight, relationships	526
Bird's Nest			→	Force, shape, transfer of weight, relationships	527
Sideways Circle			→	Force, transfer of weight, relationships	527

Figure 27.45   Two arm hang. Jump up, grasp bar with forward grip and arm extended. Hold position for several seconds.

Variations:
1. Hang and raise knees up as far as possible.
2. Keep legs straight, then raise them forward and upward.
3. Hang and change position of legs: spread; one forward, one reversed; crossed; aerial walking; etc.
4. Hang and release one hand.

Figure 27.46   Body swing. Jump up and grasp bar, with palms facing forward. Swing body backward and forward.

Variations:
1. Grip bar, with palms facing away or use a mixed grip.
2. Swing and reverse directions by gradually changing grips and direction.
3. Swing and change position of legs: swing to tuck, swing with right leg extended forward and left leg extended backward.
4. Swing and bring toes up to touch the fingers, then return.

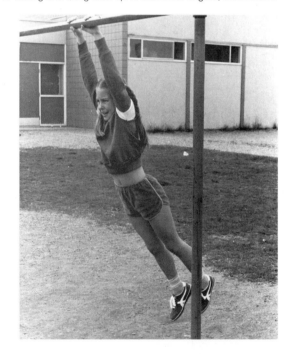

Figure 27.47 Hand walk. Begin at one end of the bar facing the opposite end. Jump up, grasp the bar with hands facing each other. Travel to the other end using a hand-over-hand movement.

Variations:
1. Repeat above in a backward movement.
2. Hand walk with legs in different positions—tucked, straddled, etc.

Figure 27.48 Hang like a monkey. Jump up and grasp the bar, with the palms forward and the hands a few inches apart. Swing the right leg up and over the bar, resting the heel on top. Bring the left leg up and over the right leg and rest the back of the left leg on top of the right foot.

Variations:
1. Pull chest to bar.
2. Shift leg to side, pointing to the floor, and so on.
3. Travel forward and backward by sliding hands and feet along the bar.

Figure 27.49 Arm and leg hang. Jump up and grasp the bar with palms facing forward. Draw one leg through arms and around the bar. Hang with the arms straight and the lower leg extended forward.

Variations:
1. Change legs and repeat.
2. Lift one hand off the bar, then re-grasp.
3. From this position shift toward each side and return.
4. From the hanging position, raise the chin to the bar and return.

Figure 27.50 Double leg hang. Jump up and grasp the bar with the palms facing forward and the hands about shoulder-width apart. Draw both legs up and over the bar, drop the knees over it, and rest the back of knees firmly against the bar. Keep the knees bent and release grip. Reach up, grasp bar, and return to the starting position.

Variations:
1. Twist the body toward each side.
2. Change position of arms.
3. With a spotter, swing back and forth.

Figure 27.51 Skin the cat. Jump up and grasp the bar with palms facing forward. Draw both legs up and through the arms and over until the legs are extended downward. Return to the starting position.

Variations:
1. From the reverse hang position, release grip and drop to the ground.
2. From the reverse hang position, change position of the legs—straddle, crossed, etc.

Figure 27.53 Front support. Jump up and take a front support position, with the arms straight and hands on top of the bar. Jump down.

Variations:
1. From the front support position, push off with the arms and jump slightly upward and backward.
2. From the front support position, adjust body to balance on the stomach, with arms extended sideways.

Figure 27.52 Pull-ups. Jump up and grasp the bar with a front (palms facing forward) or reverse (palms facing backward) grip. Pull up body until chin is above the bar.

Variations:
1. Change grip and repeat.
2. Chin with legs in various positions: with knees bent, with legs straight, with legs parallel to the ground, or with toes above the bar.

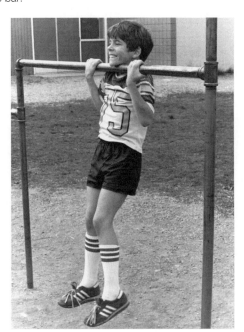

Figure 27.54 Roll over barrel. Jump up and take a front support position, with arms straight and hands on top of bar. Bend at the waist, drop head forward, roll over the bar, bring legs down, and release grip.

Variations:
1. Roll over, with one leg leading the other.
2. Roll over and raise straight legs above the bar, hold, lower, and continue rolling movement.

large apparatus activities

Figure 27.55 Scramble over fence. Jump up and take a front support position with arms straight and hands on top of the bar. From this position, bring right, then left, leg over the bar and sit on the top with arms extended sideways.

Variations:
Change position of arms—one forward and one backward, behind the head, etc.

Figure 27.57 Inverted hang. Jump up and grasp the bar with palms facing forward, and hands about shoulder width apart. Draw both legs up and under the bar. As the legs pass over the bar they are extended upward and close to the bar until the body is perpendicular to the mat.

Variation:
Once in an inverted position, extend legs sideways.

Figure 27.56 Single knee swing. Jump up and grasp the bar with palms facing forward. Draw one leg through the arms and around the bar. Point opposite leg toward the sky then swing it forward and downward and continue swinging back and forth.

Variations:
1. Change legs and repeat movement.
2. Swing to a sitting position on the bar. (Use a spotter until the performer demonstrates control throughout the movement.)

Figure 27.58 Knee circle. Begin sitting on the bar with a reverse grip. The right leg is over the bar with the knee bent. The left leg is under the bar extended and pointed down. Shift the weight upward and forward, circle the bar and back to the original position.

Variations:
1. Reverse grip and perform a backward knee circle.
2. Change leg positions and repeat movement.

chapter 27

Figure 27.59 Bird's nest. Jump up and grasp bar, with palms facing forward. Draw both legs up and through arms. Drop legs over the bar, resting back of knees firmly against the bar. Simultaneously shift lower legs backward and fully arch the back until the back of the heels rest against the bar and arms are extended.

Variations:
1. Remove one leg and extend it backward.
2. Bring legs back through the arms, then extend legs upward into an inverted hang.

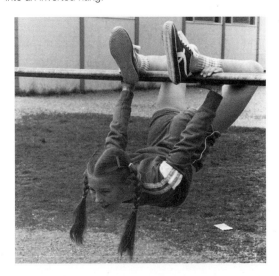

Figure 27.60 Sideways circle. Begin sitting on the bar with one leg on each side and legs locked. The arms are straight with the hands grasping the bar in front and close to the body. Fall sideways and try to complete a full circle.

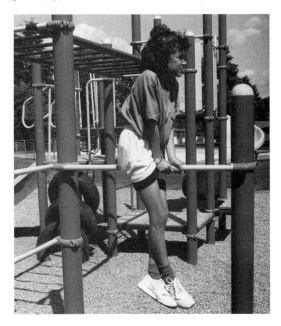

Applying Movement Skills

Proficiency on this apparatus depends upon a child's level of arm and shoulder girdle strength and endurance. Movement challenges can be designed to allow children with minimal levels of fitness to perform movements within their own level of ability. The same challenge also allows the more fit child to execute movements that involve the highest level of fitness and motor ability. The following examples illustrate how movement challenges are applied to this type of apparatus.

1. "How many different ways can you get on and off the bar?"
2. "Can you hold onto the bar and make two different shapes?"
3. "See if you can balance with part of your body on the apparatus and part on the ground."
4. "Discover two different ways of moving across the bar."
5. "Can you balance on the top of the bar and make a curled, stretched, or twisted shape?"
6. "Can you balance with parts of your body above and parts below the bar?"
7. "Is it possible to hold the bar, swing, and jump off?"

Horizontal Ladder

Activities performed on the horizontal ladder are similar to horizontal bar activities. Both require a great deal of strength and endurance of the arm and shoulder girdle muscles. Therefore, follow the progression of skills in table 27.6 and do not require *full travels*—that is, all the way across the ladder—until sufficient strength and endurance are developed. As a starting point, require the children to make it one quarter of the distance. Increase the number of rungs each day until the children reach the full distance without undue stress (figures 27.61–27.65).

Figure 27.61 Inverted push-ups. Grasp rung with palms facing forward, swing legs upward and over the rung. Hook heels over the rung then raise chin to the rung. Repeat movement several times then return to starting position.

Variations:
1. Hook only one leg over the rung and repeat movement.
2. From the inverted hang position, release one hand and twist body toward each side.

Table 27.6 Horizontal Ladder

Name of Stunt	Developmental Level			Movement Concept	Page
	I	*II*	*III*		
Two Arm Hang	→→			Force, shapes, relationships	523
Body Swing	→→			Force, shapes, transfer of weight, relationships	523
Arm and Leg Hang		→→		Force, transfer of weight, relationships	524
Double Leg Hang		→→		Force, transfer of weight, relationships	524
Pull-ups		→→		Force, shapes, transfer of weight, relationships	525
Inverted Push-ups		→→		Force, transfer of weight, relationships	527
Single Rung Traveling		→→		Force, transfer of weight, relationships	528
Rung Travel Sideways		→→		Force, transfer of weight, relationships	528
Side Rail Travel		→→		Force, transfer of weight, relationships	529
Double Rail Travel			→→	Force, transfer of weight, relationships	529
Skin The Cat			→→	Force, transfer of weight, relationships	525

Figure 27.62 Single rung traveling. Climb up one end of the ladder, rest feet on the top step, and grasp each side pole with one hand. Reach forward and grasp the second rung with one hand, palms facing forward, and the third rung with the other hand. Simultaneously shift the body forward toward the forward hand and release the back hand. Continue forward, grasping the next rung. Repeat the movement with the opposite hand and continue traveling forward to the opposite end.

Variations:
1. Change position of legs as you travel—knees tucked, legs straddled, or one leg in front of the other.
2. Double Rung Travel: Begin with both hands on one rung. Swing forward and backward and, at end of a forward swing, release both hands and regrasp the next rung with both hands.

Figure 27.63 Rung travel sideways. Begin with hands on separate rungs and body facing sideways. Shift right hand to same rung as left hand, then shift left hand to next rung. Continue pattern to end of ladder.

The following safety hints require continuous reinforcement. Before the children begin to play or practice stunts on the apparatus, take a few minutes to stress the following:

1. Check the apparatus before pupils are allowed to perform stunts.
2. Stand close to performers while they are attempting a difficult stunt in order to help them and to prevent accidents.
3. Require pupils to stand at least five feet from the apparatus while waiting for their turn.
4. Allow only two pupils on the ladder at the same time.
5. Require that the second pupil not begin a stunt until the first child is at least halfway across the ladder.
6. Require pupils to travel in the same direction.
7. Require that two parts of the body be in contact with the apparatus during the performance of all movements.
8. Do not permit children to touch or hinder a child who is performing a stunt.

chapter 27

Figure 27.64 Side rail traveling. Travel along one side rail, using a hand-over-hand movement.

Variations:
1. Change position of legs as you travel.
2. Repeat movement backward.

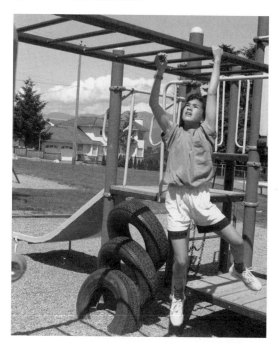

Figure 27.65 Double Rail Traveling: Grasp both side rails with the palms of both hands facing in, and swing to a hanging position. Travel forward by sliding one hand forward, then the other. Do not release the grip. Slide the hands the full length of the ladder.

Variation:
Repeat movement backward.

Individual Activities

The stunts listed in table 27.6 are arranged according to their approximate level of difficulty.

Applying Movement Skills

The horizontal ladder is similar to the horizontal bar in that both require sufficient strength and endurance to perform even the simplest movements. As this apparatus normally has side structures with two or more rungs, all parts should be incorporated into several movement challenges. The sample challenges listed below illustrate how the sides and overhead ladder are used in movement tasks.

1. "Can you balance with part of your body on the side of the apparatus and part on the overhead ladder?"
2. "How many different ways can you hang from the ladder?"
3. "See if you can hold onto a rung and swing." "Can you swing and make different shapes?" "Can you swing and land from a forward or reverse swing?"
4. "Can you 'balance' on top of the ladder?" "Can you balance on three parts?" "Can you balance on three parts and show me a twist in your body?"
5. "Discover three different ways of moving across the apparatus."

Climbing Frame

One of the most significant contributions to the elementary school gymnastic program has been the development of new climbing apparatus (figure 27.66). This apparatus has been specifically designed to provide more challenging tasks than the traditional gymnastic apparatus. The climbing frame is mounted on a wall with a variety of supplementary attachments, such as beams, poles, ladders, and planks.

Individual Activities

The stunts listed under balance beam, climbing ropes, horizontal bar, and ladder can be performed on the various parts of this apparatus. This apparatus offers an additional feature in that planks, ladders, and poles can be mounted at different levels and angles from the floor to the apparatus, thus providing an extra challenge for each stunt.

Applying Movement Skills

This apparatus should also be seen as a logical extension of the gymnasium in developing moving concepts and skills. The following examples illustrate how this apparatus can be used as an effective instructional laboratory. The skills

Figure 27.66 Nissen wall gym.

learned through the teacher's movement challenges help the children learn to use the apparatus in a constructive, safe, and creative way.

1. "Find a place on the apparatus and show me how many different ways you can balance on your spot."
2. "Can you move across the apparatus using different parts of your body?"
3. "See if you can climb up and down the apparatus using your hands and feet."
4. "Can you move through the apparatus and show a low, medium, and high position?"
5. "One partner leads and the other follows. Make up a sequence involving a transfer of weight and a change of direction."
6. "Find a spot on the apparatus with your partner. Can you develop a matching sequence including a stretch, curl, and twisted shape?"

Outdoor Apparatus

In the past few years, there has been a major change in the type of outdoor apparatus being constructed on elementary school playgrounds. Commercial equipment, such as Big Toys, are replacing the more traditional swings, steel climbing frames, and horizontal ladders. This apparatus has been designed to complement the creative and exploratory nature of young children. The general design provides more levels, angles, and holes for young children to jump off, balance on, and crawl through (figures 27.67 and 27.68). Creative playgrounds described in chapter 7 are also part of this trend. Natural materials, such as large tree roots and boulders, and discarded building materials or equipment, such as giant sewer pipes and old trucks, are now seen on numerous playgrounds throughout North America.

Many of the movement challenges suggested under horizontal bar, ladder, and climbing frame can be applied to a variety of commercial and natural outdoor apparatus (figure 27.69).

Teachers who are hesitant to use the indoor and outdoor apparatus suggested in this chapter should recognize one of the basic characteristics of the Movement Education approach: Children taught through this approach will not attempt a movement task on any apparatus until they feel mentally and physically ready. If the teacher follows this approach, accidents should rarely occur.

Figure 27.67 "Can you move across the apparatus, using different parts of the body?"

Figure 27.68 "See if you can climb up and down the apparatus, using your hands and feet."

Figure 27.69 Matching sequence.

Using Large Apparatus to Teach Academic Concepts and Skills

In previous chapters, physical activities were used as a medium through which a variety of academic concepts and skills were taught. The following sample poems illustrate how a child's experiences on large apparatus was used as the subject or focus for creative writing. This goes far beyond using physical activities to enhance a single concept or skill. Movement experiences on very exciting and challenging apparatus provide a strong vehicle for children to express personal thoughts and feelings through the written word. These poems also reveal the child's understanding and attitude about herself and her movement experiences.

Climb up the climbing wall,

Then do a swift turn on the box,
Do an interesting roll on a mat,
Flip and twirl over the bars,
Even though I'm scared,
I dare to do a flip!
The world is turning upside down,
And then I land perfectly!
I climb up the ropes,
I put hand over hand,
I am being daring and risky,
But I do it anyway.

Tristane (grade 4)

Gymnastics

Risky, daring,
Outrageous fun,
I have now accomplished it and I'm done,
The dangerous jumps, the freaky flips,
I never gave up,
I tried my best.
Practise, Practise,
It makes me feel proud,
That since I practised,
I did it well.
I feel great,
I feel secure.

Katie (grade 4)

Going over

Going under
Going way up to the top,
Going through too.
I don't know about you,
But I like travelling.
Do you?
I like P. E.
Don't you?
Going all around,
Going through the bars,
Slithering up the ropes like a snake,
We climb the ropes so high.
I hope you like climbing,
Because I do.
I jumped way up in the air,
So might you, too.
I hope that when you get there,
Nobody gets hurt.

Ryan (grade 4)

large apparatus activities

The poems are examples from a long-term project designed to integrate physical education with writing.[1] The results of this study indicated that children, at both primary and intermediate levels, improved their thinking skills, showed a significant increase in their enjoyment of physical education, and demonstrated improved communication skills. In addition, children became more critical of their own work and more willing to take risks in their writing and physical endeavors. Further, their poetic writing served to reinforce the movement vocabulary as well as extend their thinking into the aesthetic domain. The predominant use of poetic writing reinforced the connection between writing and movement experiences. Finally, the integration of writing and physical education provided children with an intrinsic link to learning in the cognitive, affective, and physical domains.

Selected References

Cooper, P. (1989). *Teaching Basic Gymnastics: A Coeducational Approach,* Second Edition. New York: Macmillan Publishing Co.

Corbin, C. B. (1972). *Inexpensive Equipment for Games, Play, and Physical Activity.* Dubuque, IA: Wm. C. Brown Publishers.

Hall, T. (1984). *Inexpensive Movement Material.* Byron, CA: Front Race Experience.

Ryser, O. E. and Brown, J. R. (1988). *A Manual of Tumbling and Apparatus Stunts.* Dubuque, IA: Wm. C. Brown Publishers.

1. Sahli, J. (1993). *Making a Meaningful Connection: The Integration of Physical Education and Writing.* Unpublished Thesis, Burnaby, Simon Fraser University.

PART 7

Dance and Movement Activities

Part 7 has been organized in a slightly different way from the game and gymnastic sections. Chapter 28 describes the basic rhythmic skills that are used in game, gymnastic, and dance activities. Chapter 29 includes the most popular singing games and folk dance activities for developmental levels I, II, and III. Chapter 30 describes several approaches to teaching creative dance activities to children in the primary and intermediate grades ■

28

Rhythmic and Movement Activities

Rhythm is the ability to repeat an action or movement with regularity and in time to a particular pattern. It is an essential ingredient of all movement, whether throwing a ball, dodging a player, or dancing a polka. Rhythm can be spontaneous, as when a young child makes up a jumping pattern without any musical background or directions imposed by the teacher. The rhythmic activities described in this chapter, however, are more structured in nature and direction, relating to the performance of a variety of body movements in time to a specific musical accompaniment.

The material in this chapter has been arranged to assist children (latter phase of developmental level I through developmental level III) in acquiring a basic understanding of the elements of rhythm and the ways the elements can be combined with a variety of game, dance, and gymnastic movements. Once children understand the elements of rhythm, they can learn other dance activities with greater speed and usually with a very positive attitude. The basic approach of gradually moving from individual to partner to group activities is used. This gradual process of joining younger children in a relaxed and creative manner provides the necessary stepping-stone to folk and creative dance activities for upper elementary school boys and girls. Once the teacher has read this chapter, she will also be able to incorporate many of the ideas into future folk and creative dance units. In addition, rhythmic activities may also be integrated into numerous game and gymnastic activities ■

Understanding the Elements of Rhythm

Music and dance have one basic element in common—both are performed within rhythmic structure. Within this structure, the underlying beat, meter, and tempo provide direction and emphasis to the song or to dance movements. All of the following elements of rhythm are interrelated and affect dance movements. They can be introduced to children in a meaningful way through the rhythmic activities described in this chapter.

Underlying Beat

Perhaps the simplest and most important element of rhythm is the underlying beat of the musical accompaniment. Children can feel the steady pulsation of their heartbeat. Each beat of the heart has the same strength, or intensity, and recurs with the same amount of time between each beat. The normal heartbeat of a child at rest is about 72 beats per minute, spaced evenly throughout the one-minute period. After vigorous activity, the child's pulse rate increases to about 120 beats per minute. The heart is still beating with an even rhythm, but faster and with a shorter interval between each underlying beat. Like a person's heartbeat, the underlying beat in music is the steady sound, or pulsation, heard or felt as music is played. The underlying beat may be slow, with long and even intervals between each beat, or very fast, with corresponding shorter intervals.

In dance, we move "in time" with the musical accompaniment when each foot, hand, or body movement synchronizes with each successive beat of the music. For example, when children clap their hands or stamp their feet to each beat in the song "Row, Row, Row Your Boat," they are keeping in time to the rhythm of the song. Moving in time to the underlying beat is perhaps the most important prerequisite to all dance activities.

Measure

A measure is an equal grouping of underlying beats. As illustrated in the figure below, four quarter notes are grouped between two bar lines and repeated for three measures.

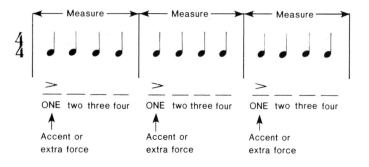

Accent

Accent is the extra force, or stress, given to certain beats in a measure. In the previous figure, the accent is on the first beat in each measure. To children, the accent is heard as a louder beat of the first note or as singing the first word of the measure louder than the other words in the measure. The purpose of accenting music and movement is to provide variety and excitement to all types of dance activities. Accenting is also used to help children change direction, such as "change direction after every fourth step" or shift to another movement pattern such as "alternately shift from a walk to a run after every fourth beat." In these examples, the emphasis given to the first beat in each measure provides a signal for children to shift to the next movement.

Time Signature

Time signature is the numerical symbol placed in front of written music to explain the underlying rhythm within a measure. The top number of this symbol indicates the number of beats to a measure, whereas the bottom number denotes the kind of note that will receive *one beat*. Four of the most common meters used in the elementary dance program are described here.

4/4 METER: *Denotes four beats in each measure*

In the 4/4 meter, each quarter note receives *one* beat, producing an even four-count meter rhythm. If a child were walking "in time" to this 4/4 meter, he would *step, step, step, step* evenly within each measure in a moderate walking speed. Since there are four beats, the child would always start each new measure on the same foot. The 4/4 meter is an *even rhythm*, with each underlying beat receiving full note value. This meter can be used with the following steps: walk, run, hop, jump, leap, and schottische.

2/4 METER: *Denotes two beats in each measure*
The accent is on the first and third beats, and quarter notes get one beat.

2/4
Rhythm
pattern

S Q S Q | S Q S Q

Accent

On first and third beats

The 2/4 meter is an *uneven rhythm* and is a combination of a *long* and a *short* beat. This meter is used with the following steps: skip, slide, gallop, polka, two-step, and bleking step.

3/4 METER: *Denotes three beats in each measure*
The accent is on the first beat, and quarter notes get one beat.

The 3/4 meter is an *even rhythm,* with each underlying beat receiving full note value. This meter is used for the waltz, mazurka, and varsoviienne.

6/8 METER: *Denotes six beats in each measure*
The accent is on the first and fourth beats, and eighth notes receive one beat.

The 6/8 meter is an *uneven rhythm* and is a combination of a long and a short beat followed by another long and short beat within each measure. This meter is used for the skip and gallop.

Tempo

Tempo is the rate of speed of the music or movement. In musical accompaniment, the tempo can be slow, moderate, or fast, or it may increase gradually from slow to fast.

In folk and creative dance activities, it is important for children to feel and understand the difference among moving slowly, moderately, and very quickly. It is also important for each child to sense different speeds of the same music and to learn to adjust movements to the new tempo of the music.

Rhythmic Pattern

Rhythmic pattern is the grouping of sounds of the song or instrumental music to correspond to the underlying beat of the music. To illustrate, in the song "Ten Little Indians," the sounds of the music are of different durations in order to provide the rhythmic pattern. The words follow the rhythmic pattern, and the rhythmic pattern corresponds to the underlying beat of the 2/4 meter of this music.

Phrase

In music, a phrase is a natural grouping of measures that gives a feeling of a complete musical thought or idea. The rhyme "Baa Baa Black Sheep" extends through the second measure

in order to complete a "musical sentence." Musical phrases are used in folk and creative dance activities to complete a series of movements before repeating them or before starting a new series of movements.

4/4 | Ba Ba Black Sheep | Have you any wool?

Intensity

Intensity refers to the amount of force exerted in a movement or sound. In movement, intensity is recognized as the feeling of heaviness or lightness. In sound, children hear loud and soft sounds in the musical accompaniment.

Teaching Procedures

The structure of a rhythmics lesson is similar to that of the game or gymnastic lesson described in previous chapters. Each rhythmic lesson normally has an introductory activity, a second skill development activity, and, third, closure. The basic progression used to teach the elements of rhythm is from individual to partner to group activities. The following sample lesson illustrates how to introduce the underlying beat, measure, and accent.

Sample Lesson: Beat, Measure, and Accent

Main theme   Moving to the underlying beat
Subthemes   Measures and accents
Progression   Individual to partner to group activities
Music   Any fast, popular record with a 4/4 beat

Part 1: Introductory Activity

Class members sit in a scattered formation on the floor, with their legs crossed.

1. Have the children clap in the following ways (without music).
   a. Clap knees four times, repeating measure (1, 2, 3, 4; 1, 2, 3, 4; etc.).
   b. Clap hands four times, repeating measure.
   c. Tap the floor four times, repeating measure.
   d. Make up combinations of four claps on knees, then four taps on the floor, and four claps with the hands (figure 28.1).
2. Have the children listen to "music" for the 4/4 meter (four beats per measure) and the accent on the first beat.
3. Repeat 1a through 1d with music.

Figure 28.1 Clap to the beat.

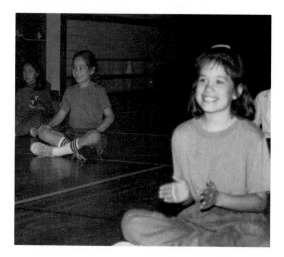

Figure 28.2 Hop to the rhythm.

Additional Ideas Once the class understands the meaning of the underlying beat and can clap four times within each measure according to the musical accompaniment, other combinations can be attempted in this introductory part of the lesson or at the beginning of a second, third, or fourth lesson, stressing the elements of rhythm:

1. Snap fingers.
2. From a standing position, slap different parts of the body.
3. From a standing position, shake one part of the body. Shake the right hand 1, 2, 3, and 4. Add other parts of the body; shake the right hand and the right leg.
4. Move parts of the body to the rhythm of the music. This could include bending, stretching, swinging, or twisting.
5. Perform locomotor movements to the rhythm of the music—walk, run, hop, or jump (figure 28.2)

Part 2: Skill Development

In the initial phase of the second part of the lesson, partners develop simple matching routines with the movements learned earlier.

1. Partners sit on the floor, cross-legged and facing each other. One child begins with four claps on whatever part of his body he chooses; his partner follows. The first performer chooses another part of his body and repeats, with his partner copying him. Continue with two more parts of the body. After the fourth part of the body, ask the partners to work together and perform the four clapping movements simultaneously on the four parts of their bodies.
2. Join partner clapping: Partners sit cross-legged, facing each other, and tap four times on the floor, then four times to each other's hands (figure 28.3), then four times to own hands (figure 28.4).

Figure 28.3 Clap four times to each other's hands.

Figure 28.4 Then clap four times to own hands.

chapter 28

Figure 28.5 Include a twist.　　**Figure 28.6** Side-by-side or back-to-back.

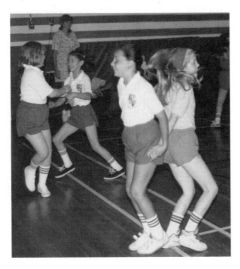

ones first presented to individuals, then to partners. These are as follows:

1. In your group of four, sit cross-legged, facing the center of the group. Without music, clap hands four times, tap floor four times, then hands again for four counts.

2. Repeat with music.

3. Make up a routine, with each child tapping the floor, then all clapping hands, then tapping the floor again. "Next time, when you clap hands, place your hands to the side and clap hands with the players on your right and your left." This should be enough to get each group started on its own routine.

3. Repeat 2 from a standing position, substituting tapping the floor with tapping or shaking one's own body parts or snapping fingers.

During the various activities of this part of the lesson, consciously stress *accenting* the first beat of each measure. That accent should also be used to signify the start of a new movement or a change in position or direction. If the latter two elements are emphasized, the meaning of a measure also becomes clear to each student.

Additional Ideas　As soon as the class understands the idea of matching clapping movements, the number of combinations becomes almost unlimited. Following are some possibilities to try here or leave until the next lesson:

1. Alternative hand clapping—tap the floor, clap one opposite hand, clap two hands.

2. Alternate a hand clap and a finger snap.

3. Include a turn, twist, or shift of the body after each measure (figure 28.5). This might include four clapping movements, followed by four steps around in a circle, then back to four clapping movements.

4. Develop matching routines (side-by-side or one behind the other), with a walk, run, hop, jump, or leap step (figure 28.6).

5. Combine locomotor movements with clapping, shaking, or snapping fingers.

6. Include a change of direction or level in these routines.

Arrange the class into groups of four. Since this may be the first group experience with this type of rhythmic exercise, it is wise to go slow at the start to allow each child to feel comfortable and to be successful with your challenges. The first challenges should be similar to the

If the children are receptive and at ease, allow them to make up their own sitting, standing, or moving routine in their own group of four. If more help is needed pose challenges, keeping them sitting on the floor, then from a standing position, and finally involving locomotor movements.

Part 3: Closure

Discuss measure, underlying beat, and accent.

Rhythmic Activities with Small Equipment

Small equipment is used with rhythmic activities in two ways. First, the equipment, such as a rope or hoop, can be used as a focal point or obstacle to move in and out of, around, or over. Second, the equipment, such as a hoop or ball, can be held or manipulated as an extension of the rhythmic movements of the body. Swinging a hoop and bouncing a ball to a rhythm are examples of the latter.

Begin by teaching hand or foot movements without equipment so that the children learn the basic movements and rhythmic patterns. Once these are acquired, introduce equipment to the routine or movement pattern.

Inflated Balls

Ball bouncing is particularly useful in helping children learn to move in time to the underlying beat of music. Any inflated ball can be used. Slow and fast tunes can be used in all of the following individual, partner, and group tasks.

Individual Tasks

Begin bouncing with one hand to the underlying beat of the music. Add the following challenges:

1. Change hands.

2. Bounce to one knee.

3. Bounce the ball around your body.

4. Bounce the ball with another part of your body (elbow, foot, etc.).

5. Bounce the ball and change direction—forward, backward, and sideways.

6. Bounce the ball and change levels—high, medium, and low.

7. Bounce, clap hands, bounce, and turn around.

8. Introduce a skipping rope. Place the rope on the floor in a curved or zigzag pattern. Develop tasks that require a bounce and a change of direction around or across the rope.

Partner and Group Tasks

The children can participate in various partner routines such as (1) matching bounces, (2) following the leader, (3) contrasting routines (one high and one low), and (4) bouncing and exchanging the ball on certain beats of the music. Group routines involving four or more players can also be developed by most children in the intermediate grades—for example, "Make up a routine with four players that includes four different bounces, a change of direction, and a change in level."

Individual Ropes

Basic rope-jumping skills and several ideas relating to the development of individual and partner routines were presented in chapter 26, however, no reference was made to musical accompaniment. The following challenges can be performed to musical accompaniment (any current popular tune that has a good beat).

The following examples illustrate the variety of ways a rope can be used in rhythmic activities by an individual or by two or more players.

Individual Tasks

Choose a record with a good 4/4 meter for the following individual tasks:

1. Place the rope on the floor in any pattern desired (straight, curled, or zigzag). Make up a routine of moving back and forth over your rope (figure 28.7). If the children feel the 4/4 even rhythm, they should use a walk, run, jump, hop, or leap step in their routine.

2. Keep the same rope pattern, but change the record or tape to a 2/4 or 6/8 meter. Pose the challenge, "Now make up a new routine, moving back and forth or around your rope." The uneven 2/4 or 6/8 rhythm should encourage children to use a skipping or sliding step in their routine.

Partner and Group Tasks

1. Develop a matching routine with your partner, using even rhythm and including a two-foot basic and a hop step (figure 28.8).

Figure 28.7 Move back and forth over the rope.

Figure 28.8 Include a two-foot basic and a hop step.

2. Make up a rope-skipping routine, with one partner following the other. (Use uneven rhythm.)

3. Place one rope on the ground and make up a matching routine with your partner, using a 2/4 meter (figure 28.9).

4. Have the children place two ropes on the floor and repeat task 1.

5. In groups of four, make up a matching routine in any pattern you like.

Rhythm or Lummi Sticks

Rhythm or lummi sticks* are extremely useful in developing the elements of rhythm. The sticks are approximately ten to twelve inches long and can be made from one-inch doweling or old broomsticks. The sticks are held between the thumb and fingers near the lower third of the stick (figure 29.10).

*Lummi sticks and records can be purchased from Educational Activities, Inc., Box 392, Freeport, NY, 11520.

Figure 28.9 Place one rope on the floor and make up a matching routine.

Figure 28.10 Hold sticks between the thumb and fingers.

Individual Tasks

The first tasks presented should give each child an opportunity to learn how to tap the sticks to the rhythm of the music and how to shift from one tapping movement to another. Challenges can include the following simple routines:

Sitting Cross-Legged or on Knees

1. Tap the floor four times, tap the sticks together four times, tap the right or left leg four times, and so on.
2. Make up a routine, tapping the floor in front, to the side, and behind you (figure 28.11).
3. Make up a routine that includes tapping, throwing, and catching the sticks and then another tapping movement.
4. Repeat 1, 2, and 3 to a 4/4 musical accompaniment.

Once the children can tap the sticks together, on a part of the body, or on the floor, the sticks can be used to teach accent, intensity, and different meters in a very enjoyable way. Try the following challenges.

Figure 28.11 Make up a routine.

5. Repeat 1 and 2, making the first beat in each measure louder than the next three beats.
6. Still sitting cross-legged or kneeling, tap the sticks together on the first beat, then tap the body (thighs, stomach, etc.) the next three times. Continue pattern.
7. Repeat 5 and 6 with the same musical accompaniment as 4.
8. Repeat 5 and 6 with a 2/4 musical accompaniment, tapping the first beat with the two sticks and the second against the body.

Standing

9. Develop a routine of tapping the sticks in front, to the side, behind the back, and against the body. Use a 4/4 and a 2/4 or 6/8 musical accompaniment to emphasize even and uneven rhythms.
10. Develop a routine involving walking, running, hopping, or jumping and tapping the sticks to the 4/4 even rhythm of the musical accompaniment.
11. Develop a routine involving skipping or sliding and tapping the sticks to a 2/4 or 6/8 uneven rhythm of musical accompaniment.

Partner and Group Tasks

The first partner activities should begin with both players sitting about two feet apart in a cross-legged position, facing each other. This position encourages the players to develop routines using the floor for tapping, as well as the partner's sticks. Following are a few sample routines:

1. Without music, hit sticks on the floor, hit both sticks together in front, hit with both arms sideways, hit floor.
2. Without music, partners hit sticks to the floor, hit their own sticks together, exchange right sticks, then exchange left sticks.

rhythmic and movement activities

3. Repeat 1 and 2 with a 4/4 or 2/4 musical accompaniment.

4. Without music, numerous calistheniclike and other rhythmic routines can be developed with two players standing face to face, side by side, or back to back.

5. Repeat 4 with same musical accompaniment used in 3.

6. Group activities can also be developed with sets of three or more children. Once the children have learned the basic tapping skills and have had rhythmic experience with hoops, balls, and skipping ropes, they will develop creative rhythmic routines with lummi sticks quickly and enthusiastically.

Hoops

Hoops can be used in two ways with rhythmic activities: (1) when placed on the floor, they become an obstacle or focal point to maneuver in and out of, around, or over and (2) when held or manipulated, they can help children move their bodies or parts of them to the rhythm of a drumbeat or music.

Several standardized movement skills described in chapter 26 can be performed in time to musical accompaniment. These skills and the ones provided in the following paragraphs illustrate the versatility of hoops, as well as their effectiveness in teaching the elements of rhythm.

Individual Tasks

Have each child place his hoop flat on the floor. Present challenges, such as the following, that involve locomotor skills and a change of direction.

1. "Make up a jumping routine, moving in and out of your hoop." Later, add other challenges such as "in and out, around, and over." (Use even rhythm, 4/4 or 3/4 music.)

2. Use two or more hoops on the floor and repeat 1.

3. Introduce ball bouncing with a hoop.

Many twirling and movement skills can be done with a hoop. The following provide a basic starting point. Use uneven rhythm—2/4 or 6/8 music.

1. "Can you twirl the hoop on your body to the rhythm of the music 'Summer Place'?" Later, substitute back, arm, wrist, leg, or foot.

2. "Can you throw and catch the hoop, keeping in time to the rhythm of the music?"

3. "Develop a routine of swinging, jumping, and twisting."

Partner and Group Tasks

In partners, twirling, throwing, catching, and nonlocomotor skills can be incorporated into a variety of interesting and challenging matching, contrasting, and follow-the-leader routines.

1. Develop a series of challenges involving partners, using one or more hoops and musical accompaniment with an uneven rhythm.

2. Repeat the challenge, using partners, one or more hoops, and locomotor skills performed with an even rhythm accompaniment. (Run, walk, hop, jump, and leap.)

3. Repeat 1 or 2, adding a ball or other small equipment to the original challenge.

Partner activities can be modified easily to add one or more children to each task.

Task Cards

Task cards can be applied to individual, partner, or group rhythmic activities with equal success. The following example illustrates the type of information that should be written on the cards.

Six to eight cards with different tasks (but the same music) should be used. Divide the class into small groups. Each child reads the challenge and then develops his own routine. Thus, there are several different types of routines rather than variations of one task. Various levels of ability can be accommodated by designing cards ranging from very simple tasks to challenges requiring greater skill and creative ability.

When equipment is unavailable for every child to perform a particular activity, use task cards and the station work technique. In the following example, the class is divided into four groups and then subdivided into partners. Each set of partners reads the challenge, then develops a matching routine. Any marching tune can be used for all stations. Allow four to five minutes for the partners to develop their routines, then put on the tune. If time permits, rotate the groups to their next station and repeat the process.

Station 1: Hoops. Make up a matching sequence with your partner that includes three different twirling movements, a pause in your routine, and a change in direction.

Station 2: Individual ropes. Make up a matching routine that includes three different steps.

Station 3: Utility balls. Develop a bouncing routine, with one partner leading and the other following.

Station 4: Lummi sticks. Make up a matching routine that includes a change of direction and a change in level.

The activities presented in this chapter should not be seen as a separate unit of dance. Rather, as was stated earlier, rhythmic activities should be integrated into game, gymnastic, and dance units. This can be done through periodic rhythmic warm-up activities and an occasional complete lesson of rhythmics interspersed within a game or gymnastic unit.

Selected References

Fleming, G. A. (1990, Revised). *Children's Dance.* Reston, VA: AAHPERD.

Harris, J. A., Pittman, A. M., and Waller, M. S. (1988). *Dance Awhile,* Sixth Edition. New York: Macmillan Publishing Co.

Murray, R. L. (1975). *Dance in Elementary Education,* Third Edition. New York: Harper and Row Publishers.

Stinson, S. (1988). *Dance for Young Children: Finding the Magic Movement.* Reston, VA: AAHPERD

29

Traditional and Contemporary Dances

All structured dances performed in the elementary school can be broadly classified as traditional and contemporary dances. The classification includes singing games and traditional dances of past cultures, as well as the contemporary dances of this generation. In this chapter, the first two sections have been organized to cope with the unique differences among the three developmental levels. The first section describes the basic steps, dance positions, and movement designs used in the dance program. The next section, "Teaching Dance Activities," provides suggestions relating to teaching folk and square dance activities using both structured and exploratory methods of instruction. The final section describes traditional and contemporary dances for all age levels. A glossary of terms is included in this section, as well as information about record companies and selected references ■

Dance Steps, Dance Positions, and Movement Designs

All traditional and contemporary dance activities use individual locomotor skills, such as walk, run, and jump, or combinations of skills such as slide, skip, two-step, or waltz step. The main individual and combined steps used in this dance program are described under "Dance Steps." The next section, "Dance Positions," describes and illustrates the various ways partners or groups of dancers hold onto each other as they perform a dance. Finally, the various ways a dancer moves in relation to a partner or other performers, such as meeting and parting, are illustrated under "Movement Designs."

Dance Steps

The following seven basic locomotor steps and four combination steps are used in one or more of the three developmental level dance programs.

Walk

A walk may vary from a basic heel-toe walking action to a shuffling movement from ball of foot to ball of foot. In most dances with an even rhythm, the accent, or emphasis, is on the first beat.

Run

A run may vary from a slow heel-toe run to a fast and vigorous running action from ball or toe of foot to the opposite ball or toe.

Rhythm: Even
Meter: 4/4

Hop

The hop is a basic springing action from the ball of one foot to the ball of the same foot.

Rhythm: Even
Meter: 4/4

Leap

A leap is a basic springing action from the ball of one foot to a landing on the ball of the opposite foot. A slight or exaggerated knee bend on each landing is followed by a lowering of the heel.

Rhythm: Even
Meter: 4/4

Jump

The jump is a basic springing action from the balls of both feet to the balls of both feet, with a slight overexaggerated knee bend. The heel normally comes down after the ball of the foot has made contact with the floor.

Rhythm: Even
Meter: 4/4

Skip

A skip is a step and a short hop on the same foot, shifting to a step and a hop on the opposite foot. In most dances with an uneven rhythm, the accent is on the first and third beats.

Rhythm: Uneven
Meter: 2/4 or 6/8

Two-Step

The two-step used in folk and square dances is a combination of a step forward on the ball of the left foot, then a closing action of the right to the left foot (weight is briefly taken on right foot), then a step forward on left foot. Repeat for the next measure, but begin on right foot.

Rhythm: Uneven						
Meter: 2/4						
underlying beat	>1̇ L	2 R	3 L	>1̇ R	2 L	3 R
stepping action	step	close	step	step	close	step
or	walk	together	walk	walk	together	walk
		first measure			second measure	

Polka

The polka step is similar to the two-step, with the addition of a hop in the combined sequence of steps. The first measure begins with stepping left, while the next begins with stepping right, alternating this action throughout the dance.

Rhythm: Uneven
Meter: 2/4

underlying beat				
stepping action	L step	R close	L step	L hop

Dance Positions

The various dance positions described and illustrated in figures 29.1 through 29.7 are used in one or more of the three developmental level dance programs.

Movement Designs

The movement designs in figure 29.8 are the various ways two or more dancers meet, greet, and part. They are used in simple singing games, as well as in folk and square dances.

Figure 29.1 Open position: facing forward, with inside hands joined.

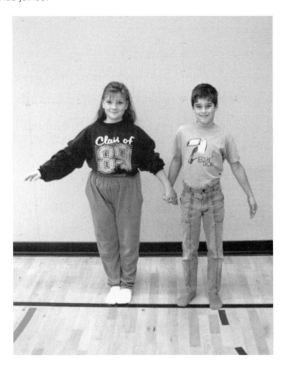

Figure 29.3 Closed position. Stand facing each other, with boy's right arm around girl and his hand resting under her shoulder blade. He holds girl's right hand in his left. Girl's left hand rests on his right shoulder.

Figure 29.2 Schottische, or conversation, position. Stand side-by-side, with girl on boy's right side. Boy's arm is behind girl's back and his hand is on her waist. Girl's left hands rests on boy's right shoulder.

Figure 29.4 Skaters, or promenade, position. Partners stand side-by-side, facing forward. Girl is on boy's right. Boy's right arm is over girl's left, and both hold right hands and left hands together.

chapter 29

Figure 29.5 Shoulder-waist position. Stand facing each other, with boy's arms outstretched and both hands holding girl's waist. Girl places her hands on boy's shoulders.

Figure 29.7 Varsovienne position. Stand side-by-side and facing forward. Girl is on boy's right. Boy's right arm is behind girl's shoulders and holding her right hand just above her right shoulder. Boy holds girl's left hand in his, about chest high.

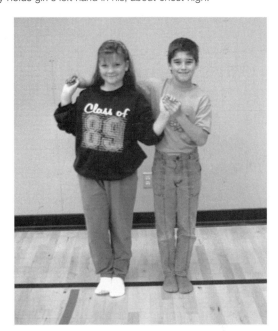

Figure 29.6 Two-hand facing position. Stand facing each other, with elbows bent and holding each other's hands.

Figure 29.8 Movement designs.

a. Meeting

b. Arching

c. Passing

d. Weaving

e. Starring

f. Swinging

Teaching Dance Activities

Dance activities for an elementary school physical education program begin with the simple singing games enjoyed by early primary children. During the next two developmental levels, children are introduced to a wide variety of folk dances from around the world. These dances can be taught in a systematic manner or through an exploratory or problem-solving approach.

Teaching Folk Dances

As suggested earlier in this book, there is no one best method of teaching that will work for all occasions. This is particularly true with the problems normally associated with teaching folk dance to children in developmental levels II and III. In many instances, these children lack a strong dance background, coupled with having been taught in a more formal or structured way. Differences in physical and social maturity and other important multicultural factors also must be considered when teaching folk dance activities to these older children. With these considerations in mind, the following suggested progression can be used as a starting point for each teacher to develop her own approach.

1. Acquire a general knowledge of the culture from which the dance originated for presentation to the class, perhaps selecting dances that represent some of the cultures or ethnic backgrounds of the children.

2. Review the music, dance steps, and movements of the dance prior to teaching it. Be confident and at ease so you can show genuine enthusiasm.

3. Start with children sitting near the music. Present the background information about the dance in relation to the class's interest and maturity. Make it meaningful to the children.

4. While sitting, play the music and have them tap out the beat, as this helps them become more familiar with the music.

5. While sitting, demonstrate the dance, or parts of it, with students. It is also helpful to teach your better students before the class demonstration to ensure they feel comfortable and the movements are correct.

6. Arrange the class into teaching formation for the dance. If it is a single circle dance, stand two steps inside the circle, demonstrate, move to another part of the circle, and demonstrate. Students tend to mirror what they see, so they will normally forget to reverse the foot movements and direction. When teaching children in front of you, do not turn around and demonstrate the step or movement. Mirror demonstrate; while facing the class, if you move your right foot, say to the class, "Move your left foot."

7. Have each student walk through the first step (later it may require a partner or group movement) and in a slow tempo. Move to the correct tempo as soon as possible.

8. Have the class repeat this part with music. Call out rhythmic cues.

9. Teach the next part of the dance in the same fashion.

10. Have the class dance the first and second parts consecutively with the music and your cues.

11. Teach each part in a similar way until all parts have been learned.

12. After the last part has been learned, have the class walk through the entire dance in the proper tempo.

13. Repeat the entire dance with music and your rhythmic cues. Gradually reduce your rhythmic cues, increase the volume of the music, and let children enjoy the dance.

Teaching Singing Games

Most primary singing games are individual or partner activities; however, both types are performed within a group situation. Since five-, six-, and seven-year-olds are basically individualistic, the singing games presented in this chapter can be performed individually while the children are in a line, circle, or scattered pattern. With practice and maturity, children progress to more advanced singing games involving intricate patterns and group participation.

Teaching singing games to children in the primary grades, particularly to five- and six-year-olds, should be an enjoyable experience for teachers and a creative experience for children. The children's uninhibited behavior and joy of movement make singing games an appropriate activity. Once they learn the words, they will provide their own accompaniment and an infinite variety of interesting and creative versions of each singing game.

Since early primary children vary widely in maturity, motor ability, and interests, no single method of teaching will prove successful with this type of activity. Each teacher should experiment with several approaches until she finds the one most suitable to her own style of teaching, usually a combination of techniques. The following suggestions may be helpful:

1. Use a form of musical accompaniment that permits you to work freely with the children, such as commercial records or a tape recording of your own piano accompaniment.

2. Give the name of the singing game and its origin, and mention something about the customs of the people. Illustrate by showing motion pictures, slides, or photographs of the people.

3. Teach the words of the singing game first. Children should practice singing the song until they have nearly memorized it.

4. Teach the basic steps of the singing game after the children have learned the verses.

5. Combine the basic steps with the words and music.

6. Combine the basic steps with the words and music, and begin with a whole class formation (i.e., large circle). Then progress to smaller groups.

7. Attempt to create a permissive atmosphere in which children feel free to express their own ideas and movements.

Through singing games, children learn to walk, run, skip, or perform a combination of these basic dance steps to musical accompaniment. When they can move rhythmically to music, they can create their own singing games. Allow them to develop their own dances to favorite nursery rhymes or songs. For example, "Sing a Song of Sixpence" and "I Saw a Ship a Sailing" have simple phrases and rhythmic melodies that provide the necessary ingredients for new singing games. In addition, children may wish to write their own verses about animals, spaceships, or special events and then try to apply them to musical accompaniment. Finding the appropriate music usually becomes a joint venture for the teacher and class. The table of additional singing games and available records later in this chapter will be of some assistance. Children should also be encouraged to create their own music. Perhaps, too, some children may be fortunate enough to have a teacher with a musical background and the talent to write musical accompaniments to fit the verses they write.

Teaching Square Dances

American folk dances include mixers, couples, longways, circles, and square dances that have been developed in North America during the past few hundred years. Of all these American folk dances, square dances have become the most popular with upper elementary school children, perhaps because of the simplicity of the steps and the enjoyment of participation.

The following suggestions will help teachers present various types of square dance patterns. A list of terms used in square dancing is provided in the glossary at the end of this chapter.

1. Emphasize fun and enjoyment rather than perfection of every skill.

2. Teach all square dance movements from a circle formation, with each girl standing to the right of her partner.

3. Select square dances that involve simple patterns, and introduce them at a slow speed.

4. Teach the dance by calling the dance patterns first without music and then with it. Once the dance is learned, you may continue to call your own dance or use a record with the calls included.

5. The majority of square dancing is done with a shuffle step rather than a run or hop. Emphasize a smooth and graceful slipping action, landing on the ball of the foot rather than on the heel.

6. The success of square dancing depends, in part, on keeping the square of four couples symmetrical and the partners parallel. Constantly check to see that children maintain the square and partners do not wander away from each other.

7. Encourage children not only to call their own dances, but also to create their own sequences of square dance figures.

Teaching Creative Folk Dance Activities

The traditional and contemporary folk dances that have been taught to upper elementary school children are rich in cultural heritage. These dances have normally been taught to children formally, with the steps, formations, and gestures of each dance introduced systematically. However, contemporary approaches to teaching elementary school physical activities use more individualized instructional techniques and more exploratory and problem-solving methods to cope with the characteristics, needs, and interests of this age group. The material that follows is an attempt to introduce a more creative approach to teaching folk dance activities. The next section describes the five basic elements of folk dance, followed by a suggested approach for teaching each of these elements in a systematic yet creative manner.

Elements of Folk Dance

Although there are marked differences in the steps, body gestures, and styles between one dance and another, all dances, regardless of age or cultural origin, are made up of five basic elements. The first element, as illustrated, includes the *steps* performed in the dance. Second, dancers move in a specified *direction*. Third, dancers move through a particular *pathway*. Fourth, dancers have a certain *relationship* to each other as they move through the dance. Finally, all dances are performed from a line, square, or circle *formation*. Each element is clarified in the following pages.

Element 1: Steps

The following seven locomotor steps (walk, run, hop, leap, jump, skip, and slide) represent the basic ways children move in folk dance activities. Most of these skills are acquired long before children reach the intermediate grades. Therefore, the emphasis in this dance program is to acquire different styles of performing each locomotor movement; to move gracefully and in time to the rhythm of the music; and to shift tempo, intensity, or other rhythmical skills to meet the challenge and enjoyable subtleties of each dance activity.

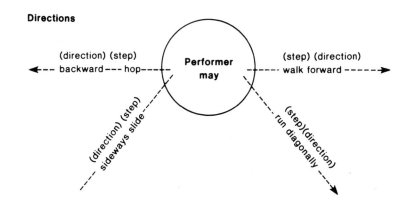

Directions

(direction) (step)
← backward --- hop

(step) (direction)
walk forward -----→

(direction) (step)
sideways slide

(step)(direction)
run diagonally

Element 2: Direction

All folk and square dance activities require performers to move in either a forward, backward, sideward, or diagonal direction. These are the simplest directions children may move in while performing the basic dance steps.

This diagram illustrates how the second element is added to the first element. For example, a child may walk (element 1) forward (element 2) or slide (element 1) sideways (element 2). The concept of "right-left" may be simplified for young children by placing a colored band on one wrist. The lesson plans in the next section illustrate how elements are added sequentially from one lesson to the next.

Element 3: Pathway

The third element common to all folk dance is the pathway of movement. A pathway may be described as a pattern of movement—straight, curved, or zigzag. In the diagram, each pathway has been added to element 1 (steps) and element 2 (direction). Note how directions and pathways relate to each other in folk dance movements.

Pathways

(pathway)
zigzagging

(step)
backwards ← --- run
(direction)

Now, a Performer may . . . .

(step) (pathway) (direction)
walk, straight forward ---→

(step)
slide

(direction)
sideways

(step) (direction) (pathway)
hop, diagonally and straight

(pathway)
curved

traditional and contemporary dances

Element 4: Relationship

Element 4 includes two ways dancers relate to each other. The first is the dance position and the way two dancers hold each other throughout the dance. The second type of relationship is the manner in which each performer moves in relation to his or her partner or other performers in the dance. The following is a list of the most common dance positions and movement designs:

Dance positions (review figures 29.1 through 29.7)	Movement designs (review figure 29.8)
Open	Meeting
Closed	Arching
Skaters	Passing
Two-hand facing	Weaving
Shoulder-waist	Starring
Schottische	Swinging
Varsovienne	

Performers may:

in a skater's position (element 4: relationship)
walk eight steps (element 1: steps)
straight forward (element 2: direction, and element 3: pathway)
change to a shoulder-waist position (element 4: relationship) and swing their partners (element 4: relationship).

Element 5: Formation

The fifth element of folk dance includes three formations in which folk and square dances are performed: line, circle, and square formations.

Formations

Line		Circle		Square		
X	X	X X		X X		
X	X	X	X	X		X
X	X	X X		X		X
X	X			X X		
X	X					
X	X					

(relationship)
Performers may . . . in promenade position,

(steps) (pathway) (direction)
walk straight forward for eight counts, then prome-

(relationship)(formation)
nade around the hall.

Teaching the Elements of Folk Dance

The approach suggested here is a continuation of the rhythmic approach presented in the previous chapter. Hence, it is assumed that children understand the elements of rhythm, such as *even* and *uneven rhythm, accent,* and *underlying beat,* and can recognize and apply these rhythmic elements to a variety of game, dance, and gymnastic movement skills.

In the previous section, the five elements of folk dance were described. These elements, illustrated in figure 29.9, can be introduced to children *sequentially* in an informal and relaxed manner through five interrelated stages. To illustrate, in lesson 1, the central theme is to move (walk, run, hop, jump, or leap) in time to an even musical accompaniment. In the introductory activities children will need to be introduced to the movement activities (central theme) involved in the folk dance. Depending on the complexity of the movements and the developmental level of the children and their familiarity with the movements, the introductory activities will need to be adjusted accordingly. It may be beneficial and necessary to introduce the children to the movements without music to begin with, and to go through the movements with "nonlocomotor actions" to ensure the children understand what is required. Once the movement actions are understood, music can be added. Individual, partner, and group activities then focus on the central theme from the beginning to the end of the lesson. Subthemes, such as changing speed or level, provide a little variety and a review of previously acquired movement skills. Although children may change direction within each movement task, specific references to directional movements are deliberately left out of this lesson. A combination of direct and indirect teaching styles will be required to teach the elements of folk dance. All steps and actions should be taught separately so that children can practice one or two movements at a time, without the worry of coordinating with a partner or group. The "part-whole" method of instruction progresses to partner and group work, moving the child gently along the learning stages continuum.

Lesson 1: Steps

Main theme Moving to even rhythm
Subtheme Change of speed and level

I. Introductory activities
   A. Individual introduction to walking, running, hopping, jumping, and leaping (may be simulated through nonlocomotor practices to ensure that early cognitive phase of learning is addressed)
   B. Individual walking, running, hopping, jumping, and leaping to 4/4 musical accompaniment
   C. Add change of speed and level to above challenge.

Figure 29.9 Introducing the elements of folk dance.

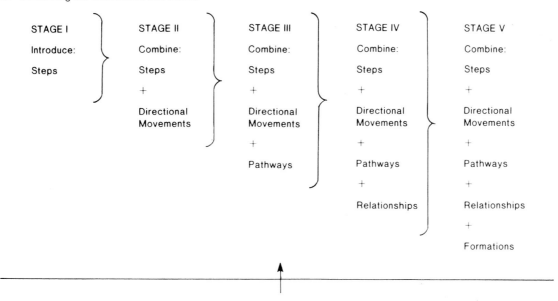

NOTE: Each of the five stages above progresses from:

Individual
to

Partner
to

Group Activities

II. Development
  A. In partners: "Make up a matching sequence that includes a run, hop, and jump and two changes in level." Use 4/4 musical accompaniment.
  B. In partners: "Develop a routine that includes clapping, twisting, shaking, running, and hopping steps." Use 4/4 musical accompaniment.
  C. In groups of four: Repeat B with four children in each group standing in a line for both challenges.
III. Closure
  Discuss meaning of measure, even rhythm, and tempo.

In lesson 2, the central theme of the lesson emphasizes the second element, *direction.* This lesson follows the same pattern established in lesson 1, beginning with individual, shifting to partner, then changing to larger group activities. Subthemes of even and uneven rhythm and changing speed provide variety as well as a review of previously introduced skills.

Lesson 2: Directional Movements

Main theme   Directional movements
Subthemes   Moving to even and uneven rhythm, change of speed

I. Introductory activities
  Repeat A and B of lesson 1, adding a change of direction to each respective challenge.

II. Development
  A. "Make up a sequence that includes a run and a hop, two changes of direction, and a clapping and shaking movement." Use 4/4 musical accompaniment.
  B. In partners: "Begin with one standing behind the other. Create a routine that includes a skip and slide, moving sideways and diagonally, and a change in speed." Use 2/4 musical accompaniment.
  C. In groups of three: "See if you can make a routine that includes one locomotor skill performed to an even musical accompaniment and three changes in direction." Use 4/4 musical accompaniment.
  D. In groups of four: "Make up a routine that includes uneven rhythm and a change of direction." Use a 2/4 musical accompaniment.
III. Closure
  Discuss uneven rhythm and directional movements.

At the completion of lesson 2, each teacher should consider such factors as the tone of the class, segregated or voluntary mixing of boys and girls for partner and group activities, and level of skill before planning the next few lessons. Some classes may need one or two more lessons that stress directional movements and help develop more positive interpersonal relationships before progressing to stage III. Hence, the number of lessons required to reach and complete the challenges in stage V depends on these factors and the progress that is made from one lesson to the next. Once children learn the basic elements of folk dance through this informal and creative approach, they develop a very positive attitude toward folk dance activities.

Dances for Three Developmental Levels

All traditional and contemporary dances described in this section are grouped according to developmental level. The main dance emphasis for each level is briefly outlined. Since there is such a wide variation in dance backgrounds and local multicultural interests, teachers should use the information in table 29.1 as a general sample of appropriate dances for each level. Other supplementary dances may be more appropriate for some teaching situations. Schools with one or more dominant ethnic groups should attempt to incorporate their dance heritage into the program.

Most of the developmental level I folk dance activities are singing games that usually involve a circle formation and simple steps or movement patterns. These singing games are part of the dance heritage of every country. They are, in essence, the forerunners of the more complicated traditional and contemporary dances. As such, they provide a foundation on which the more advanced dances can be built. Because of the cultural and historical significance of these dances, primary teachers should take time to provide interesting materials relating to their origin, the customs of the people, and the meaning of various dance movements. This information can be presented in many ways, such as reading stories and poems about the people; displaying pictures, dolls, and other articles; and showing a film about the country.

The dance activities of developmental level II shift toward a variety of folk dances performed in different formations and involving more complex dance steps and movement patterns. At this level, children learn to perform many movements, such as swings, arching, heel-toe, and the bleking step, in relatively long and often vigorous dances.

The dance program for developmental level III involves everything from simple mixers to folk dances that involve complex steps such as the waltz, polka, schottische, and two-step. These dances require more skill and form than the dances in the previous developmental level. Also, the introduction to square dance activities provides a repertoire of dances that this age group enjoys.

Table 29.1 Singing Games, Folk and Square Dances

Name of dance	Type of dance	Origin	Formation	Dance skills	Movement concepts to stress	Page
Developmental level I						
Baa, Baa, Black Sheep	Singing game	English	Single circle	Walk, stamp, bow, curtsy, turn	Change of direction, shapes	558
Bluebird	Singing game	American	Single circle	Skip	Change of direction, strong and light	558
Loobie Loo	Singing game	English	Single circle	Walk, skip, slide	Moving into space, change of direction	559
Farmer in the Dell	Singing game	English	Single circle	Walk, clap	Change of direction, relationships	559
Let Your Feet Go Tap, Tap, Tap	Singing game	English	Double circle	Skip, clap	Change of direction, strong and light, relationships	560
Hokey Pokey	Singing game	American	Single circle	Turn, nonlocomotor movements	Moving into space, shapes, strong and light	560
Sally Go Round the Moon	Singing game	English	Single circle	Walk, run, skip, slide	Change of direction, level and speed	560
Danish Dance of Greeting	Folk dance	Danish	Single circle	Clap, stamp, run	Change of direction and speed, strong and light	561
Ring Around the Rosy	Singing game	English	Single circle	Walk, skip	Change of direction and levels	561
The Muffin Man	Singing game	English	Single circle	Walk, clap, skater's position	Moving into space, change of direction	561
Did You Ever See a Lassie	Singing game	Scottish	Single circle	Walk, pantomime	Change of direction, relationships	562
How D'ye Do My Partner	Singing game	Swedish	Double circle	Skip, bow, curtsy	Change of direction, relationships	562
Children's Polka	Folk dance	German	Single circle	Slide, run, hop	Moving into space, strong and light	563
Round and Round the Village	Folk dance	English	Single circle	Skip, bow, curtsy	Change of direction, levels	563
Ach Ja	Folk dance	German	Double circle	Walk, slide, bow, curtsy	Change of direction, relationships	564
Oats, Peas, Beans, and Barley	Singing game	English	Single circle	Walk, skip, pantomime	Change of direction, relationships	564

Table 29.1 *Continued*

Name of dance	Type of dance	Origin	Formation	Dance skills	Movement concepts to stress	Page
Developmental level II						
A-Hunting We Will Go	Folk dance	English	Two lines	Skip, arch	Moving through space, change of direction, relationships	565
Jolly Is the Miller	Folk dance	English	Double circle	Walk, pantomime	Moving into space, change of direction, relationships	566
Shoo Fly	Folk dance	American	Single circle	Walk, swing, turn	Moving into space, change of direction, relationships	566
Bleking	Folk dance	Swedish	Single circle	Step, hop, bleking step	Moving into space, strong and light, relationships	566
Skip to My Lou	Folk dance	American	Single circle	Walk, skip, swing	Moving into space, change of direction, relationships	567
Paw Paw Patch	Folk dance	American	Double line	Walk, skip, clap	Moving into space, relationships	567
Pop Goes the Weasel	Folk dance	American	Double circle	Walk, skip	Moving into space, levels, relationships	568
Cshebogar	Folk dance	Hungarian	Single circle	Walk, skip, slide	Change of direction, levels, strong and light	568
Greensleeves	Folk dance	English	Double circle	Walk, star, over and under	Change of direction, relationships	569
Glowworm Mixer	Folk dance	American	Double circle	Walk, run, do-si-do	Change of direction and pathways, relationships	569
Little Brown Jug	Folk dance	American	Double circle	Slide, swing	Change of direction, relationships	569
Hora	Folk dance	Israeli	Single circle	Side step, step swing	Change of direction, relationships	570
Troika	Folk dance	Russian	Triple circle	Run, stamp, arch	Change of direction and speed	570
Grand March	Folk dance	American	Line	Walk	Change of direction, relationships	571
Oh Susanna	Folk dance	American	Single circle	Walk, slide, do-si-do	Moving into space, change of direction, relationships	571
Developmental level III						
Schottische	Folk dance	Scottish	Double circle	Schottische step	Change of direction, relationships	572
Badger Gavotte	Folk dance	American	Double circle	Slide, two-step	Change of direction, relationships	572
Sicilian Circle	Folk dance	American	Double circle	Walk, chain	Change of direction and pathways	573
Virginia Reel	Folk dance	American	Line	Walk, skip, swing, do-si-do	Change of direction and pathways, relationships	573
Solomon Levi	Square dance	American	Square	Walk, swing	Pathways, relationships	574
Oh Johnny	Square dance	American	Square	Allemande left, walk, swing	Pathways, relationships	574
Ace of Diamonds	Folk dance	Danish	Double circle	Walk, swing	Change of direction, force, relationships	574
Seven Jumps	Folk dance	Danish	Single circle	Step-hop	Change of direction, relationships	575
Norwegian Mountain March	Folk dance	Norwegian	Triple circle	Run, waltz, turn under	Change of direction, relationships	575
Alley Cat	Folk dance	American	Scattered	Touch step, turn, jump	Change of direction, force	576
Korobushka	Folk dance	Russian	Double circle	Schottische step	Change of direction, relationships	576
Klumpakojis	Folk dance	Lithuanian	Double circle	Walk, stamp, polka step	Change of direction and pathways, relationships	577
Red River Valley	Square dance	American	Square	Walk, swing, do-si-do	Change of direction and pathways, relationships	577
Heel and Toe Polka	Folk dance	American	Double circle	Polka step	Change of direction and pathways, relationships	578
Oklahoma Mixer	Folk dance	American	Double circle	Walk, two-step	Change of direction, relationships	578
Rye Waltz	Folk dance	American	Double circle	Slide, waltz step	Change of direction, relationships	578
Tinikling	Folk dance	Philippine	Line	Tinikling step	Change of direction and speed, relationships	579

traditional and contemporary dances

Baa, Baa, Black Sheep (Level I)

Musical Accompaniment
Childhood Rhythms, Series 7, No. 701
Folkcraft 1191

Formation: Single circle, with girls to right of boys and all facing center

Skills: Stamp, bow and curtsy, turn, and walk

Measures	Song	Action
1	Baa, baa, black sheep,	Stamp three times.
2	Have you any wool?	Shake fingers.
3	Yes sir, yes sir,	Nod head twice.
4	Three bags full.	Hold three fingers up.
5	One for my master,	Turn right and bow or curtsy.
6	One for my dame,	Turn left and bow or curtsy.
7	And one for the little boy	Turn around.
8	Who lives in the lane.	Face center and bow or curtsy.
9–12	*Chorus:*	Join inside hands and take sixteen steps counterclockwise.

Variations

All join hands and take eight slides to the right, then eight slides left. Raise hands and take four steps into the circle and four steps out. Repeat four in and four out. Drop hands and skip sixteen steps counterclockwise.

Bluebird (Level I)

Musical Accompaniment
Folkcraft 1180

Formation: Single circle facing center with hands joined forming arches, and one child standing under one arch as the "bluebird"

Skills: Skip

Measures	Song	Action
1–16	Bluebird, bluebird through my window,	The bluebird skips in and out of the arches all around the circle, and at the end of the song, stops behind a circle player.
	Bluebird, bluebird through my window, Bluebird, bluebird through my window, Oh Mary*, I am tired.	
	Chorus:	
1–12	Take a little boy (girl) tap him on his shoulder. (Repeat three times)	During chorus, the bluebird taps both hands lightly on the front child's shoulders. Old bluebird keeps hands on new bluebird's shoulders as she repeats the skipping action in a trainlike fashion in and out of the arches.
13–16	Oh Johnny* (Jenny*), I am tired.	Repeat entire song and chorus, adding one child at a time until all are chosen.

*Substitute name of each chosen child.

Loobie Loo (Level I)

Musical Accompaniment
Folkcraft 1184
Childhood Rhythms,
Series 7, No. 706
Bowmar Singing Games,
Album I, No. 1514

Formation: Single circle facing center with hands joined

Skills: Walk, skip, slide

Measures	Song	Action
	Chorus:	
1–2	Here we go Loobie Loo,	Circle left, using eight walking, skipping, or sliding steps.
3–4	Here we go Loobie Light,	Circle right eight steps.
5–6	Here we go Loobie Loo,	Everyone drops hands and faces the center.
7–8	All on a Saturday night.	
	Verse No. 1:	
1–2	I put my right hand in,	Place right hand toward center of circle.
3–4	I take my right hand out,	Turn, place right hand away from circle.
5–6	I give my hand a shake, shake, shake	Shake hand.
7–8	And turn myself about.	Turn in place.
	Repeat chorus after each verse.	Repeat action of chorus.
	I put my left hand in, etc.	Repeat each verse according to the movement suggested.
	I put my both hands in, etc.	
	I put my right foot in, etc.	
	I put my left foot in, etc.	
	I put my elbows in, etc.	
	I put my shoulder in, etc.	
	I put my big head in, etc.	
	I put my whole self in, etc.	

Farmer in the Dell (Level I)

Musical Accompaniment
Folkcraft 1182
Victor 21618
Bowmar Singing Games, Album II

Formation: Single circle facing center with hands joined, one child, the "farmer," in the center of the circle

Skills: Walk and clap

Measures	Song	Action
1–2	The farmer in the dell,	All walk right around the circle, singing verse while the farmer looks about for a wife.
3–4	The farmer in the dell,	
5–6	Heigh-ho! the cherry-o,*	Continue to walk around the circle as the farmer chooses a wife, who joins him at the center of the circle.
7–8	The farmer in the dell.	
9–10	The farmer takes a wife,	Repeat procedure as directed.
11–12	The farmer takes a wife,	Repeat procedure as directed.
13–14	Heigh-ho! the cherry-o,	Repeat procedure as directed.
15–16	The farmer takes a wife.	Repeat procedure as directed.
	The wife takes a child, etc.	Repeat procedure as directed.
	The child takes a nurse, etc.	Repeat procedure as directed.
	The nurse takes a dog, etc.	Repeat procedure as directed.
	The dog takes a cat, etc.	
	The cat takes a rat, etc.	
	The rat takes the cheese, etc.	Children in the center crowd around the "cheese" and clap their hands over the cheese's head, while circle players stand still, clap hands, and sing verse.
	The cheese stands alone.	
	The farmer runs away, etc.	Continue walking as the farmer, then wife, and so on, leave the center of the circle.
	(Repeat for each player as he leaves center of circle.)	Note: Cheese remains and becomes the new farmer.

*This song may be sung "derry-o," "dairy-o," or "the dearie-o."

Let Your Feet Go Tap, Tap, Tap (Level I)

Musical Accompaniment
Folkcraft 1184
Lloyd Shaw E-7

Formation: Double circle with partners facing each other, boys on the inside and girls on the outside circle

Skills: Skip and clap

Measures	Song	Action
1–2	Let your feet go tap, tap, tap	Tap foot three times on tap, tap, tap.
3–4	Let your hands go tap, tap, tap	Clap hard three times on tap, tap, tap.
5–6	Let your fingers beckon me.	Partners back to each other.
7–8	Come dear partner, dance with me.	Partners join hands and face counterclockwise.
	Chorus:	
1–2	Ta, la, la, la, la, la, la	Children skip around circle singing chorus.
3–4	Ta, la, la, la, la, la, la	
5–6	Ta, la, la, la, la, la, la	
7–8	Ta, la, la, la, la, la, la	

Hokey Pokey (Level I)

Musical Accompaniment
Folkcraft 6026
Capitol 2427
McGregor 6995

Formation: Circle facing center

Skills: Turn and nonlocomotor skills

Measures	Song	Action
1–2	You put your right foot in,	Place right foot in circle.
3–4	You put your right foot out,	Take right foot out of circle.
5–6	You put your right foot in,	Place right foot in circle.
7–8	And, you shake it all about.	Shake right leg.
	Chorus:	
1–2	You do the hokey pokey,	During the first three lines, children raise hands over head and wiggle their bodies as they turn around in place.
3–4	You do the hokey pokey,	
5–6	You do the hokey pokey,	Clap hands three times.
7–8	That's what it's all about.	

Repeat song and action for:
(1) Left foot
(2) Right arm
(3) Left arm
(4) Right elbow
(5) Left elbow
(6) Head
(7) Right hip
(8) Left hip
(9) Whole body
(10) Back side
(11) Any other part of body

Sally Go Round the Moon (Level I)

Musical Accompaniment
Folkcraft 1198
Victor 45–5064

Formation: Single circle facing center with hands joined
Skills: Walk, run, skip, or slide

Measures	Song	Action
1–2	Sally, go round the moon,	Walk, run, skip, or slide around the circle. On the word "boom," all jump into the air and clap hands or perform any movement they wish.
3–4	Sally, go round the stars,	
5–6	Sally, go round the chimneypots,	
7–8	On a Sunday afternoon—Boom!	
	Repeat above.	Repeat action in opposite direction.

Danish Dance of Greeting (Level I)

Musical Accompaniment
Folkcraft 1187
Merit Audiovisual 1041

Formation: Single circle of couples facing center, the girl on the right side of the boy

Skills: Clap, stamp, bow, curtsy, turn, and run

Measures	Action
1	Clap hands twice and bow, or curtsy, to child on the other side (neighbor).
2	Clap hands twice, turn and bow, or curtsy, to partner.
3	Stamp on the right foot and then on the left.
4	Turn around in place with four running steps.
5–8	Repeat actions 1–4.
9–12	All join hands and circle to the right with sixteen short running steps.
13–16	Repeat action to the left.

Ring Around the Rosy (Level I)

Musical Accompaniment
Folkcraft 1199

Formation: Single circle, girls to right of boys, facing center with hands joined

Skills: Walk and skip

Measures	Song	Action
1–2	Ring around a rosy	Keeping hands joined, circle left. All stop, face center, sneeze twice, then drop to squatting position on word *down*.
3–4	A pocket full of posies,	
5–6	At choo, at choo*	
7–8	All fall down.	
9–10	The cow's in the middle	All stay in squat position, sing verse and jump up at end of verse.
11–12	Lying down to rest.	
13–14	Around the king, around the queen	
15–16	We call jump up.	

*Other words, such as *tish-a, tish-a; hush-a, hush-a; ashes, ashes;* or *one two three,* can be substituted.

The Muffin Man (Level I)

Musical Accompaniment
Folkcraft 1188

Formation: Single circle facing center with one child (the "muffin man") in the center

Skills: Walk, clap, skaters' position

Measure	Song	Pattern
1–2	Oh, have you seen the muffin man,	Children join hands and circle to the left using a walk or a slow skip step and singing the first verse.
3–4	The muffin man, the muffin man,	
5–6	Oh, have you seen the muffin man,	
7–8	Who lives across the way.	
9–10	Oh, yes, we've seen the muffin man,	Children in circle stand facing center and clap hands while singing "The Muffin Man." The child in center chooses a partner from circle and brings him or her back to center (in skaters' position). This child becomes the new muffin man while the old partner returns to circle.
11–12	The muffin man, the muffin man,	
13–14	Oh, yes, we've seen the muffin man,	
15–16	Who lives across the way.	

Teaching Suggestions

With large numbers of children start with two muffin men in the center of the circle. Substitute "Drury Lane" as an English version.

Did You Ever See a Lassie (Level I)

Musical Accompaniment
Folkcraft 1183
Lloyd Shaw E-4

Formation: Single circle facing center with hands joined, one child in the center of the circle

Skills: Walk and pantomime

Measures	Song
1–2	Did you ever see a lassie, ("laddie" when boy is in center)
3–4	A lassie, a lassie,
5–6	Did you ever see a lassie
7–8	Go this way and that?
	Chorus:
9–10	Go this way and that way.
11–12	Go this way and that way.
13–14	Did you ever see a lassie
15–16	Go this way and that?

Action

All join hands and walk eight steps to the left, swinging joined hands, then eight steps back.

All stop, release hands, face the child in center and imitate his or her movements. Repeat singing game with a new leader in the center.

Teaching Suggestions

Once the children have learned the basic movements, have them create impressions such as birds, animals, and mechanical toys. And instead of walking, have them walk using swinging and swaying, stamping, and clapping.

How D'ye Do My Partner (Level I)

Musical Accompaniment
Folkcraft 1190
Lloyd Shaw E-3

Formation: Double circle with partners facing, girls on the outside circle

Skills: Bow, curtsy, skip

Measures	Song
1–2	How d'ye do my partner,
3–4	How d'ye do today?
5–6	Will you dance in a circle?
7–8	I will show you the way.
	Chorus:
9–10	Tra, la, la, la, la,
11–12	Tra, la, la, la, la,
13–14	Tra, la, la, la, la,
15–16	Tra, la, la, la, la.
	Repeat song.

Pattern

Boys bow to partners.
Girls curtsy to partners.
Boy offers hand to partner.
Join inside hands and turn counterclockwise.

With joined hands, skip around the circle. At the end of the chorus, girls move one position forward to new partners.

Children's Polka (Kinderpolka) (Level I)

Musical Accompaniment
Folkcraft 1187
Lloyd Shaw E-7

Formation: Single circle with partners facing, both arms extended sideward and hands joined

Skills: Slide, hop, and run

Measures	*Action*
1–2	Take two slides toward center and step lightly three times.
3–4	Take two slides away from center; step lightly three times.
5–8	Repeat action of measures 1–4.
9–10	Slap own knees once, clap own hands once, and clap partner's hands three times.
11–12	Repeat action of measures 9–10.
13	Hop, placing right heel forward, place right elbow in left hand, and shake finger three times.
14	Repeat action of measure 13 with left foot.
15–16	Turn in place with four running steps and step lightly three times.

Teaching Suggestions

To help children learn the dance pattern, count in this manner:

Step, step, tap, tap, tap. Repeat.
Slap, clap, clap, clap, clap. Repeat.
Hop, one, two, three. Repeat.
Turn around now, tap, tap, tap.

Round and Round the Village
(Go In and Out the Windows) (Level I)

Musical Accompaniment
Folkcraft 1191

Formation: Single circle with all facing center and hands joined, one or more players are outside the circle

Skills: Skip, bow, and curtsy

Measures	*Song*	*Action*
1–2	Go round and round the village,	Circle children join hands and walk clockwise, while outside players skip counterclockwise.
3–4	Go round and round the village,	
5–6	Go round and round the village,	
7–8	As we have done before.	
1–2	Go in and out the windows,	Children in circle stand and raise arms to form arches (windows) while outside players weave in and out.
3–4	Go in and out the windows,	
5–6	Go in and out the windows,	
7–8	As we have done before.	
1–2	Now go and choose a partner,	"It" skips around the inside of the circle, stops, and bows or curtsys in front of a partner he or she has chosen.
3–4	Now go and choose a partner,	
5–6	Now go and choose a partner,	
7–8	As we have done before.	
1–2	Now follow me to London,	"It" skips around inside the circle, followed by the new partner. Circle players skip in the opposite direction.
3–4	Now follow me to London,	
5–6	Now follow me to London,	
7–8	As we have done before.	
1–2	Shake hands before you leave me,	The circle players remain in place, clap their hands, and sing while inside players shake hands and bow or curtsy. The chosen player(s) then goes to the outside of the circle while other players return to the circle.
3–4	Shake hands before you leave me,	
5–6	Shake hands before you leave me,	
7–8	As we have done before.	

Ach Ja (Oh yes!) (Level I)

Musical Accompaniment
Childhood Rhymes VII
Lloyd Shaw E-2

Formation: Double circle with partners facing counterclockwise, boys on inside, girls on outside with inside hand joined

Skills: Walk, slide, bow, and curtsy

Measures	Song	Action
1	When my father and my mother,	Walk forward eight steps, then drop hands.
2	Take the children to the fair,	
3	Ach ja,	Partners bow to each other.
4	Ach ja.	Boys bow to girl on right. Girl curtsys.
5	They haven't any money,	Repeat actions 1–4 for 5–8.
6	But it's little that they care.	
7	Ach ja,	
8	Ach ja.	
	Chorus:	
9–16	Tra, la, la, tra, la, la, tra, la, la, La, la, la, la Ach ja, Ach ja.	Partners face each other, then take four slide steps counterclockwise, swinging their arms to the side and back on each step. Repeat four slide steps clockwise. Partners bow and curtsy, then the boy steps to the left to meet the next girl. New partners bow and curtsy.
	Repeat song.	Repeat dance.

Oats, Peas, Beans, and Barley (Level I)

Musical Accompaniment
Folkcraft 1182
Folk Dancer MH 1110-A

Formation: Single circle facing center with hands joined, one child in the center of the circle is the "farmer"

Skills: Walk, skip, and pantomime

Measures	Song	Pattern
1–2	Oats, peas, beans, and barley grow,	Farmer in center stands while children in circle walk left, taking small steps. Circle players stop, point to the farmer, shrug, turn right, and stamp their feet.
3–4	Oats, peas, beans, and barley grow,	
5–6	Do you or I or anyone know	
7–8	How oats, peas, beans, and barley grow?	
1–2	First the farmer sows his seed,	Children in circle stop, face the center, and all dramatize the words of the song.
3–4	Then he stands and takes his ease.	
5–6	Stamps his foot and claps his hand.	
7–8	And turns around to view the land.	
1–2	Waiting for a partner,	Children in the circle skip left as the farmer skips around inside the circle and picks a new partner. The farmer and new partner skip around inside the circle.
3–4	Waiting for a partner,	
5–6	Open the ring and choose one in.	
7–8	While we all gladly dance and sing.	
	Chorus:	
1–8	Tra, la, la, la, la, la, Tra, la, la, la, la, la, Tra, la, la, la, la, la, la, Tra, la, la, la, la, la.	The two farmers continue to skip inside the circle while the others join hands and circle left. "Old farmer" joins the ring and "new farmer" repeats pattern.

Name of dance	Skills	Formation	Origin	Record source
Peas, Porridge, Hot	Turn, run	Circle	English	Folkcraft 1190
Popcorn Man	Skip, jump	Circle	American	Folkcraft 1180
Mulberry Bush	Walk, skip, turn, pantomime	Circle	English	Bowman A–1, Folkcraft 1183
Ten Little Indians	Walk	Circle	American	Folkcraft 1197
London Bridge	Walk	Circle	English	Bowmar 36–A(2) RCA 45–5056
Hickory, Dickory, Dock	Run, stamp	Circle	English	Victor 22760
Little Miss Muffet	Walk	Circle	English	Childhood Rhythms Series 7, No. 703
I Should Like to Go to Shetland	Gallop	Circle	English	Folkcraft 1190
Jump Jim Joe	Run, jump	Circle	American	Folkcraft 1193 RCA 45–6182
Chimes of Dunkirk	Skip	Circle	English	Folkcraft 1190
Thread Follows the Needle	Walk	Line	English	RCA 22760 (E–87) Pioneer 3017
Turn the Glass Over	Walk, turn	Circle	English	Folkcraft 1181
Nixie Polka	Polka step	Circle	Swedish	Folkcraft 5785
Rig-a-Jig-Jig	Walk, skip	Circle	American	Folkcraft 1199
Sing a Song of Sixpence	Walk	Circle	English	Folkcraft 1180 RCA Victor 22760
Bingo	Walk, grand	Circle	American	Folkcraft 1189
Carousel	Slide, draw, step, stamp	Circle	Swedish	RCA 45–6179 Pioneer 3044–A
Hansel and Gretel	Heel-toe step, skip	Circle	German	Folkcraft 1 RCA 45–6182
Hinky, Dinky, Parlez Vous	Walk, do-si-do, promenade	Square	American	Folkcraft 1059

Dances for Developmental Level II

A-Hunting We Will Go (Level II)

Musical Accompaniment
Folkcraft 1191
Victor 45–5064
Childhood Rhythms,
Series 7, No. 705

Formation: Two parallel lines (longways set) facing each other, girls on one side and boys on the other

Skills: Skip, arch

Measures	Song	Action
1–2	Oh, a-hunting we will go,	Head couple joins inside hands and skips down between the lines to the foot of the set.
3–4	A-hunting we will go,	
5–6	We'll catch a fox and put him in a box,	Head couple turns around, changes hands, and skips back to the head of the set.
7–8	And then we'll let him go.	
		All other players clap hands while head couple skips down and back.

Chorus:

1–2	Tra, la, la, la, la, la, la,	Head couple skips around the left side of the set, followed by other couples. When the head couple reaches the foot of the line, it forms an arch under which all other couples pass. Head couple remains while the second couple becomes the head couple.
3–4	Tra, la, la, la, la, la,	
5–6	Tra, la, la, la, la, la, la, la, la, la,	
7–8	Tra, la, la, la, la, la.	

Repeat dance with new head couple.

Jolly Is the Miller (Level II)

Musical Accompaniment
Folkcraft 1192
Lloyd Shaw E-10

Formation: Partners form a double circle facing counterclockwise with girls on the inside; one player, the "miller," stands in the center

Skills: Walk and pantomime

Measures	Song
1–2	Jolly is the miller who lives by the mill,
3–4	The wheel turns around of its own free will,
5–6	One hand in the hopper and the other in the sack,
7–8	The hub steps forward and the rim steps back.

Action

Couples join inside hands and walk counterclockwise while singing the song. During the second line, children in the inner circle extend left arms sideward to form a mill wheel. On the last word of the song ("back"), partners drop hands and the inner circle steps forward while the outer circle steps backward. The extra player tries to secure a partner during this exchange. The child without a partner goes to the center.

Repeat dance with new partner.

Shoo Fly (Level II)

Musical Accompaniment
Folkcraft 1185

Formation: Single circle with girls on the boys' right, hands joined, and all facing the center of the circle

Skills: Walk, swing, and turn

Measures	Song	Action
1–2	Shoo, fly, don't bother me,	Walk four steps forward, swinging arms.
3–4	Shoo, fly, don't bother me,	Walk four steps backward.
5–6	Shoo, fly, don't bother me,	Walk four steps forward, swinging arms.
7–8	For I belong to somebody.	Walk four steps backward.
	Chorus:	
1–2	I feel, I feel,	
3–4	I feel like a morning star,	
5–6	I feel, I feel,	
7–8	I feel like a morning star.	

Partners join hands and walk around each other in a clockwise direction. Repeat. On the last "morning star," the boy raises his left hand and turns his partner under his arm. The girl is now on the boy's left. The girl on the boy's right becomes his new partner.

Join hands and repeat dance.

Bleking (Level II)

Musical Accompaniment
Folkcraft 1188
Lloyd Shaw E-9

Formation: Single circle with partners facing; boys face counterclockwise, girls face clockwise; partners extend their arms forward at shoulder height and join hands

Skills: Bleking step, step, and hop

Measures	Action
1–8	Hop on left foot, extend the right heel forward, keeping the right leg straight. As this movement takes place, thrust the right arm forward and pull the left arm back (count one). Continue for seven more counts, changing the lead foot on each count.
9–16	Partners face each other, extending arms sideways and joining hands. Boy begins with his right foot, girl with her left foot. Partners begin to turn in place by taking seven step-hops in a clockwise direction and end with a stamp on the last count. As the children turn in place, their arms move in a windmill action up and down with each step-hop.

Repeat dance in counterclockwise direction.

Skip to My Lou (Level II)

Musical Accompaniment
Bowmar Singing Games Album 3, No. 1522-A
Folkcraft 1192
Folk Dancers FD 34

Formation: Single circle with partners side by side and the girls on the boys' right

Skills: Walk, skip, swing, and promenade

Measures	Song	Action
	Verse No. 1:	
1–2	Boys to the center, Skip to my Lou,	Boys walk four steps forward and four steps backward.
3–4	Boys to the outside, Skip to my Lou,	
5–6	Boys to the center, Skip to my Lou,	Repeat.
7–8	Skip to my Lou, my darling.	
	Verse No. 2:	
1–2	Girls to the center, Skip to my Lou,	Girls repeat patterns as described above.
3–4	Girls to outside, Skip to my Lou,	
5–6	Girls to the center, Skip to my Lou,	
7–8	Skip to my Lou, my darling.	
	Verse No. 3:	
1–6	Swing your partner, Skip to my Lou, (three times)	Partners join hands and swing or skip in place.
7–8	Skip to my Lou, my darling.	
	Verse No. 4:	
1–6	I've lost my partner now what'll I do, (three times)	Release hands. Girls walk forward, boys turn and walk in the opposite direction.
7–8	Skip to my Lou, my darling.	
	Verse No. 5:	
1–6	I've got another one, prettier too, (three times)	New partners promenade counterclockwise to original position, with the girls on the boys' right.
7–8	Skip to my Lou, my darling.	Repeat dance with new partner.

Paw Paw Patch (Level II)

Musical Accompaniment
Folkcraft 1181
Victor 45–5066

Formation: Columns of four to six couples with partners facing forward (to the head of hall)

Skills: Walk, skip, clap, and cast off

Measures	Song	Action
1–2	Where, O where is sweet little Sally?	First girl turns right, casts off, circles clockwise, and goes once around the set with sixteen skipping steps, and back to place. Everyone else remains in place, clapping and singing the song.
3–4	Where, O where is sweet little Sally?	
5–6	Where, O where is sweet little Sally?	
7–8	Way down yonder in the paw paw patch.	
1–2	Come on, boys, let's go find her,	First girl takes the first boy's left hand and leads line of boys around the set. Boys may join hands. Girls in line clap hands. All finish in place facing the front.
3–4	Come on, boys, let's go find her,	
5–6	Come on, boys, let's go find her,	
7–8	Way down yonder in the paw paw patch.	
1–2	Pickin' up paw paws, putting 'em in her pocket,	Partners join hands and follow first couple once around to the right. First couple turns away from each other, with the boy going left and the girl going right, and skips to the foot of the line. The rest of the line moves one place forward.
3–4	Pickin' up paw paws, putting 'em in her pocket,	
5–6	Pickin' up paw paws, putting 'em in her pocket.	
7–8	Way down yonder in the paw paw patch.	Repeat entire dance with each new "first" girl leading.

Pop Goes the Weasel (Level II)

Musical Accompaniment
World of Fun, M–104–B
Folkcraft 1329
Victor 45–6180

Formation: Double circle in sets of four children, girl on partner's right; couples facing clockwise are couples number 1, while couples facing counterclockwise are couples number 2

Skills: Walk and skip

Measures	Action
1–4	Join hands in a circle of four and circle left with eight skipping or sliding steps.
5–6	Walk two steps forward, raising joined hands, then walk two steps backward, lowering hands.
7–8	Number one couples raise their joined hands to form an arch as number two couples pass under. Number two couples continue forward to meet new partners.
	Repeat dance.

Variation

Formation: Three children form a set, with two children joining inside hands. The third child stands in front with his back to the other two, extends his hands back, and holds the outside hands of the other two. All three face counterclockwise in a large circle.

Measures	Action
1–6	All sets skip around in a large circle.
7–8	On "pop," the child in front skips backward under the raised inside hands of the back couple and continues backward, meeting the couple behind him.
9–14	Repeat measures 1–6.
15–16	Repeat measures 7–8.

Cshebogar (Level II)

Musical Accompaniment
Folkcraft 1196
Lloyd Shaw E–15

Formation: Single circle of couples with hands joined; couples face the center with the girl on the boy's right side

Skills: Walk, skip, slide, and Hungarian turn

Measures	Action
1–4	Take seven slide steps to the left, and end with a jump on both feet.
5–8	Take seven slide steps to the right, and end with a jump on both feet.
9–12	Take four walking steps to the center, raising your hands high as you go. Take four walking steps backward to place in circle, lowering your hands as you return.
13–16	Face partner and place right hand on his or her waist. Raise left arm, pull away from partner, and skip around him or her. (This is a Hungarian turn.)
17–20	Face partner, join hands with arms held at shoulder height. Slide four steps slowly toward the center of the circle, bending toward the center as you slide. Boys start with left foot and girls with right foot.
21–24	Four step-draw steps outward (step-close-step).
25–28	Two draw steps in and two draw steps out.
29–32	Do the Hungarian turn again, then repeat entire dance.

Greensleeves (Level II)

Musical Accompaniment
Folkcraft 6175
Lloyd Shaw E–11

Formation: Double circle facing counterclockwise. Boys are on inside; girls on outside with inside hands joined. Couples are numbered 1, 2 alternately, around the circle to form sets.

Skills: Walk, star, over and under

Measures	Call	Action
1–8	Walk	Starting with left foot, take sixteen walking steps.
9–12	Right-hand star	Each set of two couples forms a right-hand star and takes eight walking steps clockwise.
13–16	Left-hand star	Form a left-hand star and take eight walking steps counterclockwise. At the end of the star, couple 1 is in front of couple 2 and both are facing counterclockwise.
17–20	Over and under	Couple 1 bends low and takes four steps backward as couple 2 raises joined hands and takes four steps forward ("turning the sleeves inside out"). Repeat with couple 2 moving backward and couple 1 arching and moving forward.
21–24	Over and under	Repeat 17–20.

To change this dance to a mixer, couple 2 moves forward on the last four steps of measures 23–24.

Glowworm Mixer (Level II)

Musical Accompaniment
MacGregor 310-B
Windsor 4613-B

Formation: Players form a double circle and all face counterclockwise, boy on inside circle holding the girl's left hand in his right

Skills: Walk, run, and do-si-do

Measures	Action
1–4	Promenade counterclockwise with eight walking steps.
5–8	Promenade clockwise with eight walking steps.
9–12	Pass right shoulders, back-to-back, then step back to place (do-si-do).
13–16	Turn to the right, face new partner, and do-si-do with eight running steps.

Little Brown Jug (Level II)

Musical Accompaniment
Columbia 52007
Folkcraft 1304A
Imperial 1213

Formation: Double circle with partners facing each other, girls on the outside circle, hands joined and raised to shoulder height

Skills: Slide and swing

Measures	Action
1–8	Boy touches his left heel to side, then his left toe next to his right foot. Repeat movement. Take four slide steps to the left. Girls start with outside foot and do the same.
9–16	Repeat measures 1–8 with four slides to the right.
17–24	Clap own thighs four times, then own hands together four times.
25–32	Partners clap right hands together four times, then left hands together four times.
33–40	Hook right elbows with partner and skip around in a circle with eight skipping steps.
41–56	Repeat clapping sequence of measures 17–24 and 25–32.
57–64	Hook left elbows and repeat turns.

Hora (Level II)

Musical Accompaniment
Folkcraft 1110
Folk Dancers MH 1052

Formation: Single circle with arms straight and hands on shoulders of dancers on either side

Skills: Side step, step swing

Measures		**Action**
1.	"Right, cross"	Step sideward with the right foot.
		Step sideward with left foot and place behind the right foot.
2.	"Right, swing"	Step sideward with the right foot.
		Hop on the right foot and swing left foot forward across the front.
3.	"Left, swing"	Step sideward with the left foot.
		Hop on the left foot and swing right foot forward and across the front.

Teaching cues: Moving toward the left.

```
  R      L      R      L      L      R
Right, Cross, Right, Swing, Left, Swing
```

Troika (Level II)

Musical Accompaniment
World of Fun M105
Folkcraft 1170

Formation: Circle of "threes" (one boy in middle of two girls, one girl in middle of two boys, or all boys and all girls), facing counterclockwise

Skills: Run, stamp, and arch

Measures	*Call*	**Action**
1–4	Run Forward	Run sixteen steps forward.
5–6	Outside Under	Center and inside partner raise joined hands, forming an arch, and run in place while the outside dancer, with eight running steps, moves in front of center dancer, under the arch, back around the center dancer to starting position. Center dancer unwinds by turning under the arch.
7–8	Inside Under	Repeat with inside dancer turning under.
9–12	Circle Left	Sets of three join hands and take twelve running steps, ending with three stamps in place.
13–16		Repeat twelve running steps to the right, ending in a reformed line and with three stamps in place.

As a Mixer:
During the last figure, the center dancer moves forward while the other dancers stamp three times in place.

Grand March (Level II)

Musical Accompaniment
Any marching record

Formation: Boys line up on one side of the room and girls on the other side; all face the foot of the room; the teacher stands in the center of the end line at the head of the room

Skills: Walk

Call	Action
Come down the center in twos.	March to meet partners at the foot of the room. As the couples meet, they turn, join hands, and march down the center to the head of the room, where the teacher is standing to give directions.
Two right and two left.	The first couple turns to the right, the second to the left, and so on.
Come down the center in fours.	When the two head couples meet at the foot of the room, they hold hands and walk four abreast down the center.
Four right and four left.	When children reach the front of the room, they divide again, with four going to the right and four going to the left, and so on.
Come down the center in eights.	When the lines of four meet at the front of the room, they join hands to form a line of eight abreast. The lines of eight march to the head of the room and halt.

Note:
This process may be reversed, with lines of eight dividing into columns of four. The columns of four march back to the other end of the room, where the two columns merge into one column of fours. The fours divide at the head of the room, and so on, until all are back to the original position of one couple.

Variations

From "Come down the center in fours," separate into twos, then call: "Form arches," or "Over and under."

First couple forms an arch and the second couple tunnels under. Third couple forms an arch and the fourth couple tunnels under. Continue this pattern.

First odd couple arches over the last couple in line and then under the next and so on down to the front of the line.

Oh Susanna (Level II)

Musical Accompaniment
Folkcraft 1186
Lloyd Shaw E-14

Formation: Partners standing in a single circle facing center, with hands joined, the girl on the boy's right side

Skills: Walk, slide, do-si-do, promenade

Measures	Call	Action
1–8	Slide to the left and slide to the right.	All take eight sliding steps to the right and eight sliding steps to the left.
9–12	Forward and back.	All take four steps to the center and four steps back.
13–16	Girls forward and back.	Release hands. Girls walk four steps toward the center of the circle and four steps back. Boys stand in place and clap hands.
17–20	Boys forward and back.	Boys go to center while girls clap hands.
21–24		Do-si-do with partners.
25–28		Do-si-do with corner girls.
29–32		Everyone promenades around the circle.

traditional and contemporary dances

Name of dance	Skills	Formation	Origin	Record source
Irish Washerwoman	Walk, swing	Circle	Irish	Folkcraft 1135
Teton Mountain Stomp	Walk	Circle	American	Windsor 4615
Kalvelis	Polka, stamp, skip	Circle	Lithuanian	Folkcraft 1418
Bingo	Walk, R, grand	Circle	American	Folkcraft 1189
Crested Hen	Step, hop	Threes	Danish	Victor 6176
Bridge of Avignon	Skip	Double circle	French	Folkcraft 1191
Teddy Bear Mixer	Walk	Double circle	American	Lloyd Shaw E-3
La Raspa	Bleking step	Scattered	Mexican	Folkcraft 1119
Crested Hen	Step-hop	Triple circle	Danish	Folkcraft 1134

Dances for Developmental Level III

Schottische (Level III)

Musical Accompaniment
MacGregor 4005
Folkcraft 1101
Imperial 1046

Formation: Double circle with partners facing counterclockwise, boys are on the inside circle and holding partners in an open dance position

Skills: Schottische step

Measures	Action
1–2	Partners start with outside feet (boy's left, girl's right), run forward three steps, and hop on outside foot and extend inside foot forward.
3–4	Begin with inside foot and repeat action.
5–6	All perform four step-hops in place.
	Repeat the first six measures as often as desired or substitute the following variations for measures 5 and 6.

Variation 1: Ladies Turn

Boys take four step-hops in place and girls turn under their arms. On the next turn, reverse movements, with the boys turning under the girls' raised arms.

Variation 2: Both Turn

Partners drop hands and dance four skip-hops in place, turning away from each other (boy turns left, girl turns right) on the first step, and ending in the starting position on the fourth step-hop.

Variation 3: Wring the Dishrag

Partners join hands about waist high and both turn under raised arms and continue around and back to the starting position.

Badger Gavotte (Level III)

Musical Accompaniment
MacGregor 610B
Folkcraft 1094

Formation: Double circle with couples facing counterclockwise; partners join hands, girl on the boy's right side

Skills: Slide, two-step, and closed dance position

Measures	Action
1–2	Begin with the outside foot (boy's left, girl's right), walk forward four steps, face partner, join hands, take three sliding steps to the boy's left, and touch the right toe behind the left foot.
3–4	Repeat measures 1 and 2 in the opposite direction.
5–8	Change to a closed dance position and take eight two-steps progressing counterclockwise, with the boys starting with the left foot and the girls with the right foot.
	Repeat dance until music ends.

chapter 29

Sicilian Circle (Level III)

Musical Accompaniment
Windsor A7S4A
Folkcraft 1115, 1242 (with calls)
Methodist 104

Formation: Circle of "sets of four" with couple facing couple, girl on the boy's right side

Skills: Walk, ladies chain, right and left through

Measures	Call	Action
1–4	Now everybody forward and back.	Join inside hands with partner. Take four steps forward toward the opposite couple and four steps backward to place.
5–8	Circle four hands around.	Join hands and circle left with eight walking steps and finish in original places.
1–4	Ladies chain.	Ladies chain across and back with the two girls changing places. The boy takes the approaching girl's left hand in his left, places his right arm around her waist, and pivots backward to reface the opposite couple.
5–8	Chain the ladies back again.	The girls return to their original positions with the same movement.
1–4	Right and left through.	Right and left with opposite couple, over and back. Walk forward to opposite couple's place, passing right shoulders, then, keeping side by side as though inside hands were joined, turn half around as a couple (man turns backward while lady turns forward), and reface opposite.
5–8	Right and left back.	Repeat the same movement, returning to original place.
1–4	Forward and back.	Forward and back.
5–8	Forward again, pass through.	All walk forward eight steps, passing opposite by right shoulder, to meet new couple.
		Repeat dance with new couple.

Virginia Reel (Level III)

Musical Accompaniment
Burns, Album J. No. 558
Lloyd Shaw E-12
Folkcraft 1249

Formation: Six couples in file formation with partners facing each other, boys on the caller's right

Skills: Walk, skip, swing, do-si-do, and cast off

Measures	Call	Action
1–8	Bow to your partner, go forward and back. Go forward and back again.	Players take three skips forward, curtsy or bow, then skip back. Repeat.
9–12	Now forward again with right hand swing, and all the way back.	Partners hold right hands, turn once around, and then back.
13–16	Now forward again with left hand swing, and all the way back.	Partners join left hands, turn once around, then back.
1–4	Now forward again with a two-hand swing, and all the way back.	Partners join both hands and turn clockwise and back.
5–8	Forward again with a do-si-do.	All partners do a do-si-do.
9–16	The head two sashay down the middle and all the way back to the head of the set.	Head couple joins hands and slides down the center of the set and back.
17–24	Cast off, with boys going left and girls going right.	All face the caller, with the boys' line skipping left and the girls' line skipping right, ending at the foot of the set.
25–32	Form an arch and all pass through.	The head couple meets at the foot of the set, joins hands, and raises them to form an arch. The second couple leads the other couples through the arch and moves to the head of the line to become the new head couple.
		Repeat dance with each new head couple.

Solomon Levi (Level III)

Musical Accompaniment
MacGregor 007-4A (with calls)

Formation: Square of four couples numbered counterclockwise, girl on the boy's right side

Skills: Walk, swing, and allemande left

Measures	Call	Action
1–4	Everyone swing your honey; swing her high and low.	Swing partner.
5–16	Allemande left with left hand, and around the ring you go. A grand old right and left. Walk on your heel and toe and meet your honey, give her a twirl, and around the ring you go. Sing chorus.	Left hand to corner, walk around corner back to partner. Extend right hand to partner, left to next girl, alternating right and left hands until partners meet. Give partner a swing and promenade.
1–8	Oh Solomon Levi, tra la la la la la Oh Solomon Levi, tra la la la la la.	Promenade around set. Repeat dance with couples two, three, and four leading. After couple number four completes its turn, have all four couples separate and repeat dance.

Oh Johnny (Level III)

Musical Accompaniment
MacGregor 652A (with calls)
Folkcraft 1037

Formation: Square dance set with girls on boys' right; all join hands

Skills: Walk, swing, allemande left, do-si-do

Measures	Call	Action
1–4	All join hands and circle the ring.	All couples move to the right in walking steps.
5–8	Stop where you are and give your honey a swing.	In closed dance position, swing partners.
9–12	Swing that little gal behind you.	Boy swings girl on his left.
13–16	Now swing your own.	Boy swings girl on his right.
1–4	Allemande left with the corner gal.	Turn to corners, give left hand to corner girl, walk around her, and return to partner.
5–8	Do-si-do your own.	Fold arms and pass right shoulder to right shoulder around partner and back to corner girl, who becomes new partner.
9–16	Now you all promenade with your sweet corner maid, Singing, "Oh, Johnny, oh, Johnny, oh."	Everyone promenade. Repeat dance.

Ace of Diamonds (Level III)

Musical Accompaniment
Folkcraft 1176
Methodist M-102

Formation: Double circle with partners facing

Skills: Walk and swing

Measures	Action
1–4	Clap hands once, stamp on left foot, then hook right elbows with three polka or six skipping steps.
5–8	Clap hands once, stamp on right foot, hook left elbows, and repeat swing.
9–12	Partners face each other with hands on hips. Inside dancers start backward with left foot; outside dancers move forward with right foot. Both take four steps.
13–16	Partners reverse directions for four steps.
17–24	Join inside hands, hop on inside foot, and polka counterclockwise around the circle.

Seven Jumps (Level III)

Musical Accompaniment
Merit Audio Visual: 1043
Methodist M-108

Formation: Single circle with hands joined

Skills: Step-hop

Measures	Action
1–8	Beginning with left foot, take seven step-hops, then jump and land with feet together on the eighth beat.
9–16	Face clockwise, start with right foot and take seven step-hops, then jump and land on both feet, facing the center.
17–18	Drop hand, place hands on hips and raise right knee high, then stamp foot on floor and join hands.
1–18	Repeat measures 1 to 18; however, do not join hands.
19	Raise left knee, stamp foot, and join hands.
1–19	Repeat measures 1 to 19, but do not join hands.
20	Kneel on right knee, stand, and join hands.
1–20	Repeat measures 1 to 20, but do not join hands.
21	Kneel on left knee, stand, and join hands.
1–21	Repeat measures 1 to 21, but do not join hands.
22	Place right elbow on floor and cheek on right fist, then stand and join hands.
1–22	Repeat measures 1 to 22, but do not join hands.
23	Place left elbow on floor and cheek on left fist, then stand and join hands.
1–23	Repeat measures 1 to 23, but do not join hands.
24	Place forehead on floor, stand, and join hands.
1–16	Repeat measures 1 to 16.

Norwegian Mountain March (Level III)

Musical Accompaniment
Folkcraft 1177
Victor 45-6173

Formation: Circle in sets of three children, all facing counterclockwise; the "set" is composed of one boy in the center and slightly in front of two side girls; the boy holds the girls' inside hands and the girls join outside hands, forming a triangle

Skills: Waltz and turn under

Measures	Call	Action
1–8	Waltz run.	Start on the right foot and take eight running waltz steps (twenty-four steps). All should accent the first step of each measure, and the leader should occasionally glance over his right and left shoulders at his partners.
9–10	Boys under.	Boy moves backward with six running steps under the arch formed by the girls' raised arms.
11–12	Left girl under.	Girl on the boy's left takes six steps to cross in front of and under the boy's raised right arm.
13–14	Right girl turns.	Girl on the boy's right takes six steps to turn under the boy's right arm.
15–16	Boy turns.	Boy turns under his own right arm to original position.
		Repeat dance.

Alley Cat (Level III)

Musical Accompaniment
ATCO 45-6226
Columbia CL-2500

Formation: Scattered with all facing the same direction

Skills: Touch step, turn, jump

Measures	Action
1	Shift right foot to right and touch toe to floor.
2	Close right toe to left foot.
3	Shift right foot to right and touch toe to floor.
4	Close right foot to left and shift weight to right foot.
5–8	Repeat 1 to 4 with left foot.
9–12	Repeat 1 to 4 with right foot being extended back and returning to side of left foot.
13–16	Repeat 1 to 4 with left foot extending back.
17–18	Raise right knee up in front of left knee; repeat.
19–20	Raise left knee up in front of right knee; repeat.
21	Raise right arm in front of left knee.
22	Raise left knee up in front of right knee.
23–24	Clap hands and jump a quarter turn to the right.
	Repeat dance, making a quarter turn toward the right during the last measures of each dance.

Korobushka (Peddler's Pack) (Level III)

Musical Accompaniment
Folkdancer MH 1059
World of Fun M108
Folkcraft 1170

Formation: Double circle, boys on outside with both hands joined

Skills: Schottische step

Measures

Part I:

Action (Schottische)

Measures	Action
	Directions are for boys. Girls begin on opposite foot.
1–2	Beginning with left foot, boy takes one schottische step away from center; girl moves backward starting on her right foot.
3–4	Repeat action toward center with boy beginning with his right foot and moving backward while girl starts on her left foot and moves forward.
5–6	Repeat 1–2.
7–8	Both hop three times on support foot (boy's left, girl's right). On the first hop, point toe forward; on second, point toe sideward; and on third, close to support foot. Boy clicks heels together on last movement.

Part II:

Action

Measures	Action
1–2	Release hands and each partner, beginning with the right foot, does a schottische step toward the right.
3–4	Start with left foot and return with one schottische step to face partner.
5–6	Join hands and step-hop forward to partner (balance together), then step-hop backward (balance back).
7–8	With hands still joined, both start on right foot and change places with three walking steps.
9–16	Repeat 1–8.

Klumpakojis (Clumsy Footed) (Level III)

Musical Accompaniment
Folkcraft 1419
RCA Victor EPA 4142

Formation: Double circle, facing counterclockwise, boys on inside, girls on outside with inside hands joined

Skills: Walk, stamp, polka

Measures

Part I:

Action (Walk)

1–4

Directions are for boys. Girls begin on opposite foot.

With inside hands joined and free hand on hip, take eight brisk walking steps counterclockwise.

5–8

Release grip, turn left, reverse directions, change hands, and take eight walking steps clockwise.

9–16

Face partner, join right hands, right elbow bent and left hand on hip. Partners walk eight steps around each other in a clockwise direction. Join left hands, left elbow bent, right hand on hip and take eight steps around each other in a counterclockwise direction.

Part II:

Action (Stamps, claps)

1–4

No action for counts 1, 2, 1, 2, then stamp three times for second measure. No action for counts 1, 2, 1, 2, then clap own hands three times for fourth measure.

5–8

Shake right finger at partner for counts 1, 2, and 3, and hold on count 4. Shake left finger at partner for counts 1, 2, and 3, and hold on 4. Clap right hand of partner, then turn solo counterclockwise in place with two steps. Face partner and stamp three times in place.

9–16

Repeat 1–8.

Part III:

Action (Polka)

1–8

Take Varsovienne position. Starting with left foot, take sixteen polka steps counterclockwise. On the last two steps, release hands and boy moves forward to meet new partner.

Red River Valley (Level III)

Musical Accompaniment
Imperial 1096
MacGregor Album 8 (with calls)
Folkcraft 1056

Formation: Square of four couples numbered counterclockwise, girl on the boy's right

Skills: Walk, swing, and do-si-do

Measures	Call	Action
1–4	All join hands in the valley.	Everyone joins hands.
5–8	And circle to the left and to the right.	With joined hands, walk four steps left and back four steps to the right.
1–4	And you swing the girl in the valley.	Boys swing corner girls (girl on the boy's left).
5–8	Now swing the Red River Gal.	Boys return to their own partners and swing them.
1–4	Now you lead right down the valley.	Number one and number three couples walk to couples on their right and join hands in a circle.
5–8	And you circle to the left, then to the right.	Walk four steps to the left and back four steps to the right.
9–12	Two ladies star in the valley.	Girls star with right hands (join right hands) in the center of the set and walk once around clockwise.
13–16	Now swing with the Red River Gal.	Boys swing partners.
1–4	Same couples to the left down the valley.	Couples number one and three walk to their left and join hands with new couples.
5–8	And you circle to the left and to the right.	Walk four steps to the left and back four steps to the right.
9–12	Now two gents star in the valley.	Boys star with their right hands and turn once around clockwise.
13–16	And you swing that Red River Gal.	Everyone swings with his partner. Repeat entire dance with two side couples taking the active part. Instead of a star, do-si-do the second time, elbow swing the third, and so on.

Heel and Toe Polka (Level III)

Musical Accompaniment
Burns, Evans, and Wheeler
Album 2, No. 225
Folkcraft 1166
MacGregor 400B

Formation: Double circle, with partners facing counterclockwise; open dance position with girl on boy's right side

Skills: Polka step

Measures	Call	Action
1–2	Heel and toe.	Partners touch outside heels forward and bend backward slightly. Touch toes of outside feet backward, bend forward slightly, and take three running steps forward (heel and toe, and step, step, step).
3–4	Heel and toe.	Repeat 1–2 with inside foot.
5–8	Heel and toe.	Repeat measures 1–4.
9–16		Partners face each other, the boy places his hands at the girl's waist and the girl places her hands on the boy's shoulders. All polka around the circle in a counterclockwise direction.

Oklahoma Mixer (Level III)

Musical Accompaniment
Folkcraft 1035
Methodist World of Fun 102
MacGregor 400

Formation: Double circle of couples, with girl on boy's right; take the Varsovienne position, with the left foot free

Skills: Walk, heel-toe, and two-step

Measures	Action
1–2	Begin with the left foot and take two, two-steps.
3–4	Begin with the left foot and take four walking steps forward.
5–8	Repeat measures 1–4.
9–12	Place the left heel forward and to the left, then the left toe opposite the right foot. Hold left hand, release right. Girls walk to the center of the circle in front of the boys as the boys move to the outside of the circle. The girls finish facing clockwise; the boys, counterclockwise.
13–16	The boy does a right heel and toe and takes three steps in place. The girl does a right heel and toe and walks to the boy behind. Repeat dance with new partner.

Rye Waltz (Level III)

Musical Accompaniment
Folkcraft 1103
Imperial 1044

Formation: Double circle with boys in the center facing girls; partners take an open dance position

Skills: Slide and waltz step

Measures	Action
1–4	Boys extend left toe to the side and return to inside of right foot. Repeat point and close. Girls perform the same movement with the right foot. Girls take three slide steps to the boys' left and touch right toe behind left foot.
5–8	Repeat in opposite direction.
9–16	Waltz around the room, with boys using their right shoulders to lead.

Tinikling (Level III)

Tinikling is a very exciting Philippine folk dance depicting the movements of the long-legged, long-necked tinikling bird, which is similar in appearance to the crane, heron, and flamingo. In the tinikling dance, the "bird" moves around two persons, who sit on the floor and manipulate two nine-foot-long bamboo poles in an attempt to trap the bird's legs. The poles are placed about two feet apart on two blocks of wood.* The players holding the bamboo poles slide them across the boards and strike them together on count one. On counts two and three, they lift the poles about an inch off the boards, open them about one foot apart and tap them twice against the boards. The musical accompaniment is a 3/4 waltz meter with a distinct "strike, tap, tap" rhythm throughout the dance.

Several basic tinikling steps can be performed individually or in combination. Once children learn to perform the following stepping movements, they soon will develop combinations and routines.

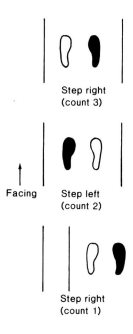

Step right
(count 3)

Facing   Step left
(count 2)

Step right
(count 1)

Basic Step

Two dancers begin in a standing position, facing each other on opposite sides of the poles. Each dancer's left side is closest to his pole. With the 3/4 rhythm, one step is performed outside the poles as they are hit together and two steps inside the poles as they are tapped twice on the blocks. The rhythm pattern is step right (outside poles), step left (inside poles), step right (inside poles), step left (outside left side), and continue back. After the basic side step is learned, the following variations can be attempted.

*Bamboo poles or 1-to-1½-inch wooden dowels can be used. Standard two-by-four lumber can be used for the blocks.

Figure 29.10 Straddle jump.

Figure 29.11 Forward and back. (© James Shaffer)

Straddle Step

The dancer performs two jumps with feet together inside the poles and a straddle jump when the poles are brought together (figure 29.10). The rhythm pattern is out-in-in.

Forward and Back

The dancer stands facing the poles. The movement consists of a step forward with the right foot inside the poles, followed by a step forward on the left foot. As the poles are brought together, the dancer takes a step forward on the right foot to the opposite side. The pattern is reversed on the next measure, with a step back on the left foot, a step back on the right foot, and a step back to the original position on the left foot (figure 29.11).

traditional and contemporary dances

Name of dance	Skills	Formation	Origin	Record source
Mayim	Walk, hop, grapevine	Circle	Israeli	Folkcraft 1108
Hop Morr Anika		Circle	Swedish	Victor 4162
Road to the Isles	Walk, schottische	Couples	Scottish	Imperial 1105A
Hinkey Dinkey	Swing, promenade	Square	French	Folkcraft 1012 (with call)
Let's Square Dance	Walk	Square	American	Victor 3001
Hohsey Square Dance	Walk	Square	American	MacGregor (Album 4618)
Chester Schottische	Schottische	Circle	American	Folkcraft 1101
Miserlou	Walk, grapevine	Circle	Greek	Merit Audio Visual 1046
Jessie Polka	Two-step, polka step	Couples	American	Folkcraft 1071
Put Your Little Foot	Varsovienne	Couples	American	Folkcraft 1165
Varsovienne	Varsovienne	Circle	American	Folkcraft 1034
Hot Time	Walk, swing, allemande	Square	American	Folkcraft 1037
Ten Pretty Girls	Walk	Circle	American	World of Fun 113
Cotton Eye Joe	Polka	Free	American	World of Fun 118
Brown Eye Mary	Walk, skip, promenade, allemande	Circle	American	Folkcraft 1186
Five Foot Two	Two-step	Double circle	American	Folkcraft 1420

When the class has learned the basic steps and pole movements, the poles can be arranged in a variety of patterns to allow the children to move in different directions. A few examples are shown in the following diagrams.

Resource Information

1. *Suggested records*
   a. "Special Folk Dances" (Tinikling, Carinosa, Czardas, Vengorka and Tarantella in 3/4 meter), RCA Victor, EPA–4126
   b. "Alley Cat," ATCA 45–6226
   c. "No Matter What Shape," Liberty Records, 55836
2. *Film*
   Tinikling—the Bamboo Dance (16 mm), Martin Moyer Productions, 900 Federal Avenue East, Seattle, WA

Single file

Crossed formation

Square formation

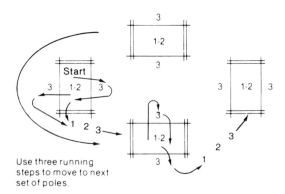

Use three running steps to move to next set of poles.

Glossary of Terms

The following words and phrases occur frequently in folk and square dances for children in the intermediate grades.

Active couple(s)
The couple(s) designated to start a dance or to whom a part of the dance is addressed.

Advance
To move forward, usually with walking steps.

Allemande left
From a circle or square formation with all dancers facing the center, the boy joins his left hand with the girl on his left and walks around counterclockwise and back to his starting position.

Allemande right
Same as allemande left but in the opposite direction.

Arch
Two dancers join inside hands and raise arms to form an arch.

Balance
In square dancing, the usual movement following a "swing your partner." Partners face each other, join right hands, and step back with weight on the left foot and the right heel touching in front. Both partners may also bow slightly.

Banjo (right parallel) position
Variation of closed position in which boy and girl make a one-eighth turn counterclockwise to a diagonal position.

Bow and curtsy
The bow, performed by the boys, may be a simple nod of the head or an elaborate and pronounced deep bend of the trunk. The curtsy, performed by the girls, may be a simple nod of the head or an elaborate and pronounced deep bend of the knees and a graceful sideward extension of the dancing costume.

Break
Release hands.

Chain (ladies chain)
In square dancing, the girls move across to the opposite couple, extending their right hands to each other as they pass, then their left hands to the opposite boy. The boy places his right hand behind the girl's back, grasping her right hand, and turns her one full turn counterclockwise.

Circle
Dancers join hands and move toward the right or left.

Clockwise
The same direction as the hands of a clock.

Closed position
Partners face each other, with shoulders parallel and toes pointing forward, the boy's right arm around the girl, with his hand on her lower back. The girl's left hand and arm rest on the boy's upper arm and shoulder. The boy holds the girl's right hand in his left.

Corner
When facing the center, the boy's corner is the girl on his left and the girl's corner is the boy on her right.

Counterclockwise
The opposite direction as the hands of a clock.

Divide or split the ring
Active couples pass through the opposite couples.

Do-si-do
These words mean "back to back" and usually involve two persons who are facing each other. The two dancers walk forward; pass right shoulders; without turning move to the right, passing back to back; and then walk backward to the starting position.

Elbow swing
Partners face each other, hook elbows (left or right), and turn with small steps.

Even rhythm
The beats in a rhythm pattern are given the same value.

Forward and back
This figure involves dancers facing each other. Both sides advance four steps forward (or three steps and a bow) and take four steps backward.

Grand right and left
This is a weaving pattern and usually follows an allemande left. Face partner and join right hands, pass and give left hand to the next dancer, and continue weaving around set.

Grapevine
A step toward the left side (count 1), step right behind left foot (count 2), step left to side (count 3), then step right foot in front of left (count 4).

Head couple
In square dancing, the couple nearest the music or caller.

Home
The starting place at the beginning of a dance.

Honor
Salute or bow to partner or other dancers.

Open position
Partners stand side-by-side, facing the same direction, with inside hands joined.

Opposite
The person or couple directly across the square.

Polka
A hop on right foot, step forward on left, close right to left, then step forward on left.

Promenade
This is the skaters' position in which partners stand side-by-side and face the same direction. The girl stands on the boy's right. Partners join left hands about waist high, then join right hands above the left arms.

Sashay
The American term for the French "chassé." These are sliding steps sideward.

Separate
Partners leave each other and move in opposite directions.

Square
Four couples, with each forming one side of a square.

Star or wheel
Two or more dancers join right hands in the center of the set and walk forward or backward as directed.

Swing
This is a rhythmic rotation of a couple with a walking step, buzz step, two-step, or skip. The swing may be a one-hand, two-hand, elbow, or waist swing.

Tempo
Rate of speed at which music is played.

Record Sources

The following list of record companies covers musical accompaniment for all singing games and folk and square dances taught in the elementary school program. Teachers can order company catalogs and be placed on company mailing lists.

Bob Ruff Records
8459 Edmarce Ave.
Whittier, CA 90605

Dance Record Distributers
(Folkcraft Records)
12 Fenwick St.
Newark, NJ 07114

Educational Activities Inc.
P.O. Box 382
Freeport, NY 11528

Educational Record Sales
157 Chambers St.
New York, NY 10007

Folk Dances Record Service
P.O. Box 201
Flushing, NY 11520

Hoctor Products for Education
159 Franklin Turnpike
Waldwich, NJ 07463

Kimbo Records
P.O. Box 477
Long Beach, NJ 07740

Lloyd Shaw Foundation, Sales Division
12225 Saddle Strap Row
Hudson, FL 33567

Selected References

CAHPER. (1983). *Folk Dance in the Elementary School.* Ottawa, Ontario: CAHPER Publications.

Evans, J. (1981). *Let's Dance.* Toronto, Ontario: Can-Ed Media.

Harris, J. A., Pittman, A. M., and Waller, M. S. (1988). *Dance Awhile,* Sixth Edition. New York: Macmillan Publishing Co.

Mynatt, C. V., and Kaiman, B. D. (1975). *Folk Dancing for Students and Teachers.* Dubuque, IA: Wm. C. Brown Publishers.

Snider, M. (1980). *Folk Dance Handbook.* North Vancouver, B.C.: Hancock House Publishers Ltd.

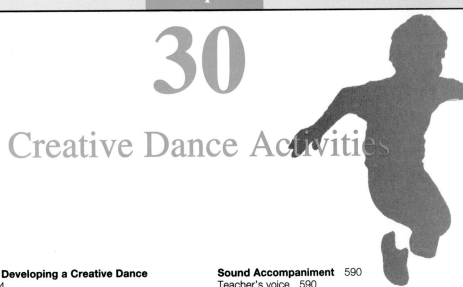

Creativity cannot exist in the abstract, and neither can creative teaching. As teachers, we want children to be able to feel and express their ideas through movement; we want them to be creative. However, no child can be imaginative or creative without a vocabulary of words, concepts, and ideas. Neither can a child express a creative movement without a vocabulary of movement skills and an awareness of various forms of internal and external stimuli.

Our task in enhancing the child's creative process is twofold. First, we must recognize the level of cognitive and motor development of the age group we are teaching. Primary children, for example, have a limited vocabulary and capacity for abstract thinking. Their world of ideas is very small; they normally demonstrate "being like" or "imitation of" in their first attempts at creative movements.

However, boys and girls in the intermediate grades have a rich vocabulary, as well as interest in exploring abstract ideas and the capacity to carry out these ideas. Their movement vocabulary has also expanded far beyond the basic locomotor skills to personal reservoirs of complex movement skills and motor patterns.

Our second task in enhancing the creative process is to develop an approach or format that can be used to encourage children to develop their own creative ideas and to express them through movement. In parts V and VI, Laban's four movement elements of body awareness, space awareness, qualities, and relationships were used as a framework to teach movement concepts and skills. This chapter will use these four elements of movement as the basic structure for developing a creative dance program for all three developmental levels ■

Structure for Developing a Creative Dance Program

All movements performed by a child can be analyzed according to the specific body actions that are involved (body awareness), the effort (qualities), the space (space awareness) within which a movement takes place, and the position (relationships) of the body to equipment or other performers (figure 30.1). This is illustrated in figure 30.3. In gymnastics, as described in chapters 25, 26, and 27, all movements can be taught according to this classification system. However, since the emphasis in gymnastics is primarily the efficiency and utility of movement, descriptive terminology, such as *swirl, hasty,* and *retreating,* are not used. In creative dance, the emphasis is on self-expression demonstrated through movement. This requires additional expressive words to explain and stimulate creative movements.

Choose a Theme

The theme a teacher chooses for a creative dance program should be based on several important considerations. The starting idea should be exciting and meaningful to the children. For example, the theme of "spaceships" would appeal to the imaginations of seven-year-olds. Another reason for this choice is that outer space and astronauts offer unlimited possibilities for young children to develop their creative talent in planning and expressing their ideas through movement. In short, from the child's point of view, the theme must be meaningful and stimulating; from the teacher's point of view, it must be practical as a vehicle to increase the child's creative expression through movement (figure 30.2).

Brainstorm

The next step in the process is to decide what elements of the chosen theme should be included in the program. Carrying through with the previous example, ideas that could be developed are shown in

Figure 30.1 Relationship to the floor or other performers.

Figure 30.2 Choosing a theme.

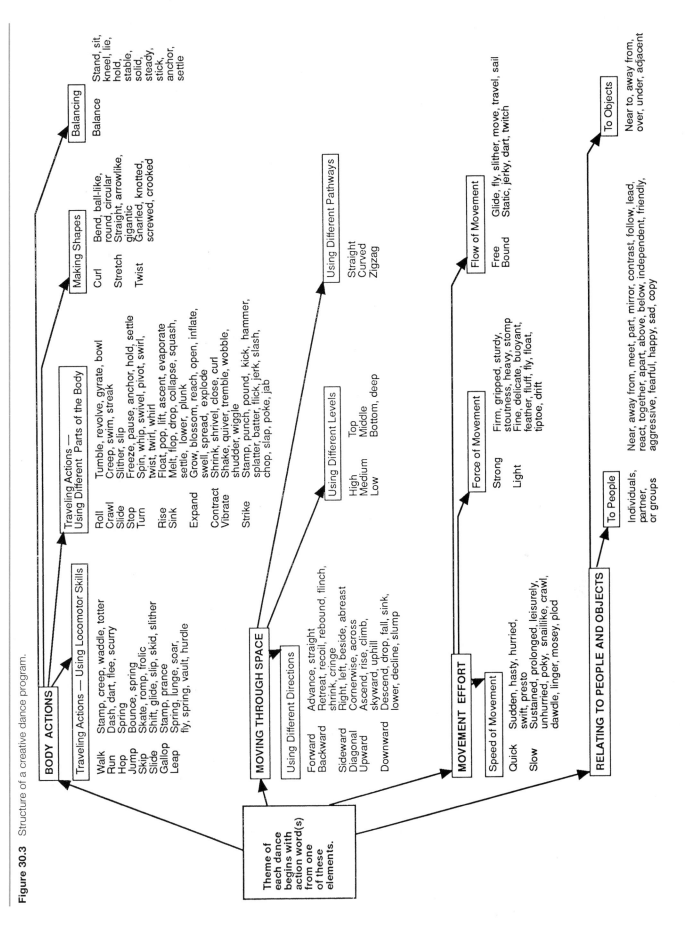

Figure 30.3 Structure of a creative dance program.

BODY ACTIONS

Traveling Actions — Using Locomotor Skills

Walk   Stamp, creep, waddle, totter
Run   Dash, dart, flee, scurry
Hop   Spring
Jump   Bounce, spring
Skip   Skate, romp, frolic
Slide   Shift, glide, slip, skid, slither
Gallop   Stamp, prance
Leap   Spring, lunge, soar,
      fly, spring, vault, hurdle

Traveling Actions —
Using Different Parts of the Body

Roll   Tumble, revolve, gyrate, bowl
Crawl   Creep, swim, streak
Slide   Slither, slip
Stop   Freeze, pause, anchor, hold, settle
Turn   Spin, whip, swivel, pivot, swirl,
      twist, twirl, whirl
Rise   Float, pop, lift, ascent, evaporate
Sink   Melt, flop, drop, collapse, squash,
      settle, lower, plunk
Expand   Grow, blossom, reach, open, inflate,
      swell, spread, explode
Contract   Shrink, shrivel, close, curl
Vibrate   Shake, quiver, tremble, wobble,
      shudder, wiggle
Strike   Stamp, punch, pound, kick, hammer,
      splatter, batter, flick, jerk, slash,
      chop, slap, poke, jab

Making Shapes

Curl   Bend, ball-like,
      round, circular
Stretch   Straight, arrowlike,
      gigantic
Twist   Gnarled, knotted,
      screwed, crooked

Balancing

Balance   Stand, sit,
      kneel, lie,
      hold,
      stable,
      solid,
      steady,
      stick,
      anchor,
      settle

MOVING THROUGH SPACE

Using Different Directions

Forward   Advance, straight
Backward   Retreat, recoil, rebound, flinch,
      shrink, cringe
Sideward   Right, left, beside, abreast
Diagonal   Cornerwise, across
Upward   Ascend, rise, climb,
      skyward, uphill
Downward   Descend, drop, fall, sink,
      lower, decline, slump

Using Different Levels

High   Top
Medium   Middle
Low   Bottom, deep

Using Different Pathways

Straight
Curved
Zigzag

MOVEMENT EFFORT

Speed of Movement

Quick   Sudden, hasty, hurried,
      swift, presto
Slow   Sustained, prolonged, leisurely,
      unhurried, poky, snaillike, crawl,
      dawdle, linger, mosey, plod

Force of Movement

Strong   Firm, gripped, sturdy,
      stoutness, heavy, stomp
Light   Fine, delicate, buoyant,
      feather, fluff, fly, float,
      tiptoe, drift

Flow of Movement

Free   Glide, fly, slither, move, travel, sail
Bound   Static, jerky, dart, twitch

RELATING TO PEOPLE AND OBJECTS

To People

Individuals,   Near, away from, meet, part, mirror, contrast, follow, lead,
partner,   react, together, apart, above, below, independent, friendly,
or groups   aggressive, fearful, happy, sad, copy

To Objects

Near to, away from,
over, under, adjacent

**Theme of
each dance
begins with
action word(s)
from one
of these
elements.**

Figure 30.4 Ideas for themes.

Figure 30.5 Brainstorming.

Figure 30.6 Simulate the take-off.

figure 30.4. Each of these ideas, such as "astronaut movements" or "spaceship movements," could be covered in a single lesson or over many lessons. The length and scope depend on how the idea is developed by the teacher and her class (figure 30.5). In this example, spaceship movements are selected as a general idea, then reduced to a shorter theme of "travel to the moon," as illustrated in the accompanying lesson.

Select Movement Actions

Since the theme of the accompanying lesson is travel to the moon, it involves a takeoff (figure 30.6), movement through space, and a landing. The main theme of the lesson is pathways and a subtheme is speed. Many words can be used to stimulate the takeoff, flight through space, and landing on the moon (table 30.1). These ideas are developed in the second part of the lesson.

Plan the Structure of the Dance

During the third part of the lesson, children begin to integrate the concepts and skills learned in part II into a creative dance. The structure of their dance should include a beginning (takeoff), a story or adventure (moving through space), and an ending (landing). For young children, a form of accompaniment, such as a percussion instrument, a poem, or taped music, is used to move the dance through each stage of development.

A teacher cannot anticipate the success of any creative dance lesson. If the class has not had experience in this type of activity and the teacher is trying this type of lesson for the first time, at first each lesson may seem isolated. Gradually, however, as children build a repertoire of movements and learn to think and move in creative patterns, each lesson will appear to be too short. The teacher will also develop

chapter 30

Lesson Plan for Travel to the Moon

Things to emphasize	Sample lesson	Teaching points
Part I: Introductory activity		
Stress general vigorous activity.	Listen to the drum beat (show, slow, quick, and stop).	See if children can keep in time to drum beat.
Stress one or more movement concepts of lesson.	Travel through space in time to the drum beat. Stop when the drum beat stops.	See if children change speed and stop with control.
Introduce musical accompaniment.	Travel and stop while moving "in straight lines". . . "now curved pathways."	Repeat activities with musical accompaniment.
Part II: Skill development		
Begin to develop main theme of lesson.	Show how rocket develops burst of speed (vibrate, shake).	Play tape recording of a spaceship launch. Discuss ways to show motor warming up, weightlessness, re-entry, how spaceship speeds up and slows down.
Begin to expand movement vocabulary.	Show how rocket takes off after countdown (slow, sustained, strong, swift).	
Encourage children to select and repeat movement.	Show how spaceship moves and stays in orbit around earth.	Look for and encourage early signs of selecting and repeating movement.
Encourage children to develop simple sequences.	Leave orbit to new destination heading for the moon.	
	When reach new destination, orbit the moon and slow down.	
	Land on the moon.	
Part III: Dance composition		
Apply concepts and skills from part II to a dance sequence.	Practice takeoff, orbit the earth, travel to the moon, orbit the moon, and land on the moon.	Help students who find difficulty in developing their own sequence.
Add relationship to a partner.	Work with partner and develop a twin launch.	Encourage children to share each other's ideas.
Allow time for practice and refinement.		
Allow time to perform for class.		
Part IV Closure		
Cover main theme.	Discuss elements of dance.	Allow children to decide what theme(s) might be possible for the next two or three lessons.
Discuss future lessons derived from this theme.	Discuss other possible lessons with another space theme.	

Table 30.1   Movement Possibilities

Body actions	Moving through space	Movement effort	Relation to people and objects
Walk	Forward—advance	Quick—sudden, swift	People: near, far, meet, part, together, apart, above, below
Run	Backward—recoil	Slow—sustained	Objects: near, away, inside, outside, over, under
Leap—soar, fly	Upward—ascend, rise, climb	Strong—heavy	
Slide—glide	Skyward	Light—fly, float, drift	
Stop—anchor, hold	Downward—descent, fall, lower, decline	Flow—glide, fly	
Turn—spin, swirl, twirl	High—top		
Rise—float, lift	Medium—middle		
Sink—drop, settle, lower	Low—bottom		
Expand—reach, open, inflate, explode	Straight, curved, zigzag		
Vibrate—shake, quiver, tremble, shudder			
Strike—flick, jerk, slash, poke, jab			

Figure 30.7 Sharing ideas.

greater powers of observation and more effective uses of her voice, percussion instruments, and all other forms of musical accompaniment. The consequence will likely be a central theme, beginning with the first lesson and carried throughout subsequent lessons. When this occurs, the format will emphasize the last portion of the lesson to allow the children maximum freedom to create, refine, and express their feelings and ideas through creative dance movements. Finally, provide time at the end of the lesson for children to perform their dances and to share their ideas with other members of the class (figure 30.7).

Stimuli

The previous section provided one way to teach a creative dance program using Laban's basic elements of body awareness (actions), body effort (qualities), space, and relationships. These aspects of movement are the paints of the painter or the notes of the musician. The ways in which body movements are joined together by individuals, partners, or groups should result both from the teacher's guidance and the children's creativity. Creative movements can be further enhanced by the effective use of a wide variety of meaningful stimuli, such as objects, stories, and paintings. Whatever external stimulus a teacher uses should be both within the bounds of the children's understanding and potentially rich in forms of expression. The examples in table 30.2 have proved appropriate for elementary school children. The following sample lesson also illustrates how a teacher can approach the class and build several creative dance lessons from one central idea.

Primary Program Sample Lesson (Level II)

Lesson   Clouds and nature
Basic theme   Interpretive movements
Formation   Multiple (scattered, line, and circle)

Table 30.2   Stimuli for Creative Movements

Stimuli	Developmental level		
	I	II	III
Balloons	X		
Fairy tales	X		
Animals	X	X	
Pictures	X	X	
Witches	X	X	
Fire		X	
Thanksgiving		X	
Weather (snow, wind, etc.)	X	X	X
Trees and plants	X	X	X
Stories and poems	X	X	X
Journeys	X	X	X
Marionettes	X	X	X
Mechanical objects (robots)	X	X	X
Rubber bands	X	X	X
Clay	X	X	X
Wire	X	X	X
Sports		X	X
Astronauts	X	X	X
Halloween	X	X	X
Fall (leaves, rain, frost)	X	X	X
Winter (cold, snow, wind)	X	X	X
Christmas	X	X	X
Spring (growing, unfolding)	X	X	X
Easter (searching, drawing, painting)	X	X	X
Water (solid, liquid, gas, flowing)	X	X	X
Insects	X	X	X
Space (planets, stars, travel)	X	X	X

The purpose of this lesson is to stimulate light and heavy movements, with emphasis on the quality rather than the direction of the response. A short discussion should precede this lesson to familiarize children with new words and the concept of clouds as part of nature. This can be done through class discussion or stories and poems about clouds.

Additional Suggestions

Reorganize the class into partners or small groups and pose questions that require a group effort to express the movement. For example, ask partners to interpret two thunderclouds moving toward each other. Continue the lesson, emphasizing soft and heavy movements. For the conclusion, discuss the movements, or play a record and allow the children to interpret the music.

Additional Resource Material

The sample lesson can assist in developing a basic approach to teaching creative or interpretive movements. Numerous other methods and techniques can be used with equal

Suggested teaching procedure	Possible responses from children
1. Movement introduction Have children sit in a scattered formation on the floor. The following questions and discussion will provide the stimulus for the interpretive movements: 　a. Think of coming to school on a nice, warm day, when the sky is filled with pretty white clouds. What do the clouds look like? 　b. If you could touch a cloud, what do you think it would feel like? 　c. If you were a big cloud, what would you do on a nice, warm day? 2. Interpretive movements 　a. Let's all move about the room as if we were clouds in the sky. 　b. To indicate light movements: Can you run very lightly on your tiptoes? 　c. What else is soft and light and makes you feel like moving as you did? 　　Introduce musical accompaniment: tambourine, triangle, or song bells. 　d. Can you move your arms and your whole body very softly and lightly while I play the triangle? (Vary the speed, but always keep the intensity very soft.) 　e. Seated in scattered formation: We have talked about light and soft things and moved so we felt that way. What is very different from softness? 　f. What can you think of that is the opposite of soft, fluffy clouds? 　g. Move around the room again, but this time we will be heavy and hard. (Use drum or blocks for accompaniment.)	1. Movement introduction The responses to your questions will be tangible objects that are familiar to this age group. 　a. Mashed potatoes, cotton candy, or cotton balls 　b. Soft and fluffy like whipped cream or Daddy's shaving cream 　c. Sleep, fly around and look at everyone, ride with the wind 2. Interpretive movements 　a. Running; romping; moving on tiptoes; or making heavy, pronounced steps 　b. Running lightly, swinging or swaying, and so on 　c. Kitten, bunny, feathers 　d. Children may remain in the same spot or shift about the room, with light, expressive movements. 　e. Stones, big and fat, heavy, rough 　f. Giants, elephants, sledgehammer 　g. Heavy pounding with feet and clenched fists, dragging arms to imitate elephant walk

success. Table 30.3 contains possible animal, mechanical, and nature movements that can be used as an additional source. The movements can be performed with the musical accompaniment listed.

The following list of recordings have been recommended by leading dance specialists as appropriate accompaniment for many of the creative dance activities listed in table 30.3.

Bowmar Records, 622 Rodier Dr., Glendale, CA, 91201.

1. *Children's Rhythms in Symphony.* Music of great composers for creative and interpretative movement.
2. *Rhythm Time,* No. 1 (023) and No. 2 (024). Music for basic movement.

Educational Activities Inc., Box 392, Freeport, NY, 11520.

1. *Authentic Afro-Rhythms: Early Elementary Through College.* Selection of rhythms from Africa, Cuba, Haiti, Brazil, Trinidad, and Puerto Rico.
2. *Rain Dance and Canoe Dance.* Selection of drums and chants.

Folkways Scholastic Records, 907 Sylvan Ave., Englewood Cliffs, NJ, 07632.

1. *Sounds, Rhythms, Rhyme, and Mime For Children,* FC 14504. Music and rhymes related to African culture.
2. *Sounds of New Music,* FX 6160. Orchestra sounds associated with farmyard scenes, factory, and space.

RCA Records, 1132 Avenue of Americas, New York, NY, 10036.

1. *Adventures in Music.* A twelve-album series for grades one to six. Excellent music resource for all types of creative dance activities.

The Dimension 5 Records, Box 185 Kingsbridge Station, Bronx, NY, 10463.

1. *Electronic Records for Children.* A selection of exciting and interesting electronic musical recordings.

The following companies, in addition to those mentioned above, provide catalogs and listings of musical selections appropriate for elementary school creative dance activities.

Educational Record Sales, 157 Chambers St., New York, NY, 10007.

Phoebe James Products, Box 134, Pacific Palisades, CA, 90272.

Kimbo Education Record Co., Box 477, Long Branch, NJ, 07740.

Hoctor Educational Records Inc., Waldwick, NJ, 07463.

S and R Records, 1609 Broadway, New York, NY, 10017.

Children's Music Center, 5373 West Pico Blvd., Los Angeles, CA, 90019.

Table 30.3　Resources for Developing Creative Movements

	Types of movement	Musical accompaniment
Animal movements		
Bear	Heavy, slow walk; run; climb	Drum (slow), woodblock, claves
Camel	Slow, bouncy walk; carry object	Drum (uneven)
Elephant	Heavy, slow, rocking walk; lift object	Drum (slow, heavy)
Frog	Hop, jump, bounce, bend	Drum (short, quick)
Worm	Curl, bend, stretch	Scraper
Monkey	Fast crawl, bent-knee jumps	Woodblock
Rabbit	Jump, bend, run, sniff	Woodblock
Soldier	Crawl, run, march	Drum, drum rolls
Tall person/short person	Bend and stretch, bent-knee walk, tiptoe walk	Drum (fast and light, heavy and slow)
Cat	Cautious walk, run, play, stretch	Woodblock, sticks
Chicken	Choppy, quick walk; scratch; peck; flap arms	Woodblock (short, quick)
Raggedy Ann/Andy	Loose, floppy walk; swing; bend	Drum, tambourine
Giant	Slow, heavy walk and run; exaggerated movements	Drum (heavy and slow), cymbals
Horse	Gallop, prance (knees high), walk, carry rider	Woodblock
Butterfly	Light, sustained movements; use of arms; soft runs; skips	Gong, cymbals
Mechanical movements		
Bulldozer	Push, bend, walk, show effort	Drum, scrapers
Dump truck	Bend and stretch, lift, locomotion, show effort	Drum
Lumber loader	Bend and stretch, lift, slow and sustained, show effort	Drum
Washing machine	Twist, roll, bounce	Scraper, drum
Ditchdigger	Bend and stretch, push and lift, show effort	Drum
Lawn sprinkler	Twist, turn, bend, stretch	Shakers, maracas
Top	Twist, turn, run, skip, walk, fall	Scraper, cymbals, gong
Clock	Locomotion (percussive), swing and sway (stiff)	Woodblock
Percolator	Rise and fall, jiggle and bob (loose and floppy)	Woodblock (accelerating beat)
Pop-up toaster	Rise and fall, bend and stretch, hop, jump	Woodblock, drum
Airplane	Rise and fall, sustain arm movements with running	Drum (vibratory beats)
Typewriter	Walk, hop, jump (short, quick), bend, stretch	Woodblock, triangle, bell
Nature movements		
Wind	Use of arms, turn and smooth run, bend and stretch while running	Drum, tambourine
Rain	Rise and fall, bend and stretch, shake	Drum, maracas
Flower	Bend and stretch, swing and sway	Drum, tambourine
Bee	Swing and sway, whip and slash with arms and trunk	Drum, tambourine
Sun	Rise and fall, bend and stretch, big and small movements	Gong, cymbals
Cloud	Sustained, smooth movements; tiptoe walks and runs; swing and sway	Cymbals, drum
Shadow	Darting walks and runs, bend and stretch, strike and dodge	Drum, woodblock
Moon	Rise and fall, bend and stretch, sustained locomotion	Drum
Wave	Rise and fall, skip, swing and sway, dynamic falls	Drum (loud and soft), cymbals
Fire	Strike and dodge, jump, turn, hop, stretch	Drum (first slow, loud, and soft)
Smoke	Rise, turn, swing, sway, run, skip, stretch	Cymbals, tambourine

Sound Accompaniment

The value of a sound accompaniment to a creative movement is judged on its ability to stimulate and enhance a child's imagination and creative movements. The proper selection and application of sound accompaniment are critical to the success of a creative dance program. Some of the more important considerations relating to the teacher's voice, percussion instruments, recorded music, and classmade instruments follow.

Teacher's Voice

All teachers are aware of the effect of their voices in the classroom, activity room, and gymnasium. In creative dance, however, the manner and tone of a teacher's speaking voice can become important stimuli in evoking creative movements. Simply speaking softly to children can encourage slower, lighter movements. Similarly, speaking sharply in a loud voice or drawing out the words provides sufficient stimulus for another type of movement response.

Figure 30.8 Effective use of percussion instruments.

When a teacher adds other characteristics to her voice, such as hissing, clicking, or humming sounds, the mood and action of the dance is directed in a variety of ways. The reservoir of sounds a young performer can make should also be exploited to the fullest, since such sounds provide an equally important stimulus.

Percussion Instruments

Various percussion instruments are useful in a creative dance program (figure 30.8). The drum, tambourine, and cymbals are ideal when teaching children to move in time to the beat and tempo of a musical accompaniment. Perhaps the drum is the most useful in the initial stages of teaching creative dance; however, the following percussion instruments are also valuable:

1. Banjo drums
2. Improvised drums—large and small containers such as coffee tins and plastic containers with plastic or cloth covers
3. Tambourine
4. Woodblocks—solid or hollow
5. Rhythm sticks—varying in size from $\frac{1}{2}$ inch by 6 inches to $\frac{1}{2}$ inch by 12 inches
6. Castanets
7. Coconut shells
8. Cymbals
9. Triangle
10. Bells—assorted sizes, individual and on a strip of cloth
11. Shakers—may be made with gravel, beans, or sand

Recorded Music

The use of recorded music in any creative dance program needs little elaboration. What a teacher and class select depends on the availability of records or tapes. The general availability of tape recorders suggests another inexpensive and flexible way of adding musical accompaniment to the dance program. If tape recorders are used, a format should be established for recording music and for classifying and storing school tapes.

Classmade Instruments

When a teacher or class makes inexpensive equipment, it is normally due to financial reasons. The suggestions that follow are based, to a very minor degree, on available finances and, to a major degree, on the positive effects of making one's own musical instrument.

Getting children interested in creative dance is a difficult task for many classroom teachers. No simple list of teaching suggestions will work for every teacher. However, when children make their own musical instruments, a very positive attitude develops, both toward the instruments and toward using them to accompany their creative dance movements.

The instruments shown in figures 30.9a–c can be made by children from grades two to six. In the process of making their own instruments, children learn to use a variety of tools and materials. Each child's instrument must make a sound that pleases him, his peers, and the teacher. The enjoyment children receive from creating their own percussion instruments varies; some enjoy making and decorating the instruments, whereas others simply like to hear their own musical accompaniment. Whatever the reasons, the classmade instruments shown in appendix B are easy and fun to construct and provide a reservoir of enjoyable and useful instruments.

Using Creative Dance Activities to Teach Academic Concepts and Skills

Academic subjects such as language arts, art, and music can be integrated with creative dance activities in a variety of ways. Drawing and painting pictures of a dance sequence (figure 30.10) or writing a story or poem to be expressed in a creative dance expands a child's ability to express ideas in an artistic and creative way. The following examples illustrate how creative dance can be used as a medium to enhance concepts and skills in language arts, art, and music.

1. Create songs or musical accompaniment for creative dance activities.
2. Construct musical instruments that can be used in creative dance activities.
3. Draw symmetrical and asymmetrical shapes of the body, then include these shapes in movement sequences.

Figure 30.9 Classmade instruments.

a

b

c

Figure 30.10 Artistic expression can be derived from physical activities.

4. Interpret songs, sounds, and musical scores through creative movement.
5. Study native or Eskimo cultures, including hunting, farming, and other aspects, that can be portrayed through creative movement activities.

Selected References

Benzwie, T. (1991). *A Moving Experience: Dance for Lovers of Children and the Child Within.* Reston, VA: AAHPERD Publications.

Boorman, J. (1969). *Creative Dance in the First Three Grades.* Don Mills, Ontario: Longmans Canada, Ltd.

———. (1971). *Creative Dance in Grades Four to Six.* Don Mills, Ontario: Longmans Canada, Ltd.

CAHPER. (1988). *Creative Dance.* Ottawa, Ontario: CAHPER Publications.

Fleming, G. A. (1976). *Creative Rhythmic Movement: Boys and Girls Dancing.* Englewood Cliffs, NJ: Prentice-Hall Inc.

———. (1990). *Children's Dance,* Revised Edition. Reston, VA: AAHPERD Publications.

Joyce, M. (1980). *First Steps in Teaching Creative Dance to Children.* Palo Alto, CA: Mayfield Publishing Co.

Lewte, G. (1982). *No Handicap to Dance: Creative Improvisation for People With and Without Disabilities.* London: Souvenir Press.

National Dance Association. (1990). *Guide to Creative Dance for Young Children.* Reston, VA: AAHPERD Publications.

———. (1988). *Dance Curricula Guidelines.* Reston, VA: AAHPERD Publications.

———. (1990). *Dance Resource Guide.* Reston, VA: AAHPERD Publications.

Stinson, S. (1988). *Dance for Young Children: Finding the Magic in Movement.* Reston, VA: AAHPERD Publications.

Wall, J., and Murray, N. (1994). *Children and Movement,* Second Edition. Dubuque, IA: Wm. C. Brown Publishers.

Zurulnik, A., and Abeles, J. (1985). *Resource List for Children's Dance.* Michigan Dance Association, 300 Bailey St., Room 201, East Lansing, MI, 48823.

Appendixes

Videotape Series D: Teaching Elementary School Physical Education

Series D consists of four videotapes designed for use in preservice and inservice physical education programs for elementary school teachers. Each videotape describes class management techniques, organization of content, and teaching strategies.

Videotape No. 1: *Teaching Game Activities*

This videotape describes how game activities are organized and taught to children who fall within three developmental levels of motor ability. Suggestions relating to class organization, lesson plans, and the use of various direct and problem-solving teaching strategies are provided for each developmental level.

Videotape No. 2: *Teaching Gymnastic Activities*

Two contemporary types of gymnastic activities are currently being taught to elementary school children. *Teaching Gymnastic Activities* describes the similarities and differences in content and teaching strategies used to teach educational and Olympic gymnastics. Ideas and suggestions are also provided on how to integrate these two approaches according to the interest and background of the children in each developmental level.

Videotape No. 3: *Teaching Folk Dance Activities*

Folk dance activities have traditionally been taught through a series of stages to allow children to learn each dance in an orderly and progressive manner. This videotape illustrates how children in the primary and intermediate grades first learn how to keep time to a music accompaniment, as well as the meaning of a measure, an accent, tempo, and a musical phrase. From here, scenes illustrate how children learn singing games, folk dances, and square dances through a progressive series of steps. The latter part of this videotape illustrates how young and older children learn to modify the dances they have learned by adding new steps, directions, and movement patterns.

Videotape No. 4: *Teaching Creative Dance Activities*

Creative dance activities can be taught through direct and problem-solving methods and by using a variety of stimuli such as photographs, stories, poems, and visual presentations. This videotape discusses the value and importance of a creative dance program and describes the basic steps that are followed when guiding young children to interpret ideas and feelings through creative dance activities. Laban's elements of movement are stressed throughout this videotape, as are the limitation, or problem-solving, methods of teaching.

Inexpensive Equipment

1. Skipping Ropes
2. Horizontal Bar
3. Wands
4. Vaulting Box
5. Jumping Boxes
6. Plastic Hurdles
7. Jumping Pit
8. All-Purpose Game Bat
9. Sand Blocks
10. Tambourines
11. Wooden Nail Keg Drum
12. Metal Drum
13. Plastic Plant Pot Drum
14. Rattlers
15. Jingle Bats, Bands, Pin-Ons, and Sticks
16. Coat Hanger Racquets
17. Beanbags
18. Markers and Scoops
19. Hoops
20. Bowling Pins

1. Skipping Ropes

To Cut Ropes

1. Measure the desired length of rope.
2. Wrap tape around the rope 5 inches above and below the cut mark (plastic tape preferred, adhesive acceptable).
3. Place rope on small wooden block and cut rope in middle of taped area.

To Store Ropes

1. Since there may be three or four different lengths of rope, dip the ends of the ropes in different colors of paint to represent short, medium, and long lengths. (Dip about 6 inches.)
2. A simple way to store ropes is across or over a bar as shown. The standard can be of any design, with the top bar about 4 feet off the floor.

3/8″ to 1/2″ rope

Tape wrapped around rope

White   Red   Blue

2. Horizontal Bar

General Features

The horizontal bar can be made for an approximate cost of fifteen to twenty dollars. It is designed for efficient assemblage and storage. The bolt, as shown in detail B, prevents the bar from rotating while stunts are being performed. The bar is held firmly to the upright standard with a fixed $2^3/_4$-inch washer on the inside and a washer and bolt as shown in detail D. For efficient storage, the side support shown in detail A may be drawn upward.

Designed by Bill Bressler
Drawn by Gary Sciuchetti

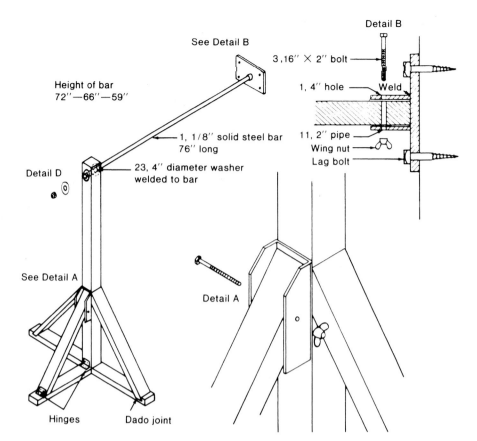

See Detail B

Height of bar
72″—66″—59″

Detail B

3, 16″ × 2″ bolt

1, 4″ hole   Weld

11, 2″ pipe
Wing nut
Lag bolt

1, 1/8″ solid steel bar 76″ long

23, 4″ diameter washer welded to bar

Detail D

See Detail A

Detail A

Hinges   Dado joint

3. Wands

General Information

A set of wands (see chapter 26 for appropriate lengths) may be made from old broomsticks. Cut off each broomstick at the desired length and round both ends. Dip the end of each set of wands in different colors of paint to facilitate each selection.

Red   Blue   Black

Color code for different lengths

Container for storage
(use spare garbage can)

4. Vaulting Box

Corner joint detail

3'3''

14''

4'0''

PLAN

Use 3/4 fir plywood.
All joints to be glued and screwed

Canvas
Sponge rubber
Padding
Felt
Top

Make opening to suit size
of walking plank or balance bench

2'' × 2'' fir
to be used
at all
corners
and at
centers

12''

8''

8''

8''

8''

4'6''

1''

4''

FRONT ELEVATION

SIDE ELEVATION

Finish: Wiped white rez stain-shellacked and varnished

5. Jumping Boxes

General Features

The jumping boxes shown here can be made for approximately fifty dollars, depending on the number of boxes and the size of each. A minimum of three for each set is recommended. *Do not* cover top with rubber matting or cloth material. Sand all corners and, if desired, paint or varnish.

18"

18"

Grip holes

30"

Rectangular Boxes

Rectangular Jumping Boxes

Sizes (Approx.)
30" x 18" x 18"
32" x 20" x 20"
34" x 24" x 24"

*Sizes permit boxes to be stacked for storage.

Materials:
3/8" to 1/2" plywood
Construction: Reinforce all corners with brackets.

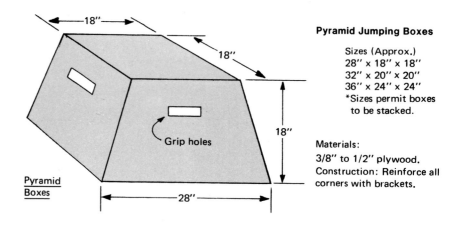

18"

18"

18"

Grip holes

Pyramid Boxes

28"

Pyramid Jumping Boxes

Sizes (Approx.)
28" x 18" x 18"
32" x 20" x 20"
36" x 24" x 24"

*Sizes permit boxes to be stacked.

Materials:
3/8" to 1/2" plywood.
Construction: Reinforce all corners with brackets.

6. Plastic Hurdles

Materials

1. 1-inch plastic pipe
2. 90-degree elbow fittings
3. Velcro strips
4. Wood or webbed crossbar

Velcro

How To Make

1. Cut two 29-inch, two 14-inch, and one 28-inch pieces of plastic hose.
2. Insert glue in ends of elbows, then insert pieces of plastic hose as shown in the diagram.
3. Attach velcro strips on crossbar and at different heights on the vertical posts.

7. Jumping Pit

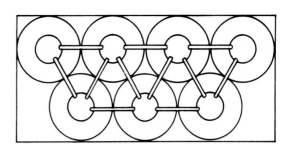

How to Make

Rubber tubes are placed on the ground, as shown in the diagram, and tied together. A tumbling mat is then placed on top of the tubes. This provides a safe and comfortable landing surface. The jumping pit can be used indoors or outdoors.

8. All-Purpose Game Bat

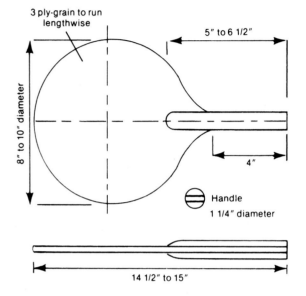

Materials

1. 1/4-inch good quality plywood
2. 1/2-inch fir strips
3. Sandpaper and glue

How To Make

1. Cut out circular bat and paddle handles.
2. Sand surfaces and round edges.
3. Glue handles.
4. Varnish or paint surfaces.
5. Tape handles for extra strength and better gripping surface.

9. Sand Blocks

Materials

1. Two blocks of wood (approx. 4 inches by 6 inches by 1 inch)
2. Sandpaper or emery paper (different grades)
3. Thumbtacks, glue, or screws
4. Thread spools or knobs

How to Make

1. Cut blocks of wood.
2. Sand surfaces and round edges.
3. Glue or screw on handle.
4. Cover bottom surface with sandpaper and tack each end. Use different grades of sandpaper or emery paper to make different sounds.
5. Decorate as desired.

10. Tambourines

Materials
1. *Pie plate tambourine:* Old pie plate, safety pins, bells or strings, and bottle caps or roofing discs
2. *Ping-pong bat tambourine:* Old table tennis bat, nails and bottle caps, or roofing discs
3. *Stick tambourine:* Stick (6 inches by 1 1/2 inches by 3/4 inch) and bottle caps or roofing discs

How to Make a Pie Plate Tambourine
1. Make nail holes around outer edge of pie plate. Sand rough side of nail hole.
2. Attach safety pin and bell to each hole, or attach string and bottle caps (two per string) to each hole.
3. Decorate as desired.

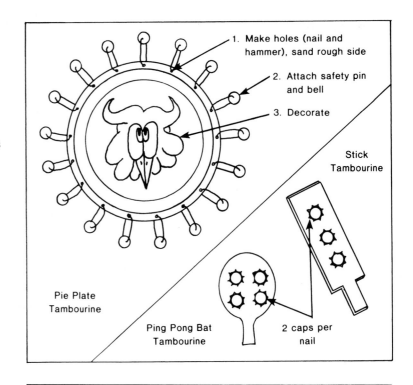

1. Make holes (nail and hammer), sand rough side
2. Attach safety pin and bell
3. Decorate

Stick Tambourine

Pie Plate Tambourine

Ping Pong Bat Tambourine

2 caps per nail

11. Wooden Nail Keg Drum

Materials
1. Nail keg (or any wooden container that has not been waterproofed or sealed)
2. Medium and fine sandpaper
3. Tacks (upholstery tacks)
4. Paints
5. Floor seal
6. Muslin, nitrate solution

How to Make
1. Sand with medium, then fine sandpaper.
2. Paint outside surface of keg with floor seal. Add a second coat after twenty-four hours.
3. Apply one coat of flat white paint. (If still darkish, add another coat after twenty-four hours.)
4. Decorate keg with bright enamel paints.
5. Cut muslin (or sailcloth) about 2 inches larger than top of nail keg.
6. Place muslin on top, drawing evenly down sides, and place thumbtacks 1 inch below top rim.
7. Start above tacks and wind colored yarn around keg and work down to cover ends of muslin. Tuck yarn under last row and tie.
8. Apply five or six coats of nitrate solution to muslin and yarn. Allow each coat to dry thoroughly.

Note: Drum beaters. A drum stick can be made by wrapping a soft cloth (cotton, wool) around end of dowel. Cover with leather, muslin, or sailcloth, and wrap with heavy cord.

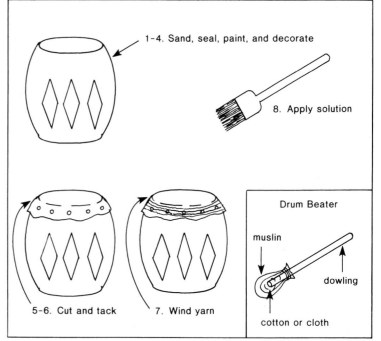

1-4. Sand, seal, paint, and decorate

8. Apply solution

5-6. Cut and tack

7. Wind yarn

Drum Beater

muslin

dowling

cotton or cloth

12. Metal Drum

Materials

1. Metal can (paint, coffee, etc.)
2. Inner tubing or rubber sheeting
3. Wire and yarn
4. Paints

How to Make

1. Remove top and bottom lids; remove any paper and soak to dissolve dirt and/or glue.
2. Apply one or two coats of flat white paint, then decorate with bright enamel paint (keep decoration toward the middle, as the outside 2 inches will be covered with tubing).
3. Cut two rubber sheets 2 inches larger than opening. Puncture holes 1 inch in from outer edge and about 2 inches apart. Lace twine through holes.
4. Place first sheet over top end and wrap twine 1 inch below top of rim. Repeat on bottom.
5. Pull top and bottom laces tight and tie.
6. Tie a twine to top lace, then to bottom, and zigzag lace around drum. This will hold both ends tight.

13. Plastic Plant Pot Drum

Materials

1. Plastic plant pots of various sizes
2. Masking tape
3. Muslin or sailcloth
4. Paint and yarn

How to Make

1. Seal drain holes with masking tape. Apply two or three strips over each hole.
2. Apply one or two coats of flat white paint.
3. Cut a circle of muslin to cover top plus sides and 1 inch under bottom edge.
4. Cut out triangles evenly spaced around circumference of cloth circle. Fold remaining ends down $1/2$ inch and sew to form $1/2$-inch hem open at both ends.
5. Lay cloth over top, down sides, and under bottom edge. Lace heavy twine through hems of the ends, pull, secure, and tie.
6. Wrap yarn around upper edge and just below vertical lines.
7. Apply five or six coats of nitrate solution to all muslin and yarn. Allow each coat to dry thoroughly.
8. Decorate as desired with enamel paint.

14. Rattlers

Materials

A rattler can be made from any container that can be easily sealed and that permits a variety of material to move freely inside the container:

1. A tennis ball container with rice or dried peas
2. A wooden matchbox with peas, rice, or sand
3. A plastic vinegar bottle with marbles or nuts with shells on
4. Plastic tubing (11/2-inch) with seeds

Note: The rattling sound of any container is determined by a combination of the size, shape, and material of the container combined with the nature of the rattling material. Experiment with different materials in each container to find the most appealing sound.

How to Make

1. Where necessary, clean container and remove all labels.
2. Place materials inside and seal opening. For tubes, cover ends with plastic or cloth and wrap with masking tape.
3. Decorate with paper, string, or paint.

15. Jingle Bats, Bands, Pin-Ons, and Sticks

Materials

1. *Jingle bats:* Coat hanger, tongue depressors, masking tape, six to eight bells, string
2. *Jingle bands:* 6- to 8-inch cloth bands, four or five bells, string
3. *Jingle pins:* Bells in sets of three or four, string, safety pin
4. *Jingle sticks:* 8-inch stick, two circle-head screws, six bells, string

How to Make

See diagrams and modify each type of jingle instrument to the available materials and creative abilities of the children.

16. Coat Hanger Racquets

Materials
1. Coat hangers
2. Nylon hose
3. Masking tape

How To Make
1. Straighten the hanger hook.
2. Bend hanger into a diamond shape.
3. Slide hanger into the hose, pull tightly, and twist loose ends around the handle.
4. Tape handle, bend half of the handle back, and retape whole handle.

1.

2.

3.

4.

17. Beanbags

Beanbag

Materials
1. Scrap cloth, such as denim or canvas
2. Beans

How To Make
1. Cut 6 1/2-inch squares.
2. Sew up three sides.
3. Fill beanbag with beans (use a commercial beanbag to determine the amount to put into each bag).
4. Sew up fourth side.

18. Markers and Scoops

Materials
1. One-gallon plastic jugs
2. Scissors or carpet knife
3. Sandpaper

How To Make
1. *For field markers*
   a. Fill one-third of jug with sand.
   b. Place different color tapes on markers or paint for use as field or goal markers.
2. *For scoops*
   a. Trace cutting line with marking pencil or pen.
   b. Cut off lower section and sandpaper edges.

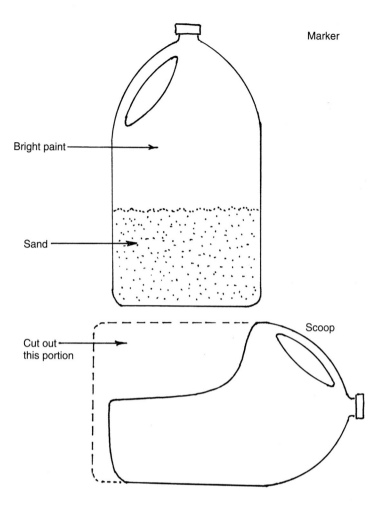

Marker

Bright paint

Sand

Cut out this portion

Scoop

19. Hoops

Materials
1. 1/2-inch plastic water pipe
2. 1/2-inch doweling
3. Tacks or staples
4. Glue

How To Make
1. Cut hose into 7-foot, 10-inch sections (makes 30-inch hoops).
2. Cut 3″ pieces of doweling.
3. Place glue inside both ends of the hose.
4. Insert 3-inch doweling and staple or tack each end to the doweling.
5. Tape over doweling area of the hose.

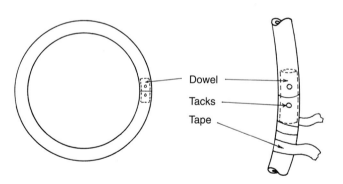

Dowel

Tacks

Tape

20. Bowling Pins

Materials

1. Discarded tenpin bowling pins (contact your local bowling alley for used pins)
2. Saw and sandpaper
3. Paint

How To Make

1. Cut off lower two inches of the pin and sandpaper rough edges.
2. Paint and/or number each pin.

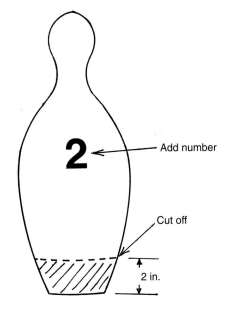

Add number

Cut off

2 in.

Apparatus, Equipment, and Supply Companies

Centaur Products Inc.
6855 Antrim Ave.
Burnaby, B.C., Canada, V5J 4M5
(604) 430–3088
General apparatus and equipment

Flaghouse
18 West 18th St.
New York, NY 10011
(212) 989–9700
General apparatus and equipment

Gerstung Manufacturers
6310 Blair Hills La.
Baltimore, MD 21209
Small equipment and rhythmic gymnastic supplies

G.S.C. Athletic Equipment
600 North Pacific Ave.
San Pedro, CA 90733
(213) 831–0131
General apparatus and equipment

Gym Closet
2511 Leach Rd.
Rochester Hills, MI 48057
Small equipment, balls, mats, paddles, parachutes, and other supplies

Laurentian Gymnastic Industries Ltd.
15 Melanie Dr.
Brampton, Ontario, Canada, L6T 4K8
(416) 791–5757
Climbing apparatus

Mosier Materials
61328 Yakwahtin Ct.
Bend, OR 97702
Parachutes, juggling scarves, balls, scooters, and other supplies

Nissen Corp.
930 27th Ave. SW
Cedar Rapids, IA 52406
(319) 365–7561
Apparatus and mats

Passon's Sports
1017 Arch St.
Philadelphia, PA 19107
(800) 523–1557
General apparatus, equipment, and supplies

Porter Athletic Equipment
9555 Irving Park Rd.
Schiller Park, IL 60176
(708) 671–0110
Gymnastic apparatus

Sidney Larrer and Co.
5315 North Lincoln Ave.
Chicago, IL 60625
(800) 526–1300
General apparatus, equipment, and supplies

Sportime
2905 Amwiler Rd.
Atlanta, GA 30360
(404) 449–5700
General apparatus and equipment

US Games Inc.
Box 360874
Melbourne, FL 32936
(800) 521–2832
Small equipment and parachutes

Wolverine Sports
745 Circle
Box 1941
Ann Arbor, MI 48106
(313) 761–5690
General apparatus and equipment

Glossary

The following words and phrases occur frequently in the instructional and extra-class physical education program. (Note: A separate glossary for folk and square dance terms are provided in chapter 29.)

Accent (p. 536)
The emphasis given to a beat in a series of beats in a measure.

Accident (pp. 158, 162)
An unforeseen event occurring without the will or design of the person whose act causes it.

Active lifestyle (pp. 8, 12)
A lifestyle which includes physical activity as a regular part of daily routines.

Activity independence (pp. 8, 12)
To be physically active through self-desire and not reliant on another person.

Act of God (p. 160)
A situation due to forces beyond the control of the defendant.

Advance (pp. 546, 554, 581)
Move forward, usually with walking steps.

Aerobic exercise (p. 171)
Exercise performed with an adequate supply of oxygen.

Agility (p. 434)
The ability to shift the body in different directions quickly and efficiently.

Agility apparatus (p. 505)
All types of indoor and outdoor climbing apparatus.

Anaerobic exercise (p. 171)
Exercise performed in the absence of oxygen.

Apparatus work (pp. 478, 506)
The second part of a gymnastic lesson. Also, the second part of a Movement Education lesson, concerned with the application of movement ideas to large and small apparatus.

Arch (pp. 550, 581)
Two dancers join inside hands and raise their arms.

Asthma (p. 221)
A condition of the lungs that causes labored breathing and wheezing.

Asymmetry (p. 473)
A position or movement characterized by the unevenness of opposite parts of the body. Using a line drawn through the vertebral column, all twisting, curling, or held positions in which greater stress is given to the limbs on one side are asymmetrical positions.

Atrophy (p. 186)
A reduction in size.

Attack (p. 323)
Players who are designated as forward line players.

Attacking team (pp. 313, 323)
The team that has possession of the ball; also known as the offensive team.

Away (p. 398)
The number of players who have been put out ("one away").

Backcourt (p. 382)
The half of the basketball court farthest from the offensive basket.

Bag (p. 398)
Base.

Balance (pp. 40, 78, 466)
The ability to maintain a stationary position or to perform purposeful movements while resisting the force of gravity. Also, the ability to hold the body in a fixed position. (The common expression is "weight bearing.")

Baseline (p. 382)
The endline of a basketball court.

Bases loaded (p. 398)
Runners on every base.

Basket (p. 382)
Circular goal located on the backboard.

Baton (p. 405)
A short, round stick passed between members of a relay team.

Beat (p. 536)
The constant, steady pulsation in a movement or musical accompaniment.

Block (p. 353)
One or two defensive players jump up at the same time as the spiker, with their hands raised and facing the oncoming ball.

Blocking (p. 346)
A legal method of stopping an opponent.

Boarding (p. 329)
Holding a player against the wall.

Body awareness (pp. 38, 466)
The way in which the body or parts of it can move (stretch, bend, twist, and turn).

Body composition (pp. 20, 182)
The relative percentage of fat to other tissues of the body.

Body mechanics (p. 78)
The efficient and effective use of the body in maintaining good alignment and performing daily tasks.

Body of a lesson (p. 106)
The major part of a lesson where the skill or concept to be learned is emphasized.

Bound flow (p. 44)
A momentary pause in a sequence of movement.

Box (p. 398)
The specific area marked and designated as the catcher's area, the batter's area, or the coach's area.

Brainstorming (p. 584)
Dance ideas developed by a teacher and her class.

Breach of duty (p. 158)
A teacher who fails to conform to her required duties to her students.

Buzz (p. 546)
The weight is held on one foot while pushing with the other foot.

Calisthenics (pp. 189, 233)
Conditioning exercises designed to improve physical fitness.

Cardiac output (p. 170)
The volume of blood the heart pumps out each minute.

Cardiorespiratory endurance (p. 187)
The ability of the heart and lungs to sustain activity.

Cardiovascular fitness (p. 182)
The efficiency of the heart, lungs, and blood vessels.

Center (p. 382)
The middle position on the forward line, usually played by the tallest player on the team.

Center of gravity (pp. 22, 78)
The point on the body around which the weight of the body is equally distributed.

Cerebral palsy (p. 219)
Neurological impairment caused by damage to the motor areas of the brain.

Circuit training (p. 199)
Repeating one or more exercises as many times as possible within a time limit.

Classroom games (p. 226)
Games, relays, and contests that can be played in the classroom.

Clean the bases (p. 398)
Hit a home run, with one or more teammates on bases.

Cleanup (p. 398)
The fourth, and usually the strongest, hitter in the batting order.

Clockwise (pp. 397, 581)
In the same direction as the hands of a clock.

Closure (pp. 107–8)
A short review session at the end of the lesson.

Command (p. 127)
A teaching method in which the teacher controls the subject to be learned and how it is to be learned.

Concept (pp. 10, 37, 150, 231)
The degree of meaning a person possesses about an experience.

Continuity (pp. 44, 422)
Movements following each other in succession.

Contra or longways (p. 554)
Couples standing in a long line, with boys on one side and girls on the other.

Contributory negligence (p. 160)
Failure of an injured party to exercise due care and concern for her own welfare.

Cooperation (p. 294)
Two or more individuals working together toward a common goal.

Cooperative game (p. 293)
A game stressing one or more elements of cooperative behavior.

Corner (pp. 325, 337)
When the defending team causes the ball to go over the endline, the attacking team is awarded a free hit from the nearest corner of the field.

Corner kick (p. 325)
A placekick awarded to the attacking team after the defending team has sent the ball over its own goal line.

Counterclockwise (pp. 393, 581)
In the opposite direction as the hands of a clock.

Crease (p. 337)
The semicircular area around the goal area.

Creative dance (p. 235)
The expression of ideas and feelings through unstructured movement.

Creative games (p. 251)
Games invented by children.

Creative playground (p. 118)
A unique arrangement of outdoor apparatus (commercial or locally constructed).

Creativity (p. 10)
The degree of inventiveness of a movement.

Criterion-referenced test (p. 142)
A measure of a person's performance evaluated against a qualitative standard.

Cumulative record (pp. 141, 175)
A method of plotting a child's performance (skill or physical fitness items) at the beginning and end of each year.

Curl (p. 39)
An action that flexes or bends the body or its parts.

Curriculum (pp. 4, 6, 91)
The total experience within the physical education program that is provided for all children.

Dance position (p. 547)
The relative body and hand position of one dancer to another.

Declarative knowledge (pp. 74, 152)
Theoretical knowledge associated with knowing what to do in order to perform a motor skill.

Defensive team (defense, defending team) (pp. 313, 324)
The team that does not have possession of the ball.

Developmental (p. 18)
The systematic and progressive acquisition of concepts and skills.

Diamond (p. 398)
The area inside the four bases.

Diaphysis (p. 23)
The center of bone growth located in the middle of the long bones.

Dink (p. 353)
A deception drop volley executed from a spiked position.

Direct free kick (p. 324)
A free kick from which a goal may be scored directly.

Direct method (p. 126)
A teaching method in which the choice of the activity and how it is performed is entirely the teacher's.

Discipline (p. 136)
A form of control imposed internally by an individual or externally by another person in control of the learning environment.

Dodge (pp. 56, 333)
A means of evading an oncoming tackler.

Double elimination tournament (p. 241)
A consolation bracket added to a single elimination tournament to assure that each team plays at least two games.

Double play (p. 398)
A defensive play by the fielding team, resulting in two outs.

Down (pp. 349–50)
A method of starting play after the ball has been stopped. In football, each team is given four downs to advance the ball ten yards.

Down syndrome (p. 215)
Moderate retardation caused by a genetic factor.

Dribble (pp. 312, 331)
A means of advancing the ball or puck with a series of short taps.

Drive (pp. 332, 372)
Hit the ball from a moderate to a long distance. Also, a quick dribbling movement toward the opponent's basket.

Dual activities (p. 294)
Cooperative and competitive activities between two children.

Duration recording (p. 144)
Recording the amount of time an event takes place.

Earned run (p. 398)
A run scored as a result of an offensive play and not as a result of an error committed by the defensive team.

Endurance (p. 182)
The ability to continue a muscular effort or movement over a prolonged period of time.

Entry activity (p. 106)
Free practice time prior to the beginning of a lesson.

Epilepsy (p. 219)
A condition of the nervous system characterized by seizures and convulsions.

Epiphysis (p. 23)
The center of growth located near the ends of the long bones.

Equipment (pp. 117, 121, 155, 161)
Relatively permanent material or apparatus that lasts, with repeated use, from five to ten years.

Error (p. 398)
A mistake committed by the defensive team.

Established duty (p. 158)
A duty a teacher has to her pupils.

Evaluation (p. 141)
The subjective and objective assessment of program effectiveness and student progress.

Event recording (p. 143)
Recording the number of times an event takes place.

Exceptional child (p. 207)
A child who deviates from the normal intelligence, physical health, motor ability, or behavioral characteristics of the average or typical child.

Extraclass program (p. 246)
A cooperative and competitive program between two or more schools.

Extrinsic motivation (p. 136)
The desire to complete a task in order to gain an external reward.

Fair ball (p. 398)
Any legally batted ball that is touched or lands in fair territory.

Fan (p. 398)
A player who misses the third strike.

Fast break (p. 382)
A situation in which the defensive team gains possession of the ball and moves it into a scoring position before the opposing team can recover into a defensive position.

Feedback (pp. 72, 77)
A process of receiving information about one's performance.

Feint (pp. 313, 333)
A deceptive movement to mislead an opponent.

Fielding (p. 390)
Gaining possession of the ball or puck.

Flexibility (pp. 184, 190)
The range of movement of a joint.

Flick (p. 333)
A method of putting the ball or puck into the air.

Flight (p. 41)
The ability to propel the body into the air.

Float (pp. 50, 201)
An interval or period during a long run in which the runner has a relaxed stride, with no increase or decrease in speed.

Flow (p. 44)
The ability to link one movement to another with control and harmony.

Folk dance (pp. 238, 550)
Dance patterns of past cultures.

Force (pp. 44, 85)
The degree of effort or tension involved in a movement.

Forced out (p. 393)
A defensive player in possession of the ball touches a base before a runner who is forced to move to that base.

Forward and back (pp. 579, 581)
This figure may involve one or more dancers facing each other. Both advance four steps forward (or three steps and a bow) and four steps backward.

Foul (p. 324)
An illegal act, such as tripping or holding an opponent, which results in a direct free kick being awarded to the nonoffending team.

Foul ball (p. 398)
A hit ball that lands outside of fair territory.

Free hit (p. 336)
A hit awarded to the opposing team after a breach of the rules.

Free throw (p. 383)
An unguarded shot taken from the free throw line. If successful, the shooting team scores one point.

Frontcourt (p. 382)
The part of the basketball court nearest each team's goal.

Front runner (p. 50)
A runner who performs best when ahead of opponents.

Fundamental motor skills (p. 47)
Locomotor, nonlocomotor, and manipulative skills and movement patterns.

Gallop (p. 55)
A sliding movement performed in a forward direction.

Games of low organization (p. 249)
Such activities as relays, tag, and simple team games that involve one or more basic skills and a minimum of roles and playing strategies.

General space (p. 42)
The physical area in which a movement takes place.

Growth (pp. 18–19)
An increase in size.

Guided discovery (p. 129)
A teaching method in which the teacher guides the learner through a series of activities.

Hash running (p. 414)
A team race, with markers and hidden directions located along the route.

Heading (p. 312)
Playing the ball by striking it with the head.

Health-related physical fitness (p. 188)
The ability to perform activities without undue fatigue and to show resistance to the development of disorders that limit one's functional capacity.

Heart rate (p. 172)
The number of times a person's heart beats in one minute.

Heats (p. 412)
Preliminary track-and-field events to determine who will compete in the final events.

High sticking (p. 337)
Raising the stick above shoulder level.

Hike (p. 342)
The movement of the ball from the center player to the quarterback.

Hitter (pp. 355, 361, 364–65)
Spiker.

Home (pp. 552, 581)
The original starting place of a dance.

Honor (pp. 552, 581)
Salute or bow to one's partner or to other dancers.

Hop (p. 53)
Transfer weight from one foot to the same foot.

Humanism (p. 4)
A philosophy that asserts the dignity and worth of human beings and their capacity for self-realization through reason.

Hyperopia (p. 218)
Farsightedness; distant objects can be seen clearly but nearby objects appear blurred.

IEP (Individualized Educational Plan) (pp. 10, 210)
A systematic plan to meet the needs of special needs children.

Illegal contact (p. 349)
Any contact of the ball in which it comes to a visible resting position.

Indirect free kick (p. 324)
A free kick from which a goal may not be scored directly.

Indirect method (p. 129)
A teaching method that allows the children to choose the activity, as well as how and what they will perform within the activity.

Individual games (p. 249)
Low-organization games played by one person with or without small equipment.

Individualized learning (p. 126)
A system of teaching that adapts to each learner's abilities, needs, and interests.

Infield (p. 398)
The playing area within and immediately adjacent to the diamond.

Infringement (p. 324)
An illegal act, such as being offside, that results in an indirect free kick being awarded to the nonoffending team.

In loco parentis (p. 158)
Acting in the place of the parent.

Inning (p. 398)
A division of the game in which both teams play until each has three players out.

Instructional unit (pp. 102, 251)
The organization of material around a central activity or theme of instruction.

Instructional variety (p. 131)
Refers to the variability or flexibility of instructional delivery during a lesson.

Intensity (pp. 186, 537)
The quality or force of music or movement.

Interschool athletics (p. 247)
Competition between schools in team and individual sports.

Interval recording (p. 144)
The systematic observation of events, conducted at various intervals of time.

Intramural program (p. 238)
Competitive or club activities offered during nonclass time, on a voluntary basis, and within the jurisdiction of one school.

Intrinsic motivation (p. 135)
An internal desire to achieve a given standard or goal.

Introductory activity (p. 106)
The first part of a lesson, which involves a general warm-up and lasts for approximately three to five minutes.

Isometric exercise (p. 186)
Contraction of muscles involving a push, pull, or twist against an object that does not move.

Isotonic exercise (p. 186)
Contraction of muscles that involves both shortening and lengthening the muscle fibers.

Jog (pp. 201, 441)
A slow, easy run.

Journal (pp. 151, 153)
A personal written record of a child's lived experiences.

Jump (p. 51)
A light transfer of weight from one foot or both feet to both feet.

Jump ball (p. 382)
A situation in which two opposing players simultaneously gain possession of the ball, and the referee tosses it up between the two players.

Jump shot (p. 372)
A shot taken while the player has both feet off the floor.

Kickoff (p. 323)
A short kick taken by the center forward at the center of the field. The kickoff is used to start the game, at halftime, and after each goal is scored.

Kyphosis (p. 174)
A marked curve of the upper back.

Ladder tournament (pp. 239, 241)
A tournament that uses a ladder to advance positions; players on lower rungs may challenge players on one or two rungs above them.

Lap (pp. 402, 412)
One complete circuit around the track.

Lateral (p. 342)
A sideways pass of the ball.

Lay-up (pp. 372, 380)
A shot taken close to the backboard. The ball is released off one hand and gently placed over the rim or against the backboard to allow it to rebound into the basket.

Lead-up game (p. 249)
A game that involves one or more concepts and skills of a major team sport.

Leap (p. 51)
A light transfer of weight from one foot to the other foot.

Learning disabilities (p. 214)
Inherited conditions that cause mild or moderate learning difficulties.

Lesson plan (p. 106)
A flexible daily plan that includes objectives, content, organizational procedures, teaching cues, evaluation, and references.

Level (p. 42)
The relative position of the body or any of its parts to the floor or apparatus. Level may be applied to either stationary activity or position.

Liability (p. 158)
A violation of an obligation to perform a duty.

Limitation method (p. 128)
A teaching method in which the choice of the activity or the way it is performed is limited by the teacher.

Linear motion (p. 84)
A movement in which the body or an object as a whole moves in a straight line.

Locomotor skills (pp. 47–48)
Basic motor skills involving a change of position of the feet and/or a change of direction of the body.

Lordosis (p. 174)
An exaggerated forward curve of the lower back.

Mainstreaming (pp. 13, 209)
Placing disabled students into the regular physical education program.

Malfeasance (p. 159)
An unlawful act resulting in injury or an adverse effect on a person.

Maturation (pp. 18, 24)
The general progress from one stage of development to a higher, more complex stage. Maturation occurs as a function of time and is independent of experience.

Measure (p. 536)
A repetitive grouping of underlying beats.

Method (p. 126)
A general way of guiding and controlling the learning experiences of children.

Misfeasance (p. 159)
Improperly performing a lawful act.

Modified teaching unit (p. 104)
A unit of instruction that emphasizes one type of activity and provides a minor focus on one or more other activities.

Movement design (p. 547)
The way two or more dancers meet, greet, and part during a dance.

Movement Education (pp. 10, 37, 77, 94, 150, 463)
An approach to teaching physical education, which uses Laban's four elements of movement as the content and stresses exploratory teaching strategies.

Movement ideas (pp. 37, 463)
A movement concept related to one or more of the basic elements—qualities, body awareness, space awareness, and relationships.

Movement training (pp. 37, 463)
The second part of a Movement Education lesson, which is concerned with the development of movement themes and activities.

Multiple teaching unit (p. 104)
A unit of instruction that includes two or more activities.

Muscular endurance (p. 182)
The ability of the muscular system to sustain performance.

Muscular strength (p. 182)
The ability of the muscles to overcome resistance.

Myopia (p. 218)
Nearsightedness; distant objects appear blurred, whereas nearby objects are seen clearly.

Negligence (p. 158)
An act, or the absence of one, that falls below the legal standard for the protection of others against unreasonable risk or harm.

Net recovery (p. 358)
A fair move to play the volleyball after it has been hit into the net by a teammate.

Neuromuscular skills (p. 69)
Motor skills under the voluntary control of the brain.

Nonfeasance (p. 160)
Failure to perform a required act.

Nonlocomotor skills (pp. 47, 57)
Movements of the body performed from a relatively stable base.

Norm-referenced tests (p. 142)
A test battery that uses quantitative data to serve as a standard by which individual performances are measured.

Novelty track meet (p. 413)
A track and field day in which children participate in a variety of novelty events.

Obesity (pp. 20, 181)
A condition characterized by excessive bodily fat tissue.

Obstacle course (p. 200)
An arrangement of small and large equipment designed to improve physical fitness and skill development.

Obstruction (p. 324)
When a player runs between an opponent and the ball.

Offense (offensive team) (pp. 313, 323)
The team that has possession of the ball.

Offside (p. 324)
When a player is illegally in the opponent's half of the field and there are fewer than two opposing players in front of the player at the moment a teammate plays the ball in a forward direction.

Olympic meet (p. 239)
A tournament that includes a number of individual, dual, and team events.

One-on-one (p. 378)
A situation in which one offensive player tries to outmaneuver one defensive player.

Open (pp. 548, 581)
Partners stand side-by-side, with their inside hands joined. Girls stand to the boys' right.

Opposite (pp. 552, 581)
The person or couple directly across the square.

Out (p. 398)
The retirement of a batter after three strikes. Also, a base runner who is caught or forced out.

Outfield (pp. 391, 398)
The fair territory located beyond the infield.

Overload (p. 186)
A performance of an exercise or activity that requires the individual to exert more than a normal effort.

Pace (p. 404)
The rate of speed the runner sets for a particular distance run.

Passing zone (pp. 405, 412)
An area on the track within which the baton must be passed.

Pathways (p. 42)
Directional routes that are straight, curved, or zigzag.

Pattern (p. 37)
The arrangement of a series of movements in relation to shape, level, and pathway.

Penalty kick (p. 324)
If a foul is committed by the defending team within the penalty area, the attacking team is given a direct free kick from the twelve-yard mark, directly in front of the goal. All other players must be outside the penalty area until the kick is taken.

Perceptual-motor response (p. 217)
The process of perceiving a stimulus and translating it into a motor response.

Personal Activity Log (PAL) (pp. 151, 154)
A personal journal to record a child's activity patterns and to establish future goals.

Personal space (p. 42)
The area around an individual that can be used while keeping one part of the body in a fixed position on the floor or apparatus; also known as limited space.

Phrase (p. 537)
A group of measures that fit together into a meaningful whole.

Physical awkwardness (p. 222)
A term used to describe children who do not suffer from any known neuromuscular disorder, yet exhibit poor motor coordination and fitness.

Physical education (pp. 6, 10, 94)
The part of the educational process that contributes to the physical, emotional, social, and mental development of each child through the medium of physical activity.

Physical fitness (pp. 6, 182)
The degree to which a person is physically able to function.

Physically gifted (p. 207)
Possessing a unique talent or ability in physical fitness.

Physically handicapped (p. 208)
Suffering from a disease or physical disability.

Pinch hitter (p. 398)
A substitute hitter.

Pivot (p. 374)
A player who has possession of the ball may move one foot while keeping the other foot in contact with the floor.

Play day (p. 246)
An interschool event in which children from two or more schools play on the same team.

Pole position (p. 413)
The inside, or curb, lane of the track.

Pop-up (p. 395)
A high fly ball that lands in or near the infield.

Portfolio (p. 153)
A purposeful collection of children's work that shows both progress and achievement.

Post (p. 380)
The post player is normally a pivot player positioned near the key with his or her back toward the basket.

Posture (p. 173)
The relative alignment of the body segments.

Power (p. 186)
The ability of the body to apply a maximum muscular contraction with the quickest possible speed.

Probing (p. 134)
Encouraging students to elaborate upon a given answer.

Procedural knowledge (pp. 74, 152)
The knowledge required to physically perform a motor skill.

Proximate cause (p. 159)
A situation in which the teacher's behavior is the main factor causing injury to a student.

Punt (p. 345)
A kick performed by dropping the ball and contacting it with the top of the foot before it touches the ground.

Pyramid tournament (p. 242)
A form of competition in which participants are arranged in a pyramid structure. Players are permitted to challenge others in the row above.

Qualities (pp. 43, 468)
How the body can move. It is the ability to move quickly or slowly, the ability to perform light or heavy movements, and the flow with which one movement is linked to another.

RBI (p. 398)
Runs batted in by a player.

Rebound (pp. 373, 379)
A shot attempted at the basket that falls back into the court area.

Reflection (p. 142)
A process of personal self-evaluation used for the purpose of improvement.

Relationship (pp. 45, 470)
The position of the body in relation to the floor, apparatus, or other performers.

Relay activities (pp. 405, 412)
Activities that involve a race between two or more participants or teams.

Respiratory rate (p. 170)
The number of times an individual inhales in one minute.

Resting heart rate (p. 172)
The number of times a person's heart beats per minute while in a quiet state of resting.

Rhythmic (p. 189)
Performing a variety of body movements in time to a specific rhythmic accompaniment.

Rotary motion (p. 84)
A movement that traces out an arc or circle around an axis or fixed point.

Round-robin tournament (p. 241)
A tournament in which every player plays every other player in the tournament.

Run (pp. 49, 411)
A transfer of weight from one foot to the other, with a momentary loss of contact with the floor by both feet.

Safety (pp. 226, 330, 387, 402, 414, 512)
When a defensive player in possession of the ball is trapped behind his or her own goal line. The attacking team is awarded two points.

Safety training (pp. 228, 330, 387, 402)
Teaching children to move and land safely and efficiently. In a broader context, it refers to the individual's safety on or around apparatus and to the individual's concern for the safety of other participants.

Scoliosis (p. 174)
A lateral curvature of the spinal column.

Scoop (p. 333)
A method of raising the ball into the air.

Scratch (p. 398)
A foul committed by stepping over the scratch line.

Scrimmage line (p. 349)
The line on which each down begins. The defending team must remain behind this line until the ball has left the center's hands.

Self-image (p. 9)
The feeling and/or opinion a child has about himself or herself.

Sequence (pp. 103, 422, 554)
A series of movements performed in succession.

Set shot (p. 372)
A shot taken from a stationary position.

Setup (pp. 358, 361)
This is normally the second hit by a team and is directed to a forward player, who then may attempt a spike or a volley over the net.

Shape (pp. 38, 467)
The image presented by the position of the body when traveling or stationary.

Side out (p. 365)
A violation committed by the serving team.

Singing games (p. 235)
A form of folk dance considered to be a forerunner of the more complicated traditional dances.

Single elimination tournament (p. 241)
A tournament in which a player or team is eliminated from further competition after one loss.

Skill development (p. 106)
The second part of a lesson.

Skinfold calipers (p. 183)
An instrument used to measure amount of body fat.

Skip (p. 54)
A combination of a long step and a short hop, with the lead foot alternating after each hop.

Slide (p. 55)
A combination of a step and a short leap, which can be performed forward, sideways, or backward.

Slow learner (p. 215)
A child whose IQ is between 70 and 90.

Sociogram (p. 153)
A technique used to study the relationships within groups.

Solid teaching unit (p. 105)
An extensive period of instruction devoted exclusively to one type of activity.

Space (p. 41)
The area in which a movement takes place.

Spatial awareness (pp. 41, 469)
The ability to move the body or its parts in specific directions.

Specificity of skill (pp. 76, 186)
The differential ability of an individual to acquire and perform physical skills and movement patterns.

Speed (p. 43)
The ability to perform successive movements of the same pattern in the shortest period of time.

Spike (pp. 361, 364–65)
A ball hit downward into the opponent's court.

Spiral (p. 341)
A forward pass in which the football moves with a spiral action, with the point of the ball leading.

Sports day (p. 247)
An interschool competitive event in which teams represent their own schools.

Square (pp. 554, 581)
Four couples, each forming one side of a square.

Square dance (p. 552)
A type of American folk dance.

Stance (p. 344)
The starting position of a football player.

Star or wheel (pp. 554, 581)
Two or more dancers join right hands in the center of the set and walk forward or backward as directed.

Station work (pp. 114, 213, 250, 402)
A technique of organizing the class into small working units.

Steal (p. 398)
A player advances to another base after the ball leaves the pitcher's hand and before the infield player can tag the advancing player with the ball.

Stimuli (p. 588)
Objects, stories, or paintings used in a creative dance lesson to stimulate movement ideas.

Strength (p. 182)
The amount of force a muscle or group of muscles can exert.

Stretch (pp. 39, 190)
Move the body or parts of it from a flexed to an extended position.

Stride (p. 405)
The distance between the right and left foot imprints on a track. The measurement is made from the toe of the back foot to the heel imprint of the lead foot.

Structure (p. 130)
Structuring refers to helping children organize where lesson content fits into their own learning experiences.

Success rate (p. 132)
The rate at which a child understands and correctly completes tasks.

Supplies (p. 121)
Materials that are expendable within one or two years.

Swing (p. 57)
A rhythmic rotation of a couple with a walking step, buzz step, two-step, or skip. The swing may be a one-hand, two-hand, elbow, or waist swing.

Symmetry (p. 463)
In Movement Education, symmetry describes a movement or balance position in which both sides of the body would look identical if an imaginary line were drawn through the middle of the body.

Tackle (pp. 313, 333)
A method of getting the ball away from an opponent.

Task cards (pp. 114, 214)
A technique in which instructions or challenges are written on cards.

Teaching formation (p. 114)
A specific way of organizing the class such as line, circle, or shuttle patterns.

Team teaching (p. 125)
The organization of teachers and students into instructional groups that permits maximum utilization of staff abilities.

Technique (pp. 126, 134)
Part of a method.

Tempo (p. 537)
The rate of speed of music or movement.

Theme (pp. 472, 584)
A central movement idea.

Time (p. 43)
The speed with which a movement takes place (quick, slow, sudden, or sustained).

Time on task (p. 131)
The amount of learning time devoted to the task by a student.

Tort (p. 158)
A legal wrong.

Touchback (p. 350)
When a defensive player intercepts the ball behind his or her own goal line and places it on the ground rather than attempting to run it out over the goal line. One point is awarded to the attacking team.

Touchdown (p. 350)
When a member of the attacking team carries the ball over the goal line or a teammate catches a ball while in the end zone. The attacking team is awarded six points.

Tournament (p. 239)
A method of organizing small and large groups for competition.

Throw-in (p. 312)
A two-hand overhand free throw awarded to the team that did not cause the ball to cross over the sideline.

Trapping (p. 310)
Stopping the ball using any part of the body except the hands.

Traveling (pp. 47, 383)
Moving in various directions by transferring weight from one part of the body to another. Also, a player who takes more than one step with the ball without dribbling it.

Turn (p. 59)
A rotation of the body and loss of the initial fixed point of contact (e.g., turning in a full arc).

Twist (p. 59)
One part of the body is held in a fixed position on the floor or apparatus and the rest of the body is turned away from the fixed position (e.g., twisting the trunk to the side and back).

Underlying beat (p. 536)
The steady pulse of a musical accompaniment.

Varsovienne position (p. 549)
The boy stands slightly behind and to the left of his partner. While both are facing the same direction, the girl raises both hands to about shoulder height and the boy joins his right hand with the girl's right hand and his left hand with the girl's left hand.

Volley (p. 309)
A type of kick in which the ball is contacted while it is in the air.

Walk (pp. 48, 411)
A rhythmic transfer of weight from one foot to the other. One foot is always in contact with the ground. Also, this occurs when four balls are called on the batter, who advances to first base.

Weight (pp. 19, 40, 466)
The degree of muscle tension involved in the production of a movement, or the maintenance of a static position involving tension.

Wellness (pp. 12, 167, 176)
A positive way of life that involves seeking and maintaining the highest level of health and well-being.

Wide (p. 39)
An action that moves the arm or legs away from the trunk.

Zone defense (pp. 374, 382)
A type of defense in which the defensive players are assigned specific areas of the court to guard.

Index

Game Activities

Dance Activities

Gymnastic Activities